What Leading Professionals Say About
The Complete Investment and Finance Di...

"The bull market of the 1990s has sp... ...w
investors and new investment produ... ... ...
Finance Dictionary serves as a ...
changing times."

—JACK HYZER, President, ...llas, Texas

"Howard Bonham is an investme... ...al in the highest sense of
the term. You get it right from the ...se's mouth. I only wish I had
authored this book that is so sorely needed by anyone who is a serious
investor or a student of the market. Mr. Bonham's book is a gigantic
accomplishment. Everyone should have a copy."

—DONALD W. HODGES, President, First Dallas Securities,
Hodges Capital Management, Inc., Dallas, Texas

"In our fast-paced investment world, keeping up with the terminology
is a necessity. *The Complete Investment and Finance Dictionary* is a
tremendous resource that's needed to stay ahead."

—BILL CHAPMAN, First Vice President and Investment Officer,
Dain Rauscher, San Antonio, Texas

"For those of us who quaver at the mention of regression analysis and
zero-beta portfolios but must talk with people who actually understand
what they mean from time to time, *The Complete Investment and
Finance Dictionary* is a book to keep at your fingertips."

—KATE THOMAS, Features Editor, *Hart's Energy Markets*,
Formerly business columnist, *The Houston Post*, Houston, Texas

"In this interesting book, Howard Bonham provides a dictionary of
investment terms that the average investor is likely to encounter,
explaining them with clarity and at times with a light touch. The book
should help to unravel some of the arcane jargon of the financial world
and make it understandable to today's investor."

—EDMUND A. MENNIS, CFA, Author, *"How the Economy Works,"*
Palos Verdes Estates, California

"Howard Bonham's new book, *The Complete Investment and Finance Dictionary*, should be close at hand for any professional, academician, serious investor or student of investing; in short, an excellent investment handbook."

—ROGER H. JENSWOLD, Chairman/Chief Investment Officer,
Roger H. Jenswold & Company, Inc., Houston, Texas

"Wall Street uses its own jargon. In a business where communications is absolutely essential, a misunderstanding can be costly. Howard Bonham's *The Complete Investment and Finance Dictionary* can be a useful reference source to help investors avoid the pitfalls of assuming an understanding of an investment term. The book is well done and useful to investors and brokers."

—DONALD C. POTTS, President & CEO,
Capital Institutional Services, Inc., Dallas, Texas

"Very comprehensive! The financial reader can rely on the *The Complete Investment and Finance Dictionary* to provide meaning or insight on nearly every investment phrase or concept he or she comes upon. The dictionary should be a big help to the average person seeking to learn more about investing."

—JEFFREY BEACH, CFA, Principal, Equity Investments,
Hanifen, Imhoff Inc., Denver, Colorado

"*The Complete Investment and Finance Dictionary* provides investors with keen insights in a compendium of important guides to financial markets."

—DILLARD SPRIGGS, President, Petroleum Analysis Limited,
New York, New York

"I perused . . . *The Complete Investment and Finance Dictionary* with great interest. While there are several financial dictionaries on the market, in today's complex, global marketplace the focus on clear definitions and examples exclusively aimed at investors makes *The Complete Investment and Finance Dictionary* a welcome addition. It is certainly a valuable resource that belongs on the bookshelves of both investment professionals and individual investors . . ."

—PAVAN SAHGAL, Editor in Chief, *Global Investment Technology,* and *Global Investment Magazine*, New York, New York

ADAMS

The Complete
Investment
and Finance
Dictionary

The most thorough and
updated reference available

HOWARD BRYAN BONHAM, CFA

Adams Media
Avon, Massachusetts

To my wife, Nancy, with love and admiration

Published by
Adams Media, an F+W Publications Company
57 Littlefield Street, Avon, MA 02322. U.S.A.
www.adamsmedia.com

ISBN: 1-58062-372-7

Printed in Canada.

J I H G F E D

Library of Congress Cataloging-in-Publication Data
Bonham, Howard Bryan.
The complete investment and finance dictionary /
by Howard Bryan Bonham.
p.   cm.
ISBN 1-58062-372-7
1. Investments--Dictionaries. 2. Finance--Dictionaries.
3. Investments--Handbooks, manuals, etc.
4. Finance--Handbooks, manuals, etc. I. Title.
HG4513 .B66   2001
332'.03--dc21   00-065003

This book is available at quantity discounts for bulk purchases.
For information call 1-800-289-0963.

How to Use This Dictionary

This book is written to serve as both a financial dictionary and a guide. **Specifically, it explains key topics in finance, accounting, law, economics, estate planning and business, and how they interact and apply to making effective investment decisions.** There is a "how to" slant to many of the investment topics. There is also a modicum of humor in order to provide contrast and emphasis as well as fun, hopefully. It is present to enhance the learning of what is often a complex but hugely important body of knowledge for achieving financial success. The information included is that which is considered useful in a climate of diverse business conditions and changing securities markets. The content strives to provide meaningful insights into short-term versus long-term investing, aggressive versus conservative investing, and offensive versus defensive investing. In other words, the assumption is that the reader wants information on financial topics for lifetime applications—an investor for all seasons.

Because the Internet promises to become such a unifying force in the workings of global securities markets—not to mention accelerated foreign trade initiatives—the dictionary incorporates many international topics, especially those pertaining to securities markets and currencies. Whenever possible, valuable Internet addresses pertaining to investing smarter are included, because the treasury of important electronic information useful to curious investors is often obscured by a blizzard of promotional hype. For the discerning Internet investor the motto should be "Viewer Beware."

When one topic expands on another or is related conceptually, there is a cross-reference to the alphabetical listing. By visiting the suggested term, the reader can develop broader insights into important financial subjects. In most cases, she or he can judge the degree of understanding desired, and exercise the reference options accordingly. In today's dynamic societies, energized even more by the stunning advances in electronic communications, barriers are falling like Berlin Walls in business transactions between countries and cultures as well as between professional disciplines. **A modern investor is well advised to possess an awareness of a wide range of fields applicable to finance and investing, from Alphas to Zeitgeist Industries, as presented herein.**

Finally, there has been a diligent effort to connect readers with helpful as well as rewarding financial addresses, both physical and virtual locations on the Internet. Also, there are important telephone numbers and e-mail addresses. This location coverage does not apply to just the investment sites of interest, but also to connections to securities regulators and government entities that provide information useful to investors. Dictionary topics also include connections to publications, associations, and private groups that further the interests of investors. Today there is more information available to investors than ever before in history, and readers are urged to learn to pursue that which makes sense and discard the chaff.

Unlike winning in lotteries and casino wagering, achieving financial and investment goals represents something more than capricious from Lady Luck. Rather, success is the result of intelligent planning, including previewing and reviewing decisions and actions along the way at regular intervals. Such focus is a huge challenge in today's dynamic, time squeezed society that bombards us constantly with digitized images and sounds. Unfortunately, most of these are spinning like tops beyond usefulness in financial planning. In response, what you will find on these pages are concise insights into clear thinking on perhaps the most important secular subject to Americans today— financial independence.

—Howard Bryan Bonham
Houston, Texas

Acknowledgments of Information Sources

The author wishes to express appreciation to the following
sources of information.

Brokerages, Private Firms, Institutions, and Government Agencies

American Bankers Association
Association for Investment Management and Research
Bureau of Economic Analysis (within the U.S. Department of
Commerce)
First Dallas Securities
Institute of Chartered Financial Analysts
Moody's Investors Service
NASDAQ
National Association of Securities Administrative Association
National Association of Securities Dealers
SAFECO Mutual Funds
Standard & Poor's Corp.

Books, Periodicals, and Subscription Services

Accountants' Handbook. Ronald Press
American Demographics
Barron's Financial Weekly
Business Conditions Digest (from the U.S. Department of
Commerce)
Calculator Analysis for Business and Finance. Texas
Instruments, 1977.
Canes, W. Stansbury, and Stephen D. Slifer. *The Atlas of
Economic Indicators: A Visual Guide to Market Forces and
the Federal Reserve.* Harper Business, 1992.
Downes, John and Jordan Elliot Goodman. *Dictionary of Finance
and Investment Terms.*
Economic Report of the President. U.S. Government Printing
Office.
The Economist
Federal Reserve Bulletin
Financial Analysts Journal
Financial Handbook. Ronald Press.
Forbes Magazine

Fortune

Garner, Bryan, Editor. *Black's Law Dictionary*.
    West/Wadsworth, 1999.

*Global Investing: The Journal of Money Management, Trading,
    and Global Asset Services*

Houston Chronicle

How the Economy Works. New York Institute of Finance.

Institutional Investor

Investor Direct

Kohler, Eric. *A Dictionary for Accountants*. Prentice Hall.

The New York Times

Oil & Gas Investor

Petroleum Finance Week

Principles of Accounting. Prentice Hall.

Smart Money

Statistical Abstract of the United States. U.S. Department of
    Commerce.

Statistical Methods. Barnes & Noble.

Survey of Current Business (from the U.S. Department of
    Commerce)

Texas Economic Quarterly

USA Today

Value Line Investment Survey

The Wall Street Journal

Internet Sources

AARP Webplace: *www.aarp.com*

American Stock Exchange: *www.amex.com*

Barra Portfolio: *www.barra.com*

Barron's Online Financial Dictionary: *www.barrons.com*

Bloomberg Online (Financial Market Reports):
    www.bloomberg.com

BusinessWeek online: *www.businessweek.com*

c|net Investor: *http://investor.cnet.com*

CBS MarketWatch: *www.cbsmarketwatch.com*

CIA WorldFactbook: *www.cia.gov/*

Co-op America: *www.coopamerica.com*

Contingency Analysis: *www.contingencyanalysis.com*

Discount Stock Brokers Ranked by Don Johnson:
    www.sonic.net/donaldj/

Dow Jones Markets: *www.dowjones.com*

DRIP Investor: *www.dripinvestor.com*
Edgar Online: *www.edgar.com*
Electronic Traders Association: *www.eletronic-traders.org*
Elliott Wave Charting Association: *www.wavechart.com*
Equity Analytics, Ltd: *www.equityanalytics.com*
European Monetary Institute: *www.ecb.int/emi/emi.htm*
Federal Reserve Bank of St. Louis: *www.stls.frb.org*
Financial Accounting Standards Board: *www.fasb.org*
Financial Web: *www.financialweb.com*
Gomez Advisors, Inc. *www.gomez.com*
Government Accounting Standards Board:
    http://accounting.rutgers.edu/raw/gasb
H.L. Camp & Co.: *www.programtrading.com*
Individual Investor Online: *www.iionline.com*
IndustryWeek: *www.industryweek.com*
Instinet Brokerage: *www.instinet.com*
International Monetary Fund: *www.imf.org*
Investment Counsel Association of America: *www.icaa.org*
Investorama: *www.investorama.com*
Kiplinger Online: *www.kiplinger.com*
KPMG Peat Marwick, LLP: *www.kpmg.com*
London Stock Exchange: *www.londonstockex.co.uk*
Maxwell Shmerler & Co.: *www.msco-cpa.com*
MoneyLine: *www.moneyline.com*
The Motley Fool: *www.fool.com*
Multex Investors Network: *www.multexinvestor.com*
NASDAQ Trader: *www.nasdaqtrader.com*
NetVest: *www.netvest.com*
New York Stock Exchange: *www.nyse.com*
Organisation for Economic Co-operation and Development
    Statistics: *www.oed.org/statistics*
Pace University Online: *www.pace.edu*
P.V. Viswanath's Home Page:
    http://webcomposer.pace.edu/pviswanath/
PCWorld: *www.pcworld.com*
Pension Benefit Guaranty Corporation: *www.pbgc.gov*
Petersen Hastings Investment Management:
    www.petersonhastings.com
Quicken Online: *www.quicken.com*
University of Alabama School of Business (Ted Bos's page):
    http://bos.business.uab.edu
Securities Industry Association: *www.sia.com*

Securities Transfer Association, Inc.: *www.stai.org*
Securities and Exchange Commission Online: *www.sec.gov*
Southern General Financial Group: *www.sgfgroup.com*
Smart Money: *www.smartmoney.com*
Stat-USA Internet: *www.stat-usa.com*
Stock Sense: *www.stocksense.com*
Technical Analysis, Inc.: *www.traders.com*
U.S. Treasury Department Online: *www.treasury.gov*
University of Toronto Library: *www.library.utoronto.ca*
University of Virginia Online Library: *www.virginia.edu/lib.html*
T.D. Waterhouse Securities, Inc.: *www.tdwaterhouse.com*
World Bank Group: *www.worldbank.com*
Yahoo! Finance: *http://finance.yahoo.com*

Individuals

Jim Barlow, columnist
Scott Burns, columnist
James Flanigan, columnist
Mark Hulbert, columnist
Gary Klott, columnist
Edmund A. Mennis, economist
Robert Metz, columnist
Howard L. Nations, attorney at law
Floyd Norris, columnist
Peter Passell, columnist
Eric Tyson, columnist

Aa

"A" shares. See **"B" shares.**

AAII. Abbreviation for **American Association of Individual Investors.**

Abandonment. In securities law, the relinquishing of all legal claims, rights, or title to specific securities by the owner's ignoring their existence or refusing to act in ways expressing ownership of them. Most often this condition occurs in the case of shares left in a brokerage account where efforts to locate the owners over several years have been unsuccessful. A court order is required to make such securities transferable. Usually such securities revert to the state, under **escheat** when declared abandoned. Other types of property besides financial assets are subject to abandonment—real estate, copyrights, leases, patents, contracts, and trademarks.

ABC Agreement. When a brokerage buys a seat or membership on the NYSE for an employee, usually a broker or trader, their agreement as to the disposition of that seat, if the employee leaves the firm. This is a critical contract because only individuals can be members of the NYSE. Upon leaving, the employee's options are: (1) transferring the membership to another employee; (2) selling the seat, giving the proceeds to the employer; and (3) retaining the membership, and buying another for the firm's designated employee.

A-bond. See **Z-bond.**

ABS. Abbreviation for **asset-backed securities.**

absorbing cost or **eating cost.** In accounting for the financial results of a business operation, a cost that is treated as an expense in the current fiscal period so that earnings are reduced. The alternative is to pass through the cost to customers in the form of a price increase. In so doing, the additional cost of operating is also collected in the revenues, thus protecting the operating margin. Having to absorb costs occurs in highly competitive industries such as the airlines, where an increase in prices can cause a loss of customers. One airline might try to pass through an increase in jet fuel, for example, only to be forced to lower its fares again because competitors absorbed the higher fuel costs.

abusive tax shelter. Any scheme that defers or escapes income taxes by actions that are taken for no reason but to escape the taxes, in the eyes of the Internal Revenue Service. Most often, the abuses occur through the use of limited partnerships and trusts. For example, the IRS might declare a limited trust created to allow taxpayers to deduct from ordinary income the losses from drilling an oil well that was abandoned earlier as a dry hole an abusive trust. In such a case, taxpayers who participated often must pay back taxes, interest on those taxes, and a penalty. *See* **abusive trust.**

abusive trust. A trust established solely for the purpose of tax avoidance, as defined by the Internal Revenue Service. The term is a reference to a strategy of taxpayers who place assets such as their homes, businesses, or marketable securities into various trust arrangements in order to avoid paying income, self-employment, and estate taxes. The IRS considers this practice illegal.

accelerated amortization. 1) The paying off of a debt faster than originally planned, often under the terms of a penalty clause that adds fees to the amount the borrower must pay. To a limited extent, these penalties reimburse the lender for less income because of the resulting shorter borrowing period. 2) The charging off against income of a depreciating or depleting asset faster than originally planned or faster than the asset is actually being used up, usually to shelter income against income taxes. *See* **accelerated depreciation.**

Accelerated Cost Recovery System. See **accelerated depreciation.**

accelerated depreciation or **Accelerated Cost Recovery System (ACRS).** Under Internal Revenue Service guidelines, the decreasing of the book value of an asset rapidly by increasing annual depreciation charges to income (and additions to depreciation reserves) at a rate faster than normal or under straight-line depreciation. The higher depreciation allowances granted by tax law reduce taxable income by increasing tax deductions in the early years of an asset's economic life, and yet increase cash available for reinvestment or distribution to the owners. However, the procedure should be considered tax deferral, since income taxes will rise quickly once an accelerated depreciation schedule is used up. A strategy of aggressive financial management is to continue purchasing assets that can be depreciated rapidly, thereby perpetuating the higher tax deductions. For federal income tax purposes under ACRS, assets placed in service after 1980 and before 1987 can be depreciated over a three-, five-, or 10-year period. For assets placed in service after 1987, the modified accelerated cost recovery system (MACRS) usually applies. *See* **declining balance depreciation, Modified Accelerated Cost Recovery System (MACRS),** and **straight-line depreciation.**

acceleration clause. 1) A clause in a bond indenture enabling the borrower or issuer to pay off the outstanding balance of the debt early, sometimes incurring penalty payments in the process which reimburse the lender, to a limited degree, for the foreshortened interest income schedule. 2) In a loan agreement or bond indenture, a clause that enables the lender to demand immediate payment of the loan outstanding if payments or certain conditions are not maintained by the borrower.

acceleration principle. In macroeconomic theory, the expansive effects upon aggregate spending for plant and equipment caused by increases in aggregate consumer demand during a business cycle.

acceptance ratio. The percentage of bonds sold of those offered for sale in a period, usually referring to municipal bonds.

ACCESS Internet Magazine. See under **Web Sites for the Inquiring Investor.**

accommodative monetary policy or **easy money policy.** A reference to the stance the Fed takes when it acts to increase funds available to member banks for lending. The Fed usually follows this course to stimulate business by increasing the money supply for investment and purchases or to lower interest rates by increasing funds for lending, or a combination thereof. Generally, the central bank will not take this action if the chances that it will cause unacceptable inflation are high. *See* **monetary policy.**

account aggregator. An Internet service that gives users information on their online accounts, usually of a financial nature, at one Web site. Users provide the central site with their user IDs and passwords of their various accounts, which enables the site's software to search the Internet and retrieve the target information, through a technique called "screen scraping."

account, brokerage. An investment firm's information base about a customer and a record of the customer's transactions. For Corporate, Partnership, IRA, Trust, or Estate type accounts, alternative forms should be requested. In the latter type accounts, the brokerage firm wants to make sure the applicant has the legal standing to conduct securities transactions for the name on the account. Some main elements of an account application are an Authorization/Signature, Customer Agreement, and a Margin Agreement/Loan Consent, which are addressed under their own topics. Other forms, including options applications, are usually requested. *See* **Authorization/Signature (Brokerage), Customer Agreement (Brokerage),** and **Margin Agreement/Loan Consent (Brokerage).**

account closed or **books closed**. See **closing the books.**

account executive or **registered representative** or **financial advisor.** A stockbroker or stock salesman, working at an investment firm and usually registered with state and/or federal regulatory agencies, who is responsible for a customer's transactions.

account form of balance sheet. See **Balance Sheet.**

account payable. A financial item in a company's accounting system that is owed and payable, usually within 90 days or sooner. Most often, it represents a bill from a vendor requesting payment for products shipped or services performed that were or will be used in the day-to-day operations of the business. It is considered a good test of solvency, if the value of these items is exceeded by the value of short-term assets most of the time. Otherwise, borrowing money constantly will be required to carry on operations.

account receivable. A financial item in a company's accounting system that will be converted into cash or near cash within 90 days or sooner. Usually it represents a bill, sent to a customer by a vendor of products or services used in the day-to-day operations of the customer's business, that is expected to be paid. Sometimes in a large operation a reserve for doubtful accounts, based on a percentage, will be subtracted from the total amount due, to reflect the company's experience with nonpayment of accounts receivable. In a test for solvency, a company's accounts receivable and cash and near cash should exceed accounts payable, most of the time. Otherwise, the company will need to constantly borrow money to stay in business.

accountant. An individual who practices accounting on a professional basis. *See* **Certified Public Accountant.**

accounting. The practice of organizing both current and expected receipts and disbursements from business transactions into useful categories and time periods for the interpretation, in monetary terms, of past events and future expectations. One should remember that the practice of accounting is a system of conventions for explaining the results of a business enterprise, rather than a system of fundamental truths. Illustrative of this point are the many riotously funny accounting stories in circulation. *See* **generally accepted accounting practices (GAAP).**

accounting value method of management performance. In measuring the investment performance of corporate management, placing the emphasis on the company's growth in earnings or stockholders' equity. This is the traditional way. For an alternative way, *see* **economic value added.**

accounts. In the system of allocating and reporting the results of a business enterprise for a fiscal period, those categories for reporting transactions that go into the preparation of financial statements such as income accounts, expenses accounts, capital accounts, or reserve accounts.

accounts receivable factor. A financial services firm that buys "accounts receivable" from a vendor of goods or services, at discounts to the face values of those receivables, so that the vendor acquires current working capital in exchange for the receivables.

accounts receivable turnover. In judging how quickly the accounts due of a business are being collected and thereby converted to cash useable in operations, the quotient found by dividing annual sales by the average of beginning accounts receivable and ending accounts receivable. If annual sales are $10,000,000, and average accounts receivable are $850,000, the turnover is 11.7 × ($10,000,000 ÷ $850,000 = 11.7). This is another way of showing that the average receivable is collected in less than a month, usually a very acceptable rate.

Accredited Investor. A special category of investor recognized under the SEC's Regulation D. Such an investor can be excluded from the maximum of 35 investors allowed for the financing of a Private Limited Partnership. This allows more investors and more capital to be raised for the partnerships, since in effect more than 35 can invest. The definition of such an investor is one who has a net worth of at least $1 million or annual income of at least $200,000; or, one who puts at least $150,000 into the partnership, with that amount not representing more than 20% of the investor's net worth. In using this regulation, investment bankers for a partnership could raise $1 million from 35 nonaccredited investors and $1 million from one accredited investor, thus doubling the capital investment with relative ease.

accretion, bond discount. See **amortization, bond.**

accruals. Monies payable or receivable, applicable to a specific time period.

accrued interest. The amount of money owed to an investor, such as a bondholder, but not yet paid. *See* **plus accrued interest.**

accrued market discount. The increments in value of a discounted bond each year as it nears its maturity date, when the full par value will be paid to the bondholder. These increments are calculated as deferred interest by bond issuers. *See* **amortization, bond.**

accumulated deficit. A description of the stockholders' equity when it is a negative amount, meaning that a company's operations, an asset write down, or a nonrecurring event charged directly to the shareholders' equity account has caused the amount left for stockholders to become negative. However, in the case of a corporation or limited partnership, this condition does not mean the stockholders are liable for the deficit, unless they have caused the deficit through some illegal corporate activity. It means that the book value of the assets less the book value of the liabilities is a negative amount and that the company is probably insolvent and must either arrange for a capital infusion or the forgiveness of debt or face bankruptcy. This condition is the negative counterpart to a capital surplus. *See* **Balance Sheet.**

accumulating discount. See **amortization, bond.**

accumulated dividend. The amount of money a corporation owes to stockholders, usually holders of cumulative preferred stock, because the dividends were not paid in a prescribed manner. When such a stock is sold, the price usually includes the accumulation per share.

accumulation area. A period of several days or more in which a stock sells within a narrow price range, because purchases are offsetting sales. This situation usually occurs after a popular stock has lost favor with investors temporarily, frequently because of negative financial or operating news, and has fallen in price to a level where investors become interested again and commence buying. They do so in the belief the company is getting back on the track that attracted them in the first place. It is a reference point commonly used in charting stocks. *See* **chart.**

acid test or **quick ratio.** The ratio of current assets minus inventory to current liabilities, which should be 1.5-to-1 at least, unless the company has extraordinarily good credit and can borrow short-term money easily because of other factors.

acquired surplus. In accounting for an acquisition using a pooling of interest methodology, that portion of the capital accounts of the surviving company not represented as capital stock.

acquisition. The purchase of a company's assets and liabilities by another company, in exchange for the purchasing company's stock, debt securities, or cash. Sometimes, certain assets and/or liabilities are excluded and are dispensed with in some other fashion. For example, an unwanted business might be spun off or sold beforehand. Technically, an acquisition involves the absorption of the assets and liabilities, without an exchange of stock—strictly a purchase for debt or cash—whereas an exchange of the common stock of one company for that of another is a merger of ownership, involving executives and business infrastructures as well as assets and liabilities. Mergers suggest a new star is born, but in the "lean and mean" corporate culture of today, nervous executives know that a merged company is often a purged company.

"across the board." A reference to a directional move in stock prices that affects most issues.

"acting as principal." A phrase to describe a broker buying or selling securities for his customer as an independent businessman, making profit as a middleman, rather than as an agent. In reports of transactions on registered exchanges, a customer must be informed when his broker is acting as principal.

active crowd. The group of bond brokers dealing in corporate bonds on an exchange.

active market. A securities market scene in which there is rapid trading of stocks or bonds, in general or in one security. *See* **volume.**

active stock. Shares of a common stock issue that are being traded often, at a high volume in relation to normal trading, making it easy to get a quotation or details of a current sale. *See* **liquidity.**

actuary. An official of an insurance company who is trained in a special type of statistics called actuarial science. As such, that person is responsible for calculating the risk factors in underwriting various types of insurance and annuity programs. These calculations are based on company experience as well as industry tables. From the calculations come the bases for setting premiums, establishing reserves, and paying dividends. *See* **annuity.**

Adelaide, Stock Exchange of. A stock exchange in Australia. Address: 55 Exchange Place, Adelaide, S.A. 5000.

Adjustable Rate Mortgage (ARM) or **Variable Rate Mortgage (VRM)**. A mortgage contract calling for a periodic adjustment of the nominal interest rate, and therefore the mortgage payments owed by a buyer of real estate to a lending institution. The adjustment is based on an established and independent interest rate index, such as one on U.S. Treasury bills. Usually the mortgage agreement calls for periods of adjustment every one, three, or five years. The purpose of this type of financing arrangement is to allow property buyers or mortgagors to benefit from declining interest rates, which are likely to occur sometime during a typical mortgage, due to the relatively long repayment period. The risk is that the buyer will guess wrong and at some adjustment point interest rates will rise, allowing the institution to raise the payments due. The ARM allows the property buyer to second-guess interest rate cycles, which is exactly what lending officers must do. However, the experience level favors the lending institution. *See* **ARMS Securities.**

adjustable rate preferred stock (ARPS) or **floating rate preferred stock** or **variable rate preferred stock.** A type of preferred stock that pays a variable dividend rather than a fixed one, a dividend that is usually paid quarterly and pegged to some money market index, such as the U.S. Treasury Bill rate. Because the dividend yield is constantly being adjusted to a more stable basic rate, this type of preferred stock is less volatile than others.

adjusted for stock dividends and splits. A phrase indicating that past earnings and dividends per share attributable to a common stock have been adjusted to reflect their historic levels relative to a recent stock dividend or stock split, thus an adjustment to show past earnings or dividends per share as though the number of shares outstanding then were the same as currently or as they will be after a forthcoming stock dividend or stock split. This is done in order to prevent investors from assuming erroneously that changed earnings or dividends per share resulting from increased or decreased shares reflect only operating results.

For example, if Split Personality, Inc. effects a 2-for-1 split of its 2,000,000 shares outstanding, past or pre-split earnings per share would be halved in order to compare with the current results and compensate for twice as many shares outstanding presently. This exercise is accomplished by dividing past earnings by the ratio of shares currently outstanding to the number outstanding in the past period: 2,000,000 shares ÷ 1,000,000 shares = 2. Otherwise, current earnings per share would appear to be declining or stagnant, only because more shares are outstanding currently. No adjustment is made for shares issued for additional capital, since the capital infusion is expected to contribute to additional earnings growth and comparisons with the unadjusted past are more realistic.

Adjusted Gross Income (AGI). In filing federal income taxes, the amount of income on which the taxpayer's **Standard Deduction** is based and subtracted, leading to the final phase in the calculation of the income tax due for a taxable year. To arrive at the AGI, the taxpayer begins with total income or receipts received—singularly or jointly with a spouse—reduced by costs such as employee business expenses, deductions for loses on income property, specific types of losses from sales or exchanges of property, charitable and philanthropic contributions, the deduction for child care by working wives, IRA and other retirement plan payments, alimony payments, capital loss deductions up to $3,000, expenses for rents and royalties, one-half of self-employment tax liability, health insurance premium deductions for the self-employed as well as operating losses, and interest penalties for premature withdrawals from certificates of deposits. In the adjustment process, the object is to modify gross earnings for benefits and penalties in the Tax Code. *See* **Gross Income.**

adjustment bonds. New bonds issued in lieu of defaulted bonds, which are more lenient to a debtor who is usually experiencing financial difficulties.

administrator. A court-appointed estate manager in the absence of a will or competent executor.

admitted assets. In the financial reports of financial institutions that are regulated, those assets that authorities allow to be evaluated and used in furnishing proof of institutional net worth or solvency. This concept is especially important in the case of insurance companies, because such institutions tend to invest in longer-term securities often not possessing high degrees of liquidity. States, which regulate insurance companies, specify what types of assets can be admitted in filings or audits. Insurance companies can own "nonadmitted" assets, such as second mortgages on real estate loans or certain common stocks, but this practice weakens their financial report (net worth), since the excluded assets cannot contribute to the company's financial rating as can investment-grade securities. An insurance management might speculate at times under the rationale that the nonadmitted assets could rise in esteem to an admitted status or might appreciate in value to a point where their sale would represent a cash gain, which is always admissible—and sometimes miraculous.

"admitted to regular dealings." A phrase signifying a security (stock, bond, warrant, right, and so on) can be traded on an exchange through regular channels and procedures.

ADR. See **American depository receipt.**

ad valorem tax or **ad valorem duty.** Meaning "according to the value" in Latin, this is a tax on property or a duty on imported goods. It is calculated on the basis of the value of goods or property at the point of the levy.

Advance-Decline Ratio. See **technical indicators.**

advance refunding. The act by a debtor of **refunding** a long-term bond before its maturity.

adverse opinion. In a company's financial statements, such as those in the annual stockholders' report, a statement by the independent auditor that the financial statements do not accurately reflect the company's financial position or operating results. This opinion is much more critical of the document's presentation than a **qualified opinion**, which calls attention to limited defects. Investors should be extremely wary of investing in a stock representing a company that has gotten an adverse opinion.

advised line. See **line of credit**.

Aerospace and Defense stocks. Those stocks representing companies engaged in the development and manufacture of equipment for air and space travel as well as the development and manufacture of such equipment used for military purposes. *See* **industry stock group.**

affiliate. 1) A company associated with another company through the ownership of up to 50% of the latter's common stock, representing a relationship in which the latter retains a certain degree of independence in its management as compared with a subsidiary. Ownership of more than 50% of the affiliate's common stock would make that company also a **subsidiary**. 2) A company associated with another company through operating or marketing agreements, under which each is bound to fulfill the terms of a working relationship designed to benefit each party. 3) Two separate companies that are subsidiaries of a third company. 4) Under banking laws, an entity owned by a bank through stock ownership; or owned by the bank's shareholders, or with officers who also are members of the bank's board of directors. 5) In filing a consolidated income tax return under the U.S. Federal Tax Code, a parent company and the associated companies in which it owns 80% of the voting stock. 6) Under the Investment Company Act, a company in which an investment company owns 5% or more of the former's voting securities.

affiliated person or **control person.** Under securities laws, any person who can exercise a high degree of influence in the management of a corporation. This includes members of the board of directors, elected corporate officers, other influential corporate officers, and investors owning 10% or more of the voting shares. Also included are persons who can affect corporate policies through such individuals, such as members of their families or close business associates.

affiliated transaction. A transaction between a brokerage firm and a mutual fund that it owns. Such a transaction is covered by the **Investment Company Act of 1940,** which proscribes a brokerage trading with a mutual fund subsidiary or affiliate. The unethical trading practices of the 1930s, when securities were dumped by brokerages on mutual funds they owned, gave rise to this act. In order to carry out an affiliated transaction today, a special exemption must be granted by the SEC.

affinity investment scheme. Under SEC enforcement guidelines, an illegal operation in which investors with common interests or heritage, such as Hispanic persons, are the target of perpetrators who take advantage of the former's lack of expertise or language comprehension, in order to defraud or mislead them into making questionable investments.

"affluenza." A facetious reference to the ambition to get rich quick in the stock market that gripped the United States during the bull market of the 1990s.

after-tax income or **earnings.** The amount remaining in the revenue stream—after deducting all the costs and expenses of doing business, interest, other income and deductions, and taxes—for payment of preferred stock dividends or contingent debt payments. If there are none of the latter securities, the amount is available for common stockholders, either as dividends or reinvestment in the business. In the case of the latter, the monies are transferred to special capital accounts to indicate they were not part of the original investment.

against the box, selling. A phrase to describe a short sale by an investor who already owns shares identical to those she is selling short. The investor anticipates that the price will drop, at which time she will buy the stock in the market to make delivery on her short sale. The shares in her "safety box" are held for long-term appreciation or they can be used, if necessary, to cover her short sale. For example, if the shorted shares go up in price—an event very traumatic for a short seller who is the "bearest" of the bears—she might decide to use the shares already owned for delivery, rather than lose money in buying shares at the current market price for delivery.

agency. In contract law, the basic legal framework for one party to act on behalf of another party to effect some legitimate outcome, usually for a fee or commission. In the securities business it is the essence of brokerage arrangements, and its use and misuse form the basis for most misunderstandings in securities transactions. Generally, an agent or broker takes no risk personally for the change in value of securities purchased or sold for a client or the principal. Nor does the broker take title. And the principal's intentions always must be adhered to. The broker's compensation is a percentage of the value of the transaction, before applicable taxes and regulatory fees. When a customer gives a broker the right to buy or sell securities at will, the agency relationship has escalated into that of a power of attorney, which must be written and notarized. *See* **arbitration.**

agency securities (GSEs). Those securities issued by entities created and sponsored by the federal government to provide low-cost borrowing to important sectors of the U.S. economy. In 1999, agency bonds amounted to $1.4 trillion, 10.2 % of the total bond debt in the United States. These securities are issued by agencies that are either owned privately but chartered publicly or agencies related to the federal government. They are not required to register with the SEC. Furthermore, they are exempt from state and local income taxes. Currently there are eight issuers of securities that are privately owned but chartered publicly. Securities issued range from short-term notes to bonds. With the exception of Farm Credit Financial Assistance Corporation, none of these are backed by the full faith and credit of the U.S. government. However, since they are associated with the U.S. government, the best credit in the world today, the securities all possess an element of extra security. Created by Congress to reduce borrowing costs, they include sectors like farmers, students, and homeowners.

Issuers of these securities are: the Federal Farm Credit Bank System, the Farm Credit Financial Assistance Corporation, the Federal Home Loan Bank, the Federal Home Loan Mortgage Corporation, the Federal National Mortgage Association (FNMA), the Student Loan Marketing Association (SLMA), the Financing Corporation (FICO), and the Federal Financing Bank.

The other category of agency securities—entities related to the federal government—have used the Federal Financing Bank for their funding needs since 1973. Except for the Private Export Funding Corporation and the Tennessee Valley Authority, these agencies are backed by the full faith and credit of the U.S. government. The agencies are: the Export-Import Bank (EXIMBANK), the Commodity Credit Corporation (CCC), the Farmers Housing Administration (FHA), the General Services Administration, the Government National Mortgage Association (GNMA), the Maritime Administration, the Private Export Funding Corporation, the Rural Electrification Administration (REA), the Rural Telephone Bank, the Small Business Administration (SBA), the Tennessee Valley Authority (TVA), and the Washington Metropolitan Transit Authority.

aggregate option exercise price. When a trader wants to take delivery on an optioned security, rather than merely speculate on the fluctuating option values, the number of units in a put or call contract (100 typically) times the exercise price. The calculation does not include the premium or price of the option, which has already been paid. Illustrating, a June put option on 100 ZIP at 50 would have an aggregate exercise price of $5,000 (100 shares × $50 per share), before the expiration date in June.

In the case of debt instruments, such as U.S. Treasury bills and bonds, the aggregate exercise price is calculated in a similar manner. The number of units (10 often, but this number can vary) is multiplied by the face value of the optioned security

($10,000 often, but this can vary) times the option price. For example, the aggregate option price of a call option on U.S. Treasury January 95 would be $950,000 on or before the January expiration date (10 bonds × $10,000 per bond × the 95% exercise price). *See* **premium, option.**

AGI. Abbreviation for **Adjusted Gross Income.**

AIM. Abbreviation for **Alternative Investment Market.**

airline alliances. In the air transport industry, the most basic alliance is an interline alliance or agreement between two or more carriers to accept the tickets and baggage of the others. There is also a code-share or block-share or tactical alliance, in which the marketing carrier buys seats from the operating carrier, and resells them at whatever price it wants. Another type is a strategic or commercial or multilateral alliance, in which participating carriers can offer single check-in procedures for connecting flights, share lounges, and frequent-flyer reciprocity. When certain airlines have been granted anti-trust immunity (ATI) by a government, they may coordinate fares and schedules, share revenues, and use one another's equipment, free from anti-trust charges.

Airlines. Those stocks representing companies engaged in transporting passengers and freight in the United States and abroad, on a scheduled basis. *See* **industry stock group.**

air pocket stock. A reference to a stock that falls rapidly immediately after negative financial or operating news. Stocks lacking broad liquidity are apt to fall into this category because no buyers can be found continuously.

aktiengesellschaft (AG). The German word for a stock company.

Alabama Securities Commission. Regulator of state securities laws in the state of Alabama. Address: 770 Washington Street, Suite 570, Montgomery, AL 36130. Telephone: (205) 242-2984.

Alaska Department of Commerce & Economic Development, Division of Banking, Securities & Corporations. Regulator of state securities laws in the state of Alaska. Address: Post Office Box 110807, Juneau, Alaska: 99811. Telephone: (907) 465-2521.

Alberta Stock Exchange. A stock exchange in Canada. Address: 300 5th Avenue, SW, 21st Floor, Calgary, Alberta Canada T2P 3C4. *See* under **Global Investment Market.**

Alcoholic Beverages. Those stocks representing companies producing products of distilled spirits for public consumption. *See* **industry stock group.**

alien corporation. A company incorporated or domiciled in a country other than the one in which it operates. Sometimes it is referred to as a "foreign corporation," but technically, under U.S. laws, a foreign corporation is one operating in a state other than the one of its incorporation.

All-American team. The right stuff! Those hustling, no-nonsense securities analysts who through hard work, meticulous attention to detail, relentless cultivation of corporate managements, and timely buy and sell signals have inspired institutional money managers to elect them to *Institutional Investor*'s annual team of research all-stars, and, in so doing, have added to commission revenues, underwriting fees, trading profits, big-buck bonuses, and all-around serendipity at their respective brokerage firms.

ALLEXPERTS.COM. Expert answers to questions, including investments. *See* **Web Sites for the Inquiring Investor.**

"all or none" (AON). An order to buy or sell securities under which the broker is instructed to fill the entire order or none of it. This stipulation in the order usually assures that the investor buys or sells enough of the security to accomplish a predetermined price goal or purpose.

All Ordinaries Index (ORDS). The primary stock price index in Australia, composed of 330 of the most active stocks listed on the Australian Stock Exchange (ASX), excluding non-Australian listings. It includes 23 component indexes of industries represented by those shares. The index was begun

December 31, 1979 and is the equivalent of the Dow Industrials, the Nikkei Dow and the *Financial Times* 100.

alliance, marketing. An agreement by two or more companies (but usually two) with complementary products or services to utilize the sales effort of one to sell products or services of the other(s). It is a less structured relationship than an affiliation in that neither party acquires ownership in the other. Each has the opportunity to enhance profits through increased revenues without incurring significant expenses. Aside from the products or services one is helping to market for the other for a share of the revenues, there is no real mutual business interest. An example would be an alliance where a car manufacturer provides its customer base to an automobile insurer for advertising and marketing purposes by the latter and to offer insurance coverage to new car buyers. The expanded value to its customers aids car sales and revenues for the auto maker as does its share of the insurance revenues. The insurer gets a database of new prospects and a selling effort by car dealers, without the expense of adding employees.

allied member. A special category of membership of the New York Stock Exchange, usually a general partner or stockholder of a member, who is not personally a member and is not allowed on the trading floor.

alligator spread. In the options markets, a reference to high commission costs that practically eliminate trading profits, even when the markets move in the anticipated manner.

all-star fund. A mutual fund in which several highly regarded portfolio managers run a portion of the fund.

alphabet stock. Various common stock categories issued by the same corporation, usually with identical privileges and voting rights but with differentiating names like "D" stock, "E" stock, "F" stock, etcetera. This stock is generally issued to be used in the acquisition of another company, but one whose identity management wishes to retain in a separate stock trading market. Sometimes it is issued in a restructuring or recapitalization or to create a tracking stock. The best known of this type are the

General Motors (GM—NYSE) "H" shares, issued when GM acquired Hughes Aircraft and combined it with its own electronics effort. As the "H" shares suggest, GM "H" shares represent equity in high technology electronics, and it is technically a tracking stock. *See* **classified stock** and **tracking stock.**

alpha stocks. On the International Stock Exchange of the United Kingdom and the Republic of Ireland, the most important stocks in terms of size and trading volume.

Alpha Value. 1) In the statistical analysis of stock prices, the percentage return experienced by a stock during a period attributable to company operations rather than general stock market activity. The higher the value, the better the stock should perform on its own merits, regardless of the stock market mood. For instance, an Alpha of 1.50 indicates that a stock could rise 50% in a period when the stock market change is zero. Statistically, the Alpha is the average change over a lengthy period, independent of the market. This characteristic highlights one of the dangers of relying on Alphas entirely—their lack of permanence. The Alpha might be 1.50 in one five-year period and 1.15 in another, indicating it has lost some independence in performance. *See* **Beta Value.** 2) In the analysis of mutual funds, the Alpha Value measures a fund's performance in relation to its Beta Value during a three-year interval. In doing so, light is thrown on how much of the fund's performance is derived from fund management ingenuity (Alpha Value) and how much from general market performance (Beta Value).

alternate minimum tax (AMT). The application of special income tax rates if certain tax benefits result in a regular income tax that is lower than the tax applicable if those benefits were added back to taxable income. Examples of benefits would be deductible property taxes, interest on home mortgage payments, job-related expenses, and exercising stock options. Its purpose is to raise taxes, in cases where tax benefits and exemptions have reduced taxable income significantly. The AMT tax rate is 26% if AMT income is $175,000 or less and 28% for income above that amount. Instead of disallowed deductions, there is an exemption of $45,000 for married couples filing jointly,

$33,750 for single individuals, and $22,500 for married couples filing separately. For changes in 2001, see **Economic Growth and Tax Relief Reconciliation Act.**

alternative investment. A reference to a financial commitment to a nonsecurity or nonconventional investment by a professional money manager. Examples are private equities and venture capital positions. This move is an effort to enhance investment performance by buying into more speculative situations. Until recently, the initial stake in these investments was high, in most cases out of reach of the average non-institutional investors. But now there are some within the reach of smaller investors, usually requiring $250,000 to $500,000 up front. The table below lists some Internet sources of information on alternative investments.

INTERNET SOURCES OF INFORMATION ON ALTERNATIVE INVESTMENTS

Name	Web Address
Asset Alternatives	*www.assetnews.com*
Buyouts	*www.sdponline.com*
Cambridge Associates	*www.cambridgeassociates.com*
Independence Holdings	*www.independencefund.com*
Managed Account Reports	*www.marhedge.com*
Spectrum Group	*www.spectrem.com*
Tremont Advisers	*www.hedgeindex.com*

Alternative Investment Market (AIM). Established in 1995, a securities market operated by the London Stock Exchange to meet the special financial needs of small, new, and growing companies. There are 307 companies listed, with 30 of them from outside Great Britain. Since its inception, total market capitalization has expanded to £5.83 billion, and £1.65 billion of new capital has been raised. AIM places no restriction on market capitalization, operating history, continuity of management, or portion of shares in public hands. It focuses on financial disclosure principles, suggesting investors buy securities based on careful analysis, and recognizing the higher risks of stocks trading in this market. Companies joining AIM are assisted by a nominated advisor from a firm of corporate finance advisors, approved by the LSE. The advisor is responsible for due diligence compliance, assists the company in preparing admission documents, and furnishes guidance on AIM rules. The advisor must remain available to counsel the corporate directors, in complying with financial obligations, after admission to the marketplace. Generally, there are less strenuous trading rules than on conventional exchanges. The range of companies includes hi-tech, bio-tech, IT, restaurants, leisure, manufacturing, and engineering, with market capitalizations from £2 million to over £200 million, though most fall between £5 million and £15 million. More than 70% of the companies traded have two or more market makers in their stocks. *See* **Web Sites for the Inquiring Investor.**

Alternate Minimum Tax (ATM). The application of special income tax rates if certain tax benefits result in a regular income tax that is lower than the tax applicable if those benefits were added back to taxable income. Examples of benefits would be deductible property taxes, interest on home mortgage payments, job-related expenses, and exercising stock options. Its purpose is to raise taxes in cases where tax benefits and exemptions have reduced taxable income significantly. The AMT tax rate is 26% if AMT income is $175,000 or less and 28% for income above that amount. Instead of disallowed deductions, there is an exemption of $45,000 for married couples filing jointly, $33,750 for single individuals, and $22,500 for married couples filing separately. For changes in 2001, see **Economic Growth and Tax Relief Reconciliation Act of 2001.**

Aluminums. Those stocks representing companies engaged in the manufacturer of aluminum and aluminum products. *See* **industry stock group.**

amateur or **outsider.** An investor not close to last-minute and comprehensive market information. Some disillusioned investors feel their broker is just such a person.

amended registration. A change made in pertinent corporate information by an underwriter and/or issuer of a proposed security that is registered with the Securities and Exchange Commission. Usually this is done at the request of the Commission because of a deficiency in the data or because the issuer wants to report a recent material corporate development.

American Arbitration Association. A public service nonprofit organization offering resolution services for disputes to businesses, attorneys, and individuals. Web site: *www.adr.org. See* **arbitration.**

American Association of Individual Investors (AAII). An association founded to arm individual investors with investment knowledge that will help them to manage their assets more effectively, emphasizing online resources. There are 175,000 members. Web site: *www.aaii.com.*

American Depository Receipt (ADR) or **American share.** A negotiable certificate, usually representing foreign securities deposited in an American bank for safekeeping, used for trading purposes in that security.

American rights. Subscription rights to buy additional American Depository Receipts, in representation of foreign stock shares. *See* **rights offering.**

American Stock Exchange (ASE) or **"Curb"** or **Amex.** A U.S. national exchange, founded in 1836, with 125 member firms presently. In recent years, it has specialized in trading options. There are 832 domestic issues and 64 foreign issues listed for trading, representing 771 companies. In the beginning, its brokers began trading securities along a street curb in New York City, hence the nickname "curb." It is a companion exchange with NASDAQ. Address: 86 Trinity Place, New York, NY 10006-1881. Telephone: (212) 306-1000. Fax: (212) 306-8376. *See* under **Global Investment Market**.

American warrants. Certificates that show evidence of subscription rights to additional American Depository Receipts.

Amex. Abbreviation for the **American Stock Exchange.**

Amex Index. A composite stock price index comprising all the shares listed on the American Stock Exchange.

amortization. 1) A financial program to systematically pay off the principal of a contractual obligation. 2) The allocation of a cost or charge to offset revenues in successive financial reporting periods until the total cost or charge is accounted for; or, the allocation of a portion of nonoperating profit or income in successive fiscal periods until the entire profit or income is accounted for. 3) **amortization, bond.** The apportionment to successive fiscal periods of the premium paid or discount received in purchasing a bond, thus more correctly reflecting the value of the net income accruing from the bond as its maturity draws nearer. Technically, a bond premium is amortized and a discount is accumulated, or accreted. Under the straight-line method of bond amortization, the discount or premium is spread evenly over the remaining term of the bond.

The premium or discount is divided by the remaining interest periods in determining the amortization amounts. In effect, these amounts are added to or subtracted from the bond investment account as the bond interest is adjusted by the amounts.

Amsterdam Stock Exchange—Amsterdam Effectenbeurs. A stock exchange in the Netherlands. Address: Beursplein 5, P.O. 19163, 1012 JW Amsterdam. Telephone: (31) 20 523 4567. *See* under **Global Investment Market**.

AMT. Abbreviation for **Alternate Minimum Tax.**

analysis, stock. A professional evaluation that leads to an opinion about the worth to investors of stock representing a company. It is based on the company's past and future profit-making ability, net asset value, and other business factors in relation to competitors in the same industry operating under similar economic conditions. The analysis can also be useful in appraising other securities issued by the company. In many cases, analysis adjusts the reported financial statements to accentuate a company's investment values and progress. An analysis is more of a memo than a document or sales piece, as is a stock report, but it is the core of the data and embodies an explanation of the investment professional's convictions about what course of action investors should take in regard to a stock issue. Often it is used internally or presented verbally. *See* **stock report.**

analyst, securities. An individual who practices securities analysis on a professional basis. *See* **Chartered Financial Analyst.**

anchoring. In applying the new discipline called behavioral economics to investing, the tendency of an investor to retain her original idea about a stock, say its earning power, even after events indicate this conviction is irrational.

"and accrued interest." See **plus accrued interest.**

Andean Pact. A trading bloc in South America comprised of Bolivia, Colombia, Ecuador, Peru, and Venezuela, with a total population of 72.5 million persons.

angel fund. An investment group, usually organized as a partnership or limited partnership, that invests Seed capital or beginning capital in start-up companies, usually in a technological sector such as providers of Internet products and services. Angel investors take a stake in less defined business plans than, say, venture capitalists and are known as "hand holders," until the fledgling is flying on its own. However, this financing concept is strictly short-term, often for less than a year. Early on they usually try to sell the idea to a full-fledged venture capital firm in exchange for an equity share. In essence, the angels are doing what friends and relatives often do—furnish capital and moral support for a great idea limited by a vague business plan. An angel fund can be thought of as a gateway to venture capital with permanent capital connections. *See* **venture capital fund.**

Annual Report Online. See **Annual Report to the Stockholders.**

Annual Report to the Securities and Exchange Commission. See **Form 10-K Filing.**

Annual Report to the Stockholders. A formal published report to the shareholders of a corporation by its top management, most prominently the Chairman, Chief Executive Officer (CEO), Chief Operating Officer (COO), and Chief Financial Officer (CFO), and tacitly approved by the board of directors, reflecting and commenting on the financial and operating progress of the enterprise during the most recent fiscal year. The report includes long-term aspects and, usually, audited financial statements and a message from both the chairman and chief executive officer—if that executive is a different person—and the chief operating officer. With the advent of the Internet, there are really three annual reports now: the hard copy printed version mailed to the stockholders and other interested parties, the SEC 10-K Filing, and the online version that appears on company home pages or on Web sites featuring annual reports as a series of links. From an investor's standpoint, there are several elements that an informative annual report should include. These examples are not exhaustive, certainly, but are a bare bones minimum. They are included in what the SEC requires in the 10-K, in some form. Also, language and style may vary in the stockholders' version and the online variety, but the information and data shown below should be present in wording or spirit. Look up the main elements in topic form elsewhere in this book. The important elements are as follows:

1. Auditor's Report or Statement with a message that the company's results are accurately reflected in the financial and operating statements, and if not, what the irregularities are.
2. Business Profile of the Company, including scope of operations, changes in markets served and nature of the competition;
3. Capital Stock Information, including price patterns over recent quarters, dividend policy, and restrictions on capital stock, if any;
4. Corporate Directory of Executive Officers and Directors of the corporation, sometimes including brief biographical sketches;
5. Financial and Operating Data, including two-year comparisons, when possible, of Balance Sheet, Income Statement,

Cash Flow Statement, Statement of Stockholders' Equity, and footnotes amplifying those statements;

6. Letter or Message to Stockholders, including a summary of operating experience of the company in the recent period;

7. Management's Discussion and Analysis (MD&A), including detailed recap of results and explanations for the past two years;

8. Pending Litigation or Contingencies—items that could affect the integrity of the financial statements or future prospects of the company, when applicable, information that is sometimes incorporated in the footnotes of the Financial and Operating Data;

9. Selected Financial and Operating Statistics for five to 10 years, when possible, so that historical comparisons can be made;

10. Stockholder Information, including information on time and place of annual meeting, the company's registrar and transfer agent—usually a bank that administers stock clerical matters—and information on how to obtain an annual report or 10-K report and the person to contact at the company regarding stockholder inquiries.

annuitant. The person who receives payments from an annuity contract, but not necessarily the owner of the contract. The owner of the contract could name another as beneficiary to receive payments, or the buyer of the contract could make the beneficiary also the owner. *See* **annuity.**

annuitize. To commence receiving a series of payments from the value accumulated in an annuity program. For example, upon retirement most investors can elect to receive a lump sum or periodic payments from the plan sponsor. The latter choice would be to annuitize the fund. *See* **annuity.**

annuity. An investment program in which an annuity underwriter makes one or a series of payments to a beneficiary or recipient, the annuitant, on specific date(s) under a contract, in consideration of receiving a sum or series of payments previously. The beneficiary can be the purchaser of the contract, who is usually the owner, or one whom that person designates. Sometimes this type of contract is called a guaranteed investment contract. It usually includes a death benefit but this feature varies with plans. The annuity landscape is broad and filled with many different programs. In this explanation, much has been simplified, in the interest of brevity and an overview understanding. For retirement planners, annuities are attractive because the income taxes from them is deferred until distributions begin. Technically, an annuity should not be considered an investment, because the principal is used up during the period of payments to the annuitant. On the contrary, investment capital is intended to be preserved, although this objective is usually not guaranteed, and sometimes is not even remotely likely. *Caveat Emptor!* Although there are many types of annuities, a popular contract in an investment context is one to finance a future education for a child, while the child is young. This would be called a deferred annuity.

Let's say two parents, Frankie and Johnny, forecast that they will need $40,000 for college expenses when their three-year-old son, Smarty, begins college in 15 years. How much of their dot-com mutual fund shares should they sell today in order to make a payment to the That's Life Insurance Co. to purchase an annuity contract which will pay them $40,000 when it reaches maturity in 15 years?

Suppose the actuaries at the insurance company assume the investment officers can invest the money for Frankie and Johnny (and millions more) at an 8.5% annual compounded interest rate. A "present value of one" formula could represent this plan, called an "annuity certain," as represented below. The plan would require the couple to sell shares worth $11,765 presently and purchase an annuity to accomplish their goal. The many annuity tables and computer and calculator programs that calculate various aspects of financial math—Present Value, Future Value, Interest Rate, and Time Period—make actually doing the math cumbersome today, so we need not dwell on that. Suffice it to say that what the investor is doing, in this case, is calculating what amount of money needed today, invested at 8.5%, will grow to $40,000 in 15 years.

In the interest of clarity, we have assumed that Frankie and Johnnie want a lump sum of $40,000 at the start of Smarty's college years. Realistically, they would probably elect to receive four equal payments, in the 15th, 16th, 17th, and 18th years of a contract, covering their son's college years. By electing installments, the couple could save $1,312, since the total initial payment, or annuitized amount for four years, decreases. This is because their money is earning interest longer.

How scientific is such a program? The $40,000 future college costs present considerable uncertainties over 15 years. But estimating such costs from a general inflation forecast would be a start. As to the assumed interest rate of 8.5%, the insurance guarantees the contract so it bears the risks. But the investor must ascertain that the insurance company is financially sound and able to pay the annuity, even if interest rates turn against it. Firms like A. M. Best & Co. and others rate insurance companies as to their abilities to meet their financial obligations. Most insurance agents and companies can provide investors with specific ratings as can industry analysts. If not, *Caveat Emptor!* Think of all the things that can happen to disrupt the continuity: wars, recessions, inflation, natural disasters, faulty management, and so on. Nevertheless, a respectable plan is better than apathy, and increases significantly your chances of success in financial endeavors. *See* **variable annuity.**

PRESENT VALUE FORMULA

$$PV = [\, 1 \div (1 + i)^n \,] \times FV$$

where:
PV = Payment for annuity;
i = Interest rate or .085;
n = Term or 15 years;
FV = Future value or expected college costs of $40,000
or

$PV = [\, 1 \div (1.085)^{15} \,] \times 40,000$ or
$PV = [\, 1 \div 3.4 \,] \times 40,000$ or
$PV = .294 \times 40,000$ or
$PV = \$11,765$

annuity, certain. An amount paid to an annuitant over a preset time period. The amount and dates of payments are guaranteed by the insurance company. If the annuitant dies before the contract matures, that person's beneficiary receives the remainder. *See* **annuity.**

"anti-advertising." A reference in general to ways to promote the use of products and services outside of traditional paid media advertising such as TV, newspapers, radio, and periodicals. Examples would be PR campaigns, sweepstakes, dot-com presentations, and personal promotions. These forms of marketing have grown in popularity as advertising rates in traditional formats have climbed rapidly, and there has emerged for distributors of products and services the need to reach niche markets.

anticipated by the market or **discounted by the market.** A reference to outcomes which are foreseen and acted upon by investors collectively so that present stock prices of related companies are affected rather than future ones. There is an insightful old saw about the stock market: "The market does not lie." Essentially, this means that the consensus of investor opinions will be correct about the outcome of a string of events as the outcome approaches, because of the constant adjustments that investors can make through buying and selling in the auction process. In academic circles, the effect is referred to as an efficient market. Thus, because investors can constantly change their opinions, there is a tendency for the market to anticipate future events.

For example, if a general upturn in business activity is expected, voluminous stock buying will generally drive prices upward from four to 10 months beforehand. For this reason, the Bureau of Economic Analysis (BEA) of the U.S. Department of Commerce officially considers stock prices one of the **leading economic indicators** of business activity in the United States. Reflecting on the fallibility of economic forecasting, however, is the waggish remark by detractors that the leading economic indicators have predicted five of the last three recessions.

WHAT THIS COUNTRY NEEDS!

Some Washington watchers attribute the following remark to President Harry S. Truman. The 33rd president became exasperated by the propensity of his economists to hedge their forecasts with the phrase, "On the other hand." Finally the no-nonsense President said with Missouri crispness, "What this country needs is more one-armed economists!"

---

antidilution provision. In the case of a convertible security, such as a warrant, share of preferred stock, or convertible debenture, a provision that protects the holders of such securities from losing their proportionate equity in the capital structure of a corporation if and when they convert the securities into common stock at a later date. This is accomplished by adjusting the conversion rate or price in proportion to the stock change. For example, suppose that when it was issued a $1,000 debenture including an antidilution provision could be converted into 50 shares of common stock, or at a conversion rate of $20 per share ($1,000 ÷ 50 = $20 share). Subsequently, the board of directors splits the stock 2-for-1. If no adjustment is made, the bondholder's equity would then be only $10 per share, because twice as many shares are outstanding. Therefore, the debenture conversion rate is halved to $10 per share, enabling the investor to receive 100 shares and $1,000 of equity per debenture as originally agreed. Usually, investors can count on such a provision, but it is important to check it out.

"antidumping" rules. See **"dumping."**

antitakeover or **poison pill strategy.** Any resolution passed by a board of directors designed to thwart efforts by outside parties to gain corporate control through stock purchases and consequently vote themselves or their allies to the board. Such measures usually call for the issuance of additional stock to existing shareholders, who are presumably friendly to current management. In effect, this strategy prevents the outside investors from ever being able to gain control of the corporation and oust current management, whom they might consider ineffective. By the same token, such a strategy might prevent corporate raiders from gaining control of the corporation and using its resources for their own selfish interests. A more extreme version is the dead-hand poison pill, which can only be revoked by the board that created it. In recent years, several institutional investors have engaged in corporate politics in an effort to eliminate such strategies from corporate governance. In Delaware, where many large corporations are chartered, courts have recently declared these strategies illegal.

Anti-trust Immunity. A government's promise not to charge members of an industry with anti-monopoly or anti-trust violations, even though the latter are sharing information in a way that makes them less competitive. The government's purpose usually is to protect or economically aid a vital industry which might be weakened without the immunity. *See* **airline alliances.**

anti-trust laws. U.S. laws, including the Sherman Act (1980), the Clayton Act (1914), and the Robinson Patman Act (1936), with numerous amendments, which make illegal the restraint of trade between states, and also, prevent interlocking directorates, price-cutting to freeze out competition, exclusive selling contracts, and charging different prices to customers. These laws are administered by the Antitrust Division of the United States Department of Justice in Washington, D.C. There has often been criticism over applying these laws, which were designed for "smokestack" America, to the electronic age now unfolding. In recent years, the Justice Department has placed a greater emphasis on protecting the consumer from price increases in implementing these laws, rather than preventing price gouging as a result of monopolistic practices. When a company dominates 70% of a market, it is considered to be vulnerable to the anti-trust laws.

"apocalypse stocks." Stocks representing equities in companies that could benefit or suffer from a global catastrophic event. Before you pooh-pooh this idea as too callous, know that there are actually public stocks available in these areas and that from time to time they are recommended by those gentle captains of Wall Street. Investors who buy these might be called clinically-depressed bears, but it takes all kinds to make a market. Here are some macabre examples.

- For investing in germ warfare, buy stocks making respiratory products
- For investing in a meteorite striking earth, buy meteorite insurance
- For investing in a nuclear accident, buy nuclear risk insurance and eye protection companies

Applied Science Stocks. Those stocks representing companies engaged in the manufacture of products resulting from scientific research and development. *See* **industry stock group.**

appraisal rights. In the case of a merger or acquisition, the rights of the shareholders of the company being acquired, or the target company, to establish the fair market value of their shares. Sometimes they must settle the matter in a court of law. Often the higher price makes the effort worthwhile, however.

a priori. In a statistical business model, the use of prior events as a basis for forecasting a future event. For example, an equation that correlated the level of a stock market index in the current year, the dependent variable, with corporate profits in the preceding year, the independent variable, would be based on a priori reasoning. This association between the two variables would be a lead-lag relationship.

arb. See **arbitrageur.**

arbitrage. 1) The simultaneous buying of securities on one exchange and selling them on another at a price advantage. For instance, a trader might suspect that after the close of the New York Stock Exchange, Hoopla, Inc. is going to issue a blockbuster announcement that it will open a chain of stores featuring sports shoes called Rooks for chess players. Fully expecting the big news to create incremental buying of Hoopla shares, the trader buys 1,000 shares on the NYSE for $5 per share and then sells it on the Pacific Coast Exchange, which is open three hours later, for $6 per share, making a nifty $1,000 profit. 2) The buying of a security currently convertible into another one or a derivative at a price advantage, because the former is selling for less than the latter on an equivalent basis. For example, an arbitrageur might buy a convertible debenture of Jason's Basins, Inc., convertible into 100 shares of common stock or at $10 per share, for $1,000 and sell 100 shares of the stock for $12 per share. She could convert the debenture to stock to make delivery on the sale. Her trading profit would be $2 per share, or $200 ($12 – $10 × 100 shares). *See* **derivatives.**

arbitrageur or **arb.** A professional trader who engages in arbitrage.

arbitration. The settlement of business disputes between investors and brokers by a panel of generally three impartial members, usually mandated by an agreement effected when an investor opens an account. Findings are binding on both parties and generally are issued within one year. Although broker associations administer proceedings, rules of arbitration are approved by the Securities and Exchange Commission.

Archipelago. A reference to what is called by organizers the first electronic stock market in the United States, created by the combination of the Archipelago company, an electronic trading network, and the Pacific Exchange, fourth busiest stock exchange in the United States in securities volume, into a new corporation. Pacific Exchange will own 10% of the new entity. The exchange will trade securities listed by New York Stock Exchange, NASDAQ, and American Stock Exchange.

arithmetic mean. An average or typical value that tends to describe a set of data, giving an equal weighting to each item in the data set. Due to its ease of computation, this is the best known and most popular of the averages used in business and finance.

Here's how you can use it. Suppose a stock you have your eye on has increased earnings per share over the past five years as follows: + 5%, + 7.5%, + 9.7%, – 3.2%, + 12.9%. What has the average gain been? Substituting: (5 + 7.5 + 9.7 – 3.2 + 12.9) ÷ 5 = 6.4% average earnings increase per year. As you can See, no year is considered more important than the others in the computation. *See* **geometric mean** and **weighted mean.**

Arizona Corporation Commission, Securities Division. Regulator of securities laws in the state of Arizona. Address: 1300 West Washington, 3rd Floor, Phoenix, AZ 85007. Telephone: (602) 542-4242.

Arkansas Securities Department. Regulator of securities laws in the state of Arkansas. Address: Heritage West Building, 201 East Markham, 3rd Floor, Little Rock, AR 72201.

Arizona Stock Exchange. A national stock exchange in the United States, operated as an electronic auction market. All stocks listed on the NASDAQ National Market and national stock exchanges are traded. Address: 2800 N. Central Avenue, #1230, Phoenix, AZ 85004. Phone: (602) 222-5858. *See* under **Global Investment Market**.

ARM. See **Adjustable Rate Mortgage.**

ARMS Index. A short-term traders' index, consisting of the average volume of issues declining in price divided by the average volume of issues rising in price. The index is calculated for the NYSE, the AMEX, and the NASDAQ markets individually. When the quotient is under 1.0, it indicates the market action is predominately in stocks rising in value. When over 1.0, it indicates the market interest is focused on stocks declining in value. This could also be called a bull-versus-bear index.

arms-length transaction. A transaction between two or more parties in which the parties have no economic interest in the outcome for each other. It is a timely concept when it is important to avoid the appearance of a conflict of interests. For example, when the CEO of a company wants to sell a company asset to his kid brother, who is the CEO of a business rival, he could procure the services of an independent broker to sell the asset after ascertaining a fair price and terms. In this way, the seller could avoid a charge of a conflict of interest from his board of directors.

ARMS Securities. Abbreviation for adjustable-rate mortgage securities. These are securities representing a proportionate ownership in a package of adjustable rate residential mortgages. Although the securities are backed by the collateral values of the real estate, the yields can fluctuate due to the adjustable nature of the underlying mortgage payments.

arrearage. The amount of money by which a security that is contracted to make distributions, such as a bond, or morally committed to pay, such as a preferred stock, is behind on the amounts of the payments. This condition can cause bonds to be in default and in the case of cumulative preferred stock can restrict dividends on the issuing company's common stock. In some cases, other restrictions can be activated, such as a restriction on borrowing money when arrearage exists.

Articles of Incorporation. The initial and basic document in the pathway leading to the creation of a corporation. In effect, it is a petition to the government of a state, usually to its secretary of state, in which the founders request that they be allowed to establish a corporate entity domiciled in that state. Included in the articles are the name of the business enterprise, although corporations exist for nonbusiness purposes also; the address; the purpose of the enterprise; the number and type of authorized shares; and the names of the directors. If the state approves the articles, it issues the founders a Certificate of Incorporation (after verifying that the check for the incorporation fee clears the bank). These two documents comprise the corporate charter, a state's inherent prerogative. After incorporation, the founders draw up the Corporate Bylaws, which outline the internal management procedures to be followed, and the board of directors approves them.

ascending triangle. See **price patterns.**

ascending wedge. See **price patterns.**

ASE. Abbreviation for **American Stock Exchange.**

Asian Development Bank. An economic development financial institution whose capital stock is owned by 40 member countries in the Asian and Pacific regions of the world and 16 outside the region. The bank began operations in 1966 and was reorganized in 1995. Besides loans, the bank makes equity investments and promotes investment of public and private capital for developmental purposes. Special attention is given to the needs of the smaller or less-developed states, although consideration is given to the overall development of a region. The bank borrows funds for its operations from world capital markets. Address: 6 ADB Avenue, Mandayulong 0401 Metro Manila, Philippines. Telephone: (632) 632-4444. Fax: (632) 636-2444. E-mail: www@mail.asiandevbank.org. Web site: *www.asiandev bank.org/index.html.*

Asian dragons. A group of countries in Asia that have shown dramatic economic growth since World War II, especially in the 1980s and 1990s, based on aggressive risk-taking, low wages, a hard-work ethic, political and financial patronage, and aggressive marketing worldwide. The group includes China, Indonesia, Malaysia, Japan, the Philippines, South Korea, and Thailand. Hong Kong is also sometimes included. However, in late 1997 overextended debts accompanied by faltering foreign exchange rates for their currencies created global financial panic that caused investors who sustained heavy stock market losses to change their tunes about each of these economies from "Puff, the Magic Dragon" to "Tuff!, the Tragic Dragon."

Asian (financial) flu or "yellow fever." The turmoil in worldwide securities markets caused by the financial problems in Asia, especially among the Asian dragons, in the late 1990s.

asked price. See **offer.**

assessable security. A reference to a security that can obligate its holders to pay a charge or assessment for certain financial obligations of the issuing company. In certain cases, common stock of banks and insurance companies fall into this category. However, in realistic terms, when such a vital institution runs into financial problems, regulators move swiftly to merge that company into a stronger one or reach some other solution.

asset. A valuable resource (physical or intellectual) that represents short-term value or long-term value. It can be a piece of equipment, property and plant, legal right, cash, or a near-cash item owned by a business enterprise. In its broadest sense, the asset is currently used or being held to make money in the normal course of business. Usually, the value of an asset is estimated at the face value, in the case of financial instruments, or at market value, or it is carried at the original cost less depreciation or depletion reductions, in the case of long-term items, on financial reports. When assets have been owned for several years, their stated or book values can be misleading. This is so because price inflation or deflation or technical obsolescence may have changed the worth of the asset, yet this is not reflected in the carried value. You might call such an asset's carried value "virtual reality." *See* **admitted asset, Balance Sheet, hard asset,** and **soft asset.**

asset accretion or **resource accretion.** The enhancement in value of a company's resources through expansion, acquisition, or natural growth, such as in the aging of wines or whiskies for sale in the future.

asset allocation. In managing an investment operation, the selection of resources such as securities to reflect the objectives and risk tolerance of the program. Periodic cash flow requirements, principal stability and growth, and asset remainder are key elements to consider as investments are selected with probabilities of fulfilling the objectives.

A rule of thumb for allocating the asset mix in a retirement account is to subtract the retiree's age from 100 to get the percentage of the total amount for common stock investments. For example, when Fred Fearless is 30, he would invest 70% in common stocks for retirement $(100 - 30 = 70\%)$; when 50, he would invest 50% $(100 - 50 = 50\%)$, and when 63, he would invest 37%. The idea here is that retirement resources should be in less risky or less volatile assets, and probably in more income-bearing assets, the closer retirement is. When a person is in prime working years, she can make adjustments in earning power to adjust for changing living expenses; but, when she is retired, her retirement assets are less flexible as to the value base, while she is more likely to incur the less predictable expenses of aging.

asset allocation, rule of thumb for. See **asset allocation.**

asset-backed securities (ABS). Securities offering packaged loans or accounts receivable for investment income and as collateral for the principal. Examples are notes backed by a batch of consumer sales contracts, such as automobile installment loans originally generated by banks. In mid-1999, bonds of this type amounted to $700 million, 5.0% of the total bond debt in the United States.

asset management account. An omnibus account at a financial institution, combining banking and investment services, in which the owner may deposit money, write checks, make credit card charges, use debit cards, and buy and sell securities, including the use of margin loans. In addition, a customer receives a monthly statement, showing activity in the account.

asset play. A reference to a stock that is attractive because of the value of the underlying assets, rather than operating prospects such as growing markets, reduced costs, or technological developments. In effect, a bona fide asset play means an investor is able to buy a share of stock with an intrinsic value greater than its current market price. For example, assume the Drilling for Dollars Oil Company shows its unproved properties, purchased five years ago, at their original cost. Since that time, an oil and gas boom has engulfed the region in which they are located. Consequently, the company is receiving bids daily worth many times more per acre than the books indicate they are worth. This discrepancy might result in making the stock's real value or breakup value more than its stock market price.

asset protection trust. A trust instrument created to protect a person's assets from legal judgments and divorce decrees, sited in certain offshore jurisdictions like the Cook Islands in the South Pacific and Nevis in the Caribbean Sea, because they allow the creators of trusts also to be the beneficiaries.

asset value per common share. In securities analysis, a reference to the worth of a common share in terms of monetary equivalence. It is calculated by adding total assets, subtracting liabilities and the liquidating values of preferred stocks and other securities senior to the common stock, and dividing the remainder by the number of shares outstanding, less treasury shares. This valuation is usually compared to the stock's market price to get an idea of how realistic the market price is. Suppose that on Big Bucks Corporation's balance sheet, total assets amount to $100 million and total liabilities (not including stockholders' equity) to $50 million, with no senior equity securities. There are 10 million shares outstanding, net of treasury stock. The asset value per share is $5 ($100,000,000 − $50,000,000) ÷ 10,000,000 shares.

assign. To sign a document as an owner of personal or real property (assignor), such as a stock certificate, indicating its transfer to a new owner or owners [assignee(s)].

assignment. In the trading of derivatives, the notice to the issuer or seller of an option that the holder or buyer has exercised his right under the option agreement to buy or sell the underlying security at the specific **strike price.**

associate membership. A special category of membership on some exchanges that allows nonmember investment firms to share in trading commissions on orders traded by members of that exchange. Sometimes limited trading privileges are also granted. The New York Stock Exchange has no associate memberships.

Association for the Taxation of Financial Transactions for the Aid of Citizens (ATTAC). An organization, predominantly in the countries of western Europe, that espouses a tax on foreign currency and international financial transactions within the European Union to insure that booming trade globalization benefits citizens in general. Although the tax, called a "Tobin tax," on financial transactions would be distributed for the common good, James Tobin, the American economist who first proposed such a tax, originally advocated the levy as a way to rein in rampant foreign exchange speculation. To be effective, the tax would need to be unanimously applicable to transactions in multiple currencies, since the omission of one or more would draw all trading to such places.

Association of Investment Management and Research (AIMR). A professional organization of more than 30,000 securities analysts, portfolio managers, strategists, academics, consultants, and other investment specialists in 70 countries, with a mission of serving its members and investors through education and sustaining high standards of professional ethics and conduct. Address: 5 Boar's Head Lane, Charlottesville, VA 22903. Telephone: (804) 980-3668. Web site: *www.aimr.org.*

Association of Stock Exchange Firms. An association of investment firms and individuals holding seats on the New York Stock Exchange.

"at a discount." A phrase describing: 1) A bond or share of preferred stock selling beneath its liquidation value. 2) A closed-end investment company or mutual fund share selling beneath its asset value. 3) A common stock share selling beneath its asset value or breakup value. 4) A convertible debenture or share of preferred stock selling for less than its conversion value, usually because investors are pessimistic about the outlook for the stock obtainable under the conversion privilege. In that case, the typically lower interest or dividend rate, because there is an **equity kicker,** is forcing the price down and yield up. Investors are concentrating on income from interest payments or dividend distributions rather than growth from equity participation for the present.

"at a premium." A phrase describing: 1) A bond or share of preferred stock selling above its par or liquidation value. 2) A closed-end investment company or mutual fund share selling above its asset value. 3) A common stock share selling above its asset value or breakup values. 4) A convertible debenture or share of preferred stock selling above its conversion value, usually because investors are optimistic about the outlook for the stock obtainable under its conversion privilege. Even though the interest or dividend yield is lower, the **equity kicker** has raised the price of the security. Investors are concentrating on the equity potential.

Athens Stock Exchange. A stock exchange in Athens, Greece. Address: 10 Sophocleous Street, Athens 10559. *See* under **Global Investment Market**.

ATI. Abbreviation for **Anti-trust Immunity.**

ATTAC. See **Association for the Taxation of Financial Transactions for the Aid of Citizens.**

at the close order. A reference to a securities market order that must be executed in its entirety at the closing price or the order is canceled.

at the market. An order to buy or sell a specified quantity of securities at whatever price is prevailing when the order reaches the place of trading.

at the money. An option contract in which the strike or exercise price of the underlying security is equal to its current trading price.

at the opening market order. A reference to a securities market or limit order that must be executed in its entirety at the opening price or the order is canceled.

auction contest. The opening up of a buyout effort by one buyer to all interested parties, usually at the invitation of the target company's management, who have accepted the inevitability of a buyout and want to get the highest price.

auction market. A specific place (exchange) where certain securities are traded by public bids to buy and offers to sell securities, under established procedures and rules, through brokers acting both as commissioned agents and independent businessmen. With the advent of the Internet, there is a growing electronic stock market—a virtual stock exchange, if you will—but the SEC does not recognize it as an official exchange. That will likely change. *See* **exchanges.**

auction rate preferred stock or **Dutch auction preferred stock** or **money market preferred stock.** A preferred stock issue on which the dividend is variable, and the dividend is established every seven weeks by bids in a **Dutch auction** on shares face-valued between $100,000 and $500,000.

audit trail. A sequential record of how a corporate transaction is accounted for or entered in the books, from the initial entries to the final ones. Using this path, any transaction can be traced to its source for verification purposes.

audited books. Those financial statements verified as to accuracy by professional accountants, using generally accepted standards. A statement to that effect, when appropriate, appears with financial documents that have been so audited. Although most companies employ internal auditors who attempt to encourage the use of acceptable accounting methods, the real responsibility of presenting full disclosure to investors rests with the outside auditors. They base their audits on sampling technique of the corporate accounts, in most cases.

The auditing procedure is a contentious one today because corporate management hires the outside auditors, which means it can also fire them for reaching conclusions about the condition of the enterprise not acceptable to or hostile toward management. Under present business conditions, it is unclear for whom the outside auditors work: managers, stockholders, or the investment public at large. Recent legal decisions seem to favor the stockholders, however. But there is no doubt who pays the auditors—corporate management, who want to look good to stockholders.

Key parties who rely on audited financial documents—managers, stockholders, analysts, investors, and so on—have been instrumental in creating the **Financial Accounting Standards Board** (FASB, pronounced "Fazbee"), which considers various accounting alternatives and sets down accounting guidelines for all accountants to adhere to in auditing books and preparing financial statements. The Securities Exchange Commission recognizes standards adopted by the FASB as appropriate. The board walks a narrow line between satisfying management, who generally want reports to reflect their glorious accomplishments, and investment professionals, who want reports to tell it like it is—at least, as long as they have a financial interest. The result has been that certain critical procedures in reporting are left optional by the board, which causes some confusion and hardship. Accounting fraud cases account for 67% of securities law suits. *See* **independence of auditors.**

Auditor's Statement in Annual Report. A brief statement by a company's outside, independent auditor that the company's results are accurately reflected in the financial and operating statements of the company, according to generally accepted accounting procedures, or if not, what the nature of the irregularities are. *See* **audited books.**

"Aunt Millie." A slightly derisive phrase referring to a public buyer of stock who owns only a few stock shares and does not trade regularly, as compared to more sophisticated institutional investors, brokerage professionals, active semiprofessionals, and traders.

AUSDAQ. An electronic trading system in Australia, operated much like the NASDAQ system in the United States.

Australian Stock Exchange. See under **Global Investment Market.**

Authority Bond. A type of bond that is issued to raise money to construct and develop some public project that has been authorized by a state legislature. Usually, the project takes the form of a corporation or government agency. Revenues from the use of the project's facilities are expected to pay the bond interest and principal when due. Most ports and airports in big cities are financed by this type bond. It is very similar to a revenue bond, because of its narrow source of revenues. Bonds providing the greatest bondholder security are those where the legislature has given bondholders special protection.

Authorization/Signature(s) Agreement, Brokerage. The last section of the application form to open a brokerage account, in which the applicant agrees to the general conditions of maintaining and trading in an account. This includes the concurrence to settle certain disputes by arbitration as referenced in the Customer Agreement. *See* **Account (Brokerage), Customer Agreement (Brokerage),** and **Margin Agreement/Loan Consent (Brokerage).**

authorized stock. The number of shares, representing units of fractional ownership in a corporation, that a corporation can legally issue to investors or others, usually in order to raise capital to carry on the corporate business. That number is established in the company's corporate charter and can be adjusted by amending the charter in the state of incorporation. Authorized stock should not be confused with **outstanding stock.** The latter is the number of shares that the corporation has actually placed in the hands of investors or others, through a public or private offering or a special presentation of stock. A corporation usually stipulates in its charter more shares than are immediately needed for distribution, in order to be prepared for a merger opportunity, or some other special opportunity, in which the stock would be useful.

automatic common exchange securities. Debt securities linked to the price of a company's common stock, although not necessarily the common stock of the debt issuer. The debt holder can usually exchange the debt for a specific number of the common shares or an equivalent cash value at maturity. As the collateralized common stock price rises, the carrying value of the debt liability is increased on the issuer's books to reflect the current value of the common stock, either in cash or exchanged common stock. It is good accounting practice for the issuer to account for the increased debt liability as unrealized charges to current income.

automatic investment plan. A program that allows an investor to accumulate and/or withdraw money automatically. Often, these plans can save an investor money, since the company sponsoring the plan does not need to spend additional time in the decision processes. In addition, some plans allow participants to withdraw specific amounts at regular intervals. This feature is useful for retirees. Basically, these plans are available through the following sponsors:

1. Payroll deductions by employers and purchase of U.S. Savings Bonds. *See* **Series E Savings Bond.**
2. Payroll deductions by employers or self-employed in defined contribution IRA plans and use of money to purchase various investment fund shares. Company plans are known as 401(k) plans, self-employed plans are Keoghs, nonprofit and educational plans are 403(k)s and federal and other government plans are 457s. Sometimes employers match employee contributions to these plans. *See* **Individual Retirement Accounts.**
3. Dividend reinvestment plans or DRIPS offered to shareholders by corporations, usually at price discounts and other savings. *See* **Dividend Reinvestment Plan.**
4. Dividend and capital gains reinvestment programs offered by mutual funds. *See* **mutual fund.**
5. Debit of a specific amount from a savings or checking account and purchase of mutual fund shares on a regular basis. *See* **mutual fund.**

Auto Parts. Those stocks representing companies engaged in the manufacturer of replacement parts for the automotive industry. *See* **industry stock group.**

Autos or **Automotives.** Those stocks representing companies engaged in the manufacture of automobiles and trucks, generally light trucks. *See* **industry stock group.**

available short stock. Shares of stock that an investor may borrow from her broker to make delivery on a short sale. It is a broker's responsibility to find out if stock is available for borrowing before completing a short sale.

average cost. The arithmetic mean or average price an investor pays for several shares of stock bought at different times.

average deviation or **mean deviation.** In statistics or in measuring the volatility of stock prices, the calculation of the average dispersion or scatter about the central tendency of the price changes for one or more stocks. It is used in measuring the risk of selected stocks, as measured by their volatility. For the preferred measure of risk, *see* **standard deviation.** *See* **range, variance,** and **volatility.**

average down. To buy desired stock shares whenever the price drops, thus lowering the average cost over time.

Average Duration of Unemployment. See **Economic Indicators.**

average number of shares outstanding. A phrase indicating that the earnings per share of a common stock are based on the average number of shares outstanding during the fiscal year, rather than the actual number at year-end. Generally, this average is used in a company's financial reporting and is calculated because scenarios such as a new stock issue at the end of a fiscal year would distort realistic earnings per share by making them appear too small. This could occur because the return on capital from the new stock issue would not be given ample time to impact earnings in proportion to the increase in shares.

For example, assume Jason's Basins Corp., the premier maker of hot tubs that boldly advertises, "No investor takes a cold bath in our tubs," reports net earnings at the end of its fiscal year ending December 31 of $3,000,000. Furthermore, the company sold 500,000 shares of new common stock on November 1 for $12.50 per share, or a total of $6,250,000, resulting in 2,500,000 shares outstanding on December 31. That means the company would report $1.20 per share ($3,000,000 / 2,500,000), based on the actual shares outstanding at the close of the current fiscal year. Last year the company earned $2,500,000 or $1.25 per share, based on 2,000,000 shares outstanding.

Obviously, this procedure can lead to a distortion, since the $6,250,000 of new capital, less underwriter's fees, has not been used meaningfully in establishing results for the latest fiscal year. Let us say, in a spirit of magnanimity, that Jason's management regularly earns a return on equity of 15%. In a full year of its use, the $6,250,000 capital infusion could earn $937,500 or $0.38 per share.

The lack of opportunity to generate such earnings is the problem we are addressing. The manifestation of the distortion appears in the illusion that earnings per share have declined from one year to the next, whereas, in effect, the additional shares have caused the apparent decline. Adjusting each year for the average number of shares outstanding partially corrects the distortion and enables a more realistic inquiry into the investment success of the corporation. A weighted average is used, and the time-weighted shares of 2,083,333 obtained is divided into the $3,000,000 net income, producing adjusted earnings of $1.44 per share. This is $0.19 or 15.2% over the prior year, and a much fairer presentation of results.

Average Prime Rate. See **Economic Indicators.**

average, statistical. The average concept is one of the most important in the business of investing. It represents a typical value that tends to describe or quantify a group or universe of data. Additionally, it provides a basis for interpreting extreme or extraordinary data. It is a measure of the value of a central tendency in a group. The most important averaging techniques are: the arithmetic mean, the median, the mode, the geometric mean, and the quadratic mean. The weighted average is a refinement of the arithmetic mean. There is much controversy about which averaging techniques to use. Even statisticians disagree. Most investors use the arithmetic mean, because it is the simplest to construct. The extreme values are generally eliminated, which is a problem if there are many of them. The median is also simple to construct, and the extreme values do not distort the central tendency so much. The mode is also less affected by extremes and can be estimated by inspection. But it is limited when the number of data points grows large. The geometric mean tends to minimize extreme values, but it is relatively difficult to compute and not used often. The quadratic mean embodies many effective characteristics, but it is also relatively difficult to calculate. *See* **weighting.**

average, stock. See **stock averages.**

average up. To sell shares of a stock in which a liquidation of all of the stock is planned ultimately, by selling whenever its price rises, and thus raising the average realization.

Average Weekly Claims, Unemployment Insurance. See **Economic Indicators.**

Average Weekly Hours, Manufacturing. See **Economic Indicators.**

average yield to maturity. The arithmetic mean of annual yields on a bond from the time of an investor's purchase to the maturity date. The purchase discount, or premium, is accumulated, or amortized, over the remaining life of the bond in figuring the yield. For example, suppose an investor buys a $1,000 bond for $950 that pays $50 or 5% annually in semi-annually interest payments, having five years until maturity. In computing each annual yield, 20% of the $50 discount, representing one-fifth of the remaining bond life until maturity, is accumulated to the $950 purchase price, so that the first year annual yield is $50 divided by $960 or 5.21%. In the second year after purchase, the $50 discount is divided by $970 for a 5.15% yield, and so on until $50 is divided by $1,000 to yield 5.00%, in the last year. Then the yields are divided by five to calculate the average yield to maturity. *See* **amortization.**

averaging. See **dollar cost averaging.**

"away from." A phrase in reference to a security's price that is a specific amount greater or lesser than a basis price. For example, an odd-lot price is executed ⅛ or ¼ away from the following round-lot price.

Bb

"B" shares. Mutual fund shares that carry no front-end sales load but do charge commissions and higher annual management fees than "A" shares do. Typically, these shares have redemption charges if they are liquidated within six to eight years. Brokers receive bigger sales commissions—usually 3% to 4%—from selling big-dollar amounts of these shares to customers than front-end charges would represent, because they do not discount the commissions for sizable purchases of the shares, as is done in the case of "A" shares carrying front-end loads. In one representative fund, the sales load starts at 5.25% for a $5,000 investment but drops to 3% at $100,000 and more as the amounts get larger. *See* **break points.**

B2B stocks. See **business-to-business stocks.**

B2C stocks. See **business-to-customer stocks.**

Baby Bells. A reference to the seven regional operating companies that American Telephone & Telegraph (AT&T) was required to divest itself of under a U.S. Circuit Court consent decree in 1984 connected with an antitrust legal suit. Originally, the seven companies had exclusive rights to offer local telephone service in their respective geographic regions of the United States but could not enter long-distance markets or manufacture communications equipment. The original parent, AT&T, was precluded from entering local markets. However, with passage of the Telecommunications Act of 1996, the court order was modified by allowing the seven to enter long-distance markets and AT&T and other long-distance carriers, such as WorldCom/MCI and Sprint, to provide local services. The original seven have been reduced to four, with the mergers of Bell Atlantic (mid-Atlantic states) and Verizon (Northeastern states); SBC (Southwestern states) and Pacific Telesis (Western states) and Ameritech (Midwestern States). The other two Baby Bells are BellSouth (Southern states) and U.S. West (Rocky Mountain States).

Baby Boomers. That generation of Americans, who were born between 1946 and 1964, the dynamic post-WWII years in America. After the war, the pent-up desires for family formations generated the births of 75.8 million Americans. These citizens are now passing through their most productive years and are exerting record amounts of investment activity. The investment ethos will continue strong, because as they continue through their peak earning years they are concerned about retirement and are stashing huge sums of money into retirement IRAs, (k) Plans, Keogh Plans, annuities, and other investment packages. The effect is expected to energize investment activity for the next 25 years.

baby bonds. Bonds representing debt of less than $1,000, usually with a face value of $100. For quoting information, See **quote (2).**

back-testing. See **data mining.**

backing and filling. A phrase describing a quick upturn of market prices followed by a gradual decline toward starting levels as buyers lose some but not all of their interest in stocks.

"bad boy" clause. A reference to a provision in an agreement with a top executive of an organization that states that any special financial favors promised to that person, such as in a **"top hat" pension plan,** will be canceled in the event that she or he commits some act, such as a felony.

balance of payments. An economic arrangement for showing movements of currencies, capital, and gold, or other reserve resources between countries, in settlement of their transactions with one another during a specific period, usually a year. There are three types of balance of payment accounts: current, capital, and gold. Any of these can reflect a surplus or deficit, but a country's overall payments can still be in balance, since that is the objective of the system. It is like a corporation's Source and Applications of Funds Statement in this respect: It explains how operations were financed. The current account includes transactions of goods and services, the capital account represents investments, and the gold account includes movements of gold.

An analysis of a country's balance of payments is indicative of its relative financial status in the international community, and can often foretell the future direction of its currency's foreign exchange value and its interest rates. If a country is running a negative current account—importing more goods and services than it is exporting—and settling this deficit with gold shipments, it is only a matter of time until its gold reserve is precariously low, a situation that will impair the country's ability to continue importing. However, if its leaders and businessmen can induce foreigners to invest in their industries, thereby transferring scarce foreign reserves to that country, the country can "balance its payments," and possibly continue importing excessively. This illustrates why the overall balance of payments must be analyzed to draw inferences about a country's status. Of course, this balancing strategy is the scenario recommended to a developing country. Even so, a country balancing its payments with gold or capital is operating on borrowed time, economically. *See* **balance of trade.**

balance of trade. A country's surplus or deficit in the trading of its output of goods and services among foreign countries. Generally, it is desirable that a country maintain a positive or favorable balance of trade and services, meaning that it exports goods and services more valuable than those it imports in a period. The opposite situation is a negative or unfavorable trade balance. The prime calculation is made on transactions involving manufactured or processed goods or natural resources—automobiles, computers, telecommunications switch gear, oil, and so on. Technically, that is the balance of trade basis. But of equal and growing importance in the measure of international trade is the export and import of services—banking, brokerage, insurance, and others. It is the net trading balance between the total of physical goods and useful services that determines a nation's financial condition internationally.

When a nation maintains a positive trade balance, its currency is in high demand. This tends to enhance that currency's exchange rate and lower borrowing rates. Its output is popular, so traders want its currency. For the same reason, investors want its debt issues. On the other hand, when a country maintains a negative or unfavorable balance of trade, the exchange rate of its currency is depressed and its borrowing rates are high. After all, that country has flooded foreign exchange markets with its currency because it buys so much relative to what it sells, and it probably has borrowed a great deal, so its interest rates are high. Basically, international traders do not want anymore of that currency in any form. However, keep in mind that Lower Transylvania can import twice as much value in goods as it exports, but export three times as much value in services as the goods represent, and have a favorable overall balance of trade and international financial position.

Balance Sheet or **Statement of Financial Condition.** A detailed statement of the financial condition of a business enterprise at the close of a fiscal period, showing the components of assets, liabilities, equity capitalization, and net worth or stockholders' equity. The eventual object of the balance sheet is to measure a company's financial worth by an arrangement that subtracts liabilities from assets to calculate the net worth, or negative net worth in certain cases, as a rough indication of its value in monetary terms. However, this should be considered only an approximation, since assets are usually carried at depreciated, depleted, or amortized book values rather than market values, and debt indentures are not always fully described or are described only in the footnotes. There are also items like stock warrants and options, which only show up in the footnotes but which bear on the financial condition. Actually, the footnotes are nearly as important as the main body of the balance sheet, because many of the controversial accounting treatments are described there.

An apt metaphor for the balance sheet is that it is a snapshot of a company's financial condition at a moment in time. It is one of the four financial documents that regularly appear in corporate annual reports, and often in their interim statements. There are two formats used in preparing balance sheets—the account form and the report form. In the account form, which is the most popular, assets are presented on the left side of the page and liabilities and owners' equity on the right. In the report form, current assets appear at the top of the page with current liabilities directly below and subtracted and owners' equity next, in a columnar form. *See* **Cash Flow Statement, Income Statement,** and **Statement of Shareholders' Equity.**

Balance Sheet Leverage. See **Financial Leverage.**

balanced budget. A program of planned cash outlays balanced by cash receipts during a fiscal period. *See* **capital budget** and **operating budget.**

balanced fund. A mutual fund owning a portfolio of both growth and conservative securities, usually consisting of common stocks for growth and preferred stock and bonds for income and conservatism.

balanced investing. The maintenance of a predetermined relationship among security values in a portfolio by constantly selling those overvalued and buying others undervalued. For example, if a portfolio were balanced between 50% bonds and 50% common stock, and stock values reached 70%, enough stock would be sold and reinvested in bonds to restore the 50-50 balance.

balloon. A final payment on a debt instrument, such as a bond or mortgage, that is larger than the others in the debt service schedule. This is arranged between the lender and the borrower when the borrower is expecting an unusually large cash inflow at the end of the amortization period or when the borrower intends to refinance the loan balance. A loan that includes a balloon payment is often called a partially amortized loan.

balloon interest. The higher interest rate applying to the portion of serial bonds that matures late in the repayment schedule.

balloon maturity. A reference to a bond issue or other long-term debt, in which larger amounts of interest are due in the final years of the repayment schedule.

ballpark figure. An estimate of a stock's financial prospects, such as earnings expectations, based on preliminary information or incomplete data.

bang for the buck, more. An expression meaning that the purchase of a certain stock generates more investment leverage than many others. It can be a reference to characteristics like a stock's greater income stream or greater exposure to a business that is currently hot. In essence it suggests that the stock should produce a greater investment return than other ones being considered. For example, a stock giving investors a 5% yield and a high growth P/E multiple gives more bang for the buck than a stock with an equal P/E multiple but no dividend.

bank discount basis. See **discount yield.**

Bank Holding Company Act of 1956. A federal act, amended in 1966, 1970, and 1999, that established a barrier between commercial banking, securities underwriting, and insurance underwriting in response to aggressive acquisitions and expansion by TransAmerica Corp. Congress believed the possibility of underwriting losses was too risky for banks. Under this law, a bank holding company that owns two or more banks or other bank holding companies must register with the Board of Governors of the Federal Reserve System. Thereafter, it is called a registered bank holding company. This act was amended by the Financial Service Modernization Act of 1999. *See* **Financial Service Modernization Act of 1999** and **Glass-Steagall Act.**

bank holding company. See **Bank Holding Company Act of 1956.**

bank line. See **line of credit.**

Bank of Japan. See **BoJ.**

banker's acceptance. A short-term note that does not bear interest but is sold at a discount and pays its face value at maturity. In this way, the holder of the certificate of debt collects interest. Usually, these notes originate to facilitate foreign commerce. Instead of paying cash, an importer might instruct her bank to issue a letter of credit. Upon receipt of the letter, the exporter draws a draft from the importer's bank and discounts the draft at his bank, which sends it to the issuing bank. That bank "accepts" it and guarantees payment at maturity. There is an active market in these securities among banks, money market funds, corporations, and institutional investors. These securities are guaranteed both by the issuer and accepting bank.

Banking Act of 1933. See **Glass-Steagall Act.**

bankrate.com. A Web site featuring information on bank and finance matters for consumers. *See* **Web Sites for the Inquiring Investor.**

bankruptcy. The condition when a person, partnership, corporation, or municipality is unable to pay its debts as they become due, and is entitled to take benefit of state or federal bankruptcy laws. A filing for bankruptcy can be involuntary—instigated by creditors—or voluntary—instigated by the insolvent party. The word "debtor" is now used, instead of "bankrupt," under the federal code. Under that code, revised in 1978, Chapter 7, which can be personal or of a business nature, is in the nature of a liquidation proceeding and involves the collection and distribution to creditors of all the debtor's nonexempt property to satisfy claims, by the court-appointed bankruptcy trustee. Under Chapters 11, 12, and 13, on the other hand, the court seeks reorganization and a new beginning, rather than liquidation. Creditors look to future earnings of the debtor, rather than property liquidation, to satisfy claims.

Banks. Those stocks representing companies engaged in commercial banking activities. *See* **industry stock group.**

Bar chart or line chart. A graphic representation whereby daily, weekly, or monthly high and low prices for a stock are depicted by vertical lines, joined together at the opening and closing prices; chartists believe these charts are most useful when maintained on a daily bases. Charts can be kept by hand, purchased from services in hard copy, or downloaded electronically, and they can be annotated by the chartist. There are sometimes two scales on a chart. One measures a stock's prices and the other its trading volume for the period observed. Another method annotates trading volume at significant levels. In charting stocks, prices should be adjusted for stock splits and significant stock dividends. It is a good idea to indicate on the chart when these events took place. Charting is a method of using a graphic market analysis of a stock as opposed to technical analysis or fundamental analysis. The patterns formed by the recorded price ranges, together with volume analyses, are used by chartists in determining timing of stock purchases and sales.

Bar charting is more precise than point-and-figure charting, so it is more difficult to construct and maintain than a **point-and-figure chart** is. The passage of time and trading volume receives more prominence in the bar chart, while a point-and-figure chart lends itself to more customized notations. However, both types often ignore fundamental values in interpreting investment timing signals, and are considered a "black art" by some orthodox market professionals. The main criticism directed at relying on charts is that they are highly subjective and draw conclusions ex post facto. *See* **price formations.**

barbell portfolio. See **barbell strategy.**

barbell strategy. As a bond investor, to make disproportionately large commitments to both near-term and long-term maturity dates, constructing a barbell portfolio. This strategy is useful when the investment manager expects the long-term bonds to perform better than the intermediate ones, due to the current structure of interest rates and future expectations. The near-term batch provides cash flow for administrative and investment needs as well as safety.

Barcelona Stock Exchange. See under **Global Investment Market.**

bargain hunter. An investor who holds cash until he finds a stock so cheap that the dividend represents a high yield; it is a stock with an extremely low price/earnings multiple or its price is significantly under its book value. He buys feeling that the high dividend yield, low price/earnings multiple, or discount to its book value will attract other buyers, driving up the stock's price.

bargain stock. A stock selling for such a low price that its dividend represents an extremely high yield or its earnings represent an extremely low price/earnings multiple, in relation to stocks with similar risks and earning power.

***Barron's* Confidence Index.** A ratio using the *Barron's* (financial weekly) average of the yield of 10 of the highest grade bonds over the yield of 10 intermediate-grade bonds, expressed as an index. In theory, if the ratio or index gets smaller, investors are putting increasing amounts of money into high-grade bonds and shunning lower-grade bonds, thus showing diminished investor interest in more speculative investments. Conversely, if the index gets larger, speculative interest is stronger. The purpose of such an index is to gauge investor optimism or pessimism about the economy, on balance, since investment commitments to bonds usually reflect long-term expectations. *See* **flight to quality, flight to safety, and TED Spread.**

Barron's Online. See under **Web Sites for the Inquiring Investor.**

barter, corporate. At the dawn of commerce, the prevalent method of exchange was for a buyer to trade something, presumably something of value, for the seller's product. As nations created media of exchange—pelts, furs, gold, silver, and diamonds at first, and later money, as represented by currency and coins—bartering for goods and services all but disappeared in the economies of industrialized societies. However, in the decade of the 1990s, there has been a revival of this practice, especially among Internet companies who sell advertising space. Specifically, these are companies that sponsor Web sites for profit. In 1999 bartering revenues accounted for an estimated 10% to 15% of revenues for this industry group, with one leading company reporting 24% of revenues were from barter. In the case of Internet companies, the main item for barter is advertising, a $693 million market for Internet companies. As a portion of total revenues, bartering has doubled in three years. Many financial and investment experts have a problem with this practice. When a company sells products or services for something other than money (such as credit), no direct cash flow or earnings is created from such revenues. Only indirect cash flow from sales resulting from the bartered advertising results. And since many stock valuation models are based on these items, distortions can occur.

The SEC requires that companies break out bartering revenues, when the latter account for 10% or more of a company's revenues. But many companies do not mention them in media earnings reports. In many cases investors must probe SEC filings thoroughly to find them mentioned. A company that has received a service such as advertising for providing products or services should account for them by showing such revenues, say $10 million worth, as revenues, and $10 million in advertising expense. Defenders of the practice claim the double-entry accounting makes the procedure legitimate, since margins are reduced. But detractors consider the revenues "fluff," since they might not produce any hard money sales.

base. *See* **forming a base.**

bash. To criticize or exaggerate a stock's shortcomings on the Internet or imply that it is extraordinarily overvalued because of specific or general events—past or future—in the hope of making a personal gain by the stock transactions that ensue. *See* **investment sites.**

basic earnings per share. A replacement in reporting rules, adopted by the Financial Accounting Standards Board in 1997, for "primary earnings per share." A minor adjustment in "fully diluted" earnings per share was also made. Under the new rules, "basic earnings per share" ignores potential dilution, while "dilution per share" will continue to reflect maximum dilution. However, accountants are required to furnish vital information such as potentially dilutive contracts in financial statements. In effect, the new rules transfer the burden of assessing potential dilution from statement preparers (accountants) to statement users (analysts and investors).

basis book. A book of schedules that convert bond quotes into dollar amounts. *See* **bond.**

basis of exchange. The rate at which one security can be converted into another.

basis point. A measure equal to one-hundredth of 1% (.01%); so 25 basis points is one-quarter of 1%; 50 basis points is one-half 1%; 100 basis points is 1%. Basis points are used in describing changes in bond quotes.

basis price. See **bond basis.**

bath, accounting. A reference to the management action of allocating heavy business expenses or losses to a particular accounting period, eliminating them in one fiscal period—usually in a quarter or a restatement of prior annual results—so as to prevent them from causing uncertainty in the future about how and when they will affect corporate performance. It is a business metaphor for cleaning up the books, with respect to certain items that have negative connotations. It is not necessarily a reference to an illegal procedure, although it is sometimes questioned on the grounds of its appropriateness, from an accounting viewpoint, and on ethical grounds. In some remote cases, there can be culpability because of fraud.

An example of taking an accounting bath would occur if Magicians, Inc., a renowned acquirer and savior of distressed companies, negotiated to buy Jams, Inc. for cash. Before the closing, the management of Jams, following the accord, charged its earnings with a $100 million write-down of assets, creating a $50 million operating loss for the quarter. It took a bath! After the acquisition, financial comparisons with prior results would be salutary for Jams and, through association, Magician, because of the big loss. Furthermore, the written-down assets would require less depreciation expense in future periods, leaving more for earnings, also to the credit of Magician. This comeuppance would likely improve the marketability of Jams should Magician wish to dispose of it. Besides that, the bath likely would improve Magician's stock price, because Jams's earnings would enhance its own financial performance with the pro forma statement of its earnings including Jams's results. As long as the assets written down were truly overvalued in terms of the market value for those assets, the scheme was legal, albeit opportunistic. The write-down could have occurred over a longer period, but that would not have created the dramatic recovery the Magicians wanted.

bath, stock market. A reference to a huge loss in the stock market.

BEA. Abbreviation for **Bureau of Economic Research.**

bean counter. In the corporate culture, a reference to an executive who guards expenses fiercely, often to the detriment of business creativity; a cost cutter who enjoys wielding the money ax and one who is often brought in to cure a losing operation.

bear. An investor who is selling stock in anticipation of the stock price going lower, in a climate of generally falling stock prices. *See* **selling short.**

Beardstown Ladies or **Beardstown Business and Professional Women's Investment Club.** The most famous investment club in the United States, with a membership of 15 ladies in Beardstown, Illinois. It was formed in 1983 and gained notoriety through writing investment books extolling their simplistic, common sense methodology of selecting stocks for performance. The most successful book, and a 1995 bestseller—*The Beardstown Ladies Common Sense Investment Guide*—claimed the club had achieved a 23.4% investment return from 1984 to 1993, exceeding that of investment professionals and the S&P 500 Index, the latter returning 14.9% during that period. However, in computing the return, the ladies counted the $25 assessment contributed per member each month as an investment. By most counts, the mistake was an honest error. (Or, was it a newfangled Ponzi scheme?) An audit showed their actual return was 9.1%. The average age of the ladies is 70. The club is credited greatly with the enormous popularity of investment clubs; they have grown from 13,000 in 1994 to 34,000 today.

bearer bonds or **coupon bonds**. Bonds that are not registered as to a specific owner and pay interest to the current holder. The interest and principal when due are paid to whoever has possession of the bonds; no endorsement is required for ownership of such bonds to change. Interest is collected by clipping coupons from the bond and presenting them to the bond issuer's paying agent, usually a bank. Bearer bonds may usually be exchanged for registered bonds, but often there is a charge of from $2 to $5 per bond.

bearing interest. The automatic accrual of interest payments to a holder of a bond or other security.

bear market. Trading in securities dominated by sellers who force prices down through heavy offerings of stock for sale. Short selling is prevalent. *See* **selling short.**

bear raid. An effort by stock speculators to manipulate the price of a stock by selling large amounts of the shares short, driving down prices, and then purchasing the stock at the lower prices. This practice is illegal and is the reason for the uptick and zero plus tick rules pertaining to short selling, promulgated by the SEC. Those rules stipulate, under an uptick, that a short sale can only be executed when the last price was higher than the previous one or, under a zero plus tick, was unchanged but higher than the previous different price.

bear trap. A period following a big market selloff in which stock buyers are fooled into thinking the selloff is over because of a general rise in stock prices. They begin buying what are considered undervalued shares, only to find another market downturn makes them overvalued.

behavioral finance. The growing field of study that suggests current financial theories, emphasizing quantitative concepts, are not explaining today's stock prices and that more attention should be given to the behavioral sciences.

Beige Book. Nickname for the Federal Reserve report called *Summary of Commentary on Current Economic Conditions by Federal Reserve Districts.* The report is prepared by the Federal Reserve Bank of St. Louis and published eight times per year. Each Federal Reserve Bank gathers anecdotal information on current economic conditions in its district through reports from bank and branch directors and interviews with key businessmen, economists, market experts, and other sources. The Beige Book summarizes this information by district and sector. Web site: *www.federalreserve.gov/FMOC/BeigeBook/2001.*

Beirut Stock Exchange. See under **Global Investment Market.**

bellwether stock. A common stock issue that persistently leads stock market price trends because of the significance economically of the corporation it represents, its reputation as a reflector of general business conditions, its close association with special economic conditions, or simply because investors believe its price movements are significant to the market's direction.

beneficial owner. An investment firm's customer who is the actual owner of a stock holding, in terms of economic benefits, even though the stock is registered in the firm's name.

Bermuda tax shelter. A loophole in the U.S. Tax Code that allows domestic property and casualty insurance companies to relocate to Bermuda or be acquired by companies domiciled there, resulting in an avoidance of U.S. income taxes. The law allowing this was unused until 1999, when six American insurers moved their headquarters to Bermuda or were acquired by companies there. In the year 2000, Congress took up the issue. A bill was introduced to eliminate this loophole, on the basis of its providing unfair competition to domestic companies are diverting millions of dollars from the U.S. Treasury.

BestCalls.com. A Web site for investors featuring corporate conference call schedules, including upcoming and archived calls. *See* **Web Sites for the Inquiring Investor.**

best efforts. A reference to agreements by investment bankers or dealers to buy from corporations issuing only as many shares of stock in a new issue as they can sell to the public.

"best execution." A phrase on an order making it the obligation of a brokerage firm to extend every effort to negotiate the best possible trade for a client.

Best Rating. An appraisal of an insurance company, in terms of its capacity to meet financial obligations, produced by A. M. Best Co. *See* **annuity.**

beta stocks. On the London Stock Exchange, those stocks considered second-tier equities, in terms of relative size and trading volume.

Beta Value. 1) In the statistical analysis of stock prices, the percentage return experienced by a stock during a period attributable to general stock market activity. A Beta Value is the covariance of a stock in relation to the market in general, represented by the

S&P 500 Stock Index. The closer to "one" the value is, the more it moves with the stock market. Conversely, the closer to "zero" the value is, the less it moves with the stock market. A Beta can be positive or negative. It is indispensable in weighting a portfolio to a stock market index. By selecting stocks with a Beta of one, the portfolio manager can anticipate that the performance will mirror the index. In using Betas, it is imperative that they be chosen from recent analyses, because Betas, like Alphas, lack stationarity. That is, they do not stay the same. Therefore, to make sure the association is relevant, use recent studies. 2) Another valuable use of Betas is to establish the volatility of stocks, which is another way to describe their risks, in relation to the stock market generally. A Beta of 1.50, for example, suggests a stock is twice as volatile as one with a Beta of 1.25, in terms of the S&P 500 Stock Index. Therefore, in terms of the market, it can be considered twice as risky. One generalization is in order: investors who are conservative should be choosing stocks with low Betas, less risky, while those who are speculators ought to be in stocks with high Betas, more risky. *See* **Alpha Value.**

Beverages—Alcoholic. Those stocks representing distillers and distributors of beverages containing alcoholic spirits. *See* **industry stock group.**

Beverages—Non-alcoholic. Those stocks representing companies making and distributing beverages containing no alcoholic spirits. *See* **industry stock group.**

beyond-the-box-business. A reference to a manufacturer's strategy to expand its revenue base by offering customers add-on services and products that augment the basic product sold. For example, some computer makers also offer Internet services, financing of purchases, warranties, and instructional sessions, all for fees or subscriptions. In this manner, manufacturers can expand revenues even though sales of the main product are flat.

BHAG. (Pronounced "Beehag") Abbreviation for "big, hairy, audacious goals." This is a nickname used in management theory to designate the setting of very ambitious, long-term corporate goals, which by their grandiose scope can transform a company into a more serious competitor. Generally, the time frame for the strategy is considered 25 to 30 years, with intermittent sub-goals or checkpoints along the way, say every 10 years. Although ambitious, the goal must be attainable to be legitimate. For example, an announcement by Land Rush Properties, Inc. of Death Valley to attract the Winter Olympics of 2024 would not be a bona fide BHAG.

bid. 1) The amount an investor or dealer will pay for a unit of a security, usually restricted to the round lot quantity established for trading. 2) The amount an underwriter offers to pay a bond issuer for a quantity of bonds, stated as the average annual percentage of the face value of the bonds that the issuer must pay as interest. Bids are reported as the average annual interest cost to the bond issuer or original seller over the life of the bonds. For example, if 4.965% is the lowest bid on interest costs by an investment underwriter on a new bond issue, that is the lowest annual interest cost of each $1,000 bond obtainable by the borrower through the sale of the bonds. This annual interest cost should not be confused with the coupon interest rate or contracted interest rate, which might be 5%, in the example. The 4.965% is the average interest cost agreed to at the time the bids are taken, which adjusts the 5% rate to the current rate of return demanded by investors on that type of bond.

The issuer will still pay 5%, or $50, interest annually to future bondholders, but he receives a premium or an amount over $1,000 for each bond from the underwriter, which brings his real interest cost down to 4.965%. If investment funds had been scarcer when the bids were taken, the borrower might have gotten less than $1,000 per bond from the underwriter, so that the average cost would have been the 5% contract rate plus the amount of the discount under $1,000, averaged over the life of the bonds, something like a 5.125% interest cost.

When the underwriter offers the bonds to the public, he quotes them at a lower interest basis to the buyer, which reflects a price above what he had to pay for the bonds. The differential represents his profit. Of course, that's in the best of all worlds. If interest rates suddenly rise steeply, bond prices fall steeply, and the dealer is wondering why he ever got into the bond business.

bidding block. A reference to the process of financing new bonds through competitive bids from underwriters. *See* **rejected bid.**

"bid wanted (BW)." A phrase indicating that a stockholder wants to sell shares, and will entertain bids. However, the prices bid are considered negotiable. This type of message usually appears on stock quotation sheets.

Big Bang. The name describing the deregulation of securities markets in London on October 27, 1986. This event helped clear the way toward a world financial marketplace. In terms of significance, it would rank in importance with **May Day** in the United States.

Big Blue. Nickname for IBM Corporation and stock.

Big Board. 1) A blackboard or electronic panel where transactions on the New York Stock Exchange are reported. 2) Nickname for the New York Stock Exchange.

"big box" retailers. A facetious reference to strip shopping centers and malls, where large retail stores with lots of floor space and many departments dominate shopping activity. The term has risen from comparisons with Internet stores or "virtual" retailers. Detractors of big stores believe they are going out of style, and that Internet shopping will replace them in shopping importance.

bigdough. A reference to a Web site with a database of money managers. *www.bigdough.com.*

Big Five. The nickname for the five largest accounting firms in the United States in terms of annual revenues. One or another of them performs the accounting and auditing functions for most domestic corporations, attesting to the accounting adequacy of their clients' annual reports and other documents. Besides that, they do consulting work for clients. It is the latter service that is raising questions over their possible conflict of interest. Many believe is difficult for the auditor to remain objective when judging a company that has retained the auditor as a consultant.

The five firms are: Accenture, PricewaterhouseCoopers, Deloitte & Touche, Ernst & Young, and KPMG Peat Marwick.

big spread. *See* **wide spread.**

Big Three. The collective nickname for the three biggest automobile manufacturers and distributors in the United States—Chrysler, Ford, and General Motors. The importance of these auto makers in terms of their influence on the economy has made them an important gauge of economic conditions. However, as globalization of domestic industries picked up steam in the second half of the twentieth century, auto makers from around the world began joint venturing in manufacturing and marketing projects. Outsourcing has become important, in place of vertical integration. In 1998 Chrysler merged with Daimler-Benz, the German industrial giant. As a result the Big Three is less defined than it once was, and certainly less of the economic barometer it once was. But the cyclical group is still important for investors, especially as to providing clues of cyclical changes. *See* **outsourcing** and **integrated company.**

big ticket items. 1) In describing consumer purchases by their importance in terms of relative prices, those articles that are in the high end of the price range for consumer goods. Usually those purchases involve some form of consumer debt, as in an installment sales contract or mortgage contract, and are represented by durable goods or those expected to last more than three years. Houses, automobiles, heavy appliances, and boats are examples. They are important to economists and industrial analysts, because a change in the trend for such a product is a better indicator of a change in general business conditions than a change for lower-priced items. This is because consumers are more inclined to go into debt when optimistic about their futures; and are likely to reduce debt when they are pessimistic. 2) Broadly speaking, the term also refers to capital-spending projects which require some form of external financing, such as bonds, to accomplish. Refineries, pipelines, cable networks, and science laboratories are examples.

big uglies. Those stocks representing companies that are basic manufacturers and processors, so called, partly in jest, because their facilities are big, noisy, and often emit pollutants. Examples are: steel plants, refineries, paper mills, tire plants, electric utilities, and rock and roll concerts.

Bilbao Stock Exchange. See under **Global Investment Market.**

bill and hold. As a vendor of goods, to record sales on a product(s) that has not been shipped and for which no payment is required for a period of time exceeding normal trade practice. This accounting practice is considered misleading, because the revenues are not recorded in the appropriate period and the earnings resulting from the premature transactions are fictitious. Presumably, the order could be canceled at a later date. The Securities and Exchange Commission is tightening surveillance of companies that engage in the practice.

bill of exchange. A phrase describing a bank draft in international transactions. *See* **draft.**

BINGO. A nickname for a Non-Governmental Organization that has grown in resources and sophistication so as to take on the configuration of a private corporation. Such an organization often is a multinational trading organization, with trading, management, and advertising expertise. Although such an entity retains the mantle of charitable operations, in reality it can be a private contractor to governments to supply them needed materials and services. Usually, it operates under a tax umbrella, so that it competes effectively with avowed profit enterprises.

black chip stock. 1) A stock representing a corporate management that has recently lost favor with investors, usually because of policies that have led to financial reversals or static operations, which have impeded anticipated earnings growth. 2) In relation to South Africa, a stock representing a company that is implementing the ownership and management of corporate affairs by Blacks as part of the transition away from past apartheid policies.

blacked-out "quiet period." A reference to a time before or after a new securities issue when the underwriting and distribution syndicate is so large that no or hardly any investment firms are publishing information on the company, in observance of the "quiet period." The "quiet period" is a time in which pending events have caused traditional sources of corporate information to withhold data, due to legal considerations. See **"quiet period."**

Black Friday. 1) A name given to certain Fridays in financial history on which have occurred monetary panics or stock market collapses. Financial panics commenced on Fridays in 1869 and 1873; a stock market crash took place on a Friday in 1929 and ushered in the depression of the 1930s. 2) A name given to the Friday after Thanksgiving for retailers, if business is slack.

black glasses. A reference to the viewpoint of an investor reading financial information, usually about shares of stock in a company out of favor with investors, with an overly-negative bias. This can lead to unwarranted pessimistic assumptions about future prospects, followed by a missed opportunity in purchasing an under-priced stock. *See* **rose glasses.**

Black Monday. 1) A reference to Monday, October 19, 1987, when the U.S. stock market dropped precipitously. The DJIA plunged 508 points and sent ripple effects around the world. There was a general concern with federal budget deficits, high stock prices, and international problems. Program trading was also blamed. 2) Also known as **Bloody Monday,** a reference to the huge selloff of U.S. stock prices on Monday, October 27, 1997, when the DJIA fell 554 points. It was prompted by deteriorating economic conditions in Southeast Asia, Russia, and Japan, as well as high stock valuations in the United States.

Black-Scholes model. The algebraic formula used to price options and other derivative securities, developed by mathematician Fisher Black and economists Myron S. Scholes and Robert C. Merton in 1973. Until then, it was very difficult to deal with the variables that might affect the price of an option. Accordingly, the volume in the option business was minuscule. The Chicago Board Options Exchange, the first exchange specializing in options, opened as the model was published. The model was immediately adopted and hardwired into pocket calculators, enabling the traders to price options quickly. The options market has grown explosively since then. With modifications, the formula can also be applied to pricing many contracts whose values depend upon future events, such as other types of options, futures, derivatives, and insurance policies.

"blanked out." A phrase describing a lack of trading in a stock during a market session.

blind pool. A securities offering by a limited partnership in which management has not disclosed the exact properties to be purchased. In evaluating such an arrangement, investors should consider the track record of the management. Most often, this situation accompanies real estate financing. On the other hand, a **specific pool** lists information about the assets to be purchased.

blind trust. A legal arrangement, created and documented by an instrument of trust, in which certain assets, such as securities, are placed under the absolute management of an independent party, usually a fiduciary institution such as a bank or money management firm. The purpose of the trust is to separate the owner(s) of the assets from the management of the assets, usually because that person(s) could have a **conflict of interest** in that the interest in the assets might take precedence over some duty or obligation. The trusts are also useful in preventing the appearance of a conflict of interests. They are used a great deal in government appointments, to enable the appointee to render objective decisions in policy matters. Sometimes an officer of a corporation might be compelled by the board of directors to place securities that represent competitors in a blind trust, in order to avoid the conflict in his job. The essence of the trust's plausibility is that the trustee may dispose of the assets in question as a part of its investment strategy, so that the beneficiary no longer knows what assets are in the portfolio.

block alliance. See **airline alliances.**

block of stock. A large number of shares of a stock accumulated for a single trade.

Bloomberg Online. See under **Web Sites for the Inquiring Investor.**

Bloomberg Web Site. See under **Web Sites for the Inquiring Investor.**

blue chip stock. A stock that has paid a consistent dividend and grown earnings at least moderately or at an average rate over several years, and is not totally dependent on general economic conditions for future growth.

blue sheets. See **National Daily Quotation Service.**

blue sky laws. Those state regulations that outline requirements for securities issues and sales that are intrastate in nature. The expression came from the remark of a judge who said a certain stock was as valuable as a "piece of the blue sky."

Board. 1) Short version of Board of Directors. **board.** 2) A chalk board or electronic panel where market transactions are recorded.

board marker. A brokerage employee who transfers market prices from the ticker tape to a blackboard.

Board of Directors. Those persons elected by the stockholders of a corporation, under conditions set out by its articles of incorporation and bylaws, to establish general policies and a continuing direction for the enterprise. The directors, usually three or more, elect a Chairman, who is their liaison with the executive officers of the corporation. The latter group is the top management team that runs the business daily and makes quarterly reports to the Board on progress. Generally, besides the Chairman, the team includes the President and/or Chief Executive Officer, the Chief Operating Officer, and the Chief Financial Officer. Often, other officers are included. Usually, but not exclusively, it is the Chairman and the management team who bring business updates to the Board, and respond to their questions about operations. The Board approves the hiring of certain senior management employees, approves operating and capital budgets, approves mergers and acquisitions, and takes up other "big picture" questions as they occur. While directors may also be employees, there is a growing recognition that directors need to be independent of the Chairman and senior management, because they represent the stockholders, and should be ready to act in advancing their interests.

Board of Directors, mutual fund. Under SEC rules promulgated in 2000, a majority of the board of mutual fund companies must be independent, in order to protect investors from conflict of interests by directors, improve the board's position in dealing with a fund's management, and establish higher profiles of directors to ascertain their independence. Independent fund directors are expected to protect investors' interests and maintain a fund's integrity. Duties involve approving fees, monitoring financial performance, and preventing questionable practices. Other recent rules include:

- Current independent directors must nominate new independent directors rather than fund managers or fund advisors.
- Attorneys representing independent directors must also be independent—not associated with fund management of close affiliates.
- Fund companies must disclose basic information concerning fund's directors, including information about possible conflicts of interest. They also must reveal directors' ownership of shares in the company's group of funds.

Board of Governors, Federal Reserve Bank. The supervisory body of the 12 Federal Reserve banks, consisting of seven members, appointed by the president of the United States and confirmed by the Senate for a term of seven years. Terms are staggered.

board room. 1) The area where brokerage customers watch the quote board or tape. 2) The conference room in a corporate head-quarters where the board holds its quarterly and special meetings.

Bogatá Stock Market. See under **Global Investment Market.**

bogus. A description of a fake security or financial document.

bogus bank (Web). A reference to a banking scam on the Internet. These fraudulent schemes are based on trying to entice persons at a Web site to send money for deposit, usually by offering to paying exorbitantly high interest or charging unusually low loan rates. In addition, the scam usually makes the Web site take on the appearance and name of a legitimate banking operation. To verify an Internet bank's legitimate existence, check the Federal Deposit Insurance Corporation's Web site: *www.fdic.gov* and find out if the cyberbank is legally chartered. Also, check to See if a physical address is shown as opposed to a post office box number. Finally, a legitimate cyberbank is likely to have its own domain in its Internet address.

boiler plate. A reference to the standard auditor's statement in a financial document that vouchsafes that a company's financial reports to the public are representative of its actual condition or operating results. *See* **audited books** and **Auditor's Statement in Annual Report.**

boiler room. An unethical and often illegal place where salesmen use high-pressure techniques over long-distance lines to sell worthless or near-worthless securities.

BoJ. Nick name for Bank of Japan, that country's central bank that is similar to the U.S. Federal Reserve Bank.

bolsa. The Spanish word for stock exchange.

bolsa or **Bolsa Mexicana de Valores.** The stock exchange in Mexico.

Bombay Stock Exchange. See under **Global Investment Market.**

bond. A certificate representing long-term debt, usually in the amount of $1,000, with principal, maturity date, and interest rate shown on its face, issued by a corporation or government entity to raise money to fund long-term projects. A bond does not represent ownership, as does stock, and offers no opportunity for the investor to increase his or her interest income above that of the stated terms. Interest payments, which are usually made semiannually to bondholders, and the principal when it is due are fixed obligations of the issuer and must be paid, if the issuer is to remain solvent.

The terms of the bond, such as financial restrictions placed on the issuer or penalties to the issuer for prepaying the bond, are called the indenture. Insurance companies and banks, as well as some other institutional investors, invest their reserves largely in bonds, because they can accurately predict the resulting income stream from the bonds. Since a bond represents a promise to repay a specified amount at some future date, plus a percentage of that amount in interest annually or semiannually, the financial standing of the issuer determines a bond's investment merit and relative value among other bonds.

Also, the issuer often pledges valuable property as collateral to the bondholder, which can be sold to pay interest and principal if these obligations are not met. It is an investment truism that the longer a bond's maturity, the more sensitive its price is to fluctuating interest rates. This is because a bond's price is constantly adjusting to the investment return investors demand in the capital markets. In a bond's case, the investment return is a combination of interest payments received and the appreciation or discount represented by the change from its cost when the face value is paid at maturity. The greater the number of years in which the current cost must make such an adjustment, the more sensitive the bond's price will be to interest rate changes. *See* **corporate bond, Treasury bond, municipal bond**, and **debenture.**

bond amortization. See **amortization (3).**

bond averages. Those daily indexes of price changes in different categories of bonds that are published as averages. *See* **Dow-Jones bond averages** and *New York Times* **bond averages.**

bond basis or **basis price.** A figure reflecting the average yield of a bond, taking into account its cost, its contractual interest rate, and the years or months to maturity, used as a method for pricing or quoting the bond. This basis figure can be translated to a dollar value by using a basis book or by multiplying it by 10. For example, a 6% bond maturing in 10 years even and selling on a 7.25% average yield basis is priced by the basis book at 91.22. When multiplied by 10, this figure gives a dollar price of $912.20 per $1,000 bond, a discount of $87.80, which compensates the investor at the bond's maturity date for accepting a nominal interest rate (6%) at a time when rates are higher currently.

bond department. A commercial bank division that buys and sells bonds for the bank's account or for resale.

bond discount. The amount for which a bond is selling beneath its **par value.**

bond house. An investment firm that underwrites new bond issues, usually municipals exclusively.

Bond Market Association. A business association that speaks for the bond industry, advocating its positions in governmental, regulatory, and marketing affairs worldwide, with foreign firms comprising 20% of its membership. Its membership includes securities firms and banks that underwrite, trade, and sell debt securities. The association's Web site is especially useful to investors, because it accesses prices and yields on municipal bonds, and provides a gateway of links to prices and yields on most other types of bonds. Address: 40 Broad Street, New York, NY 10004-2373. Phone: (212) 434-8400. Fax: (212) 440-5260. Web site: *www.bondmarkets.com.*

Bond Market Association Online. See under **Web Sites for the Inquiring Investor.**

bond quote. See **quote (2).**

bond scale. A schedule of average yields for each year of maturity of serial bonds, based on their public offering price and interest each year.

bond table. A tabulation of investment and trading information for corporate, municipal, U.S. Treasury, and U.S. agency bonds, usually found in newspapers. Although data for each bond market is presented in different tables, much of the information is similar. For example, in the case of zero bonds, the numberal "0" would appear in the coupon column of the municipal table. Remember—for U.S. Treasury bonds, fractions are 32nds. For the meaning of terms and symbols, refer to the glossaries, usually found at the end of tables.

CORPORATE BOND TABLE

(1) BosCelts 6s38	(2) 9.2	(3) 22	(4) 65³⁄₈	(5) +¹⁄₄

Explanations:

(1) name of issuer/Boston Celtics paying 6% of the par value and maturing in 2038

(2) current yield of 9.2%, based on the interest rate and closing price of bond

(3) volume on last trading day was $22,000 in bonds

(4) closing price of $653.75 (65.375 × 10)

(5) change in price of $2.50 (.25 × 10)

MUNICIPAL OR TAX-EXEMPT BOND TABLE

(1) IssueNevada GO Bonds	(2) Coupon 5.00	(3) Maturity 5-15-28	(4) Price 97¹⁄₈	(5) Yield to Maturity

Explanations:

(1) issuer/state of Nevada general obligation bonds

(2) interest rate is 5% of par value

(3) maturity date is May 15, 2028

(4) price is $971.30 (97.125 × 10)

(5) yield to the maturity date is 5.19% annually

U.S. TREASURY BOND AND NOTE TABLE

(1) Rate	(2) Mat. Date	December 02	(3) bid	(4) Ask	(5) Chg
5.13			$101^{14}/_{32}$	$101^{15}/_{32}$	0.06

Explanations:

(1) interest rate is 5.13%

(2) maturity date is December 2002

(3) a buyer will pay $1,014.38 per bond (101.438 × 10)

(4) a buyer is willing to pay $1,014.69 (101.469 × 10)

(5) change in price of $0.06 per bond

(6) yield of 4.25% based on bid price

bonus issue. Free capital stock distributed to a company's shareholders in a ratio to the number of shares already owned, as a reward for investing in the company. This is a practice in Australia, Canada, the United Kingdom, and certain European countries. It resembles a stock dividend in the United States, and represents a symbolic act in that no new corporate wealth is created, as is the case when stock is sold.

book, broker's. A personal tabulation that a broker maintains, along with current securities positions, of those investors that are considered likely prospects to continue the professional relationship established, regardless of the broker's business affiliation. It reflects potential future business, and is really what an employer wants to review in considering hiring prospective, experienced brokers.

book value, asset. The value of an asset shown on a corporation's books or in preparing its balance sheet. This amount is usually based on the original or historical cost, less depreciation or depletion or obsolescence charges, and often is not a true current or replacement value.

book value per share—common. The stated or par value of the common stock added to the surplus or retained earnings accounts and divided by the total number of common shares. This value is significant when compared with the amount a share costs currently, since it sometimes indicates an undervalued or overvalued market price. In practice, the book value is keyed to the historical cost of a corporation's resources, while the current market price is keyed to the prospective values of the resources. It must be remembered that every company is a candidate for a sale to new owners, and the book value is the starting point for establishing a worth.

books. 1) The accounting records of a business. 2) The record of sales in a new securities underwriting by the syndicate manager.

books closed or **accounts closed.** See **closing the books.**

boom. A period of strong business expansion, usually in reference to the general economy, but it can also apply to regions.

Boston Stock Exchange (BSE). A U.S. national securities exchange, founded in 1834. It has over 200 members and trades approximately 2,000 securities, with 160 primary companies listed. Address: 100 Franklin Street, Boston, MA 02110. Phone: (617) 235-2000. Fax: (617) 235-2200. Web site: *www.bostonstock.com. See* under **Global Investment Market.**

both ends of the list. A reference to long-term bonds (maturing in 15 years or more) and near-term bonds (maturing in five years or less), especially U.S. Treasury bonds.

Botswana Stock Exchange. See under **Global Investment Market.**

bottom. A reference to a low point in the stock market generally or the price of a security during a specific period.

bottom fishing. As an investor, searching for and buying stocks that are attractive based on their fundamental values after a significant stock market selloff. The bottom fisher or bargain hunter focuses on intrinsic values like discounted book values and high dividend yields, rather than opportunities in individual stocks, and usually buys stocks she would only consider seriously because the selloff has lowered most prices drastically.

bottom-up decision strategy. In making decisions about the most attractive securities to buy or sell, the use of analyses and research on individual companies, in making selections of specific securities. This technique is based on the assumption that a close look at the outlook for many companies will yield the best investment results. *See* **top-down decision strategy.**

bottom out. In the case of a stock falling in price, to reverse that trend and stabilize in price, setting the stage for a rise in price.

bourse. The French word for stock exchange.

boutique. A research-oriented investment firm that specializes in one or more industry groups. In order to justify economically the narrow scope, such a firm usually selects popular industries with stocks having big-market capitalizations. In this way, it can generate big share and commission volumes. Although written reports are prepared, a great deal of the brokerage business is done through analysts' personal visits to institutional clients.

Bowie or **royalty bonds.** Bonds backed by future royalties on publishing rights and master recordings, named after the rock singer David Bowie who was the first issuer of such asset-backed bonds.

box. An expression for a place where securities are in safe-keeping, usually referring to an investment firm's depository.

box maker. A reference to makers of personal computer housings or the containers for the configuration of microprocessors, chips, and other hardware that constitute a personal computer. The other entities in the personal computer industry are peripheral equipment makers and software makers. Examples of box makers are Dell, Compaq, Gateway, and IBM. Examples of peripheral makers are Imation Zip drives, Hayes modems, and UMAX scanners, while examples of software makers are Microsoft, Corel, and Intuit.

Brady bonds. Securities issued by certain foreign countries in need of financial assistance under a plan developed in 1989 under Treasury Secretary Nicholas F. Brady in the Bush administration, in which the bonds are backed by U.S. Treasury bonds. Those countries had defaulted on international debt. The purpose was to reduce their foreign bank loans outstanding.

brain power. A phrase describing the scientific prowess of a company's research and development staff. In applied science stocks, it has replaced to a certain degree the traditional book value as a measure of stock value.

branch office. An investment office affiliated with a stock exchange or NASDAQ member, connected to its main office and other branches by electronic communication devices.

Brazil Commodities & Futures Exchange. See under **Global Investment Market.**

breadth, market. The extent to which the stock market participates in a price movement, in terms of the ratio or percentage of issues trading on an exchange or in a market. The greater the breadth in a move, the more confidence investors can have in its perseverance or duration. Generally, experts believe that when two-thirds or 65% of shares trading move in the direction of a market index, the breadth is significant and indicates the direction will last for a time. *See* **Advance/Decline Ratio** under **technical indicators.**

breakaway gap. See **gap (1).**

breakeven point, corporate. A level of units sold, and therefore revenues, at which the costs of operating are met. Above this level earnings could result and under it losses could result. In calculating the breakeven point, the revenues should be those from ordinary operations, like ordinary store sales or automobile sales, otherwise the breakeven point could be skewered by extraordinary transactions in a certain period. It is a critical level, since a level too high means breakeven is out of reach, as are earnings consequently, and the enterprise is likely to be unsuccessful from an investment point of view.

breakeven point, investment. A securities sale price that just covers the original cost of the investment, the commissions, fees, interest if appropriate, and taxes, when known reasonably well. The object is to determine at which point an investor begins to receive a return or makes money.

breaking the syndicate. In the underwriting of securities, the dissolution of the formal underwriting syndicate as a force that sustains the market support for a new security issue. Afterwards, its members can dispose of the issue without restrictions. Usually, the selling group disbands 30 days before the underwriting syndicate, although these conditions are spelled out in each underwriting agreement. The reason the selling group is relieved first is that its selling concession or fee is lower.

breakout. A deviation in a stock price from a series of similar price transactions into a sudden price move up or down. Traders, especially chartists, watch for these deviations as indicators that if they occur on the downside, it is a selling signal, while their occurrence on the upward side is a buy signal. *See* **chart.**

break points. In a mutual fund's front-end sales load structure, those levels of investment at which discounts in the load apply. For example, if the load starts at 5% on investments up to $10,000 and drops to 4.5% from $10,000 to $50,000, and 4% from $50,000 to $100,000, the break points are 4.5% and 4%.

breaking a leg. An expression describing the abrupt cessation of an upward price trend by a security or market average, followed by a sharp downturn in prices. In the theater, a good actor "breaks a leg." In the stock market, a bad actor "breaks a leg."

"breaking the spread." A term of derision for a market maker in a stock quoting a price that is above the current bid price or below the current asked price, although the prices are supposed to be set by natural supply and demand forces in a competitive market.

bridge bank. A banking facility, usually created and funded by a government, to alleviate a banking system overburdened by nonperforming loans—those loans behind in interest payments and/or principal repayments 90 days or more—in one or more commercial banks within the system. This is accomplished by the bridge bank's assuming troubled loans and selling them to other lenders at deep discounts, in order to compensate the buyers for the risk of not getting paid back in many cases. The new note holders then try to collect and retire the debts. Often the process includes closing or consolidating the inefficient banks in the system. It is the final disposition of a banking crisis, one that frequently goes hand-in-hand with general troubles in a nation's economy.

bridge financing. In investment banking parlance, the capital advanced toward keeping a project going until permanent, long-term financing is arranged. Commercial banks, institutions, and private investors usually provide bridge financing for periods of one to three years.

Broadcast Media. Those stocks representing companies owning facilities and resources enabling them to disseminate television and radio programming over licensed public channels. *See* **industry stock group.**

broad tape. A nickname for the machine over which a hard copy of financial news is printed. It is usually located in brokerages, operating throughout the business day. It derives its name from the wide paper on which it prints, compared with the narrow ticker tapes or narrow electronic windows.

Broker, About Your. Internet information source on broker reputations. *See* **Web Sites for the Inquiring Investor.**

broker, stock. A businessman who arranges for the exchange of securities between investors, strictly on a commission basis. Many brokers also act as principals or independently at times, rather than agents. And so "broker" has the connotation of a general securities salesman. *See* **securities salesman.**

broker holder of record. An investment firm holding stock in its name, even though the stock is technically owned by a customer. *See* **beneficial owner** or **safekeeping of securities.**

brokerage. A firm equipped with communications facilities and information to buy and sell securities for customers. *See* **full-service brokerage.**

brokerage window. In a self-directed retirement account, such as a 401(k) plan, a provision that allows an enrolled employee to invest some of the funds contributed in a broad array of mutual funds and securities, through the use of a brokerage outside the financial sources used by the employer or sponsor in administering the program. The main element of uncertainty about allowing this discretion is whether doing so is an abrogation of the plan sponsor's fiduciary responsibilities under ERISA. However, the practice is becoming more popular in the United States. In 1995, fewer than 1% of plans allowed brokerage windows, while 7% did so in 1999.

brokers loan. A bank loan to a securities dealer or broker, pledged by securities and usually collectible on demand.

brown fields. A reference to abandoned industrial sites that have degraded the surrounding soil, fauna, and environment, due to toxic or otherwise objectionable wastes. Sometimes the degrading continues after the site has been closed. Usually, such sites have been used for processes that use large quantities of certain chemicals, minerals, or radioactive materials.

BSE. Abbreviation for **Boston Stock Exchange.**

Bucharest Stock Exchange. See under **Global Investment Market.**

bucket shop. An extinct operation in which a broker did not enter a customer's order immediately, but held the order for a possible price change in order to make a personal gain. Although the bucket shop no longer exists as a category of securities business, its spirit is often present in otherwise legitimate operations. For example, when a broker holds a power-of-attorney in a customer's account and is acting as principal, she might hold a customer's order to sell shares until she can buy them at a cheaper price and pocket the difference.

Budapest Stock Market. See under **Global Investment Market.**

budget. 1) **Operating budget**. An estimation in advance of revenues and allocation of expenses over a fiscal operating period, in order to provide a model for achieving certain financial results.

2) **Capital budget.** An estimation in advance of cash receipts and cash disbursements, in order to provide a model for carrying out planned capital improvements during a fiscal period.

Buffett, Warren E. See **"Oracle of Omaha."**

Building Materials. Those stock representing companies engaged in manufacturing materials used in construction projects, usually materials for buildings, as opposed to construction engineering projects themselves. *See* **industry stock group.**

Building Permits, New Private Housing Units. See under **Economic Indicators.**

"bulge bracket." In the highly competitive business of bond underwriting, the top three positions in terms of business volume. This bracket is the most profitable per bond.

bull. An investor who is buying stock in anticipation of the price rising for that stock, in a climate of generally rising stock prices.

bullet bond. In connection with a "put" bond issue, that portion of the package that is sold as a straight bond in the cash bond market. *See* **put bond.**

bullet strategy. As a bond investor, a strategy to commit disproportionately large amounts of money to bonds with intermediate maturity dates of two to 10 years. This can be effective in maximizing performance when the Federal Reserve is actively lowering interest rates.

Bulletin Board (OTC-BB). The stock quoting service for over-the-counter stocks with small capitalizations, operated by the National Association of Securities Dealers. There are 6,400 companies listed. The only requirements for listing are sponsorship by a brokerage firm and filing financial statements with regulators; however, there are exceptions to the latter requirement. It is the most loosely-regulated of the national markets, where over $5 billion worth of trades occur annually, and listed companies are not required to file financial results with the SEC. Real time quotes, last sale prices, and volume information are posted but often a brokerage controls the market for a stock.

It is among the trading in these stocks that fraud is most likely, because a great deal is not known about the companies. Only one market maker must certify that it has current financial information. *Caveat emptor!*

bullion. Precious metals like gold or silver processed in the form of ingots, bars, or plates. It is a reference to quantity of a metal rather than a value, so that some specification of content is in order. Most often it is used in shipments between countries, to satisfy their balance of payments requirements.

bullion coins. Coins containing precious metals such as gold and silver. Their intrinsic value depends on the content of the metal in each coin. There exists a global market of brokers and dealers that buy and sell bullion coins. The Web site of one such dealer: *www.washingtonmint.com. See* **Eagle, American Gold; Krugerrand, South African;** and **Maple Leaf, Canadian Gold.**

bull market. A market in which securities prices are rising for several months, in an atmosphere dominated by optimistic buyers.

bull up a stock, to. To exaggerate the potential value of a stock in order to stimulate sales commissions, trading profits, or capital gains.

bunch orders, to. In the management of a large number of odd lot orders on an exchange, to execute them in batches in order to get the best prices and expedite their execution.

"burden of proof is on the bulls." In market trading where no price trends are obvious, but rather one in which prices are up one day and down the next, an expression meaning that if the market is to take a prolonged higher price trend, the buyers (bulls) must do more than talk optimistically. They must begin buying, thereby actually raising prices through increased stock demand. It's a variation on the challenge, "Put your money where your mouth is!"

Bureau of Economic Analysis (BEA). An agency of the U.S. Department of Commerce with the mission to produce and distribute accurate, timely, and relevant economic statistics that provide governments, businesses, households, and individuals with a comprehensive picture of economic activity in the United States. Among its many economic account series, probably the most important is the National Economic Accounts, which provide quantitative data and text on production, distribution, and use of the nation's output, such as gross domestic product (GDP). The agency also prepares estimates of the country's tangible wealth and input-output tables that show how various industries interact with one another. The Regional Economic Accounts provide estimates and analyses of personal income, population, and employment for regions, states, metropolitan areas, and counties. The International Economic Accounts encompasses the international transactions accounts or balance of payments and estimates of U.S. direct investments in foreign countries and foreign investment in the United States. The agency's monthly record—*Survey of Current Business*—pulls together the estimates, analyses, and research into one package.

Bureau of Economic Analysis Online. See under **Web Sites for the Inquiring Investor.**

Bureau of Labor Statistics (BLS). An agency of the U.S. government that is a collector and supplier of economic and business statistics; a division of the U. S. Department of Labor.

burn rate. In the case of a start-up business venture, the amount of money being spent in order to keep a business going in excess of revenues it is generating. For example, if total monthly expenses are $500,000 and revenues are $250,000, the burn rate is $250,000 per month. Venture capitalists like to feel the burn rate will decline on a consistent basis before committing money to a new project. But sometimes they get burned.

Burst Basket execution. A contrived trading program in which floor specialists, acting in the aggregate as a market maker, purchase or sell the component stocks required for execution of a specific basket trade.

Business and Company Profile in the Annual Report. A descriptive overview of the company appearing in the annual report. This section describes the corporation's scope of operations, including products and services offered and corporate resources employed in carrying on its business. Also included are changes in the company's markets served as well as the nature of the competition. If the company enjoys a dominant market position, it is usually mentioned. There is usually a reference to the concentration of the company's business, in terms of revenues, in a few customers, or a high degree of dependence on a few suppliers. For the investor, this section indicates the staying power of the company, if business activity slows.

business cycle. 1) A period of alternating high and low general business activity—in such activities as capital expenditures, industrial production, sales, and profits—in which an expansion occurs in the first phase, followed by a contraction of such activities to or below the levels of the previous trough in the second phase, after adjusting for the effects of seasonality, trend, and irregularity on those levels. A complete cycle goes from a trough to a peak to the ensuing trough, or from a peak to a trough to the ensuing peak. Since 1945 there have been nine business cycles in the United States, lasting 61 months on average. The current business cycle that began as a trough in March 1991 is still in effect after 104 months. Since 1854 in the United States, contractions have gotten shorter, while expansions have gotten longer. The longest expansion since 1945 lasted 106 months. The longest contraction since 1945 was 16 months. Business cycle reference dates are established by the National Bureau of Economic Research, Inc. 2) In a manufacturing operation, the length of time (usually several months) required for raw materials to be acquired, converted into finished products, and placed in the hands of sellers.

Business Inventories and Sales Report. A report for economists and industry analysts that is released by the Bureau of the Census of the Department of Commerce mid-month. It is less important than some of the other economic indicator reports because most of the data has appeared already. The only new information this report introduces is retail inventories. The importance of the report is that business inventories are a significant part of GNP and they can signal the future of the economy. Business inventories are a leading indicator, while business sales are considered a coincident one. However, because of the recent trend to minimize business inventories, the level of inventories or the ratio of business sales to inventories is becoming less important as an indicator of changes in economic activity. The source of the data in this report is a monthly survey of manufacturers' shipments, inventories, and orders; and from wholesale and retail trade surveys. Changes in Business Inventories and Sales do not influence securities prices greatly, and when they do, the results are unpredictable.

business model or **business plan.** As the top management of a company, the blueprint selected for operating the business enterprise. A good model usually is profitable and based on adherence to strict disciplines or policies that seem likely to gain market share over competitors. There can be unique features to it, such as a way to keep inventory costs low or effective cross-selling arrangements. It is the ability to develop and implement successful plans that makes top management valuable to a company and able to command high P/E multiples.

business portfolio. A description of the diverse operating companies or divisions that a company owns or controls as differentiated from securities owned.

business-to-business (B2B) stocks. Stocks representing companies serving e-commerce companies, through providing software and services that enables the latter to transact business with e-vendors.

business-to-customer (B2C) stocks. Stocks representing companies serving e-customer companies, through providing software and services that enable the latter to transact business with e-customers.

Business Week Online. See **Web Sites for the Inquiring Investor.**

bust the trade, to. Between brokers, to cancel a completed securities transaction. Usually, no money is exchanged.

"buy." A stock recommended for immediate purchase by an investment firm, and one appearing on its recommended list. This is the most popular commentary on a stock, because it is optimistic and opens avenues for corporate finance business for the firm. Approximately three quarters of investment firm recommendations are "buys."

buy area. See **resistance area.**

buy in, to. To buy the same securities a second time because of a failure of the seller to deliver the securities in the first trade. Under New York Stock Exchange regulations, if the buyer pays less, the original trade is canceled; if he pays more, the original seller (or member) must make up the difference.

BUYandHOLD.com. A Web site that offers investors a long-term stock accumulation program, with a minimum stock purchase of $20 and charge of $2.99 per purchase. The site also features investment information and news. This is a similar program to the Dividend Reinvestment Plans that many corporations offer investors. *See* **Dividend Reinvestment Plan** and **Web Sites for the Inquiring Investor.**

buyback, stock. The term describing a strategy by a corporation's management, usually the board of directors, to purchase shares of its common stock in the market. Usually, a program or plan will be authorized for management to buy back a certain number of shares. The typical reasons for doing so are varied but usually involve one of the following objectives. By allocating capital to such a plan, (1) management can enhance the values per share for the remaining stock in public hands, such as earnings per share, asset values per share, stockholders' equity per share, cash per share, and so on, although technically, the stock purchased should be retired to reduce shares outstanding; (2) by buying back stock, the supply is reduced which might improve its stock market price for acquisitions and new stock issues;(3) fewer shares remain in public hands which could give management more control of corporate direction through more insider stock ownership; (4) stockholders' equity is increased, raising the ratio of equity to debt, thus laying the groundwork for more borrowing, except when borrowing money to buy back the stock stymies this result or creates more additional interest expense than the earnings increment; (5) management demonstrates its belief in the investment prospects of the company, thus attracting other new capital to the shares or new creditors to the company; (6) share dilution from exercised stock options could be minimized. To be a successful strategy, management should buy its stock at a reasonable price. Otherwise, book value per share might be reduced, since the purchase is recorded in the capital accounts of a corporation, and is calculated by reducing the asset values by the liability values and the capital account values. For this reason, most companies reserve the strategy for periods of depressed stock prices. One effect that is always positive is on earnings per share. No matter what is paid for the stock, the reduced shares will increase earnings from operations, except for the exception in (4) above. For this reason, investors should be careful in examining a company that increasing earnings per share is based on growing markets and operations rather than decreased shares.

buying climax. The point in securities trading when demand drives the price of a stock sharply upward, then diminishes suddenly, leading to reduced prices until sustained demand again forms for the stock. Many experts claim a general buying climax precedes a bear market.

buying power. The maximum market value of additional listed securities that can be purchased with the excess funds available in a margin account because of market appreciation of securities already in the account. *See* **margin account.**

Bylaws of a Corporation. The rules adopted by the board of directors of a corporation for its operations and management within the scope of its charter after approval by the original stockholders. *See* **Articles of Incorporation.**

BVRM–Regional Stock Exchange (Africa). See under **Global Investment Market.**

Buenos Aires Stock Exchange. See under **Global Investment Market.**

Cc

CA. Abbreviation for **Chartered Accountant.**

cabinet crowd or **inactive crowd.** The bond brokers on the New York Stock Exchange who file their orders so that trading among themselves can be carried on without their presence.

CAC 40. A stock price index of the 40 most active stocks listed on the Paris Bourse.

cafeteria employee retirement plan. A retirement program for employees that offers variable features, in the form of securities, life insurance, savings, and so on. In effect, such a pension benefits plan allows for an adjustment in each employee's assets and insurance coverage, from monthly contributions to changes for new financial responsibilities and goals, at appropriate points along a career path. Usually, an employee can elect to adjust the plan asset mix once a year.

cafeteria office policy. A method of locating employees by an employer, whereby the employee is given the choice of working out of a central office of his or her home. Usually, the bare essentials are provided, such as a computer, desk, and a chair.

CAGR. Abbreviation for compounded annual growth rate.

Cairo & Alexandria Stock Exchange. See under **Global Investment market.**

California Department of Corporations. Regulator of securities laws in the state of California. Address: 3700 Wilshire Boulevard, Suite 600, Los Angeles, CA 90010. Phone: (213) 736-2741.

call, bond. The right of the issuer of a bond to redeem bonds from holders at a specified premium over par value, beginning several years after their issuance and lasting for a specified period after the first call date. A call prerogative is mentioned in the bond indenture as well as the offering prospectus.

call, options. A written contract to buy 100 shares of a specified stock at a certain price by a stated date, usually in 30, 60, or 90 days or six months. The buyer of a call anticipates a rise in that stock's market value, so he ensures that he can buy cheaply by exercising his call option and then sells the shares for a profit at the future market price after the cost of the call and commissions is deducted. The commission is not paid until the call is exercised. Call options are traded over-the-counter and on the Chicago Board Options Exchange, the American Stock Exchange, and the Philadelphia Stock Exchange.

callable bonds. Those bonds that are redeemable by the issuer at any time with given notice, usually for a specific amount. The purpose of a callable clause is to enable the issuer to eliminate the bond debt if earnings are good or issue new bonds at lower interest costs if that is possible. *See* **noncallable bonds.**

call date. See **call, bond.**

called. A description of a securities issue being redeemed before maturity by the issuing corporation, under preset conditions.

call loan. A commercial bank loan that is repayable on demand. *See* **street loan** and **broker's loan.**

call of bonds. A redemption of bonds by the issuer by payment of the principal before maturity, often accompanied by a premium or penalty to the bondholder.

call price of bonds. The amount of money a bond issuer agrees to pay to bondholders if the bonds are paid off or redeemed before maturity. For example, if bonds are callable at 103, multiply 103 × 10 for the callable price of $1,030—a $30 premium on a $1,000 bond.

call price of preferred stock. The amount of money a corporation agrees to pay preferred stockholders per share in the event the corporation decided to eliminate certain preferred stock by buying it back. The call price is generally higher than the issue price to induce long-term investors with the capital gain in the case of such a call. Generally speaking, it is unwise to pay more for a share of preferred stock than its call price, because the callable option can often be exercised before the new owner can resell the stock, causing a market loss.

call protection. As a bond investor, a period of time in the term of a bond issue when the issuer cannot buy back or redeem the bonds. In many cases the protection is for the life of the bond, in other cases the protection can end in several years, 10 most often, after which the debtor has a right to buy back bonds. It is important for an investor to explore the protection available, because an early redemption could lower interest income when the redemption funds are reinvested. *See* **bond, call.**

CALPERS. Acronym for California Public Employees Retirement System.

Canadian Dealer Network. An electronic stock market for small-capitalization stocks, operated by the Toronto Stock Exchange.

cancel an order. To withdraw an order before it has been accepted by either buyer or seller or their agents. Thus, there has been no actual transaction before the cancellation. *See* **bust the trade.**

canceled stock. Stock reacquired by a corporation and retired. Such stock is not reissuable.

Capacity Utilization Estimate, Federal Reserve. An important report for economists and analysts, released by the Federal Reserve Board mid-month in conjunction with its Industrial Production Report. The report estimates the capacity utilization of the nation, by measuring the extent to which capital facilities are being used in the sustainable output of goods. Capacity utilization is the ratio of the index of industrial production to a related index of capacity. Although there is variability, there is a connection between capacity utilization and inflation, which is the primary reason the report is significant. The measure reflects low volatility and is reasonably easy to predict. When changes in capacity utilization are up, fixed income securities tend to go down, common stocks tend to move up, and dollar exchange rates remain neutral. *See* **Industrial Production Report.**

CAPE. Abbreviation for **Cash-Adjusted Price/Earnings ratio.**

capital, corporate. That money or other assets turned over to a corporation by investors in exchange for a representative ownership in the corporation; or, money from operating profits allocated to a surplus account after the completion of a fiscal period.

capital, invested. The amount of money stockholders have invested in a corporation as represented by the capital surplus and retained earnings accounts, plus the stated, or par, value of the stock outstanding. Along with other surplus amounts, "Earned Surplus," or "Retained Earnings," is included because technically it could have been distributed to stockholders and is considered part of their investment. *See* **Return On Invested Capital.**

Capital Asset Pricing Model (CAPM) or **Time Value of Money Model.** The most widely used formula for establishing the present value or how much to pay today for an investment unit, whether represented by a share of stock, a parcel of real estate, an oil well, a commercial airliner, a professional football team, or virtually any going business. Basically, the formula sets a discounted or present value on a future stream of payments to an investor. This amount is the ideal investment price, if the investor wants to earn the named return, and the other assumptions in the model are accurate. In its applications to common stock pricing, it should be regarded as a rational approach to an investment cost rather than an exact prediction. Usually, the stream of payments is the residual of revenues less operating disbursements, or it could be dividends. The present value is deliberately set less than the future value to enforce the idea that the use of money over time should earn a return and that the investor therefore must pay less today for that future stream. The special attraction for this formula is that it relies on cash flows, meaning that it is applicable in comparing investments subjected to differing accounting conventions. However, there are many variants of cash payments. As global investing becomes more prevalent, this feature will become increasingly important. The formula appearing below is simplistic but useful.

$$NPV = FV \div (1 + i)^n$$

where:

NPV = Net present value of the company's cash flow in three years;

FV = Future Value of that cash flow;

i = Interest or return expected by investor;

n = Number of periods used in discounting cash flow.

Let's simplify this "Greek" with an example. You are interested in a spicy company—Scandal Promotions Inc., a Washington, D.C. think tank—that sometimes gets bored with public policy and creates ribald stories about politicos. Its stock is quoted at $3 per share. You decide to consider holding shares for three years and want to figure how much to pay. Analysts indicate the cash flows in three years will be $10 million, judging Washington hijinks can be counted on to keep the company busy at least that long. You decide the 8.5% that common stocks have returned over the past 50 years, in excess of the risk-free or pure interest rate, plus the additional 25% volatility of this sizzling stock as represented by its Beta of 1.25—the average return and the Beta together comprising the premium over the risk-free return—is the least you can accept from such a risque adventure, over the next three years. Thus, you can calculate the acceptable return as: 8.5% plus 1.25 times that average stock return to account for the additional risk, plus 5.1% for the U.S. Treasury bill interest rate or the pure interest rate for a total target return of 5.7% (8.5 × 1.25 + 5.1 = 15.73). This becomes your hurdle discount rate —the stock's future cash flow has got to be discounted that much to justify the risk.

There are 1.5 million shares of Scandal Promotions issued and outstanding. Substituting in the formula: ($10,000,000) ÷ $(1.157)^3$ or (1.55) equals $10,000,000 ÷ 1.55, or $6,451,613, which is the present value, or DCF, for that stream of future cash flows. Dividing that by shares outstanding of 1,500,000 establishes a present value for the cash flow of $4.30 per share. On the basis of these bare facts, the stock seems underpriced by

$1.30, since it can be bought for the present value—at your hurdle rate of 15.7%—or less.

capital assets. Those assets that can create products or services of material value purchased for long-term service and that are not sold in the normal course of a company's business. Examples are machine tools—such as lathes, grinders, and drill presses— plastic extrusion machines, metal stamping machinery, steel rolling machinery, and so on. The cost of capital assets is shown by depreciation charges each fiscal period, reducing revenues by the portion of the asset's useful life used up, rather than showing the entire cost as an expense that period.

capital budget. A formal plan, usually written, specifying how and when capital equipment or assets will be purchased, usually for the ensuing five years. Usually, it includes construction of facilities, Research & Development, advertising in certain cases, modification of plant and equipment, purchase of machinery, and so on. *See* **operating budget.**

Capital Consumption Adjustment (CCA), Commerce Department. An adjustment made by the Department of Commerce (DOC) in calculating the true value of the Gross Domestic Product (GDP), or total output of the United States in a fiscal period. The adjustment represents the total value, or cost, of the economic lives of capital assets used up in producing the GDP, and results in the Net National Product (NNP). The rationale for making the adjustment is that there can be no national product unless that capital consumption is considered and accounted for. Generally the allowance is between 10% and 15% of GDP. When various taxes are then subtracted, the difference becomes National Income (NI). Technically, the adjustment is made for the difference in depreciation as valued in determining the income reported for income tax filings and "economic depreciation." Economic depreciation is based on applying the value of consistent accounting or economic service lives and straight-line depreciation, related to capital replacement costs. It is equal to the capital consumption from tax returns plus or minus the DOC's estimate of consumption of fixed capital. In the United States the Commerce Department reports profits both before and after it makes this adjustment. For the other principal adjustment, See **Inventory Adjustment Allowance.**

capital consumption allowance, corporate. See **depletion allowance** and **depreciation allowance.**

capital controls. The name of the action taken when governments control the buying and selling of foreign currencies in their jurisdictions, usually during times of financial crises.

capital expenditure. An outlay for a long-term plant or equipment, as opposed to spending for normal operating costs. It represents an expenditure increasing the long-term value of company property and productivity, and their costs or Book Values are accounted for in the balance sheet under Plant & Equipment or a similar heading. When a piece of capital equipment is added to a corporation's resources, its total cost does not reduce earnings in that fiscal period. But each year a portion of its cost is charged to the Depreciation, Depletion & Amortization accounts to reflect its lower value due to wearing out or obsolescence

The important point about capital spending is that each unit of property and equipment increases profits more than the expense of its DD&A, maintenance, interest, and operation decreases them. It's got to improve the bottom line to justify itself economically. Suppose the Batmobile Corp. board of directors decides to purchase 10 metal drill presses to make bigger holes for the laser zappers in the front fenders. It appropriates $2 million, and the presses are installed, increasing the Property, Plant, and Equipment accounts by $2 million. Assuming they have a useful life of five years and a salvage value of $100,000 and the accountants use straight-line depreciation, in each full year $380,000 is charged against revenues to account for their wearing out, producing a lesser book value. At the end of the economic life, the equipment is financially worthless, even though it might still be useable. The latter point is important in the event it is used beyond the accounting life, because in the ensuing periods, no DD&A expenses reduce the revenue stream. The result is higher earnings or profit

($2,000,000 − $100,000 = $1,900,000 ÷ 5 = $380,000 depreciation each year.)

capital formation. The accumulation of money or capital goods, with which other goods and services can be produced, so that a chain of economic activity is set in motion. For a country, the result is usually a rise in the standard of living for the inhabitants. The source of the capital can be from internal savings or external investment. It is the essential of a dynamic economic society.

capital gain. 1) Long-term capital gain. For federal income tax purposes, the appreciation on the sale of property not part of a taxpayer's regular business inventory held for a period of at least 12 months and one day. It is the difference in the selling price of the property and its adjusted purchase price. The tax rate on such a gain is 20%, or 10% for those in the 15% ordinary-income tax bracket. 2) Short-term capital gain. The same sort of gain but on property held less than 12 months and one day. The tax rate is the ordinary income rate up to 35%. Capital losses can be used to offset gains before the computation of taxes. In the case of realizing a long-term gain on a home sale, there is a $500,000 and $250,000 tax exclusion for taxpayers filing jointly and singly, respectively. For changes in 2001, see **Economic Growth and Tax Relief Reconciliation Act of 2001.**

capital gain distribution. See **capital gain dividend.**

capital gain dividend. The payments distributed to a shareholder by a mutual fund from its trading gains in securities, rather than from dividend and/or interest income. The shareholder has a tax liability based on how long the mutual fund owned the shares sold from which came the capital gains distributed—over 12 months is a long-term gain, under 12 months a short-term gain. Note that the tax liability is not based on how long the taxpayer has owned the mutual fund shares. Usually, the mutual fund sends each shareholder a statement at the end of a year specifying which portions of distributions are from income and which part from capital gains. The shareholder then includes each, or losses if present, in his personal tax filing. *See* **capital gain.**

capital gains tax. See **capital gain.**

capital goods industries. Those industries representing a sector engaged in making machinery, materials, and equipment used in manufacturing. *See* **sector.**

capital growth. The appreciation of assets in which funds are invested because of a firm's expanding physical facilities and/or profitable use of those assets.

capital intensive. A reference to an industry in which component companies require a concentration of capital assets to compete effectively. This means a great deal of heavy physical plant and equipment—machinery, buildings, transport equipment, and so on—must be purchased or leased. Consequently, such companies borrow a great deal and are more sensitive to interest rates. Usually, their Balance Sheets display sizable portions of fixed assets and debt. Costs such as debt service, maintenance, and amortization of assets are more dominant in operations than labor costs, for example. In investment analysis, they are said to be heavily-leveraged, which means that stockholders can earn disproportionately more when revenues are high than when they are moderate or low. This follows because most of the costs are relatively fixed—depreciation, depletions, lease payments, interest payments, administrative, and so on—and do not reduce income available for stockholders much more in busy periods than in slow ones. These industries tend to be cyclical, with wide earnings swings. However, the capital intensity makes it more difficult for competitors to enter. Examples of capital-intensive industries are Refining, Steel, Chemicals, and Mining. *See* **labor intensive.**

capitalism. An economic system which advocates the ownership of a country's capital, land, and labor by individuals or business enterprises who are free to use these resources in satisfying their material wants.

capitalization or **capital structure** or **invested capital.** 1) In the financial description of a corporation, the amount of money invested at present, and how it is represented as between securities outstanding—common stocks, preferred stocks, and bonds—and retained earnings, or deficits and capital surplus. There can be classes of each component, such as Class A and Class B common stock, senior and junior preferred stock, mortgage bonds or debentures, and restricted and unrestricted retained earnings. In the traditional measure of capitalization, book and face values are used, so that common stocks are considered at par values or issued values, preferred stocks at par, preference or stated values, and debt at face values or the amounts owed.

In examining a corporate structure for investment purposes, you are interested in how much of the revenue stream and net worth can be claimed by each component of the capitalization, or what the position of each is in the event of a calamity, interruption in business, insolvency, or dispute among investors about their rights in extreme events such as mergers. In most industries, companies tend to maintain reasonably similar portions or ratios of these components, for once the conventional wisdom establishes the propriety of a structure, it is much easier to sell new securities when in compliance, so to speak. Also, the structure has a track record. It works!

Another basis for differentiation in capital structure is in the stage of corporate development: Young companies tend to use more equity financing and reinvest earnings, because the growth potential is higher, a quality stockholders love. Mature companies rely more on debt, because revenues are more predictable, a quality lenders love. There is a basic flaw in only considering this type of capitalization analysis—it depends on book values, which by convention are historical and overlook current financial dynamics. The next topic overcomes this flaw to an extent, but is not free of other ones.

2) Total shares outstanding multiplied by the current price of a share, which is more accurately the market capitalization or market cap. When this product is combined with other equity securities and debt to represent the capital structure, greater emphasis is placed on current values or "going concern" values. This follows because stock buyers have appraised the current and future value of the shares, regardless of what the book values are. When this concept is used, often a company with a

high debt ratio becomes one with a moderate or low debt ratio. And lenders feel better also, for if they have to take control of operations for nonpayment, they know the assets are likely worth more than the Balance Sheet indicates. *See* **ratio.**

capitalization or **gross capital.** The total amount received from the sale of bonds, preferred stock, and common stock by a corporation, at a given point in time.

capitalize an expenditure, to. To include the benefits received from a purchase as an asset in the Balance Sheet.

capitalize earnings, to. To set a present value on a stock based on a multiple of its future earning rate; i.e., if a share is expected to earn $2 in a year and is selling at $30, it is capitalized at 15 times its future earnings. Technically, any method in which the earnings stream, both present and future, is used to establish a stock value is a capitalization of earnings.

capitalize fixed charges, to. To determine the total amount of debt represented by annual interest charges by dividing an assumed or known interest rate into the charges; for example, $200,000 worth of bond interest at an 8% rate would represent $2,500,000 of debt ($200,000 ÷ .08).

Capital Leverage. See **Financial Leverage.**

capital loss. The loss on a sale of property not part of a taxpayer's business inventory. Under Internal Revenue Service regulations, a private taxpayer can deduct $1,000 per year of net capital loss (after deducting gains) from regular income over the years until the loss is used up. For taxpayers in a tax bracket above 35%, generally, it is more advantageous for tax purposes to incur losses in one year and long-term gains in another, since if only losses are taken, taxable ordinary income taxed up to 39.6% is reduced. On the other hand, when losses are used to offset long-term gains, the loss is used to reduce a source of income on which the maximum tax is only 20%, a waste of the capital loss. A corporation is limited to five years in using a capital loss to offset future income.

capital market. The prevailing rate of return that investors demand as reflected by yields on long-term securities, usually considered those coming due in over one year, although purists will argue that from one to five years represents an intermediate market. Definitively, the capital market is considered transactions in long-term securities—bonds, debentures, preferred stock, common stock, mortgages, for example—while the **money market** is considered transactions in short-term securities and instruments—Treasury bills and notes, commercial paper, banker's acceptances, certificates of deposit, or broker call loans, for example. The defining principle is that long-term securities are issued to raise money to build permanent resources, while short-term securities are issued to raise money to operate day-to-day, although there are many overlapping functions by each one. Psychology, money supply, habit, and competition for funds are significant factors as money shifts from one type of investment to another and, in doing so, establishes interest rates for each term or maturity.

The premiums and discounts on securities reflect how a set interest or coupon rate on its face can be adjusted to current investor demands, by decreasing or increasing its actual yield. The interest rate on the issue date of a security is a fixed interest amount or cost only to the issuer, as the security matures, and a fixed yield only to the investor who holds the security until maturity. To all other investors, the interest rate varies from day to day as the price of the security changes.

capital stock. The value given various stock issues on a company Balance Sheet, usually not reflecting the common stock's real value, but more likely reflecting the most favorable tax treatment at the time of incorporation. *See* **common stock.**

Capital Stock Information in Annual Report. The purpose of this section of the annual report is to provide information about the capital stock, usually common stock. It includes the quarterly range in the company's stock price over two or more years as well as the trading symbol and market in which the stock trades. In addition, information about a change in the capital stock status is shown. Often there will appear information as to restrictions on the common stock, such as dividend restrictions imposed by debt covenants. *See* **Annual Report to the Stockholders.**

capital structure or **capitalization.** The division of the money invested in a corporation between common stock, preferred stock, and bonds, stated in dollar amounts. The surplus accounts or net worth are included in the common stock tier of capital. Basically, the capital structure reflects the investment personality of a corporation. That is, the lower the debt layer, including lease contracts, in relation to the common stock, the less financial risk involved, because low debt means low fixed financial obligations. A high preferred stock tier suggests a risk in the middle of the spectrum. There are preferred dividends that take precedence over common share earnings, but they can be passed, in most cases, until times improve. On the other hand, extremely low debt can mean a company lacks growth potential, since revenues are not increasing rapidly enough to service growing debt and there is no opportunity to exploit leverage. There is a great deal of variance among industries. *See* **financial leverage** and **financial structure.**

Capital Surplus or **Contributed Surplus.** On a corporation Balance Sheet or the capital surplus exhibit, the difference between the par value, or stated value of the outstanding stock, and the amount received from its sale or issue.

Capital Surplus Statement. A document showing the capital surplus of a corporation, usually appearing in the annual report, and often combined with the Statement of Shareholders' Equity.

capital turnover. A ratio of the total revenue per year of a business divided by the amount invested in it as an indicator of how quickly it can generate investment return.

CAPM. Abbreviation for **Capital Asset Pricing Model.**

Caracas Stock Exchange. See under **Global Investment Market.**

carry-back. See **net operating loss (NOL) carry.**

carry-forward. See **net operating loss (NOL) carry.**

"carry trade." A global financial strategy of borrowing funds in one currency, say the Japanese yen in 1997, converting the funds to invest in securities in another currency where higher interest rates prevail, say U.S. Treasury bills, and later selling the securities to convert back and repay the loan. The higher interest payments, which more than cover the costs of debt service, are pocketed, and the proceeds from the sale of the investment are converted back and used to repay the debt. The key to a successful "carry trade" is that there is a high enough interest rate differential and that the weaker currency does not reverse itself and appreciate against the currency of the investment during the holding period. When this happens, the conversion back to the original currency can eliminate the benefits of the higher interest income. In addition, the value of the securities purchased can diminish, also spoiling the strategy. *See* **gold carry trade** and **yen carry trade.**

CARS. Nickname for **Certificate for Automobile Receivables.**

cartel. A combination of industrial companies, usually at an international level, calling for limitation of output, dividing up the market, and maintaining pricing agreements.

Casablanca Stock Market (Morocco). See under **Global Investment Market.**

cash account or **"type I" account.** The traditional and most-popular account with an investment brokerage firm. A cash account is available to most investors, either by placing an order for securities and paying for or delivering them by the settlement date or by depositing cash for future trades. Some brokerages require advance deposits of several thousand dollars. In either case, financial and personal information is requested, and most brokerages will extend privileges based on the customer's credit standing. In cases where an investor is not known, a brokerage might require funds deposited in advance of making a purchase or securities deposited in advance of their sale. The latter caveat is especially true in online trading, which is characterized usually by more customer anonymity than face-to-face transactions.

When required to keep a cash balance, it is important that a brokerage firm gives an investor access to a money market fund, into which idle cash is transferred at regular intervals. This transfer is called a "sweep." It provides a return on the investor's cash, while it is waiting to be used. *See* **margin account** and **option account.**

Cash-Adjusted Price/Earnings Multiple (CAPE). The adjustment of the conventional **Price/Earnings Multiple** of a company possessing a great deal of cash and/or other liquid assets, to reflect that the cash or liquid portion of the stock is worth exactly that amount, while the operating-firm portion should be capitalized or estimated on some other basis. By subtracting the cash per share from the stock price and dividing that figure by the trailing four quarters EPS, an adjusted operating P/E Multiple or CAPE is calculated. Adherents claim this rationale more nearly describes how much the true P/E Multiple is, since the liquid assets are not contributors to corporate long-term earnings and are excluded from the capitalization of earnings.

To illustrate, suppose Batman Productions, Inc. makes masks, capes, and skin-tights for Batman aficionados the world over. The CFO is a curmudgeon, demanding that half the corporate assets be in cash or short-term Treasuries. The street estimate for Batman Productions (symbol: BAT), priced at $50 on the NYSE, is $8.50 per share. The Heroes & Villains analyst at Stern Bears Brokerage calculates the cash, or highly liquid value behind the stock, is $5 per share. By subtracting the cash value from the stock price, s/he gets $45, which when divided by the earnings estimate, concludes that the Cash-Adjusted Price/Earning Multiple, or CAPE, is 5.3x. (($50-$5) = ($45 ÷ $8.50) = 5.3x). That would compare to a Price/Earnings Multiple of 5.9x, before the adjustment. ($50 ÷ $8.50 = 5.9x). As you can see, the stock appears cheaper, when only the results of operating assets are valued.

cash balance pension plan. See **pension plan.**

cash burn rate. See **burn rate.**

cash contract or **cash trade.** A stock exchange transaction calling for delivery of and payment for the securities the same day instead of allowing the regular waiting period.

cash cow, corporate. A reference to a subsidiary or division that generates significant cash flow during a fiscal period, often supporting or subsidizing other divisions that are either start-ups, contributing nothing, or losing money. Usually a cash cow counts on regular revenues, and has the advantage of low, reasonable expenses. An example is a natural gas or crude oil pipeline, which has a 20-year life, low maintenance, and long-term demand for its volume of products.

cash-dividend preferred stock. That preferred stock specifying a cash amount for dividends rather than a percentage of the par value.

cash earnings. See **cash flow.**

cash equivalents. Those commercial bills, notes, securities, and other property readily convertible (in from 90 days to six months) into money.

cash flow. A stream of monies composed of net income plus items charged as expenses and allocated to an accounting period but not actually paid out and less items credited as income but not actually received as cash. It is really a statement of the change in cash position from the prior period to the current one and includes items from both the Income Statement and the Balance Sheet. These items include depreciation and depletion allowances, amortization of intangible assets, deferred taxes and other accounting charges that do not represent actual cash outlays but are considered a cost of doing business during that period, and proportionate shares of income allocated in activities like joint ventures. It is an important source of funds because internal reinvestment funds come from this accumulation. See **Balance Sheet, Cash Flow Statement, Income Statement,** and **Statement of Shareholders' Equity.**

cash flow ratio. The ratio of cash flow to sales, expressed as a percentage. This elaborates on the pretax profit margin by only deducting direct operating expenses from gross earnings before calculating the percentage, thus clearly indicating a company's operating ability to generate a money flow. *See* under **ratio.**

Cash Flow Statement or **Sources and Applications of Funds Statement.** That portion of a financial report that provides detailed information on the actual amount of cash receipts received by a company in a given fiscal period less the actual cash disbursements made. It reports on real cash transactions rather than allocated income and expenses. *See* **Balance Sheet, Cash Flow, Income Statement,** and **Statement of Shareholders' Equity.**

cashier. An employee of an investment firm authorized to write checks to customers and supervise securities accounting.

cash-only market. An announcement that trading in a certain issue that day is only on a cash basis, meaning delivery and payment for the securities is required on the day of the trade.

cash or deferred option profit sharing plan (CODA). A 401(k) plan in which an employer designates either a portion of pay or a specific amount that an employee may elect to take in cash or to defer all or in part.

cash position or liquid position. A situation in which a percentage of an investment portfolio is in cash or near cash, for example, 50% cash position. This does not mean, however, that there is currency strewn about the office, but that the cash is represented by short-term Treasury bills and notes or other highly liquid, safe securities.

cash trade. See **cash contract.**

Cassandra myth. In Homer's writings, there was a reference to the beautiful Trojan princess, Cassandra, to whom the god Apollo gave the gift of prophecy. However, when she refused his sexual advances, he put the curse on her that her prophecies all would be of disaster and would come true, but nobody would understand them or believe her. The investment community has adopted the myth in a modern twist that pokes a little fun at erudite forecasters of market gloom and doom, suggesting that their gloomy forecasts will come true but that they will be unable to convince their clients to take action, thus leaving them to the same fate the less prophetic suffer.

Cassandra's Revenge. See under **Web Sites for Investing Women.**

catastrophe or **disaster bond.** A bond instrument in which some portion or all of the principal is forfeited, if a specific natural disaster—earthquake, flood, hurricane—occurs within a certain period. On the other hand, interest is usually guaranteed. These bonds are issued by insurance companies, which See them as ways of reinsuring certain potentially catastrophic risks. Generally, the odds of catastrophes occurring are once in 100 to 250 years. The odds of occurrence and the portion of principal at risk form the basis for ratings assigned such bonds. Usually, the bonds are below investment-grade bonds in quality and, consequently, usually are priced to yield three to five basis points above investment-grade corporate bonds.

CATS. Abbreviation for **Certificates of Accrual on Treasury Securities.**

Caveat Emptor. A Latin phrase and legal concept standing for "Let the buyer beware." Since it implies that a buyer (investor) has a responsibility to check out products and services in a transaction, except in items where warranties apply, it is probably the most important phrase in a successful investor's vocabulary.

CBOE. Abbreviation for **Chicago Board Option Exchange.**

C-bond. See **Z-bond.**

CBS Market Watch Online. See under **Web Sites for the Inquiring Investor.**

CBT. Abbreviation for the **Chicago Board of Trade** ceiling. *See* **resistance area.**

CCI. Abbreviation for **Consumer Confidence Index.**

CCA. Abbreviation for **Capital Consumption allowance.**

CCL. Abbreviation for the **Colorado Springs Stock Exchange.**

CEA. Abbreviation for **Council of Economic Advisers.**

"Centennial-type" mutual fund or **swap fund.** A mutual fund in which an investor can exchange individual stocks for shares in the mutual fund without paying a capital gains tax immediately on the stock he is exchanging. If an exchange is made, the investor will pay a capital gains tax when he redeems his fund shares. The tax-cost basis of his fund shares is the cost of the securities exchanged. The fund shares received by the trader represent ownership of the miscellaneous securities exchanged by investors in the fund, which might be a collection of good and bad investment values, so certain caution should be exercised in investing in such a mutual fund. Professional investors have usually not taken part in accumulating the total fund portfolio.

Center for Financial Learning, GE. A web site offering investors information and advice on retirement planning, estate planning, managing taxes, building a financial plan, and so on. *See* **Web Sites for the Inquiring Investor.**

Center for Research in Security Prices (CRSP). A research facility at the University of Chicago Graduate School of Business, which maintains the most comprehensive collection of standard and derived securities data available for the NYSE, AMEX, and NASDAQ stock markets. The center maintains historical data spanning a period from December 1925 to the present day. It was founded in 1960 by James H. Lorie and Lawrence Fisher, professors at the University of Chicago Graduate School of Business, to advance research on securities markets. Products and services are available to academic and commercial users on a fee basis. Address: 752 South Wells Street, Suite 800, Chicago, IL 60607. Phone: (773) 702-7467. Fax: (773) 702-3036. Web site: *http://gsbwww.uchicago.edu/research/crsp.*

Central Limit Order Book. A central registry of limit orders and prices for popular publicly-traded stocks. Such a record is the objective of securities regulators in the United States, especially as electronic investing is fragmenting the historic trading patterns.

central market. Under federal legislation that took effect in June 1975, a system whereby all markets in which listed stocks are traded compete with each other in offering the best prices for securities.

Central Registration Depository (CRD). A computer database maintained and operated by state securities regulators and the National Association of Securities Dealers. The latter group is the brokerage community's self-regulatory organization. The database provides information related to the registration status of brokers and firms and disciplinary actions taken against either. It's a good idea to check this record when dealing with unknown securities brokers or salesmen. Public disclosure hotline: (800) 289-9999.

century bonds. Corporate bonds with a maturity date of 100 years.

CEO. Abbreviation for **Chief Executive Officer.**

certificate, stock. (1) An affidavit of ownership of a specified number of corporation shares. Certificates are valuable documents and are often printed in secret inks to prevent counterfeiting. If lost, most corporations require the stockholder to post a fidelity bond before replacing them. (2) A negotiable certificate representing a deposit of stock with a pending change in its condition.

Certificate for Automobile Receivables (CARS). Pass-through securities backed by packaged automobile installment loans originally generated by banks and paying interest from those installments. *See* **pass-through securities** and **asset-backed securities.**

Certificate of Accrual on Treasury Securities (CATS). A type of **zero-coupon bond** backed but not actually issued by the U.S. Treasury, and sold at a deep discount. Certain investment firms are permitted to issue or sponsor these securities, which are backed by the U.S. Government and U.S. Treasury securities. No interest payments are made on these STRIPS periodically as is done in the case of conventional bonds. Instead, interest is accumulated for bondholders and paid at the maturity of the bonds. Under IRS regulations, even though bondholders receive no interest until the accumulation of total interest at maturity, they are subject to filing **imputed interest** income each year, on the accumulated amounts they would have received if the zero-coupon bonds had been conventional bonds. Because the interest liability is imputed on this type of bond, they are recommended for tax-sheltered programs, such as retirement plans. This is because in such programs there is no tax liability until the plan is used by the investor, usually at retirement, when income tax rates are usually lower. There is no interest liability on such plans during contribution years, imputed or otherwise.

Certificate of Incorporation. See **Articles of Incorporation.**

Certificate of Participation. A form of municipal equipment lease.

Certified Financial Planner (CFP). A person who advises others on achieving long-term financial goals, either for a fee or on a commission basis. In order to use the designation, the licenSee has demonstrated experience and a commitment to education and ethics applicable to a professional financial planning practice. Address: Certified Financial Planner Board, 1700 Broadway, Suite 2100, Denver, CO 80290-2101. Phone: (303) 830-7500. Fax: (303) 860-7388. Web site: *www.cfp-board.org.*

Certified Management Accountant (CMA). An individual who has past experience and educational requirements in the field of management accounting in Canada. Management accounting is specialized beyond the bounds of traditional accounting. Its objective is to provide management with dynamic information for making operating decisions and developing strategies for business success. Part of the accreditation program is to facilitate updating of skills. There are 28,000 CMAs in Canada. Web site: *www.cma-canada.org.*

CFA. Abbreviation for **Chartered Financial Analyst.**

CFD. Abbreviation for **Contract for Difference.**

CFP. Abbreviation for **Certified Financial Planner.**

CFO. Abbreviation for **Chief Financial Officer.**

CFY. Abbreviation for **current fiscal year,** when appearing with financial or operating results that are usually associated with the first three quarters. After these, the reference most likely becomes LYE for "latest fixed year."

CFYE. An abbreviation for "current fiscal year ending," when followed by a date.

chaebol. Types of business structure in South Korea in which a parent company owns many subsidiaries. The parent is often vertically-integrated but not necessarily so, and is family-owned. Samsung is the largest one in South Korea, the world's eleventh largest economy, with 58 subsidiaries. The 30 largest of these business organizations account for one-half of South Korea's industrial output. The business form resembles the conglomerate in Western economies.

chain-weighted index or **Fisher index.** The measure of change in economic data which is calculated from a moving average of current and recent observations rather than a more historic, fixed-price base period. The U.S. Bureau of Economic Analysis (BEA) converted to a chain-weighted basis for several key economic series in 1997. The result has been a more moderate degree of estimates of changes in series like the Consumer Price Index and Gross Domestic Product. This is because when the more recent and moving data is used as the base, rather than a previous base year, which could be as much as 10 years prior, the effects of rapidly declining prices is recorded significantly in the changes. The effect is particularly noticeable in cases of high-technology products like computers, which tend to decrease in price as the high research and development costs are amortized. For example, in a chain-weighted price change, from Year 1 to Year 2 is 4.0%, and from Year 2 to Year 3 is 5.0%, the annual changes are chained as follows: Year 1 = 1.00, Year 2 = 1.04 (1.0 × 1.04), and Year 3 = 1.09 (1.00 × 1.04 × 1.05).

Chairman of the Board. The top executive officer of a corporation who is elected by the stockholders' deputies, the board of directors, to supervise the affairs of the enterprise. This officer presides at all quarterly board meetings, and is empowered to call special meetings to consider matters like acquisitions, mergers, and lawsuits. *See* **Board of Directors.**

"change." A reference to the fractional portion of a stock quote, which can be as low as one-sixteenth of a dollar. For example, 10^{1}/_{16}$ or $10.0625 in decimal form, might be expressed as "10 dollars and change" in a fast-moving stock report. As decimal quotes establish their presence in the United States, there will probably be a greater tendency to do this, because decimalization will produce 100 fractional portions or 100 cents in the fractional portion of a quote.

channel stuffing. Shipping large volumes of merchandise to distributors in a fiscal period in order to book large revenues and profits quickly. This accounting practice is considered misleading, because the goods can be returned to the producer, thus requiring adjustments to the accounts that were over-stated. Basically, the practice of booking sales to distributors is allowed under present accounting rules, if a reasonable estimate of returns is also reported and deducted from the gross amounts. The Securities and Exchange Commission is tightening surveillance of companies that engage in the practice without providing a reasonable estimate of returns.

charge off, to. To subtract an expense or cost, usually an unusual one such as the loss of a patent or copyright that is valuable, from current earnings or a surplus account or asset account in the current fiscal period. Also, the effect can be accomplished on historical results by restating financial statements. The transaction both increases expenses and reduces the monetary value of resources, through accounting entries, in the applicable fiscal period. This action is a major one, usually requiring the acquiescence of top management.

Charitable Remainder Trust. A trust created as a result of an irrevocable gift to a charitable organization, a gift the economic benefits from which the charity does not actually receive until the donor dies or the gift "matures," in the parlance of financial giving. A donor gets a tax deduction for the gift immediately, but not for the entire amount since the charity will not receive proceeds immediately. The allowable deduction is based on the age of the donor(s) and on prevailing interest rates, established by the IRS. A donor receives payments for life and may decide how assets are invested.

Charitable Remainder Annuity Trust (CRAT). A type of **Charitable Remainder Trust,** in which the donor(s) receives a fixed sum annually, or more frequently, to be not less than 5% of the fair market value of the assets placed in trust (as established by the IRS).

Charitable Trust. A type of trust arrangement in which property placed in trust must be used for charitable purposes.

chart. A graphic representation of a stock's successive price movements. Often these movements form definite patterns; when a stock's price deviates from the pattern, chartists claim it is a key signal in that the resulting price upturn or downturn can be measured by the pattern before the deviation and the trading volume during the deviation.

Actually, a chart enables an investor to picture the price trends of a stock in relation to volume and other factors more dramatically than statistics alone. Charting can be elaborate, including notations on obscure technical factors, or simply a price record of a stock and its volume of trading. A great deal depends on how much the chartist wants to include, how much he wants to See graphically of a stock's past price movement so that he can more intelligently predict future prices.

Basically, there are two types of charts—**bar charts** and **point and figure charts.** Although the formulation of investment policies based on charts alone overlooks vital financial information about the corporations involved, it is claimed this technique does offer insight into advantageous market timing, since most stock prices move in cycles or at least patterns. The chartist maintains a record of what shareholders did in the past when a stock was at a significant price level and feels that they will react in a predictable manner when the price returns to that level. Basically, he feels they will either sell or buy on balance and the resultant price move, or breakout, will be obvious if he has recorded price, time, and volume factors as well as other events like splits and extra dividends as the price has reached this level before. His prime objective is to know immediately how much a price will change once it has pierced a significant price level. *See* also **gap** and **price formations.**

Charter, Corporate. A document issued by a state or the U.S. government granting rights to corporations to engage in business under certain conditions within that jurisdiction. *See* **Articles of Incorporation.**

Chartered Accountant (CA). A designation for an individual specially trained and experienced in all phases of public accountancy, and one who has passed qualifying exams and been approved by the Institute of Chartered Accountants in the country of practice. Besides educational training, Chartered Accountants must demonstrate a high degree of professional service and integrity. It is the counterpart in the United Kingdom to the Certified Public Accountant in the United States. The designation is prevalent in countries of the original British Commonwealth.

Chartered Financial Analyst (CFA). An individual who has demonstrated knowledge and techniques of sound investment management through successfully passing three examinations and fulfilling experience requirements over a minimum period of five years. The program is administered by the Institute of Chartered Financial Analysts. *See* **Institute of Chartered Financial Analysts.**

Chartered Investment Counselor (CIC). A designation formed so that excellence and experience in the investment counsel profession might be better recognized. The charter was designed to recognize the special qualifications of persons employed by member firms of **The Investment Counsel Association of America, Inc.** (ICAA) whose primary duties are consistent with section 208(c) of the Investment Advisors

Act of 1940, pertaining to use of the term "investment counsel." Also, sections I and II of the Association's Standards of Practice highlight the professional responsibilities and qualifications required of designees:

- An investment adviser is a fiduciary and has the responsibility to render professional, continuous, and unbiased investment advice oriented to the investment goals of each client.
- To enable a member firm to serve its clientele effectively, its investment and managerial personnel should be individuals of experience, ability, and integrity.
- Candidates are required to hold the Chartered Financial Analysts designation.

Web site: *www.lwnweb.com.ima.cma.htm.*

chartist. One who uses stock price charts for aid in investment timing.

Chemicals. Those stocks representing corporations manufacturing chemical products for industrial and personal products. *See* **industry stock group.**

Chicago Board of Exchange. See under **Global Investment Market.**

Chicago Board of Options Exchange (CBOE). A national securities exchange, founded in 1975, listing option contracts on 1,100 stocks. Average daily volume in first half of 1998 was 796,000 contracts. It plans to merge with the **Pacific Coast Stock Exchange.** Address: 400 South Lasalle Street, Chicago, IL 60605. Phone: (312) 786-5600.

Chicago Board of Trade (CBOT). The largest futures and options trading facility in the world. Average daily volume is approximately 2 million contracts, covering commodities, interest rates, and bond futures and options on futures for financial indexes, commodities, and Treasuries. It plans to consolidate some operations with Chicago Mercantile Exchange. Address: 141 West Jackson Blvd., Chicago, IL 60604-2994.

Telephone: (312) 435-3500. *See* under **Global Investment Market.**

Chicago Mercantile Exchange (MERC). A national securities and commodities exchange in the United States, founded in 1874, specializing in futures and option contracts. It has 2,725 members, representing 79 firms. Address: 30 South Walter Drive, Chicago, IL 60606. Phone: (312) 930-3457. *See* under **Global Investment Market.**

Chicago Stock Exchange. A U.S. national exchange founded in 1882. It became the Midwest Stock Exchange in 1949 and resumed under its present name in 1993. It is the second largest stock exchange in the United States in terms of trade and share volume, with 4,000 companies listed. Address: 440 S. Lasalle Street, Chicago, IL 60605. Phone: (312) 663-2980. Fax: (312) 663-2396. Web site: *www.chicagostockex.com.*

Chicago Tribune Online. See under **Web Sites for the Inquiring Investor.**

Chief Executive Officer (CEO). That corporate officer responsible for recommending programs and policies affecting a corporation to the board of directors and for implementing those approved through his authority to manage the enterprise. The CEO is usually the president or the chairman of the board.

Chief Financial Officer (CFO). That corporate officer responsible for the management of the accounting systems, cash flow, and long-term financial objectives of a corporation. The CFO is usually the financial vice-president, comptroller, or treasurer.

Chief Information Officer (CIO). That corporate official who is responsible for developing and managing information technology resources in a company, while fostering comprehensive technology direction that furthers business objectives of the company. Usually, such a person is required to be trained in electronic information technology.

Chief Operating Officer (COO). That corporate officer responsible for the day-to-day operations of a corporation as laid out by the direction established by the board of directors and delegated to the CEO.

Chilean Electronic Stock Market. See under **Global Investment Market.**

"Chinese trading." A critical term levied by traders in an over-the-counter stock at one who attempts to negotiate an independent price for that stock, after there has been an understanding about the price or an established way to set the price.

"Chinese Wall." A reference to the operating barriers—conceptual more than physical—between the departments of an investment brokerage firm so that the personnel and files of the investment banking, corporate finance, trading, sales, and research departments do not intermingle. Since the investment banking and corporate finance departments have access to nonpublic information related to clients, it would be unfair to the general investment public if that firm's trading, sales, and research departments gained advance knowledge of such information, since they could exploit it in their activities. By the same token, when a research department analyst is preparing a report on a stock and that opinion is likely to have a material effect on the price of the stock when the report is issued, it would be unfair to the general investment public for the trading and sales departments to have advance knowledge of that impending event. For example, a trading department might adjust its inventory of the stock in question to avoid a loss or to make a profit when the report comes out. Rule 10b-5 of the Securities and Exchange Commission calls for the "Chinese wall" to be maintained. Some other rules also touch on this point. And several exchanges have similar rules.

Although it is not as well documented, this partition is also mandated and maintained between the appropriate divisions of other financial institutions, such as a bank or insurance company. The wall separates personnel and records possessing nonpublic information about public corporations from research, trading, and portfolio management functions of that institution. The same reasoning is present. For example, if in a commercial bank the corporate banking department has access to nonpublic data on a NYSE company that is required to furnish such data as part of a loan covenant, and that company's stock is included in the bank's pension funds under management, the nonpublic knowledge could advantage the pension fund managers at the expense of the investment public.

churn accounts. As a broker, to constantly prod customers to trade their holdings without fundamental investment reasoning.

CiberCentro for Latinos. A Web site featuring advice, news, and chat rooms for Latinos, in English, Portuguese, and Spanish. *See* **Web Sites for the Inquiring Investor.**

CIC. Abbreviation for **Chartered Investment Counselor.**

CIO. Abbreviation for **Chief Information Officer.**

CIN. Abbreviation for the **Cincinnati Stock Exchange.**

Cincinnati Stock Exchange (CIN). A national securities exchange. Address: 49 E. Fourth Street, #205, Cincinnati, OH 45202. Phone (312) 786-8803.

circuit breakers. Internal systems and procedures that halt trading on stock exchanges in cases of extraordinary imbalances of buy and sell orders. These imbalances can cause prices to plunge, suddenly wiping out billions of dollars in stock values. Consequently, the SEC and stock exchange officials have established critical points in changes in the DJIA as flash points. When the index drops a specific amount, controls are set in motion to reinstate order in the markets. The following circuit breakers are in effect on the NYSE:

- In the case of a 10% decline in the DJIA, trading will be halted for one hour. When the DJIA rallies at least 10%, the restrictions come off.
- In the case of a 20% decline, trading will halt for two hours. When the DJIA rallies at least 20%, no trading restrictions are in effect.
- In the case of a 30% decline anytime, trading will stop for the rest of the day. When the DJIA rallies at least 30%, there are no restrictions.

- In addition, a 900-point drop in the DJIA will cause a halt for one hour if the decline takes place before 2:00 P.M.; for 30 minutes before 2:30 P.M.; with no action between 2:30 P.M. and 4:00 P.M. On a 1,750-point decline, trading will stop for two hours if the decline happens before 1:00 P.M.; for an hour if before 2:00 P.M.; for the remainder of the session if between 2:00 P.M. and 4:00 P.M. A 2,650-slide will postpone trading for the rest of the session. The point magnitudes are adjusted quarterly, based on the DJIA closing prices in the previous month, rounded to the nearest 50 points. The percentages are adjusted on the first of January, April, July, and October.

classified stock. Common stock issued by a corporation with specific differences in regard to shareholder privileges and voting rights. *See* **class of stock.**

class of stock. A particular category of corporate stock with specific rights and limitations. Usually, corporate management issues classified stock to make an acquisition or raise new equity capital. There are differences in shareholder privileges and voting rights, usually, among classified stocks issued by the same corporation. For example, Mitchell Energy classified Dev/ "A" (MND.A – NYSE) stock is voting but Mitchell Energy Class "B" (MND.B – NYSE) is nonvoting. Most often, classified stock bears the name "A," "B," or "C." There are 2,080 classes of stock, including common and preferred, listed for trading on the New York Stock Exchange representing 1,567 corporations. *See* **alphabet stock.**

Clayton Act of 1914. See **antitrust laws.**

clearance transaction. The surreptitious practice of buying stock through one broker and selling immediately through another if its market price rises, letting a securities "factor" finance the transaction. If the stock does not rise in value, the buyer never appears to make payment to the first broker, who is left with the purchased stock.

clearing house. 1) In securities management, an exchange agency that records trading balances between member firms. 2) In banking, an agency that records withdrawals and additions between member banks.

CLEC. An abbreviation for **competitive local exchange carrier.**

"click" investing. See **online investing.**

CLOB. Abbreviation for **Central Limit Order Book.**

close contracts. To settle the buy and sell accounts between member firms of an exchange.

closed corporation. A reference to a corporation's stock that is held entirely by a few people who refuse to sell to the public at large.

closed-end investment company or **closed-end investment trust.** A company organized to invest in securities, operating under the Investment Company Act of 1940, with a restricted number of shares. Some closed-end investment companies are listed and the selling prices of their shares are determined by supply and demand. Often shares trade at less than their asset value, or at a discount, and often at more than asset value or at a premium. If the shares are listed, regular exchange commissions apply. *See* **quote (1).** If not listed, the regular over-the-counter quoting system applies. *See* **quote (4).** *See* **mutual fund** or **investment trust.**

closely held or **tightly held.** A reference to a corporation's stock that is almost entirely held by a few people who are reluctant to sell it even at reasonable prices.

close the books. To announce the completed sale of all shares of a new offering to the public and the absorption by the market at the public offering price.

closet indexing. As a mutual fund portfolio manager, investing most of a fund's resources in stocks that comprise most of the stocks in a particular stock market index, with a similar weighting to their weighting in the index, investing the slight remainder in other stocks or more of the index stocks. The fund still charges standard management fees to fund shareholders, despite providing very little active fund portfolio management.

CMA. Abbreviation for **certified management accountant.**

CMO. Abbreviation for **Collateralized Mortgage Obligation.**

CNBC Business News Online. See **Web Sites for the Inquiring Investor.**

Coalition of Black Investors (COBI). A Web site featuring advice and news for black investors. *See* **Web Sites for the Inquiring Investor.**

coda alliance. See **airline alliances.**

Coincident Indicators. See **Economic Indicators.**

Coffee, Sugar & Cocoa Exchange. See under **Global Investment Market.**

COLA. Abbreviation for **Cost of Living Adjustment.**

collapsible corporation. In tax law, a business enterprise operating under a corporate charter, created with a view to selling the corporation or distributing its assets before a substantial part of its potential taxable income is realized.

collar. 1) An option package—a type of derivative—underwritten by a securities firm or bank and designed for an over-the-counter stock in which a corporate executive foregoes some of the upside potential in his stock for the promise of cash if the shares happen to decline in value. 2) A commodity hedge transaction in which one party is required to make payment to the other party if the average NYMEX reference price for a commodity falls below the floor price for the transaction, and the latter party is required to make payment to the first party if the average NYMEX reference price for any settlement period rises above the ceiling price in the contract. 3) A fall in an index price to a predetermined level that temporarily stops program trading on an exchange until buy and sell orders become more balanced. Its purpose is to halt stock price collapses that are sudden and based on emotional selling. In February 1999, restrictions made collars become effective on program trading when the Dow Jones Industrial Index moves 2% in either direction.

collateral loan. A commercial bank loan with securities or other assets pledged as security in case the borrower cannot repay the money. Banks may loan money on unlisted securities as well as listed, whereas national exchange brokerage houses may only loan on listed securities.

collateral trust bonds. Those bonds pledge by property held in trust.

collateral trust notes. Those short-term financial obligations pledged by property held in trust.

Collateralized Mortgage Obligation (CMO). A bond that is backed by many mortgage contracts, arranged by maturity dates and yields into classes, or tranches, that determine the pay out schedules of the bonds. These bonds can mature in several months up to 20 years. The various tranches mature at different intervals and pay different interest rates. Usually, the bonds are guaranteed by a government entity, such as the **Federal Home Loan Mortgage Corporation** (Freddie Mac) and **Government National Mortgage Association** (Ginnie Mae) as well as other issuers. Because of the guarantee and generally high quality of the mortgages therein, these bonds are considered investment quality by the rating services. Even so, if mortgage rates decrease significantly, a spate of refinancing by mortgagors in the batch could cause a premature payout to bondholders. Freddie Mac CMOs are issued in minimum denominations of $25,000.

collective bargaining. Those negotiations on hours, wages, profit sharing, insurance, retirement benefits, and so on between representatives of management and organized groups of employees.

college prepaid tax plan. A program created by certain states that enables a taxpayer to defer all earnings from the plan's resources, accumulated for the college education of a child, until withdrawn for tuition payments. At the later date, they are taxed at the lower rates of the child/student, for state and federal income tax purposes. The state creating the program guarantees the accumulating amount will be adequate or nearly so to meet future tuition costs in that state. The proceeds can only be used in schools of that state, unlike college savings tax plans. Tax experts point out that these plans are managed very conservatively, in order to vouchsafe the availability of funds; and, therefore, money might be more efficiently invested in other education plans. The portfolios are also less flexible than in other programs. *See* **college savings tax plan.**

college savings tax plan. Allowed by the IRS beginning in the mid-1990s, a tax-deferred plan now established by 23 states, including Connecticut, Iowa, Maine, New Jersey, New York, and Rhode Island, with the list growing each year. A taxpayer can accumulate funds for a child's education through investment in securities such as mutual funds, money market funds, stocks and bonds, differing in each state and handled and managed by investment firms. Portfolios can be adjusted for the changing circumstances of beneficiaries of plans. The investment earnings are not taxable, under federal or participating states, until withdrawal later at the child/student's lower tax rate. In certain states, the investment return when used appropriately is excused completely from tax liability. Some states, most notably New York, also allow deductions on state income tax filings for contributions to such plans. Unlike college prepaid tax plan versions, the plan assets can be used for college tuition anywhere. *See* **college prepaid tax plan.**

Colorado Division of Securities. Regulator of securities laws in the state of Colorado. Address: 1580 Lincoln, Suite 420, Denver, CO 80203. Phone: (303) 894-2320.

combine. See **complex.**

combined or **overall coverage.** The ratio of earnings, before bond interest but after taxes, divided by the combined interest and preferred dividend requirements. For an industrial company, four times is satisfactory; for a utility, three times.

coming out. See **coming to market.**

coming to market or **coming out.** 1) A reference to a new security issue being readied legally and financialyl for public sale.

2) A phrase describing when a new security issue will be available for public sale when followed by a date; for example, "The bonds are coming to market on June 8." 3) "Coming to market at" or "Coming out at" A phrase describing at what price a new security issue will be sold to the public when followed by an amount; for example, "The stock is coming to market at $12 per share, the price to investors."

command and control management structure. A reference to a corporate style of management that depends on a chain of command and established corporate policies in the communications and operations that run a company. Top executives relay instructions and receive feedback through assistants and supervisors. Opponents of the method charge that misunderstandings and miscommunications result from the tedious flow of information. Usually, there is no crossover between different departments—finance, engineering, research, marketing, and so on—in planning and implementation. This concept thrived through most of the twentieth century with the dominance of mega-corporations in the business world. In the technological revolution of the late twentieth century, a management emphasis on speed and idea sharing evolved that lends itself better to the smaller entities that are dominating new business formation in the early twenty-first century. It is called **flat management structure** and is an extension of the cost cutting and emphasis on "leanness" that began in the fiercely competitive 1990s.

commercial alliance. See **airline alliances.**

Commerce Department. See **Department of Commerce, U.S.**

Commercial and Industrial Loans. *See* under **Economic Indicators.**

commercial paper or **paper.** Those short-term certificates of indebtedness that are sold at percentage discounts from their face value, placed as collateral for loans, or held until they are paid off.

commingled investment account. An investment portfolio supervised by a bank and acquired with funds exchanged by investors for units of participation in the plan. In effect, the bank acts as mutual fund manager. However, under present laws the bank is exempt from various provisions of the Investment Company Act.

commission. A percentage of the market value of a securities sale or purchase paid to a brokerage firm, one-fifth to one-third of which generally goes to the broker. The commission on listed stocks is generally about $1\frac{1}{2}\%$. Since May 1, 1975, exchange members can no longer charge uniform commission rates but must negotiate their own charges with customers, a regulation that has generally led to lower rates for institutional investors and higher ones for individuals. Commission rates are becoming more negotiated as online brokerage gains market share. Some online brokerages charge flat commission rates, in some cases as low as under $10 per transaction. Of course, that rate does not buy a customer an extravagant Christmas gift. Most old line brokerages charge per share prices to large investors, amounts calculated from the firm's cost per share transaction, with some profit thrown in. *See* **override** and **sales load.**

commission house. *See* **brokerage house.**

commission house broker. *See* **floor broker.**

Commitments and Contingencies Section of the Annual Report. That section of a company's annual report that discusses certain arrangements in effect or events that might occur that could affect the financial or operating results of a company in the future, either positively or negatively. By extension, such items could affect investment performance. Examples are items such as long-term leases, perhaps representing abandoned facilities that are drains on cash but not producing income and tax liens by the IRS for amounts that would penalize the company's results materially in the future. On the positive side, there may be items such as leases of facilities at below market prices, giving the company a competitive advantage; lawsuits that represent extraordinary gains for the company when adjudication is finished; or tax appeals that could result in favorable rulings that would refund monies to the company. Often these items appear as a subsection of the Consolidated Notes to the Financial and Operating Statement Section. *See* **Annual Report to the Stockholders.**

Commodity Credit Corporation (CCC). See **agency securities.**

Commodity Futures Trading Commission (CFTC). The federal regulatory agency, created by Congress in 1974, that administers the Commodity Exchange Act. Its primary charge is to monitor the futures and commodity options markets, looking for and preventing commodity price distortion and market manipulation, and to protect the rights of consumers who use the markets for either commercial or investment purposes in the United States. The free-wheeling derivatives market is regulated by the Commission. Its mandate was renewed and expanded in 1978, 1982, 1986, and 1992. Under its jurisdiction are 255 commodity brokerages, 49,318 sales persons, 9,007 floor brokers, 1,164 floor traders, 1,291 commodity pool operators, 2,514 commodity trading advisors and 1,389 introducing brokers. Address: Three Lafayette Center, 1155 21st Street, Northwest, Washington, D.C. 20581. Phone: (202) 418-5080. Fax: (202) 418-5525. Web site: *www.cftc.gov.*

Commodity Futures Modernization Act of 2000. A bill before Congress that would attempt to clarify complex legal and regulatory questions concerning trading securities and commodities by global corporations and multinational banks. As the bill is now worded it would also settle some regulatory conflicts between the SEC and CFTC and establish futures trading in individual stocks.

common market or **trading bloc.** The commerce that results from an agreement between several countries to promote trade between themselves, usually erecting tariffs against goods from other countries and calling for political policies that will stimulate free flow of goods between the member countries.

common share. See **common stock.**

common stock or **capital stock** or **common share.** The collective form of ownership of a corporation in the United States. Common stock is divided into many equal shares and usually entitles a stockholder or owner to vote on major corporate issues and for directors, proportionate to shares owned. Usually, shareholders are entitled to a proportionate share of additional common stock if they wish to purchase it. Otherwise, they are entitled to the rights, which they may sell. It has no guaranteed dividend, but shareholders are entitled to profits when directors declare such a distribution to shares outstanding. However, this may be done only after debts and preferred stockholders are paid. A common share is considered a residual security in that a shareholder has last claim on profits and assets in the event of liquidation. *See* **ordinary share.**

common stock ratio. The ratio of the par, or stated, value of common stock, plus surplus, to the total capitalization, expressed as a percentage. Approximately half of capitalization should be in this category, in a well-situated industrial company. For all manufacturing companies in the United States, the average common stock ratio was 43% for most of the 1990s.

common trust fund or **pooled trust fund.** A fund belonging to several owners that is held by a bank as trustee and pooled for investment purposes. The fund is managed like an individual trust fund, with all owners sharing in the income, and invested at the bank's discretion. The practice allows institutions to manage small bequests more efficiently.

Communications Equipment Makers. Those stocks representing companies engaged in the manufacture of equipment used in voice, data, and video communications. *See* **stock industry group.**

Communications Software & Services. Those stocks representing companies making and distributing computer software and offering services for communications applications. *See* **industry stock group.**

"communicopia." An expression coined on Wall Street, signifying the panorama of companies contributing to the transmission of audio, video, and data signals and the convergence of these businesses into communicatons, entertainment, programming, and electronic commerce. It refers to the huge array of stocks available for investors, and the potential for high market gains from owning the right ones. (It is Wall Street's Horn of Plenty.)

Community Reinvestment Act (CRA). A Federal act, passed by Congress in 1977 and amended in 1995 and 1995, that encourages depository institutions like banks and savings and loan entities to help meet the credit needs of the communities in which they operate. This charge includes the credit needs of low- and moderate-income neighborhoods, and is based on policies associated with safe and sound banking practices. Compliance is based on periodic exams of credit institutions by supervisory agencies like the Federal Reserve Board, Comptroller of the Currency, the Federal Deposit Insurance Corporation, and the Office of Thrift supervision. The leverage on the institutions to carry out the spirit of the act is found in actions taken in response to the application for deposit facilities, including mergers and acquisitions. This act was amended in 1999 by the **Financial Services Modernization Act of 1999.**

company stock purchases or **reacquired stock.** Those purchases of its own stock by a corporation in the open market through requests for tenders or by negotiated purchases of large blocks for any of the following reasons: (1) to have stock for option and employee purchase plans, (2) to provide for mergers or acquisitions, (3) to have stock for payment of stock dividends, or (4) to reduce shares outstanding and increase earnings-per-share. Reacquired stock is not considered treasury stock.

compensation package. A reference to the total amount of money and derivative securities values that a company pays to a top executive, usually stated on an annual basis. It includes annual salary, option grants, stock grants, automatic raises, bonuses, and incentive payments, and sometimes other emoluments, such as insurance and living expenses. A monetary value is placed on the various categories for the year in the calculation of a compensation package. In deciding what the mix of the compensation should be, executive pay consultants and directors are guided by the relative attractiveness of each category, at that point in time, so that the emphases change. For example, when the company's stock is enjoying a rise, stock options and stock are popular, as they were in the late 1990s. In some very generous practices of corporate governance, an executive might be reimbursed for any loss in the stock's value beneath the exercise price or anticipated price. However, this practice is coming under accounting scrutiny, and may be treated as an expense in the future.

When high flying companies, like the dot-coms in the 1990s and early 2000s, slow down, other incentives grow in popularity with boards, programs like bonuses and incentive payments. For investors, excessive use of stock grants and stock outright can cause future dilution, both of stockholders' equity and earnings. A company issuing stock, even though it is restricted, at a 5% rate annually must increase earnings by that amount, just for earnings per share to stay flat. In the case of an executive paying an exercise price for stock, the return on that payment must at least equal the increase in shares, in order for earnings per share to remain even. Obviously, there is a point of diminishing returns for investors, including executives, in continuing extravagant accelerating compensation packages too long. *See* **repricing, stock options** and **under water.**

competition, economic. A commercial environment in which there are efforts by disassociated sellers or buyers to do business by offering the most attractive financial terms to customers.

competitive bidding. The making of offers to pay an issuer a special amount for securities by each of several underwriters of syndicates who want to sell the securities to the public at a profit.

competitive local exchange carrier (CLEC). (Pronounced "See-leck") A reference to one of the many new startup companies that have entered the local-service telephone markets since the Telecommunications Act of 1996 allowed competition with the **Baby Bells,** who had enjoyed regional monopolies since 1984.

complex or **combine.** A union of two or more companies' assets for a specific business purpose without a legal merger.

composite average. A stock average combining representative price changes of industrial, railroad, and utility stocks.

composite table. A stock quotation table showing the daily ranges of stocks based on trading on several national exchanges, including NASDAQ and Instinet furnished to newspapers by Associated Press and United Press International.

composite yield. The average yield of all the stocks in a stock average.

compound the annual growth rate, to. In analyzing corporate performance, to measure the increase in a business series—such as earnings per share, shareholders' equity, or oil reserves—between a beginning date and ending date as though it had compounded regularly over each division, such as fiscal quarters or years, in that time frame. In reality, most business series are mercurial, so the procedure can be somewhat misleading. But the concept does link to the basic nature of a business enterprise, which is to employ each period's resource gains toward accumulating more numerous ones in the future. In cases where a series has not fluctuated a great deal in growth, the procedure is more valid. Certainly, most managements would like to compound corporate growth in a predictable manner. For example, Shaky Sam's, Inc.'s earnings per share are as follows: 1995/$0.25, 1996/$0.50, 1997/$0.30, 1998/$0.25, 1999/$0.75, 2000/$0.70. The symbolic compounded annual growth rate is 22.9%, measuring the $0.25 in 1995 to $0.70 in 2000 as though it occurred over five annual compounding periods of 22.9% each. However, the average earnings growth is 84.7%, calculated by adding each annual change in earnings and dividing by five. Actually, in this case, the compounding principle actually describes the growth function more realistically.

compound earnings, to. To measure a company's earnings growth over a period by expressing the annual gains as a set rate of percentage increases over each previous year. A company that is compounding earnings faster than the national average is considered a growth company. *See* **compound the annual growth rate.**

compound interest, to. To add successive interest payments to the principal to form the base for figuring the next interest accumulation or payment; thus, interest is paid on the principal plus cumulative interest in each successive period. This method is applied to savings accounts by most savings institutions, although the compounding periods vary to differentiate an institution from competitors or to attract new deposits. In reality, there is little difference in a future value that has compounded one time during a year or one time quarterly. The formula for compounding interest is the foundation for investment planning, whether in a savings account or an investment. The formula or derivatives of it are used for calculating such vital matters as growth of savings, growth of corporate earnings, growth of insurance reserves, and growth of pension plan reserves. It is the formula that makes our planet go, in a financial sense. In the formula below, interest is compounding on an annual basis. *See* **compounding periods, compounding rate, continuous compounding, interest,** and **simple interest.**

$$FV = PV \times (1+i)^n$$

where:
FV = Future amount;
PV = Present value or beginning amount;
i = Interest rate;
n = Number of compounding periods.

For example, if a depositor opens a savings account with $1,000, compounding at 5% annually, calculated annually, and s/he plans to leave it five years, then s/he could count on:

$$FV \text{ (Deposit)} = \$1,000 \, (1+i)^n$$
$$= \$1,000 \, (1.05)^5$$
$$= \$1,000 \times 1.28 \text{ or}$$

FV = $1,276, which is the value in five years of $1,000 compounded annually.

compounding periods. In a formula calculating the compounding of a present value or principal amount over time, the number of times in a year that the compounding function is carried out. If it is done more often than once a year, say twice or four times, the basic rate is divided by the compounding frequency to get the annualized or fractional rate. *See* **compound interest** and **compounding rate.**

compounding rate. In a formula calculating the compounding of a present value or principal amount over time, the basis percentage of that amount or rate of interest, stated on an annual basis, that is added to that amount in each compounding period. In estimating the compounding rate or substituting into the rate in calculations using the formula, the annual rate is adjusted for fractions of one year. In this way, a 6% annual rate becomes a 3% semiannual rate (6 ÷ 2 = 3) and a 1.5% quarterly rate (6 ÷ 4 = 1.50). *See* **compound interest.**

comptroller, corporate. A corporate officer who supervises the accounting system and its implementation within a company.

Comptroller of the Currency, U.S. A federal office established in 1863 as a bureau of the Treasury Department. The Comptroller is appointed by the president and confirmed by the Senate for a term of five years. The office, technically called the Office of the Comptroller of the Currency, supervises the national banking system, with a staff of over 1,800 bank examiners who examine more than 2,500 banks within the Comptroller's jurisdiction. However, the **Federal Reserve System** overSees bank holding companies. Basically, the office charters, regulates, and supervises national banks—banks chartered by the federal government—to ensure a safe, sound and competitive national banking system that supports the citizens, communities, and economy of the United States. Also, the office is an excellent source of U.S. banking data. Web site: *www.occ.treas.gov.*

Computer Software & Services. Those stocks engaged in designing and producing computer software and servicing its use. *See* **stock industry group.**

concentrated fund. A mutual fund representing a portfolio of approximately 30 stocks, rather than 100 or so that is typical. This structure allows money managers potentially to focus on exceptional opportunities, and thus increase performance, instead of diversifying and likely achieving average performance at best. In effect, it is a nondiversified fund. Such a fund can also be used to achieve special investment results, such as highest-possible dividend yield.

concept stock. A stock that seems poised to receive financial impetus from a new way of thinking in society, rather than improved operating fundamentals. Examples are stocks associated with the abatement to global warming.

concession. See **selling concession.**

conduct remedy. A legal solution to anti-competitive behavior, involving forbidding certain kinds of business behavior such as intimidating rivals of their customers. *See* **structural remedy.**

Conference Board, The. An important business association and research network, linking executives from different companies, industries, and countries. Founded in 1916, it is a nonprofit, non-advocacy organization with more than 2,300 members worldwide. Its two primary purposes are: (1) to improve the business enterprise system, and (2) to enhance the contribution of business to society. There are more than 1,600 members, connecting more than 1,000 senior executives from 20 European countries. Major subjects such as finance, human resources, external affairs, operations, and strategy are addressed. The broader network includes more than 335 companies throughout Asia, Latin America, the Middle East, Africa, and the Caribbean in 41 countries. Two important research reports produced by the Board are the Consumer Confidence Index and the Leading Economic Indicators. Address: The Conference Board Inc., 845 Third Avenue, New York, NY 10022-6679. Phone: (212) 759-0900. Fax: (212) 980-7014. Web site: *www.conference-board.org.*

Conference Board of Canada. Address: 255 Smyth Road, Ottawa, Ontario, KIH 8M7, Canada. Phone: (613) 526-3280. Fax: (613) 526-4857. Web site: *www.conferenceboard.ca.*

Conference Board of Europe. Address: ChauSee de La Hulpe, 130, Box 11, B-1000 Brussels, Belgium. Phone: (32) 2 675 5405. Fax: (32) 2 675 0395. Web site: *www.conferenceboard.org/ TCBEurope/europe.cfm.*

confirmation. A customer's notice of a security transaction.

confirmed line. See **line of credit.**

conflict of interest. In a business sense, a reference to unethical profiteering or the appearance of the potential for unethical transactions by a corporate officer having a financial interest in two or more companies dealing with each other. One remedy for this problem is the creation of a **blind trust.**

congeneric corporation. A corporation that controls and guides subsidiaries or divisions in similar profit pursuits. In the current financial lexicon, it refers to control corporations in the financial sector. An example would be an insurance company that owns banks, leasing companies, investment companies, and so on. *See* **conglomerate.**

conglomerate. A corporation organized to pursue economic opportunity in diverse industries. Planning and control are centralized in a small top-management group. These flexible executives usually function like managerial consultants, with operations being decentralized into profit centers. Conglomerates are eager to acquire other corporations, usually financing the acquisition program through the issue of debt or equity securities to buy the companies. Hopefully, in the program consolidated earnings per share will be increased, making the market price of the conglomerate's stock worth more and consequently available for more acquisitions at advantageous levels. In combining assets and earning power of acquired corporations, the **pooling of interests** accounting technique is usually practiced. The underlying growth concept is the successful acquisitions practiced by the management. Growth through acquisitions is considered as feasible as a line of consumer durables or nondurables. *See* also **free-form management.**

Connecticut Department of Banking. Regulator of securities laws in the state of Connecticut. Address: Securities Division, 260 Constitution Plaza, Hartford, CT 06103. Phone: (203) 240-8230. Phone: (800) 831-7225.

connectivity. A reference to the Internet-created concept in which business is conducted through partnerships and short-term alliances, rather than under long-term business arrangements. It represents a combination of virtual entities, like one-man business shops, in which entrepreneurs use the Internet to join together to accomplish some specific task and then disband, with most of the parties looking for another such connection. This new business model is changing dramatically the way global business is done, although there is a tendency for the connectivity to take place in countries sharing similar language, laws, and monetary systems. As an example of the dramatic changes occurring in the business architecture, the Small Business Administration (SBA) in the U.S. estimates that the portion of the U.S. work force employed by *Fortune* 500 companies has dropped by one-half over the past 30 years.

On the other hand, the SBA expects the number of single-person shops to increase to 7 million firms by the year 2005. The Internet is ushering in the age of independent entrepreneurs, mobilizing under connectivity. The success of these independents will be more associated with their ability to network with others, such as industry leaders, suppliers and other independent contractors, through high-tech communications, than with a relationship with one large company. With so many independent contractors vying, costs should come down. Success in using connectivity will require a Web site that puts the independent in the loop with kindred business interests. Also required is the realization that information must be shared in order to be valuable.

consent dividend. A dividend that a stockholder consents to leave with the corporation for its use, but one that he agrees to report for personal income taxes.

consolidated note. A short-term obligation backed by the good faith and assets of several debtors, although only one security issue represents the debt. For example, Federal Home Loan Banks issue notes that "are the joint and several obligations of the Federal Home Loan Banks."

consolidated statements. The combination of subsidiary and parent data in financial statements.

consolidation. A fusion of the assets of two or more corporations of similar size into a complete new company. At least one-half, and sometimes two-thirds, of the shareholders in each of the companies must approve. Shareholders of the acquired company also have "appraisal rights." This means they are entitled to the fair market value for their shares. Often, there is a disagreement between the acquiring firm and the shareholders of the firm(s) being acquired, which sometimes does not get settled legally for years.

consolidation area. A range of market price fluctuations for a stock, with limits close together.

consolidation merger. A type of corporate **merger** in which a dominant corporate player merges with or otherwise acquires a smaller entity or places the target company into its established operations. Usually at least one-half and sometimes two-thirds of corporate shareholders must approve a merger or consolidation.

consolidator. A company that buys smaller companies, usually in the same or similar industries, for valuations (for example, price/earnings multiples) under current stock market prices. The buyer often effects savings through cost cutting and other means and then sells the combined companies in a public offering at much higher market valuations. *See* **roll-up.**

constant dollar formula. See **formula investing.**

constant dollar index. See **fixed-weighted index.**

constant ratio formula. See **formula investing.**

Construction Spending Report. Compiled by the Bureau of the Census of the Department of Commerce on the first business day of the month for the two previous months, a report for economists and industry analysts that represents nearly 20% of GNP. It measures the value of construction put in place in current dollars during the course of a month. There are sections of the report comprised of nonresidential construction (3% of GNP), residential construction (5% of GNP) and construction spending by state and municipal governments (11% of GNP). Another reason for the report's importance is that construction and auto sales tend to lead the economy into and out of recessions. Thus, the report contains predictive data, although the data is highly volatile. One of the weak points is that the report lacks currency. Several sources contribute to the data in the report, government and private. When Construction Spending rises, there is little effect on fixed income securities, common stocks, or dollar exchange rates.

Consumer Confidence Index (CCI). A monthly index gauging the general optimism of U.S. citizens, published by The Conference Board on the basis of its survey of 5,000 households. The report consists of two parts: (1) the Present Situation Index, and (2) the Expectations Index. The Consumer Confidence Index hit its all-time high of 142.3 in October 1968. That is measured from the level in 1985, the base year, during which the CCI is considered to be 100. By contrast, the Index was 106.8 in early 2000. Unlike most business indicators, the CCI does not measure monetary or financial prospects, but the intangible of public exuberance about their financial prospects. This level of "feel good" is important, because consumers account for 70% of the spending in the U.S. It should not be regarded as a mathematical trend or cycle, but irregular shifts in optimism and pessimism.

consumer credit. The extension of the privilege of future payment to consumers purchasing in retail outlets.

Consumer Installment Credit to Personal Income ratio. See under **Economic Indicators.**

Consumer Price Index (CPI). A measure of relative changes in the prices of selected goods and services bought by middle-income city families, compiled by the Bureau of Labor Statistics (BLS). Until 1997, the BLS assigned 100 to a base year, and when average prices changed, the index reflected the percentage; for example, an index of 150 meant that current prices were 150% of the base period, up 50%. Economists recommend a revision of the base period and commodities used in such an index every 10 years. For the modern version of the CPI, see **chain-weighted price index.** *See* also **Consumer Price Index (CPI) Report** and **Producer Price Index.**

Consumer Price Index (CPI) Report. Issued by the Bureau of Labor Statistics of the Department of Labor in the second half of the month, an important report for economists and analysts that is considered the most important measure of inflation in the U.S. The CPI gauges consumer prices for a basket of popular goods and services. It is an index, meaning current prices are compared to a base level. The latter is updated regularly as are the items in the basket of goods and services every 10 years. Technically, there are two CPIs—the CPI-U or price levels for urbanites and the CPI-W or price levels for wage and clerical workers. The CPI includes imported goods. However, it is not as comprehensive as some other inflation measures, like the Implicit Deflator. When the Consumer Price Index increases, fixed income securities tend to decrease, common stocks tend to decrease, and dollar exchange rates vary. *See* **Consumer Price Index.**

Consumer Price Index for Services. See under **Economic Indicators.**

contagion. A reference to the chain reaction experienced among related currencies and countries when a major world currency is devalued by a leading country's government, in response to its economic problems. Such a phenomenon occurred in Southeast Asia in the late 1990s.

Containers—Metal & Glass. Those stocks representing companies turning out cans and glass for storing and marketing beverage products. *See* **industry stock group.**

Containers—Paper. Those stocks representing companies making and distributing cardboard boxes. *See* **industry stock group.**

contingency reserves. Those liquid resources held for unexpected spending.

continuous compounding. The process of calculating compound interest on a continuous basis over a fixed time period, rather than at certain intervals during the period, such as at the end of each quarter. In a theoretical sense, the argument is made for this method that it is more appropriate in the investment process because money borrowed or loaned is usually put to work on projects operating on a continuous basis. In actuality, there is not a significant difference in the results in the compounding system used—the rate and time period are much more important—but many institutions that pay interest continuously compounded believe the technique sounds more rewarding and advertise it to attract depositors. *See* **compounding.**

Check it out! Marsha and Marvin Max deposit $5,000 to Full Throttle Savings. They are attracted by the continuous compounding feature of its certificates of deposits and safety. Currently the Thrift pays 5.25% annually. M&M expect to leave the Present Value of $5,000 for five years. How much will it grow to? The Future Value would be $6,501.96, which is $44.22 more than had the $5,000 been compounded each year at the 5.25% for five years; $12.17 more than had it been compounded each quarter. Every little bit helps.

contract. 1) An agreement between a seller and buyer to exchange a security that is widely traded in the market for a price. 2) An agreement between a seller and a buyer to exchange a class of securities before they are issued for a price, in which case the securities are traded on a "when-issued" basis.

Contract for Difference (CFD). In the United Kingdom, ownership of a virtual share of stock as opposed to physical ownership, traded on a margin basis. Usually the margin is 20% of the underlying stock value. Although the share can be purchased on margin, the investor participates in the full price movements of a share. The primary benefits of trading CFD shares are direct cost savings and flexibility. The investor is not liable for stamp duty, which is currently 0.5%, because shares do not actually change hands. Secondly, the investor can sell stock short, to take advantage of downward stock prices.

contract rate. The fixed annual interest rate a bondholder will receive stated as a percentage of the principal due at a bond's maturity. This rate does not indicate the actual **yield to maturity,** since no consideration is given to the cost of the bond to the bondholder, which determines the actual yield. *See* also **market rate.**

contractual investment program. A mutual fund plan whereby much of the sales load for investing over a specified period is deducted in the initial years.

contrarian. An investor who generally eschews the popular stock groups of the day in favor of neglected, overlooked ones that have prospects for a recovery and subsequent investor popularity. The mindset is one that identifies an investment consensus in regard to stocks in an industry, country, or sector, and then analyzes whether there is a rational argument for investing in the opposite direction.

Contributed Surplus. See **Capital Surplus.**

contributing share. A share only partly paid for, in Australia, Canada, the United Kingdom, and certain European countries, and one which requires certain future payments on specific future dates, or alternatively in certain cases, forfeiture of the share.

contributory retirement or **pension fund.** A plan accumulating from the contributions of both an employer and employees. *See* **pension plan.**

control person. See **affiliated person.**

convergence trading. In the parlance of derivative markets, the search by investors or speculators for two or more securities whose prices generally move in association with each other, in the same direction. When securities deviate from past trading patterns, usually identified by a computer model, the investors or speculators buy or sell those securities expected to adjust in the future in a manner that will make money. For example, electric utility bonds usually rise in price when interest rates decrease, because nearly all bonds rise when interest rates fall to adjust the yield to lower current investor demands and because utilities are capital intensive to the extent that lower interest rates mean higher cash flow, or more bond safety, other factors remaining equal. Let's say White Knuckle Speculators, Inc. has detected a convergence between interest rates and electric utility bond prices whereby the bonds rise from 3% to 5% whenever interest rates decline 1%. Then the White Knuckle's model detects an anomaly!—Megawatt Electric, Inc., 7% bonds of 2010 have not adjusted in price. White Knuckles buys the bonds, expecting a near-term gain when the bonds do adjust.

conversion. 1) The exchange of one security for another. 2) The exchange of a put for a call, or vice versa.

conversion parity. The market price at which a convertible bond or debenture or preferred stock is equal to the market value of the stock into which it can be converted. To determine if a convertible bond is selling at its conversion parity, divide its principal due at maturity by its conversion price, giving the number of shares into which the bond can be converted. Next, divide the bond's market price by the number of shares just found. If the quotient equals the market price of one share, the bond is selling at its conversion parity. If the quotient is less, it is selling at a discount. If the quotient is more, it is selling at a premium. For a preferred stock, divide the par value or stated value or liquidating value by the number of shares into which it can be converted. Then determine premium, parity, and discount in the same manner as for a convertible debenture. *See* **discount (2)** and **premium (2).**

conversion price. The exchange rate into common stock of a convertible bond or preferred stock, based on a price per common share. For example, a bond might be convertible into stock at $100, or 10 shares per $1,000 bond.

conversion ratio or **conversion rate.** The number of shares of common stock for which a convertible bond or preferred stock share can be exchanged, based on a specific number of shares per bond or preferred share. For example, a $1,000 par value bond might be convertible into 20 shares of stock or converted into stock at the rate of $50 per share (1,000 ÷ 20).

convertible debenture. A bond that a holder may exchange for common stock, usually in the issuing company, under conditions set forth in the indenture agreement. Although this type of debenture resembles other debentures, the common stock feature often dominates the pricing rather than the interest yield, and sometimes these debentures are junior to straight debentures. When investors are buying the common stock, driving prices higher, the convertible debenture rises proportionately. At the same time, the yield declines. When the common stock slides in price, so does the debenture, but the yield rises. Investors who espouse this type of security believe they are invested in an income-producing equity, while enjoying a floor provided by the yield if the stock falls precipitously in value. *See* **bond, bond tables, conversion, conversion parity, conversion price, conversion ratio,** and **reset.**

convertible discount. See **discount.**

convertible-preferred-share placement. A security having preferential claims on dividends and assets, and convertible into common shares in the same company at a floating conversion price so that as the common stock's market price gets lower the convertible shareholder gets more common shares. Such a security is usually placed privately. It is marketed for companies seeking capital infusion during the initial years of research and development, when revenues are scarce. This type of security gained some ill repute in the 1990s, because certain shareholders allegedly tried to drive the price down, and therefore their conversion price down, by short selling the stock.

convertible preferred stock. A preferred stock that a holder may exchange for common stock, usually in the issuing company, under conditions set forth in the issuing agreement. This type of preferred stock has the same characteristics as other preferred stocks, except the common stock conversion feature tends to dominate the pricing of the security. When the common stock is popular, it forces the convertible's stock price up and the yield down. And when the common stock loses favor, the converse happens. Sometimes the dividend on such a security is lower and the position in the capital structure is junior, however, because the investor gets the conversion privilege. Regular investors in convertibles believe they get the best of two worlds—dividend income and an equity participation in a corporation whose prospects they like. *See* **stock tables, conversion, conversion parity, conversion price,** and **conversion ratio.**

convertible premium. See **premium.**

convertible stock. A class of common stock that the holder may exchange for another class, usually for common stockin the same company, for a specified conversion price and under conditions set out at the time of issue. This privilege is usually granted by the board on an issue when it is difficult to attract investors but the corporation does not have the cash flow to support convertible preferred stock or a convertible debenture. *See* **stock table.**

convoy system. A method of managing a country's financial institutions so that they move in tandem or in unison, and are quickly helped by the government when they develop problems or need new capital.

COO. Abbreviation for Chief Operating Officer.

cooperative or **mutual company.** See **stock company.**

cook the books, to. As a manager of a corporation, to cause incorrect data to be recorded in certain accounts, which misrepresents the true nature of corporate results.

"cookie jar" accounting. A strategy by corporate management of allocating current revenues to future accounting periods, in order to minimize unattractive results for investors and to smooth out reported long-term results. This is accomplished through the use of "reserve accounts," to which deferred revenues are posted in a current period, and which reduce reported revenues in that fiscal period. Presumably, they are already high so that creates no investor relations problem. When current revenues are weak in some later period, the reserve account is reduced or reversed, with the result that current revenues are increased. The increased revenues mean that more of the company's overhead costs are absorbed, allowing more income flow to the bottom line. The practice is not a generally accepted accounting procedure, since under that convention revenues, as well as other operating accounts, should be recorded in the period in which they occur.

Copenhagen Stock Exchange. See under **Global Investment Market.**

core inflation. A reference to rises in the cost of living that are endemic to an economic system, thus likely to be permanent or long-term in duration. Such increasing cost-of-living forces can be increases in wages and other benefits under labor contracts, capital costs, import tariffs, and so on. They are "sticky costs," not easily rescinded and, therefore, more likely to cause permanent inflation than price increases that are temporary or seasonal in nature, such as food prices. *See* **headline inflation** and **inflation.**

corner. To purchase the available supply of a stock.

corporate bond or **corporate.** A debt instrument issued by a private corporation, usually for a term of 10 years or more. They have similar characteristics to bonds generally, with certain differences. In the first place, they are fully taxable at all levels of government. Also, they are priced and traded on exchanges. In the agreement with the lenders, or in the indenture, they pledge to maintain a sinking fund into which bonds are slowly paid off with cash deposits or with bonds purchased in the market, whichever is cheaper for the issuer. Bonds in a series mature at the same time. Their par value is generally $1,000, although junior bonds for less, even $100, have appeared on the scene at times. In mid-1999, these bonds amounted to $2.5 trillion,

19.2% of the total bond debt in the United States. *See* **bond** and **bond tables.**

corporate culture. The attitude created by a company's top management, in relation to the business ethics and other business policies practiced by the company's employees. Some cultures are very casual, while others are very structured. Generally, new companies engaged in research and development of leading edge technologies reflect the former. Companies engaged in more traditional products and services tend to epitomize the latter. Attitudes and practices involving attire, work schedules, competition, chain-of-command, employee participation in decisions, promotions from within and workplace manners are examples of characteristics that comprise a corporate culture. When two or more companies merge, clashing corporate cultures can offset the economic advantages of the merger. For this reason, cultural compatibility is an important consideration in examining the prospects for an effective merger.

Corporate Directory in the Annual Report. The page or pages in a company's annual report that list the corporation's board of directors and executive officers, sometimes including brief biographical sketches. Usually, the company's address and communications addresses are shown. For investors, this can be an important page. Generally, when the board is comprised of persons who are business or professional leaders, it is implied that the company desires an association with ethical leaders. It is no guarantee, but such a group is probably also stockholder friendly, a positive trait for prospective investors. On the other hand, there is no guarantee that such an illustrious group is highly competent to run the affairs of the corporation extremely well. A modern fact of corporate governance is that professional managers run the show, at least until they have run it into the ground. Directors are usually selected for prestigious backgrounds—often providing window dressing—but a well-connected group is certainly preferable to one with Mafia ties. There are few guarantees in stock investing today, but energetic well-informed directors and top executives are a big plus. *See* **Annual Report.**

corporate governance. A description of the manner in which those persons entrusted with carrying out a corporation's objectives do so. Usually, the objectives are spelled out in the corporate charter and extended by official policies of the board of directors. The term does not describe management efficiency, which is more a function of how everyday business is conducted, but describes how corporate executives, including the chairman and the board of directors, conduct themselves in hiring corporate officers, auditors, attorneys, and consultants, and in approving policies, business, community objectives, and budgets.

They can be highly moralistic and ethical or avaricious and morally questionable in acting as stewards for the investors. For example, Sam Goodman, chairman of the Apricot Computer Company, Inc., hires Steven Idle, his son-in-law, as president and chief executive officer. In addition, he employs his uncle's accounting firm, Cook, Euwer & Books, as auditors. And not wanting to offend anyone in the family, he orders Steven Idle to employ a cousin, Zola Spinner, as a public relations consultant. The lack of independence and objectivity possibly created by this case suggests questionable corporate governance.

corporate income tax rate. The portion of corporate net income taxable in a fiscal year, under the U.S. and state tax codes. As in the case of the personal income tax, the tax is graduated for corporations. The District of Columbia and every state except Michigan, Nevada, Texas, Washington, and Wyoming levy corporate incomes taxes.

corporate raider. 1) An individual who converts corporate funds to his personal use, usually while in an official position such as president or chairman of the board. 2) A corporate official who causes a rise in the market price of his corporation's stock, usually by spreading rumors, in order that he can sell his stock at a profit without a regard for the corporation or its other owners or creditors. 3) An investor who gains control of a corporation by buying its severely underpriced stock, selling off the assets for profits, and ignoring the long-term role of the enterprise.

corporate welfare. In a broader sense, the term refers to any government financial favoritism to a business entity, such as by a municipality or state, to lure that entity into locating a facility within the geographic area of the government body. Examples are property tax abatement to a new business facility and free land and site preparation for a new facility. These subsidies are popular with voters because they create jobs and revenues. However, they are often unfair to competitors that have to pay for what the new facilities are granted as incentives.

corporates. Abbreviation for those bonds issued by corporations.

corporation (corp.). A legal entity, created under laws of a state to engage in a specified business or other activity, having continuous life, limited liability of stockholders, a charter, and several owners. Many shares of stock, representing proportionate ownership and control of the corporation and earnings through election of directors, are sold to investors who may keep them or resell them. Large sums of money, invested with limited financial liability, can be raised through a corporate structure, making it advantageous over proprietorships and partnerships. It is the advent of the modern corporation, with its fluidity of stock ownership, that has made possible the huge popularity of stock markets in the industrial nations of the world.

corporation account. An investment firm's record of securities transactions in a corporation's name, after it has submitted proper resolutions to an investment firm indicating an authority for certain officers to negotiate security transactions.

corporation records. A corporation's permanent records including the charter, by-laws, elections, stockholder meetings, directors meetings, resolutions, and stock issuances and transfers.

corporation tax. A levy on the income of a corporation. Under federal tax laws, the tax amounts to 34% on income. The tax is criticized because stockholders pay an income tax on dividends, which are usually part of the corporation's taxable income, creating double taxation on the corporation's net income distributed to stockholders.

correction. A return in the stock market to more realistic prices after excessive selling or buying. In Wall Street terms, a correction is approximately a 10% move. In everyday parlance, the term applies more to a downward price adjustment. In some ways, the term is a misnomer, since the price adjustment really means that a totally new valuation for prices has occurred or a revised outlook by investors has gained ascendancy.

correspondent. A person or organization that maintains continuous business relations with another. In the investment business, a correspondent is a firm or individual who ultimately transacts orders for exchange members who have no floor brokers, or one who transacts foreign orders for domestic firms.

cost of goods manufactured or **materials cost** or **raw materials.** Payments made for goods to be improved upon through manufacturing.

cost of goods sold. Those payments made for an inventory of goods to be sold.

Cost of Living Adjustment (COLA). An automatic adjustment in wage agreement, retirement plans, and certain debt securities in which the benefits or interest payments are adjusted upward for changes in general prices, usually measured by the Consumers Price Index.

cost-of-living index. See **Consumers Price Index.**

cost or **market.** A reference to a method of inventory valuation of goods used in manufacture based on their cost or market value, whichever is lower.

cost-plus inflation. Rising general prices caused by increases in the costs of supplying goods, rather than overheated demand for them, although the two phases are interactive. When demand rises some, it drives manufacturing costs higher. These higher costs, in turn, are passed on to merchants and consumers, and the cycle is perpetuated. *See* **demand-pull inflation.**

costs. See **expenses, cost of goods sold** and **cost of goods manufactured.**

couch potato. An investor who avoids as much personal decision making as possible in selecting securities, instead buying shares of stock index mutual funds or bond mutual funds.

Council of Economic Advisers (CEA). A council in the U.S. Office of the President, created under the Employment Act of 1946, that advises the president on the formulation of national economic policy to promote employment, production, and purchasing power under free competitive enterprise. In particular, the CEA performs the following functions: (1) assists and advises the president in the preparation of the annual Economic Report; (2) gathers timely and authoritative information concerning economic developments and trends to analyze and interpret policies; (3) develops and recommends policies to the president; and (4) makes reports and studies the president might request.

countercyclical credit policy. A central bank and government policy of stimulating the economy in recessions and depressing it in booms by influencing bank credit (Federal Reserve's authority) and controlling federal spending (Congressional authority).

coupon. 1) A detachable piece of paper on bearer bonds that is mailed or presented to a paying agent for interest collection. 2) A reference to the interest payment to which a bondholder is entitled.

coupon bonds. Those bonds with attached coupons that are detached and presented for interest payments on certain dates, often called bearer bonds.

cover a short sale. To buy securities for delivery on a short sale.

CRA. Abbreviation for **Community Reinvestment Act.**

cramming. The entry into e-tailing by a brick-and-mortar company by duplicating its existing business procedure and product line in the new Internet operations, thus overlooking the unique possibilities inherent in Internet merchandising. Crammers are trying to emulate the margins and other results they have garnered in their traditional businesses. The practice is considered one of the leading causes for failure in e-tailing.

crapshoot. A slang term meaning to invest continually in cheap stocks with little chance of appreciation in the hope that someday one will skyrocket in market value.

crash. A severe and precipitous downturn in business activity, securities prices, and so on.

crash program. A company's all-out effort to accomplish a goal abnormally fast.

CRAT. See **Charitable Remainder Annuity Trust.**

CRD. Abbreviation for **Central Registration Depository.**

creative financing. A somewhat facetious term describing the raising of money from sources in such a way that the availability of the funds depends on the occurrence of a chain of improbable events or the participation of a few reluctant investors who are likely to gain disproportionate profits or some other advantage, in relation to others in the deal. It is usually a deal that requires a lot of imagination and patience to put together. For example, if Melt Down Electric Power needs $200 million to build a new generating plant, its investment banker could suggest selling first mortgage bonds in that amount. On the other hand, suppose the banker knows that bond investors will not commit the money for nuclear facilities, especially to a borrower of Melt Down's reputation. Voila! The MBA problem solvers in the corporate finance department get the call. They get together one evening, pass around the pipe, and concoct this scheme. Melt Down will form a subsidiary—Deals, Dice & Drinks Casinos—that will issue $250 million in unsecured convertible bonds, use $50 million to build its first 10 casinos, and lend $200 million to Melt Down for its power project. But the financing depends on Deals, Dice & Drinks becoming licensed to operate casinos in five states. That means DD&D will have to prove its CEO had ancestors who were members of the Outrage tribe, distant cousins to the Osage. Could be a difficult search, according to consulting headhunters. That's creative financing!

credit balance. The amount owed to a customer by an investment house through the sale of stock or dividend accruals.

credit crunch. A contraction of funds available for lending in a country or economy, usually due to a shortage of funds caused by competing demands—public or government versus private demands, for example—and usually affecting both consumer and business lending. A shortage of credit can restrict business expansion and liquidity of assets to an extent that investing in the affected country is curtailed. The importance for investors is that the growth of companies is damped, generally speaking. Central banks—in the United States the Federal Reserve System—are usually the most recommended remedy, using their capacities to increase commercial bank reserves.

critical mass. A reference to the point at which a company can achieve specific objectives, either through acquisition, capital expenditure, internal growth, or some other means of reaching a commanding size. Usually, it is the attainment of a size large enough to secure advantageous financing, develop effective products, broaden manufacturing facilities, or gain marketing prominence. For example, Wee Woeful Waffles, Inc. makes and distributes frozen toaster waffles. Its marketing VP, Ike Idea, has tried for five years to get the Big Guy Eats & Treats grocery chain to stock its waffles in their freezers. But Big Guy says space is reserved for vendors who can supply at least three products, in order to develop brand volume. So . . . Wee Woeful acquires Sugarless But Tasty Pastries, maker of frozen donuts and frozen cheesecakes, for common stock. Now Wee Woeful can supply three frozen products. Voila! The company has attained critical mass.

"crony capitalism." A reference to the style of capitalism in some Pacific Rim countries, most notably Indonesia under President Suharto in the financially-troubled 1990s, in which the government grants favored franchises and licenses to family members and political allies. The practice creates de facto monopolies and can lead to inefficiencies and corrupt business practices.

cross-border merger or acquisition. A business combination involving companies domiciled in different countries, but usually operating in the same industry.

cross-border trading. A reference to providing investors with access to 24-hour securities trading by establishing a single order book for the most popular 1,000 or so stocks internationally, allowing trading in those stocks that corresponded to daytime business hours in progressive time zones around the world. In this manner, trading would be continuous in certain stocks. For example, trading could move from the United States to Tokyo to Europe and back to the United States as a new business day commenced, allowing investors to get executions through the night while allowing exchange employees to get some sleep.

cross marketing. The practice of two or more companies, but usually just two, jointly advertising or using facilities to sell dissimilar products and services. Although products and services are different, they appeal to similar buyers. The result is that marketing costs are reduced, sometimes by half. The joint use of mailing lists and advertising pages are examples.

crossing orders. A reference to a floor broker settling one of his buy orders with one of his sell orders, or vice versa.

crossover. See **moving average crossover.**

CRSP. Abbreviation for the **Center for Research in Security Prices.**

Cuba (CyberCuba) Securities Exchange. See under **Global Investment Market.**

CUBEs (QQQs). A type of derivative securities that represents a microcosm of the NASDAQ 100 stock index, an index of 100 stocks many call the New Economy market, since it includes tech equities such as dot-coms, telecommunications, and bio-tech issues. They are purchased by investors as a unit of ownership in an investment trust that holds a portfolio of common stocks that closely tracks the price performance and dividend yield of the NASDAQ, although dividends are infrequent in these emerging companies. These securities began trading in 1999 on the AMEX, becoming its most traded security in early 2000.

"cum rights." A description of a stock purchase which includes certain subscription rights.

cumulative preferred stock. A type of preferred stock on which specified dividends accrue even though they are not paid in one or more years. Before any dividends are paid to common stockholders, thereafter, the total accrued dividends must be paid to the holders of the cumulative preferred stock.

Cumulative Quarterly Income Convertible Preferred Securities (QUIPS). A relatively new category of preferred security marketed by Goldman, Sachs & Co., in which a trust is created to issue preferential units or QUIPS that are backed by junior debentures issued to it by a corporation raising capital in the stock market. The units pay quarterly distributions to holders of the QUIPS on a cumulative basis, as long as the trust receives interest payments on the debentures. The QUIPS are redeemable by the trust when the corporation redeems the debentures and are convertible into common stock if not redeemed. Like a preferred stock, they have a specified liquidation value. Like a bond, they have a specific maturity date and value.

cumulative voting right. The right of common stockholders to concentrate all of their votes on one candidate for the board of directors, rather than being required to spread their votes by voting for a candidate for each vacancy on the board. This feature often enables stockholders with fewer shares to elect one or two directors, since those opposing their choice might spread their votes. *See* **proportional representation** and **statutory voting right.**

Curb. 1) The nickname for the **American Stock Exchange,** originating from its original meetings on a street curb. 2) A blackboard or electric panel where transactions of the American Stock Exchange are recorded.

"curbs" or **"collars," program trading.** Restrictions on **program trading** whenever the DJIA moves 50 points or more higher or 50 points or more lower than the closing price on the preceding day, imposed by the NYSE. The curbs remain effective until the DJIA moves to within 25 points of the previous day's close or until the close that day at 3:00 P.M. CST. When a curb is in effect, program selling can only be executed on an uptick and program buying on a down tick. *See* also **"sidecars"** and **"circuit breakers."**

"curbs in." A designation by the business news TV network CNBC that trading curbs are in effect.

currency. Any accepted medium of exchange.

currency board. A monetary authority, created by a government, that issues notes and coins convertible into a foreign anchor currency or commodity. Usually, the anchor currency is that of the country's richest or strongest trading partner. The currency or commodity is called reserve currency. Holders of the monetary authority's coins and notes may convert into the reserve currency at a fixed rate and on demand. In effect, the board sets a country's foreign exchange rates, instead of relying on a central bank to manage exchange rates and create money. Under such a plan, a country promises to keep enough foreign currency, usually the anchor currency, on hand to pay off all holders of its currency. A currency board system goes a step further than the traditional fixing of exchange rates, in which a government pledges to exchange the local currency for a foreign currency at a preset rate. Under the board, the government in effect subverts general economic development to a stable exchange rate. It's a subtle distinction but one very important to international investors who are interested in the preservation of their principal. As a system of managing foreign exchange, countries used boards mostly in the nineteenth century. Then in the twentieth century, central banks became popular. However, in the 1990s, currency boards regained popularity in response to investor demands for protection as a rash of financial problems among debtor nations occurred.

current account balance. In international trade, the difference between what a country pays to foreigners for goods and services and other miscellaneous items purchased and the amount it receives from foreigners for exports of goods and services and other miscellany sold, usually during a fiscal quarter or year. *See* **balance of payments** and **balance of trade.**

current assets. That cash or valuable properties convertible into cash within 90 days to a year.

current dollars or **nominal dollars.** In reporting an economic or business time series, such as the Gross Domestic Product (GDP) or Corporate Earnings over a span of months, quarters, or years, the use of the actual values that occurred in each observation. Sometimes these values are not realistic in terms of measuring whether they have sustained the same buying power that existed in a prior base period or in measuring how much of the change is due to changes in output. They are adjusted to reflect the equivalent buying power compared with the base period. When this is done, the results are called real dollars or inflation-adjusted dollars. *See* **real dollars** or **inflation-adjusted dollars.**

current fiscal year (CFY). A reference in a financial report to the fiscal year currently in progress as opposed to the one just completed, called the latest fiscal year (LFY).

current liabilities. Those accounts, debts, or services payable within 90 days.

current ratio or **working capital ratio.** The ratio of current assets to current liabilities. A 2.5-to-1 ratio is considered desirable for industrial companies. This is a quickie solvency ratio, when a company is unable to borrow money to pay bills.

current return. See **current yield.**

current yield or **current return.** The current annual income from a security, stated as a percentage of its current cost. For example, annual income of $50 on a bond costing $910 is a 5.50% yield ($50 ÷ $910). Current yield is important to investors contemplating the purchase of a stock or bond, whereas yield based on the past cost is important to an investor already owning the same stock or bond.

CUSIP. A system developed by the American Bankers Association (ABA) and maintained by the Standard & Poor's Service Bureau for uniquely identifying every security that is actively traded in the securities industry with a standard nine-character number. In addition, the system applies standard abbreviations to the legal description of the issuer in order to also standardize descriptions. These standard numbers and descriptions are used by virtually all sectors of the securities industry, and are critical for the accurate and efficient clearance and settlement of securities as well as back-office processing.

custodian. 1) A buyer and or supervisor of a related minor's account under a state's Uniform Gift to Minor's Act. 2) In an investment trust arrangement, a trustee who must carry out the decisions of others in managing the trust's portfolio.

custodian account. Any securities in the name of a minor related to the purchaser under a state's Uniform Gift to Minor's Act.

Customer Agreement (Brokerage). The basic understanding between a brokerage firm and its customer regarding business procedures in force between the two parties. There follows a sample Agreement, one used by a NYSE member firm with its identity removed. *See* **Account (Brokerage), Authorization/ Signature(s) Agreement (Brokerage),** and **Margin Agreement/Loan Consent (Brokerage).**

CUSTOMER AGREEMENT

In consideration of (Brokerage name removed) accepting and carrying for me one or more accounts, I hereby understand and agree that:

1) Legal Capacity to Enter Into Agreements—I am at least the age of 18 years and am of full legal age in the state in which I reside. If I am an employee, member or partner of any security exchange or

member firm thereof, of any corporation a majority of the stock of which is owned by any exchange or a broker/dealer I have so indicated on the account application. I also agree to notify you promptly if I should later become employed in any of the capacities cited above.

2) Definitions—Applicable Rules and Regulations—The terms "securities," "options," or "other property," as used herein, shall include money, securities and commodities of every kind and nature and all contracts and options relating thereto. All transactions shall be subject to the rules, customs and usages of the exchange, market or clearing house where executed, and to all applicable federal and state laws and regulations.

3) Orders, Executions and Statements—Reports of the execution of orders and statements of my account shall be deemed accepted by me if you have not received written objections from me within five days with respect to the former and 10 days with respect to the latter after transmitted by you to me. You may execute any transaction authorized by me on any exchange or other market where such business is then transacted. You may reject any order I place with you in your sole discretion. I understand that you reserve the right to refuse, and assume no responsibility for, orders sent through the mail for the purchase or sale of securities or other investments. I also understand that if I request the transfer or registration of foreign securities, I may be responsible for any transfer fees charged to you.

I understand that you direct customer orders in equity securities to exchanges and market makers based on an analysis of their ability to provide rapid and quality executions. These market participants guarantee that all customer orders are executed at a price equal to or better than the displayed national best bid/best offer. Your policy also assures that these market participants provide your customer orders with price improvement and limit order protection. I further understand that you may receive remuneration for directing customer orders to these market participants, the source and amount of which is available upon written request.

4) Deposit of Equity—Consent to Recording—I understand that you reserve the right to require full payment or an acceptable equity deposit prior to the acceptance of any order. I understand that you may tape record telephone conversations with customers in order to permit you to verify data concerning securities transactions.

5) Payment of Indebtedness Upon Demand—I shall at all times be liable for the payment upon demand of any debit balance or other obligations owing in any of my accounts with you; and, I shall be liable to you for any deficiency remaining in any such accounts in the event of the liquidation thereof, in whole or in part, by you or by me, and, I shall make payments of such obligations and indebtedness upon demand.

6) Security for Indebtedness—All securities and other property whatsoever which you may hold, carry or maintain for any purpose, in or for any of my accounts, whether individually or jointly held with others, are subject to a lien in your favor for the discharge of all the indebtedness of me to you, and I hereby grant to you a continuing lien, security interest and right of set-oft in all such property and securities whether now owned by me or hereafter acquired. You may hold securities and other property as security for the payment of any liability or indebtedness of me to you, and you shall have the right to transfer such securities and other property in any of my accounts from or to any other of my accounts, when in your judgement such transfer may be necessary for your protection. In enforcing your lien you shall have the right to sell, assign, and deliver all or any part of the securities or other property in any of my accounts when you deem it necessary for your protection. You reserve the right to close transactions in my account if you believe there is inadequate security for my obligation or upon an event which in your opinion jeopardizes my account. You shall have all rights of a secured party under the Uniform Commercial Code.

7) Costs of Collection—The reasonable costs of collection of the debit balance and any unpaid deficiency in my accounts, including attorney's fees incurred by you, shall be paid or reimbursed by me to you.

8) The Laws of New York Govern this agreement and its enforcement shall be governed BY THE LAWS OF THE STATE OF NEW YORK; shall cover individually and collectively all accounts (Cash, Margin, Option or other) which I may open or reopen with you; and shall inure to the benefit of your successors, whether by merger, consolidation or otherwise, and assigns and you may transfer my accounts and my agreements to your successors and assigns, and this Agreement shall be binding upon my heirs, executors, administrators, successors and assigns.

9) Agreement To Arbitrate Controversies—

- Arbitration is final and binding on the parties.
- The parties are waiving their right to seek remedies in court, including the right to jury trial.
- Pre-arbitration discovery is generally more limited than and different from court proceedings.
- The arbitrators' award is not required to include factual findings or legal reasoning and any party's right to appeal or to seek modification of rulings by the arbitrators is strictly limited.
- The panel of arbitrators will typically include a minority of arbitrators who were or are affiliated with the securities industry.

I agree that any controversy relating to any of my accounts or any agreement that I have with you will be submitted to arbitration conducted only under the provisions of the Constitution and Rules of the New York Stock Exchange, Inc. or pursuant to the code of the Arbitration of the National Association of Securities Dealers, Inc. Arbitration must be initiated by service upon the other party of a written demand for arbitration or notice of intention to arbitrate. Judgment, upon any award rendered by the arbitrator, may be entered in any court having jurisdiction. No person shall bring a putative or certified class action to arbitration, nor seek to enforce any pre-dispute arbitration agreement against any person who has initiated in court a putative class action; or who is a member of a putative class who has not opted out of the class with respect to any claims encompassed by the putative class action until: (i) the class certification is denied; or (ii) the class is decertified; or (iii) the customer is excluded from the class by the court. Such forbearance to enforce an agreement to arbitrate shall not constitute a waiver of any rights under this agreement except to the extent stated herein.

10) Losses Due to Extraordinary Events—You shall not be liable for loss caused directly or indirectly by war, natural disasters, government restrictions, exchange or market rulings or other conditions beyond your control.

11) Joint and Several Liability—If there is more than one owner of the account, then obligations under this agreement shall be joint and several.

12) Separation of Provisions—If any provision or condition of this agreement shall be held to be invalid or unenforceable by any court, or regulatory or self-regulating agency or body, such invalidity or unenforceability shall attach only to such provisions or condition. The validity of the remaining provisions and conditions shall not be affected thereby, and this agreement shall be carried out as if such invalid or unenforceable provision or condition were not contained herein.

13) Presumption of Receipt of Communications—Communications may be sent to me at my address given in the New Account Application as a mailing address, or at such other address as I may hereafter give you in writing and all communication so sent, whether by mail, telegraph, messenger, or otherwise, shall be considered delivered to me personally, whether actually received or not.

14) SEC Rule 14b—i(c)—Communication Between Companies and Shareholders—You will release my name, address, and security positions to requesting companies in which I own shares that are held in my account, unless I notify you in writing that I object.

15) Credit Information—I authorize you to make inquiries for the purpose of verifying my creditworthiness and to provide information regarding my performance under this agreement to credit reporting agencies and to your affiliates. I understand that, upon my request, you will tell me whether a credit report was requested and provide the name and address of the agency that furnished it.

I understand that any alteration to this Agreement will be ineffective to relieve me of my obligations hereunder.

customer hub. A reference to an Internet group that offers goods or services to many buyers that are transacting business with only one or a few vendors, using a seller of many products or a storefront. *See* **vendor hub.**

customer safekeeping. See **safekeeping of securities.**

Customer's Loan Agreement. The written understanding between a customer and broker, laying out the procedures for the customer maintaining a margin securities account and allowing the broker to use the customer's securities for general margin purposes. *See* **Account (Brokerage), Authorization/ Signature(s) Agreement (Brokerage),** and **Customer Agreement (Brokerage).**

Customer's man. The original name for a **registered representative**.

cybersquatting. The practice of registering Internet domain names, with the objective of selling them to others who might derive a marketing advantage from the linkage between that name and their corporate image. It is popular for media companies to use letters and words in their names in their Internet addresses, such as *www.sjmercury.com* for the *San Jose Mercury News.* Cybersquatters anticipate which popular companies will want to exploit an available domain name, and reserve it, planning to sell it to the logical user at a profit.

cybervestor. An investor who uses the Internet for trading securities, usually common stocks, through the facilities of one of the 100 Internet brokers. Frequently, these investors focus on quick profits in speculative stocks, using day trading brokerage facilities. It is the fastest growing stock market, accounting for 15–25% of retail stock trading. When stock market volume is heavy, there is some evidence these traders have difficulties getting timely executions.

cycle. 1) The return of a stock to an original price after several months above and several months below that price, although the order might be reversed. 2) In business, the return of sales, production, profits, and so on, to a previous level after several months above and below that level.

cyclical high. The high period of business activity for a company in a **cyclical industry**.

cyclical industry. An industry in which there are alternating industry-wide slowdowns and expansions in capital expenditures, production, sales, and profits.

cyclical low. The low period of business activity for a company in a **cyclical industry.**

cyclical stock. A description of stock that rises and falls pricewise with the business cycle or in lock step with some other macro event, displaying patterns of activity. This association is because the company—or perhaps the industry in the case of a corporate behemoth—that such a stock represents depends for most of its growth in earnings on upturns in general business activity. By the same token, business cycle contractions can create losses in the stock's results. For that reason, when maximizing investment results, the best time to purchase a cyclical stock is just before or in the early stages of an economic and business expansion, when earnings and dividends will likely be robust. The best time to sell it is just before a contraction begins. This feat is more difficult than it sounds, because signals preceding critical turning points in a cycle are usually not entirely clear in the early stages.

Generally, the corporate management of a cyclical stock cannot do many things externally to improve its results, since demand is derived from general business activity. Instead, management emphasizes tight internal controls and economies of scale, such as raw materials sourcing. One exception to this impediment to internal self-improvement is improving market share through product and service improvement. That sort of market penetration in these industries generally requires several years, however.

In a dynamic economy, some of a cyclical stock's growth is from trend, but most of it comes from successive economic expansions that peak at a higher level each cycle. That recurring surge provides investors a long shelf life usually, compared to a high-growth rocket that burns out in a few years. On the other hand, some cyclical stocks are stagnant or actually deteriorating as they move through successive cycles. Characteristically, a cyclical stock at the bottom of business activity begins adding sales in successive years, until the peak is reached. Then revenues begin tapering off until the trough is reached once more. That is a complete cycle.

Note that cyclical fluctuation is not the same as seasonal fluctuation. The former moves in a direction over several years, while the latter rises and falls at the same time annually. Steel manufacturing is cyclical; Christmas card publishing is seasonal. Usually a cyclical stock can be characterized by high levels of capital investment and moderate to large labor intensity. Consequently, when output is high, marginal unit costs are low.

That truism explains why unit margins and earnings improve, with the full production that accompanies a business cycle expansion. From an investment point of view, there is a long-term advantage to a cyclical stock. The demand for the product made is recurring, in peaks and valleys. Thus, it has staying power, perhaps over many cycles, that a growth equity sometimes lacks, due to a limited demand horizon. *See* **growth stock.**

Dd

D & B. 1) Abbreviation for **Dun and Bradstreet.** 2) An abbreviation for a Dun & Bradstreet credit report.

daily trading limit. The maximum amount that a class of commodities or derivative securities, such as interest futures, is allowed to rise or fall in a day, as ordered by an exchange.

daisy chain. A reference to stock traders trading shares in a way that manipulates the volume and price of a security in order to drive the price up, after which they sell their holdings to those sucked in by the scheme. This is a violation of U.S. securities laws.

Dar es Salaam Stock Exchange (Tanzania). See under **Global Investment Markets.**

data mining. A reference to the tendency for stock market pundits and stock pickers to ferret out historical data and information on a batch of stocks, usually a large database universe, and apply a filter or strategy that indicates the prices of certain of those stocks are attractive, at least in the present. The problem with the technique is that often there is no meaningful association between the past and present in long-term stock price patterns, even though the hypothesis or selection is back-tested for recent times. Back-testing is the process of hypothetically trying out a decision-making strategy over the market's recent behavior, in order to See if it would have provided an advantage in stock selection.

Date of Record. See **Record Date.**

"dawn raid." A reference to a corporate raider's order to a broker to buy all the shares available of a specific stock at the opening of the market. The object is to acquire a pivotal amount of the target stock before its management is aware of the plot.

DAX. See **Frankfort DAX Index.**

day loan or **morning loan.** A bank loan to a brokerage firm to finance the purchase of certain securities, conditioned on their delivery by the clearing late that day. When delivered, they become the collateral for the loan, which then becomes an ordinary broker's call loan.

day order. An order to buy or sell units of a security that expires at the end of the trading day unless canceled or executed first. Technically, all orders are day orders, unless they are good-till-canceled.

day trader. An individual investor who buys and sells stocks rapidly at a computer keyboard, which is usually furnished in the trading room of a day trading firm. But trading can be from wherever special telephony equipment and software is installed for a day trader, including a home or office. Their objective is to make money on many fractional changes in prices, although they are likely not averse to making money on big price changes also. Some sell securities short, an indication that day trading is merging conceptually with other forms of trading. These traders hold no securities beyond a day, unlike most investors who are more long-term oriented.

There are approximately 5,000 day traders and 62 day trading firms in the United States, and day trading now accounts for about 15% of the NASDAQ trading volume. Day traders have access to the NASD-sponsored Small Order Execution System, or SOES, which pushes orders of 1,000 shares are less to the top of the execution line so that small investors can get executions at spreads advertised by market makers in stocks.

The day trader tries to make money at the bid and offer spreads between stocks, and pays much lower commissions and costs than conventional investors do. Sometimes, in the case of individual traders, the trading facility requires a deposit up front, ranging from $5,000 to as much as $50,000, to cover the day trader's potential losses. In addition, there are suggestions that some trading firms arrange loans for customers. Although some day traders are profitable, a regulatory survey in 1999 found that most lose money. *See* **Electronic Communications Network.**

day trading firm. A business site specializing in furnishing a
place and the electronic equipment for customers to engage in
trading securities, on a short-term basis, electronically. These
firms are usually members of the National Association of
Securities Dealers (NASD), which gives its customers market
information on many stocks listed on the NASDAQ exchange,
as well as some foreign exchanges. In some cases the firm is a
participant in an Electronic Communications Network (ECN),
which provides customers access to trading securities with the
other participants in the ECN. In the firm's business site generally are up to as many as 100 computer desks, where customers
view securities trading information on the computer screen. The
firm usually requires a deposit when an account is opened,
sometimes of several thousand dollars. Afterwards, it charges
customer usage fees, transactions fees, and fees for other services provided. Frequently, customers are not allowed to leave
overnight securities balances.

The firms lend money to customers for trading purposes,
from which they receive interest. In addition to lending money
to customers for regular trading, day trading firms provide
margin loans to customers. The New York Stock Exchange and
the National Association of Securities Dealers have approved
proposals to place special margin requirements on day traders.
Under these proposals, customers who practice day trading
would be required to maintain a minimum in their margin
accounts of $25,000 at all times. The proposal has been sub-
mitted to the Securities and Exchange Commission for
approval. Currently, the requirement is $2,000. Besides that
proposal, the securities groups have proposed that the traders
who qualify for margin trading be allowed to borrow up to four
times the equity balance, versus two times currently. Also, customers borrow money from one another, but on a personal
basis. The ethical and political body of day trading firms is the
Electronic Traders Association. Because there has been a proliferation of such firms in recent years, it is recommended that day
traders seek advice on the reputations of firms and industry
practices, through chat groups, bulletin boards and personal

inquiries. *See* **day trader, Electronic Communications Network,** and **Electronic Traders Association.**

DCF. Abbreviation for **discounted cash flow.**

"dead cat bounce." A reference to a stock that has not appreciated in value in a long while suddenly moving up in price. The inference is that something external to company operations is the cause, such as a broad market upturn. Basically, the expression implies that the stock's recovery simply recaptures some of its prior loss as investors become more optimistic about prospects for the market in general. Consequently, investors should expect no more meaningful appreciation, after the sudden reflexive price upturn. This expression is also applied to an economic recovery that represents a return to a prior level of macro activity such as Gross Domestic Product, after an external force caused a brief decline.

dead-hand poison pill. See **antitakeover strategy.**

deal. An underwriting agreement between a corporation or other capital user and an investment banker to bring to market a new securities issue, including terms of the financing.

dealer. A securities businessman who buys over-the-counter securities for his own inventory, profiting or losing on selling them later. *See* **securities salesman.**

dealer concession or **selling group concession.** The profit to an investment firm from sales of the securities in an underwriting in which it has not invested but securities of which it has agreed to sell, a portion of which goes to the salesman.

"Dear John" memo (DJ). A reference to a notice from a brokerage that an online trader got none of the shares requested in an initial public offering.

death future or **viatical settlement.** A gallows humor nickname for an investment in which the death benefits of a terminally ill person are purchased in a lump-sum, usually for 50–80% of those death benefits. Under federal legislation, the prepaid cash amount is tax free, when certain stipulations are met. Investors who buy such a policy collect on the face value when the insured dies. The difference in the amount paid and the death benefits collected constitutes the yield, which can be highly unpredictable due to variable life expectancies. Technically, such an agreement is called a viatical settlement. Although the SEC has expressed an interest in regulating these investments, it has not gained legal jurisdiction. Instead, the investments are regulated by the insurance commissioners of states in which they are legal.

death tax. A nickname for inheritance tax. *See* **inheritance tax.**

debenture. A long-term debt certificate, paying interest, secured by the general credit of the issuer rather than a specific piece of property as is the case with a mortgage bond. *See* **bond.**

debit balance. The amount owed to a broker or dealer in a margin or regular account.

debt. A contractual obligation between two or more parties to pay a specific sum of money or installments of a sum, usually including interest payments, at certain dates and places in the future or on demand.

debt capacity. As judged by investors in debt securities, a company's ability to take on initial debt or additional debt by issuing new debt securities. The restriction or limit is determined by the level and constancy of annual transactions such as revenues and the amount of that flow available to apply to paying off all or part of debt expense or interest and debt retirement. Besides the current picture, the long-term trend is considered by creditors. Sometimes the capacity is structured, such as a requirement in a bank loan covenant that the company must maintain a 75/25 equity/debt ratio, or the shareholders' equity must always be at least 75% of total capitalization.

debt ceiling or **debt limit.** The maximum amount of money that a bond issuer can owe, usually in reference to a municipal borrower. Since the limit has usually been established by referendum it must be increased in the same manner.

debt financing. The raising of capital by a corporation through the sale of bonds or some other form of borrowing.

debt limit. See **debt ceiling.**

debt retirement. See **retirement, debt.**

debt service requirements. The principal and interest due annually on bonds. Credit analysts usually make sure these required payments are generously covered by the debtor's cash flow.

decimal pricing. The use of decimals in quoting prices of securities, rather than fractions as was done historically before the year 2000—10.50 instead of 10½ and 10.25 instead of 10¼—on tapes and stock tables. This procedure is the trend in global stock markets, in the pursuit of clarity in securities trading. Decimal trading has been introduced on the New York Stock Exchange, the American Stock Exchange, and NASDAQ in the United States and on most major exchanges in the world. However, there are pockets of securities markets, like certain futures and options trading, where the conversion is taking longer. In the United States, the SEC was the driving force behind the adoption of decimal pricing, beginning in 1997. By the end of 2001, the conversion to decimal trading will be mostly completed in the United States. Besides the argument that decimal pricing would improve clarity in trading, it is contended that decimals will give investors more opportunities, since there will be 100 prices per dollar at which a security can trade, rather than selected fractions as was the historical system. In other words, a penny is the new minimum trading fraction. Under the new method, stocks are priced to four decimals and rounded to two. However, U.S. Treasury bonds will continue to trade in whole numbers and 32nds, which together multiplied by 10 gives the price of the bond. A bond quoted at 100.12 is worth $1003.75 (100 plus $^{12}/_{32}$ or 100.3750 x 100 or 1003.75). *See* **fractional pricing.**

declare a dividend. As a corporation's board of directors, to appropriate eligible funds for dividend distribution to stockholders in a formal action. Generally, dividends must be paid out of operating income as opposed to capital surplus or paid-in surplus accounts, unless it is a liquidating dividend. *See* **liquidating dividend.**

declining balance. See **depreciation allowance.**

Deductible IRA. An investment retirement account in which the investor's contributions are deductible from taxable income, in filing income taxes. *See* **Individual Retirement Account.**

deep-discount bond. A reference to a bond that will mature in the distant future and that carries a low contracted interest rate in relation to current rates obtainable by investors on the same quality of bonds. The result is that the bond's current market value is at a sharp discount under par to enable investors to realize a similar yield to maturity as they would on bonds paying the current interest rate. This realization of a comparable yield to maturity results from amortizing during the bond's remaining life the gain over purchase price that will be received when the bond matures at par. Since the bond's remaining life is several years at a low interest rate, the purchase price must be discounted substantially to produce a gain at maturity large enough to increase through amortization the average annual yield (contracted rate plus amortized discount) in all the remaining years to maturity.

For example, a 25-year bond with a contracted rate of 3% might sell for par, or $1,000, at the time of issue. However, if five years later the yield to maturity obtainable in the market on a comparable bond were 5%, the market price of the former bond would decrease to $749 to compensate investors for the lower nominal rate, in which case it would be a deep discount bond.

deep-discount brokerage or **broker.** An investment firm offering trading services only to investors, using the electronic technology of the Internet. Because of low overhead expenses, trades are provided for as little as $7.95 per 100 shares. It is a bare bones service. Although there is controversy over the adequacy of trading services provided, indications are it is adequate except in extremely high volume sessions. Sometimes links are posted to research services, but there is usually a subscription fee or charge for their products. *See* **full-service brokerage** and **discount broker.**

deep pockets. A reference to a company or investor with plentiful cash or near-cash resources, an important factor for investors in trying to forecast who will win a bidding contest in a stock buyout or merger.

defensive stock. A stock whose price remains firm in a faltering market, usually because the product it represents is essential to consumers, and they will continue to buy it even in recessions. If the yield on such a stock is reasonable and the dividend seems likely to continue, the stock's market value will often increase as money pulls out of uncertain stocks and flows into businesses with more predictable profits. *See* **money-rate issues.**

Deferred Annuity or **Deferred Payment Annuity.** An annuity plan in which payments to the annuitant are delayed for a number of investment periods, such as when college expenses begin in the future for a parent. *See* **annuity.**

deferred charges. Those current money outlays that apply to future periods. Since they are not actually due currently, they often appear as assets on a Balance Sheet.

Deferred Compensation Retirement Plan. Of all the retirement plans, this one is applicable to the most employers. It can be used by state and municipal governments, tax-exempt nonprofit entities, and profit-oriented businesses. Through salary contributions on a pretax basis, employees can make payments. The tax status of the contributions turns on whether the plan is qualified or nonqualified for tax deferrals, under IRS rules. A deferred compensation plan (IRC Section 457) is advantageous to employers in the following situations:

- Organization has many highly compensated employees and only a few not highly compensated.
- Organization has many employees whose benefits are limited by IRC Section 415.
- Organization is for profit or nonprofit.

deficit. An excess of money outlays or charges over revenues, in an accounting period.

deficit financing. The spending of borrowed money or past earnings as opposed to current revenue.

defined asset fund. A pool of capital invested in securities that are representative of a certain financial or capital category, such as municipal bonds or common stock. *See* **unit investment trust (UIT)** or **unitrust.**

defined benefit pension or **traditional pension** or **fixed benefit plan.** A pension plan under which a company pays a set amount monthly to a plan participant after a pensioner's retirement. The amount is based on that worker's wages and seniority. Such plans are partly insured by the federal government in the event of losses of principal.

Defined Contribution Retirement Plan. A pension or retirement program under which an employer promises certain contributions to a plan but not the ultimate benefit. The beneficiary is the principal contributor to the fund and bears all the risks, in the event of losses. Success of the plan depends on the worker's ability to save and the quality of the investment management. These are the most popular type of 401(k)s.

deflation. A state of inactive business in a country's economy, generally accompanied by lower producer, consumer, and stock prices.

Delaware Department of Justice. Regulator of securities laws in the state of Delaware. Address: Division of Securities, State Office Building, 820 N. French Street, 8th Floor, Wilmington, DE 19801. Phone: (302) 577-2515.

delayed delivery. The presentation of securities sold to a brokerage later than the typical three days, after the transaction date. *See* **delivery date.**

delayed opening. A postponement of a stock's initial trade on an exchange, usually because massive accumulations of buy or sell orders would create a disorderly market. During the delay, brokers attempt to offset the buy orders with sell orders or vice versa.

delivery. The presentation of recently sold securities, which are in legal form and ownership, to an investment firm by the seller.

delivery date. The required date on which a seller must deliver securities to the brokerage, usually three days after the transaction date unless prearranged by the seller. In this case the delivery can be 3 to 60 days—called a seller's option—and sometimes the purchaser's price is adjusted.

Delphic forecast. A reference to the technique of forecasting by taking a survey of expectations espoused by a panel of experts concerning a future event, such as a stock index's closing price for the year. The predictions of the others in the survey are reviewed by each contributor, after which each one makes adjustments to his or her predictions. A composite or average of the modified predictions is adopted by those needing the information, since the consensus of the probabilities is considered more likely to occur than any of the individual opinions. The key to this type of forecast being reliable is that the experts advance independent opinions, based on a high level of expertise, rather than ones that emanate from the same source.

demand area. See **resistance area.**

demand-pull inflation. A general increase in prices caused by a shortage of goods, rather than an increase in the costs of supplying the goods.

Department of Commerce, U.S. (DOC). A department of the federal government, headed by a cabinet-level secretary. Its mission is to promote job creation, economic growth, sustainable development, and improved living standards in the United States. It accomplishes these by working in partnership with business, universities, communities, and workers, in a three-pronged program that includes:

1. Building for the future and promoting U.S. competitiveness in the global marketplace by strengthening and safeguarding the nation's economic infrastructure;

2. Keeping America competitive with cutting-edge science and technology and an unrivaled information base;

3. Providing effective management and stewardship of the nation's resources and assets to ensure sustainable economic opportunities.

Among its many important divisions are the Bureau of the Census, **Bureau of Economic Analysis,** National Oceanic & Atmospheric Administration, Patent and Trademark Office, and the Economic Development Administration. Telephone: (202) 482-4883. E-mail: opaosec@doc.gov. Web site: *www.doc.gov.*

Department of Commerce, U.S., Online. *See* under **Web Sites for the Inquiring Investor.**

depletion allowance or **capital consumption allowance.** An accounting charge to income and deduction from revenues to allow for the using up of the worth of certain assets, such as oil, coal, and copper, so that money needed to replace them will be available from the reserves accumulated in each period from the charges and deductions from revenues. Usually, these deductions are not subject to income taxes over the period of depletion.

Depository Institutions Deregulation and Monetary Control Act. A federal act of 1980 promoting deregulation and greater flexibility of financial institutions. Its key provisions were:
- Phased out regulation of interest rates for banks and thrift institutions
- Authorized interest-bearing checking, demand deposit accounts for financial institutions
- Permitted stock brokerages to offer checking accounts
- Mitigated state usury laws on home mortgages on amounts exceeding $25,000
- Authorized second mortgages
- Stopped geographical restrictions on mortgage lending.

depreciation allowance or **capital consumption allowance.** An accounting charge to income and deduction from revenues to allow for the wearing out of the worth of certain assets, such as machinery, buildings and trucks, so that money needed to replace them will be available from the reserves accumulated in each period from the charges and deductions from revenues. Usually, these deductions are not subject to income taxes over the period of depreciation. There are several methods of depreciation in use among corporations. They break down into two basic types: straight-line and accelerated. In the former, it is assumed the asset wears out at the same rate each period, while in the latter, it is assumed that depreciation is greatest in the early periods. Note that the accelerated methods do not necessarily reduce federal income taxes by allowing bigger deductions in the early years. These methods defer taxation because in the later years there is less deduction available than in the straight-line method. The accelerated methods should, therefore, be considered as a tax deferral method. In the double-declining balance method, sometimes called the 200% declining balance, twice the amount of the straight-line rate is charged, or 40% of the asset value is charged each year. There is also a 150% declining balance, which is calculated on the same basis

depression. A state of severe contraction of business activity, in which general prices decrease, consumer income drops, supplies of goods and services exceed demand, unemployment goes up, inventories stack up, and construction activity contracts. There is a decrease in consumer and business confidence. There is an increased avoidance of risks and investment projects are canceled. The last worldwide depression occurred in 1930. Perhaps as harmful as the economic hardship that takes place is the political turmoil unloosed as desperate people often follow ambitious and misguided demigods.

derivative. A financial instrument that has a value and return keyed to or derived from an underlying stock, bond, commodity, or other resource. They are loosely regulated, compared to full-fledged securities, by the Commodity Futures Trading Commission. Furthermore, there are disputes about the scope that commission's regulation may cover. Since 1987, the derivatives market has grown from approximately $865 billion to $37 trillion. There are two primary kinds of derivatives, called "plain vanilla" derivatives: options and "forward" types. The latter type includes forwards, futures, and swaps. As to the differences, an option gives the holder the right to buy or sell an underlying resource, while a "forward" type is a definite commitment by the holder to buy or sell an underlying resource. Derivatives may be listed on exchanges or traded privately over-the-counter, between institutions. Under an FASB standard that became effective in 1999, companies must show the fair-market values of derivatives on their Balance Sheets. And under certain conditions, they must adjust their reported earnings to reflect changes in the derivatives' values.

derivatives-disclosure rules. Those rules promulgated by the SEC to enable investors to better understand the risks that ownership of financial derivatives by investable companies entails. Derivatives include options, futures contracts, and swaps. The rules require that disclosure of financial risks be measured in one of three ways: (1) providing a table that shows the fair values and contract terms of contracts, (2) analysis showing the potential loss or gain arising from changes in interest rates or other market rates or prices, and (3) value-at-risk calculations that illustrate the potential loss from market movements with a certain likelihood of occurrence. The methods of actual accounting for derivatives is the province of the FASB.

derivative security. In many respects, such as in trading, this is like a regular bond, but its return is derived from factors other than just interest rates. For example, returns on structured notes might change with variance in stock prices, commodity prices, foreign exchange rates, and so on.

descending triangle. A price pattern made by recorded high-high-low bars on a stock bar chart or Xs and Os on a point-and-figure chart. Chartists look at the magnitude of the rise at the backside of the triangle, believing that the drop after the breakout will be similar. If the rise on the backside is $10 per share, look for a decline of $10 after the breakout. *See* **price patterns.**

descending wedge. A price pattern made by recorded high-low-close bars on a stock bar chart or Xs and Os on a point-and-figure chart. Chartists believe that the closer the trading range at the bottom of the wedge becomes, the greater will be the decline after the breakout. *See* **price patterns.**

detachable warrant. See **warrants.**

deterioration. See **market deterioration.**

devaluation. A planned reduction in the value of a monetary unit. For instance, if a country's money unit is based on an amount of gold, a devaluation, or making of each money unit worth less gold, means foreign creditors can get less gold with their balances of that money, either in bank deposits or investments. This diminution in exchange value applies to a conversion into other foreign currencies as well.

development expenses. Those outlays required to ready a product for market. Often these expenses are accumulated and capitalized, appearing on a Balance Sheet as "Deferred Charges" and deducted from or amortized against the earnings of future accounting periods to offset revenues from the product's sales in the appropriate periods.

DEWKS. In marketing parlance, an acronym for "dually-employed with kids." This term is a reference to two income producers in a family with children. Usually, such people have more disposable income than one-worker families, and are prime prospects for children's items, educational products, and services and investment products and services.

DIAMONDs (DIAs). A type of derivative securities that represent a microcosm of the Dow Jones Industrial Average, an index many call "the stock market." They are purchased by investors as a unit of ownership in an investment trust that holds a portfolio of common stocks that closely tracks the price performance and dividend yield of the DJIA. These securities began trading in 1998 on the AMEX.

DIFF or **Euro-rate differential.** A futures contract trading on the Chicago Mercantile Exchange that is based on the spread in the interest rate between the U.S. dollar, the German mark, the British pound, and the Japanese yen.

digerati. A reference to the intellectual and financial elite, such as CEOs of Internet success stories, in the digital age.

digest a gain, to. In reference to most investors trading in the stock market, to accept an unexpected gain in stock price, so that a wave of selling and depressed prices does not follow because of apprehensive profit takers who are selling. Usually, good financial news has justified the higher level of prices.

dilution of equity. In reference to the ownership in a corporation, a reduction in the asset value or earning power represented by each share because of the issuance of new stock by a corporation without a proportionate increase in resources, or, a decrease in assets without a decrease in stock outstanding.

diminishing balance or **declining balance.** A reference to any one of several accounting methods for depreciation whereby the value of an asset is reduced by a fixed percentage each year. *See* **depreciation allowance.**

DINKS. In marketing parlance, an acronym for "dual income with no kids." This term is a reference to two income producers in a family with no children. Usually, such people have more discretionary income and are prime prospects for high-priced luxury goods and services. They are also receptive to investments.

directed shares or **"friends and family shares."** A reference to shares of stock in an initial public offering (IPO) or secondary offering that are allocated to certain persons at the request of the issuer. The recipients on the list get the right to buy a specific number of the shares at the offering price immediately before the offering to the public. They have the extra benefit of not having to hold their shares for a specified time, as do insiders and members of the underwriting group. Instead, they may sell their shares any time, providing many with the quick profits that can follow an IPO. This practice has become more popular in recent years, having grown from a typical allotment of 1% to 5% of the total shares offered in the early 1990s to 5% to 10% in the late 1990s. Although the business purpose was to reward business partners, customers, and prospects of the issuer, the practice has taken on the trappings of awarding status symbols and quick money to acquaintances for many managements. In other words, it has become a headache for many, especially the underwriters who must administer the distributions.

direct placement. See **private placement.**

direct investing. See **direct stock plans.**

direct stock market. A reference to the use of the Internet by start-up companies in raising new capital, by soliciting funds from small investors. Technically, these companies might elect to contact prospective investors using some other method besides the Internet, such as personal contact. The important point is they deal directly with investors, rather than through investment bankers or securities underwriters. The middleman is eliminated, making a new financing less costly, with more going to the company and, therefore, to the investors.

direct stock plans (DSPs). Programs initiated and operated by public corporations to sell their stock directly to investors, saving the latter brokerage commissions and fees in the process, and assuring investors direct ownership of stock rather than street name ownership. In addition, the investor receives notices, reports, and dividends directly from the corporation. Corporations engage in these programs to enable themselves to develop a type of stock distribution to their liking. Many corporations sell additional shares to existing stockholders for a flat price rather than by a number of shares. Consequently, a small number of shares can be purchased. Sometimes the companies offer shareholders dividend reinvestment plans that also allow investors to accumulate additional shares, without commissions and fees. The SEC regulates these programs as well as reports and communications with investors. Online sources of information on direct stock investing are: Netstock Direct Corporation at *www.netstockdirect.com;* Drip Investor at *www.dripinvestor.com*; No-load Stock Insider at *www.noloadstocks.com. See* **Dividend Reinvestment Plan.**

directors. See **Board of Directors.**

dirigiste economics. A reference to economic policies, especially in regard to international trade, that are considered obsolete, in terms of promoting growth within state economies. In a modern sense, the term refers to a rejection of the conventional economics prescription for emerging countries of low debt and government controls, emphasizing stability, in favor of an emphasis on freer financial markets and market development for a country's exports as a way to achieve economic growth.

dirty stock. A stock that cannot be delivered in an acceptable manner.

disaster bond. See **catastrophe bond.**

disclaimer or **hedge clause.** A brief statement, but sometimes not so brief, appended to an investment report, stock letter, or document that makes an effort to disassociate the issuing firm, usually a brokerage firm or investment banker, from the responsibility of warranting the accuracy of the report's contents or recommending the purchase of securities through its contents. As the propensity to litigate for personal injury has grown in our society, the scope of disclaimer clauses has increased. There are now disclaimers or hedges in a report or sales memorandum against the appearance of guaranteeing financial results, investment suitability, impartiality, and absence of conflict of interests, to name a few. In cases where the investment firm or securities salesman has a financial interest in securities mentioned in a report, such information should also disclosed, to disclaim that the report is impartial.

Besides trying to establish that the issuer bears no responsibility for accuracy or false assumptions related to the report, the disclaimer basically is an effort to make a full disclosure of any colorations that a report might contain in favor of the publisher's interests, such as optimistic projections when the publisher has received stock warrants or stock options in the subject company, in exchange for issuing the report. The spirit of the disclaimer is to observe the SEC mission of providing complete information, or transparency, as that agency calls it, in order that investors can make informed decisions. There tends to be a significant difference between traditional Wall Street hedge clauses, where the content addresses more general prejudices against investor interests that arise in the normal course of the securities business, and online disclaimers, where the contents address specific disclaimers, such as unsuitability of the security for certain investors and remuneration for the support of a security.

discount. 1) The amount under face, or par, value for which a bond or preferred stock is selling. *See* **money market.** 2) The amount under asset value for which a closed-end investment company share is selling. 3) **convertible discount.** The amount under the conversion value for which a convertible bond or preferred stock is selling. To determine if a convertible security is selling for a discount or premium, calculate how much the convertible common equivalent would cost per share by dividing the convertible preferred stock current cost by the obtainable shares of common stock. Subtract that cost from the current price of the common stock. If the result is a plus amount, the conversion represents a discount; if a minus amount, it is a premium. To illustrate, assume the convertible preferred stock of JazzMe, Inc. is selling for $100 per share. Furthermore, each share is convertible into five shares of common stock, which is currently priced at $25 per share. The convertible equivalent of the preferred stock is $20 per share ($100 ÷ 5). Subtracting that from $25 per share gives a $5-per-share discount. In other words, it would cost an investor $5, or a 25% discount, less per share to buy the shares through purchasing the convertible preferred stock and exchanging it for five shares of common stock. However, it is important to remember that giving up a preferred dividend might offset the discount somewhat, and should be considered. *See* **premium.**

discount brokerage or **broker.** A brokerage firm that offers only limited trading services to investors. Usually, only actual transaction services are provided, so that investors are expected to bring some degree of knowledge and planning relative to their trades to the table. However, there is a growing tendency for other services, such as research, to be furnished. This often occurs in the form of links to Internet materials or third-party research reports. The fewer services provided enable the discount broker to charge lower commissions than the full-service counterpart. These commissions can be as low as $29.95 per 100-share trade. However, investor accounts are not usually monitored as closely, at least in the cases where a diligent **full-service brokerage** is involved. There is a controversy over whether a discount broker can provide even the equivalent trading capabilities of a full-service broker. Evidence suggests that the service from either is similar, except in cases of high-volume crises, when full-service firms have an advantage in getting off trades. *See* also **deep-discount brokerage.**

discounted cash flow (DCF) or **present value of money.** The amount of money required today to grow into a specified future sum, assuming that the present fund will be invested at a specified rate of interest for a given number of years. It is the amount an investor needs to invest in the present to accumulate a definite future sum, given the interest rate obtainable and the number of years the money can be left in the investment. *See* **annuity** for present value formula.

discounting the market. The taking into account of anticipated financial events by investors so that present stock prices are affected rather than future ones. Thus, investors discount the impact of expected events on future security prices by acting immediately, so that when the event comes about there is little effect on stock prices.

discount rate, FED. A reference to the interest rate charged by the Federal Reserve Bank for short-term loans to members and other banks, made at the discount window and collateralized by government securities when other securities deemed eligible, meaning extremely high quality. This rate is considered the floor on bank interest in the United States, since members and other banks key their prime rate to it.

discount rate, present value. That annual rate of return or interest applied to a future amount of money or principal in a present value formula that will convert that future amount to the sum required today to satisfy the equation, in the specified time. The discount rate or interest rate is actually the payment to the investor for the use of the money and the risk of losing the money. In the case of a common stock, the discount factor required varies with (1) the inflation rate, (2) the supply and demand pressures on the stock, and (3) the risk of loss. Establishing the required discount rate usually begins with the no-risk rate of return, defined as the U.S. Treasury 90-day bill rate. Next, the investor adds a factor that reflects the return from common stocks generally and the Beta Value or volatility of price movements of the stock under consideration in relation to the average for common stocks—the risk premium.

discount window. A reference to the process established by the Federal Reserve Bank by which members and other banks may obtain short-term loans from the Fed at a closely monitored interest or discount rate. Loans are not automatic and, in fact, are discouraged by the Fed, except when a bank's reserves are short and need to be replenished.

discount yield. The yield on a security sold on a discount basis, such as a U.S. Treasury bill. Sometimes this method of calculating yield is referred to as bank discount basis. The formula to calculate is: (Discount ÷ Face Value) × (360 ÷ days until maturity). For example, let's say an investor can purchase a $10,000 Treasury bill for $9,500, maturing in 180 days. What is the annualized yield or rate of return? Substituting in the formula: $(500 ÷ 10,000) × (360 ÷ 180) = .0500 × 2 = .10$, or 10%.

discretionary account. A securities account operated under the customer's consent for the broker or dealer to trade his securities without prior approval.

discretionary income. That portion of a consumer's income not committed to buying essentials such as lodging, food, and utilities. It is closely followed by economists because its magnitude often represents new spending that can stimulate the economy.

discretionary order. A customer's order for a specific security to be bought or sold and for what amount, which his broker may execute when he feels the timing is right.

discretionary trust, investing. A mutual fund or unit trust not limited to investing in a specific type of security.

discretionary trust, legal. A personal trust that allows the trustee to manage the assets in the trust and decide when to distribute income to the beneficiaries.

disinflation. A description of the slowing down of general prices increases, usually caused by a slowdown in economic activity, so that producers can not raise prices readily for fear of losing sales. Note that this is not deflation, when prices actually decrease, but a slower rate of inflation.

disintermediation. In an economy, the movement of savings or investment funds away from institutions such as banks into higher-yielding securities in the public markets, such as the general money market.

disinvestment. As a company, the selling or otherwise disposing of assets without replacing them or not maintaining assets that wear out or are used up.

Disposable Income. Under the system of National Income Accounts, that portion of Personal Income remaining after personal taxes and certain fees have been deducted. It is available for spending or saving and is watched closely by economists as a gauge of consumer buying power. *See* **discretionary income.**

"disposition effect." Based on studies by Terrence Odean, assistant professor of finance at the Graduate School of Management at the University of California at Davis, the tendency of investors to sell stock in which they have a profit rather than those in which they have a loss. The reason apparently is because investors try to avoid taking losses, even when it might alleviate income taxes for them, in the hope that the losing stock might turn into a winner. Inadvertently, they do the opposite of the professional advice: "Cut your losses short, and let your profits run."

"dissed." As a public company, criticized severely in public by a securities analyst.

dissolution. An agreement by stockholders, or a court decree, which sets into motion the sale of a corporation's assets or the distribution of them to shareholders, after creditors' claims are satisfied, initiating the end of a corporation's life.

distress sale. A sale of property, including securities, under the pressure of having to raise money to satisfy claims.

distribution, securities. The management of a sale of a large block of stock, often over one million shares, through a group or syndicate of brokers. The object is to sell the stock with as little effect on the price as possible. It is a process of looking for buyers of the stock, without attempting to sell the issue.

distribution in liquidation. See **return of capital (3).**

District of Columbia Services Commission. Regulator of securities laws in the District of Columbia. Address: Securities Division, 450 Fifth Street NW, #821, Washington, DC 20001. Phone: (202) 626-5105.

ditto (do). The term used in a newspaper listing of securities quotes when the same company, but a different class of its securities, is being reported.

diversification. 1) The entrance of a company into new business fields. 2) The commitment of investment funds into varied types of businesses or geographic regions, for example, bonds, preferred stocks, or common stocks in several unrelated industries, to protect against stock market losses caused by industry-wide downturns. 3) The commitment of investment funds frequently, so that the probability of more successes is enhanced over time.

diversified fund. A mutual fund that invests shareholders' money in several different companies and industries. *See* **diversification (2).**

divestment. The transfer of assets by a corporation to another owner(s), either through a sale or spin-off, usually under a court order or because the corporation wants to merge with another company and is required by regulatory agencies or the Justice

Department to shed assets that would jeopardize consumer interests or be monopolistic before the merger.

dividend. 1) A fund paid proportionately to corporate stockholders out of earnings or sale of assets. Various classes of stock in a corporation might participate in the dividend fund differently, but the distribution to each class is proportionate to the number of shares in that class. Most dividends from corporate earnings are paid quarterly, and the last quarterly payment is considered to be the indicated dividend rate (multiply by four to get the annual dividend). Extra dividends from asset sales or from extraordinary earnings are paid when convenient and are not considered regular dividends. For quoting information, See **stock table.** 2) Those payments to policy holders by mutual insurance companies to distribute surpluses. Unless a policy is paid-up and the cost of insurance to the policy holder has been recovered, these dividends are not taxable, but are treated as a partial return of premiums. 3) Those payments to shareholders from building and loan associations, mutual savings banks, and credit unions. These payments are treated as interest income and do not enjoy a dividend exclusion for federal income tax purposes.

dividend capture. The practice of systematically buying stock shares a few days before their ex-dividend dates or the dates when new buyers are not entitled to the most recently declared dividends. The object is to buy them cum-dividend, or with dividend, early enough so that the coming dividend has not been fully reflected in the price, hold them until the ex-dividend date when their price will drop by the dividend amount, and then sell the shares when they rise to their level prior to the dividend period. In doing this, the investor counts on getting the dividend plus a small gain to cover trading expenses.

dividend coverage. The number of times earnings exceed the dividend requirement of a common stock after subtracting senior dividend requirements. The measure indicates relative safety of a dividend when the coverage is at least two. The ratio was 1.7 times in the late 1990s for the average U.S. corporation.

dividend credit. A credit allowed on certain dividend income in filing income taxes.

dividend discount model. A mathematical model that uses a stock's future dividends in computing the present price to pay for a share of that stock. This is very similar to the methods used in pricing bonds, capital projects, and common stocks using other discounting methods, except that assumed dividend flows are used rather than other cash inflows. Basically there are three approaches: (1) assuming constant dividends in the future, (2) assuming dividend growth at a constant rate in the future, and (3) assuming dividend growth at variable rates of growth. The formula assuming a constant dividend growth follows:

DIVIDEND DISCOUNT MODEL

(Assuming Constant Dividend Growth)

$$P_S = D_S (1 + g) \div (r-g)$$

where:

P_S = Present value of stock;

D_S = Present dividend;

g = Annual rate of dividend growth;

r = Discount rate of return assigned to stock risk

Let's do it. You are looking at buying shares of Morning After, Inc., a leading maker of aspirin tablets, for $25 per share. It is a company that has demonstrated steady earnings growth of approximately 7.5% annually, on a compounded basis, over the years. The dividend payout ratio has remained 50% long enough to assume it will continue to do so. Consequently, dividends are also growing at 7.5%. The dividend this year has grown to $2. You plan to hold the stock five years and expect a return of 15%, or .15 (discount rate). How much should you pay for a five-year holding period? Substituting: The current dividend ($2) × (1 + .075, or 1.075) = $2.15, divided by the .15 discount rate minus the .075 (7.5%) dividend growth rate produces a present stock value of $28.67, using this model. Since you can buy the stock for $3.67 less, the model suggests it would be a good holding for five years, given your expectations.

"dividend-on." A description of a stock purchase that includes its recently declared dividend. *See* **dividend payout.**

dividend payout. The ratio of cash dividends paid on common stock divided by earnings on common stock, expressed as a percentage. It represents the amount of income earned that management chooses to pass along to the owners of the business. Historically, in the United States industries have paid out on average 55% of profits; utilities 70%; and growth companies much less, if anything, since they reinvest most of their earnings on the tools of growth. For all U.S. corporations, the average dividend payout was 60% of net income in the late 1990s.

Dividend Reinvestment Plan (DRIP). A program carried out for the stockholders by certain corporations in which cash dividends are used to purchase additional shares or fractional shares, on the dividend payment date. Sometimes the reinvestment is at a discount to the current market stock price. Many companies also allow stockholders to buy additional shares. Usually, the company administers the program without charges or with only nominal fees to participants. Several Web sites provide assistance, such as *www.dripcentral.com* and *www.netstockdirect.com.*

dividend return or **dividend yield.** The annual dividend per share divided by the current price of the company's stock, expressed as a percentage. This ratio is very mercurial, in line with the ups and downs of the stock market, but during the 1990s, the average annual yield on stocks in the S&P 500 Stock Index was 2.5%.

dividends-per-share—common. The total dividend declared and distributed by the board of directors of a corporation on the common stock in a year, divided by the number of shares outstanding.

divisive reorganization. The division of a corporation through choice or under directive from an antitrust suit into two or more separated corporations. *See* **spin-off, split-up, split-off.**

DJ. Abbreviation for a **"Dear John"** memo.

DJIA. Abbreviation for **Dow-Jones Industrial Average.**

DOC. Abbreviation for **Department of Commerce.**

Dodd, David. Coauthor of the classic book on applying quantitative methods to buying and selling common stocks, *Securities Analysis. See* **"Graham-Dodd."**

"dog." Slang term for an ignored stock with low trading volume.

"dog and pony show" or **"road show."** The somewhat facetious names for the repetitious presentations before interested investors in key financial cities that companies planning initial public offerings must conduct, in meeting the "due diligence" requirements of the SEC and other regulatory bodies.

Dogs of the Dow. The 10 top-yielding stocks in the Dow Jones Industrial Average.

Dogs of the Dow Strategy. A portfolio strategy aiming to trade for those stocks in the Dow Jones Industrial Average with the 10 highest yields each year.

dollar bond. A bond denominated and redeemable in U.S. dollars issued outside the United States.

dollar cost averaging. The buying of a fixed dollar amount of stock shares at regular intervals so that more shares are bought at low prices, fewer at high, resulting in an average cost that is lower than the average price. In an eventual rising market, this mathematical advantage guarantees the average cost of the shares will be less than their current market value. Dollar cost averaging is recommended for long-term investors who want to avoid continual decisions regarding timing in their purchases of a quality stock that seems destined for market gains. The system also limits losses since more shares of a stock are bought as its price drops, thus reducing the average cost, as compared to a system of buying in quantity at a high price, paying a high average cost.

As was mentioned, the great benefits of dollar cost averaging occur in the long term when the price begins rising.

While studies show losses are unlikely if a plan can be continued, the principle of dollar cost-averaging is valid only if the shares accumulated are sold above the average cost to the investor, which necessitates a price upturn toward the end of the accumulation period. The New York Stock Exchange recommends dollar cost averaging in its Monthly Investment Plan, as do mutual funds stressing systematic accumulation of shares.

dollarization. A reference to the adoption by a country of the American dollar as its official medium of exchange. The decision to do so by a government is usually due to a failure of its national currency system, followed by a search for a stabilizing influence on its economy or because there are close trading ties or political ties with the United States. As a matter of policy, the U.S. is ambivalent about the practice. The most recent conversion to the dollar was by Ecuador in the year 2000. Panama did so in 1903. Other countries using dollarization are Liberia and some small Pacific Island governments. There has been much discussion about Latin and South America converting to the dollar. The argument for doing so is the advantages of doing so in promoting regional trade, economic stability, and other common interests. Arguments against the conversion are a loss of sovereignty and financial flexibility. Among hemispheric countries carrying on significant trade with the United States and considering the conversion are Mexico, Argentina, and Peru.

domicile. The place where a corporation is incorporated, usually the state, as opposed to its headquarters address. Often a company incorporates in one state because of tax, franchise, or political advantages but operates in another because of operating or marketing advantages.

donated stock. Shares of the fully paid capital stock of a corporation, contributed to it without consideration. The par value is carried in a "Donated Surplus" account at par value.

Donated Surplus Account or **Donated Capital.** A special Shareholders' Equity account to which contributions of stock of a corporation, gifts, and cash are credited. *See* **Capital Surplus.**

dot-com stock. A reference to a stock that represents a category of dynamic new stocks that began appearing in the late 1990s, through IPOs by new corporations designed to exploit the Internet medium for selling products and services. Most often, they are created as start-ups, joint ventures, or mergers, and they are vendors offering a wide range of products and services. In fact, the most outstanding characteristic of the group is the extraordinary range of products and services offered—books, videos, groceries, gourmet foods, toys, games, and so on. They specialize in niche markets, quite often. The nickname for these stocks originated from the Internet protocol requiring use of a ".com" after their domain name, or name for doing business. They epitomize the virtual store. An example is "egghead.com." A complete Internet address is usually something like *www.broccoli.com*. Because the Internet concept of vending, or e-tail as it is called, is new and untested, these stocks tend to sell at exorbitant prices when commonly used evaluation techniques are used in analyzing them. For that reason, promoters of the stocks developed intriguing measures such as "eyeballs per month," or "unique visitors per quarter," or "questions per day," or "hits per quarter." These measure the number of Web surfers that land on the company's page. They are suspect as analytical tools, because they reflect no financial transactions. Often the companies in question are reporting no earnings and/or cash flow. *See* **proxy valuation.**

double bottom. A price pattern made by recorded high-low-close on a stock bar chart, or Xs and Os on a point-and-figure chart. Chartists believe the repetitive bottoms, especially on high volume, indicate the stock is a bargain at that price and will experience buying support there. *See* **price patterns** and **resistance area.**

Double-Declining Balance. See **depreciation allowance.**

double taxation. A term used by critics to describe the present federal income tax laws pertaining to corporations. Under current laws, net income of a corporation is taxed plus the income of stockholders receiving dividends from that net income, which amounts to two income taxes on the same income. This situation has caused many corporations to issue stock dividends rather than cash, since a dividend receiver can hold the stock 12 months plus a day and get a more favorable capital gains treatment. *See* **corporation tax.**

double top. A price pattern made by recorded high-low-close bars on a stock bar chart, or Xs and Os on a point-and-figure chart. Chartists rationalize the repetitive tops indicate the stock is overpriced at that level, which will cause selling pressure there in the future. The top is seen as a resistance price level. *See* **price patterns.**

double witching hour. The last hour of stock market trading on the third Friday of all months except March, June, September, and December, when stock options and stock index options contracts expire. The effect often triggers heavy buying and selling of options, futures, and the underlying stocks. *See* **triple witching hour.**

doubtful or **delinquent account.** An account receivable on a company's books that has not been paid and is past due the payment date or time followed by trade practice. Usually, a trade account—one representing a transaction typical of others in the industry—is due in 30 days from the invoice date. Keeping accounts receivable current is one of the most important functions of effective management. It contributes to a company's solvency or insolvency. Often the greatest product or service on the planet can become troubled because customers are not paying bills on time. One way to ascertain how effective receivables are managed is to maintain an "aging schedule." This is an analysis that breaks down all accounts receivable into categories of how long they have been due or how long they have been outstanding. The categories are: current or under 30 days from billing, past due by 1–30 days, past due by 31–60 days, past due by 61–90 days, and past due by over 90 days. In the schedule, the amount in each category is shown as a percentage of the total due. Trade practice varies, but a good rule of thumb is that 75% or higher of the total due should be current or past due by only 1–30 days. Studies show that the longer accounts are past due, the greater the chances of nonpayment, so managements are well advised to keep collections current.

"dough." A slang expression for money.

Douglas Gerlach's Invest-O-Rama Online. See under **Web Sites for the Inquiring Investor.**

Dow Jones bond averages. Those daily price averages of 10 first grade rail bonds, 10 second grade rails, 10 utilities, 10 industrials, and a composite average of all 40 bonds compiled by Dow Jones & Co. *See* **bond averages.**

Dow Jones Business Directory. A Web site that rates online brokers, based on measures such as execution of customer's orders, research availability, account services, and so on. *See* **Web Sites for the Inquiring Investor.**

Dow Jones Composite Average. A stock "average" or index that measures price changes in three major economic sectors in the United States. It is comprised of those 65 stocks in the combined Dow Jones Industrial Average, the Dow Jones Transportation Average, and the Dow Jones Utility Average.

Dow Jones Industrial Average. The oldest and most famous of the stock market "averages," and one that measures price changes of 30 blue chip stocks in mathematical terms having no direct relation with actual prices of the stocks used in the process; thus, the popular habit of referring to this "average" as a dollar-and-cents or percentage figure is erroneous. It is actually a sophisticated index of price changes in the market for industrial-type stocks, representing large and important companies in the U.S. economy. The "average" takes into account the effect of dividends, stock splits, and other actions on the prices of stocks used by Dow Jones & Co, the compiler of the index. Stocks included are changed to maintain a representative industrial cross section to the index.

In the 1990s the composition of the index has been changed three times. The most recent one became effective with the opening of markets on November 1, 1999. This change moved the index away from companies that "make things" in the direction of companies that "do things." The latest entries were Microsoft, Intel, Home Depot, and SBC Communications.

Originally, 12 closing prices of 12 industrial stocks were added and divided by 12 to get an actual average. Over the years the procedure has been mathematically refined and made to measure the effects of stock splits and dividends on included stock prices. This is accomplished by calculating the regular average on the day before a stock used is to split, for instance. Then, the stock prices are added again, this time with the split stock listed at its new price. The total is divided by the regular average just taken, resulting in a new divisor that is divided into the total price after the split to get the new "average."

The Dow Jones industrial "average" is computed using only about 2% capitalizations of stocks listed on the New York Stock Exchange; therefore, it is considered inadequate as a market indicator by many experts. But since investors in general emphasize this "average," its movement must be followed as a clue to future investor actions. To illustrate calculation of the "average," suppose the value of the 30 industrial stocks is $1,800, giving an average price of $60. After halving the price of a stock scheduled to split 2-for-1 the next day, the total price is found to be $1,750. Dividing the regular average of $60 into $1,750, a new divisor of 29.2 is found. This is divided into $1,750 to get a new average of 59.9.

Dow Jones Markets Online. See under **Web Sites for the Inquiring Investor.**

Dow Jones Transportation Average. A stock "average" or index that measures price changes in the transportation sector of the U.S. economy. It is comprised of 20 stocks, representing airline, railroad, and trucking companies. *See* **Dow Jones Industrial Average.**

Dow Jones Utility Average. A stock "average" or index that measures price changes in the utility sector of the U.S. economy. It is comprised of 15 stocks, representing natural gas, electric power, and power companies. *See* **Dow Jones Industrial Average.**

Dow theorist. A strategist of the stock market who evaluates the general outlook for securities prices according to the Dow theory.

Dow theory. A theory of stock market analysis based on 200-day moving averages of the Dow Jones Industrial Average and Dow Jones Transportation Average. According to the theory, the market is in an upward trend if either average advances above a previous significant high followed by the other average. If they fall below a former significant low, the market is in a downward trend. It does not predict how long basic trends will continue.

down. See **off.**

downgrade. As an investment firm, to lower the expectations and investment attractiveness of a stock on its recommended list. Downgraded stock postings are often clothed in euphemistic terms—such as "market performer" or "accumulate on price weakness," in order to avoid offending the company's management and consequently losing corporate finance business in the future.

downscale buying. The buying of securities at intervals as the market price declines, in the belief that the lower prices are temporary; the opposite of pyramiding.

downside. A reference to a general drop in securities market prices during a trading session.

downside risk. A reference to the vulnerability of a security to a sharp fall off in market price. Usually it is accompanied by an estimate of the potential lower price, based on some quantitative measure such as a P/E multiple of Asset Value. For example, suppose that over a period of five years the Spinner Yo-Yo Corp. has never sold under 10 times its annual earnings. Currently priced at $20, its EPS estimate for the current year is $1.50. The downside risk could be said to be $5 per share. *See* **upside potential.**

downsize, to. As a strategy of corporate management, to shrink a company's size through asset sales, spin-offs of divisions, retirements of facilities, and often a formal restructuring, certainly an informal one. A reduction in products and services and employees usually accompanies these moves. The object is to eliminate nonstrategic businesses and to reduce operating costs and enhance profitability. *See* **nonstrategic assets.**

downstream. A reference to the traffic of matters such as money, accounting, and control from a parent corporation to its subsidiaries.

downtick. A decline in the trading price of a stock, versus the previous transaction in that stock.

draft. A written order from one person (drawer) to a financial institution (drawee) calling for payment of a sum of money in cash to a third party (payee). A bank account check is a draft. *See* **bill of exchange.**

drain reserves. Policies set in motion by the Federal Reserve System that result in a reduction in the U.S. money supply. The central bank accomplishes this by three measures: (1) selling bonds at attractive prices, causing bond dealers to buy them and thus reduce their bank balances; (2) increasing reserves requirements, making member banks increase reserves with Fed banks; and (3) raising the borrowing rate for member banks, so that they are inclined not to borrow money from the Fed but, rather, to decrease loans to maintain an ample supply of funds.

DRIP. See **Dividend Reinvestment Plans.**

Drucker, Peter F. An American management consultant and author who is considered the father of modern management. He is the author of 31 books on a variety of social and economic topics and two novels. He pioneered the examination of management as its own entity, and formulated a professional discipline for those wishing to pursue it as a career. Before that, management was regarded as a group of professional skills such as finance and accounting.

drugs. See **pharmaceuticals.**

drying up. A description of an active market that is losing investor interest, resulting in lower volume and prices.

DSPs. See **direct stock plans.**

due bill. An affidavit signed by a seller of securities promising to deliver property to which the buyer is entitled, usually in the future.

due date. In the case of a debt instrument, such as a bond, the date on which the balance must be paid.

Due Diligence. The procedures required by regulatory authorities of companies issuing new public stock, related to the disclosure of all significant information to investors. Actually, there is more than regulatory oversight requiring this practice. Brokers and underwriters working in a stock are expected to familiarize themselves with the issuing company and other matters connected to the deal. Failure to do so creates potential lawsuits against them by investors who followed the advice of the professionals. The procedure is so important that most companies appear in several financial markets, in order to answer questions from securities analysts, institutional investors, and brokers. *See* **"dog and pony show"** and **prospectus.**

Duff & Phelps, LLC. An investment bank founded in 1932 that provides financial advice, opinions, and valuations to clients; represents sellers and buyers of middle-market companies; raises equity, senior debt, and mezzanine capital for middle-market and emerging companies; and provides advisory services on public offerings. Web site: *www.dufflc.com.*

dull market. A reference to the stock market when trading is quiet with modest price fluctuations.

"dumping." Under international trading agreements, the exporting of goods to foreign countries at a price below what they cost to manufacture in the exporting country. In exports to the United States, that condition is determined by the Department of Commerce. In making that determination, the department includes a profit as a legitimate part of the costs. If aggrieved domestic companies that compete with the imported products suffer "material harm," according to an independent agency, prohibitive tariffs can be imposed. This process is considered flawed by many experts, because it can become a long-term retaliation that is in reality protectionism for inefficient domestic companies or industries. These critics suggest instead invoking the "safeguard" clause of most international trade agreements for dealing with a sudden influx of cheap foreign exports. Under this concept, an independent agency must judge that "serious harm" has resulted from the dumping—a higher threshold of economic injury than "material harm"—and the resulting import tariffs are temporary and must be phased out. If they are not phased out, reparations must be paid to the domestic producers. In this way, the exporters are not penalized unduly, and retaliatory measures are not invoked against the importing country.

Dun and Bradstreet (D & B). A worldwide credit rating organization and provider of other business information. Web site: *www.dnb.com.*

durable goods. A reference to industrial products that have a relatively long useful life—over three years—for example, automobiles, furniture, and such. Also, goods that require no further processing are sometimes called durable. *See* **Durable Goods Orders Report** and **nondurable goods.**

Durable Goods Orders Report. A report released in the second half of the month by the Bureau of the Census of the Department of Commerce detailing data on new orders for durable goods, orders, and the accumulation of order backlog. In compiling the report, analysts perform a 10% sample of manufacturers and include only firm or legally-binding orders. Economists and industry analysts use the report to evaluate and anticipate the health of the manufacturing sector. Because it is such a volatile series, partly because of aircraft and defense expenditures, non-defense orders are extracted and analyzed separately as a harbinger of capital spending. The latter spending is significant in estimating GNP. Durable goods forecasting is very difficult. When durable goods orders increase, fixed income securities tend to drop in value, common stocks tend to rise, and dollar exchange rates are not affected. When durable goods orders decrease, fixed income securities tend to rise, common stocks fall, and dollar exchange rates are independent.

durable power of attorney. A form of the power of attorney designation, whereby the agent, or person named to possess a power of attorney, shall continue in that capacity in the event the principal or grantor of the power becomes disabled. *See* **power of attorney.**

duration of a bond or bond portfolio. A measure of the weighted average life of the interest payments and the return of principle upon maturity of a bond or bond portfolio. This measure is usually a shorter period than the time until maturity, and relates more to the cash flow schedule for an investor from bond investments. *See* **maturity.**

Dutch auction. 1) A procedure in which the issuers of securities ask holders of the securities to name a price at which they would sell them back to the issuer. It resembles a prearranged tender offer, in many respects, because the issuer can accept all or a fraction of those offered back. The purpose of the maneuver is to reduce or eliminate a certain class of securities, reduce debt, or get better terms through issuing another security. 2) A procedure in which the underwriter of a new issue of stock requests bids from investors on how many shares they want and at what price per share. After bids are in, the underwriter begins allocating shares from the highest bid down, until all shares are allocated. However, the actual price every investor pays is the lowest bid price. According to investment bankers partial to this pricing method, it saves underwriting fees. They are usually about 5% of the issues total value, or gross, rather than the more conventional 7%. From the company's standpoint, one disadvantage is that the IPO is not as likely for the frequent big bounce after the offering, because many investors interested in the shares have already bid on and gotten stock. 3) A procedure in which the price of a security is gradually lowered to the level required to draw investor bids, at which price it is sold. This is the method used by the Treasury Department in selling Treasury bills.

Dutch auction preferred stock. See **auction rate preferred stock.**

dynamic hedging. As the broker for a worried equity portfolio manager who is buying put options from the broker's firm to protect her portfolio from a loss, the practice of limiting risk by selling stock or futures to offset the potential requirement to buy stock from the portfolio manager. In other words, it is hedging against hedgers.

dynamic pricing. A reference to a vendor offering random price discounts to buyers or offering to sell merchandise at varying discounts, tailored to special needs of buyers. In the case of random discounts, the vendor is testing the market, in order to establish a price for a product or service. This practice is prevalent in merchandising on the Web.

Ee

EAFE Index. A stock price index of European, Asian, and Far Eastern stocks, maintained by Morgan Stanley investment bankers. These stocks are selected for liquidity and industry diversification. The index is considered a barometer for international stock performance. Also, financial futures and options contracts are derivatives of this index.

Eagle, American Gold. A gold coin issued in $5, $10, $25, and $50 denominations by the United States in 1986, used by investors for investing in gold conveniently. The coins contain $1/10$ ounce, $1/4$ ounce, $1/2$ ounce, and 1 ounce of gold, respectively, 22 karat quality. The Roman numeral dates changed each year until the early 1990s, when Arabic became the style. On one side is a modified rendition of the Augustus Saint-Gaudens classic $20 gold design of 1907–1933. On the reverse side appears a contemporary design by Mrs. Miley Busiek. Like all bullion coins, these are sold initially for the value of the gold therein, plus a premium to cover the costs of manufacturing, marketing, and distribution. At the present time, they are the only gold coins the United States Treasury permits to be included in tax-deductible retirement programs, such as IRAs. *See* **Krugerrand, South African** and **Maple Leaf, Canadian Gold.**

early withdrawal penalty. The reduction of principal when an investor withdraws the resources from an investment or securities account. In most IRAs and in Certificates of Deposit there is a penalty for early withdrawals.

Earned Surplus. On a financial statement, the name for a cumulative special account that is created by transfers from net income each year.

earnings or **net profit, profit, net earnings.** On an income statement, the amount remaining for stockholders—both preferred and common—after deducting from total revenues discounts and returns, the cost of goods sold or materials used, operating expenses, interest, and taxes during an accounting period. Note that when the "net" amount is arrived at, both cash and accounting expenses have been applied, so that amortization expenses or accounting charges such as the depletion of a resource affect the bottom line as much as direct expenses like salaries and wages. *See* **cash flow.**

earnings available for fixed charges. See **fixed charge coverage.**

earnings before interest, taxes, depreciation, and amortization (EBITDA). A phrase indicating that a company's net earnings results have been adjusted by adding back interest expense, income taxes, and depreciation and amortization of assets. Securities analysts make this adjustment to focus on how well managements have performed in corporate operations alone, without regard to market-sensitive expense items such as interest, external measures such as income taxes, and noncash, accounting charges such as amortization of assets. Those items are not reflective of how effective managements have met the challenges within their day-to-day control or how well they have generated EBITDA earnings. While the comparisons can be useful in establishing how well a company manages its internal operations, it is impossible to escape the fact that financial and tax management are also very important in evaluating a stock. This is the sort of concept that usually develops when stock market exuberance has pushed traditional methods of stock evaluation—P/E multiples, dividend yields, price-to-book values, present values of future cash flows, and so on—higher than historic levels suggest is prudent. Consequently, creative research departments begin emphasizing items like BITDA/multiples, which are by definition lower, making stocks seem cheaper.

earnings-per-share—common. The balance of earnings available for dividends on the common stock or other elective corporate needs after all legitimate obligatory expenses have been paid or incurred. These include accounting charges such as depreciation, depletion, and amortization or special charges to income. Next, preferred stock dividends are subtracted. The portion of the revenue stream remaining is reserved for common stockholders, either in the form of dividends or reinvested in the corporation.

However it is used, the amount is divided by the shares of common stock outstanding, to calculate the portion for each share. Common stock is called a residual security. Coverage should be at least $1.50 to $2.00 for every $1.00 of established dividends, for a stock to be considered a bona fide income stock. In the 1990s the earnings coverage on the average dividend in the United States was $1.60 for each $1.00 of dividend paid.

earnings-per-share—preferred. The ratio of net income available before common stock dividends are considered divided by the number of shares of preferred stock. This indicates how many times preferred dividends were earned. A preferred stock is well covered, if dividend payments on the common, over a five-year period, average upwards of one to three times preferred dividend requirements. Another measure is that earnings available for preferred dividends be seven times fixed charges plus twice the preferred dividend.

Earnings Report. A company's quarterly or annual memorandum of financial and operating results, released at the end of each fiscal period. This report is briefer and more readable than the formal documents, such as the 10-Qs and 10-Ks, filed with the SEC. It is mailed to shareholders, brokers, and media. Generally, a less glossy version comes out earlier for the media and brokers. Besides these, there are even briefer versions that go on news wires, which are usually the first versions issued and the ones that affect stock prices the most.

earnings yield. The reciprocal of the price/earnings ratio or the quotient obtained from dividing the P/E multiple into 1. In securities analysis, it is an effort to compare a P/E multiple more directly with yields on other securities and investments in general by converting it to a reciprocal. For example, when a common stock's P/E multiple of 20 is converted to its reciprocal of .05 it is said to be yielding 5% ($1/20$) × 100. This is often more comprehensible for investors, because a stock's price can then can be compared more directly with yields on preferred stocks, bonds, certificates of deposit, and so on. A stock's P/E multiple of 50 × could only seem like half a hundred, maybe not too expensive, but the reciprocal earnings yield of 2% ($^1/_{50}$) × 100 could seem very expensive when the savings deposit rate is 5%, unless they are doubling every five minutes!

EARNINGSWHISPERS.COM. An investors Web site featuring corporate estimates from securities analysts. *See* **Web Sites for the Inquiring Investor**.

EASDAQ Stock Market. Abbreviation for Europe Association of Securities Dealers Automated Quotation System, a smaller European counterpart to NASDAQ. It is an independent electronic stock market for rapidly growing companies, established in Brussels in 1996 by 60 financial institutions from 12 countries. Under a special agreement with the SEC, American companies can offer initial public offerings of their stocks through EASDAQ without registration with that agency. However, that exchange must safeguard against the distribution of those IPOs in the United States. There are 30 stocks listed on EASDAQ at present. *See* under **Global Investment Market.**

easier market. A reference to the stock market when prices are lower in quiet trading.

easy money. A reference to low interest rates on borrowed funds. Interest rates move in cycles, as a function of general business activity, and so the expense of borrowing in the form of interest is a relative notion. From 1980 to 1996 in the United States, the prime rate ranged from 6.00% to 15.26% on an annual basis, with 8.99% the arithmetic mean.

easy money policy. 1) A Federal Reserve Bank policy of making money available to the public at low interest rates through the following monetary actions: lowering rates on money loaned to commercial banks, which can be loaned to their customers; reducing the reserves member banks must have at the Federal Reserve Bank to back loans, thereby freeing more money for customer loans; accepting more commercial paper from member banks as collateral for banker loans (rediscounting); buying securities through the Federal Open Market Committee, which increases commercial bank customer deposits, and therefore the money base; and persuading member banks to ease money through its role as central banker to the system. 2) A Federal Government policy of making money available to the public at low interest rates through the following fiscal actions: reducing income taxes through reduced rates or increased credits, usually in conjunction with an effort to stimulate the economy; establishing low-interest loans for various purposes; creating large scale projects that generate jobs, again in conjunction with efforts to stimulate the economy; encouraging new capital formation from foreign investors; and exerting pressure on the Federal Reserve Board to implement an easy money policy.

eating costs. See **absorbing costs.**

EBITDA. Abbreviation for **earnings before interest, taxes, depreciation, and amortization.**

EBITDAM. Acronym for Earnings before Interest, Taxes, Depreciation, Amortization and Marketing Expenses. This concept was concocted as Internet stocks were introduced and popularized. It is the traditional cash flow measure, with a company's marketing expenses added, in an effort to rationalize investing in stocks that have not commenced earning money, usually due to huge marketing outlays in relation to an undeveloped revenue base. By building up cash flow in this manner, proponents of such stocks hope to produce a positive price ratio, such as Price/EBITDAM. *See* **EBITDA** and **EBITDAX.**

EBITDAX. The EBITDA level of earnings plus exploration expenses, in the case of oil and gas companies. The additional add-back is justified by adherents on the grounds that management did not have to spend that money, and, therefore, it could have been available for other purposes. Never mind that management did have to spend the money to remain in business. The concept is more applicable to establishing a company's capacity to pay fixed charges.

ECN. Abbreviation for **Electronic Communications Network.**

E-commerce. The standards, regulations, and technology established for buying and selling products and services online.

econometrics. An approach to economic analysis based on formal quantitative analysis. Mathematical models are used to develop models for the behavior of economic variables such as demand, supply, interest rates, capital formation, and so on, with the object of generating scenarios for various assumptions in an economy and what consequences they could have for others. For example, forecasting budget surpluses for the United States involves the use of econometrics.

Economic Calendar: The Dismal Scientist. A Web page updating important economic and business events and data. *See* **Web Sites for the Inquiring Investor.**

Economic Growth and Tax Relief Reconciliation Act of 2001 (HR1836). The most significant revision of the U.S. Tax Code in 20 years, enacted by the 107th Congress in May 2001 and signed by the President in June 2001, it is estimated to be a $1.35 trillion tax reduction. Although some of the bill's provisions are retroactive to January 1, 2001, most are phased in as well as phased out over a nine-year period. The act expires in nine years, thus its provisions must be considered temporary, unless reinstated by a future Congress and president. Most changes made by the act are only adjustments to the prior code. Its major features are listed below. *See* **Tax Relief Act of 1997.**

- Reduction in marginal tax brackets. Beginning July 1, 2001, top bracket of 39.6% drops to 35% by 2006; 36% drops to 33%; 31% to 28% and 28% to 25%; 15% remains the same; and a new 10% bracket is added, retroactive to the beginning of the year, and applies to first $6,000 of taxable income for single taxpayers and $12,000 for married couples filing jointly.
- Expansion of $500 per child credit to $600 in 2001, $700 in 2005, $800 in 2009 and $1,000 in 2010. The credit also could be used by workers earning slightly more than $10,000 per annum, even when owing no income taxes.
- Beginning in 2005, a phasing down of the marriage penalty, which now causes higher taxes for half the married couples filing jointly than if they were filing individually.

- Phasing out of the estate tax. The act gradually raises the exemption and reduces the rate. The exemption of $675,000 will climb to $1 million in 2002 and stair-step up to $3.5 million in 2009. The highest tax rate of 55% on estate assets will immediately decline to 50%, and to 45% by 2007. In 2010 the estate tax will be repealed, while gift taxes will continue.

- The $2,000 per annum allowance for contributions to IRAs or individual retirement accounts will rise to $3,000 in 2002, $4,000 in 2005, and finally to $5,000 in 2008. Afterwards, it will increase in $500 increments to compensate for inflation.

- The $10,500 per annum allowable contribution to 401(k), 403(k), and 457 tax-deferred retirement savings plans sponsored by employers will rise to $11,000 in 2002, $12,000 in 2003, $13,000 in 2004, $14,000 in 2005, and $15,000 in 2006. Afterwards, maximum contribution is indexed for inflation.

- Taxpayers will be allowed to deduct up to $5,000 in college tuition, although that benefit will disappear in 2005.

- For tax-related education savings accounts, contributions allowed are raised from $500 to $2,000 per annum.

- Beginning in 2002, savers over age 50 can contribute an additional $500 to IRAs and $1,000 per annum afterwards. For employer-sponsored plans like 401(k)s, those savers over fifty years of age can contribute an additional $1,000 in 2002, $2,000 in 2003, $3,000 in 2004, $4,000 in 2005, and $5,000 in 2006 and afterwards.

- Raises the maximum amount of income that can be counted as a base for retirement benefits.

- Discontinues the **Alternative Minimum Tax (AMT)** until 2006.

Economic Indicators. Those quantitative signals that indicate the condition of the U.S. economy, in terms of business cycles. For analysis of business cycles, the National Bureau of Economic Research has established that certain economic series or events precede a change in the general direction of business—Leading Indicators—or accompany the change—Coincident Indicators—or trail the change—Lagging Indicators. The relationships have been tested historically. These series are watched, both singularly and collectively, as clues to the business outlook and general health. From the analyses, the federal government bases fiscal policy, and the Fed bases monetary policies. *See* **Leading Economic Indicators Index.** The short list of these indicators follows:

U.S. ECONOMIC INDICATORS

Indicators	Economic Activity	Unit
1) Leading	Average weekly hours, manufacturing	Hours
	Average weekly claims unemployment insurance	Volume
	Manufacturers' new orders, consumer goods, materials	Dollars
	Vendor performance, slower deliveries diffusion index	Percent
	Manufacturers' new orders, nondefense capital goods	Dollars
	Building permits, new private housing units	1,000s
	Stock prices, 500 common stocks	S&P
	Money supply, M2	Dollars
	Interest rate spread, 10-year treasury bonds less federal funds	Percent
	Index of consumer expectations	Percent
2) Coincident	Employees on nonagricultural payrolls	Millions
	Personal income less transfer payments	Dollars
	Industrial production	Index
	Manufacturing and trade sales	Dollars
3) Lagging	Average duration of unemployment	Weeks
	Inventories to sales ratio, manufacturing and trade	Ratio
	Labor costs per unit of output, manufacturing	Percent
	Average prime rate	Percent
	Commercial and industrial loans	Dollars
	Consumer installment credit to personal income	Ratio
	Consumer price index for services	Percent

Source: The Conference Board

economic policy. See **fiscal policy** and **monetary policy.**

economic profit. A measure of true operating profits after all costs, including the cost of debt and the opportunity cost of equity capital, are deducted. This concept differs from accounting profit in that equity opportunity costs, or how much the equity resources could earn employed elsewhere, are used to evaluate management's skill rather than only direct costs such as interest, wages, rent, and so on.

economic substance, doctrine of. In tax matters, the principle established by judges and courts that if a transaction's only purpose is to avoid taxes, it is without economic purpose and can be ignored in tax calculations. The doctrine is applied most often to questionable tax shelters.

economics. The study and measure of how human beings acquire their physical needs and wants, with particular emphasis on the social system evolved to do so.

economic value added (EVA). A concept for measuring what can be termed opportunity costs in order to determine which corporate projects boost shareholder values more than would assured returns in more passive investments. It is derived by subtracting the average interest cost of capital employed during a period from net after-tax return-on-equity. This amount can then be compared with a yardstick assured return, such as U.S. Treasury bonds, to judge management's decision on how it spent capital. If the EVA is not greater than the yardstick return, the corporation has paid opportunity costs, since the latter return was higher and guaranteed. For example, if net income represents a 15% return on equity, the capital costs are 7%, and the assured return is 5%, the EVA is 3% ($15\% - 7\% - 5\% = 3\%$). If U.S. Treasuries are yielding 5%, management has earned a 3% premium over opportunity costs, and has added economic value of 3%.

economies of scale. A reference to the economic situation when by increasing the volume of production of a product, the cost of producing each unit decreases. This occurs when a large portion of the costs are fixed or relatively fixed—rent, labor, utilities, general, and administrative—so that when more total units are manufactured, total costs go up disproportionately less, since they are spread over many more products. This axiom is the basis for mass production in industry, and was the linchpin of the Industrial Revolution in the late 1800s and early 1900s. There is a point, however, when costs get too high in relation to the capacity of the productive facility, and dis-economies of scale set in. This situation can occur when lots of overtime labor is needed, machinery breaks down through lack of maintenance, extra floor space has to be rented, and so on. Investors should look for manufacturing stocks where unit costs are going down as demand for the product rises, a situation that often means greater earnings for a company.

Economist Online, The. See under **Web Sites for the Inquiring Investor.**

EDGAR. Abbreviation for **Electronic Data Gathering, Analysis, and Retrieval system.**

EDGAR Online. A Web site featuring subscription access to corporate SEC filings. *See* under **Web Sites for the Inquiring Investor.**

Educational IRA. See **Individual Retirement Accounts.**

effective date. In the registration of a public securities offering with the SEC, that date on which the filing has been acknowledged by the SEC as fundamentally adequate to allow an investor to make a decision on the information made available. Note that the SEC does not accept the filing as proof of its investment merit, but only that certain information is made available to the public. Often a filing must be amended. On the effective date, which generally takes from 30 to 90 days after registration, underwriters may begin the distribution process. *See* **"quiet period."**

effective par value. The par value equivalent of a no-par preferred stock, assigned by dividing the dollar dividend by a realistic yield on such a security, considering what yield is required for such a security to have investment attraction. For example, a preferred stock dividend of $2 could be divided by 5% ($2.00 ÷ .05), assuming that 5% is the going rate for yields on that type of investment. This gives an effective par value of $40 for comparative purposes. This exercise can often be useful in estimating the liquidating value of a no-par preferred.

effective price. The round-lot sale price on which an odd-lot price is based.

effective rate. The actual yield on a debt security, based on its contractual or coupon or nominal rate of interest paid and the price paid for the bond, as opposed to buying the security for the face value or value at maturity. There are several ways to calculate bond yields, depending on the investor's time horizon and particular investment goals. *See* **Yield to Call** and **Yield to Maturity.**

effective tax rate. The annual payment for federal income taxes divided by the taxable income. This calculation is important for investors in the case of corporations, because there are several taxable categories or brackets, basically, and getting into a lower one can improve cash flow. So, by determining the percentage of taxable income a company actually pays, one gets a better look at how deft the management team is in minimizing its taxes as compared to others in its peer group. Items such as tax deferrals, tax credits, net operating loss, and carry forwards come into play in this matter. To illustrate, suppose Stealth Industries, Inc. reports Taxable Income of $10 million and federal income taxes paid of $1.5 million, the effective tax rate is 15% (1.5 ÷ 10) × 100. Since the company's taxable income places it in a 35% tax bracket, management's tax planning would seem effective. *See* **corporate income tax.**

Efficient Market Theory (EMT). A description of the hypothesis that in a broad stock market in which all news that would affect stock prices is generally known by both buyers and sellers of stock, at any given time stock prices reflect realistic values. This concept is an integral part of the "random walk" theory, and explains why, under that theory, future price movements will move in a random manner, since the movements will be based on news not yet disclosed to the public. According to adherents of this theory, this explains why forecasting individual stock prices accurately, in a general sense, is impossible. *See* **random work theory of stock market.**

efficient portfolio. A portfolio of stocks that is constructed so that the maximum return expected is commensurate with the level of risk expected. The object of such a portfolio is that the investor is not exposed to any unnecessary risks, in the form of volatility, in striving to reach the goals of the investment return. The actual construction is done using statistical tools such as standard deviations, variances, and covariances.

EFTA. Abbreviation for **European Free Trade Association.**

"e-lance economy." A business architecture in which large corporations increasingly hire small entrepreneurial firms to perform special business projects on a temporary basis. Once a project is completed, the team disbands. Many observers believe this will be the prevailing corporate landscape of the future. The descriptive name for such firms comes from their promotion and exposure over the Internet, combined with the "freelancing" concept of working. The movement is already growing as the Internet expands into a vast electronic marketplace. The "e-lance" firms, with sometimes as few as 10 employees, promote their goods and services on the Internet, for a fraction of the costs that conventional physical locations would require. This is usually augmented by other promotional methods, such as personal contacts. While the projects can be economically rewarding for them, they are often prohibitive for large corporations. Adding these groups as permanent employees is expensive, because of the embedded costs in relation to the brevity of the tasks.

"e-lance firm." A small entrepreneurial firm, sometimes with less than 10 employees, that specializes in a discipline or skill that large companies need on a temporary basis. The descriptive name for such firms comes from their promotion and exposure over the Internet, combined with the "freelancing" concept of working. Such firms are hired for a specific task, at much less than the large company would pay to hire permanent employees for the job. *See* **"e-lance economy."**

e-lancer. A principal or employee of an **e-lance firm**. See also **e-lance economy.**

elasticity of supply and demand. A reference to how sensitive buyers are to price changes in a product, as reflected by changes in their purchases, or how sensitive sellers are to price changes in a product, as reflected by changes in their production. When a buyer increases purchases as prices decrease, that demand is said to be elastic. When a buyer decreases purchases as prices increase, that demand is also said to be elastic. When a seller increases production as prices increase, that supply is called elastic. When a seller decreases production when prices increase or remain the same, that supply is called inelastic. Think of supply and demand as rubber bands. When they change shape trying to accompany price changes, they are elastic and responsive. If they break and cannot change shape, they are inelastic and not responsive.

Certain products and services are inherently elastic, and vice versa. The products that are mostly sold when economic times are good are elastic, because in good times when prices tend to be high they sell well, but in slow times they slacken the pace, even when prices are lowered. Often, they are not necessary products. Investors might want to avoid stocks representing these products in recessions. On the other hand, products such as medicines tend to maintain demand, whether prices increase or decrease, because medicines are necessary and the demand tends to be inelastic. That is why certain stocks—medicines, utilities, advertising, fuels, foods—are considered defensive stocks.

election of a stop order. The occurrence of a market sale that turns a securities **stop order** into a market order; for example, a sale at 140 would elect a sell stop at 140⅛ or 140.12.

Electric Companies. Those stocks representing companies providing electric power. *See* **industry stock group.**

Electrical Equipment Manufacturers. Those stocks representing companies engaged in the manufacture and servicing of heavy electrical apparatus and equipment. *See* **industry stock group.**

electronic board. An exchange quote board with prices posted electronically.

Electronic Communications Network or ECN. A network of investment institutions and securities broker-dealers, operated by companies such as Bloomberg Tradebook, Reuters' Instinet, and Datek Online Holdings, that coordinates online securities trading between the institutional investors and the securities broker-dealers on the network for a fee. The networks match orders posted anonymously between institutions and broker-dealers. There are 50 such trading networks in the United States, with greater trading volume than the American Stock Exchange and the five regional markets in total. It is estimated these networks comprise 25% of NASDAQ trades today. These networks must make available to public investors network quotes that are better than those on regular auction markets. This SEC requirement is an effort to give large and small investors equal investment opportunities.

Electronic Data Gathering, Analysis, and Retrieval System (EDGAR). The electronic data gathering, analysis, and retrieval system that performs automated collection, validation, indexing, acceptance, and forwarding of investment information submissions by companies and others who are required by law to file forms with the U.S. Securities and Exchange Commission (SEC). Its primary purpose is to increase the efficiency and fairness of the securities market for the benefit of investors, corporations, and the economy, by accelerating the receipt, acceptance, dissemination, and analysis of time-sensitive corporate information filed with the regulatory agency.

Not all documents filed with the SEC by public companies are available on EDGAR. Companies were phased into EDGAR filing over a three-year period, ending May 6, 1996. As of that date, all public domestic companies were required to make their filings on EDGAR, except for filings made on paper because of a hardship exemption. Third-party filings with respect to these companies, such as tender offers and Schedules 13D, are also filed on EDGAR.

However, some documents are not yet permitted to be filed electronically and consequently are not available on EDGAR. Other documents are filed on EDGAR voluntarily and consequently may or may not be available on EDGAR. For example, Forms 3, 4, and 5, which are security ownership and transaction reports filed by corporate insiders, and Form 144, which is a notice of proposed sale of securities are filed on EDGAR at the option of the filer. Similarly, filings by foreign companies are not required to be filed on EDGAR, but some of these companies do so voluntarily. Until recently, this was also the case with Form 13F, the reports filed by institutional investment managers showing equity holdings by accounts under their management. However, on January 12, 1999, the SEC issued a rule to require electronic filing of the form as of April 1, 1999.

It should also be noted that the actual annual report to shareholders, except in the case of investment companies, need not be submitted on EDGAR, although some companies do so voluntarily. However, the annual report on Form 10-K or 10-KSB, which contains much of the same information, is required to be filed on EDGAR. EDGAR filings are posted to their Web site at least 24 hours after the date of filing.

Electronics. The popular name for growth stocks of companies in the development, manufacture and marketing of memory chips, microprocessors, switches, transistors, and diodes and in technologies such as infrared, microwave, and related fields. The word is not a valid industry classification, since it is too broad and includes products from cheap radios to expensive space and telecommunications equipment. For a truer growth stock classification, see **Applied Science Stocks.**

Electronics—Defense. Stocks representing those companies engaged in the design and manufacture of equipment and systems used in national defense. *See* **industry stock group.**

Electronics—Instruments. Stocks representing those companies engaged in the manufacture of electronic instruments. *See* **industry stock group.**

Electronic—Semi-conductors. Stocks representing those companies engaged in the manufacturer of electronic equipment for computers and other electronic-operated products. *See* **industry stock group.**

Electronic Traders Association (ETA). An association of order-entry firms, proprietary trading firms, related companies, vendors, and individuals. It provides an opportunity for individual investors to trade securities electronically through the NASDAQ Stock Market Small Order Execution System and SelectNet, and through electronic communications networks (ECNs) as well as electronic systems sponsored by other exchanges. In addition, ETA promotes the interests of the industry in Washington, D.C. by engaging policy makers about the benefits of electronic trading. Its mission is to ensure that policies adopted in Washington represent the interests of the electronic trading industry and of small public investors nationwide. It encourages price competition and investor fairness and confidence in the market. Besides educating the media and policy makers about the industry, it represents electronic trading in rule-making and other regulatory proceedings at the Securities and Exchange Commission and other federal agencies. Address: 1800 Bering, Suite 750, Houston, TX 77057. Phone: 713.706. 3300. Web site: *www.electronic-traders.org.*

Electronic Trading Network. See **Electronic Communications Network** and **Primex Trading.**

eligible paper. That commercial paper owned by member banks of the Federal Reserve System, that the Federal Reserve will discount in order to build up the members' reserve balances as a method of expanding commercial loans throughout the system.

E-line Financials. See **Web Sites for the Inquiring Investor.**

Elliott Wave Theory. A reference to a theory formulated by R. N. Elliott in 1939 that stock market prices change along certain patterns or waves, in response to a natural progression of shifts in the psychology of investors, acting en masse. The shifts take place as greed and fear dominate investor moods. Basically, the theory suggests that stock prices move in a pattern of five waves up and three waves down, forming a complete cycle of eight waves. However, there are intermediate stages. Theorists analyze "A" and "C" waves to predict price ratios, based on numbers from the Fibonacci series. Patterns adjusting stock prices to market trends are called "corrections." Other theorists have adopted Elliott's work to modern stock markets.

embezzlement. The fraudulent conversion of money or property to the use of one to whom it is entrusted.

e-money. A Web program that enables customers to perform financial transactions online immediately, view their account status, and transfer funds.

emotional selling. A wave of stock selling triggered by psychological factors, such as gloomy international events, presidential election uncertainties, and so on. The events do not justify the selling pressures in economic and business senses.

Employee Retirement Income Security Act of 1974 (ERISA). The federal statute setting up the procedures for ensuring the safety and fairness of most private pension plans in the United States. The law also created the **Pension Benefit Guarantee Corporation,** and provides for easier access by employees to pension benefits and for their mobility when employees change employment. Three federal agencies or federally sponsored agencies promulgate regulations that are used to implement the law. They are the Department of Labor, the Internal Revenue Service, and the Pension Benefit Guaranty Corporation. In order for a plan to be qualified, and therefore receive tax benefits, it must provide employees with rights in the following categories:
1. Disclosure must be afforded participants on the basic plan and other documents furnished on request.
2. Coverage of a certain portion, but not necessarily all, employees.
3. Participation by employees who meet plan requirements.
4. Vesting—participants who work specified periods earn nonforfeitable rights to pension on retirement.
5. Benefit accrual to participants for all years of participation in a plan.

6. Nondiscrimination in favor of higher-paid and older employees.

7. Survivors' benefits for widows and widowers, although this benefit can be waived if both spouses agree.

8. Benefits for divorced spouses must be paid, when so directed by a special court order.

9. Distributions to participants must follow their requests as to timing and form of payment.

10. Fiduciary standards are imposed on plan managers and investment managers.

11. Appeals of benefit denials are provided for those denied benefits, first to the plan managers and then the courts.

12. Remedies by courts are provided under ERISA for violations of the law.

13. Noninterference with benefit rights by managers, because of discharges, layoffs, plant closings, or other unlawful means.

14. Reporting of detailed financial and actuarial information to the IRS, which may be made available to participants is required regularly.

Employee Stock Ownership Trust or **ESOT.** A program expanded under the Employee Retirement Income Security Act of 1974, under which a corporation may elect to set aside profits or shares of its stock for the benefit of employees. In the case of a qualified plan, the directors can declare such an allocation, under a trust arrangement, that is tax-deductible to the corporation and on which taxes are deferred until an employee's share is distributed to him. Not only can employees be rewarded, but corporate management can buy shares of stock outstanding with untaxed income; in effect they can fund a pension plan with no cash outlay.

employee stock purchase plan. (ESPP). See **qualified stock purchase plan.**

Employment Report, Monthly. An important report to economists and analysts issued early each month by the Bureau of Labor Statistics of the Department of Labor. It is the first complete look at the economy each month and is used in forecasting other economic indicators. In the report, data is presented on employment, average workweek, and hourly earnings for virtually every sector of the economy. When the results in the report rise, fixed income securities usually decrease, common stocks rise, and dollar exchange rates also rise. When the report goes down, fixed income securities go up, common stocks and dollar exchange rates fall.

Employees on Non-Agricultural Payrolls. See under **Economic Indicators.**

EMT. Abbreviation for the **Efficient Market Theory.**

endgame. The strategic plan devised by the management of a company to keep itself viable and competitive in the final phase of working out intense problems or pressure on its operations or marketing. This differs from an **exit strategy** in that it envisions a continuation of the company's business at hand on a long-term basis under the best possible circumstances, whereas an exit strategy suggests a total withdrawal from a deteriorating situation under the best possible terms. For example, companies like Microsoft, AT&T, and IBM, that have been under intense scrutiny and pressure on antitrust grounds from the U.S. Department of Justice, must develop endgames as new operating environments are created in which they must compete effectively.

end-of-the-week liquidation. A reference to the increased selling of stocks on Fridays because of the apprehension market traders have about news events developing while the markets are closed over the weekend, preventing them from reacting until Monday's opening when prices could be drastically affected. This selling is extremely heavy if unfavorable news seems likely over a weekend.

endorsement. 1) The signature affixed to the back of a check or negotiable instrument by the party to whom the payment indicated on its face is being made, which makes the instrument transferable to another party. *See* **qualified endorsement.** 2) In the case of a security certificate, the signature of its owner affixed to its back, making it transferable, as in the case of a delivery on the sale of stock.

endow, to. In establishing the financial means for an enterprise to operate, the commitment of resources, such as securities, that will provide regular cash flow to that end.

endowment. A permanent gift of resources benefiting a person or institution. Usually, the resources are converted to some format, such as securities, that will produce operating income for the benefiting enterprise.

energy industries. See **sector.**

Engineering & Construction. Those stocks representing companies engaged in building and assembling parts for massive public and private projects. *See* **industry stock group.**

"enhanced" S&P 500 funds. Mutual funds that invest in a core of established company stocks but also include growth and undervalued shares in their portfolios in an attempt to exceed the performance of the index funds with a minimum of additional risks. In tinkering with the portfolio components, these fund managers emphasize long-term performance. They believe that adding to the index fund's performance by just 1% or 2% is worth pursuing, because of the compounding effects of increments over the years. One of the characteristics of the enhanced funds is that turnover rates are higher, possibly leading to more capital gains distributions for shareholders. This can produce more tax liability, a situation that might negate higher investment performance.

enhanced thrift program. A 401(k) plan in which an employer offers all or a portion of an employee's contribution.

enter an order. To transfer a directive to buy or sell securities via wire to an exchange.

enterprise resource planning software. Software packages and applications that coordinate a manufacturer's complete business operation.

Enterprise Value (EVA) A reference to the stock market valuation of a corporation, found by multiplying the company's shares outstanding by its current share price less cash and plus current debt. In a sense, this result is the current investor, both equity and debt investor, estimate of the company's value. Cash is deducted, because that is an actual value.

Entertainment. Those stocks representing companies engaged in producing and presenting products and services used in public entertainment. *See* **industry stock group.**

entrepreneur. A person who likes to create and launch one or more new business entities, usually using venture capital until it is feasible to sell public stock. The entrepreneur is not committed to a certain type of business, at least in the beginning, but concentrates on where the most attractive economic opportunities are. Once s/he spots a business opportunity, s/he raises capital and puts in place a rudimentary work force, who are quite often also entrepreneurs. Once the business is airborne, often the main entrepreneurs sell their interests and look for another startup opportunity. Sometimes the entrepreneur(s) are technically-trained professionals who form a business to develop a product, such as a medicine. Although the entrepreneur may sell an up-and-running startup to another company, the true entrepreneur wishes to operate his or her own business unit in the beginning. The reward for such a person is a large portion of the business earnings or the capital gain from its sale. *See* **intrepreneur.**

equilibrium price. In a market economy, the price when the supply of goods or services matches the demand for them.

Equipment Leasing Partnership. A limited partnership formed to raise money for the purchase of capital equipment—such as airplanes, tankers, railroad cars, super computers, ships, and telephony equipment—and the leasing of it to operating companies for use in their businesses. Partners earn income from the lease payments in proportion to the shares of the partnership they own and can save money on their personal income taxes through the use of certain expenses of the partnership, such as depreciation and other amortization. Limited partners are free of additional liability in the venture unless they overstep their authority in some manner or act irresponsibly. The general partner acts as manager of the partnership and, as such, is the key in making the venture successful. This person has to arrange for leases of the equipment, usually prearranged before the actual partnership financing, and keep the equipment fully working in order for the investment to make the returns originally forecast. The limited partners have recourse to the general partner if that party does not perform according to the partnership agreement.

equipment trust bond or **equipment trust certificate.** A bond secured by physical assets held in trust. The bonds are usually issued by shipping companies, railroads, airlines, and so on, who need the equipment for their operations and who pay the interest and principal amounts from general corporate revenues. But if these payments are not forthcoming, the bondholders have claims on the collateralized equipment. However, as a practical matter, most creditors would rather work out some remedial plan than take title to the equipment. Title to the equipment resides in the trustee, usually a bank, until the bonds are paid off. The trustee is responsible for monitoring the terms of the trust indenture, including the proper maintenance of the equipment and the financial condition of the operators of the equipment.

equipment trust certificate. See **equipment trust bond.**

equity. 1) A customer's cash interest in a margin account after the sum borrowed from an investment firm to buy stock has been deducted from the stock's current market value. 2) A certificate of ownership in a corporation. 3) The financial claim to mortgaged property that the debtor has; the amount is found by reducing the loan balance from the market value of the property.

equity base. The market price of a stock multiplied by the shares outstanding. Generally, a large equity base in relation to the actual stockholders' book equity, or book value, means the shares are overpriced because of a speculative market. But there is another spin to this situation. The excessive price could also reflect investors' belief that management will grow the corporation fast, thus increasing stockholders' equity and, in turn, the book value.

equity capital. See **owners' capital.**

equity financing. The raising of money for a corporation by issuing and selling stock, versus debt financing.

equity-indexed annuity. A financial instrument issued by insurance companies that guarantees investors a fixed minimum return over the term of the contract while protecting the principal by keying investment reserves fractionally to a stock market index. However, the annuitant gets only a portion of the stock gains and usually no dividends.

equity ratio. A stock's equity base or stock market capitalization divided by the shareholders' equity. If the equity base is $500,000,000 and the shareholders' equity is $100,000,000, the equity ratio is 5, or 5-to-1. It's another way of measuring how many times book value the stock is selling. If the ratio is high, say, over 10–to–1, there is an indication the market price of the stock is too high in relation to the tangible value of the shares, but there are usually other considerations. That's why there's a stock market!

e-reporting. A reference to the publication and disclosure of corporate financial information on the Internet, through company Web sites or business information sites. Since this forum for the dissemination of financial information is growing in popularity, international groups are studying whether the present ad hoc approach should be supplanted by a more structured and standardized one, for the sake of clarity to investors.

ERISA. See **Employee Retirement Income Security Act.**

eroding prices. Those market prices that are gradually declining.

escalator clause. A clause in a wage contract, retirement benefit, or interest payment providing for automatic adjustment of wages, in relation to changes in living costs, usually defined by a price index such as the CPI. *See* **COLA.**

escheat. Under a requirement by various state laws, turning over the assets in dormant customer accounts to the appropriate state authority by a bank or brokerage firm, after a specified number of years have passed. These properties are considered abandoned under law. However, they may be reclaimed by the legitimate owners or their heirs. States are required to communicate the existence of escheated assets to the public, through media advertising, principally. The assets subject to the laws of escheat include both securities and cash balances in accounts.

escrow agent. A financial institution, usually a bank, appointed by a company intending to buy a large block of stock in another company to receive tendered shares in the latter company from stockholders wishing to sell. The shares are held in escrow because their purchase at a specific price is usually contingent upon a minimum number being presented for sale to the escrow agent. *See* **tender.**

escrow deposit. A reference to a deposit of funds or a commercial instrument with a disinterested party until fulfillment of certain conditions.

E-shares. Those stocks that represent companies providing products and services to Internet users. Examples are Internet Service Providers, Internet software products, and Internet auction marketeers. Although there are few success stories financially in this pioneering technology group, it is early in the electronic revolution. The group will continue to grow in investment importance. For that reason, the stocks must be considered by investors, although selecting correct choices is extremely difficult at present.

e-sign bill. See **Federal Electronic Signature in Global and National Commerce Act.**

ESOT. Abbreviation for **Employee Stock Ownership Trust.**

estate. That real or personal property that can be passed to heirs. *See* **inheritance** and **inheritance task.**

estate account. Those brokerage transactions in the name of an estate. An attorney should be consulted before such an account is opened.

estate planning. The allocation of an individual's disposable funds into insurance, savings reserves, and investments, with an eye to protecting against emergencies while accumulating assets for future security. *See* **retirement planning.**

estate tax. See **inheritance tax.**

ETA. Abbreviation for **Electronic Traders Association.**

e-tail. The buying of consumer goods and services on the Internet. Another name for electronic retail.

ETF. Abbreviation for **exchange-traded fund.**

ethical drug industry. Those makers of drugs used for prescriptions.

E-trading. Buying and selling stocks through a broker who offers services principally on the Internet. Usually, investors get executions at discount commissions. Research and ancillary investment services are not always offered. *See* **Internet investing.**

Eurex Trading System. A fully electronic exchange for the trading of financial derivatives conducted through a telecommunications network of computer terminals. From its trading center in Frankfurt, Germany, the system links over 300 participants in Germany, Switzerland, Amsterdam, England, Finland, France, Spain, and the United States. The **euro** is used in settling accounts. Plans are in place for expansion into Asia. Web site: *www.Eurexchange.com/entrancehall/index.html.*

euro. The single currency of 11 members of the **European Union.** These countries are: Austria, Belgium, Finland, France, Germany, Ireland, Italy, Luxembourg, the Netherlands, Portugal, and Spain. The conversion rates between the currencies of the participating countries are fixed between themselves as well as against the euro. Until the year 2002, the euro will have limited use. In 2002 it will begin to replace the national currencies of the union as euro currencies and coinage are circulated. In mid-2002 only the euro will be circulated. There will be seven euro currency notes and eight euro coins. *See* **European Central Bank.**

eurodollar. U.S. currency deposits or reserves residing outside the United States, primarily in European banks, and used often in settling international payments.

EURO GLOBEX. An agreement that allows members of MATIF and MONEP in France, MEFF in Spain, and MIF in Italy to trade each other's contracts from their own workstations across interconnected electronic trading platforms. *See* **Global Investment Market.**

Euroland. A reference to the geographic boundary of the European Union which forms a one-currency financial and trading marketplace nearly as large as the United States. Presently it includes 11 states of the 15 official members of the union. Because of the central bank and official currency, the **euro,** there are no longer opportunities for speculators or investors to exploit the differences in the former exchange rates and, to a lesser extent, interest rates. In general, investing in the region will become more a process of company selection as in the United States.

Euronext. A planned European stock exchange, scheduled to open by the end of the year 2001. It will combine the French, Dutch, and Belgian exchanges, and will be dominated by the Paris Bourse. To be incorporated in the Netherlands, the exchange will list 1,300 companies, with a market value of $2.2 trillion. That would make it the biggest exchange in the euro-trade zone, which does not include the United Kingdom. After its formation, it will be the second-largest exchange in Europe and the sixth largest in the world.

European Central Bank (ECB). Under the Treaty of Maastricht establishing the third stage of European economic and monetary union beginning in 1999, the central bank of the union. As such, it will play a similar role to the U.S. Federal Reserve Bank in that it will control the basic money supply, supervise foreign exchange operations and be responsible for establishing a system for payments and settlements between financial institutions.

European Economic Community (1957) or **European Common Market.** A disbanded common market composed of France, West Germany, Italy, Belgium, the Netherlands, Luxembourg, and Great Britain. This organization was the genesis and the predecessor of the **European Union** of today.

European Free Trade Association (EFTA-1960). A disbanded common market composed of Sweden, Norway, Denmark, Switzerland, Austria, and Portugal. Finland was an associate member. These members have joined the present **European Union.**

European Union (EU). A group of European countries working together on common concerns—economics, environment, water quality, commerce, finance, government, agriculture, and so on. Presently the union has 15 member states with over 370 million citizens, although members are presently at varying degrees of participation. Members include: Belgium, France, Germany, Italy, Luxembourg, the Netherlands, Great Britain, Denmark, the Irish Republic, Greece, Portugal, Spain, Austria, Finland, and Sweden. The group grew from the **European Economic Community,** founded in 1957, and merged with the European Free Trade Association of the Scandinavia region of Europe. Other countries either hope to join the EU or form close ties. They are: Bulgaria, Cyprus, the Czech Republic, Estonia, Hungary, Latvia, Lithuania, Poland, Romania, Slovakia, Slovenia, and Turkey. The treaty establishing the EU is known as the Maastricht Treaty of 1992. This union is the most advanced yet in Europe and is governed by a parliament, council, and president. Over time, it promises to become a major economic force in world trade, rivaling the United States and Japan. The EU issues its own currency, the **euro.** It will become the most integrated common market of the 21st century among free countries, although the lack of a common language will be somewhat constrictive.

EVA. Abbreviation for **economic value added**.

evangelist. As a corporate CEO, to spend an inordinate amount of time on promoting the company's technological advances or innovative ideas to the public rather than the financial and operating performance to investors. In many ways, such an executive becomes an industry spokesperson for companies on the leading edge of a new industry. The person tries to promote the company's stock as an indicator of future success.

evergreen financing. The use of short-term bank loans that are continuously extended or increased rather than repaid, to pump capital into a business enterprise that the bank wants to keep solvent.

excesses. A reference to excessive buying or selling of securities often without good reason, leaving their prices vulnerable to movement in the opposite direction. *See* **overbought, oversold** and **correction (1).**

excess margin funds. The excess over margin requirements which could be withdrawn in cash from a margin account, bearing in mind that the New York Stock Exchange and brokerage house minimum requirements must be met after such withdrawal.

excess profits tax. A tax on corporation profits that exceed a specified level or on profits that exceed those of previous years. *See* **corporation tax.**

exchange. A specific location where buying and selling of securities occurs, complete with incidental clerical functions. Membership and acceptance of a code of business ethics is usually a prerogative for trading privileges on an exchange. Note: Exchange members buy and sell for themselves or for their customers, not the exchange. They trade securities either as agents or brokers, on a commission basis, or as principals, independent vendors making money as middlemen in buying and selling to customers.

exchange acquisition. The purchase of a large block of stock on the floor of an exchange, usually through solicitations of sell orders by brokers, at a set price and for a special commission paid by the purchaser.

exchange agent. A corporation's fiscal agent, usually a bank or trust company, appointed to supervise a special exchange of shareholders' stock.

exchange distribution. The sale of a large block of stock on the floor of an exchange, usually through solicitations of buy orders by brokers, at a set price and for a special commission paid by the seller.

exchange offer. An offer by a corporation to exchange a class of its stock for stock in another corporation in a merger effort. Usually, investment firms are authorized to solicit acceptances of the exchange offer.

exchange rate. The conversion ratio of a national currency into another one. *See* **foreign exchange rate.**

exchange, stock. A specific location where buying and selling of securities occurs, complete with incidental clerical functions. Membership and acceptance of a code of business ethics is usually a prerogative for trading privileges on an exchange. Note: Exchange members buy and sell for themselves or for their customers, not the exchange. They trade securities either as agents or brokers, on a commission basis, or as principals, who are independent vendors making money as a midpoint in buying and selling to customers. When an exchange includes members domiciled in different countries, there can be different methods for transacting securities, because of different laws and conventions in the countries. Otherwise, exchange rules apply to each member equally. In the year 2000, the 10 largest exchanges in the world, in terms of stock trading capitalized, were the New York Stock Exchange ($11.5 billion), NASDAQ ($5.1 billion), Tokyo ($4.3 billion), Osaka ($2.9 billion), London ($2.8 billion), Euronext ($2.2 billion), Frankfurt ($1.4 billion), Toronto ($800 million), Milan ($705 million), and Zurich ($674 million). Note: **Euronext** is scheduled to open in 2001.

exchange—traded fund (ETF). A form of mutual fund that trades on an exchange, currently mainly on the American Stock Exchange, which invests in diversified securities representing market indexes. The funds provide investors with low annual management expenses and efficient tax strategies. However, they are bought and sold through brokers, so there is a commission involved. There were nearly $25 billion in assets in their portfolios at the end of 1999, a rise from $2.4 billion three years prior. Unlike conventional mutual fund shares, ETF shares can be bought throughout the trading sessions, can be bought on margins, sold short or bought or sold at a limit. These funds typically invest in indexes like "Spiders," "Webs," and "Diamonds." Since dividends are reinvested quarterly or monthly, in cash management the ETFs are slightly behind conventional mutual funds that reinvest dividends daily. There is a distinct tax advantage for institutions in purchasing these fund shares in that they can exchange their shares for the underlying stocks in an ETF, escaping any capital gains tax in that generation of trading.

exchanging. See **refunding.**

exchanging checks or **swapping checks.** A reference to the brokerage practice of requiring a customer to make payment for a stock bought before he is given a check for the sale of the same stock.

ex-distribution or **without distribution.** A reference to a trade in which a stock buyer is not entitled to a stock distribution such as additional stock resulting from a stock split.

ex-distribution date. The date on which a stock sells **ex-distribution.**

ex-dividend or **without dividend.** A reference to a trade in which a stock buyer is not entitled to a recent dividend.

ex-dividend date. The date on which a stock sells **ex-dividend.** On this date the market price is usually lower by the dividend amount. Open buy and sell stop orders in a stock on the ex-dividend date are usually reduced by the dividend amount. Ex-dividend dates are usually three business days before the record date.

execution. The completion of an investor's offer to sell with a buyer's acceptance, or vice versa, usually done through brokers.

executor or **executrix (female).** The person charged with carrying out terms of a will by its maker. As such, the person accumulates the assets, settles taxes, pays off debts of the estate, and distributes the remainder to heirs, according to the will. The responsibility ends when the estate matters are settled, as determined by a probate court, usually in a period of one to three years. Family members, trusted friends, attorneys, and banks usually serve as executors or executrixes.

exempt marginable securities. A category of listed securities not requiring regular margin when they are purchased on credit.

exempt securities. Those securities that are excepted from the provisions, except for the fraud provisions, under the **Securities Act of 1933.**

exempt shorts. A category of listed securities not requiring an uptick before selling them short.

exempt transactions. For exempted distributions under the Securities Act of 1933, See **registration.**

exercise. To act on a right provided for in a securities contract. An example is an options contract, in which the investor has the right to buy or sell an underlying security or commodity at a specified price for a limited time. When the investor takes action to do this, the right is exercised.

exercise notice. A broker's notice to the Options Clearing Corporation that a customer intends to exercise a right to buy or sell the underlying stock in an options contract.

exercise price. That price at which a share of stock or unit of a commodity underlying an options contract can be bought (called) or sold (put) during a limited period, usually three, six, or nine months for options. An example would be a put contract to sell 100 shares of Whoopee! Corp. for $25 per share for six months. Note that the option itself also has a price, called a premium, when purchased.

exhaustion gap. See **gap (3).**

ex-interest. A reference to an income bond sale in which the buyer is not entitled to the interest recently declared.

ex-interest date. The date on which an income bond sells **ex-interest,** following a declaration of interest to the bondholders.

exit costs. A reference to those costs or charges that will result from a corporation's plan to discontinue a business activity. In order to record such costs, a corporation must show they meet the following criteria, according to the SEC:

- Costs pertain only to the discontinued operations
- Costs are not established to generate revenues after the commitment date to exit the activities
- Costs are either (1) incremental to other costs incurred prior to the commitment date for the exit, and directly result from the exit plan; or (2) result from an existing contractual obligation prior to the commitment date and they will continue after the exit plan is completed. *See* **exit plan.**

exit plan. Under SEC regulations pertaining to when a business entity may show a corporate restructuring charge from discontinuing the use of certain resources, a plan by the restructuring corporation establishing the commitment to the discontinuance and elimination of the resources by its top management or board of directors. The plan must delineate its termination date and confirm the corporation's intentions to support the plan's progress with detail similar to operating and capital budgets. Usually, a restructuring charge is taken after a corporate merger. Details of the plan should appear in the MD&A section of the company's annual report. *See* **exit costs.**

exit strategy. A reference to an investor's plan to withdraw from a financial commitment by taking certain actions if specified events occur within a predetermined time frame. Usually, it is a reference to a principal's intention to call off a plan to acquire a company if certain adverse things happen. In doing so, the investor would hope to realize either a financial gain or suffer only a minimal loss. Whether one is buying a few shares of common stock or a multimillion-dollar company, there should be a clear plan to complete the investment operation. The completion would occur when investment expectations are fulfilled or thought to be no longer likely. In the case of common stock, it might be when the price reaches a certain level, in terms of the P/E ratio or dividend yield. A disciplined investor, who wishes to maximize performance, often would rather sell and reinvest than hang in for one long uncertain period. Remember, the long term is a series of short terms. In this context, the long term is a period during which the economic fundamentals for a stock have deteriorated. *See* **endgame.**

exotic option. An option with a unique underlying asset or unique terms or conditions.

exotics. A reference to derivative contracts that are unique, custom designed for the parties involved. Since they are relatively complex as to potential financial gains and losses, they usually are more risky than conventional or "plain vanilla" derivatives. *See* **total-return swap.**

exotic swap. A complex variety of swap whose return is derived from a formula that may include numerous factors, such as multiple indexes or financial assets.

expected outcome. See **risk/reward expected outcome.**

expected return. In economic terms, a consensus among investment experts of the percentage rate at which the stock market will grow in value, usually expressed on an annual basis. Both dividends and capital appreciation are included in the estimation. The amount estimated is used as the discount factor in a present value formula, which uses the future income stream from stocks to calculate the present value of the market. Often, this is called the true expected return. It is important in that its acceptance establishes an important valuation model for stocks, in general. When the expected return in stocks is not in sync with their real growth rate, then investment planning lacks predictability.

expenditure. The purchase of goods or services for a company's long-term improvements or operations. Such purchases are usually treated as amortized capital assets on company records and financial reports. Their value is reduced by a predetermined depletion, depreciation, or obsolescence expense in each fiscal period, which gives an accounting for the "using up" of the assets. In this way, the systematic amortization is the expense, rather than the initial outlay. One problem with this technique is when the replacement of the asset is rising in cost faster than the amortization installments are accounting for the using up. This means it has actually cost more for a company to operate than the financial statements reflect. For this reason, the FASB requires that public companies with inventories and fixed assets exceeding $125 million or total assets of more than $1 billion show the effects of inflation in their conventional reports. *See* **inflation accounting.**

expense. To treat an outlay of money as an operating expense during a fiscal period, deducting it from revenues so that it appears on the accounting records as an expense, reducing profits, rather than as an asset. The item is used up in a relatively short time, and the treatment is the opposite of capitalizing an expenditure. The rationale is that its benefits are completely used up in the near term, whereas an expenditure's benefits lasts for more than one fiscal period. Note that an expense need not be a cash disbursement, but the allocation of a current or past purchase that reduces the portion of revenues carried down to earnings. For example, management could decide to expense the original cost of an asset that has become worthless. The rationale for this action is that its purchase is part of the cost of doing business, even though it will never be used.

expense ratio. In the analysis of a mutual fund's management, the percentage of fund assets represented by payments for management and operating fees, but excluding brokerage expenses and sales costs and commissions.

expenses or **costs.** Those actual payments made for goods or services used in normal business operations. As such, they are subtracted from revenues in calculating earnings. They are recurring costs, such as labor, maintenance, and utilities, not the buying of durable items. The cost of goods for an inventory to be sold is not included. *See* **cost of goods sold.** Also, the cost of raw materials for manufacture is excluded. *See* **cost of goods manufactured.**

expiration, options. A reference to the final day of an options contract, after which it cannot be exercised and expires worthlessly.

expiration cycle, options contracts. The pattern of expiration dates used in the trading of near-term options contracts during the year. An investor can choose from one of the three cycles in which options contracts are written. Contracts can be for three, six, or nine months and expire on the last day of the month. When the first month in a cycle expires, it is dropped and the last month of that cycle is added to the cycle.

expire on close, to. To automatically cancel a limit order at the close of a market session when its price terms are not reached within the time limitation, i.e., the day, week or month. An odd-lot order in a stock that had no round-lot trades after the order was entered will expire on the close of that exchange unless there is an instruction to trade on the basis price.

export. A shipment of goods or services out of a country.

Export-Import Bank (EXIMBANK). See **agency securities.**

Export-Import Bank of the United States. An independent agency of the U.S. government that helps finance foreign sales of U.S. goods and services. In over 60 years, the bank has supported more than $300 billion in U.S. exports. Created in 1934, the bank was established under its present enabling law in 1945. It was instrumental in financing the reconstruction of Europe and Asian countries, after WWII. Primarily, the bank accomplishes its mission of stimulating American exports through: (1) making working capital loans, (2) making loans to foreign purchasers of U.S. goods and services, and (3) granting credit insurance against nonpayment by foreign buyers for political risk.

export subsidy. That financial government assistance given exporters who cannot profit against world competition. *See* **subsidy.**

ex post facto. In a statistical business model, the use of completed events as a basis for forecasting a future event. For example, an equation that correlated the level of a stock market index in the current year, the dependent variable, with corporate profits in the same year, the independent variable, would be based on *ex post facto* reasoning. This association between the two variables would be a simultaneous relationship.

expropriation. The complete acquisition without compensation of foreign-owned assets by a government.

expulsion from an exchange. The complete removal of a member from trading privileges of an exchange, usually for a violation of financial or ethical standards.

ex-right date. The date on which a stock sells **ex-rights.**

ex-rights or **without rights.** A reference to a trade in which a stock buyer is not entitled to recently declared subscription rights.

extended hours. A reference to opening an exchange for securities trading for a specified period after or before the regular daily trading session. The popularity of Internet trading after the work day has prompted exchanges to open their trading facilities during extended hours.

external factors. Those events that have no direct relationship to business prospects, but that nevertheless affect stock prices, for example, elections.

external funds. Those monies that are obtained from outside sources, for a company's capital expenditures program or capital expansion during a fiscal period. The source of the monies can be items such as stock sales, bond sales, bank borrowing, capital contributions, and so on. The higher the portion from external funds, the less conservative is the company. For conservative investors, it is frequently preferable if no more than half come from external funds except in quasi-monopolies like utilities. Otherwise, a company tends to be highly leveraged and susceptible to volatile results. *See* **internal funds.**

extra dividend. A dividend bonus, usually declared at year-end, representing extraordinary profits or the distribution of past profits out of earned surplus.

THE DESSERT FOR EXXON WAS HUMBLE PIE

The huge ballroom was packed for the Dallas Society of Securities Analysts luncheon that day. The guest presenter was Exxon, the first big company with a "New Age" name in the traditional oil and gas industry. The company had just changed its name from the Humble Oil Company, the family name of one of the founders. This was the first appearance before an analyst society since the historic name change. To add to the intrigue, a few days before the luncheon meeting, the management of Exxon and other key oil and gas companies had been raked over the coals by a committee of the U.S. House of Representatives. The House was on a vendetta, trying to attach blame to "Big Oil" for the accelerating oil prices and oil shortages of the 1970s. Harsh accusations were hurled at the cowed and surprised executives, they were charged with causing the shortages to make "obscene profits." It was a disillusioned and slightly bitter management that showed up in Dallas for the luncheon, but Exxon was making important changes and they had come to put their best foot forward. The fact that they were in Texas—heart and soul of "The Oil Patch"—was enough to instill fuzzy warm feelings in the visitors. After the main course, as dessert and coffee were served, the dignified chairman made a few remarks and opened the floor for questions. The first question broke the spell of euphoria, and brought down the house: "Mr. Chairman, if you had it to do all over again, would you change your name from 'Humble'?"

---

extranet. A reference to a corporate network of computers that is available to strategic business partners globally, on the Internet. A consortium of oil and gas exploration companies might utilize such a hookup to disseminate data on updated results of a drilling program in which all had an interest.

extraordinary item. An unusual transaction during a fiscal period that has resulted in a financial entry that needs to be explained to shareholders. Because it is a nonrecurring event, earnings are stated both before and after including the transaction so that investors can See that it does not affect basic trends. These are sizable events, like significant revenues from real estate sales, losses from employee embezzlement, a quantum writeoff of a resource, and so on. *See* **non-recurring items** and **recurring items.**

"eyeballs per month." See **"dot-com" stock.**

Ff

face value. The amount of money that the issuer or seller of a bond, note, or preferred stock owes the holder at its maturity (in the case of notes and bonds), or liquidation (in the case of preferred stocks). The interest and discounts, including discounts established in pricing the securities originally and in pricing them in the market afterwards, are based on this amount, as are the interest payments on bonds and dividend payments on certain preferred stocks. Aside from determining interest and dividend payments, the face value only has relevance at maturity, since fluctuating interest yields and dividend yields demanded by investors change the security's actual value in the securities markets constantly during its life. For example, a corporate bond might be issued for $1,000, with annual interest payments of 6.5%, or $65 annually, payable at $32.50 per half. One year later, investors might demand only 5.5% for a bond with the rating of the bond in question, so the bond would be priced in the market at approximately 118, or $1,182 ($65 ÷ .055, rounded to the nearest tenth). The yield will change often, but the face value of $1,000 will be paid to the holder at maturity, which might be 25 years away. Generally, securities have the following face values: Notes, various; corporate bonds and debentures, $1,000; municipal bonds, $5,000; federal bonds, $10,000; and preferred stocks, $100.

factor. See **accounts receivable factor** and **securities factor.**

Factory Orders and Manufacturing Inventories Report. This report, published the first part of the month by the Bureau of the Census of the Department of Commerce, includes extremely volatile data, with only limited new information for economists and industry analysts. But it does include data on orders and shipments of nondurable goods, manufacturing inventories, and the ratio of inventories to sales. Revisions of the durable goods data might appear. Coming one week after the durable goods report, its main value is nondurable data, which tend to be more stable than durable goods data. The inventory numbers are probably the most important element of this report, because they can indicate dangers when they get too large, in relation to sales. However, the inventory/sales ratio is a lagging indicator in the big picture. The data is collected from a sample of several thousand manufacturers. When factory orders rise, fixed income securities fall, while common stocks and dollar exchange rates react negligently.

FAF. Abbreviation for **Financial Accounting Foundation.**

fair rate of return. The annual rate or percentage allowed as a return on the stockholders' equity or, in some cases, the capital investment or rate base, for regulated companies such as public utilities, by state and federal agencies. In setting the allowable rate, which becomes the basis for the allowable charge for the company's product or services, commissions take into consideration total operating and capital costs for the entity regulated as well as consumer interests. (Often, commissioners are elected.) Unfortunately, or perhaps fortunately at times, politics gets into the picture. For example, suppose a state commission is conducting a rate hearing for Short Circuit Electric Corp. They decide to allow a 20% return on the company's rate base of $100 million. That would be $20 million annually. If they allow that return or decide that is the fair rate of return, the 20 million stockholders would earn $1.00 per share. But what if that return means an increase in electric rates for 10 million people in the state. The commission might vote to keep rates the same, not wanting to anger consumers, even though investors might sell the stock, forcing it downward in price. Analysts who work on regulated companies make it their business to learn whether regulatory bodies are more investor friendly or more consumer friendly. It helps them in anticipating rate trends and choosing attractive regulated investments.

fallen angels. A reference to bonds that were once investment quality but since then have lost favor because of the issuer's financial deterioration or the issuer's or guarantor's refusal to honor covenants in the bond agreement. In a sense, they have become **junk bonds,** but they did not start that way, unlike true junk bonds.

Fannie Mae. Nickname for **Federal National Mortgage Association.**

Farm Credit Financial Assistance Corporation. See **agency securities.**

Farmers Housing Administration (FHA). See **agency securities.**

far month. In trading options or futures contracts, that month which represents the farthest expiration day away.

FASB. (Pronounced "FAZ-BEE") Abbreviation for **Financial Accounting Standards Board.**

"fast-pay" or **"step-down."** A type of preferred stock designed as a tax strategy. Unlike conventional preferred stock, on the dividend distributions of which corporations and investors must pay income taxes, these preferred shares are created in an effort to avoid taxes. The method is to create a real estate investment trust to receive intended dividend distributions as tax-free interest or rent payments from a corporation. In turn, the trust pays the dividends, on which they are legally entitled to take a deduction.

favorable trade balance. The excess of exports of goods and services over imports of goods and services, in a country's international trade accounts. *See* **balance of trade.**

FDIC. Abbreviation for the **Federal Deposit Insurance Corporation.**

Fed. Nickname for the **Federal Reserve System.**

Federal Deposit Insurance Corporation (FDIC). A federally chartered insurer of deposits up to $100,000 per depositor in commercial banks and thrift institutions. This insurer also acts to prevent bank failures by making loans and buying assets, in order to effect mergers and acquisitions among problem banks. In 1989, Congress reorganized the program, creating separate divisions for commercial banks and thrift institutions, the latter agency replacing the **Federal Savings and Loan Corporation (FSLIC).** Banks pay a fee, based on their deposits, which is used to fund the insurance program.

Federal Electronic Signature in Global and National Commerce Act or **e-sign bill.** A bill enacted by Congress and signed into law in 2000, enabling companies and individuals to transact business and other matters online by using digital signatures. Such signatures would become legally binding. Although the bill raises issues yet to be resolved, such as the exact definition of a digital signature, proponents suggest that e-commerce and e-business can now broaden beyond credit card transactions to more comprehensive transactions, such as contracts. This extension is seen occurring especially in the draft stages of documents.

Federal Employees Retirement System (FERS). A retirement plan for federal employees, except military personnel, updated by the Federal Employees Retirement System Act of 1986. To be eligible for retirement benefits, a federal employee must complete at least five years of civilian employment and be 62 years old. Virtually all federal employees, including Congress, the courts, and bureaucrats are covered.

Federal Farm Credit Bank System. See **agency securities.**

Federal Financing Bank. See **agency securities.**

federal funds. Those excess reserves credited to Federal Reserve member banks that can be loaned to other member banks at relatively low interest rates for short periods. It is the interest or discount rate charged for these funds that is one instrument in allowing the Fed to control interest rates of the banking system in the United States. *See* **Federal Reserve Act.**

federal funds rate. The rate established by the Fed for the lending of federal funds by member banks.

federal gift tax. See **gift tax, federal.**

Federal Home Loan Banks. The 11 regional banks established in 1932 by savings and loan associations, building and loan associations, savings banks, and so on for making loans to its members to reloan to the public as home mortgages. *See* **agency securities.**

Federal Home Loan Mortgage Corporation or **Freddie Mac.** The mortgage-lending company created by Congress in 1970 to increase funds for home buying. It accomplishes this by purchasing mortgage loans in great quantities and packaging them for resale to investors. It is privately owned, but sponsored by the U.S. government. By adjusting its credit standards on the loans it purchases from banks, the corporation can influence the amounts of mortgage lending funds available in the United States, although it is freer from this type of political pressure than its sister mortgage underwriter, the **Federal National Mortgage Association** (Fannie Mae). *See* **agency securities** and **Collateralized Mortgage.**

Federal Housing Administration. A federally affiliated agency that insures lenders against losses on residential real estate.

Federal National Mortgage Association or **Fannie Mae.** An independent federal agency, founded in 1938, which is the biggest underwriter of home mortgages in the United States. Rather then lending directly to home buyers, it purchases voluminous packages of mortgages from banks and other lenders in the so-called secondary market, to create additional mortgage funds in the United States. By adjusting its credit requirements for the loans it buys, the association can affect the amount of mortgage funds available at any given time. In a pilot program begun in 1999 to provide more mortgage funds to home buyers with marginal credit, the association offered 30-year mortgages for up to $240,000, at 1% above the conventional rate. Many of these candidates are minorities, groups in which home ownership accelerated rapidly during the 1990s. The association is a public corporation, with a competitive earnings growth rate. *See* **agency securities.**

Federal Open Market Committee (FOMC). An adjunct committee of the **Federal Reserve System,** composed of the seven members of the Board of Governors—appointed by the U.S. president—and five bank presidents from among the 12 Federal Reserve Banks. Of those five, four rotate into positions and the fifth is the president of the Federal Reserve Bank of New York. The committee is responsible for the system's open-market operations—purchasing and selling U.S. government and agency securities. This action adjusts the amount of money available to banks and other depository institutions for lending in the United States, and thus controls the amount and interest cost of commercial credit. The committee also develops strategies to promote economic growth, full employment, stable prices, and a stable pattern of international trade and payments. It also manages the Fed's strategies in foreign currencies.

Federal Reserve Act. A Congressional Act of 1913 establishing the **Federal Reserve System.** This provides for the supervision of our commercial banking system by establishing 12 regional banks, owned by and paid for by fees from the 6,300 commercial member banks in the system. The Federal Reserve System is the central bank of the United States and supervises activities, along with the Comptroller of the Currency of the U.S. Treasury, of federally chartered banks in the United States as well as state banks that are members.

It accomplishes its oversight role in the following ways: (1) by controlling the fraction of deposits or reserves that can be loaned by each member bank it adjusts total credit available in the system; (2) by controlling the margin rates or down payment required on securities that investors buy on credit; (3) by controlling the level of interest rates through adjusting its discount rate or the funds it makes available to banks short term, on which prime rates are pegged; and (4) by controlling the level of government securities that member banks hold, through the trading activities of the **Federal Open Market Committee,** which either injects extra lendable reserves or withdraws lendable reserves from the system.

The system also exercises "moral suasion" in restricting or expanding banking activities. This is another expression for collective and personal pressure. The system is directed by a board of seven governors, appointed by the president for a term of seven years each, the chairman of which is one of the most important posts in the United States in terms of influencing business activity. There are Federal Reserve Banks in the following cities: Atlanta, Boston, Chicago, Cleveland, Dallas,

Kansas City, Minneapolis, New York, Philadelphia, Richmond, San Francisco, and St. Louis.

Federal Reserve Bank. One of the 12 member banks of the **Federal Reserve System.** *See* **Federal Reserve Act.**

Federal Reserve Board (Beige Book) Online. See under **Web Sites for the Inquiring Investor.**

Federal Reserve Board or **Board of Governors.** In the Federal Reserve System, the governing body for the goals and operations of the system. In particular, it is the seven-member board, appointed by the President, that establishes the discount rate the Fed charges other banks for overnight loans. This rate becomes influential in establishing prime interest rates charged by banks in the system. *See* **Federal Reserve System.**

Federal Reserve Regional Bank. See **Federal Reserve Act.**

Federal Reserve Regulations. See **Regulation A, Fed; Regulation D, Fed; Regulation T, Fed; Regulation U, Fed;** and **Regulation Z, Fed.**

Federal Reserve System or **the Fed.** The independent central bank and manager of **monetary policy—money supply** and interest rates—for the United States. It is composed of 12 regional banks and all federally chartered commercial banks in the United States as well as voluntary state banks. Although the **Comptroller of the Currency** supervises all national banks in the United States, the Federal Reserve supervises bank holding companies. *See* **Federal Reserve Act, Federal Open Market Committee,** and **Federal Reserve Board.**

Federal Savings and Loan Association. A mutual savings bank, operating under federal charter, created to make loans to its members (depositors) as well as general mortgage loans, distributing the profits from operations to depositors as dividends.

Federal Savings and Loan Insurance Corporation (FSLIC). A federally chartered insurer of savings accounts up to $40,000 for federal or state savings and loan associations who pay a fee commensurate with their volume of deposits.

Federal Trade Commission (FTC). A Federal agency created in 1914, empowered to prevent individuals, partners, or corporations from using unfair methods in commerce and false or fraudulent advertising in the promotion of products and to police business competition under terms of the antitrust laws. The Commission is composed of five members, appointed by the president, approved by the Senate, for seven-year terms. There are 10 regional offices to handle complaints. Consumer Protection address: Consumer Response Center, Federal Trade Commission, 6th Street & Pennsylvania Ave., NW, Washington, DC 20590. Bureau of Competition address: Office of Policy and Evaluation, Room 394, Bureau of Competition, Federal Trade Commission, Washington, D.C. 20580. Web site: *www.ftc.gov.*

Federal Unemployment Tax Act (FUTA). A Congressional statute that created a federal tax on the wages and salaries of a company, used to contribute to a trust fund that collected and distributed the receipts to the states for aid to unemployed workers. The tax rate is 0.8% on the gross salary or wages up to $7,000 annually per employee.

fee, finder's. See **find.**

"fell out of bed." A slang phrase indicating a stock's price dropped precipitously.

FICA. Abbreviation for Federal Insurance and Care for the Aged, or **Social Security** tax.

FICO. Abbreviation for the Financing Corporation. *See* **agency securities.**

fidelity bond. A form of insurance against loss from embezzlement or theft. Such bonds are popular with corporations and non-profit organizations, where key persons have access to large sums of money that is for the benefit of others. Pension funds, business corporations, and unions are examples. The premiums are priced on the risk of the business or activity, in addition to the number of employees and work locations.

FIDO. Nickname for Fidelity Management & Research Company.

fiduciary. A person acting in a position of financial trust with respect to another, usually as the result of a legal action. Examples are the executor of a will, a receiver appointed by a bankruptcy court, trustees under a trust indenture, and legal guardians appointed by courts. Most states have established standards for fiduciaries, including rules against the use of assets for personal gain and the types of assets that can be invested in. *See* **legal investments, legal list,** and **"Prudent Man Rule."**

FIFO. Abbreviation for **first-in-first-out** inventory valuation.

FIGS. See **zero-coupon convertibles, municipals.**

filling orders. A reference to the practice by an ethical investment house of selling stock that they do not recommend, but for which there is customer demand. The concept is that they might as well make the commissions or profits as another firm. The stock is usually an over-the-counter promotional issue.

final prospectus. See **underwriting agreement.**

Financial Accounting Foundation (FAF). A nonprofit organization incorporated to overSee the **Governmental Accounting Standards Board** and its advisory council as well as selecting members, providing funds, and providing general oversight of the **Financial Accounting Standards Board.** The following organizations sponsor the FAF and nominate its trustees:
- American Accounting Association
- American Institute of Certified Public Accountants
- Association for Investment Management and Research
- Financial Executives Institute
- Government Finance Officers Association
- Institute of Management Accountants
- National Association of State Auditors, Comptrollers and Treasurers
- Securities Industry Association

Financial Accounting Standards Board (FASB). The rule-making body formed in 1972, and supported by the American Accounting Association, American Institute of Certified Public Accountants, Association of Investment Management and Research, Financial Executives Institute, National Association of Accountants, and the Securities and Exchange Commission. The mission of FASB is to establish and improve standards of financial accounting and reporting for the guidance and education of the public, including issuers, auditors, and users of financial information. Although the SEC has statutory authority to establish financial accounting and reporting standards for publicly held companies under the Securities Exchange Act of 1934, it has relied throughout its history on the public sector, through FASB. *See* **Governmental Accounting Standards Board.** It is the purpose of the FASB to accomplish the following:

- Improve the usefulness of financial reporting by focusing on the primary characteristics of relevance and reliability, and on the qualities of comparability and consistency.
- Maintain current standards, to reflect changes in methods of doing business and changes in the economic environment.
- Consider promptly any significant areas of deficiency in financial reporting that might be improved through the standard-setting process.
- Promote the international comparability of accounting standards concurrent with improving the quality of financial reporting.
- Improve the common understanding of the nature and purposes of information contained in financial reports.

Financial and Operating Data in the Annual Report to the Stockholders. The section of the **Annual Report to the Stockholders** that deals with the financial and operating progress of the company. It is a chronicle of the recent financial operations of the company and a snapshot of its present financial condition. As such, the section provides audited information on such important items as revenues, expenses, earnings, cash flows, resources, debt, stockholders' equity or interest, and capital structure. In addition, the footnotes to the financial and operating statements amplify this data, sometimes adding material that describes contingencies like pending law suits. When appropriate, operating data appear, outlining the volumes of physical inputs and outputs that the corporate effort experienced during the fiscal period. In terms of insights into investment values, this is the most important of all the sections in the Annual Report for investors. It gives investors numbers to translate into pragmatic corporate progress and investment value. Often this section is introduced with a Financial Review.

When possible, two-year or three-year comparisons are present. Frequently, there is also an historical summary of financial and operating information, although this type table also can appear inside a cover or nearby. While other sections invite management editorializing and spinning, this section stresses measurements of value, at least to the extent possible in accounting convention. The important elements of this section are the following statements or schedules: the **Balance Sheet,** the **Cash Flow Statement,** the **Income or Operating Statement, the Statement of Stockholders' Equity** and, extremely important, footnotes amplifying those statements. As the caveat in this section usually says, the footnotes should be considered an integral part of the statements. It is not often, but sometimes a situation appears in the footnotes that management wants to down play, to the detriment of prospective investors. Besides the technical amplification of accounting and management procedures, this section can contain very useful information related to debt structure, corporate history or contingencies, or other significant items. *See* **Shareholders' Equity, Statement of.**

financial architecture. In reference to the international structure of financial and investment positions, a description of how transparent or apparent the risks and rewards of investing in foreign countries are. A financial architecture that is highly transparent is one where investors are fully aware of the risks inherent in foreign securities. On the other hand, one that is not transparent is obscure as to foreign financial risks and rewards. The term came to have renewed importance with the Asian financial meltdown in the 1990s. The World Bank and the International Monetary Fund are leaders in the efforts to give the architecture more clarity.

Financial Engines Investment Advisor. See under **Web Sites for the Inquiring Investor.**

financial house. A private banking institution, often a partnership, that lends money, buys equities in businesses either for retention or resale, and arranges for the financing of new business projects. Capital used for these purposes is contributed by partners, borrowed, taken from among the house's assets, or pledged by other participants of a venture. A financial house is not under the rigid banking laws of commercial banks and insurance companies and generally enters into more venturesome projects.

financial industries. See **sector.**

financial institution. A financial entity, usually chartered by a state or the federal government, that accepts money from the public in exchange for its safekeeping and related services or other financial services. Basically, they break down into depository institutions and nondepository institutions. The former include commercial banks, savings and loan companies or thrifts, mutual savings banks, and credit unions. They pay interest to depositors and invest most of the depositors' money in loans. The latter type is represented by insurance companies and pension plans. They take in money through insurance premiums or pension contributions, which they invest in a broad spectrum of investments, and in exchange they insure lives and property or provide retirement funds. Beginning in the 1980s and accelerating in the 1990s, there began a convergence of financial services by both depositary and nondepositary into single institutions. This trend is likely to continue, prompted by federal legislation allowing financial mergers.

financial intermediary. A financial institution, such as a mutual fund, commercial bank, savings and loan company, credit union, or others that serve as conveyors of the funds flowing between megasectors of the economy that have surplus funds for investment and those that have a shortage of funds. Basically, there are three sectors that are vitally affected—households, business entities, and government functions. In a sense, they use the intermediaries to channel the flow of funds between them, with households usually furnishing the funds through savings and businesses and government using the funds for their purposes. The actual flow is represented by deposits, certificates of deposit, notes, bonds, and other securities. In the process, individuals who save become investors in a huge, diversified portfolio.

financial lease. A reference to a lease contract, usually noncancellable, in which the lessor only provides the use of certain equipment or facilities over the term. All other costs and expenses, such as taxes, maintenance and insurance, are borne by the lessee.

Financial Leverage or **Balance Sheet Leverage** or **Capital Leverage.** The effect of a company's capital structure or capitalization on the earnings available for the common stockholders, as determined by the debt-to-capital ratio. When there is a great deal of long-term debt and/or preferred stock, say from 50% to 75% of total capitalization, there is a also a great deal of financial leverage on common stock earnings. This is because as revenues increase, the fixed debt payments and preferred dividends stay the same, so that the total revenue increments flow through to the common stock, except for attendant increased variable operating expenses such as labor, maintenance, fuel, and so on. When a company's stock represents a high financial leverage, it is said to be "trading on the equity." The heavy bond and/or preferred stock financing in relation to outstanding stock results in abnormally high stock earnings in periods of good business and expanding sales volume. In effect, bondholders have financed the business growth. This leaves the stockholders in an enviable position as long as revenues are increasing and are above the debt and other cost requirements.

For example, let's assume WebSloth Inc., an up-and-coming Internet search engine, has borrowed $10 million at 7.5% interest per year to expand facilities. Furthermore, say its operating profit grows to $3 million, or 25% greater, before interest of $750,000 and taxes, and $2.25 million, or 15%, after interest of $750,000 the following year. Its financial leverage is

.25 ÷ .15 or 1.7×. Another way of looking at the concept of the measurement of financial leverage is that it measures by what factor the pretax income has grown annually as a result of the borrowing.

financial page. See **market page.**

financial position. The description of the financial condition of an individual or company, for purposes of borrowing, in terms of asset values, earning power, ability to repay debts, ability to control expenses, reputation among creditors and money lenders, and, in the case of a corporation, profit making ability, or capitalization. It usually takes the form of a report for use in measuring the financial image of a corporation, when considering an investment in it. Such a report usually rates the company on the basis of general criteria, such as its ability to grow earnings considering the total corporate situation.

Financial Pyramid. A symbolic presentation of conventional investment wisdom as to the allocation of an investor's resources up and down the risk spectrum. Basically, the pyramid suggests that the prudent investor should make the cornerstone or foundation of the program the base of the pyramid. And that is where most of the resources should appear, certainly in the beginning. The pyramid structure is an excellent way to structure an investor's IRA, when it gets large enough in terms of assets. There follows a brief discussion of each tier in the pyramid, focusing on the part it plays in a long-term program and types of securities that are appropriate.

1. *High Liquidity and Safety.* At this level, resources are spent in accumulating investments with High Liquidity and Safety of Principal. This means securities that are high grade, with little chance of nonpayment, either as to dividends, interest, or repayment of principal at maturity or whenever it is timely for an investor to sell them. It also means that they are easy to sell or liquidate, because they are so desirable and because there is an active market in which they trade. The greater the chances of needing money for emergencies or an expected opportunity to occur, the greater the portion should be of assets in this category. Obviously, the

investor's age and other income potential, such as career job prospects or self-employment expectations, should be factored in. But since it is the broad base of the plan, it is the most important and, as such, ought to have something like 40% of the resources available invested in it, at a minimum.

We are talking here about savings accounts, certificates of deposit, Treasury bills and notes, high-grade bonds, high-grade preferred stocks, and high-grade commercial paper. Although an individual's circumstances should dictate the most plausible ratio allocations, the discipline of four-tenths at the bottom, three-tenths next, then two-tenths, and finally one-tenth of resources at high risk should prove rewarding over time. This will account for 100% of resources, in a very manageable and flexible way, and accomplish most financial aspirations.

2. *Income/Long-Term Growth.* The second tier of the pyramid is where the fun begins. The object of resources allocated in this bracket is to provide income, although not necessarily as high as from securities in the base of the pyramid on a yield basis, and to grow your assets, both dividends and market values. These are the securities that provide the strong possibilities of both increasing yields, based on original investments, and capital appreciation, reflecting expanding markets, revenues, and earnings. The prime examples of what fits this bill are high-grade common stocks, convertible preferred stocks, and convertible debentures. Both dividends and interest should be secure on preferred stocks and debentures; this is another way of staying well covered by cash flow available for that purpose. There should likely be income and growth present, a qualification usually associated with a track record of five years or more of accomplishing it, and there should be bona fide expectations of continuing the growth five years or more. Once again, every investor has different circumstances to consider, but 35% of resources allocated to this category would seem reasonable for most investors.

3. *Speculative.* Investment traditionalists say that when the chances of enterprise success are better than 50%, it is an

investment; when the chances are less than 50%, it is a speculation. That's not a bad guide. Much speculation has enough of an element of predictability about it that most professionals consider it in an investment context. In other words, valid speculation is close enough to the 50% probability of being successful that similar techniques are used by analysts in appraising its chances of success—such as industry trends, seasonality, price patterns, management credentials, market liquidity, and upside potential.

However, one judgmental aspect is different: The reward must be greater than the risk in terms of dollars or in whatever currency the securities are denominated. In fact, as one moves up the pyramid to the riskier heights, bigger rewards in relation to losses must always be in sight. Ideally, there should be a disproportionate reward goal. That is, if an investor estimates there is a 50% chance of trebling an investment's present value, some fraction of that, say one-third, should be acceptable as a loss. That rationale represents a risk/reward ratio of 3:1. The investor is expecting three dollars of gain for every dollar of loss. The thinking suggests that since the probability of success in such an investment is less than 50%, an investor needs to maximize the returns on the right decisions about such financial commitments to more than offset the more numerous wrong ones.

In this category of securities, there could be a mixed bag. It might include low-grade equities that are struggling but turning things around, or new entities that are not making money yet but have great prospects. New technologies and products could be present, always risky propositions. Most derivatives representing high-grade equities also would belong in this cache. They move in value reasonably close to their underlying issues, usually common stocks, which give the investor some prerogative to buy or sell at specific prices. But unlike their brethren in the second tier of the pyramid, they don't provide as much income, usually none, or capital appreciation potential, because they are so short-term oriented. A recommended ratio for these securities is 20%.

4. *High Risk.* Now we enter orbit, flying among the rank speculations—high fliers that are usually cheap in price, making them especially hard to pass up. Many of the comments made about the Speculative group are appropriate here. These securities are fraught with problems, from financial difficulties to product defects or inadequacies; sometimes they are simply unknown, an anonymity that has penalized the stock price. But this sort of flaw disappears rapidly in today's electronic market. Also, they might operate under adverse conditions, such as recent laws that make them practically illegal. Oil companies that are drilling out in the boonies, where no geologist has gone before, are prime candidates. Taking this dilemma one step further, the company might be too short of cash flow to keep going.

The common denominator of the high-risk securities is there is not much chance of success, in which case there is not much chance of a payoff on the investment. When such conditions exist, the risk/reward ratio should be even higher than is acceptable in the third tier—probably the ratio should be no lower than 10, unless an investor is feeling very lucky. This means if you buy 1,000 shares in a dilapidated gold mine that has not operated in 50 years, for $5 per share, you ought to expect to lose it all. But, if you are joyfully wrong, then you ought to be able sell the stock for $50 per share in the future. Of course other risks, like no liquidity, information gaps, and fraud, also permeate this investment fabric, so be careful. Penny stocks usually go here. In fact, anything that's too good to be true goes here.

But everybody needs to dream, and every now and then, one of these fliers takes off and the faithful become rich. As a guide, investors ought to consider in the neighborhood of something like a 10% commitment to these high-flying white chips. Another way to think about this allocation is that the portion of resources not allocated to the first three tiers belongs here. If you are looking for clues as to which companies are in the right circumstances to become anointed and blast off, here's a short list for a starter:

- Company is working in new technology that does not require regulatory approval.
- Company retains high-energy-level officers with marketing flair.
- Company officers are adept at raising capital, but are disciplined.
- Company is entrepreneurial, not trying to buck giants in the field.
- Company officers have good reputations in the business community.
- Company owns critical patent or copyright rights to exciting product(s).

Financial Review Introduction of the Annual Report. See **Financial and Operating Data of the Annual Report to the Stockholders.**

Financial Services Information Sharing and Analysis Center. A clearinghouse for uncovering threats and vulnerabilities to computer systems, created in 1999 under a presidential directive, between the U.S. Treasury and the financial services industry. It is managed by private industry and represented the second phase in the Clinton Administration's plan to create a nationwide system to combat cybercrime.

Financial Services Modernization Act of 1999. A Congressional act passed and signed into law in November 1999, by which most of the proscriptions of the Glass-Steagall Act of 1933 and the National Banking Act of 1956 against combining banking, insurance, and securities investing within a single company are relaxed. The Glass-Steagall Act was passed by the Congress in an effort to halt the speculation among financial institutions that occurred at the time of the stock market crash of 1929 and the years preceding it. The Financial Services Modernization Act allows banks, insurance companies, and investment firms to combine and market one another's products and services. Although it was promoted as a bill that would aid consumers, in terms of convenience and choices, in reality it provides U.S. financial companies with the legal framework to compete in the international marketplace that is evolving for financial products and services.

Most foreign banks have the ability to market a broad range of these products and services. Also moderated in the bill were the federal audit procedures under the Community Reinvestment Act of 1977 as amended, aimed at enforcing compliance by banks with provisions to give more consideration to minority lending. The biggest issue in the debate was over the privacy rights of customers. Under the bill, a financial company may use cross marketing for its products and services, but must get permission to provide customer information to others. It is likely legislation will be presented in the future to expand the privacy guarantees of customers. *See* **Bank Holding Company Act of 1956, the Community Reinvestment Act**, and the **Glass-Steagall Act.**

financial statements. Those documents that measure the financial condition and progress of a company over a selected period, usually quarterly and annually. Most often they include a Balance Sheet, Income Statement, Source and Application of Funds Statement, Retained Earnings Statement, Shareholders Equity Summary, Capital Surplus Statement, and footnotes.

financial structure. The composition of a corporation's total method of financing its operations. Besides the capital accounts—long-term debt and stockholder's equity—it includes short-term borrowing and accounts payable. This analysis divulges more about management's use of financial leverage. *See* **Capital Structure.**

FinancialWeb—Tools of the Trade. See **Web Sites for the Inquiring Investor.**

Financials. Those stocks representing companies—banks, insurers, and investment companies—in the sector that provides various financial services to the public. *See* **sector.**

Financials—Miscellaneous. Those stocks representing companies providing various financial services—small loans, title insurance, real estate brokerage, and so on—to the public not offered by major institutions. *See* **industry stock group.**

financier. A private businessman who organizes and participates in financial backings for business ventures, usually involving large sums of money.

financing. The raising of capital funds by a corporation by selling stocks or bonds or borrowing from a bank. *See* **equity financing, debt financing,** and **note.**

Financing Corporation (FICO). See **agency securities.**

find. A discovery by a broker in an investment firm of an underwriting deal, for which he receives a generous fee, usually at least 5% of the value of the financing package to investors.

Finnish Securities Exchange. See under **Global Investment Market.**

firewall. A reference to the effort by financial institutions to eliminate communications between the investment and banking sides of an institution, or the brokerage and banking side of an institution. Under the Glass-Steagall Act of 1933, now under attack in Congress as being outmoded, banks are not allowed to control securities brokerages or dealers. This proscription is to prevent bank deposits from being exposed to the risks of securities underwriting and trading. However, in recent years banks have been offering limited brokerage services, as the Fed and Comptroller of the Currency have made accommodations to them. And, on the other side of the coin, brokerage customers can write checks on their accounts, to a limited extent.

firm bid and offer. A definite commitment to buy (bid) or sell (offer) securities at a certain price exacted from a customer by a broker-salesman, before he locates another customer to complete the transaction.

firm commitment. In general in the securities business, a distinct pledge to take some action, made by a professional who is staking his reputation on completing the intention. It covers matters like buying and selling securities, purchasing units in an underwriting, or quoting a security's price. It can be written, verbal, or both. It is the stuff of which investment integrity is made. *See* **nominal quotes.**

firm market. A condition of the stock market when prices remain steady in active trading.

first and refunding mortgage bonds. Those bonds issued to pay off others that are near due; the refunding bonds are secured by a property first mortgage as soon as the prior bonds are paid off.

first-in-first-out (FIFO). In inventory valuation, an accounting assumption that the goods on hand were bought during the last part of an accounting period, while those used were bought first. In calculating income, this means cost of goods sold was based on prices at the beginning of the period. In periods of inflation, this approach will overstate profits because the cost of goods sold is understated, based on cheaper earlier prices.

first preferred stock. A preferred stock issue that takes precedence over the regular preferred, in the matters of dividends and liquidation rights.

fiscal agent. A representative who acts as a depository for funds, makes collections and disbursements, and so on.

fiscal policy. An economic program designed and implemented by an autonomous government, usually at the federal level, intended to effect some economic goal in a country, such as stimulating the economy during periods of recession or slowing the economy during periods of inflation, or distributing the national wealth differently. It can also be used to attract foreign investment to a country, by methods such as offering tax advantages to such capital. In the United States, the tools to accomplish these goals reside in the taxing and spending powers of Congress and, to a limited degree, by executive orders of the president.

By increasing income taxes, the government can reduce disposable income and slow down an inflationary economy. With the additional Treasury tax receipts, it can reduce the national debt, thus lowering interest rates, or authorize the new revenues to be spent for public projects, thus distributing the monies to another group of citizens. The opposite effects can also be accomplished. Of course, there are many variations and combinations of fiscal policy tools.

Fiscal policy and monetary policy can accomplish similar goals, through two distinct institutions: the federal government which determines fiscal policy through its taxing and spending powers and the Federal Reserve System which manages **monetary policy** through controlling available money and credit using the banking system. The former is more responsive to political expediencies, while the latter answers to the calls for a sound banking and monetary system. Adherents to fiscal policy are known as "Keynesians," while those advocating monetary policy in managing the health of an economy are called "monetarists." On occasion, one of these players has acted in the past to counter the efforts of the other. *See* **Federal Reserve Act.**

fiscal year (FY). The 12 consecutive months used for reporting the ending financial condition, operations, and budgeting by a business. The quarterly fiscal periods key off this date. Most companies use a calendar year as their fiscal year, ending December 31. Also, March 31, June 30, and July 31 are popular. The choice of a fiscal year depends a great deal on the nature of the business, although convention also influences decision making. For example, the construction of swimming pools is a seasonal business. Therefore, CoolPool, Inc. might decide to close its books or establish its fiscal year end as September 30, in order to include the active selling season and low inventory point.

Fisher index. See **chain-weighted index.**

Fitch Investors Service, LP. A full-service rating agency of bonds and other fixed-income securities, established in 1913, rating 70% of active state issuers of general obligation debt. Web site: *www.fitchibca.com.*

five Cs of credit. The five characteristics money lenders analyze when making a decision about lending money to a business enterprise and, to a lesser extent, to an individual. 1) Character—the entity's credit history and indications about its honesty. 2) Capacity—the physical and human capacity of the business, including management, to generate the cash flow necessary to pay its bills and the loan. 3) Collateral—the ultimate recourse of the lender, the quality and liquidity of what is pledged for the benefit of the lender, if the terms of the loan cannot be fulfilled. 4) Capital—the amount of money the borrower has or has at stake in the business, an indication of its commitment to the ongoing life of the entity. 5) Condition—the state of the industry or markets in which the enterprise competes, an effort to determine whether growth or decay is the prospect. There is no doubt that good banking practice rests on such principles, but an excess of lendable funds can make a marginal borrower more attractive.

five percent policy. A National Association of Security Dealers' recommended policy of limiting member trading profit on a transaction to 5%.

fixed annuity. A life insurance plan in which an investor pays a vendor, such as a bank or insurer, a fixed sum in advance in exchange for a guaranteed amount at a later date. The interest rate applied to the principal can be changed annually, but it can never fall beneath a statutory minimum.

fixed assets. The durable resources a company uses in conducting business, such as buildings and machinery, as opposed to tools, mineral rights, and such.

fixed-charge coverage. The number of times total fixed obligations annually will divide into the revenue stream available to pay these fixed obligations. For example, Fat Fudgies, Inc. shows net revenues of $40,000,000 available for fixed charges of $10,000,000. Thus, fixed charges are earned four times ($40,000,000 ÷ $10,000,000). The industrial average for fixed charge coverage is seven times. This is an important measure, because management cannot do a great deal to lower fixed costs—bond interest, lease payments, property taxes—in a short time, as it can to lower variable costs—wages, advertising, travel, and so on. Therefore, the fixed charge coverage must leave a cushion for slack revenue periods.

Fixed Costs or **Fixed Charges.** A company's ongoing money requirements for items such as interest, rentals, guaranteed dividends, leases, and other regular obligations of known amounts.

These charges continue no matter what the level of operations is, and are sometimes called indirect costs. *See* **Variable Costs.**

fixed-income investment. The employment of funds in securities or an enterprise in which the return, whether dividends or interest, is a fixed amount. In periods of inflation, this type of investment loses purchasing power; for example, insurance annuities, bonds, preferred stocks.

fixed-rate loan. A reference to a debt security or promissory note that bears the same interest rate throughout its term. *See* **adjustable rate mortgage.**

fixed-weighted index or **Laspeyres index** or **"constant dollar" index.** In measuring real changes in GDP, or any other series for that matter, a statistical index in which a certain period is established as the base period, along with a set of constant prices for that period, in order to value the output in every period being measured, in those prices. Because relative prices and associated patterns of purchases change over time, such a measure of GDP growth will be extremely sensitive to the base year chosen, so that a shift in the base year can have an extreme effect on the measured growth rates. This was the type of measure used by the BEA in estimating GDP until 1997, when that agency shifted to a chain-weighted index. It has long been acknowledged that measures of output that use fixed weights of a single period tend to misstate growth as one moves further from the base period. This tendency is called the substitution bias and reflects the fact that the commodities for which output grows rapidly tend to be those for which prices increase less than average or decline. *See* **chain-weighted index.**

flat bonds. Bonds trading without accrued interest. *See* **ex-interest.**

flat management structure. A reference to a corporate style of management that removes management tiers between top executives and lower-level employees in the communications and operations that run a company. This concept is an extension of the policies of cost cutting and "leanness" that began in the fiercely competitive 1990s. The ultimate goal is to make organizations capable of responding quickly to technological changes in the production and marketing of products and services. Usually, there is a team approach to getting out a product line. Teams are composed of employees from various disciplines—engineering, accounting, research, marketing— who plan a path to the goal, with modifications along the way. Proponents say employees get a sense of participation that other management forms do not engender. Besides that stimulus to employee longevity, the company benefits from the flexibility and rapidity with which decisions can be made and implemented. Corporate relationships and dress are more informal. Employees aspire to attractive stock options over high salaries. The opposite of **command and control management structure.**

flat tax system. An income tax plan in which all income levels are taxed at the same bracket or percentage rate. In recent presidential campaigns, a flat rate of 15% has been most often suggested as the one with which to start. It is the opposite of the progressive tax system. Adherents argue that as wealthier taxpayers earn more, they would keep more and thus have a greater incentive to continue earning fully. This result would stimulate the economy to the benefit of all taxpayers. It is also commended for its simplicity. On the other hand, critics argue it is regressive, in that it penalizes lower incomes more by taxing a higher portion of them, leaving less for household essentials. *See* **progressive tax system.**

flat yield curve. See **yield curve.**

Flex Option, Equity. A type of equity option designed to provide institutions and individual investors with the ability to customize their options investment strategy. Using this type of option, investors may request a date, strike, and exercise style other than those currently offered in the market place and customize an options contract to meet specific needs. These options, when approved, are backed by the Options Clearing Corporation.

flier. A highly speculative securities purchase.

flights of capital. The heavy traffic of money, metals of exchange (gold), and credit between countries for reasons other than normal financing. Most often the traffic occurs because a country's government or social system has become hostile to investors, both domestic and foreign. The results can be devaluation of its currency, nationalization of foreign investments, or expropriation of foreign assets. The flight is a universal financial exodus from a country, rather than an effort to improve the quality of investments there. It's a Red Alert! *See* **flight to quality** and **flight to safety.**

flight to quality. A reference to a change in investor attitudes, collectively, causing investment funds to flow into higher quality securities, especially in the bond markets. Although some of the characteristics are the same, this flight is not as desperate as a **flight to safety.**

flight to safety. A reference to the movement of large amounts of capital funds into higher quality securities, usually because of impending financial defaults, currency devaluations, or problems among lesser quality issues. These movements can include movements into higher investment grade issues within the same country as well as movement into foreign securities denominated in more stable foreign exchange. It's a Yellow Alert! *See* **flights of capital** and **flight to quality.**

float. 1) The number of shares of a corporation's stock that is actively being traded in the stock market. The float is not necessarily the same as outstanding stock, since it represents shares in the possession of profit-minded investors who will buy and sell the shares advantageously as opposed to investors who intend to hold the shares, regardless of the stock's price. The float is a much more finite measure of a stock's liquidity than outstanding stock and usually represents the difference between the latter and shares held by: individual trusts; dealers who intend to keep the shares for long-term profits; the issuing corporation; investors not intending to sell their shares soon, which could include institutional investors, founders of the corporation, and their relatives; or holders of large blocks of the stock. The float might be calculated as follows in a hypothetical corporation.

FLOAT OF CEMENT BLOCKS, INC.

Shares Outstanding	10,000,000
Less Shares In:	
Trust Ownership	1,000,000
Family Estates	1,500,000
Officers' Blocks	750,000
Corporate Treasury	500,000
Dealer Inventory	100,000
Total Nontrading Stock	3,850,000
Balance or Float	6,150,000

The float is especially important in measuring the liquidity of an over-the-counter-stock. Since in this type of market there is often little volume for stocks traded, the float indicates how many shares could be bought or sold without affecting the price drastically, although the number fluctuates narrowly with changing investor attitudes concerning the desirability of owning the stock. Usually, a float representing 20% or under of the stock issued reflects a tight trading market and should be considered a nonliquid investment. 2) New capital realized through stock or bond sales.

float a currency. As officials of the financial affairs for a country, to remove all trading restrictions and exchange support for the country's official currency, in order to allow it to reach its market value in world foreign exchange markets. By not exchanging the currency for others at specific rates and by allowing it to trade freely in world markets, the country's government or central bank is usually attempting to stabilize its economy, after a period of high growth and debt issuance followed by a slow down. The opposite strategy is to peg the currency to another currency or allow it to fluctuate within a band or range of exchange rates.

float an issue. To sell bonds or stocks to the public, usually with the aid of investment bankers.

floating rate preferred stock. See **adjustable rate preferred stock.**

floor. The trading area of a stock exchange.

floor broker or **commission house broker.** A broker who handles orders for his firm's customers on the floor of an exchange.

floor trader. A member of a stock exchange who trades on the floor for his own account.

Florida Office of the Comptroller. Regulator of securities laws in the state of Florida. Address: Securities Division, Plaza Level, The Capitol, Tallahassee, FL 32399. Phone: (904) 488-9805. Phone: (800) 848-3792.

"flower bond." A reference to Treasury bonds issued prior to April 1971 that when owned by a decedent at the time of his death could be redeemed at face value in satisfaction of federal estate taxes, even though they had a current market value at the time below face value.

fluctuations. Rapid changes in security prices. *See* **minimum fluctuations**.

flurry. A short period of rapid trading in a security or in the entire market, causing either higher or lower prices, generally resulting from sudden business news or a significant event, for example, a presidential election result.

focus group. In an evolving marketing program conducted by or for a vendor of consumer goods or services, a preselected sample of individuals that is representative of the consumers in the market that the vendor wants to reach. New ideas for products, services, and advertising are developed by the vendor, using opinion inputs from the members of the group.

folios. A reference to the investment product concept introduced in 2000 of enabling investors to select the stocks or stock categories for inclusion in a basket or batch of stocks, which they own directly and manage themselves. It can provide the diversification of a mutual fund, supplemented by the benefits of investors managing the shares for personal tax advantages and retirement alternatives. Usually, the brokerage charges a flat advisory or trading fee monthly. A typical amount for retail customers is $29.95.

follow-through. A continuation of a market rally after a holiday or weekend.

FOMC. Abbreviation for **Federal Open Market Committee.**

food chain, economic or **business.** A reference to a chain reaction in the business world, in which the purchases of one or more companies that supply similar materials or products are made because they are filling purchase orders from one or more companies above them in a serial process of producing or processing a final product. This is an analogy to a food chain in nature, in which every living organism is dependent for food on devouring another group or one lower in the food chain. In the business world, at the top of the chain are the major industries, usually manufacturers or processors. When the management of one decides to turn out a new product line, it sets off a sequence of buying, as many components of that product line are ordered. Automobile makers, for example, are at the top of a food chain that consumes components from steel makers, aluminum makers, plastics extruders, glass makers, textile mills, rubber producers, electronic suppliers, microprocessor suppliers, electrical equipment, and so on. When interruptions, such as labor strikes, occur at any level of the business food chain, the entire chain can be shut down. It is analogous to the effects on whales when the nourishment that feeds the sea life they consume disappear from the sea. When demand for a final product changes, the fortunes of every vendor in the chain is impacted. It is important that investors recognize the primary business food chains to appraise the risks of supply disruptions on the stocks of included companies. *See* **input-output model.**

Foods. Those stocks representing companies engaged in processing and distributing various foods for public consumption. *See* **industry stock group.**

footnotes to financial statements. Those statements and data expressed as footnotes to the financial statements, usually found in corporate annual reports, that expand on certain accounts significantly: for example, accounting policies, such as the inventory valuation method; lease obligations; depreciation schedules; debt schedule; descriptions of common stock or preferred stock classes, when appropriate; contingent liabilities; stock options issued; asset delineation; business segment analysis, and so on. Often, highly controversial items are assigned to the footnote section of the annual report by the FASB. This means the savvy investor should check them out closely. *See* **Financial and Operating Data in Annual Report.**

"footprint." In venture capital terminology, a sign that a company has established itself as one of the favorites for success, in a developing but potentially profitable technology or process. Although such a company usually represents a highly speculative investment, its head start in matters like brand recognition, marketing networks, or patent filings make it one of the most likely to achieve financial success.

Footsie Index. Abbreviation for the **FT-SE 100** or *Financial Times*-London Stock Exchange index.

Forbes Magazine **Online.** See under **Web Sites for the Inquiring Investor.**

forecast. An estimate or prediction of the magnitude of future events, usually involving a combination of statistical extrapolation and guesswork by the forecaster. It is a technique used by securities analysts, economists, credit analysts, and corporate planners developing assumptions about future conditions. For more detail, See **projection.**

forecast feedback. The tendency for a well-known forecast of some future economic or business event to materialize as predicted, because so many people believed the forecast initially that their consequential actions accomplished the predicted result. For example, if influential leaders in the investment industry forecast a downturn in the stock market, their argument might be strong enough to persuade so many investors to sell on balance that the overall market does sell off.

forecasting stock market or **valuation model, stock market.** A mathematical system for anticipating the direction and level that stock market prices in general will take in the future, or for calculating a present reasonable value for those prices. A forecasting or valuation model is a finite explanation of a complex event. It is not a perfect explanation, but a working one, and one intended to be updated as new relevant factors are observed. Adherents of forecasting models believe that they are more often correct in making investment decisions than a "seat of the pants" philosophy. A good model has been tested against historical results so that pure mathematical pedantry is rejected. It should be added that a good model need not be complicated, but it should improve your chances over time of forecasting effectively. Perhaps the most important contribution a good model makes to the investment process is to instill a disciplined approach that is not dependent on ebullient bull markets for success. Forecasting models, skillfully used, encourage rational decisions. Baron Rothschild, the legendary Paris financier, surely must have used some sort of model, for when asked how he made so much money in the stock market, he answered: "By selling too soon."

There are many stock market forecasting and valuation models, and more are being invented daily, almost as fast as financial Web sites are created. Most advanced spreadsheet software programs offer forecasting models or applications that enable the user to forecast financial events. Mathematically-inclined investors can develop their own, thereby giving themselves the added advantage of preventing a model's popular use from watering down its effectiveness, through a phenomenon called **forecast feedback.** A commitment to the time required for updating and refining the model is important. Generally, a model is an extrapolation of a trend, using a time series like a stock market index; a present or future capitalization of financial valuation measures like yields or P/E multiples; a correlation of related economic and business statistics, like corporate profits and stock prices; or a combination of the above. Today the investor can save time and energy and improve accuracy by using one of the forecasting applications in a good spreadsheet program. Software designers like Lotus 1-2-3, Mirosoft Excel, or

Corel Quatro Pro are examples. In addition, calculator makers like Hewlett-Packard and Texas Instruments offer forecasting and extrapolation programs built into their machines. With so many statistical applications available in ready-to-calculate software, it now seem prehistoric for investors to create them from scratch, unless special shadings or insights are the objectives.

As an example, one modeling technique employs stock market and capital market indices to evaluate or forecast the stock market. This model is popular with certain Federal Reserve officials and some Wall Street economists. It assumes there is a direct relationship between the yields on U.S. Treasury 10-year bonds and the rate of earnings growth of the companies comprising the S&P 500 Stock Index. The capitalizations of these major companies constitute 85% of the total stock market value, so it is a very appropriate surrogate for the stock market. In the model, the premise is made, based on prior observations, that when yields on Treasuries go up, the S&P Index will go down, and vice versa. Treasury bond prices and the S&P Price Index tend to move in opposite directions, although not simultaneously, in adjusting to yields demanded by investors. Inherent in the advocacy of the model is that stocks and bonds are in competition for investors' money. When Treasury bond yields are high, that attracts money from stocks, lowering their prices and raising their yields. When Treasury bond yields are low, money is attracted away from them into stocks, which raises yields on the former, lowering values, and jacking up stock values. Here is the equation for the EPS/Yield Model.

$$V = (S\&P/EPS_{500} \div TY_{10}) \times 100$$

where:

V = stock market value or level;

$S\&P/EPS$ = earnings per share of S&P 500 Index;

TY = yield on 10-year Treasury bond, expressed as a percentage.

Plugging in numbers to illustrate this model, when the EPS of the S&P 500 is expected to be $55 and the yield on 10-year Treasuries is 4.25%, the valuation for the S&P Index in the current year is or should be 1,294 ($55 ÷ 4.25% or .0425). If the current market is way off this mark, maybe it's time to change strategy. Note that such a model can be used to establish a reasonable level for the market currently or forecast the level, once one of the variables begins to break out of a traditional ratio with the other. Touching on the importance of testing a model, if it does not approximate market levels in the past, when the variables for the S&P earnings and Treasury bond yields are substituted, it is doubtful it can do so in the future, in which case it is a scurrilous or useless model. It is important to remember that a statistical correlation or association is based entirely on past observations. *See* **regression.**

forecasting, stock price. The attempt to predict the market price of a particular stock as of a future date, in order to estimate the capital appreciation from currently purchasing the stock. There are numerous methods of forecasting, all involving degrees of dependability; however, the following four techniques are representative and enjoy a certain prestige in the financial world, a skeptical place in which acceptance of any mathematical analytical technique is noteworthy.

1. *Earnings multiple projection.* This method has become the most popular one. In the calculations, annual earnings-per-share for a stock is estimated for the contemplated year of sale. This EPS is multiplied by the "normal" price/earnings multiple for the stock, which estimates the market price in the year of sale. In selecting a normal price/earnings multiple, a five-year average can be used, in lieu of the current one to inculcate long-term realism into what might be a currently distorted multiple. It is wise to include some slow years in the process, if possible. Future earnings can be estimated by calculating average earnings-per-share gains over a recent span, say five years, and adding that average gain to the most recent year's actual EPS. It is not necessary to include slow years in this case, because the momentum of recent years is likely to continue one year, at least.

  The validity of using P/E multiples to evaluate a stock's price has diminished, with a study issued in 1998 by Baruch Lev and Paul Zarowin of the Stern School of Business at New York University. The study indicates that over a 20-year period that covered the 1970s and early 1980s, there was a decreased correlation between earnings and stock prices, by one-half. In the study, stocks of 5,000 companies were used. The decreased correlation also applied to cash flows and book values. The authors of the study have concluded that stock price volatility has increased because investors are more uninformed on the fundamentals about their holdings, largely because of a trend toward significant and unexpected charges to income, like write-offs. Such a conclusion implies that quantitative measures like prices to earnings, cash flows, and book values have also become less important in stock decisions. One alternative to those traditional methods of evaluation, which are usually considered long term, is the rapid reaction to news by investors, news that is often not highly important in the long term.

2. *Probability analysis.* This method of forecasting is usually a computerized system that includes the construction of mathematical price-movement models to fit the stock market. These models provide for the psychological shifts of investors as well as technical market movements. Whenever a stock that is programmed deviates from the model even slightly, a probability of the price change and rate of change is established. Some advisory services advertise an 80% accuracy record.

3. *Square root rule.* Briefly, the plan is based on the theory that in periods of rising market prices equal increments are added to the square roots of stock prices, and conversely, in periods of declining market prices, equal amounts are subtracted from the square roots of stock prices. Although the idea is no longer as applicable, because stock splits have destroyed some of the proportions, many analysts claim it still has uses. For example, suppose at the beginning of a bull market Sky Rocket, Inc. common stock is priced at $36 and Whoosh! Corp. at $64. According to this theory, if Sky Rocket rises to $81 (the square root has risen from 8 to 9), then Whoosh! Corp. should rise to $49 (the square when its square root of 6 is increased by 1 to 7). Obviously, forecasting in this manner is based on every stock participating

in broad market moves, or a Wall Street version of the quote, "A rising tide lifts all boats."

4. *Beta values.* This technique of stock price forecasting has developed from statistical studies showing historically that stock price changes have a certain relationship to price changes in the total stock market as measured by a stock market index or average. For example, if a stock's Beta Value is 1.10 then the price of that stock would be expected to move 10% more than the general market; if the Beta is 1.20, it could move 20% more; if the Beta is .90, it might move 10% less; and so on. If the Beta is 0, forget it, there is no market connection. When forecasting using this technique, the forecaster must make an assumption about how much the market will change and apply the Beta value of a particular stock to this assumption. Beta values are available from sources like Value Line Investment Service. The problem in using Betas is that they are not stationary over the long term, which means that Betas change between investment periods, sometimes considerably.

foreclose, to. To set in motion legal action that will liquidate property held as security for a debt in the event of a default in payments by the debtor.

Foreign Corrupt Practices Act. A federal law enacted in 1977 forbidding the bribing of a foreign official by a representative of a U.S. corporation, in order to secure a contract. It is enforced by the SEC.

foreign crowd. Brokers dealing in foreign bonds on the New York Stock Exchange.

foreign exchange. 1) A rate of converting one currency into another. For example, in early 1998 Canadian dollars were convertible into American dollars at the rate of .6988 (Canadian) to $1.00 (United States). This meant that if a United States businessman had a check for $1,000.00 drawn on a Canadian bank, he would receive credit for only $700.00 rounded off, or 70%, from his bank. For investors, fluctuating foreign exchange rates is one of the risks in buying foreign securities. When the investor buys or sells the securities, the amount paid or received is the price of the stock in the foreign country times the conversion rate of that currency into dollars, minus trading costs and applicable taxes in the case of a U.S. investor. Conversion tables appear in many metropolitan newspapers and other media. In a free market, they are determined by supply and demand. In a regulated market, the government or central bank regulates them. There is a flip side to this risky business. The foreign exchange fluctuation, while considered a risk, can also be an opportunity. Let's say an investor in the United States buys the Mexican stock, Bull Ringers, S.A. on the Bolsa for 100 pesos per share on June 30, 1998 when the exchange rate is 0.1116 dollars per peso. The cost would be $11.16 per share, plus trading costs. Over the following year, if the exchange rate fell to 0.15555 pesos per dollar, and the investor sold, the receipts would be $15.55—a $4.49 profit per share profit from the foreign exchange conversion before trading costs. Ole! 2) A claim on a bank for a specific amount of foreign currency.

Foreign Sales Corporation (FSC). An entity formed by a U.S. exporting company in one of 32 countries and U.S. possessions designated by Congress, in order to legally avoid federal corporate income taxes on a portion of the revenues from those exports. The company directs the records for those sales through its FSC, in order to limit taxes. Popular sites for the location of FSCs are Barbados, Guam, and the Virgin Islands. This strategy saves U.S. companies $8 to $10 billion annually in income taxes. It is considered by many a blatant form of corporate welfare. *See* **Shared Foreign Sales Corporation** and **Foreign Sales Corporation Provisions of U.S. Tax Code.**

Foreign Sales Corporation Provisions of U.S. Tax Code. A set of IRS regulations that grants corporate income tax relief to domestic corporations that export through subsidiaries domiciled offshore. In order to be eligible for this tax relief, a U.S. company must engage a minimum proportion of direct costs from foreign countries, including advertising and records processing. In late 1999, the World Trade Organization (WTO) declared these provisions unlawful on the grounds they provide illegal subsidies to U.S. corporations involved in international trade. The United States has appealed the decision. If an appeal does not reverse the decision, presumably the U.S. Congress will be called on to amend the provisions or repeal them.

Form 3, SEC. A report filed with the SEC by corporate directors or officers or stockholders owning more than 10% of a company's stock, when they make their initial purchases.

Form 4, SEC. A report filed with the SEC by those filing Form 3, when they buy additional shares in the same corporation.

Form 5, SEC. For those filing forms 3 and 4, an annual report filed with the SEC of their holdings in companies covered in those forms.

Form 8-K, SEC. A report filed with the SEC by a company in the event a significant corporate event occurs before the next 8-K or 10-K is filed.

Form 10-K, SEC. The annual report that most public corporations that have issued stock traded actively in the United States must file with the Securities and Exchange commission (SEC), within 90 days of the close of the fiscal year unless an extension has been granted. The report is sometimes also sent to the stockholders, usually embellished with commentaries on the corporation's accomplishments and future expectations. Although the 10-K filing contains specific and complete items relevant to an investment decision about a company, it is not a recommendation to buy or sell securities. Rather it is intended as a document presenting information an investor needs to make a rational decision. Often a company sends a separate annual report to shareholders, which usually extols management's performance and outlook, while providing useful items relevant to the investment process. The 10-K is a cut-and-dry, no-nonsense presentation, while the shareholders' annual report is more likely an entertaining presentation of text and graphics on management philosophy and data. The 10-K requires inclusion of the following subjects: The company's business scope, resources, legal matters, stock market matters, historical financial data, stock market information, capital structure, management discussion of operations, financial statements, auditing matters, directors, management remuneration, and possible conflicts of interest among management and third parties. In extreme cases, annual reports to stockholders can be so embellished that they take on a "coffee table" status. But the reading is only as good as the results posted by the company. The **Annual Report to the Stockholders** includes most material in the SEC version, so see that topic for more details.

Form 10-KSB, SEC. The alternative SEC annual report for small companies, abbreviated but requiring much of the same information as the 10-K.

Form 10-Q, SEC. An abbreviated version of the 10-K for a fiscal quarter, filed with the SEC at the close of each of the first three quarters of a company's fiscal year. Often, this document or some variation of it serves as the stockholders' quarterly report.

Form 12B-25, SEC. A request to the SEC by a company for a delay in filing a required corporate report, like a 10-K or 10-Q. When finally filed, "NT" is affixed to the title of the delayed report.

Form 13-D, SEC. A notification to the SEC by a large investor, such as an institution, that its management intends to try to influence the corporate policies and decisions of a company of which it owns 5% or more of the stock outstanding. Most institutional investors are passive, satisfied to let managements of companies operate free of interference. This form indicates a big investor is tired of waiting for results but cannot gracefully exit the investment or believes that it could turn into a winner with some advice. It has turned active.

Form 5500, SEC. A report that must be filed with the U.S. Labor Department annually by large pension funds, disclosing what securities and other assets are in the fund's portfolio.

Form S-1, SEC. A report to the SEC by a company registering new securities, usually an initial public offering or secondary issue. There are other "S" forms used for registrations associated with mergers, employee stock option plans, and real estate investment trusts. When foreign companies make these types of registrations, the prefix is "F," followed by a number.

Form S-4, SEC. A registration and report to the SEC of information for use by a company's stockholders in deciding whether to approve or reject a merger plan.

Form-T. A filing required by the National Association of Securities Dealers including information on transactions in stocks after regular trading hours.

forming a base. A flattening-out of wide price fluctuations in securities prices until prices are firm for a period long enough for investor confidence to return and an orderly advance to begin.

formula investing. The making of investment decisions based on a predetermined dollar relationship between stocks and bonds, or stocks and savings in the case of average investors. (For purposes of this discussion, the term fixed-income asset will be used to indicate savings, bonds, debentures, notes, or any assets in which dollars invested are preserved in quantity.) Although formula investing can be simple or complex, all formulas have as their elemental objective the automatic sale of stocks when prices are relatively high and vulnerable to decline, usually as indicated by a historical stock index, and the purchase of stocks when prices are relatively low. The proceeds are converted to a fixed-income asset until stock prices decline to an established level in the same index, at which time they are reacquired with money taken from liquidation of a portion of the fixed-income investment.

The result of an effective formula is that profits are taken in a high stock market and stocks are bought cheaply when the market is low. Consequently, the hazardous practice of continuous forecasting can be modified since a formula requires systematic changes in the portfolio, although most institutions using formulas regard them as supplements to personal judgment.

There are many variations of investment formulas; however, most can be placed in the following three categories:

1. *Constant-dollar formula.* In this plan, the amount of money invested in stock is kept at a specific dollar value. Adjustments in the portfolio can either be periodic or when

a market index reaches a certain level. Of the investment formulas, the constant-dollar plan is less likely to fortify the investor against changing market situations, although it is the simplest to operate. Most experts agree that adjusting should occur when a stock index reaches a predetermined level. The reason adjustments under all the formulas need to be correlated to an index is that these indicators better signify when the entire market is vulnerable to a decline than do prices of a limited number of stocks in a portfolio.

The constant-dollar formula has two disadvantages as revealed in studies of the market: (1) The system restricts profits if begun at a low market price level, because in a bull market common stocks tend to be liquidated too early in their rises; and (2) the system depletes a modest portfolio if a high level is selected to begin, because fixed-income assets will be exhausted as they are quantitatively liquidated to buy stocks in the declining market. Thus, it is important to begin at a "normal" price level, a difficult task considering the myriad factors, psychological and economic, that affect stock prices.

2. *Constant-ratio formula.* In this plan, the dollar ratio between stocks and fixed-income assets is adjusted periodically (usually quarterly) or at certain market levels to predetermined percentages. The ratio is usually constant regardless of the market level, but it can be made to reduce stocks as the level rises. For instance, if a 50-50 balance is desired quarterly, at the close of each quarter the total value of the stock would be calculated, and enough sold or bought to restore the 50% stock portion.

Of course, a conservative investor would change the ratio to emphasize fixed-income assets; perhaps 30% stock and 70% fixed-income would be more to his liking. As mentioned above, adjustments are more effective when pegged to a market level as represented by a stock index. Many institutions adjust portfolios when an industrial stock index changes by 20% or more instead of waiting for the next quarter. Studies show that the constant-ratio formula enables the investor to participate in bull markets, while at the same time protecting him to a degree from serious price declines. Its flexibility has attracted many institutions.

3. *Variable-ratio formula.* In this plan, the ratio of stock in a portfolio is adjusted to maximize stock purchases at low prices and minimize their acquisition at high prices. There are more formulas of this type in use than any other, although many have been discontinued. (Unfortunately, formula investing seems to be abandoned in long-term bull markets.) The main difficulty with this type is that a market "norm" must be selected, i.e., a price level considered realistic. But here is a guide. A norm is a magical moment in the stock market when there is as much being said and written about the prospects for more growth as there is about prospects for slower growth. It is an emotional and psychological equilibrium as far as stock prices go. In this formula, the ratio is made to change as price levels fluctuate above and below the norm, so that a smaller percentage of stock is held as the price level ascends.

Although the variable-ratio formulas are theoretically the most complete, the accurate selection of the norm makes implementation of them challenging. Although a norm may be selected by experienced observation, there are three methods of computing a norm mathematically: the trend-line method; the moving average method; and the intrinsic-value method. Briefly, here is how each is developed:

A. The trend-line method is an attempt to project a market index several years into the future. The projection is based on economic growth rates and market tendencies; sometimes, even inflation is considered. The projection is considered to be the norm, and deviations of the actual index from the projection form the ranges or zones in which the various ratios govern the portfolio content.

B. In the moving-average method, an arithmetic average is taken of market index numbers over a reasonably long period—often the quarterly average over a 10-year period is used—dropping the first index number and adding the most recent one each time. Thus, in a norm developed from a moving average using quarters over a 10-year period, the total of quarterly numbers is divided by 40 (number of quarters). The moving average provides a more realistic norm than a fixed average because the results are continuously moving in the direction of the actual long-term price trend.

C. The intrinsic-value method was designed by analysts who believe that the level of stock prices is inherently correlated to intrinsic stock values like earnings and dividends. Some ratio is conceived measuring this correlation, which becomes the norm. One such technique for finding a norm was advanced by the dean of securities analysts, the late Benjamin Graham, who called his system the Central Value method. To calculate the norm, the investor divides the average earnings on stocks used in the Dow Jones Industrial Averages for the past 10 years by twice the current interest rate on Moody's high-grade (Aaa) bonds, and multiplies the result by 100—the result is the Central Value. Under his system, when the Dow Jones industrial "average" reaches 120% of this Value, all stocks are sold; stocks are reacquired when the average declines to 80% of the Value.

Most of the variable-ratio formulas observe the "halfway rule." This is a requirement that stocks only be purchased as the index moves away from the norm, a stipulation designed to prevent the purchase of stocks when a price level drops slightly from a questionable high level. Unfortunately, formulas that are dependent on a norm are often out of timing with the market, since indexes do not move precisely with the norm. Most analysts contend, however, that the current index eventually becomes correlated with the norm and, thus, investment actions based on deviations from this number benefit a portfolio in the long term.

Fortune 500 company. A reference to a company selected among the top 500 in the United States by *Fortune* magazine in an annual survey, on the basis of their size in several parameters. The selection is a prestigious attainment, in that the list of 500 companies is a mark of distinction among investment professionals. There are several measures used in the rankings, including sales, net income, total assets, stockholders' equity, share earnings growth for 10 years, investment return to investors for latest year, and total investment return to investors over 10 years. The survey includes separate rankings in the indicators.

***Fortune* 500 Index.** A common stock index, created by *Fortune* magazine and developed by its editors in the year 2000, that tracks stock prices of those stocks selected for inclusion in the annual tabulation by the magazine of the financial characteristics of the largest corporations in the United States. The Chicago Mercantile Exchange is licensed to trade futures and options contracts in the index.

***Fortune* E-50 Index.** A common stock index, created by *Fortune* magazine and developed by its editors in the year 2000, that tracks stock prices of companies serving the Internet economy. The Chicago Mercantile Exchange is licensed to trade futures and options contracts in the index.

***Fortune* Online.** See under **Web Sites for the Inquiring Investor.**

Forward Looking Statements in the Annual Report or **Safe Harbor.** Under the terms of the Private Securities Litigation Reform Act of 1995, statements made by management in a press release or report that involve known and unknown risks and uncertainties which may cause a company's actual results in future periods to differ materially from forecasted ones. These risks are described in the company's **Annual Report to the Stockholders** and its Form 10-K filing with the SEC.

forward price/earnings multiple. The current market price of a common share divided by its estimated earnings per share in one or more future years. Many money managers shun stocks priced at more than three times their forward earnings growth rate. For example, let's say analysts estimate that Socko Fine Hosiery, Inc., priced at $15 per share, will earn $0.50 in the next fiscal year. The forward P/E multiple is 30×. If earnings are estimated to grow 20%, compounded annually over the next three years, some investors would consider the stock attractive, since it is priced at less than the three-year growth rate (.75 of the rate). *See* **Price/Earnings Ratio or Multiple** and **price/earnings growth multiple.**

forwards. See **futures.**

401(k) Plan. A retirement plan that allows an employer to make an annual pretax contribution of up to $10,000 and an employee to contribute 15% of salary or wages. A participant vests 100% immediately in employee contributions, while vesting in the employer's contributions may be graduated over seven years. The pretax feature on contributions is very important. It allows the investor to contribute 100% of an amount that otherwise would be taxed. For example, an investor in the 28% marginal tax bracket could contribute or get a tax credit for $100 before income taxes by contributing to a plan or receive only $72 after taxes by not contributing. These plans are portable to other employers and provide a great deal of investment flexibility. Usually, when funds are withdrawn early, there is a 10% tax penalty. There are three types of 401(k) plans: (1) enhanced thrift programs, (2) cash or deferred option profit sharing plans, and (3) salary deferral savings plans. See **Individual Retirement Account.** This plan is suitable for entities in the following circumstances:

- Organization is profit or nonprofit and not a government entity.
- There are more than 25 participants.
- Flexibility in contributions is desirable.
- Matching employee contributions is an objective.
- Exclusion of part-time employees is desired.
- Selection of vesting schedule other than 100% by employer is important.
- Loan and hardship withdrawal privileges for participants are preferred.
- Employee contributions on a tax-deferred basis is objective.

403(B)(7) Plan. The equivalent of a 401(k) retirement plan for a nonprofit enterprise. It is available to public educational institutions, churches, and church-affiliated employers, and other nonprofit organizations under the Internal Revenue Code (IRC). Generally, employers organized for charitable, scientific, educational, or religious pursuits are possibly eligible, but not all of these are. Participation is voluntary. Participants in such a plan contribute by making pretax payments from their paychecks. The pretax feature on contributions is very important. It allows the investor to contribute 100% of an amount that otherwise would be taxed. For example, an investor in the 28% marginal tax bracket could contribute or get a tax credit for $100 before income taxes by contributing to a plan or receive only $72 after taxes by not contributing. Maximum contributions are spelled out in the IRC. Employers also are allowed to contribute through matching allocations. Employees vest in their contributions immediately; the employer's contribution can be graded over seven years. When employers also contribute, additional record keeping and disclosure is required. This plan might be a good choice under the following conditions:

- Entity is educational, religious, or nonprofit in nature.
- Employer wishes to match contributions.
- Employer wishes to select vesting schedule.
- Loan or hardship withdrawal privileges are desirable.
- It is an objective for employees to contribute on a tax-deferred basis.

fractional pricing. The use of fractions in quoting the prices of securities under $1.00, rather than decimals: 10½ rather than 10.50. This procedure was the historical method that lost favor as **decimal pricing** advanced. Decimal pricing, already popular in foreign stock markets, recently became the official method in the United States when the Securities Industry Association (SIA) initiated decimal trading on July 3, 2000.

fractional share. 1) A mutual fund purchase of less than a full share. Most mutual funds sell fractional shares to three digits. 2) A stock distribution, usually resulting from a stock dividend, in which a shareholder is issued less than a full share, called **scrip,** which the corporation will generally exchange for cash. 3) Under the monthly investment plan of the New York Stock Exchange, a purchase of less than a full share of stock by an investor who must accumulate 20 full shares before he is issued a stock certificate.

"Frankenstein foods." A derisive nickname for foods processed from agricultural crops that have been genetically modified. The name was chosen to suggest the potential horrific effects on humans who consume such foods. That strategy was adopted by those criticizing their use, even though the U.S. Food and Drug Administration has approved the process.

"Frankenstein stocks." A reference to stocks engaged in the agribusiness of making Seeds for crops that have been genetically engineered or modified to make plants more pest resistant, more hearty, or more productive.

Frankfort DAX Index. A stock price index of leading German companies.

Frankfurter Wertpapierbörse (FWB). See under **Global Investment Market.**

fraud. See **Internet fraud** and **investment fraud.**

fraud, securities. Acts of engaging in false representations or manipulative practices when buying or selling securities.

Freddie Mac. Nickname for the **Federal Home Loan Mortgage Corporation.**

free-carry. A reference to a situation when the interest rate to borrow money to buy a security is offset by income from the security.

freeEDGARonline. A Web site featuring free access to corporate SEC filings. *See* under **Web Sites for the Inquiring Investor.**

free-form management. A corporate managerial team heading up a conglomerate corporation. Generally, a free-form group maintains a flexible business philosophy and endeavors to emphasize return on investment rather than product orientation, in pursuing corporate acquisitions and mergers in diverse industries. These corporate planners provide financial service and advice to division profit centers in the conglomerate complex. The control and planning is centralized but the operating functions are decentralized in the divisions.

free market. A reference to over-the-counter stock prices that are determined by supply and demand for stock, rather than underwriters' bidding the price up to give the stock firm market support, as they can legally do after marketing a new issue.

free reserves. In the U.S. banking system, the amount by which aggregate excess reserves deposited by member banks in the Federal Reserve system exceed their borrowings from the Federal Reserve to meet reserve requirements.

free-riding. The practice of buying stock with expectations of paying for it out of proceeds from its sale. The New York Stock Exchange prohibits this by requiring the exchanging of checks. *See* **exchanging checks.**

free-wheeling. The description of a stock that has broken a previous high and is trading in a new price range. Analysts who chart stock prices regard the eventual price level of a stock in this situation as unpredictable since there is no automatic supply of the stock from anxious shareholders that would impede the price rise.

"friends and family shares." See **directed shares.**

front-end sales load. The charges to investors for buying shares of a mutual fund in a contractual accumulation plan payable on the initial purchases of shares, leaving small equity for the investor in cases where the plan is terminated early. A typical example would be 4% to 5% of the purchase amount. Such shares are also called A-class shares. Of the three types of sales loads—the other two are **level sale load** and **back-end sales load**—the level rate is the lowest and usually cheapest for the investor if the shares are held less than three years. In judging the alternatives, a great deal depends on the fund's performance.

front running. As a broker or trader in the securities or commodities business, the unethical and illegal practice of using information gained in advance, such as from a forthcoming research report, to take a position in a security or commodity, with the object of selling out at a higher price when the information becomes public. There is a distinction between this information and **insider information** in that the latter represents information not scheduled for public dissemination.

frozen account. A foreign financial account impounded by the government where the account is located.

frozen index fund. A fixed portfolio of stocks that does not change as a result of a fund manager's decision or because component companies are merged or liquidated in taxable transactions. There is a tax advantage to such a fund, since it distributes to shareholders only ordinary cash dividends but never taxable capital gains. In the United States a taxable investor defers capital gains present indefinitely, sometimes allowing heirs to benefit from the tax-free step-up in basis at the original buyer's death.

FSC. See **Foreign Sales Corporation.**

FTC. Abbreviation for the **Federal Trade Commission.**

FT-SE 100 Index (Footsie Index). A stock price index of the 100 largest companies listed on the London Stock Exchange, based on market capitalizations, maintained by the *Financial Times.*

FT-SE 250 Index. A stock price index of the 101 to 250th largest companies listed on the London Stock Exchange, based on market capitalizations, maintained by the *Financial Times.*

"fudge factor." In economic model building by a securities analyst, economist, credit analyst, or corporate planner, the use of intuition to adjust the statistical projection to allow for surprises or changes in the underlying data. *See* **projection.**

full disclosure or **disclosure.** The revealing of all relevant financial information about a security as it pertains to the represented company's operations, stock market performance, commissions on an underwriting or distribution of shares, sales loads, fees, and so on, as outlined by federal and state laws. In a sense, it is the process of making a company transparent to investors, so that they can make informed investment decisions about that company's securities. Companies accomplish this responsibility through media releases, visitations, and meetings. In meeting the requirements of securities laws, it is important that companies communicate the same information at the same time to the investment public. This prevents one set of investors from obtaining an informational advantage. In August 2000, the SEC made simultaneous disclosure to all shareholders mandatory. Previously, certain investors, such as large institutions, often received preferential treatment in receiving information. Most companies are complying with this regulation using simultaneous Web casts of conference calls with securities analysts. *See* **selective disclosure.**

full-service brokerage or **broker.** A brokerage business that offers investors a complete line of investment services, provided continuously by employees or partners, including: effective trading capabilities, securities research and analysis, potential to participate in new stock and bond issues, asset management, tax-sheltered investments, check-writing privileges, and other broad investment and financial planning products. Because the complete line of services requires more experts and specialists, and more administrative costs, commission costs and fees are higher than discount brokers charge. It is important for the investor to realize that the broker and the brokerage firm usually make money on every phase of the services, including trading profits on buying and selling securities for customers, but not the actual commissions, which usually are profitable during periods of high share volume. In comparing full-service brokers with others, the investor should keep in mind that full-service brokers monitor accounts regularly for potential investment action, and so there is a personal touch. A caveat to this observation, however, is that any broker's biggest accounts, in terms of asset values, get the most and sometimes only attention. *See* **deep-discount brokerage** and **discount brokerage.**

fully-diluted earnings per share. Net income available for common stock, divided by common shares outstanding, adjusted for the effects of any residual securities—warrants, options, convertibles, and so on—which could be exchanged for common stock if the holders so desired, and thus providing the potential to reduce earnings per share.

"fully-funded." A reference to a company's capital expenditures program or purchase of capital assets that is paid for by cash flow from company operations. No additional debt or equity financing is needed for the purchases or commitments.

fully-paid and non-assessable. A reference to stock for which the original subscribers paid at least the stated par value and that may not be assessed to meet obligations of the corporation in case of insolvency.

funded debt. 1) For municipalities and states, securities such as bonds or notes, on which some fund is appropriated for the payment of interest and principal when due. The appropriation can be specific or general, such as in the appropriation of future taxes or public revenues. 2) For corporations, a debt owed on money borrowed to repay miscellaneous unsecured debts or debts manifested by short-term notes or secured bonds, thus substituting a new debt for them. This new debt, the funded debt, is secured by a general mortgage, a series of bonds, or an issue of stock, usually maturing in the distant future, and frequently at a lower interest rate. 3) That debt represented by bonds or long-term notes (5 years or more).

funded pension plan. A reference to a pension fund in which monies have been designated and reserved that are adequate for meeting the current and future retirement benefit obligations of the plan sponsor or employer. Funding of plans is closely watched by the Department of Labor under ERISA. In the footnotes of annual reports, corporations are required to show the condition of their pension or retirement plans, in terms of whether it is adequately funded or not. *See* **Employee Retirement Income Security Act (ERISA).**

funding bonds. Those bonds sold to raise money to pay current debts. Thus, many short-term debts are converted into long-term bonds.

"funny money." An unflattering reference to the use of new securities with questionable value or some other noncash, ill-conceived payments by a purchaser who is trying to buy or merge another company without giving up anything of real or comprehensible value. Although it is a humorous term, there are times in frothy bull markets when "funny money" deals appear, presumably because during those periods investors become gullible and tend to believe all securities are drenched with value.

FUTA. Abbreviation for **Federal Unemployment Tax Act.**

futures or **forward contracts.** Contractual agreements to buy or sell specific amounts of interest rates, currencies, commodities, or stock indexes, at certain dates in the future for specific prices. There is presently a federal ban on trading futures contracts in individual stocks, a ban established in 1982 when regulatory standards for trading stock index futures were enacted. However, there is presently a bill before Congress allowing such trading. Neither the SEC, which regulates securities trading, nor the Commodity Futures Trading Commission (CFTC), which regulates commodities trading, will likely regulate the proposed stock futures market. Rather, an electronic trading market, much like NASDAQ, is planned. Futures trading is popular with traders because of the leverage. Usually a 5% to 10% margin is required, so that on a $50,000 contract, $2,500 to $5,000 is paid to the investment firm. If the value of the underlying entity doubles, to $100,000, the trader sells, pays off his debt of $47,500 or $45,000, and makes the difference less trading and interest costs. Usually futures contracts trade on exchanges, while forwards trade in the over-the-counter market.

FYE. Shorthand for "fiscal year ending," when followed by a date. It is used when reporting a company's financial and operating results.

Gg

G7. See **G8.**

G8. A reference to an annual meeting along with interim planning and activities by the heads of state or government of the eight major industrial democracies in the world—France, the United States, the United Kingdom, Germany, Japan, Russia, Italy, and Canada. The conclave, originally called **G7**, was formed in 1975, except for Russia which was added later, hence G8. It has consistently dealt with macroscopic management, international trade, and relations with developing countries. Matters like post-Cold War economic relations, energy and terrorism have also been of recurring concern. Beginning in 1994, the G7 and Russia met as the P8 (Political 8), following each G7 summit. The agenda of P8 excluded financial and certain economic issues.

G-37 rule. An SEC rule that prohibits bond dealers, investment executives, and their firms from donating more than $250 to state and local officials who have the power to award them underwriting business.

GAAP. See **Generally Accepted Accounting Principles.**

"GAAP." See **"Growth at Any Price."**

GAINS. See **zero-coupon convertibles, municipals.**

game theory. The theory of how intelligent individuals interact with one another in an effort to achieve their own goals. Although the theory is used mainly in economics and psychology, there are increasing applications of it to the stock market. Basically, the application is to consider investors as players in a game, and calculating how they will react to various stock market situations.

GAO. Abbreviation for **General Accounting Office.**

gap. A space caused by no overlapping of price ranges on two successive days, on a chart. A series of gaps can be classified as follows, but experts claim they are meaningful only on a daily chart.

1. Breakaway gap. A gap of two points or more with good volume after a period of stability and inactivity.
2. Measuring gap or runaway gap. Following a breakaway gap, a bigger gap that chartists claim indicates the price move is 40% to 50% complete.
3. Exhaustion gap. A gap that indicates a sudden price move is over. If after an extraordinary advance, a stock gaps into a new high range and then drops to the bottom of that day's range, the advance is probably over, according to charting devotees.

"GARP." See **"Growth at a Resonable Price."**

GASB. (Pronouced "GAZ-BEE") Abbreviation for **Governmental Accounting Standards Board.**

GATT. See **General Agreements on Tariffs and Trade.**

GDP. Abbreviation for **Gross Domestic Product.**

"geared." See **"leveraged."**

Gee Whiz! factor. A late-breaking information item on a stock that would be expected to affect the stock's price as soon as the market assimilates the news.

General Agreement on Tariffs and Trade (GATT). An ad hoc, defunct agreement of the 1940s adopted by interested countries for conducting international trade in goods, replaced by the World Trade Organization (WTO) in 1995.

General Accounting Office (GAO). Established by the Budget and Accounting Act of 1921, this independent auditing office is charged with examining all matters relating to the receipt and disbursement of public funds. The office is under the control and direction of the Comptroller General of the United States, who is appointed by the president with the advice and consent of the Senate for a term of 15 years. The primary responsibility of the GAO is to support the Congress, through audits and evaluations of federal government programs and activities. Most of these audits are made in response to specific congressional requests. The office is required to take on projects assigned by congressional chairpersons, but responds to other members when possible. There are other assignments performed under agreements with standing committees or required by law. The capacity to examine practically any government function requires a staff schooled in many disciplines. Consequently, the GAO staff includes experts in accounting, law, public and business administration, economics, social sciences, physical sciences, and others. Address: 441 G Street NW, Washington, DC 20548. Web site: *www.gao.gov.*

Generally Accepted Accounting Principles (GAAP). Those accounting conventions, guidelines, and rules recommended by the Financial Accounting Standards Board (FASB) to be used in the U.S. in the preparation of financial documents, such as balance sheets and income statements. The principles are used by the SEC in regulating domestic securities markets.

general obligation bonds. Those bonds sold by a municipality that has agreed to pay the bond interest and principal from general taxes, if necessary.

General Services Administration (GSA). See **agency securities.**

Geneva Stock Exchange. See under **Global Investment Market.**

geometric mean. An average or typical value that tends to describe a set of data. It is less impacted by extreme values among the items used in the computation than other averaging techniques. In measuring business and financial results, this trait is the main reason for its preference over the arithmetic mean. On the other hand, the fact that you cannot use negative values or a zero as the root or a negative among the items in the averaging limits its usefulness. In any series of items, it is always smaller than the arithmetic mean. *See* **average, statistical.**

Georgia Office of the Secretary of State. Regulator of securities laws in the state of Georgia. Address: Securities Division, 2 Martin Luther King, Jr. Drive, #802 West Tower, Atlanta, GA

30334. Phone (information): (404) 656-2895. Phone (complaints): (404) 656-3920.

Ghana Stock Exchange. See under **Global Investment Market.**

gift. See **gift tax.**

gift tax, federal. A federal tax on the value of gifts of personal or real property, including securities, in excess of $600,000 ($1 million starting in the year 2006). The tax ranges up to 57%, after certain allowances. A donor is allowed to give away up to $10,000 per individual each year tax free. This exclusion is indexed for inflation.

gilt-edged investment. A bond issued by a company with a continuous record of 10 to 20 years of excellent earnings and uninterrupted payments of debts.

"gimmick." A slang term for a callable and/or refunding clause of a bond. *See* **callable bonds** and **refunding.**

Ginnie Mae. See **Government National Mortgage Association.**

GIPS. Abbreviation for **Global Investment Performance Standards.**

give out. As a broker receiving an order, to turn it over to a colleague for execution.

give up. As a broker receiving an order from another broker's customer for convenience, to split an exchange commission with the regular broker.

GKOs. Short-term notes issued by Russia, denominated in rubles.

glamour stocks. That group of applied science stocks that have enormous market-gain potential if their sales and earnings increase rapidly, which keeps the market spotlight on them. These stocks are highly fluctuating, generally, because of their unpredictable earnings—past and future. But since their products emanate from new technology, the growth curve is starting at a low base and, therefore, the potential is much greater than for companies in mature industries.

Glass-Steagall Act. Named after its sponsors in the Congress, Senator Carter Glass and Representative Henry Steagall, the reference actually refers to the Banking Act of 1933. This act was partially amended by the Financial Services Modernization Act of 1999. The Glass-Steagall Act restrained commercial banks from doing investment banking business. It also provided the basis for legislation that would authorize the Federal Reserve Bank to allow banks to engage in the securities business in a limited way. The Act was deemed necessary after more than 11,000 U.S. banks failed or had to merge by 1933, during the Great Depression, reducing the number of active banks by 40%. The Act established new approaches to bank regulation—such as deposit insurance and the separation of commercial banking and investment banking—with the exception of permitting commercial banks to underwrite government-issued bonds. It is interesting to note that within two years of passage of the Act, Senator Glass led a group for its repeal, believing it was overreactive. However, no other banking legislation was passed by Congress until the Bank Holding Act of 1956.

Reflecting the hard-driving times during the 1980s and 1990s, as commercial banks became more global in scope they also moved into securities underwriting and distribution. Rather than using changes in federal law to accomplish this, they did so under the aegis of regulatory bodies, such as the Federal Reserve and Comptroller of the Currency. By 1996, there were 3,641 insured banks, or about one-third of the total, selling mutual fund shares or annuities. Of these, 115 banks sold proprietary fund shares. Assets in bank funds totaled $454 billion, 15% of the $3 trillion mutual fund market. *See* **Bank Holding Act of 1956** and **Financial Services Modernization Act of 1999.**

Global Investment Market. A reference to the unification of major securities and commodities exchanges and markets of the world into one trading presence through the facilities of the worldwide Internet. An investor can now access nearly every investment market on the planet, using a PC, a modem, and an Internet connection. What one gets is a kaleidoscope of markets, in terms of monetary size and investment products. Global exchanges represent a range of total market capitalizations from a few million dollars into the trillions. Products include equities, debt instruments, derivatives, metals, commodities, including futures contracts, in most of those markets. The cyberspace investment market is a fledgling, having accelerated in importance rapidly; consequently, it includes developing countries with rudimentary trading systems and industrial nations with more complex and sophisticated markets and traditional ways of doing business.

GLOBAL SECURITIES EXCHANGES

Securities Exchange/ Language (besides English)	Internet Address
Alberta Stock Exchange	*www.alberta.net*
American Stock Exchange	*www.amex.com*
Amsterdam Exchange	*www.aex.nl/scripts/ finance/aexhome.asp*
Arizona Stock Exchange	*www.azx.com*
Athens Stock Exchange	*www.ase.gr*
Australian Stock Exchange	*www.asx.com.au*
Barcelona Stock Exchange	*www.borsabcn.es*
Beirut Stock Exchange	*www.lebanon.com/financial/ stocks/index.htm*
Bilbao Stock Exchange/Spanish	*www.xcse.dk*
Bogatá Stock Market/Spanish	*www.bolsabogata.com.co*
Bombay Stock Exchange	*www.bseindia.com*
Boston Stock Exchange (BSE)	*www.bostonstock.com*
Botswana Stock Exchange	*http://mbendi.co.za/exbo.htm*
Brazil Commodities & Futures Exchange	*www.bmf.com.br/imdexenglish.asp*
Bucharest Stock Exchange	*www.rasdaq.ro/news/eng/new.html*
Budapest Stock Market/Hungarian	*www.fomax.hu/fmon/index.html*
BVRMB Regional Stock Exchange (Africa)	*http://mbendi.co.za/exch/brvm/index.htm*
Buenos Aires Stock Exchange	*www.bcba.sba.com.ar/cell2_a.htm*
Cairo & Alexandria Stock Exchange	*http://mbendi.co.za/exeg.htm*
Caracas Stock Exchange	*www.caracasstock.com/*
Casablanca Stock Market (Morocco)	*http://mbendi.co.za/exmo.htm*
Chilean Electronic Stock Market / Spanish	*www.bolchile.cl/portada.htm*

Chicago Board of Exchange	*www.cboe.com*
Chicago Board of Trade	*www.cbot.com/index.html*
Chicago Mercantile Exchange	*www.cme.com*
Coffee, Sugar & Cocoa Exchange	*www.csce.com/cscehome.cfm*
Copenhagen Stock Exchange	*www.xcse.dk/uk/index.asp*
Cuba (CyberCuba)	*www.cybercuba.com/*
Securities Exchange	*cubaexchange.html*
Dar es Salaam Stock Exchange	*http://mbendi.co.za/extu.htm*
(Tanzania)	
EASDAQ Stock Market	*www.easdaq.be*
Finnish Securities Exchange	*www.som.fi*
Frankfurter Wertpapierbörse (FWB)	*www.exchange.de/fwb/fwb.html*
Geneva Stock Exchange	*www.bourse.ch*
Ghana Stock Exchange	*http:ourworld.compuserve.com/*
	homepages/khaganu/stockex.1.htm
Guayaquil Stock Exchange (Ecuador)	*http://www4.bvg.fin.ec/eng/*
	beige2.asp
Helsinki Stock Exchange	*www.hse.fi/english_index.html*
Hong Kong Futures Exchange	*www.hkfe.com*
Hong Kong Stock Exchange	*www.sehk.com*
Indian Stock Exchange (India)	*www.nseindia.com*
Istanbul Stock Exchange	*www.lse.org*
Italian Stock Exchange	*www.borsaitalia.it*
JASDAQ (Japan)	*www.jasdaq.com*
Johannesburg Stock Exchange (JSE)	*http://mbendi.co.za/exjs.htm*
Kampala Stock Exchange (Uganda)	*http://mbendi.co.za/exug.htm*
Korea Stock Exchange	*http://.kse.or.kr*
Kuala Lumpur Stock Exchange	*www.klse.com.my/*
Lagos Stock Exchange (Nigeria)	*http://mbendi.co.za/exng.htm*
Lisbon Stock Exchange	*www.bvi.pt/main.shtml*
Lima Stock Exchange	*www.bvl.com.pe/homepage2.html*
London International Financial	*www.liffe.com/home/index.htm*
Futures & Options Exchange (LIFFE)	
London Metal Exchange	*www.lme.co.uk*
London Stock Exchange	*www.omgroup.com*
Ljubljana Stock Exchange (Slovenia)	*www.ljse.si/html/eng/kazalo.html*
Lusaka Stock Exchange (LuSE)	*http://mbendi.co.za/exza.htm*
(Zambia)	
Luxembourg Stock Exchange	*www.bourse.lu*
Madrid Stock Exchange	*www.bolsamadrid.es*
Malawi Stock Exchange	*http://mbendi.co.za/exma.htm*

Maputo Stock Exchange (Mozambique)	*http://mbendi.co.za/exmz.htm*
MATIF—Commodities	*www.matif.fr/N4.htm*
Mauritius Stock Exchange (SEM)	*http://mbendi.co.za/exmr.htm*
MEFF Village—Financial Derivatives	*www.meff.es*
Mexican Stock Exchange/Spanish	*wysiwyg:/main.6/* *http://www.bmv.com.mx*
MidAmerica Commodity Exchange	*www.midam.com/main1.htm*
MIF—Interest Rate Derivatives	*www.borsaitalia.it*
Minneapolis Grain Exchange	*www.mgex.com/top.htm*
MONEP– Equity & Financial Derivatives	*www.monep.fr*
Montreal Stock Exchange	*www.me.org*
Nairobi Stock Exchange	*http://mbendi.co.za/exke.htm*
Nicaraguan Stock Exchange	*http://bolsanic.com*
Oslo Stock Exchange	*www.ose.no*
Nagoya Stock Exchange	*www.iijnet.or.ip/nse-ip*
Namibian Stock Exchange	*http://mbendi.co.za/exna.htm*
NASDAQ Stock Market (U.S.)	*www.nasdaq.com/welcome.html*
New French Exchange	*www.nouveau-marche.fr/* *bourse/nm/homenm-fr.html*
New York Board of Trade	*www.nyce.com/page000.html*
New York Mercantile Exchange	*www.nymex.com/home.htm*
New York Stock Exchange	*www.nyse.com*
New Zealand Stock Exchange	*www.nzse.co.nz*
Paris Stock Exchange	*www.bourse-de-paris.fr*
Pacific Exchange	*www.pacifiex.com*
Philadelphia Stock Exchange	*www.libertynet.org/PHLX*
Prague Stock Exchange	*http://stock.eunet.cz/index_e.html*
RASDAQ Stock Market (Romania)	*www.rasd.ro*
Rio de Janeiro Stock Market/ Portuguese	*www.bvrj.com.br/paina.htm*
Russian Exchange	*www.fe.msk.ru/infomarket/* *ewelcome.html*
Russian Trading System	*www.rtsnet.ru/default.stm*
Santiago Stock Exchange	*www.bolsantiago.cl/imgles/* *index.htm*
São Paulo Stock Exchange	*www.bovespa.com.br/home_i.htm*
Shanghai Metal Exchange	*www.sh.com/exchange/* *shme/shme.htm*
Shanghai Stock Market	*www.comnex.com/stock/stocks.htm*

Singapore International Monetary Exchange (SIMEX)	*www.simex.com.sg*
Singapore Stock Exchange	*ses.com.sq*
South African Futures Exchange	*www.safex.co.za*
Spanish Financial Futures & Options Exchange (MEFF)	*www.meff.es*
Stockholm Stock Exchange/Swedish	*www.xsse.se/www/ welcome.nsf.Dokument.Index? OpenDocument*
Swaziland Stock Market	*http://mbendi.co.za/exsw.htm*
Swiss Exchange (SWX)	*www.bourse.ch/iswxhome.htm*
Sydney Futures Exchange	*www.sfe.com.au/Presentation*
Taiwan Stock Exchange	*www.tse.com.tw*
Tehran Stock Exchange (Iran)	*www.neda.net/tse*
Tel Aviv Stock Exchange	*www.tase.co*
Thailand Stock Exchange	*www.set.or.th*
Tokyo Stock Exchange	*www.tse.or.ip/eindex.html*
Tunis Stock Exchange	*http://mbendi.co.za/extu.htm*
Toronto Stock Exchange	*www.telemium.ca*
Vancouver Stock Exchange	*www.vse.ca*
Vienna Stock Exchange	*http://apollo.wu-wien.ac.at/ cgi-bin/boerse/.pl*
Warsaw Stock Exchange	*gopher://plearn.edu.pl:71/ 11/roznosci/ekonomia*
Winnipeg Commodity Exchange	*www.telemium.ca/WCE*
Zagreb Stock Exchange (Croatia)	*www.zse.hr*
Zimbabwe Stock Exchange	*http://mbendi.co.za.exzi.htm*

Global Investment Performance Standards (GIPS). Ethical standards for advancing, on a worldwide basis, the cause of fair representation and full disclosure of investment performance results. These standards were adopted by a GIPS Committee, composed of 24 investment organizations around the world. Primarily, they deal with the preferred methods of presenting portfolio performance results, and are mainly for the use of investment counselors and money managers who endorse comparisons with others on a global basis. They were introduced in 1999 by the Association for Investment Management and Research.

GLOBEX Alliance. The world's first electronic trading network for futures and options contracts, sponsored by the Paris Bourse SA (Paris Stock Exchange), the Chicago Mercantile Exchange, and the Singapore International Monetary Exchange (SIMEX). It enables the three founders to trade each other's contracts around the clock. *See* **Paris Stock Exchange, Chicago Mercantile Exchange,** and **Singapore International Monetary Exchange** in **Global Investment Market.**

GM. Abbreviation for food that has been genetically modified. This process is highly controversial internationally, with European markets resisting the importation of such foods.

GNP. Abbreviation for **Gross National Product.**

going-concern statement. A reference to the explanatory paragraph in an external auditor's opinion of a company's financial statements that is intended to inform interested parties of whether the company is viable and will continue as a "going concern." In fulfilling that purpose, it has been found to be unreliable in 50% of the cases, and accountants and financial executives have taken up the matter for study to see if possible changes should be made in the future.

"gold-carry trade." Among international investors and traders, the trading strategy of borrowing gold from a bank and selling the gold to buy securities that pay more in interest than the cost of borrowing the gold—in the United States in 1999 the differential was as much as 4% at times. When the price of gold declines, as the trader hopes it will, the trader can sell the securities and buy gold to repay the gold loan with increased money available, profiting from that difference and the interest differential. However, if the price of gold rises, the gold repayment becomes more expensive and the carry might represent a loss. In addition, the value of the securities purchased can affect the profitability of the trade. When the securities decline in value, the proceeds of their sale will buy less gold to repay that loan. If the securities appreciate, the reverse will be true. *See* **"carry trade"** and **"yen-carry trade."**

gold clause. A clause in an international financial contract calling for payment in gold.

golden handcuffs. The conveyance to key executives of valuable incentives, such as stock options, at terms so favorable as to keep the executive from leaving. Such a person is considered critical to a high performance by the board and investors in general.

golden parachute. Special retirement or severance benefits provided executives who are being displaced in a takeover by another company. In a hostile takeover, the benefits are usually voted by the target's board; in a friendly takeover, the acquiring company might do so to garner support within the takeover target.

Goldilocks economy. Generally upbeat economic activity over a sustained period, without inflationary pressures, quashing the need for monetary restraint or stimulus by the Fed or fiscal restraint or stimulus by the federal government.

"gold mine." An investment that has made money for an investor on several occasions.

Gold Mining shares. Those stocks representing companies engaged in the mining, processing, and marketing of gold. These stocks attract speculative investors whenever there is talk of devaluation of major international currencies or other unsettling economic events. *See* **industry stock group.**

gold standard. A national monetary system recognizing gold as a medium of exchange or measure of value.

good delivery. *See* **delivery.**

good-till-canceled order (GTC). An investor's order to a broker to buy or sell units of a certain security, most often at a specific price, until it is canceled or executed.

good volume. A description of active trading on an exchange as compared to average days. On the New York Stock Exchange, 25,000,000 shares per hour is very active. Active trading in an individual security makes market gain more possible. On the other hand, it can accelerate losses.

Goodwill. An intangible asset, usually representing the worth of a company's reputation, to which some companies assign a value on their balance sheets, especially when they pay more than the book value for an acquisition. In this case the excess is shown as "Goodwill" on the balance sheet, and must be amortized by annual charges to income until eliminated. However, if the acquirer uses **pooling of interests** in accounting for the purchase, no Goodwill account need be established. A company can take three to 40 years in amortizing Goodwill, depending on the nature of that asset. There is an exception to this requirement under current accounting guidelines. When the excess paid for an acquisition represents "research in process," the entire amount may be written off currently. This eliminates the long-term drain on earnings. "Research in process" is defined as research costs not yet converted into marketable products. There can be a very significant value to Goodwill. When it has never been carried on the books or has been fully amortized, it can even be considered a hidden asset. When a company enjoys a reputation for quality and/or solid value in its product line, it has a substantial advantage when introducing new products. That is Goodwill as any toothpaste maker will tell you.

Here's the way it works. Bad-DreamWorks, Inc., a movie and video production company, pays $100 million for Julio's Studios, L.P., a high-tech production facility. The net book value for Julio's is $75 million, which means Bad-DreamWorks must show $25 million on its balance sheet as Goodwill. The company's eagle-eyed accountants would determine the appropriate amortization schedule—ranging from three to 40 years—establishing the annual amortization charges. But there is a chance the $25 million can be regarded as Research in Process, since its graphic designers are immersed in a project to morph halos above the heads of all candidates for political office for TV spots. In this case, Bad-DreamWorks could deduct the entire $25 million in the year of the acquisition, and start a clean slate. Investors forgive big write-offs when they buy clean slates and unbounded hopes.

gorilla stock. A stock that combines so many important assets and dominates such lucrative markets that it has become awesome in the eyes of investors, and therefore it represents a company feared by weak managements vulnerable to involuntary buyouts or mergers.

Governmental Accounting Standards Board (GASB). Organized in 1984 by the **Financial Accounting Foundation (FAF),** GASB establishes standards of financial accounting and reporting for state and local government entities. Its standards guide the preparation of financial reports of those entities. The Foundation selects members of GASB and its Advisory Council, funding their activities, and exercising general oversight. The standards promulgated provide accountability to the public, and are the basis for investment, credit, and many regulatory and legislative decisions involving government entities.

The mission of GASB is to establish and improve standards of state and local governmental accounting and financial reporting that will (1) result in useful information for users of financial reports and (2) guide and educate the public, including issuers, auditors, and users of those reports.

Government bonds. Those long-term federal obligations—five years plus—bearing interest. The bonds are issued by the U.S. Treasury and are considered the safest investment in the United States, if not the world. The federal government can use its general taxing powers to redeem the bonds.

Government crowd. The brokers dealing in United States securities by vocal trading on the floor of the New York Stock Exchange.

Government National Mortgage Association or **Ginnie Mae.** A federal agency that offers investors mortgages guaranteed by the federal government under mortgage-interest subsidy programs to create additional mortgage funds. *See* **agency securities.**

graduated tax system. See **progressive tax system.**

Graham, Benjamin. The founder of modern securities analysis and coauthor of the seminal book on the subject, *Securities Analysis.* He advocates a logical approach to the valuation of common stocks, as opposed to buying and selling them impulsively. His advocacies include that a stock is worth the present value of its future dividends. Overall, his methodologies imposed discipline on stock decisions and established intrinsic values for stocks. Besides working on Wall Street, he was a teacher at Columbia University. Among his students was Warren Buffett, the premier investor in the United States. *See* **"Graham-Dodd."**

"Graham-Dodd." A reference to the classic book *Securities Analysis* by Benjamin Graham and David Dodd. It was originally published in 1934, and has been expanded in five editions. Nearly 1 million copies have been sold. This book was the basis for modern securities analysis, with its accent on quantitative methods to establish the evaluation of common stocks.

Gramm-Leach-Bliley Act. See **Regulatio S-P, SEC.**

gray iron castings. A reference to the industry engaged in producing automobile engine blocks, construction pipe, iron plumbing fittings, and industrial dies. These products are basic to the production of most durable goods, and orders for them reflect the level expected in the consumption of autos, appliances, and so on.

"gray list." An informal roster of corporate clients that an investment banking firm circulates among brokers, indicating that such stocks should not be traded, because a public offering or some other event is imminent, which could impact the company's stock price. Trading on such information in advance of public knowledge could make the firm's brokers "insiders," and guilty of securities fraud.

gray market. The selling of manufactured goods at a deep discount in foreign markets for later import and resale in the manufacturer's domestic market, in an unchanged condition.

grease. Exorbitant commissions paid to salespeople engaged in a fraudulent stock operation.

"Greater Fool Theory." A reference to the attitude of mindlessly buying a stock or stocks that are overpriced by historical standards, in the belief that some future buyer will pay even more for the shares without any better justification.

greenmail. A reference to a corporation or its agent buying back its common shares from one or more new stockholders who are threatening a takeover of the corporation. This practice was prevalent during the 1980s, when corporate warfare often got hostile and predatory. In response, a federal law was enacted imposing a 50% tax on any gain or other income received by anyone exercising greenmail.

green sheets. See **National Daily Quotation Service.**

"grinding." As an online trader, trying to make many small profits through executing many trades.

gross capital. A reference to total capitalization.

Gross Domestic Product (GDP). A measurement representing the broadest aggregate economic activity of a country. In current or real terms for the U.S., the total market value of the output of goods and services produced by labor and property located strictly in the U.S., but for which suppliers of resources and labor used may be either U.S. or non-U.S. residents. It is an aggregate estimated and published quarterly by the Bureau of Economic Analysis (BEA) of the Department of Commerce. GDP is part of the National Income and Product Accounts (NIPA) system in the U.S. BEA also generates special industrial GDP measures, such as auto and truck output. In January 1992, BEA substituted the GDP concept for the GNP concept, although there is not a great deal of difference in the aggregates. Globally speaking, GDP is the total market value of the goods and services produced in a nation before depreciation, depletion, and so on. It includes private, as well as government purchases, gross private domestic investment, but not net foreign investment. The table below aggregates the elements of Gross Domestic Product into its major components. *See* **Gross National Product** and **National Income and Product Accounts.**

GROSS DOMESTIC PRODUCT AND ITS COMPONENTS
($/BILLIONS)

Account	Change (%)	1999	1998
Gross Domestic Product	5.7	9,254.6	8,759.9
Personal Consumption Expenditures	7.00	6,257.3	5,848.6
Gross Private Domestic Investment	6.00	1,622.9	1,531.2
Net Export of Goods and Services (Mil)	70.8	(255.5)	(149.6)
Government Consumption, Expenditure and Gross Investment	0.01	1,529.8	1,529.7

Source: Department of Commerce (Bureau of Economic Analysis)

Gross Income. The total amount of monies received or accrued by an individual, professional group, or financial institution in a fiscal period before expenses and costs of conducting business, for professional entities, are deducted. In the case of individuals filing income taxes, it is total income or receipts in a tax year, which is modified to Adjusted Gross Income (AGI) in order to calculate taxes due. *See* **Adjusted Gross Income** and **Standard Deduction.**

gross in the business. The dollar amount of proceeds to an investment firm per share, in an underwriting or special exchange distribution. A portion goes to the salesperson.

Gross National Product (GNP). In current or real terms for the U.S., the total market value of the output of goods and services produced by labor and property supplied by U.S. residents, but for which suppliers of resources and labor used may be either U.S. or non-U.S. residents. Economists consider this and the **Gross Domestic Product** the most important gauges of economic activity in a country, because they represent the broadest measure of activity and spending. It becomes **Net National Product** after allowances for depreciation and consumption of capital are subtracted. For the U.S., GNP is estimated quarterly by the Bureau of Economic Analysis (BEA) of the Department of Commerce, and was the principle estimate of aggregate economic activity in the U.S. until January 1992, when it was supplanted by the concept of Gross Domestic Product (GDP). BEA made the substitution, in order to draw a closer comparison with international data on the subject.

The basic formula describing Gross National Product is GNP = C + I + G + X (X - M), where: C = Consumption, the most important sector in the U.S. economy, comprising 56% of the total; I = Investment, mostly real investment, like residential and non-residential construction, comprising 14% of the total; G = Government Spending, contributing 17%; (X - M) = Exports minus Imports, with Exports adding to GNP and imports subtracted from GNP. Most of the time in the U.S., imports exceed exports. A rise in GDP or GNP tends to lower values of fixed income securities and raises common stock prices and dollar exchange rates. A decline in GDP or GNP tends to raise values of fixed income securities and lowers common stocks and dollar exchange rates. *See* **Gross Domestic Product.**

gross revenues or **gross sales.** Total monies received or accrued from running a business before deductions for returns or allowances but after adjustments, discounts, sales taxes, and related excise taxes and cash discounts. It is the genesis of the revenue stream from a business enterprise that, hopefully but not necessarily, ends as income or earnings for the investors. In everyday parlance, gross sales is most often used in retail or wholesale operations, while gross revenues is most often associated with manufacturing operations.

Group of Eight. See **G8.**

Group of Seven. See **G7.**

growth. See **growth stock** and **growth formula.**

"Growth at a Reasonable Price ('GARP')." This is a reference to buying stocks at prices close to average valuations or historically in line with expected growth as defined by price/earnings multiples, book values, dividend yields, cash flow multiples, or other valuation techniques. It represents a situation in which investors can expect a reasonable rate of return from a stock investment, commensurate with the risk. *See* **GAAP.**

"Growth at Any Price ('GAAP')." This is a facetious reference to buying stocks at prices that are above average valuations or historically out of line with expected growth as defined by price/earnings multiples, book values, dividend yields, cash flow multiples or other valuation techniques. It represents a situation in which investors cannot realistically expect a reasonable rate of return from a stock investment, unless the market continues to value a stock without reference to general norms. *See* **GARP.**

growth formula. An approximated method for estimating the future profits and consequent market price of a stock. *See* **implied growth rate** and **discounted value.**

growth stock. A stock representing a company whose earnings and other investment values are growing faster than the national corporate average, and that is generally plowing its earnings into self-expansion, giving the stock great potential future value. A company whose earnings are increasing at a rate in the range of 10% to 15% or greater, compounded annually, has represented an excellent growth situation historically in the United States. As long as inflation remains moderate, that ought to be a very respectable rate in the future also. When measuring a company's growth, the financial data should be adjusted for inflation, so that the growth factors are isolated from the effects of general economic conditions. An alternative is to use an indexing system that measures physical units sold or shipped each year, but this only reveals marketing progress and not financial performance. In the early stages of a growth company's life, financial volatility should be expected, but at some point a successful company should commence a rhythm of expansion that lasts for several years. Correctly perceiving when a growth period is ending allows an investor to take money out before the stock loses its shine.

In view of the high income-tax schedule and lower capital-gains schedule, many growth companies are achieving growth by using earnings to invest in strategic assets or to buy other companies, rather than declaring and paying out dividends. Consequently, the value of the acquiring company's stock rises by the earnings value or net asset value of the acquisitions, and the stock, if held for 12 months plus a day and sold, is taxed on the lower capital-gains schedule. One of the paramount traits of a growth stock is manifested in this tendency: growth investors commit to the stewardship of the corporate managements of the stocks they own to grow their investment assets, rather than to dividend payments that they could reinvest. Of course, the personal income tax reduces the dividend income paid out of a company's earnings, so it's not a level playing field.

It is important not to confuse stock market performance with growth, although growth or prospects for it usually beget stock market performance. Growth is an investment package, usually containing actual or prospective attractive increases in revenues, earnings, corporate resources, and stockholders' equity, to name just a few important elements that should be present. Furthermore, growth should be recurring for five years or more, although the averaging concept is allowable, in these cases. Acceleration in a lesser time frame suggests that some sort of fad has impersonated growth. Bona fide growth should be based on supplying some economic need with products and services that represent new or improving ideas or technologies. Often, growth equities are found in subindustries that are developing niche markets too small for jumbo companies to enter. But one of the bonuses of discovering this genre of stock is that a jumbo will acquire the sleek greyhound, when its critical mass is big enough. This scenario is nurtured by the company's reinvestment of earnings, to stay competitive in charting new frontiers. Investors should feel that their growth stocks will be on the cutting edge for awhile, or else the high valuations those stocks typically command could disappear and spoil the chances for handsome returns in the future. *See* **capital gain** and **cyclical stock.**

GSEs. See **agency securities.**

GTC. Abbreviation for **good-till-canceled order**.

guaranteed accounts. Those brokerage accounts that have been guaranteed as to payment of debts by a third party.

guaranteed stocks and bonds. Those securities with interest and/or principal or dividends guaranteed generally by a third party's leasing of property for amounts, which will enable the security issuer to pay dividends or interest or principal to the security holder. However, sometimes a parent company will guarantee certain aspects of a subsidiary's securities, such as interest on bonds or dividends on preferred stock.

guerilla marketing. A reference to the emerging marketing technique of using personal confrontation with prospective buyers by product representatives, encompassing the use of proactive and imaginative strategies, in order to gain product recognition or increase market share over competitors. One type of guerilla marketing is the use of "street teams" to confront prospects outside, say in a line for a rock concert, and distribute samples or brochures of their employer's competitive disks or concert announcements. Another function of street teams could be to distribute written advertising or samples of food, supplemented with brief personal commentary, to those attending a festival where eating is a paramount activity. The advantages of this form of marketing over conventional kinds is that niche markets and their prospective customers can be identified, accessed, and marketed to directly. The essence of this new marketing art form is simplicity, directness, and mobility.

Guayaquil Stock Exchange (Ecuador). See under **Global Investment Market.**

guidance line. See **line of credit.**

Hh

halfway rule. See **variable ratio formula** under formula investing.

Halloween Indicator. A reference to the tendency for common stocks in the United States to increase more in market value from November through April than from May through October, as reported by Mark Hulbert in his "Strategies" newspaper column. In a study conducted by Ibbotson Associates, a research firm in Chicago, large-cap stocks returned 4.9 percentage points more, on an annualized basis, between November 1 and April 30 than they did between May 1 and October 31. In the case of small-cap stocks, during November through April they returned 18.2 percentage points more. The study covered stock prices year end, from 1925 to 1998. The results are even more impressive when one considers that the two market crashes in the period—1929 and 1987—were removed from the calculations. In a related study concluded for 36 stock markets outside the United States, Sven Bouman, a portfolio manager in the Netherlands, and Ben Jacobson, an economist at the University of Amsterdam, recently found a similar pattern. The explanation for this seasonality is that investors often sell stocks before taking vacations and buy stocks when they return. Broadly speaking, the vacation season is from May 1 to November 1.

Hang Seng Index. A Hong Kong stock index, listing stocks in that geographic region.

Hanseatische Wertfalische Hamburg. A stock exchange in Hamburg, Germany. Address: Chauenbergerstrasse 47 2000 Hamburg 11.

hard assets. In a company's portfolio of resources, usually listed in its balance sheet, those items that represent physical or mechanical objects. Examples are buildings, machinery, inventory, real estate, vehicles, furniture, and mineral deposits. From an investment viewpoint, the stated values of these assets are more reliable, because they have usually been purchased as opposed to developed internally; they have a resale value to competitors or an economic value can be calculated. However, as the U.S. economy evolves more and more to an information society, involving greater amounts of intellectual properties and other **soft assets**, the investment importance of hard assets is diminishing.

hardball. A corporate policy toward competitors that is based on aggressive tactics, such as trying to squeeze out displays of a rival's products in retailing.

hard currency. 1) Any money backed by gold. 2) Any currency freely convertible into other currencies.

Hardware & Tools. Those stocks representing companies producing equipment and tools used in small construction and repair jobs. *See* **industry stock group.**

Hart-Scott-Rodino Antitrust Improvement Act of 1976. A Federal law requiring that any corporate acquisition exceeding $15 million be filed with the U.S. Justice Department, for approval or expiration of a waiting period.

Hawaii Department of Commerce and Consumer Affairs. Regulator of securities laws in the state of Hawaii. Address: Securities Commission, P.O. Box 40, Honolulu, HI 96810. Phone: (808) 586-2730.

head and shoulders. A price pattern made by recorded high-low-close bars on a stock bar chart, or as Xs and Os on a point-and-figure chart. Chartists say the main price move after the breakout will be similar to the distance upward in the middle portion or "head" of the pattern, in the opposite direction. The same reasoning applies to a pattern with the head extending down. If the peak of the head is $20 per share higher than the breakout level, the downward decline will be $20 after the breakout. In the case of an upside down head-and-shoulders chart, the opposite reasoning would apply or a $20 increase.

"head fakes." In online trading markets, a reference to big traders trying to create the illusion of movement in a stock's price.

headline inflation. A reference to rises in the cost of living that are not endemic to an economic system, thus likely to be temporary or short term in duration. Such increasing cost-of-living forces can be increases in the prices of agricultural products, commodities like oil, or sharp reduction in supplies of specific goods. They are fragile price increases, difficult to maintain and, therefore, less likely to cause permanent or core inflation than price increases that are permanent or long term in duration. However, because they are popular consumer items, they might get a great deal of media attention, hence the name. *See* **core inflation** and **inflation.**

Health Care—Diversified. Those stocks representing companies providing a broad range of health care services. *See* **industry stock group.**

Health Care—Drugs. Those stocks representing companies making and distributing medicines and drugs for health care providers and the public. *See* **industry stock group.**

Health Care Providers. Those stocks representing companies engaged in the sector providing health care products and services. *See* **sector.**

Heavy Duty Trucks & Parts. Those stocks manufacturing large transport trucks and their replacement parts. *See* **industry stock group.**

heavy hitter. In a brokerage firm, a leading salesperson in terms of commissions generated from securities transactions. Generally, a broker with a personal share from commissions generated amounting to $1 million.

heavyweight, market. A stock representing a corporation with many common shares outstanding (100,000,000 plus), annual revenues of $10 billion or more, and backed by a strong financial position; a corporate giant; a stock with price movements considered so significant that it influences investor trading actions.

hedge. In securities trading, to offset or reduce a possible loss by buying and selling securities likely to rise and fall in opposite directions under the same conditions. By way of illustration, if a speculator decides to sell short 100 shares of Sizzle Inc. stock at a price of $50, he might simultaneously buy a call to buy 100 shares of Sizzle at $50. Then, if the stock does decline in price, say to $40, he buys to cover his short sale, pocketing $10 profit per share, less trading costs and the call price. On the other hand, if his forecast has been faulty, and Sizzle rises, he would exercise his call to buy 100 shares at $50 for delivery on his short sale, losing only trading costs and the call price.

hedge clause. See **disclaimer.**

hedge fund. A pool of investment capital, usually organized as a limited partnership. Generally, the fund consists of a relatively small group of investors who make sizable initial contributions, frequently above $100,000, and as high as $500,000 or $1 million. Since 1997, mutual funds have been allowed to sell stock short so that there are now quasi-hedge funds that only require a $1,000 initial investment. A conventional hedge fund, run by one or more general partners, uses the speculative techniques of margin buying, options strategies, and short selling to register capital gains for the fund members. Generally, hedge fund managements charge 1% to 2% of assets annually and 20% of gains. Presently the asset value of hedge funds in the United States is approximately $350 billion, where 2% of public funds, 15% of big corporate pension funds, and 33% of endowment funds make hedged investments.

hedging against inflation. In periods of rising prices, the purchase of equities that are rising in value because of potentially high corporate profits, rather than fixed income investments, which diminish in value as measured by less buying power. Inflation ultimately depresses stocks, however, so this concept has definite limitations.

Helms-Burton Act or **Cuban Liberty and Democratic Solidarity Act.** A federal act signed into law in 1996 that is designed to discourage non-American companies from doing business or investing in Cuba, when such business or investment would utilize formerly American facilities seized by the present Cuban government.

Helsinki Stock Exchange-*Helsingin Arvopapereriporssi.* Address: Fabianinkatu 14, SF 00131, Helsinki. *See* under **Global Investment Market.**

hemline indicator. The tongue-in-cheek belief that when the hemlines of women's skirts go up, so do stock prices, and when hemlines go down, so go stock prices. It's not MBA material, but at least it does not skirt the issue.

hidden asset. In the practice of securities analysis, the discovery of a resource not carried or assigned a realistic value on a company's balance sheet. This can be the justification for increasing a company's stock worth, since presumably the asset could be sold or otherwise employed for obscured gains separately or in the event of a merger or liquidation by the company owning the resource. Such resources usually take the form of real estate or securities that have escalated in value, or unexploited manuscripts, inventions, and natural resources. However, this process is tricky, and can lead to hyperbole in describing a stock. It is always possible the resources are shown at minimal values, because they are worth those or less!

high. The highest price paid for a security in a period.

high finance. A phrase describing operations in corporate financial affairs and security management on a grand scale.

high flier. A stock that is trading at an extraordinarily high price, based on a traditional valuation technique like the P/E multiple or the Price/Book Value, and one that is usually very volatile because investors are uneasy with the high unsupported price level.

High Grade Common. Those stocks representing companies with proven records of revenues and earnings growth. *See* **industry stock group.**

"high-risk" audit. In the parlance of securities regulation, a special request by securities regulators made to an auditing firm to apply special scrutiny in the audit of the books of a company under a cloud of suspicion for securities law violations. It usually accompanies a filing by the company to offer more shares to the public.

High Tech Composite. Those stocks representing the sector engaged in providing highly technical products and services in such fields as electronics and imaging. *See* **industry stock group.**

high tech industries. See **sector.**

high yield bonds. See **junk bonds.**

"hindsight bias." In a statistical analysis of an investment manager's performance, a reference to using historical data that is not germane to that manager's decisions during certain periods of the analysis horizon. In doing so, when the manager's performance is below standard, it could be attributed to a hindsight bias in the analysis. For example, a mutual fund that focuses on hot Hungarian goulash stocks in the year 2000 that is compared with one that chooses stocks randomly over the past 25 years by backwards tracking is disadvantaged by hindsight bias. Over the entire period, Hungarian goulash stocks were not hot, and most likely would not have been selected then by the epicurean's portfolio.

historical sales approach. A reference to a mutual fund sales presentation that emphasizes a period in which the general economy prospered and was reflected in the growth and income from mutual fund shares, inferring that the same thing will happen in the future. In terms of what sort of material should be included in sales literature issued by mutual funds, the SEC has come down hard on "misleading statements." For that reason, fund managements try to present a complete description of past and expected results.

historical trading range. The price range, in terms of lowest prices and highest prices, and sometimes opening and closing prices, during regular intervals—daily, weekly, monthly or yearly—since a stock's initial public offering. By studying the ranges and patterns, an investor can get an idea of how others have valued the stock over time and under various market conditions. If the stock's price moves into a new territory, it would seem logical that investor sentiment has changed, which is often a signal for the investor to buy or sell shares.

"hits per quarter." See **dot-com stock.**

"hold." A stock once recommended for purchase by an investment firm reclassified to one of retain and watch. This commentary usually is applied to a stock that has reached a full or overvalued price and one the firm does not wish to publish a "sell" on for fear of offending the company's management and consequently jeopardizing corporate finance business in the future.

holder. One who owns securities or notes.

holding company. A company whose main business activity is acquiring stock of other companies and providing direction, reporting income from the operating subsidiaries as either equity in the results or dividends. The alternative investment style is an operating company that carries on the production of goods and services directly.

Holding Company Depository Receipts. See **HOLDRs.**

HOLDRs. Acronym for Holding Company Depository Receipts, each one a bundle of 20 or so related companies representing a specific sector of the economy, such as drugs, biotech, or the Internet, bought or sold in one transaction. They are not managed, in that once the companies and amounts are predetermined, there is no change, unlike SPDRs which change with the S&P Index. An investor owns shares of each company represented in the unit and receives proportional dividends and Annual Reports. There is no management fee or sales load, just an administrative fee. They are purchased like any other equity security through a broker and are available only in 100-share round lots. One drawback is their rigidity, meaning that since no companies can be added or dropped, exciting new ones are missed and deteriorating old ones are retained. For more information, see the Web site: *www.holdrs.com.*

holiday. A day on which an exchange is closed besides Saturdays and Sundays. For example, holidays on the New York Stock Exchange are New Year's Day, Washington's Birthday, Good Friday, Memorial Day, Independence Day, Labor Day, Thanksgiving, Christmas, Martin Luther King's Birthday, and presidential election days. In addition, certain holidays can be declared if Christmas falls near or during a weekend and New York exchanges close on New York general election days.

Holt Stock Report Online. See under **Web Sites for the Inquiring Investor.**

Homebuilding. Those stocks representing companies engaged in residential construction. *See* **industry stock group.**

home run. A reference to a corporate ploy or strategy that is very successful, such as an advertising campaign that increases sales significantly.

Hong Kong Futures Exchange. Address: 605-608 Asia Pacific Finance Tower, Citibank Plaza, 3 Garden Road, Central, Hong Kong. Phone: (852) 2842-9333. Fax: (852) 2845-2043. *See* under **Global Investment Market.**

Hong Kong Stock Exchange. Address: Exchange Square, Hong Kong, (852) 5 22 11 22. *See* under **Global Investment Market.**

Hope Scholarship credit. A federal income tax credit that can provide up to $1,500 in reduced taxes per year for each student in a household in college or vocational school. The credit expires after the first two years of schooling. To claim the credit, a student must be enrolled at least on a half-time basis. There are other stipulations such as the tuition amount, scholarship funds received by the student, and the income level of the taxpayer. *See* **Lifetime Learning Credit.**

horizon analysis. In analyzing the expected results of a commitment of funds for a stock or portfolio of stocks, the establishing of a definite time frame or horizon to hold the investment and the assumed cash inflows and cash outlays involved over the time period. From that, a forecast of the imputed discount rate or the internal rate of return can be calculated to ascertain whether the investment is attractive. *See* **internal rate of return.**

horizontal integration. See **integrated company.**

Hospital Management. Those stocks representing companies engaged in providing hospital and health care services. *See* **industry stock group.**

hot deal. A new issue, usually an IPO, that will be sold to the public at a price substantially below the market value of existing shares or, in the case of an IPO, shares of similar companies, sometimes enabling a buyer to make profit immediately.

hot issue. A new issue that is rumored to have fast-rise potential.

hot line. A direct telephone line from one securities dealer to another to expedite trading, quoting, and market news.

hotel, to. As an employer, to move employees among several offices or cubicles, as a policy where many employees work at home or on flexible times, in order to avoid leasing and maintaining unnecessary office space.

Hotels & Motels. Those stocks representing companies providing hotel and motel accommodations for the traveling public. *See* **industry stock group.**

Household Furnishings & Appliances. Those stocks representing companies making residential furniture items and appliances. *See* **industry stock group.**

Household Products. Those stocks representing companies making small convenience and efficiency items for residences. *See* **industry stock group.**

"house's money." In a situation where stocks in general have risen in values and then declined, a reference to the amount of the decline that is covered or exceeded by the gains. As long as losses are offset by the gains, it is assumed that investors will not panic and bail out of the stock market, because investors' worth generally has not diminished since before the gains. The analogy is to the tendency of a casino gambler who has won money to treat ensuing losses not exceeding the gains as money belonging to the house management and, therefore, not personal losses. For example, if Laura Liberated's stocks rise by $5,000, followed by a downturn of $3,000, she figures the loss is house money, so she stays pat. On the other hand, if her portfolio drops $10,000 in value, she rationalizes she is $5,000 poorer, and might sell out. There is a certain fatalistic element to this reasoning, one that poses a riddle—if an investor only sells when losses offset gains, how does the investor make money in the market?

Housewares. Those stocks representing companies manufacturing cooking, dining, and bathroom items for residences. *See* **industry stock group.**

Housing Starts/Building Permits Report. Because housing construction is the first indicator to recover in economic expansion and the first to contract in recession, this report compiled by the Bureau of the Census of the U.S. Department of Commerce in the second half of the month is closely watched by economists and analysts. Volatility is a trait, especially in colder months. It represents a "big ticket" item, like automobiles, that consumers embrace in good times and postpone in difficult times. Starts are divided into single-family and multi-family categories. In the latter, the number of units in the project, usually apartments, translates to the number of starts. Low mortgage rates tend to stimulate starts, while high rates tend to depress them. Building permits are published at the same time. They tend to lead starts by one month, and provide clues as to the volume of starts. Upturns in housing starts tend to drive down values of fixed income securities, increase common stock prices, and do not affect dollar exchange rates. Downturns tend to raise fixed income securities, depress common stock prices, and do not affect dollar exchange rates.

Hulbert Financial Digest. A newsletter that reports on the performance of 160 investment newsletters, by tabulating how investors would have done following their advice on securities selection. It spotlights top newsletters, including investment strategies, track records, and techniques. Also, it shows graphs of their performance back to 1980. In addition, the newsletter contains articles on mutual funds and stocks shunned and favored most by mutual funds and the general investment approaches of newsletters. Telephone: (888) HULBERT. E-mail: *hfd@hulbertdigest.com.* Web site: *www.hulbertdigest.com.*

Humphrey–Hawkins Report and **testimony.** A semiannual written and verbal report on the economy and monetary policy presented to the House Banking Committee and the Senate Banking Committee of the U.S. Congress by the Chairman of the Federal Reserve Board. The practice originated in 1978 under a law sponsored by Senator Hubert Humphrey and Representative Augustus Hawkins that reinforced the Fed's mandate of promoting maximum growth, low unemployment, and low inflation. In addition, it formally established the accountability of the Fed to the Congress. *See* **Federal Reserve System.**

hurdle rate. In a formula calculating the present value of an investment that can be considered a future stream of cash flows, the discount rate that makes the sum of the future streams equal to the present value. It is the discount factor or rate of return that makes the formula or investment "work" for the investor.

hybrid fund. A public or private fund that invests in market-neutral stocks, arbitrages stock positions, and engages in "corporate governance" activities or buys fund shares that do. The objective of such managements usually is to increase returns over conventional investments over a long-term investment horizon.

hybrid security. A security issue that combines legal characteristics of both debt and equity in that both classes of capital rights must be considered in actions ordering claims on the issuer's resources, such as in bankruptcy reorganizations. When an indenture is present and the security is a convertible debenture, it is a hybrid, because the holder clearly has both creditor and equity rights. Legally, there would be a tendency to place such debentures on the low rung of debt claims and in the highest position among equity claimants.

hype. Exaggerated praise on the Internet for a stock's prospects, implying that it is extraordinarily attractive because of specific or general events, past, or future, usually from one who plans to make a personal gain by the stock transactions that ensue. *See* **investment sites.**

hypothecation of customer's securities. A pledge of securities as collateral by a customer for a margin account loan, without a transfer of title. Also, securities on deposit with a brokerage can be hypothecated by a brokerage for loans if agreed to in writing by a customer, without transfer of title. *See* **Rules, SEC #15c2-1.**

Ii

IAN. Abbreviation for **interest arrears note.**

IBCC. Abbreviation for **International Bureau of Chambers of Commerce.**

I-bonds or **inflation-indexed bonds.** See **E-Savings Bonds.**

IBRA. Abbreviation for **Indonesian Bank Restructuring Agency.**

IBRD. Abbreviation for **International Bank for Reconstruction and Development** or **World Bank.**

ICANN. Abbreviation for **Internet Corporation for Assigned Names and Numbers.**

ICFA. Abbreviation for **Institute of Chartered Financial Analysts.**

Idaho Department of Finance. Regulator of securities laws in the state of Idaho. Address: Securities Bureau, 700 West State Street, Boise, ID 83720. Phone: (208) 334-3684.

Illinois Office of the Secretary of State. Regulator of securities laws in the state of Illinois. Address: Securities Division, 900 South Spring Street, Springfield, IL 2704. Phone: (217) 782-2256. Phone: (800) 628-7937.

implied or **sustainable growth rate.** The measure of the long-term capacity of a company to grow its earnings if it is assumed Retained Earnings are reinvested at the same Rate of Return as the Return on Equity over the years, and no other capital except Retained Earnings are available during the period. This method applies a degree of realism to the process of estimating future earnings, and consequentially estimating a stock's future valuation. This is because future earnings are made dependent on management's inherent ability to grow them, without recourse to new financing or capital. The formula can be expressed in the following example:

Bigger Than Life Corp. is a manufacturer of steroids. It is a mature pharmaceutical company that distributes 50% of net income each year to stockholders in the form of dividends. Over the past five years, the company has earned 15%, or .15, on stockholders' equity. The Implied Growth Rate is 7.5% (15% × .50% of EPS after dividends = 7.5%). This exercise suggests that earnings will grow by 7.5% on average. Thus, the 7.5% can be plugged in the Future Value formula to estimate earnings per share in some future year. As you can see, this exercise measures how much the business will grow earnings retained each year, if the past is a guide. *See* **compound interest.**

Implied Rate Analysis. A reference to arriving at an estimate of the rate of return of any financial or investment item, based on informal statistical inference, rather than actual results. For example, if an analyst projects revenues of a company will double in five years to $25 million, that the after-tax profit margin will be 15% at that time, and that shares outstanding will number 2,500,000, the implied earnings-per-share would be $1.50 (($25,000,000 × .15) ÷ 2,500,000).

import. A shipment of goods received from another country.

import duty. A governmental tax collected on imported wares.

import quota. A restriction by a government, either as to value or amount, of a product that is imported.

improvement bonds. Those bonds sold to raise money for the physical improvement of existing facilities.

improvement fund. Those required annual monies, usually a percentage of the face value of bonds, that the issuer of bonds must apply to maintenance of the properties serving as collateral for the bonds. *See* **indenture.**

imputed interest. A reference to allocating an accumulation in the value of an asset, such as a discounted zero-coupon bond as it approaches maturity, to a certain period during which it represents an interest expense to the bond issuer or interest income to the bondholder. On a broader scale, whenever a compounded growth rate from the capital appreciation or depreciation for a security is inferred, the interest rate is imputed. For example, if Orbitronics, Inc., the foremost maker of space gear, rises from $10 per share to $15 per share in a period of three years, the annual compounded growth rate could be represented as 14.5%, instead of a 50% long-term capital appreciation or capital gain. In this way the capital gain in a security is made to deem like regular income receipts. This practice might seem duplicitous, but it is a method of equating different type of securities, at least in terms of investment return. However, the practice does overlook the differences in risk factors, which should be part of every comparison of investment return. *See* **zero-coupon bond.**

"in a stock." A reference to owning shares of stock in a specific corporation. Usually, it denotes a short time frame, after which the investor will replace the stock for another.

in-and-out. A reference to buying and selling securities on an exchange almost simultaneously.

in-and-out costs. See **round-trip costs, inactive crowd,** and **cabinet crowd.**

in anticipation of death. See **gift tax.**

"In-favor stocks." A reference to those stocks that Wall Street firms and investors are receptive to buying at present. The reasons can be mixed, and they can pertain to investment characteristics, such as a current stock market emphasis on high yields, making stocks that pay generous dividends popular, or to business fundamentals, like a spike in demand for products in an industry with limited productive capacity, making that group popular. The topic brings up the sometimes overlooked aspect of the stock market—marketing stocks to investors. There are modes, styles, and fashions in the pristine world of finance, just as there are in most other commercial endeavors. Once buying momentum begins for certain stocks, investors are in a go-go frame of mind toward such securities. This receptiveness encourages investment firms to ferret out new investment ideas that are similar. On the other hand, once disappointing results or performance has soured the market on certain stocks, investment firms tend to avoid recommending such stocks, at least until conditions improve.

An example of in-favor stocks was the Internet boom of the late 1990s. Nearly every aspect of the burgeoning sector enjoyed a reign of extreme stock popularity—Internet Service Providers, Cable Providers, Telephony, Internet Search Engines, Internet Portals and Gateways, and Internet Software Applications Makers, for example. This occurred even though there were hardly any earnings per share. In late 1999, when Congress seemed close to repealing the Glass-Steagall Act and amending the Banking Act of 1956—both aimed at allowing the amalgam of banking, insurance and investment firms under one business roof for the first time in 70 years—financial services stocks were in favor, over the prospects of profitable mergers impacting the stocks of affected companies.

Another example of in-favor stocks were the wildly popular oil and gas stocks of the late 1970s and 1980s. When OPEC, the international cartel of oil exporters, set production quotas and prices for oil wellhead prices in the United States nearly quadrupled. The effect was that breakup values for domestic oil and gas stocks elevated proportionately and more, in certain cases, because of expectations for future discoveries, and these stock prices were the darlings of Wall Street. When OPEC lost its cohesiveness and non-OPEC producers flooded the market with cheaper oil, the party was over. Stocks collapsed and became out of favor, until business conditions improved. *See* **out-of-favor stocks.**

in registration. A reference to the period in which a security issue is examined by the Securities and Exchange Commission before it can be sold. In an unstable market, underwriters are apprehensive during this period because a drop in the market generally can make the stock difficult to sell at an acceptable price to the issuer when it is released. The number of days a security is in registration varies with the Securities and Exchange Commission workload, the number of new issues, and the completeness of financial information pertaining to a registered security, but 90 days is probably typical. *See* **registration.**

in syndicate. The status of a new securities issue which is only partially sold and subject to market transactions by the underwriters to keep a high price prevailing, any loss from which is a syndicate promotional expense. *See* **syndicate bid.**

in the black. A description of profitable business operations.

in the market. The state of having money currently invested in popular common stocks.

in the money. The condition describing an option when the value of the underlying security is above the exercise or strike price for calls and below the exercise or strike price for puts.

in the red. A description of unprofitable business operations.

inactive crowd. See **cabinet crowd.**

inactive stocks. Those stocks trading infrequently in comparison with related ones; trading under 10,000 shares per day is considered inactive on the New York Stock Exchange.

Inc. Abbreviation for incorporated. *See* **incorporated.**

income. An increase of money or equivalent wealth over a period of time from business activity. This is a generic term and, for investment purposes, must be further delineated, since securities have varying claims to the revenue stream as it become income. *See* **earnings** or **net profit, net earnings, operating income,** and **profit.**

income bonds. Those bonds on which interest is payable only if the issuer has earned sufficient amounts. *See* **flat bonds.**

income investment. The commitment of funds into securities which provide regular income from dividends or interest, while usually providing a minimum of investment risk.

income reserved trust. A special trust whereby there is a transfer of income-producing property to a beneficiary with the stipulation that the donor will receive the income during his life. This trust is useful for security gifts to charitable organizations during a lifetime, reducing estate taxes but allowing the donor to enjoy income from the gift. An attorney should be consulted for complete information.

income statement. A detailed accounting of a company's revenues, expenses, and resultant profit or loss, during a specified period. The income statement is a rendition of the revenue stream, from sales down to income left for investors, with a view towards financial realism. However, it should not be confused with the Cash Flow Statement, since it includes many items that are not represented by actual cash inflow and outflow, but are subjective allocations of portions of the revenue stream to various income and expense categories or accounts. By including revenues and expenses, which are both cash and noncash, the income statement better explains what has happened to stockholders' equity during a specific fiscal period.

It is important to remember that there are many differences and wrinkles to allow for in reading an income statement. Some accountants like to place items in the footnotes that others prefer in the body of the document. That is why the footnotes are important. Some like to charge retained earnings or earned surplus with certain costs, while other like to place them in the expense accounts. *See* **Balance Sheet, Cash Flow Statement, and Statement of Shareholders' Equity.**

income tax. An assessment on the income of corporations, associations, and individuals levied by some states and the federal government, the latter administered by the Internal Revenue Service; established by the Sixteenth Amendment in 1913. 1) Federal personal or individual income tax. There are five marginal income tax rates levied by the federal government. However, under the present federal tax code, because of numerous deductions, credits, and exemptions, the actual number of tax rate categories is 10, on average. The District of Columbia and every state but Alaska, Florida, Nevada, Texas, Washington and Wyoming taxes individual income. For changes in the year 2001, see **Economic Growth and Tax Relief Reconciliation Act of 2001.** 2) *See* **corporate income tax.**

incorporated. The state of being a legal corporation, operating under a defined charter of organization and objectives.

incubation, mutual fund. A practice of introducing a mutual fund on a private basis, with small capital contributions by the sponsoring company and insiders. After the fund establishes a track record through aggressive investment tactics, the sponsor sells shares to the public, which has been attracted by the fund's record. The SEC examines new funds, in order to ascertain whether incubation has mislead investors about the fund's likely performance as a public, larger fund.

incubator company. An investment company that buys into emerging companies that are candidates for exceptional financial growth, because of ownership or control of promising business prospects, advanced technology or a highly-marketable product(s). These are actually venture capital firms, but ones with a highly developed sense of financial nurturing of the startup or turnaround companies they invest in. Sometimes their investment is represented by debt with an equity kicker, like stock warrants or options, but it often is represented by stock shares or partnership units. The incubator can be organized as a partnership or corporation. *See* **incubator stock.**

incubator stock. The publicly traded stock shares of an **incubator comapny.** These stocks or limited partnerships units offer public investors the opportunity to own equity in emerging companies, start-up companies, and IPOs through the incubator's stock, in a way that is usually more diversified than sole ownership of one of the incubator's holdings would be. Some incubators' portfolios represent as many as 50 entities. Also present, of course, are the risks of early investing in growth companies. Because of the financial immaturity of the entities owned by incubator companies, it is difficult to evaluate them with conventional stock appraisal methods. The most common method is to get an estimate of the total worth of the portfolio, reduce that figure by liabilities, and divide by shares outstanding. *See* **incubator company.**

indenture. A detailed agreement of the conditions of a bond issue printed on the bond certificate. It is a recitation of commitments and rights of the debtor or issuer of the bonds, including the term of indebtedness.

independence of auditors. In order to establish greater independence for external auditors who also provide other services to clients, the SEC at the close of 2000 approved the following rules which began in 2001. In doing so, the commission acted to lessen chances of conflicts of interest between an auditor performing audits used by the public for a client on a fee basis and also receiving payments for other services during the same time period.

- Place restrictions on the number of employees and family members who might have investments in or employment with the client firm.
- Require disclosure by audited firm in annual proxy statement information about other services provided by their auditors during last fiscal year, and indicate whether the company's audit committee has considered whether such services have interfered with the auditor's independence.
- Restrict auditor's internal work for the client to 40%, measured in total hours.
- Allow internal audit services by auditor applicable to operating internal audits not related to accounting controls, financial systems, or financial statements.
- Bans operation or supervision of client's information technology systems by auditor, unless certain identities and disclosures are made.
- Exempts smaller businesses with under $200 million in assets.

Independence Standards Board. A group created by the Securities and Exchange Commission and the accounting profession to address problems, such as conflict of interest, that could reduce the ability of auditors to remain objective in examining the books of clients. The board was formed in early 1997 and consists of eight members, four from the accounting profession and four from the public.

index fund. An unmanaged mutual fund which weights its equity investments in industries according to the weights of a broad stock market average, such as the Standard & Poor's 500 Stock Index, or a fund more limited in stock diversity. The purpose is to duplicate as nearly as possible the performance of the stock market or a sector thereof, thereby reducing the relative market risk as much as possible, in terms of that model. In addition, the fund saves investors money, because expensive research and management staffs are reduced or eliminated completely as well as expenses of trading securities often. Statistically, in periods exceeding 10 years, index funds outperform 75% of all mutual funds. In fact, the technique developed from the historical failure of managed funds to exceed the performance of the market through discrete stock selection. *See* **closet indexing** and **exchange-traded fund.**

index numbers. A system of measuring relative changes in prices or production by assigning 100 to a base period with which other periods are compared, usually as a percentage of change. An index number is found by calculating the average price of or total number of selected commodities during a period being compared with a base period and finding what percentage that measure is of the base value by dividing the measure of identical commodities during the base period into the current measure and multiplying by 100.

For a simplified example, suppose total production in U.S. home appliance plants for October is 950,000 units, which is established as a base period for future comparison and assigned a value or index of 100. If during November production of the same units totaled 1 million units, the November index is calculated as follows: 1,000,000 divided by 950,000 multiplied by 100 (1.05×100) which gives an index of 105. The index represents a 5% rise in production over October ($105 - 100$).

Index of Consumer Expectations. See under Economic Indicators.

index option. A put and/or call contract on an index or set of stocks representing a broad equity market, industry, or sector of an economy, country, or geographic region.

Indian Stock Exchange (India). See under Global Investment Markets.

Indiana Office of the Secretary of State. Regulator of securities laws in the state of Indiana. Address: Securities Division, 302 West Washington, #E-111, Indianapolis, IN 46204. Phone: (317) 232-6681. Phone: (800) 223-8791.

individual account. An investment account operated in one person's name.

Individual Investor Online. See under **Web Sites for the Inquiring Investor.**

Individual Retirement Account or **IRA.** Because legislation establishing tax-advantaged retirement accounts has been somewhat uncoordinated and focused on disparate political factions in the United States, there are currently four kinds of retirement programs in use. They are: 401(k) Plans, 403(k) Plans, IRAs, and Keogh Plans. There is also a hybrid type called Simplified Employee Pension–Investment Retirement Accounts or SEP–IRA accounts. An estimated 85 million Americans have investment retirement accounts. The main difference in the categories mentioned above, besides the actual tax provisions, is the nature of the creator or sponsor or the economic status of the future pensioner. IRAs can be opened by non-working spouses up to $2,000, even when the working spouse is covered under a qualified plan. Profit-oriented enterprises use 401(k)s; nonprofit enterprises use 403(k)s; states, counties, cities, and political subdivisions use 457s; and self-employed persons use Keogh and IRAs; and sole proprietors use SEP–IRAs. In the case of 401(k)s, employees may not contribute more than $9,500 annually or 20% of their salary, whichever is less. In the case of Keoghs, a business owner may contribute up to a lesser of $30,000, or 20% of net business income yearly. With self-employed IRAs, a person may contribute up to the lesser of $22,500 or about 13% of net business income.

    A salient feature of the landmark Employee Retirement Income Security Act of 1974, is that for the first time, persons not covered under a qualified employer plan were allowed to accumulate resources in an investment account for their retirement on a tax-sheltered basis. The pension legislation allowed such individuals to take a deduction from gross income for amounts contributed to accounts but the deduction could not exceed the lesser of (1) 15% of compensation or income earned, and (2) $1,500. The most recent amendments to the Act, under the Taxpayer Relief Act of 1997, expanded IRA plans and made them more complex. There is no limit on the number of IRA accounts a person may have. For changes in 2001, see **Economic Growth and Tax Relief Reconciliation Act of 2001.** *See* also summary below, and **"stretch-out IRA," Deductible IRA, Roth IRA, Nondeductible IRA, Simplified Employee Pension–Investment Retirement Account, Spousal IRA, and Education IRA.**

Summary of Individual Retirement Accounts:
1. *Deductible.* Eligible taxpayers are not participating in an employer plan, regardless of earnings. Also included are persons covered by employer plans, if they are filing joint returns and their adjusted gross income in 1998 was less than $50,000 (escalates to $80,000 by 2007); or single taxpayers whose adjusted gross income was less than $30,000 in 1998 (escalates to $50,000 in 2007). Taxes on contributions and income from retirement fund are not due until withdrawal. However, distributions before age 59 plus six months are subject to a 10% penalty. Exceptions to the penalty: withdrawals to pay for education costs and withdrawals up to $10,000 for an initial home purchase. By age 70 plus six months, distributions must get underway.
2. *Educational.* Eligible taxpayers are those filing jointly. They may contribute up to $500 per child under 18 years each year, if adjusted gross is less than $150,000 (phases out at $160,000). Taxpayers filing singly are eligible if their adjusted gross income is less than $95,000 (phases out at $110,000). Taxes are paid on contributions but income from invested funds is never taxed, if used for qualifying educational purposes. Portions of the fund not spent on education or rolled over to another family member's IRA must be distributed to the beneficiary at age 30, usually subject to a 10% penalty.
3. *Nondeductible.* Taxpayers who can afford the contribution are eligible. Taxes are paid on contributions but taxes on

income from the retirement fund are deferred until withdrawal. *See* **Deductible IRA** for other guidelines.

4. *Roth.* Taxpayers filing jointly are eligible, if adjusted gross income is less than $150,000 (phases out at $160,000). Single taxpayers whose adjusted gross income is under $95,000 (phases out at $110,000) are also eligible. Taxes are paid on contributions but retirement plan earnings are not taxed, if the account is at least five years old and the beneficiary is at least age 59 plus six months, deceased, or disabled. Penalties are excepted, when home purchase and education expenses are like those in Deductible IRA plans.

5. *Spousal.* Taxpayers eligible are working spouses not covered by employer plans, if adjusted gross income is less than $150,000 (phases out at $160,000). A non-working spouse and partner may each contribute up to $2,000 to a plan, if the working spouse earns at least $4,000. A working spouse may elect either a deductible or Roth Plan. A non-working spouse may elect a deductible, nondeductible, or Roth Plan, depending on the taxpayer's income and retirement plans.

Indonesian Bank Restructuring Agency (IBRA). The agency established by the International Monetary Fund in 1998 as a condition of a $40 billion rescue package to Indonesian banks, in the aftermath of the boom-to-bust economy experienced in that country in the 1980s and 1990s. The agency has taken over nearly 50 failed banks and has assumed equity in approximately 200 companies in its efforts to sell assets in order to rebuild the troubled banks.

industrial capacity. In economic planning, the ratio of how much of a state's manufacturing, mines, and utilities potential is in use. Between 80% and 85% is considered desirable. Economists fear that when the ratio gets above 85%, inefficiencies will develop, raising costs and causing inflation. When the ratio is below 80%, they fear that slack time will cause a recession. In the United States, the Fed releases these figures monthly.

industrial development revenue bonds or **industrial revenue bonds.** Those bonds sold by a municipality to build equipment that is leased for enough money to pay the bond interest and principal. Proceeds from bond sales are usually used to construct a building, which is leased by a corporation guaranteeing to pay rent sufficient for interest and principal payments on the bonds. The bonds are backed by the municipality contract with the leasing corporation—not the taxing power of the municipality—and are generally exempt from income taxes. This type of bond issue allows cities and counties to attract new industries, and has been criticized in those areas from which industry has been lured on the grounds that the tax-free aspect amounts to federal subsidization of industrialization of certain areas.

Industrial Production Index. An index number published by the Federal Reserve Board to measure in physical units the level of industrial production in the United States, relative to a former period, expressed as a percentage of the former periods. *See* under **Economic Indicators.**

Industrial Production Report, Federal Reserve. An important report to economists and analysts issued in mid-month by the Federal Reserve Board, that measures in index form (relative to a base year) the physical volume of output of the country's factories, mines and utilities. Collectively, these goods account for approximately 45% of the economic output in the United States Although the report omits services, it is significant because industrial production is responsive to economic activity in general. Also, it is not a volatile series, and so, relatively easy to forecast. Another feature of the report is that output is expressed in "real" terms, free of the distortions of inflation. The report is a popular tool for forecasting GNP and GDP. Surprisingly, it has little impact on securities markets. When industrial production rises, fixed income securities tend to recede, common stocks rise and dollar exchange rates are unaffected. When it falls, fixed income securities fall, common stocks drop and dollar exchange rates are not affected. *See* **Capacity Utilization Estimate.**

Industrials. The securities of manufacturing or marketing operating companies. *See* **industry stock group**.

industry. A group of companies engaged in the same or similar primary business, whether manufacturing, processing, or service, and generally competing with each other for increased market share. For investment purposes, the importance of industries is that such a structure provides a benchmark for comparing companies or stocks, in terms of financial and operating parameters. This comparison enables investors to ascertain whether they are buying shares in the best stock in the group, the riskiest, the worst, and so on. This sort of knowledge is one way to know what to expect from a stock, in terms of investment performance.

Industry structure is also important from the standpoint of research administration. It makes a great deal of sense to assign research coverage based on industries, because when an analyst becomes an expert in an industry, he adopts several stocks for coverage and merchandising. And he has a peer group with which to test ideas. On the other hand, if an analyst develops investment ideas piecemeal, he has to learn several industries in an ongoing process. The important characteristic an industry must possess is a plethora of investable ideas, although not necessarily simultaneously. As the economy becomes more specialized, industries proliferate and many disappear, the victims of obsolescence. Don't get caught in one of those!

The most detailed industry structure in the United States is the **Standard Industrial Classification (SIC),** eventually to become the North American Industry Classification System (NAICS). It is important to realize that the SIC structure is for purposes of public administration, and includes both private and public industries, huge and minuscule, while investment industries are designed to present investment-worthy ideas, exhibiting suitability for investors and liquidity. For that reason, the SIC list includes several hundred entries, whereas the average investment firm's list would be only 25 to 50. In fact, some brokerage industries are maintained to provide a showcase for corporate clients. Independent research firms, like Standard & Poor's and Value Line, usually average 75 to 100 companies in their research coverage. Some professional investors buy shares in several companies in a new, untested industry, in order to diversify their risks.

industry stock group. A sample of several companies representing the same industry, usually compiled to measure some aspect of investment performance or other benchmark in that industry. Money managers who emphasize stock groups practice a "top down" style, in which decisions are made on industry outlooks first. Company selection for sale or purchase comes next, under the assumption that companies within an industry have a high performance correlation with their industries. The alternative to this is "bottom-up" stock selection, in which company analyses come first. There are many sources of industry stock groups, which differ from the SIC Industry Codes in that the former industries are constructed for marketing purposes. Such a process can eliminate mundane industries or industries with minuscule stock capitalizations, at least until they grow enough to become investable by institutions.

inefficiencies. In the price structure of securities at a certain point in time, anomalies that exist as a result of misinformation or the lack of information by investors. This concept is based on the theory that securities markets are efficient, in that they reflect prices investors will pay for securities at a certain time. Quants utilize computer models that spot inefficiencies, and buy or sell the affected securities in order to profit from the correction that mathematically is predicted to occur. *See* **quant.**

inflated market prices. Those stock prices overvalued in terms of current and future earning power, yield or net asset value, or some other stock evaluation method, because of speculative demand.

inflation. A state of rising prices caused by intensive consumer buying and usually proportionately lesser increases in industrial output, the latter usually associated with full utilization of a country's plant and equipment. In the U.S., the Department of Labor measures inflation using various price indexes. The two most used by investors are the Consumers Price Index (CPI) and the Producers Price Index (PPI). The CPI is useful because it measures price changes in a broad array of consumer items and services at the retail level and is, therefore, a better indication of the current state of prices.

On the other hand, the PPI measures price change at the wholesale level, and is oriented towards the original or manufactured price of goods. Less volatile, its value to the investor is that it shows price trends better and sometimes foretells increases in the CPI by 6 to 12 months. Curiously, however, there is not a close relationship between short-term movements in the PPI and CPI. To a limited extent, the information in the indexes suggests whether general inflation, represented by the CPI and PPI, is heating up and, therefore, whether monetary and fiscal policy might be initiated for its control. That action, in the form of higher interest rates, could impede business growth and thus stock price gains in the process. This is the objective of the Fed, of course, when it raises interest rates. *See* **Consumer Price Index, core inflation, headline inflation, Producer Price Index,** and **stagflation.**

inflation accounting. The practice of indicating how inflation has changed the values in a company's financial statements, using a price index or price deflator. The Financial Accounting Standards Board (FASB) requires public companies with fixed assets and inventories of more than $125 million or total assets of more than $1 billion to include supplementary information in their conventional financial reports showing the effects of inflation. Usually, the effect is to lessen the value of assets, because the process increases amortization reserves or offsets to the net values of the assets. On the other hand, the procedure has less effect on the value of inventories, since they have presumably been purchased recently. The practice is more useful in periods of high inflation, when financial statements can be misleading, unlike the 1990s.

Inflation-indexed Savings Bonds or **I-Bonds.** U.S. Treasury Savings Bonds with interest paid linked to a cost-of-living price index. They are issued in denominations ranging from $50 to $10,000, maturing in 30 years. Investors may defer income tax payments on interest as long as they retain the bonds. Interest is reinvested and added to the principal amount. These bonds are exempt from state and local taxes, like all U.S. Treasury bonds. Interest payments are based on an established nominal or contractual rate issue and on changes in the inflation rate, so that interest payments rise during inflationary periods to compensate the investor for the loss of purchasing power of the principal. On the other hand, decreases in the inflation rate only reduce the adjustable rate, meaning that the bonds are protected against deflation to the extent that deflation can wipe out only the adjustable rate.

Interest payments are based on two factors: (1) A fixed-interest rate, ranging from 3% to 3.5%, established when the bonds were offered to the public in 1998; and (2) an inflation-adjusted rate. This latter variable inflation-adjusted rate is changed every six months and is based on the Consumers Price Index (CPI), maintained by the Bureau of Labor Statistics. Holders may defer tax payments on the interest until these bonds are redeemed. If the bonds are redeemed to pay for college tuition, all or part of the interest income may be excluded from income taxes. *See* **Series E Savings Bonds.**

Inflation-indexed securities. Notes and bonds, usually issued by government bodies, bearing interest income linked to the **cost-of-living index,** in the country of issue. This linkage assures an investor that his return will exceed inflation rates in that currency, over the life of the security. The U.S. Treasury issued inflation-indexed notes in 1997, initially maturing in 10 years; later they were offered to mature in five years. The Tennessee Valley Authority (TVA) and Federal Home Loan Bank followed suit soon afterwards. The U.S. Treasury issued a 30-year bond or a TIPS (Treasury Inflation-Protected Security), the first inflation-adjusted one, in 1998. Treasuries carry a fixed rate of return and a variable one that mirrors the **Consumer Price Index (CPI).** That part that is fixed is distributed as interest during the year, while the adjusted portion increases or decreases the principal. For example, a $1,000 inflation-backed Treasury might be issued paying a 3.75% interest rate. If inflation is 2.5% in that year, the 3.75% interest or $37.50 would be paid, while the 2.5% inflation adjustment would accrete to the $1,000 principal at the close of the year—making the principal due and on which the next adjustment is based $1,025. One big detriment to owning these bonds is that the inflation adjustment is taxable each year, even though not paid until maturity in the redemption.

Information Super Highway. See **Internet.**

Information Technology (IT). Within the operating framework of a company, the techniques established for developing electronic information architecture, telecommunications, data systems, and information policies and procedures. This includes client/service systems, network development and maintenance, and Internet capabilities. It is the newest and becoming one of the most important technologies in the business world.

InfoSeek: Personal Finance Online. See under **Web Sites for the Inquiring Investor.**

inheritance. That personal and real property which passes to legal heirs upon the death of the maker of a last will and testament. Personal property is represented by items such as securities, cash, valuable coins, valuable gems and jewelry, furniture, furnishing, automobiles, savings, checking accounts, and CDs. Real property is represented by land and improvements thereon, such as outlying houses.

inheritance tax or **estate tax.** A federal or state levy on the value of personal or real property inherited. The federal tax applies to estates (or gifts) in excess of $625,000, and the rates range as high as 55% of the value of the property in the estate above that amount. The exempt amount rises to $1 million in the year 2006. For a family business in an estate, the exemption increased to $1.3 million in 1999. For changes in the year 2001, see **Economic Growth and Tax Relief Reconciliation Act of 2001.**

initial margin. When buying securities partly on credit or margin, the amount of money a broker requires to be deposited when a purchase is made. *See* **margin.**

initial public offering (IPO). A phrase to describe those securities, usually common stock, that a company sells to the public the first time. In arranging for the sale, an investment banker usually works with the management of the issuing corporation and advises it on the terms and price of the offering for a front-end fee that is deducted from the selling price of each security.

The IPO fee is 7% of the IPO value most of the time. In 20% of the cases, the corporation has enough prowess to pay less.

During times of exuberant stock markets, IPOs are in great demand, because brokers and investors are looking for new names with which to participate in the optimistic market. Often demand outgrows supply, so that only a few investors can actually get the new issues. This is especially true if big institutions are vying for the stock, which has by then become a "hot issue." Little investors are threatened with extinction. However, the dissemination requirements of stock exchanges require some degree of breadth in shareholder distribution, which mitigates the financial power of the institutions. But not to worry for the little guys who miss out on a hot issue, because historical studies show that they can buy the stock cheaper by waiting a few months.

input-output model. An economic model which provides tools for a systematic analysis of the inter-industry transactions in a country, region, area, or industry. The technique was developed by Professor Wassily Leontief of Harvard University, for which he received a Nobel Prize in 1973. It has found extensive use especially in forecasting and planning, both in the short term and long term. Investment applications include estimating demands on the companies in one or more industries from sales in one or more other industries. The U.S. Department of Commerce develops and publishes input-output models of the economy every 10 years, which are available to the public through the U.S. Government Printing Office. *See* **food chain, business or economic.**

inside quote. The bid and asked price of an unlisted stock among dealers. When they quote this stock to a customer, they subtract from the bid side and add to the asked side to allow themselves a profit, unless they are transacting for a commission.

insider. Under Federal securities law: 1) An investor close to corporate financial information which could affect the company's stock price, if known publicly. 2) A corporate officer, director, or owner when such a person buys the corporation's stock and sells it within six months, and the transaction is not for a retirement plan. Under SEC regulations, when this waiting period is not observed, any profit should be turned over to the corporation. However, this penalty can only be assessed through the actions of the board of directors or a shareholder lawsuit. In the case of an IPO, a corporate director or officer must wait six months before selling shares received in the offering.

Institute of Chartered Financial Analysts. An organization founded to qualify candidates for competency in the professional practice of securities analysis. The institute supports continuing education programs and ethical conduct. Address: Association for Investment Management and Research, 5 Boar's Head Lane, P.O. Box 3668, Charlottesville, VA 22903. Phone: (804) 980-9755. Fax: (804) 980-9755. E-mail: *info@aimr.org.* Web site: *www.aimr.org/aimr/cfa.html.*

institutional mutual fund. A mutual fund in which investment selections are indexed to a popular stock index. They usually require higher minimum investment amounts, sometimes one million dollars are more, and higher investment additions but charge investors smaller management fees. Fees can be under 1.0% versus an average of 1.55% for equity funds and an average of 0.96% for fixed-income funds, according to Lipper Analytical Services. This combination usually attracts institutional investors. The object of such a fund is to emulate the performance of the stock index to which it is keyed.

Insider Information. That corporate information of such a significant nature that the knowledge of it has been construed by the Securities and Exchange Commission as giving its possessor an unfair advantage in buying or selling that company's stock. The advantage established is in relation to the public. Knowledge of this information precludes one from trading in securities of the corporation until the information is disclosed to the public or it loses its materiality, according to recent SEC cases and statements.

Insider job. A reference to rapid trading by security dealers in a particular stock to attract outside interest, differing from a wash sale in that the sales are bona fide. *See* **wash sale (1).**

insolvent. A description of a business unable to pay lawful obligations.

installment loan. A loan on which the principal and interest is paid off in installments.

Instinet. A private electronic stock trading system managed by Reuters Holdings, PLC., composed of brokers and institutional investors who trade stocks using the World Wide Web. It is one of 50 private trading networks in the United States. Combined, the networks handle about 18% of the volume in NASDAQ stocks and 3% of the volume in NYSE stocks.

However, transactions are relatively secretive, although the SEC wants to shape this market into a more transparent one. Now both Instinet quotes and trades are reported on NASDAQ. Quotes from broker members of Instinet are reported on all market quoting devices, if those quotes are better than generally available, but not those from institutional investors. The SEC will probably require all quotes to be reported, among other expansionary changes.

Conventional stock markets are regulated as exchanges by the SEC, while the Internet is regulated as a broker-dealer. Mostly, this distinction means the Internet is subjected to less capital requirements. The Instinet system is operated on a neutral basis from eight financial centers—Frankfurt, Hong Kong, London, New York, Paris, Tokyo, Toronto, and Zurich. Web site: *www.instinet.com. See* **Electronic Trading Network.**

Institute of Chartered Financial Analysts (ICFA). A professional organization composed of chartered financial analysts that fosters high professional and educational standards in financial analysis; conducts programs of research in financial analysis, and administers the examination program leading to the designation Chartered Financial Analyst. 3,794 members. Address: University of Virginia, P.O. Box 3668, Charlottesville, VA 22903.

institutional investors. Those organizations which invest funds held in the public's interest, employing professional investment managers; for example, banks, insurance companies, pension funds, and so on. As a practical matter, these investors dominate the market, because they control such huge volumes of money and securities.

Insurance, Multiline. Those stocks representing companies underwriting and selling various types of insurance policies. *See* **industry stock group.**

Insurance, Property & Casualty. Those stocks representing companies underwriting insurance coverage of real and personal property. *See* **industry stock group.**

Insurance Brokers. Those stocks representing companies engaged in marketing insurance contracts for various under-writers. *See* **industry stock group.**

intangible assets. Those assets with no physical value; for example, Goodwill, patents, copyrights, and such. However, a lack of physical dimension or value does not mean such assets can not have a great deal of monetary value. Usually, to realize the value of an intangible, some exploitation is required, such as publishing and marketing a manuscript or musical score. One salient example of an intangible asset is goodwill or reputation among buyers. When a company is sold for more than its real asset value, goodwill becomes obvious, and is shown on the balance sheet as a valuable asset. How much would a mediocre jewelry store pay for the right to call itself "Tiffany's"?

intangibles tax. A state tax levied on the income from intangible property, such as securities.

integrated company. A combination of two or more related business operations owned and operated by a single manage-ment, usually to increase efficiency or business volume. There are two forms of integrated companies: (1) Horizontal integra-tion is the combination of business operations at the same func-tional level, for example, a consumer finance company with a chain of department stores. The finance company complements the store sales and vice versa. (2) Vertical integration is the combination of related business operations at different func-tional levels, for example, a manufacturer who operates store outlets for his products. The manufacturer supplies the stores and so is integrated with the marketing level. *See* **integrated utility holding company.**

integrated utility holding company. Under the Public Utility Holding Company Act of 1935, a holding company with assets physically interconnected or capable of interconnection, and one which normally may be economically operated under a single management.

intellectual capital. A reference to the creative energies and abilities, collectively speaking, of the employees of a company. Modern management is becoming aware of the importance of fostering the development of these capacities into tools for accomplishing corporate objectives. Besides scientific and technological applications, areas like marketing and product development are increasingly emphasized. After a history of emphasizing the importance of "hard assets" in corporate success, management is turning more to human resources as tools, in which intellectual capital is included.

intellectual property. In conventional business law, a presentation which is the creation of an artist or inventor, and that is considered to possess commercial value. Book and play manuscripts, video scenarios, computer software, designs, art renderings, and so on are examples. Usually a company purchases the right to use such a property for a specific purpose, like making a movie from a book, and pays a royalty or a portion of the revenues generated by the project to the property owner, besides any initial payment for signing the contract. Intellectual properties are assets that appear on a company's balance sheet and often are understated because the property has not yet been commercially exploited. In the 1990s, as the new economy became more important in the stock market, the concept broadened. It now includes images, ideas, people, and brands that make an enterprise unique to an investor.

interactive mutual fund. A mutual fund in which shareholders can view online the securities in its portfolio currently as well as changes taking place. Also, the shareholders can make suggestions online on securities to add or eliminate.

interchangeable bond. A bond which the owner may change from a bearer to a registered bond or sometimes vice versa. *See* **bearer bonds** and **registered bonds.**

interest. A charge for the use of money, expressed as a percentage of that money on an annual basis. Usually the charge is higher if the borrower's financial position is not strong, which compensates the lender for the additional risk of nonrepayment or prolonged repayment. This differential is especially prevalent in bond financing. In general, short-term interest charges can be calculated from the following formula:

$$\text{Amount Borrowed} \times [\text{Duration of loan (Days)}] \div 360 \text{ (Days in a Year)} \times \text{Interest Rate (\%)}.$$

For example, if \$1,000 is borrowed for 30 days at 5% interest, the interest charge would be: \$1,000 × (30 ÷ 360) × .05 or \$4.17.

interest arrears note or **IAN.** When an issuer of debt is undergoing severe financial problems, a bond or note submitted to a creditor in lieu of an interest payment that is due.

interest coverage. The ratio of the revenue stream before income taxes divided by the annual interest charges. Generally, a manufacturing company's interest coverage is satisfactory at 5 times; for public utilities, 3 times. The measure is calculated before income taxes, because business interest is a tax deduction.

interest declaration. A resolution by a corporation's directors to pay interest on income bonds. *See* **income bonds.**

interest rate. The prevailing interest charge, stated as a percentage (%) or in hundredths of the principal amount, in a specific category of borrowed money.

Interest Rate Spread. See under **Economic Indicators.**

interim dividend. A dividend declared between regular dividend dates, which are usually quarterly, to spread stockholders' income more evenly throughout the year.

interim report. A brief resume of a company's financial and operating results distributed to stockholders, professional investors, the investment community, and the media. Generally, it covers a period of time less than a year, usually one fiscal quarter. However, such a report can also be a progress report on solving some company problem(s) or working out a special arrangement, like a court-mandated merger or divestiture order. *See* **quarterly report.**

interline alliance. See **airline alliances.**

interlocking directorate. A reference to membership by the same persons on more than one board of directors of affiliated corporations. When competition is reduced as a result, this practice is prohibited by the Sherman and Clayton antitrust laws.

Intermarket Trading System. An electronic linkage between the major securities markets in the U.S., whereby brokers and dealers at the various exchange sites—the New York Stock Exchange, NASDAQ, and the regional exchanges, such as the Philadelphia Stock Exchange—can route orders for stocks and other securities to each other. Under prodding from the Securities and Exchange Commission, these systems are forming the basis for an electronic marketplace that is national in scope.

intermediate bonds or **intermediates.** Those bonds maturing in 5 to 15 years.

intermediate movement. A stock price move lasting from one to six months and retracing one-third to two-thirds of the price changes in the preceding rise or fall.

internal factors. Those events which have a direct relationship to general business prospects, and which affect stock market prices, such as steel output, auto sales, business loans, and so on. Such an internal factor may, for example, be responsible for employment of many well-paid workers who buy other goods and services, thus affecting the entire economy. Or the factor may control a great deal of spending power through functions such as the lending of money.

internal funds or **internally-generated funds.** Those monies that are available, as a result of current or past operations, for a company's capital expenditures program or capital expansion during a fiscal period. The source of the monies are from items like net income, amortization expenses that do not involve outlays of cash, sale of capital assets, deferred income taxes that do not involve outlays of cash or write-downs, or write-offs of assets. Because internal funds are so important, many analysts look harder at a company's **cash flow** than its earnings, in estimating future results. Usually in a company's capital expenditures program, a portion comes from internal funds and a portion from **external funds.** The higher the portion from internal funds, the more conservative is the company. Usually, for conservative investors, it is preferable if at least half come from internal funds on an ongoing basis, except in quasi-monopolies such as utilities. Otherwise, a company tends to be highly leveraged and susceptible to volatile results.

internally-generated funds. See **internal funds.**

internal rate of return (IRR). The rate of return in a present value of money equation at which the discounted future cash flows equal the initial cash outlay. In other words, for the investor deciding how much to pay for the future streams of cash from a resource, it is the discount factor or interest rate that makes the present value and future value equal. For single investments, the Association of Management & Research (AIMR) recommends this method of computing a rate of return. It can be represented in a simplified version by the following formula:

$$R = (1 + r)^n - 1$$

where:
R = annualized rate of return;
r = percentage change in security value;

n = number of days, months or quarters the security held divided into number of those units comprising one year.

For example, let's say Walt Whiz owns 100 shares of Sudsy Beer Corp., which he bought at $5 per share three months ago. In other words, he has held the stock for one quarter. The price has hopped to $5.50 per share. Walt hates stale beer so he sells. The exponent in the equation becomes 4 (4 ÷ 1). His annualized realized return is: $(1+.10)^4$ or $(1.10) \times (1.10) \times (1.10) \times (1.10) = 1.4641 - 1 = .4641$ or 46.4%. Let's drink to that!

Internal Revenue Service (IRS). A division of the United States Treasury Department which is the collector of taxes for the U.S. government. Often, this ebullient group of Christmas elves is referred to as the Infernal Revenue Service.

International Accounting Standards Committee (IASC). An organization working toward the development of global accounting standards since 1973, standards which will facilitate the trading of foreign securities in most countries through conformed reporting conventions, full disclosure, and transparency for investors.

International Bank for Reconstruction and Development (IBRD). See **World Bank.**

International Bureau of Chambers of Commerce (IBCC). A world forum where chamber of commerce executives from industrial and developing countries and those with economies in transition can exchange experience and expertise. The IBCC also represents chambers worldwide in contacts with intergovernmental organizations and other international bodies. Address: Paris, France. E-mail: *IBCC@iccwbo.org.* Web site: *www.icc-ibcc.org.*

International Exchanges (iX). Organized in the year 2000, through a merger of the London Stock Exchange and the Frankfurt Stock Exchange, with a link to NASDAQ. It is the fourth-largest stock exchange in the world, headquartered in London.

International Monetary Fund (IMF). Created in 1944 at
Bretton Woods, New Hampshire, this organization promotes
international monetary cooperation, facilitates the expansion
and balanced growth of international trade, promotes exchange
stability, assists in the establishment of a multilateral system of
payments, makes its general resources temporarily available
under adequate safeguards to members experiencing difficulties
with a blance payments, and shortens the duration and lessens
the degree of disequilibrium in the international balances of
payments of members. The fund is sustained by member contributions, the largest of which is the U.S., with slightly under
20% of total funding. At the end of 1996, the fund had issued
$42.1 billion in special drawing rights (SDRs) to member coun-
tries with balance of payment problems. Address: International
Monetary Fund, Washington, D.C. 20431, USA, Telephone:
(202) 623-7300: Fax: (202) 623-6278.

**International Organization of Securities Commissions
(IOSCO).** An organization of global securities regulators with
the purpose of developing international standards of securities
regulation.

International Securities Exchange (ISE). The latest national
securities exchange established in the United States, approved
by the SEC in 2000 for electronic options trading. It is the first
exchange approved by the SEC since 1973, and began trading
options contracts in May 2000. Other options exchanges in the
United States are the Chicago Board of Trade, the American
Stock Exchange, the Pacific Exchange, and the Philadelphia
Stock Exchange. Backers and developers of the exchange are a
large group of brokers, headed by Morgan Stanley Dean Witter,
E*Trade, and Americatrade. Initially, the exchange listed 600 of
the most active equity options. As an electronic exchange, there
is no traditional trading floor and all trades are electronic and
anonymous. The ISE has created a regulatory division and
joined the Options Clearing Corporation, which operates under
SEC sanctions. *See* **American Stock Exchange, Chicago
Board of Trade, Pacific Exchange, Options Clearing**

Corporation, Philadelphia Stock Exchange, and **Global Investment Market.**

Internet or **World Wide Web** or **Web.** A reference to the vast collection of documents, databases, and software programs linked through telephony codes and facilities to a global network of computers. This information base and network is sometimes called the Information Super Highway. Beginning in the late 1990s this forum became the fastest growing segment for trading in investment securities, accounting for between 20% and 25% of the total retail trade in securities. This growth is occurring globally as the world moves toward one big securities market, although there are impediments to this happening completely and soon. There are language barriers, currency differences, accounting differences, and business ethics, to name but a few.

Internet Broker Scorecard. A service of Gomez Advisors' Website that ranks online brokers in such areas as phone response time and staff quality. Web site: *www.gomez.com.*

Internet Corporation for Assigned Names and Numbers (ICANN). The organization that assigns and manages the system of Internet addresses in the United States.

Internet fraud. The illegal act of spreading false and misleading information over the Internet that causes investors to suffer losses for reasons not associated with the inherent risks in the stock market. It is the fastest growing type of investment fraud, due to the ease of disseminating false or misleading information broadly and efficiently over the rapidly expanding electronic medium. Perpetrating these frauds is easily increased by the naivete of many investors who believe they are controlling their investments on the Internet, when, in reality, they are at the mercy of anonymous crooks. The Securities and Exchange Commission has the responsibility of enforcing anti-fraud provisions of securities laws in the United States. Recently, this agency has established an automated surveillance system, dedicated to coping with Internet fraud. Under this system, a "crawler" will electronically scan web sites for approximately 50 keywords that are considered potentially indicative of fraud.

A phrase such as "get rich quick" is an example. The automated surveillance system would construct a database of problem sites from scanning Web sites and public online forums, like message boards. Internet chat rooms are not included. E-mail would not be included, unless it appears in public online forums. This system, in its infancy, is likely to undergo many changes as it is implemented. The delicate balance between regulatory and privacy rights is in question, and many utilizers of the Internet object to certain aspects of the SEC's new system, on the grounds it violates privacy. *See* **investment fraud.** According to the SEC, the biggest sources of Internet fraud are:

- False claims of a big offering of a recommended stock in the near future;
- Greatly inflated financial projections or forecasts of recommended stocks;
- Untrue background or investment record of advisors;
- Advice by analysts who are compensated by stock shares in recommendations;
- Exaggerated claims of investment firm's experience in trading.

Internet funds. Mutual fund shares representing investments in companies deriving most of their revenues from Internet-based business. Some are sold strictly on the Internet. Examples are: Munder Netnet, WWW Internet, and The Internet Fund.

"Internet road show." The reference to the dissemination to the public of material investment information required by the Securities and Exchange Commission, in connection with a new public issue of stock, using the Internet as a medium for its presentation, in part. Originally, Internet presentations were considered radio or TV by securities regulators, and presentations over that medium were prohibited, since only oral statements about the security and the preliminary prospectus can be made during the period between the filing and the effective registration of the security issue or the "road show" period. But recently "no-action letters" dealing with such presentations have apparently moderated that position.

Internet stocks. Stocks representing companies deriving most of their revenues from Internet-based business. Examples are Amazon Books (retailer), Doubleclick (advertising), and Yahoo! (search engine). *See* **dot-com stock.**

"Internet time." In the lexicon of the high-tech business community, a reference to the rapidity with which events such as deal making, technological innovation, and the success and failure of companies occur.

Internet trading or **E-trading.** Stock transactions that originate on the Internet. There are nearly 100 brokerage firms that accept trades on the Internet, some of which are old-line firms. At the close of 1997, there were 3 million online brokerage customers, a number that will climb to 14 million by the year 2003, according to Forrester Research. Online commissions range from $5 per trade to more than $30, with varying degrees of assistance and research furnished. Internet trading accounts for approximately 17% of total stock trading volume in the United States A source for information on Internet brokers is the Gomez survey at *www.scorecard.com. Barron's* and *Smart Money* also publish rankings of online firms.

intervention. The preliminary steps to nationalization of foreign assets by a government.

intra-day low or **high.** The low or high set by the Dow Jones averages during a session.

intranet. A reference to a corporate network of computers and ancillary technology that uses Internet facilities and technology to access and manage internal documents. The European branches of a global marketing company might use such a system to share information on the level of inventories at each one's location in order to maintain supply availability for all customers by shipping to branches with low inventories.

intrepreneur. A person who likes to create and launch one or more new products or services, but as an employee of a large corporation. Usually a team of this sort of person is created to carry out the development of a certain commercial program.

Like the entrepreneur, the intrepreneur is often not committed to a certain type of business, but concentrates on where the management of the corporation decides the attractive economic opportunities are. Usually the intrepreneur is compensated at a higher salary rate and receiving equity in the resulting products or services or the corporation. Once the product or service is marketable, often the intrepreneurial team is disbanded. Sometimes the intrepreneur(s) are technically-trained professionals, who are selected because of their expertise. *See* **entrepreneur** and **skunkworks.**

intrinsic value. In securities analysis, the concentration on the tangible worth represented by a common stock, such as the market value of its net assets or the present value of a stream of future corporate cash flow—most likely in the form of its dividends or earnings—in selecting the most attractive stocks to buy or the most logical ones to sell. To illustrate, suppose your favorite high tech stock is Memories Are Made of This, Inc. It sells for $25 per share, and the present value of its minuscule dividend stream is only $12. Clearly the stock is overpriced, using this intrinsic value technique. The flaw of this method is that it often eliminates investing in stocks with attractive future growth potential, because operating results are immature, thus retarding current dividends and a consequential high present value.

intrinsic-value method. See **variable ratio formula** under **formula investing.**

Inventories to Sales Ratio. See under **Economic Indicators.**

inventory. 1) Those goods which are stocked to carry on a primary business objective. They are consumed in the business process. 2) The variety and quantity of security issues which an over-the-counter dealer keeps in his personal account for resale.

inventory turnover. See **sales to inventories.**

Inventory Valuation Adjustment (IVA), Commerce Department. An adjustment made by the Department of Commerce (DOC) in calculating the National Income and

Product Accounts (NIIPA) for the difference between the cost of inventory withdrawals as valued in determining profits before tax and the cost of those withdrawals valued at replacement costs. It is necessary because, under accounting practices used by businesses to determine income, inventories are often charged to cost of sales at their acquisition rather than at replacement costs. In periods of changing prices, this practice results in inventory profits or losses. In the United States, the DOC reports profits both before and after this adjustment. For the other principal adjustment, see **Capital Consumption Allowance.**

inverse numerical order. A phrase used to describe bonds which are redeemable before maturity starting with the ones farthest from maturity and working back toward the nearest.

inverted or **negative yield curve.** A long-term **yield curve** reflecting a yield schedule, usually on U.S. Treasury issues, in which there is a reversal or anomaly in the order of yields. This situation is usually caused by a shortage of investable funds in the short term and a scarcity in the long term. For example, in the case of the U.S. government, since short-term yields on Treasury bills and notes are normally lower than long-term ones on bonds, a curve showing short-term yields higher would be considered inverted, and would suggest economic events— budget deficits, refunding maturing issues, emergencies, and so on—are causing demand pressures for money or capital in the immediate future.

Investment. The converting of assets, usually money, into a security or enterprise with the objective of preserving that amount or capital as well as earning a reasonable return or percentage on it at regular intervals. In investing, even when the preservation of capital and return is not expected immediately, the investor's mind-set on the front end is that realistically both will materialize in the future. *See* **speculation.**

Investment Advisers Act of 1940 as amended. A Congressional act regulating professional investment advisers, with respect to conduct, personal disclosure, management of clients' securities, and advertising. It covers all persons who professionally advise others, either directly or in written correspondence, on the value of securities or the advisability of investing in or selling securities. The act also covers persons who disseminate for payment analyses or reports concerning securities. Exemptions are granted to newspapers and magazines of general interest and regular circulation; brokers and dealers who give advice incidental to other services and gratuitously; and banks, attorneys, teachers, and accountants who give advice incidentally, and those persons who confine advice to U.S. government obligations. Unless exempt, such advisers must register with the SEC, unless their clientele is intrastate in nature or restricted to very few persons and certain other categories. The use of the term "investment counsel" is confined to registered advisers engaged in appropriate activities. Also, the educational and working background of registrants is on file with the SEC, although the latter does not pass upon the qualifications of registrants. In a transaction with a client, a registered adviser cannot act as principal for his own account or as a broker for a third party, unless the client is notified. Registrants are required to maintain records for at least five years. Although a great deal of the registrants' records are private, the SEC can subpoena them for trials. Fines are the usual method of enforcement, although jail terms are also used. *See* **securities laws.**

investment banker. An individual, or firm, who purchases securities in big blocks from a corporation or government agency for resale to the public, profiting from the difference between the price for which the securities were purchased and the resale price. *See* **underwriter.**

investment club. A small group of investors pooling their resources and knowledge to buy securities as well as to share profits and losses from capital gains and losses. Most clubs operate on democratic principles, voting on what securities are included in the portfolio. Usually, the members take turns at researching and analyzing stocks and presenting their conclusions to the club. Besides an initial investment when the club is formed, most club assess members monthly or quarterly to grow capital for investing. Through the combination, small investors are able to share in a more diversified portfolio and obtain lower transaction costs than if they were investing alone. *See* **Beardstown Ladies, National Association of Investors Corporation,** and **World Federation of Investors Corporation.**

investment company. See **investment trust.**

Investment Company Act of 1940 as amended. A federal act regulating the activities of investment companies—mutual funds and investment trusts—and placing them under the jurisdiction of the Securities and Exchange Commission. From a regulatory standpoint, the act establishes an effort to effect the following practices:

1. honest and independent management of investment companies through restricting, in general, the portion of the board of directors who have a conflict of interest with shareholders;

2. greater participation in the management by investors and strict adherence to the fund's stated investment objectives;

3. maintenance of sound capital structures, including restrictions on debt;

4. full disclosure of financial performances to shareholders and filings with the SEC;

5. selling practices that are clear to investors up front, and the elimination of unfair tactics such as switching shareholders from one fund to another, while charging additional sales load;

6. the regulation of advertising practices by investment companies.

investment counselor. A person who advises others on the investment of funds, usually for a fee based on a percentage of the invested values, and who is registered and supervised by the Security and Exchange Commission under Investment Advisors Act of 1940 if he or she has more than 10 clients and any of them reside outside his or her state of domicile.

investment fraud. The use of false or misleading information to induce investors to buy securities that causes them to lose money not ordinarily associated with stock market risks. In the United States, the Securities and Exchange Commission and the various state securities regulators are responsible for enforcing the anti-fraud provisions of federal and state securities acts. *See* **National Fraud Information Center, Securities and Exchange Commission, Securities Act of 1933,** and **Securities Act of 1933 Amended.** Some major categories of investment securities frauds are:

- Affinity fraud. The perpetration of securities fraud directed at ethnic, professional, or religious affiliations.
- Day-trading scams. The use of exaggerated and deceptive advertising claims about trading profits by day-trading firms.
- Entertainment scams. The promotion of dubious investments in movies, TV programs, infomercials, theme restaurants, and Internet gambling.
- Financial guru fraud. The promotion of cheap or risky stocks by a national figure, using false information.
- Foreign currency scam. The promise to the average investor of big profits, which are proven to be exaggerated and unlikely, from betting on changes in various foreign currency values.
- Pump-and-dump scam. The blatant promotion of securities, in which the promoters have a financial stake, disguised as independent research in Internet junk mail, telephone calls, Internet message boards, newsletters, and other media.

To avoid fraud, follow this advice suggested by the Commodity Futures Trading Commission, the North American Securities Administrators Association, the National Consumers League, and the Securities and Exchange Commission.

1. Hang up on high-pressure callers promoting guaranteed profits from volatile stock, currency, or commodities markets.
2. Avoid any company that forecasts or guarantees profits that seem unbelievable, while promising little or no financial risk.
3. Only trade on margin after you understand how margin accounts work.

4. Maintain a skeptical attitude towards tips you get on the Internet.
5. Be suspicious of anyone who urges quick investment decisions.
6. Remain wary of exotic investments that are confusing.
7. Determine if a security you are interested in is registered with the SEC and the appropriate state securities regulator, and ask for a propsectus.
8. Inquire about account statement procedures, commissions, and fees before investing.
9. Check on an investment advisor or the securities offered by calling the appropriate local, state, or federal regulators to determine if they are registered, and if there is a disciplinary record.
10. Avoid dealing with any securities operator who will not furnish professional background details.
11. Pass up any confusing investment, because it might be confusing to dupe investors.
12. When an investment sounds too good to be true, it probably is.

investment house. An outdated term for a firm or office where securities can be traded on a commission and/or dealer basis.

investment letter stock. A stock distribution exempted from registration with the SEC under the **Securities Act of 1933** as amended but requiring a written statement from the investor to the distributor affirming that he is buying the stock for investment purposes. This affirmation implies that the investor intends to retain the stock for long-term objectives as compared with immediate stock market profits. Presumably, he has committed himself to keeping the stock two years or until his investment objectives change or corporate financial results of the stock jeopardize his investment position. *See* **registration for exempted transactions.**

investment quality stock. A stock which has stable earning power and is paying consistent dividends, yielding as well as other high-grade securities such as bonds and mortgage notes.

Generally, earnings are analyzed on a 5- to 10-year basis in analyzing a stock for investment quality.

investment sites (Web). Web sites on which investors, speculators, and frauds may post notices on a bulletin board or engage in investment chatter about stocks in a chat room. There is inherent in these formats the opportunity for unscrupulous persons to use the formats to hype or bash stocks, often for their personal gains. Erroneous information or exaggerated prospects for a stock can be presented, for instance, although legitimate information and advice also occurs. Most of the regulatory bodies are developing methods for coping with securities fraud on the Internet. The far bigger problem is chat rooms, because the comments are fleeting, while bulletin board postings go to an archive and are traceable for use in prosecutions of stock manipulation. There are four sites where most investment commentary is focused: Microsoft's *www.investor.com*; Motley Fool's *www.fool.com*; Go2Net's *www.siliconinvestor.com*; and Yahoo Inc.'s *www.yahoo.com*. *Caveat Emptor!*

investment trust or **mutual fund** or **investment company.** A financial organization that pools funds in exchange for shares in the total fund and invests in diversified securities. Trading profits and dividend income can be reinvested or distributed to shareholders. These organizations are regulated by the federal Investment Company Act of 1940. Technically, only those investment companies set up under a state trust agreement, such as the Massachusetts investment trusts, can be called trusts, but common usage has assigned the term to investment companies. There are two types of investment companies. *See* **open-end investment companies** and **closed-end investment companies.**

Investor Home: The Home Page for Investors on the Internet. See **Web Sites for the Inquiring Investor.**

Investor Relations Information Network (IRIN). See **Web Sites for the Inquiring Investor.**

Investor Relations Officer (IRO). That official in a company responsible for reporting operating and financial information to the media, analysts, and investors. In small companies, this individual is often also the Chief Financial Officer.

Investor Responsibility Research Center (IRRC). An independent, nonprofit, research firm established in 1972. It is the leading provider of unbiased research on proxy voting issues, corporate governance, and corporate social responsibility topics. The Center provides research to 400 institutional subscribers who rely on the research and analysis of its professional staff. The Center also serves governments, corporations, law firms, boards of directors, boards of trustees, the media, and others seeking independent analysis of the issues shaping corporate decision making and investment trends. Web site: *www.irrc.org*.

investorguide.com. A Web site featuring a directory of links to over 6,000 stocks, in addition to corporate news, stock quotes, research, personal finance, and so on. *See* **Web Sites for the Inquiring Investor.**

Investor's Business Daily Online. See **Web Sites for the Inquiring Investor.**

Investorville. A Web site offering investment message boards, industry and market trends, and personal finance advice. *See* **Web Sites for the Inquiring Investor.**

IOSCO. Abbreviation for **International Organization of Securities Commissions.**

Iowa Department of Commerce. Regulator of securities laws in the state of Iowa. Address: Insurance Division, Lucas State Office Building, Des Moines, IA 50319. Phone: (515) 281-4441.

IPO. Abbreviation for **Initial Public Offering.**

IPO.com. A Web site providing financial and market information on stocks that are recent inital public offerings. *See* **Web Sites for the Inquiring Investor.**

IPO Maven. A Web site providing financial and market information on stocks that are recent initial public offerings. *See* **Web Sites for the Inquiring Investor.**

IRA. See **Individual Retirement Account.**

IRIN. Abbreviation for **Investor Relations Information Network.**

Irish dividend. A facetious term for an assessment of shareholders by a corporation.

IRO. See **Investor Relations Officer.**

IRRC. Abbreviation for **Investor Responsibility Research Center.**

irregular market. A securities trading session in which normal trading patterns are upset. Usually, untested speculative issues gain along with the more popular speculative favorites while many investment quality securities are lower.

irrevocable trust. A document similar to a revocable trust designed to allow the maker to give away certain property before death, thereby having that property excluded from his or her estate taxes. These trusts cannot be changed. *See* **revocable trust.**

IRS. Abbreviation for **Internal Revenue Service.**

IRS Digital Daily, The. A Web site devoted to providing tax forms and infromation from the Internal Revenue Service (IRS). *See* **Web Sites for the Inquiring Investor.**

Islamic investing. A reference to the inclusion of investment principles in the practice of the Islamic religion, conducted by Muslims, unlike most other mainstream religions of the world. Worldwide, Muslims are able to invest between $80 billion and $150 billion, an amount that is increasing by 12–15% annually. Muslims are instructed not to invest in "sin" stocks—i.e., those that offer certain banking services, pork products, alcoholic products, and entertainment—or stocks representing companies that do not quantify earnings, such as supermarkets and advertising agencies, as well as companies that derive revenues from advertising, such as many Internet companies. To date, the Board of Islamic Law has approved 650 stocks worldwide that adhere to Islamic tenets, with a market capitalization of $10 trillion, and 14 financial service companies as suitable for their investment programs.

issue. A specific class of stock or bonds distributed by a corporation or governmental authority, in order to raise money.

issued stock. That authorized corporate stock which has been transferred to investors.

issuer. Any corporation or governmental authority which has sold to the public stock or bonds currently in force.

issues traded. The number of classes of stock, representing different corporations, which traded during a market session.

Istanbul Stock Exchange. See under **Global Investment Markets.**

IT. Abbreviation for **Information Technology.**

Italian Stock Exchange. See under **Global Investment Markets.**

IVILLAGE MONEYLIFE. See under **Web Sites for Investing Women.**

iX. Abbreviation for **International Exchanges.**

Jj

"jamming the auditor." A reference to corporate management giving its auditors inadequate time to examine the books before announcing results of operations. Often, this action is intended to cover up some irregularity in the results.

January Effect. A name given to the propensity for small-cap stocks to rise more in value than large-cap stocks, in early January of each year. According to adherents, since 1926 small-cap stocks have gained 5% more on average than large caps. One reason ascribed to this phenomenon is that year-end tax selling in the prior year has forced stock prices down, rather than investor disappointment in fundamentals, and the bargains that have resulted have attracted buyers.

January Indicator. A popular opinion among some investors that in a year the S&P 500 Stock Index rises in January, the general market will rise. Advocates claim that this tendency has occurred 88% of the time since 1950.

Japan Inc. A reference to the economic powerhouse that Japan has developed into since its defeat in WWII. In terms of its GDP, which has grown over recent years at 2.6% annually, the island country ranks as the second largest economy in the world, exceeded only by the United States. Services comprise 60% of Japan's GDP, industry comprises 38%, and agriculture 2%. Its population is 127.4 million. Much of the credit for the country's economic success is the close internal cooperation between manufacturers, suppliers, and distributors, called *keiretsu,* as well as its strong work ethic, high literacy rate, and high technology propensity.

JASDAQ (Japan). The over-the-counter electronic trading system in Japan, similar to the NASDAQ in the United States, where most small Japanese companies trade. *See* under **Global Investment Market.**

"Jewish engineering." A somewhat facetious but perhaps apropos reference to the formal study of economics, derived from the legendary reputation that members of the Jewish faith have for succeeding in business by using common sense approaches rather than the arcane principles of formal economics—such as marginal propensity to consume, accelerator effect, random walk, and Simon says: "Two giant hops forward and a stumble backwards."

"jiggles." In the online trading markets, those stocks that fluctuate in price frequently and quickly.

Johannesburg Stock Exchange (JSE). See under **Global Investment Market.**

joint account. An investment or banking account, in which two or more parties have equal rights and voice in its management. By prior arrangement, either one or all the parties may participate in making transactions altering holdings in the property in the account.

joint account agreement. In securities trading or banking, a form in which two or more parties apply to open a joint account, although only one party can be designated by the others to authorize transactions in the account. All parties owning the account must sign the form.

joint bond. A bond issued with more than one debtor responsible for payment of the debt obligations, such as bond interest and principal when due. Often a parent corporation will guarantee the debt service of a bond issued by a subsidiary, in which case they are joint debtors or issuers. However, the guarantor can be a nonaffiliated party also. Guarantors can also agree to pay other obligations for an issuer, such as dividends on a preferred stock issue.

Joint Stock Company. A hybrid form of business enterprise in the United States, combining characteristics of the conventional corporation and partnership, in which investors receive shares of stock which are freely transferable but that confer on them unlimited liability for the debts of the company. They also elect directors of the company. It differs from the usual corporation, by not providing limited liability for stockholders, and differs from a partnership by not requiring cumbersome procedures for transferring ownership shares. This type of business organization definitely has benefits: Taxes are usually lower, initial formation is easier and cheaper and there is less regulation. Even so, it is not popular in the United States. The main criticisms are these companies cannot own real estate and shareholders have unlimited liability.

"jointly and severally." In general law, a reference to the phrase included in an agreement that creates a liability for all parties entering into an obligation, either in total or separately. This phrase gives the party(s) having a claim a broader base of possibilities in pressing a claim, since that party(s) can look to one or more obligators for restitution. For example, when a bond is guaranteed by several parties, any one or all may be sued for non-performance of the contract by the bondholder(s). The inclusion of this phrase in an agreement usually adds quality to a bond indenture, especially where some large, credit-worthy companies are the creditors. The phrase creating the opposite effect—"severally but not jointly"—limits the liabilities of parties jointly and is relatively less attractive for investors.

joint tenants. Generally in securities ownership and banking, a reference to two or more parties who own the same property in a joint account. Caution should be exercised in assuming a legal joint tenancy always exists in such an account, since courts in some states have ruled both parties must contribute towards the purchase(s) of property included to create a valid joint tenancy.

joint tenancy with rights of survivorship (JTWROS). In securities ownership or banking, a joint tenancy in which the surviving co-owner(s) of property(s) inherits the entire account, upon the death of another joint tenant. Such an arrangement can by-pass the probate process, although the survivor(s) may be liable for estate taxes. *See* **joint account, joint tenants,** and **tenants in common.**

joint venture. An agreement between two or more parties to combine certain of their resources to accomplish a specific business objective, without a formal reorganization of each participant in the case of two operating companies wishing to collaborate. However, a formal structure to the joint venture usually occurs, such as a corporation or partnership arrangement, but it still operates with the narrow objectives of the joint venture. Sometimes two companies wish to blend their technologies toward some product, but do not wish to merge their companies or reorganize themselves. This restricted organization has the advantage of affording a relatively easy formation and termination of the project, when it is completed or if it is not working out well. Usually, the venture is staffed with employees temporarily assigned from each participant. Money is contributed, based on the proportion of the venture committed to by each party, or until it develops cash flow if having its own revenue stream is in the plans. For example, crude oil pipelines are constructed and operated through joint ventures, in corporate form, created by several oil companies owning oil reserves to ship through the lines. When the oil plays out, the joint venture lines are dissolved or used for some other purpose.

In the United States, the Justice Department and the Federal Trade Commission has proposed guidelines on the types of arrangements that are not in violation of federal antitrust laws. This was in response to the many companies that want to form joint ventures in purchasing, marketing, licensing, or research, but are growing more confused about the legal restraints. In the guideline proposals, the agencies recognize that the forces of globalization and technology are pressing companies to form collaborations to enter foreign markets, raise increasing amounts of capital and reduce production and other costs. The two agencies maintain that agreements among competitors to share or divide markets by allocating customers, suppliers, territories, or lines of commerce continue to be illegal. However, when companies otherwise are in competitive industries and wish to collaborate in a manner not disturbing the competitive picture, joint ventures will probably be allowed. The agencies indicated that there might be a problem if the companies, in combination, hold more than 20% of a market.

Journal. Abbreviation for *The Wall Street Journal.*

journaling. In an Internet trading firm or day trading firm, the practice by management of arranging loans between customers to finance securities trades. Often these loans bear unusually high interest rates and can be between customers who are strangers, in different branches. Because they are relatively free of regulation, abuses of securities financing laws can occur.

JTWROS. Abbreviation for **joint tenants with right of survivorship.**

judgment. In commercial law, a reference to a court's order to a defendant in a legal action, that directs the defendant to pay the plaintiff's (party bringing the claim) claim for a specific sum of money. Usually, the plaintiff is suing for money owed and due from a loan, a sale of goods or services, or damages from a breach of contract. Often the stock of a company seeking a judgment will react favorably when the outcome is likely to be successful in court.

jumbos. Those certificates of deposit denominated in a minimum $100,000 amount. They are usually acquired by big institutional investors.

junior issue. A class of stock or bonds that loses priority to one or more of a corporation's securities, in the matter of income, interest, or dividend payments, or in a liquidation distribution of assets. In a corporation's hierarchy of multiple securities, there is always one most senior and another most junior, but in evaluating the position of each, it is usually in relation to all those more senior and all those most junior. In other words, the important point is that the amount of cash flow and asset values that will be available to the category in question, in comparison with the others, is what determines how senior or junior an issue is. *See* **position, securities claim,** and **senior issue.**

junior mortgage. In mortgage financing, a debt secured by a mortgage on real property that is beneath one or more other mortgages in terms of priority in settling the lender's claim, in the event of a default by the borrower. Sometimes there is a second and third mortgage on the same property, leading to senior and junior mortgages. Mortgages are satisfied in the order of their seniority, in the event of nonperformance by the borrower. *See* **senior mortgage.**

junior refunding. The act of refinancing federal, state, or municipal bonds that mature in five years or less with bonds that mature in more than five years. Usually, this is done for one of two reasons: (1) to pay off high-interest bonds with ones costing less in interest charges and (2) to ease debt service requirements by stretching out payments, during tight financial times.

junior subordinated issue. In a multiple corporate debt structure, a debt issue that loses priority to other securities, but is senior to at least one other. *See* **junior issue** and **senior issue.**

junk bonds or **high-yield bonds.** Bonds associated with high risk, in terms of financial default or irregularity in fulfilling the terms of their indenture contracts. Because of their high risk, they usually are high-yielding bonds, relative to investment-grade bonds. This is because investors have depressed the prices in their refusal to accept lower interest rates, at least from such questionable bonds. Generally, they are debentures, or bonds without specific collateralization, such as mortgage bonds offer, and are instead repayable from the full faith and credit of the issuer. Issued by unknown or financially ailing companies, these bonds are rated BB or lower by Standard & Poor's, or BA or lower by Moody's Investment Service. Such bonds often proliferate during periods of high interest rates and tight credit, when quality differences reflected in yields tends to dim.

jurisdiction. In legal matters generally the place where units of judicial administration, such as police departments and courts, are empowered to administer laws. In investment matters, the term applies to a local, state, or federal agency responsible for establishing procedures and enforcement of laws regulating certain business operations, usually on an industry-wide basis. Because of the incursion of federal activities into public welfare issues, most of the powerful agencies in the United States are at the federal level. Examples are the Federal Food and Drug Administration (FDA), the Federal Trade Commission (FTC), the Federal Communications Commission (FCC), the

Environmental Protection Agency (EPA), and the Federal Energy Regulatory Commission (FERC). At the state level, the Texas Railroad Commission (TRC) is a powerful regulator of oil and gas, because so much of those resources are produced in that state.

Regulated industries usually enjoy some privilege for the requirement to operate under supervision, especially on the local level. For example, electric power companies are granted a monopolistic franchise to supply electricity to an area in exchange for rate regulation at the state and local level, and the federal level when its transmission lines cross state boundaries. Cable TV companies are granted a franchise to supply TV over cable within a geographic boundary in exchange for regulation of charges and programming by city councils and the Federal Communications Commission, in certain cases. For investors, it is important to know how a company representing a prospective stock relates to regulation in general, in the case of environmental law, and specifically, in the case of certain federally-regulated industries such as energy, pharmaceuticals, railroads, airlines, foods, and restaurants, to name but a few.

Kk

KA–CHING. See under **Web Sites for Investing Women.**

Kaffirs. A reference to shares representing ownership in South African gold mining companies, which are traded on the London Stock Exchange and over-the-counter as American Depository Receipts in the United States. Under law, the companies must distribute most of their earnings as dividends. Consequently, the shares provide investors with dividend income and a certain hedge against inflation. However, there are attendant political risks in South African investments, as well as gold price volatility.

kangaroos. A nickname for the **All Ordinaries Index** of Australia.

Kansas Securities Commission. Regulator of securities laws in the state of Kansas. Address: 618 South Kansas Avenue, 2nd Floor, Topeka, KS 66603. Phone: (913) 296-3307.

Kentucky Department of Financial Institutions. Regulator of securities laws in the state of Kentucky. Address: Division of Securities, 477 Versailles Road, Frankfort, KY 40601. Phone: (502) 573-3390.

Keogh Plan (H.R.10). Under the Keogh Act as amended by the **Employee Retirement Income Security Act of 1974**, a program that allows qualified self-employed individuals (and shareholder/employees of Subchapter "S" corporations) to contribute 15% of earned income or $7,500, whichever is less, toward retirement benefits, while deferring payment of federal income taxes. The plan is especially applicable to doctors, lawyers, accountants, engineers, and other self-employed professionals.

key man (woman) insurance. A reference to a life insurance policy, usually term but not always, that is purchased by a company that is also the beneficiary. It insures against economic loss from the death of an important company executive, usually the cheif executive. The purpose of the policy(ies) is to provide a sum of money to the company in the event of an executive's death that can be used to recruit a replacement, perhaps offering a bonus, or to make some other arrangement for the welfare of the company and investors. It is a vital consideration when investing in a small company, especially one built on the expertise or skills of the chief executive.

Keynes, John Maynard. See **Keynesian Economics.**

Keynesian Economics. The economic philosophy of making the government responsible to direct the economic activities of a country and to intervene in them when necessary. The result, adherents claim, will be more economic growth with greater stability. British economist John Maynard Keynes developed the blueprint for the doctrine in his book, *The General Theory of Interest, Employment, and Money,* published in 1935. It proved to be the response applied to the Great Depression in the United States and many other countries in the 1930s. He recommended the government's entry into the marketplace by controlling aggregate consumer demand through adjustments in taxing and government spending or fiscal policy. Demand is the key. He believed when it is too slight, unemployment and economic stagnation will result, and when it is too great, inflation will result. Keynesian Economics prevailed in the industrialized nations, until the last quarter of the 20th century, when a revisiting of classical economics such as Laissez-faire gained a foothold in macroeconomic planning. Keynes himself, predicted that the harsh conditions imposed on the defeated Germany by the Treaty of Versailles after WWI would inevitably lead to German rebellion. Of course, it was this national mood that swept Adolph Hitler to power and triggered WWII. *See* **Laissez-faire Economics** and **monetary aggregates.**

kickback. A practice of ill-repute and sometimes outright illegality, in which one party is paid through a return of a portion of money previously paid to another party in some transaction. It is typically begun by the party receiving the money in the first place in exchange for the business or granting favors. Example: In securities trading, if a broker gives back part of the commissions a customer was charged for trading as an inducement to continue the relationship, it would be a kickback and illegal under securities laws. This practice usually represents an ongoing relationship, whereas a payoff represents a one-time payment, with the same objectives. Kickbacks and payoffs are illegal for U.S. corporations to engage in as methods of doing business.

kicker or **sweetener.** A feature of a debt security that gives an investor an additional reason to commit money to the security, besides the interest income and maturity schedule(s) available. Usually, it takes the form of the right to convert a debenture to common equity at a predetermined price or warrants to buy common stock at a predetermined price for a specific length of time. Often the feature is an inducement for investors who otherwise might avoid such a security, either because the yield is not adequate for the risks involved or because the quality of the issuer is below standards set for both debt and equity. The sweetener is more attractive when the conversion stock price or warrant exercise price is close to the current stock market price. In these cases, the prospect's additional investment returns sooner and means a higher rate of return on the investment package. From the issuer's viewpoint, including the inducement usually means paying less interest costs while granting the company prospects for more equity and less debt in their balance sheet, a change that usually improves the balance sheet and supports more debt in the future.

kidstock. A Web site for youngsters, featuring companies that cater to that market. *See* under **Web Sites for the Inquiring Investor.**

Kiplinger Online. See under **Web Sites for the Inquiring Investor.**

knock-out option. A type of option contract that establishes a specific price in advance at which the option holder may buy the underlying position—whether commodities, stocks, or other positions—but is not obligated to do so. When the price passes through the preset price, the option expires and is worthless.

Regular options do not have a preset price and only expire when the preset time period is over. Knock-out options cost less because the chances of their being exercised is less.

"Know Your Customer" rule. A reference to the ethical standard in the securities industry requiring that brokers understand the financial condition and disposition of their customers. It is formally stated, and always inferred, by the rules of most exchanges and regulators. In particular, Article 3 under Rules of Fair Practice of NASD, stipulates that members, when recommending a transaction in a security to a customer, believe from information available that the transaction suits the needs of the customer. Financial information provided by a customer when opening an account includes such information, in most cases. *See* **Suitability Rule.**

Kondratieff Wave or **Kondratieff Cycle.** A reference to a long-term business cycle in industrialized countries, notably the United States, that spans 48 to 60 years. The theory was developed by Nikolai Kondratieff, an economist in the Soviet Union, who in 1925 published a study entitled, "The Long-Wave Cycle," for which he received a Nobel Prize. He constructed his theory after analyzing the levels of wages, interest rates, foreign trade, coal and iron production, and commodity prices in industrialized countries from the 1780s to the 1920s. He postulated that each long wave had two phases: a 25-year upturn, followed by a 25-year downturn which included a 10- to 15-year plateau of apparent recovery. Others have applied his research and theory to the late 20th and early 21st centuries. The upswing was characterized by rising prices, economic expansion, and high inflation. Eventually, prices broke, overcapacity persisted, debt was repudiated and depression set in. For the investor, it means there have been serious long-term economic problems in industrialized capitalistic economies, and it is possible there will be again. However, these cycles are slow, except for the "shocks" ending the secondary recovery plateaus of the downturns. *See* **Elliott Wave.**

Krugerrand, South African. A gold coin issued by South Africa in 1967, with a gold content of 1 ounce, 22 karat quality. It is the most widely-held gold coin in the world, used by investors to conveniently invest in gold bullion. Like other gold coins, it is sold initially for the value of gold contained therein plus a premium to cover the cost of manufacturing, marketing, and distribution. In the aftermarket, it can sell for a premium. This coin dominated the gold coin market until the late 1980s, when its high premium over other gold coins began to decrease. On one side of the coin is a depiction of Paul Kruger, first president of the Republic of South Africa from 1883 to 1902. On the reverse side appears the springbok, the official national animal of South Africa. *See* **Eagle, American Gold** and **Maple Leaf, Canadian Gold.**

Ll

L. See **money supply**.

Labor Costs per Unit of Output, Manufacturing. See **Economic Indicators**.

labor intensive. A reference to an industry in which component companies require a concentration of labor pools to compete effectively. This means that physical plant and heavy equipment—machinery, buildings, transport equipment, and so on—are not nearly as important as qualified employees. Consequently, such companies do not borrow a great deal and are less sensitive to interest rates but are affected by the level of wages. Usually, their balance sheets display leased facilities and moderate debt. Costs such as debt service, maintenance, and amortization of assets are less dominant in operations than variable costs, such as wages and salaries, training, advertising, and lease rentals. In investment analysis, they are not heavily leveraged, which means that stockholders earn proportionally more when revenues are high than when they are moderate or low. In other words, revenues and earnings tend to move by the same percentages. These industries are not tied to the business cycles, since they can be more innovative in marketing products and services. In fact, their orientation tends to be services over products. For investors, this characteristic means companies do not have large front-end money requirements. On the other hand, their relative freedom of entry means fierce competition. Examples of labor-intensive industries are Hotels, Restaurants, Entertainment, and Financial Services. *See* **capital intensive**.

Laffer Cure. A reference to the graph curve showing a relationship between productivity and reductions in marginal tax rates in the United States, used in illustrating **Supply-side Economics** during the initial years of the Reagan presidency. The curve was originated by economist Dr. Arthur B. Laffer, reputedly on a cocktail napkin in an impromptu rendition of the advantages of a tax cut in increasing tax revenues. Laffer is considered the father of supply-side economics, a concept that has been derided in recent years.

Lagging Indicators. See **Economic Indicators.**

Lagos Stock Exchange (Nigeria). See under **Global Investment Market.**

Laissez-faire Economics. The economic philosophy of allowing the business segment of a nation to operate relatively free of government interference. Considered part of classical economics, it is based on the belief that an omnipotent economic force will direct resources in and out of industrial development, according to profitability. Furthermore, this movement of resources leads to the greatest benefits for all in the society. The concept was first developed by economist Adam Smith, writing in his book, *Wealth of Nations*, in 1776. He referred to the economic force as an "invisible hand." In the nineteenth century this brand of economics stimulated the Industrial Revolution in Great Britain and the United States. However, in the twentieth century the monopolization tendencies engendered by laissez faire caused a reaction in the form of government regulation. Keynesian Economics, developed by British economist John Maynard Keynes, took over as the economic bible in the depressed 1930s. Its keystone was the advantage of government direction in the economic activities of a nation. That persisted until the last quarter of the century in the United States, when a wave of deregulation began. *See* **Keynesian Economics.**

large caps. Stocks of large companies, in terms of total stock market valuation, with stock market capitalizations of $5 billion and above (share price × shares outstanding). It is important to note that the capitalization size categories are generally relative to the level of stock prices. Stock cap groups might be smaller or larger in different market environments. Institutional and mutual fund investors have popularized the size-hierarchy technique, to enable them to coordinate their research and trading expertise with the magnitude of investment funds under management, for maximum efficiency. *See* **micro caps, mid caps,** and **small caps.**

Laspeyres index. See **fixed-weighted index.**

last-in-first-out (LIFO). In inventory valuation, an accounting assumption that the goods or materials on hand were bought during the first part of an accounting period, while those actually used were bought last. In calculating income, this means cost of goods sold was based on prices at the end of the period. In periods of high inflation, companies often elect to report financial results on a LIFO basis to minimize the distorting effects of inflation. In other words, by using the costs of recently purchased goods, operating costs are increased, and income is reduced. In this way the effect of inflation is moderated, allowing for a more objective reflection of company progress.

last sale. The price of the last market transaction in a particular stock during a trading session.

late tape. A period during which market transactions, as reported on an electronic ticker, are one or more minutes late, which necessitates that the wire operators omit the first or possibly the first two digits of a sale. However, no digits are dropped on opening sales or when it is desirable to print the full figure.

launder, to. To conceal the true origin of large amounts of cash or its equivalent, through shifting it between several banks. The source of the money is illicit, such as embezzled funds, misappropriated funds, or drug receipts. When laundering is done, usually a phony account is established to receive deposits. In the United States it is unlawful to use registered broker-dealers for such a purpose.

Law of Large Numbers. In statistics, the recognition that the greater the number of events expected in the future, the less the chances that an incorrect prediction will have disastrous repercussions. This action is especially useful in insurance underwriting. For example, if Lloyds of London insured the Titanic for $100 million in 1912 as one of 10 ocean liners insured that year, its sinking might have been disastrous, because the premium income from the others was not great enough. However, if the insurer underwrote 1,000 liners, the loss of the Titanic would have been less deleterious to Lloyds' results.

lay-off. A reference to that portion of rights to subscribe to a stock issue that are bought in the market before the expiration date by one or more investment firms, who then sell the portion these rights represent of the forthcoming stock issue to clients on a "when issued" basis immediately after the expiration date. The "when issued" stock is priced slightly under the current market price of the existing securities in the same class. After the new securities are issued, the client makes payment and the investment firm makes delivery, profiting by the difference in the price it receives and the cost of the rights in the market plus the amount paid the issuing corporation for the new security upon exercising the rights.

An investment firm begins buying rights when in its judgment the value of the forthcoming stock as represented by securities of the same class already trading will rise by the expiration date above the its costs. To the investor, the advantages of buying a stock in a lay-off is that he can purchase large quantities of the stock cheaply if the lay-off is sizeable, without affecting the market price.

"lay-up business." In the full-service, traditional brokerage industry, an easily-executed order for buying or selling a popular stock, at a high commission rate. This is the type of business that requires little time or effort by members of the brokerage, and is highly profitable. Consequently, many experts believe, it is the type of business that will be attracted to online investing, at a fraction of the commission rates.

leadership, market. See **market leadership.**

Leading Economic Indicators Index (LEI). This composite index released the last business day of the month serves as a signal of changes in the business cycle for economists and industry analysts. Historically, the index precedes the general economy in troughs and peaks and therefore is a handy tool for forecasting. There are 11 economic series in the index, each of which vary in lead time in troughs and peaks. The components are: average work week in manufacturing, initial unemployment claims, new orders for consumer goods, vendor delivery performance, orders for plants and equipment, building permits,

changes in unfilled orders for durable goods, prices of sensitive
materials, S&P 500 stock prices, M2 money supply adjusted for
inflation, and consumer expectations index. These components
are weighted in compiling the composite index. The composite
performs more reliably than any single component as an indicator. Sources of the report are various government agencies
and private groups. When the LEI goes up, fixed income securities tend to go down, common stocks rise and dollar exchange
rates rise. When the LEI decreases, fixed income securities tend
to rise, and common stocks fall as do dollar exchange rates. *See*
Coincident Indicators and **Lagging Indicators.**

Leading Indicators. See **Economic Indicators.**

league tables. Annual rankings of investment bankers on Wall
Street according to the total monetary value of investment
banking deals they participated in. The lists are compiled by
Securities Data Company of Newark, New Jersey, and are not
widely publicized. The bankers use them to market their prowess
to clients and prospective clients and often to set their fees.

LEAP. See **Long-term Equity Anticipation Security.**

learning curve. A representation on a chart of the improvement
in the results of an activity or process with the frequency of rep-
etitions or practice. In the business world, usually it is a depiction of results along a manufacturing or processing assembly
line, but the concept can also be applied to other skills, such as
preparing advertising layouts. For example, because sales have
been spotty, the advertising department of Monica's Dress
Boutiques, Inc. is charged with creating a page advertisement
each week for the apparel industry magazine—*Clothes Hoss.*
Furthermore, they are told that in order to measure the results,
advertising director Mike Mediason will record dress sales
volume each week from the chain of specialty dress stores for
12 weeks in the first quarter of 1998. Then he will construct and
publish for the Chief Executive Officer a chart showing the
learning curve of the advertising staff. Needless to say, this
chance for fame spurs on the advertising staff. They clearly

improve the advertising impact each week for 11 weeks, as measured by dress sales.

When the line flattens out in the twelfth week, the learning curve is completed. Maybe it's time to develop another campaign or advertise in a similar magazine, since the staff will likely begin well along the curve now, getting results sooner. Investors should look for evidence that a learning curve will improve results or reduce costs predictably when a company introduces new products and services. Buying such a stock in the early stages of the curve could prove profitable.

leaseback. See **sell and leaseback.**

legal age. The age at which an individual can legally enter into binding agreements and contracts without the consent of a parent or guardian. As such, that person can open a brokerage account, and make trades, pending meeting other qualifications.

legal entity. An individual or organized group that has a legal status to make agreements, binding on all parties, and carry out lawful objectives. A corporation is a legal entity, if properly constituted, and is answerable to acts engaged in by parties so empowered by its charter or bylaws. Note that a minor is not a legal entity and therefore lacks the standing to open an investment account. *See* **ultra vires acts.**

legal investment. A commitment of funds by a fiduciary, usually an institution such as a bank or insurance company, into holdings that do not violate any state or federal laws. Usually, bonds and preferred stocks appraised in the upper brackets by rating agencies such as Standard & Poor's, Moody's, or Fitch Investors Services are legal investments. The scope of "legal investment" is broader than **"legal list"** because the former concept encompasses privately placed securities and mortgages sometimes falling outside the strict definitions of a legal list but none the less legal, as well as public securities, while the latter refers to public issues or enumerated private placements. A privately placed investment must stand the test of not violating the basic laws of contract and "prudent man" fiduciary responsibility, whether or not it appears on a legal list. For example, In The Dark Insurers, Inc. could not invest funds contributed by policy holders in an M-4 tank to be used in a plot to spring Billy "The Shadow" Sutton, the notorious convicted bank robber. Among other problems, it would be an agreement calling for the commission of a crime, even though the structure of the contract might be according to "legal list" guidelines.

legal list. Those specified securities in which trustees, banks, insurance companies and other fiduciary institutions may invest funds held in a position of trust with regard to the public, according to state laws and federal regulatory agencies. Regulatory authorities compile these lists so that higher-quality debt, equity securities, and other investment instruments, such as real estate mortgages, will be invested in. The purpose is to protect payments made to the institution or trustee by the public for insurance coverage or retirement. Sometimes states allow fiduciaries to apply the **"prudent man rule,"** instead of adhering to a legal list. *See* **legal investment.**

legal monopoly. The granting of an exclusive right to a person or a company to operate a business within a specific jurisdiction, usually under the terms of a contract or franchise. The governing body of the jurisdiction regulates the grantee as to policies and rates or prices. The most common examples are utilities—electricity companies, water companies, natural gas distributors, and cable TV companies. The idea of such an anomaly in the United States at a time of free markets and capitalism is that society deems some products and services so vital to the general welfare that competition would be inefficient and counterproductive. Thus, a city, state, or municipality grants an exclusive privilege, as long as the entity is operated in a manner that serves all well, while allowing reasonable profits from operations to reward investors and attract new capital.

legal opinion. 1) In securities law, an opinion, requested by an investment banker originating a securities issue or a private financing, written by an attorney at a law firm expressing that a certain transaction or financing agreement is structured so that it meets the requirements necessary to provide investors some lawful standing or advantage they find attractive. The advantage might be a tax break, such as tax-exempt interest on municipal bonds, or a statement elaborating on the legality of a tax-free exchange of securities, or the legality of an unusual leasing arrangement, or a legal amplification of any number of prospective securities issues. Usually, the law firm employed specializes in the type of opinion requested. The opinion is an integral part of the Official Statement—the official document for investors that accompanies a municipal bond financing—or the Prospectus—the official document that accompanies most other securities issued. Without the statement, there is a serious flaw in the rights of parties to the contract. 2) A statement by an attorney general or a company's in-house general counsel on the legality of a certain transaction. In very restricted matters, such as corporate legal liabilities, these are used as legal opinions. But investors should be careful, because quite often a conflict of interest can exist between such officials and the legality commented on.

legal reserves. 1) The types of securities and other assets in which insurance companies are required to invest premiums from policy holders to protect those policy holders from unwise speculation or concentration of resources in illiquid assets by insurance managers. In other words, in order that insurance companies remain able to pay out benefits and cash values to policy holders under terms of the insurance policies, insurance regulators and legislatures establish legal reserve definitions; 2) The liquid assets in which commercial banks are permitted to invest the demand and time deposits of customers. Usually, the reserves are comprised of Treasury bills, notes, and bonds, and some quasi-government bonds. The Federal Reserve System, state banking regulators and the U.S. Comptroller of the Currency supervise reserves and loans made within the banking system.

Lehman Brothers T-Bond Index. A price index of U.S. Treasury long-term bonds, maintained by Lehman Bothers investment firm.

LEI. See **Leading Economic Indicators Index.**

Leontieff, Wassily. See **input-output model.**

lessee. A company who will lease a plant site built with proceeds from a municipality's sale of industrial revenue bonds. The quality of the bonds is determined by the lesSee's ability to fulfill the terms of the lease, enabling the municipality to repay the bond interest and principal. *See* **industrial development revenue bonds.**

letter of deficiency. A written request by the Securities and Exchange Commission for more information on a proposed issue in registration.

letter of intent or **memorandum of intent.** 1) A written agreement of intention between two or more parties having the authority to negotiate and implement such an objective, such as merging two or more companies. This is usually a preliminary document, often with conditions attached, upon which a formal contract is based and upon which other parties are invited to participate, such as two managements signing a letter of intent to merge their companies, and then taking the letter to an investment banker or commercial banker to arrange financing. In the securities business, this letter is not as binding as the final contract, since it only commits the parties to the effort. If impediments arise that could not have been anticipated, such as an inability to develop financing or the inability to win shareholder approval, where that is required under the corporate charter or bylaws, the plan is dissolved. 2) A shareholder's written statement agreeing not to sell specific shares of a company's stock for a certain period. Such stock is called "letter stock" and usually is created as part of a stock underwriting or private placement. In either case, equity kickers in the form of shares, warrants, or options are granted to investors or owners as an added inducement to do the deal. The letter is required to prevent the potential additional common stock putting selling pressure on stock prices immediately after an underwriting or financing is completed.

letter of transmittal. A form used by a stockholder to accompany stock that directs a fiscal agent to make some disposition of the stock. For example, it may be a form used by a stockholder to authorize a corporation's exchange agent to exchange the stock accompanying the form for another class offered by the issuing corporation. It could be a form to authorize an escrow agent to deposit the stock accompanying the form in order to exchange the stock for another class or to authorize the stock to be deposited to a purchaser's account if certain conditions are met, as in the case of a tender. *See* **tender and escrow agent.**

Letter or Message to Stockholders in Annual Report. Since this is the first important section of the Annual Report, it is usually upbeat. If not, then it generally explains the problems management encountered in making the year a successful one. Besides summarizing the prime events of the year under review, there is frequently some mention made of the next fiscal year, which is usually the current one and underway when the Annual Report is distributed. Most annual reports are published in March or April for fiscal years ending in the previous December. Often there is mention made of the amount that will be spent in the current year on Capital Expenditures, which has already been budgeted by the Board of Directors. New and retiring board members are mentioned. In general, this message is a written summary of what stockholders would hear at the Annual Meeting, including new corporate or business developments that will affect future operations. *See* **Letter** or **Message to Stockholders in Annual Report.**

lettered stock. *See* **tracking stock.**

level sales load. Charges that are based on an even rate annually that investors pay to buy shares of a mutual fund. A typical example would be 1% to 2% of the fund's assets represented by the shares owned. Such shares are also called C-class shares. Of the three types of sales loads—the other two are **front-end sales load** and **back-end sales load**—the level rate is the lowest and usually cheapest for the investor if the shares are held less than three years. In judging the alternatives, a great deal depends on the fund's performance.

leverage, investment. 1) A reference to the numerical amount each invested dollar returns, based on market appreciation of the security representing the investment. Leverage is found by dividing the security's sale price by its cost. For example, a stock that cost $5 and sold for $15 had a leverage of three; each dollar invested returned three. 2) A reference to the amount used in purchasing securities in relation to the borrower's equity. This is found by dividing the total cost by the borrower's equity. For example, White Knuckles Holdings, LP, a hedge fund, purchased $20 billion in securities, using $1 billion of its equity and $19 billion in borrowed funds. Its leverage was 20, or 20 to 1 ($20 billion ÷ $1 billion). *See* **financial** and **operating leverage.**

"leveraged" or "geared." A description of a business enterprise that is using debt in addition to equity capital in order to grow or maintain operations. The debt is comprised of long-term securities, unless they are convertible debentures or bank notes. Although a heavy debt burden over the long term can be hazardous to the financial health of a business, if skillfully used, it can provide benefits. This is because the interest and repayment of debt is generally fixed, suggesting that when revenues increase rapidly, capital costs remain the same, allowing the company to flow more money to the bottom line or earnings level. On the other hand, when revenues fall precipitously, capital costs can leave little or nothing for the bottom line. The measure of leverage is often expressed as the ratio of debt to total capital or the debt/capital ratio. Generally speaking, when that gets above 50%, a business is said to be highly leveraged, although that varies among industries and business conditions as well as the general financial condition of the company in question. For example, if BankDough Enterprise's total capital is $10 million and total debt is $6 million, leverage is 60% ($6 million ÷ $10 million = .06 × 100). *See* **leverage.**

leveraged buyout. A reference to the purchase of a company, often a public and well-known one, by one or more persons who use the assets of the targeted company as collateral for securing a loan with which to pay the selling owners. They repay the loan from the company's cash flow after the purchase. Since a loan is usually made before title is actually transferred in this kind of deal, it is usually made contingent on a completion of the buyout. However, since such a purchase is often based on shareholder response to a tender offer and no seller is paid until enough of the equity is committed to the sale, the lending entity can be nearly certain it will be completed when the loan is made or taken down. If extreme caution is the order of the day, a loan can be configured short term so that it can be repaid as soon as the deal falls through. Since the interest on a daily basis is usually manageable personally by characters in a leveraged buyout strategy—for instance, $137 per day on every $1 million borrowed at 5% interest—the abortion of the plan is not usually too costly for the buyers. But hey, no one likes to lose! In some cases, the buyout can be a private one, such as a group of employees buying a company and using the assets as collateral for the implementing loan, or a group buying a company, in order to take it private. In any of these cases, the company's assets pay for the buyout, so to speak. Technically, a leveraged buyout is the purchase of a company with borrowed funds from any source, such as a loan from the principals in the deal, using their personal assets as collateral. Even in this case the cash flow from the company usually pays off the loan. *See* **private, going** and **reverse leveraged buyout.**

leveraged loan. A loan to a borrower with a high amount of debt, in relation to its equity. Bank regulators consider a loan to a borrower with debt of 3.5 times equity as a leveraged loan and subject to close scrutiny. *See* **leverage.**

LFY. An abbreviation for "latest fiscal year," when joined by reporting results. It refers to the last completed fiscal year. For example, "Lil' Tex Inc. revenues LFY were $25,000,000."

LFYE. An abbreviation for "latest fiscal year ending," when followed by a date. For example, "Whammo's earnings for LFYE December 31 were $500,000."

liability. One of a group of items that represent obligations owed by a company, usually payable in money. Basically, there are two kinds of liabilities: short-term and long-term. Examples of short-term liabilities are: trade accounts payable in 90 days or less, such as bills for purchases of inventory or raw materials for selling or manufacturing operations, fuel purchases, tool purchases, furniture and fixtures bought, and services performed. Other short-term liabilities would include bank notes payable in 90 days or less, the current portion of bond interest or bond repayment, salaries and wages payable for work performed, withholding tax payments, and so on. These are items required to operate on a daily basis. Long-term liabilities are: leases, bonds or indentures issued, mortgages, deferred taxes payable, legal contingencies, and so forth. These are items required to operate over a span of several years and usually paid for over that span. *See* **Balance Sheet.**

LIBOR. Abbreviation for the London Interbank Offered Rate to borrowers of money. It is a floating rate that serves as a basis for many international lending and other financial agreements.

licensing agreement. An agreement whereby the developer of a product or manufacturing process allows another to market or use it in exchange for money or trade benefits.

lien. A creditor's right to seize property to settle a debt.

life cycle or **life style mutual fund.** A type of mutual fund that offers investors a portfolio of cash, bonds, and stocks structured to achieve a reasonable return over a specific time span. The rationale of such a program is that investors with set investment horizons can participate in a fund without worrying about adapting to disparities between personal investment objectives and the fund's holdings. For example, a 5-year life cycle fund during an expanding economy might invest heavily in cyclical stocks that would be expected to perform well during that span and high-yielding stocks and bonds. These funds are also called retirement funds. Critics of them charge that the funds are actually nothing but balanced mutual funds.

Life Insurance stocks. Those stocks representing companies underwriting and marketing various life insurance contracts and annuities. *See* **industry stock group.**

life of a bond. The number of years until the maturity date of a bond.

life style mutual fund. See **life cycle mutual fund.**

LIFO. Abbreviation for **last-in-first-out** inventory valuation.

Lifetime Learning credit. A federal income tax credit of up to $1,000 for tuition and fees after the first two years of college or vocational school. This credit is limited to one student per household, but it is applicable even if the student is enrolled for one course. *See* **Hope Scholarship credit.**

light trading. A reference to low volume of market transactions, under 100,000,000 shares on the New York Stock Exchange. However, that volume would represent heavy trading in certain other stock markets.

Lima Stock Exchange. See under **Global Investment Market.**

limit order. An order to buy or sell stock restricted as to the price at which it may be executed and/or its duration.

limited company (LC). See **limited liability company.**

limited liability. The legal restriction of an investor's financial responsibility beyond the amounts actually invested by him in a corporation or limited partnership.

limited liability company (LLC). A relatively new form of business structure, created in Wyoming in 1977, that allows more investors to participate in a combination of partnership and corporate characteristics than the more established **"S" corporation** allows. Most states authorize and charter LLCs, which can enable an investor to pass through to a personal tax filing both income and deductions from operations of the limited liability company. Although associates of an LLC are not liable for contractual obligations of the LLC, professional malfeasance or malpractice cannot be avoided under the umbrella of an LLC.

limited liability entity. Any one of several forms of business organization and ownership that provides boundaries on the legal liabilities of the owners of the enterprise in transactions with the public. These include **corporation, "S" corporation, limited partnership, limited liability company, limited liability partnership, private limited company,** and **sociedad anonima.**

limited liability partnership (LLP). A form of business organization combining the simplicity of a general partnership with the limited liability of a corporation. Partners are not liable for the errors, omissions, or negligence of the other partners, but they are liable for their own acts and for the contractual obligations of the LLP. Usually an LLP must be registered with the secretary of state and have insurance covering public liability. *See* **limited liability company** and **partnership, general.**

limited partnership (LTD). A financial structure under state statutes that has general and special partners. General partners conduct the business and have full liability of partners. Special partners invest and have limited liability as to debts, and so forth, as well as limited return on investment. *See* **partnership, general.**

limited power of attorney. See **power of attorney.**

linear regression. In statistical analysis, a representation of a line plotted through a set of data points that comes closest to all the points. Often the technique is used to forecast business trends.

line chart. See **bar chart.**

line of credit or **bank line.** An arrangement whereby a bank agrees to furnish a specific sum of money or loan to a business on a continuous basis until canceled, after a period of one year or on predetermined dates. This arrangement is not contractual but is a moral commitment and usually does not incur a commitment fee. However, compensating balances with the bank are normally required, usually 10% of the amount of the line and 10% additional of any borrowing arising from the line. If the customer is advised of the line, it is called an advised line or confirmed line; if not, but is instead a bank's policy line of credit, it is called a guidance line. Public companies often make a public announcement when lines of credit are granted them, because the lines represent good credit and banking relations. These are necessities to successful operations for most companies. Frequently, the announcements appear in annual reports and press releases. They tell investors that a bank has examined a company's financial health and is satisfied, at least during the period of the commitment.

liquidating dividend. A dividend payment from the sale of corporate assets prorated among stockholders. It can result from the dissolution of a corporation or a partial sale of assets and is considered an unearned dividend. *See* **unearned dividend and return of capital (3).**

liquidating REIT. A real estate investment trust formed by a bank or other company into which were transferred mortgages and real property. These were then liquidated in a way calculated to create a tax break. This strategy was made unlawful in a 1998 tax bill.

liquidating value. 1) The value of a share in a corporation in the event of liquidation. 2) The cash value of a share in an investment company when it is redeemed or cashed. *See* **asset value** for how it is calculated.

liquidation. 1) The sale of a corporation's assets and payment of its debts followed by a dividend to stockholders if cash remains. 2) The conversion of property into cash.

liquidity. The easy convertibility of a security into cash.

liquidity ratio. The ratio of cash and near-cash (marketable securities) to total current liabilities, expressed as a percentage. This supplements the current ratio by indicating how much immediate cash is available by excluding inventory—not always liquid—from the ratio. (Have you ever tried to sell electric fans in midwinter?) A 1-to-1 ratio or higher reflects a strong position.

liquid position. See **cash position.**

Lisbon Stock Exchange. See under **Global Investment Market.**

list. An alphabetical list of securities that are traded on an exchange.

listed securities. Those corporate stocks representing companies that have met one or more stock exchanges' financial requirements and that have listed their stock with one or more listing   **390**

exchanges for trading purposes. Certain corporations and government bonds are listed. If a stock is listed on more than one exchange, it is possible to save money by selling on the exchange located in a state with a lesser transfer tax.

listing. The placing of a security under an exchange's administration for trading purposes.

listing requirements. For examples of listing requirements, see **NASDAQ Stock Market** and **New York Stock Exchange.**

Livelink Pistripe: The Source for Business Knowledge. See under **Web Sites for the Inquiring Investor.**

living trust. See **revocable trust.**

Ljubljana Stock Exchange (Slovenia). See under **Global Investment Market.**

LLC. Abbreviation for **limited liability company.**

load. See **sales load.**

loan, subordinated. A debt that is paid after other debts in case of legally enforced payments to creditors.

loan covenants. Financial terms under which a bank makes a loan to a borrower. A violation of one or more of these standards is grounds for the bank to demand repayment of a loan.

loan extension. The granting to a borrower of additional time to repay a loan, accompanied by a new note and interest charges. Often, banks will allow business firms to extend loans indefinitely or pay them down gradually as long as the interest is paid regularly and the business assets are productive.

loan participation funds or **floating rate funds** or **prime rate funds.** Bank loans considered below investment grade that have been bundled into fund shares for sale to individual investors. These loans are usually illiquid. Because the fund manager can buy the loans at discounts, they are high yielding to the fund's shareholders, in relation to alternative short-term securities. However, the portfolio's "bad loan" assets should make an investor careful. *Caveat Emptor!*

loan value. The amount of money a lending institution will loan to a borrower based on the market value of the asset pledged as collateral. For example, a bank might loan 60% of the current market value of several shares of stock, allowing a 40% margin for market depreciation to protect itself in case of a default.

locked-in. An expression used when an investor holds a security that has grown in market value over its cost and that the investor does not want to sell, because of the income tax liability.

"lock-up agreement." An agreement made prior to a public offering of a company's shares between the issuer of those shares and certain investors receiving shares prior to the public offering that restricts the latter from selling the shares for a specified period. Usually, the locked-up shares are issued in exchange for some service, such as providing loans for operations until the public offering is sold.

"lock-up merger agreement." A tender offer condition in which the bidder for tendered shares receives an option to buy treasury shares of the target corporation at a price below the tender offer. In effect this potential to dilute the common shares can scare off other parties.

"lock-up" period. In the case of a company issuing stock to the public for the first time, the interval that company insiders agree to wait before selling any of their shares. It is usually six months, and the company makes the agreement with their underwriters to protect the latter from insider shares flooding the market and driving down share prices soon after the underwriting. It is a method by which underwriters protect buyers of a new issue as well as their own equity interests in the new issue, if any. On the other hand, insiders of companies that are publicly traded are not restricted from selling their shares after new shares are sold, but must announce such an action afterwards.

logarithmic charts. Those charts that show logarithms of values—such as stock prices or earnings—on the vertical scale, so that equal percentages of change always take the same distance up or down and, therefore, make the same slope. In this manner, viewers can get a more accurate picture of growth or decline figures. To illustrate, a line representing a stock's price rise from $10 per share to $20 would take the same vertical space and slope as a later rise from $20 to $40 per share, on a logarithmic scale. A tuned-in investor would know that the growth rate has remained the same by noticing equal slopes. On an arithmetic scale, however, the slope of the latter change would appear steeper and deceptively greater on a percentage basis, possibly misleading the investor into thinking market appreciation is accelerating.

London Club. An informal assembly of more than 600 bankers and other creditors of Russian entities that was created to negotiate with Russian officials through a steering committee about the repayment of Russian debt and interest, both recent and older, when financial problems overtook Russian states after the overthrow of the Communist regime and caused a general inability to repay debt on time. The Russian government owes about $30 billion plus over $1 billion in delinquent interest to members of the club.

London International Financial Futures & Options Exchange (LIFFE). See under **Global Investment Market.**

London Metal Exchange. See under **Global Investment Market.**

London Stock Exchange. See under **Global Investment Market.**

long bonds. In trading bonds, a reference to those issues maturing in 15 years or more.

long end. In an issue of serial bonds, those bonds that mature last.

long position. An ownership of certain securities. *See* **long sale.**

long pull. See **long-term investing.**

long-range maturities. Those bonds maturing in 15 years or more.

long-range capital gain or loss. The profit or loss resulting from the sale of a noninventory asset held 12 months and a day or longer, under IRS regulations. *See* **capital gain.**

long sale. A sale of securities that are owned by the seller, as opposed to borrowing them for a short sale.

long-term debt ratio. The amount of the long-term debt, such as bonds, and so forth compared to the total capitalization, expressed as a percentage. In an industrial concern, this debt should not be greater than one-half, preferably less.

Long-term Equity Anticipation Security (LEAP). An option contract, either a put or call, that has a life of two years or more when originally issued. LEAPS trade on exchanges, and are exchangeable into regular exchange-traded options when their remaining lives decrease to the shorter maturity ranges of regular options.

long-term investing or **long pull investing.** The investing in an enterprise for a year or longer, rather than for quick results. Even though the objective is long-term, however, the stock should be evaluated at regular intervals to ascertain the value is still present. The long term is a series of short terms, according to some money managers.

loony. Nickname for Canadian one-dollar coin.

Los Angeles Times Online. See under **Web Sites for the Inquiring Investor.**

Loss. 1) As a business enterprise, reporting more in expenses, money disbursements, or decreases in asset values than received in revenues or asset gains. 2) As an investor, the experience of receiving less upon selling or exchanging a security than the amount paid for it.

loss on small business stock. A reference to the special income tax treatment on stock in a company that qualifies as a small business whereby a loss resulting from its sale, exchange, or the stock's becoming worthless can be treated as an ordinary loss rather than a capital loss, up to $25,000 per year. This ordinary loss is allowable only on stock purchased after June 30, 1958 in a company that for five years prior to the loss realized more than 50% of its gross income from operating a business. To qualify as a small business, the company cannot be capitalized for over $500,000 or have equity of over $1,000,000, and must belong to individuals or partnerships to whom it was originally issued.

Louisiana Securities Commission. Regulator of securities in the state of Louisiana. Address: 1100 Poydras Street, New Orleans, LA 70163. Phone: (504) 568-5515.

Low Price Common. Those stocks representing less expensive, more speculative shares. *See* **industry stock group.**

Ltd. 1) A British business abbreviation for a **limited liability company**, similar to the U.S. corporations. 2) Abbreviation for a **limited partnership.**

Lusaka Stock Exchange (LuSE) [Zambia]. See under **Global Investment Market.**

Luxembourg Stock Exchange. See under **Global Investment Market.**

LYONS. See **zero-coupon convertibles, corporate.**

Mm

M1. See **money supply.**

M2. See **money supply.**

M3. See **money supply.**

Maastricht Treaty. The treaty in 1992 in Maastricht, Netherlands, between 15 Western European countries that set in motion plans for the European Union and established the **euro** as the uniform currency between those countries.

Ma Bell. Nickname for the original American Telephone & Telegraph Company, before its breakup under a court order in 1984. *See* **Baby Bells.**

Machinery. Those stocks representing companies producing machines and equipment for manufacturers. *See* **industry stock group.**

machinery industries. See **sector.**

machine tool orders. Purchases by manufacturers of heavy equipment such as drills, presses, lathes, shapers, planers, grinders, and so on. This is a key stock market indicator, since a pickup in machine tool orders forecasts increased industrial production, generally.

"macro" funds. Those managed funds that take positions in foreign currencies or base securities holdings on global trends. These funds lost popularity in the late 1990s, when the fast emerging economies of Asia and Latin America and the reorganized economies of the former USSR faltered and faced insolvencies as a result, most often, of mismanagement and over-extended debt.

It is especially a reference to global hedge funds, which attempt to maximize performance through taking short-term and mid-term positions in various foreign currencies, interest rates, derivatives, and securities, some exotic in financial nature. Often complicated trading formulas are employed in such a fund to take advantage of anomalies in worldwide trade and money flows. Beginning in 1975, these funds proliferated, with Tiger Management, Soros Fund Management, and Long-Term Capital Management excelling in performance at various times, before diminishing greatly in value toward the turn of the century.

Madrid Stock Exchange. See under **Global Investment Market.**

magnified tape. A transparent ticker tape that is magnified on a screen for brokers and spectators in a brokerage house.

mailing list. A list of an investment firm's customers or prospective customers who are mailed periodic investment information from the firm's research sources.

Maine Department of Professional and Financial Regulation. Regulator of securities laws in the state of Maine. Address: Bureau of Banking, Securities Division, State House Station 121, Augusta, ME 04333. Phone: (207) 582-8760.

maintenance costs. Expenses that are charged to keeping land, plant, and machinery in repair.

maintenance fund. Required annual monies, usually a percentage of gross operating revenues, that the issuer of mortgage bonds must set aside for repairs of mortgaged property. *See* **indenture.**

maintenance requirement. The point at which a call for money or securities is made by a brokerage, based on a decrease in the market value of securities in a customer's margin account and one leaving the customer's equity beneath a specified percentage of market value. For example, assume a maintenance requirement is 25%, and the cost of securities bought on margin was $10,000, $7,000 of which was paid for by the customer, leaving the customer's debit balance $3,000. The market value of the margin securities later drops to $3,500. The $3,500 less $3,000, which the customer owes, is $500 (his equity), which is not 25% of $3,500, or $875. A maintenance call of $375 would bring the customer's equity to $875, or 25% of the $3,500 market value.

major swing. A market price trend lasting a year or more and moving stock prices 20% or more. *See* **intermediate movement.**

"majority of issues traded." A phrase that measures daily investor confidence in stable or rising stock prices when followed by "gained," "lost," or "remained unchanged." If the majority traded gained, confidence is excellent; if the majority lost, confidence is poor; if unchanged, highly indifferent. Majorities are figured from stocks trading on an exchange or the NASDAQ quotes and are a stronger confidence measure than pluralities.

make a market, to. As a dealer, to stand ready to bid on or offer for sale certain unlisted stocks. In effect, buyers and sellers of these stocks do not have to wait for a market to materialize, giving many local stocks immediate liquidity.

maker. The party who obligates himself to pay a specified amount by signing a promissory note.

Malawi Stock Exchange. See under **Global Investment Market.**

manage earnings, to. As corporate management, to exercise control over shareholder earnings in one or more fiscal periods through adjustments to the level or methods used in operations or choices of accounting procedures. The object of such a strategy is to protect a company's stock market values or project a desirable corporate image, by "managing away" or minimizing detrimental events and results and maximizing positive ones. To a certain degree, this strategy is acceptable because of the "materiality" rule among accountants and auditors. Basically, this allows a downplaying or omission of adjustments to financial reporting that affect earnings 5% or less.

There is also a practice among managers, who are forced to show a major negative event in their reports, to throw any other known unfavorable decisions into that period too, to get the bad news out of the way. This latter attitude flies in the face of allocating revenues and expenses to the period in which they occur, a fundamental tenet of business accounting. For example, if Sculpted Results, Inc. made a big sale in the final month of their fiscal year, and its management wished to cap revenues in the period, it might arrange with the buyer to amend the order in a minuscule way and submit it on the first day of the next period so that it would affect earnings in that period. In that way, management could cause earnings to appear stable.

management, top. The executive administrative group charged with carrying out the aims and affairs of a corporation on a day-to-day basis. They are hired, unlike the members of the board of directors, who are elected by the shareholders, although often members of the Board serve as officers of a corporation. Quarterly, the management team reports on financial and operating progress to the Board, with ideas to improve, if appropriate. Functionality is emphasized over titles. It is customary to include the chief executive officer, the chief operating officer, the chief financial officer, the corporate secretary, and the heads of operating divisions and key committees as top management. Sometimes an executive steering committee or a similar group exists to plan development and direct activities, especially in large corporations. As to the board of directors, technically, they are not operating management but are policy managers. In reality they tend to go along with operating management, unless corporate affairs become hopelessly bogged down.

It is generally conceded among professional investors that the quality of top management is the most important characteristic to look for in selecting a common stock. Although there are few company managements that display a complete set of ideal traits constantly, a majority of the following ones should be present most of the time.

1. The management team should be able to put in place the strategies and controls to consistently make money. In the case of new management, prior business associations should be referred to.
2. They should be problem solvers, in the sense that they can adjust product prices and fix flaws that have hurt sales.
3. There is in place a well-articulated corporate goal or mission.
4. Management should establish the framework for a clear corporate culture, reflecting a certain orientation such as results or creativity.

5. They should value employee contributions, and build an organization that will foster achievement.

6. Top management should have an understanding of the industry and market in which they are competing.

7. The management team should be on good terms with bankers, suppliers, customers, regulatory agencies, and other important players in the industry.

8. They should have established distinct financial boundaries, such as debt and equity ratios, although these can also be goals, in developing a stable financial structure.

9. Top management should be able to assimilate different viewpoints from other employees in creating a sound corporate strategy and work out internal problems together.

Management Information Systems (MIS). The design, implementation, management, and use of information technology in companies and other organizations.

Management of Technology (MOT). A relatively new college curriculum leading to a master of science degree, offered most often by technical universities. A program usually focuses on business innovation, entrepreneurship, electronic commerce, and technology strategy. Direct company participation often takes the place of the historical case method used in **Master of Business Administration** programs. The courses are taught with an emphasis on technological challenges and opportunities. Even traditional courses such as finance have been revised. Major fields of study include Management of Technology and Innovation in Financial Services (MOTIF) and Telecommunications and Information Management (TIM).

Management's Discussion and Analysis (MD&A). This is one of the most important parts of a corporate 10-K filing and shareholders' annual report. It includes management's—usually the chairman's and president's—detailed summary of the company's significant operating and financial results for the current and prior fiscal years. It gets into the operating and financial nitty-gritty, more so than the Letter or Message to the Stockholders does. *See* **Annual Report to the Stockholders** and **audited books.**

managing underwriter. See **underwriting.**

manipulations. Those acts by securities traders designed to depress or inflate security prices to their advantage.

manufacture, to. As a business establishment, to employ and manage a work force necessary to acquire the raw materials, process them, fabricate them, and turn out new products for sale to other manufacturers or to final consumers through distribution. Often, parts of the manufacturing process, such as design or a downstream phase, is subcontracted out to others. A manufacturer sometimes employs its own sales force, and in other cases uses independent manufacturers' representatives to distribute products. *See* **remanufacturing.**

Manufacturers' New Orders, Consumer Goods. See **Economic Indicators.**

Manufacturers' New Orders, Non-Defense Capital Goods. See **Economic Indicators.**

manufacturing. Those stocks representing companies making parts, assemblies, and equipment for manufacturing that is not vertically integrated. *See* **industry stock group.**

Manufacturing and Trade Sales. See **Economic Indicators.**

manufacturing industries. See **sector.**

Maple Leaf, Canadian Gold. A gold coin issued by the Royal Canadian Mint and guaranteed by the Federal Government of Canada. It was introduced in 1996, the first minted coin comprised of 99.99% pure gold. This is 24k quality. It is issued in five weights: $\frac{1}{20}$ ounce, $\frac{1}{10}$ ounce, $\frac{1}{4}$ ounce, $\frac{1}{2}$ ounce, and 1 ounce. The national emblem of Canada adorns one side of the coin. The Maple Leaf and the Krugerrand are the most popular gold coins in the market today. *See* **Eagle, American Gold,** and **Krugerrand, South African.**

Maputo Stock Exchange (Mozambique). See under **Global Investment Market.**

margin. The amount of money a customer must deposit with a broker in order to buy or sell securities short, among those which can legally be bought or sold on margin, expressed both in money and as a percentage of the market value of these securities. The market value is determined by **Regulation T** of the Federal Reserve Board. This amount is called the initial margin. Granting credit is a good business for brokerages, because they borrow at prime, or a "broker's loan" bank rate, and lend at two or three percentage points above that rate. Also, they make money on the commissions these leveraged accounts generate.

There are actually three sources of brokerage **margin requirements**: (1) Fed requirements, (2) exchange requirements, and (3) house or the brokerage requirements. The NYSE members must receive $2,000 in value to open a margin account, and the value of stock purchased on margin must be $5 per share or more. Most other exchange member firms also make these prerequisites. The balance of a securities purchase on margin is borrowed from the brokerage. Stocks can also be used as margin. When money or acceptable stocks are used, their buying power amounts to their market value divided by the current legal credit to equity ratio in buying marginable securities. This margin, the initial margin requirement, is set by the Fed. Thereafter, on those securities, the **maintenance requirements** are set by the NASD or the brokerage firm.

For example, if the current margin requirement is 50%, stock valued at $10,000 deposited with a broker would have a buying power of 50/100ths, or 50% of $10,000, or $5,000. When an investor opens a margin account, if its equity is not at least $2,000 and 50% of the current value of the securities in the account, an initial margin call is made. Afterwards, if the equity drops below 50% of the current securities value, a maintenance call is made to bring the equity up to 50% of the securities value. However, a brokerage firm can use its own maintenance requirement, usually directed by the NASD. That current ratio is 30%. It is possible to make lots of money through margin investing, but it's not for the faint-hearted.

margin account or **"type II account."** An account with a brokerage firm that enables a customer to borrow money for additional transactions or use securities owned and deposited with the firm as collateral or margin for additional purchases. Most brokerage firms screen margin buyers carefully for financial soundness, because they are granting credit to these customers. Even if an investor does not plan margin purchases, short sales must be made from a margin account, and the same margin requirements are in effect. A **cash account** must exist before a margin account is opened. *See* also **option account.**

margin agreement. A customer's approval for a brokerage firm to pledge the securities held in the customer's margin account as collateral for bank loans by the investment firm. This is called rehypothecation of the securities. *See* **hypothecation of customer's securities.**

margin call. A brokerage firm's demand for additional deposit when the market value of stock in a new margin account is beneath the percentage maintenance requirements. *See* **margin.**

margin of profit, gross. 1) The difference between total net sales and the cost of goods sold. 2) **margin of profit, net.** The difference between total net sales and net income after all deductions. *See* **pretax profit margin**.

margin requirements. The portions of security market values that customers must furnish personally when buying them. In buying listed securities the minimum—currently 50%—is determined by the Federal Reserve Board, although brokerage houses and banks can require more when customers buy on credit. Banks generally require customers to furnish 30% to 40% in borrowing to buy high-grade over-the-counter stocks, 10% on Government and high-grade municipal bonds. Bank margin requirements are established by **Regulation U** of the Federal Reserve Board. In all cases, the lending institution can sell the security to collect the unpaid balance, and interest is charged during the loan period. All institutions that loan money for the purchase of securities base their credit on the market stability of a particular security as well as current business conditions.

margin security. A security that has been approved for inclusion in a margin account. Under **Regulation T** of the Federal Reserve Board, a margin security can be: (1) any listed security or one having unlisted trading privilege on an exchange; (2) any over-the-counter stock identified by the Fed as possessing the marketability, popularity, informational presence, and financial quality of listed securities; any over-the-counter security trading under a plan directed by the SEC in trading in the National Market System; any mutual fund or investment trust shares registered under the **Investment Company Act of 1940**; (5) any securities exempt by regulators or law from margin restrictions. IRAs, Keogh Plans, and 401(k) Plans may not use margin in buying or selling securities.

margin to the market. A phrase meaning no margin is required in buying stocks or commodities.

Marginal Efficiency of Capital for a company or **marginal productivity of capital** or **natural interest rate.** A reference to the managerial concept that only investments that return more money in the form of earnings than they cost in the form of interest are worth pursuing. It is the annual yield on the most recent addition to a company's capital assets or the annual yield on prospective additions. If the return is positive, the marginal efficiency of capital is positive; if negative, the marginal efficiency is negative or diminishing. When it begins to become positive, it indicates to management that it would pay to embrace such an investment, all other factors remaining equal. The amount of money a customer must deposit with a broker in order to buy or sell securities short, among those which can legally be bought or sold on margin, expressed both in money and as a percentage of the market value of these securities. The market value is determined by **Regulation T** of the Federal Reserve Board. However, as a practical matter, the higher the return the more competition attracted to the markets those projects represent, which ultimately has the effect of diminishing the returns while raising capital costs.

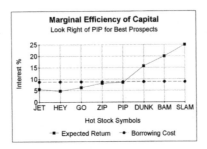

Marginal Efficiency of Capital for an economy. A reference to the tendency for the **Marginal Efficiency of Capital** to influence interest rate levels in a macro, or broad, economic sense. In the early stages of a period of marginal efficiency—returns are rising above capital costs—increasing amounts of capital become available. Finally, returns decrease or diminish, and so capital flows into lower returns available at lower costs, because the capital supply is so great.

marginal productivity of capital. See **Marginal Efficiency of Capital.**

Marginal Return on Equity (MROE). A **ratio** that reflects the progress of management in enhancing successive fiscal results through additions to shareholders' equity. It is a more sensitive barometer of financial and investment performance than simply using a company's historical average return on equity. The reason is that by using the marginal concept, the return on new equity capital is measured, whereas in using the historical average, older capital dominates the measure and, since assets representing that have often been fully amortized, higher returns naturally tend to result from current earnings. By applying MROE, the analysis answers how management is doing with the new money in the current competitive environment. Moreover, when the investor is using the MROE concept to estimate future financial results, it is more reliable in the near term. The accompanying example illustrates the concept.

MARGINAL RETURN ON STOCKHOLDERS' EQUITY

(1)	(2)	(3)	(4)	(5)	(6)
	Stockholders'	Stockholders'	Incremental Stockholders'	Increase in	Marginal Return on Stockholders'
Year	Equity ($/000)	Equity Prior Year ($/000)	Equity ($/000)	Net Income ($/000)	Equity (%)
1	125,000	100,000	25,000	2,135	8.5
2	133,260	125,000	8,260	1,112	13.5
3	145,213	133,260	11,953	1,257	10.5
4	152,750	145,213	7,537	1,155	15.3
5	157,921	152,750	5,171	916	17.7

Average Marginal Return on Stockholders' Equity 13.1

Sources for Calculating Marginal Return on Stockholders' Equity:

(2) Current balance sheet

(3) Prior balance sheet

(4) Increase in Stockholders' Equity in current balance sheet

(5) Increase in net income from current income statement

(6) Column (5) divided by Column (4).

---

marginal tax rates. In a tax code, the percentage of each additional amount of taxable income that is subject to tax. Under a 1993 bill, marginal tax rates in the United States were set at 15%, 28%, 31%, and 36%. *See* **progressive tax** and **flat tax systems.**

marital deduction. A halving of inheritance taxes by splitting the assets in an estate with a spouse. Under federal estate tax laws, one-half of the property in an estate may pass to the spouse tax-free if properly transferred in a will. An attorney should be consulted.

Maritime Administration. See agency securities.

mark to the market. As a broker who has advanced money to another one for stock borrowed in a customer's short sale, to request a return of part of the money if the stock's market value declines; the reverse would take place if the market value increased.

market. 1) A specific location where securities are traded. 2) The vast network—voice and data—of securities dealers, brokers, traders, investors, and speculators who are actively trading with each other. This concept originally referred to geographic boundaries, such as the United States or the United Kingdom. However, with the application of the Internet to investing, the market is coming to have a global context, at least among the industrialized nations. In terms of market value, the size of the market has grown dramatically. In 1980 the value of all stocks in the U.S. market was $1.4 trillion. By the end of 1997, the value had escalated to approximately $13 trillion. That is an annual compounding rate of 13.9%.

"market, the." See **market price.**

market action. The degree of price movement and volume of trading that securities demonstrate.

market activity. See **active market.**

market indicators. See **popular market indicators.**

market averages. See **bond average** and **stock average.**

market closed. 1) A reference to a signal, which is a gong on the New York Stock Exchange, for trading to stop on an exchange. 2) The situation when a trader in unlisted or over-the-counter securities stops quoting his bids and offers.

market deterioration. A general collapse of investor confidence accompanied by much lower security prices. In particular, those stocks that historically have been stalwarts in terms of resistance to panic selling—Utilities, Foods, Pharmaceuticals, for instance—fall in price, even though their dividends are safe. The investor sentiment is that sooner or later, all stocks will suffer material losses.

market indicators. See **popular market indicators.**

market leader. A popular stock that quickly reflects in price and volume changes in investor outlook because the company it represents is quick to profit from good business conditions or suffer losses in depressed business conditions.

market leadership. A reference to the tendency that some individual stocks, industries, or stock sectors have demonstrated in recent history of exerting a significant influence over how investors perceive the health of the stock market, in terms of its financial stability and prospects for the future. The direction of leadership can be negative or positive, but is the engine associated with change in stock prices at that point in time. Investors are focused on that segment of the market for instructions, speaking figuratively, on what to do—sell, buy, or stay put. When the stock market is chaotic, with prices moving erratically, the market is said to lack leadership. In this case, putting money in can be largely a crapshoot on random price fluctuations. In modern portfolio theory, stocks with Betas that are one or near one would represent market leadership. They move with the market, indeed they move the market. As the reader might guess, it is a little like the riddle of whether the chicken or egg comes first. The caveat here is that leadership stocks change with the times and corporate fortunes. Will Microsoft exert leadership after the antitrust case is settled? Betas change. Be sure an apparent market leader is not yesterday's news. *See* **Beta Value.**

market-neutral investing. A strategy of investing money in stocks that are considered undervalued, and then trying to neutralize the risk by selling short an identical value in stocks considered to be overvalued. If prices of the shorted stocks drop, the borrowed securities for the short sale can be replaced at a profit. The proceeds are used to buy short-term U.S. Treasury bills, earning a money market rate of return, which neutralizes the loss if the undervalued stocks also fall in price.

market open. 1) A reference to a signal, which is a gong on the New York Stock Exchange, for trading to commence on an exchange. 2) The situation when a trader in unlisted or over-the-counter securities gives his first bid and offer for the day.

market order. An order to buy or sell a security at whatever price current supply and demand have established.

market page or **financial page.** A daily newspaper section reporting quotes and trading news of securities and commodities, as well as other business news. *See* **bond table** and **stock table.**

market performance. A description of a stock's market behavior, emphasizing price firmness and volume. If the price has remained stable or risen, in relation to others, market performance is beneficial to investors.

"market performer." A euphemistic description of a stock's prospects by a sell-side securities analyst, usually because the analyst no longer wants to recommend the stock but does not wish to offend the company's management with an outright "sell" recommendation for fear of losing the company's corporate finance or syndicate business.

market's performance. A description of the general market behavior of all securities in a particular category, but more popularly applied to stocks listed on national exchanges, with emphasis on price firmness, volume, and stock averages. If the majority of stock prices are higher when volume is also high, the market's performance is considered beneficial to investors.

market play. See **market action.**

market price or **"the market."** A quote giving the price some buyer will pay (bid) for a security and for what price a seller will sell (offer) the same security. Before buying any security, it is important to establish that there is a continuous buying and selling of that security, a guarantee that the investment can be liquidated quickly at the best possible price. Often, the "last sale" is used in stating the market price.

market rate. The annual interest rate currently sought by bond buyers, stated as a percentage of a bond's price. This rate varies due to changes in investment money available, risks, inflation, business outlook, and so on. The contractual interest rate of a bond, which is stated as an annual percentage of the face value, is adjusted to meet the fluctuating market rate by changes in the bond's price. *See* **contract rate** and **yield to maturity.**

market research. A study of the factors influencing trading psychology of securities buyers and sellers, emphasizing future trends.

market stability. A reference to transactions with minimal price fluctuations in an obvious upward trend with good volume.

market strength. A measure of the general tone of the market using volume, prices, number of issues traded, closing price patterns, excessive fluctuations, and other factors that reflect investor confidence as a measure of future trends.

market summary. In popular usage, a description of the price movements of common stocks of national interest, emphasizing the Dow Jones averages, volume, and major industry trends and significant individual stock movements.

market valuations or **paper values.** The measure of the value of the total outstanding shares of all companies listed on an exchange as reflected by the closing prices of the small percentage of shares that trade daily.

market value added. The difference between the total value of a company's stock outstanding at current price levels and outstanding debt and the total capital invested historically. It represents the wealth created or destroyed by management. Total capital invested includes long-term debt and the book value of common and preferred stock issues. For example, if the investors of Sky's The Limit Corp. originally bought 5 million shares of common stock for $5 million, the company's retained earnings account has grown to $1 million, and its long-term debt issues have been $25 million, the total capital invested is $31 million. Let's say the stock's current price is $75 million, or $15 per share, and its debt is $5 million, or $1 per share. This makes the total market value $80 million, and means the management has added $49 million, or $9.80 per share, in wealth for stockholders ($80 million minus $31 million).

market wealth. See **real wealth.**

marriage tax or **marriage penalty.** A reference to the current higher federal income tax on taxable income earned by a married couple, both working, than on an equal amount of taxable income earned by a couple, one working. For changes in the year 2001, see **Economic Growth and Tax Relief Reconciliation Act of 2001.**

"married to a stock." A term describing an investor who refuses to sell a stock that has dropped in price, even though it is obvious the stock was not a good buy.

Maryland Attorney General's Office. Regulator of securities laws in the state of Maryland. Address: Division of Securities, 200 St. Paul Place, 20th Floor, Baltimore, MD 21202. Phone: (410) 576-6360.

Massachusetts Secretary of the Commonwealth. Regulator of securities laws in the state of Massachusetts. Address: Securities Division, One Ashburton Place, Room 1701, Boston, MA 02108. Phone: (617) 727-3548.

master limited partnership (MLP). An operating business partnership that has grown larger by rolling up other partnerships. Tax-wise there is an advantage to investing in them, or any limited partnership, for that matter, because partnership income, losses, deductions, and credits pass through to each limited partners personal tax filing. Consequently, there is no double federal taxation of the investor's income as there is when the investor receives a dividend from a corporation. There are also other tax advantages.

Master of Business Administration (MBA). A graduate degree, usually requiring 60 hours or two years of college work, that is designed to equip students with effective analytical and business knowledge in developing successful business plans and policies. Most often, the case method is employed as a teaching tool, in which historical problems and successes of actual companies are studied and learned from. Other types of degrees in this area are: Master of Management of Technology, Master of Management of Technology and Innovation in Financial Services, and Master of Telecommunications and Information Management.

match orders, to. As a broker, to seek offsetting orders for a heavy accumulation of either buy or sell orders in a stock, usually following suspended trading, invoked to maintain an orderly market in the stock in the face of sensational news about it.

matched and lost. A reference to the report to a customer on a limit order when his broker made a simultaneous bid or offer on the exchange floor with another broker and they flipped a coin to see which order was executed. It means no execution.

matched order. See **wash sale (1).**

materiality. The degree to which an adjustment to a basic accounting entry will affect earnings. Under current accounting and auditing procedures, if the adjustment to an account such as revenues will not change earnings more than 5%, it is considered immaterial and, therefore, not required to be reported in investor news releases or reports. There is a move underway at the SEC, however, to force auditors to take into account why the adjustment is omitted or played down. If the reason is to protect stock values for key employees or manage earnings, this treatment may be discouraged or disallowed in the future. *See* **manage earnings.**

MATIF—Commodities. See under **Global Investment Market.**

maturity. The date on which the face value of a financial obligation is due to be paid.

Mauritius Stock Exchange (SEM). See under **Global Investment Market.**

maximize shareholder values. The act of trying to increase the value of common stock by management, usually begun by employing one or more investment bankers (sometimes the job requires more than one!). The strategy is quite often a management response to disgruntled shareholders who have watched other stocks appreciate significantly but not the one they own. The plan is usually a short-term one, as opposed to long-term operating improvements, and can utilize asset sales, mergers, spinoffs, split-ups, joint ventures, reorganizations, and so on.

Essentially, it represents an admission that business as usual has not inspired the stock market, and that it is time to get creative.

May Day. A reference to May 1, 1975, a day on which the SEC required commission rates charged by brokerage houses to cease being uniform and become negotiated, competitive rates between each brokerage firm and its customers.

MBA. Abbreviation for **Master of Business Administration.**

m-commerce. A reference to the abbreviation for mobile commerce or electronic technology in which monetary transfers are made at the point of sale, in order that purchasers pay vendors for merchandise received through some form of digital communications. Although this technology is in its infancy, market futurists consider it likely to become popular. Most likely, it will take the form of using a wireless phone or palm organizer to order a money transfer at a vendor site, such as a vending machine, in order to make payment for a product that is delivered immediately afterwards. Payment could be made through wireless checking account transfer, credit card debit, or instructing a party to send a check.

MD&A. Abbreviation for **Management's Discussion and Analysis.**

mean deviation. See **average deviation.**

mean reversion. In statistical analysis, the tendency of a series of data to move back to its central tendency. This propensity prompts stock market data, such as average annualized capital gains, to return to an established norm. For example, if the average annualized gain for a stock index over a 25-year period is 7.5%, then current gains of 20% would be considered excessive, using the mean reversion concept. By the same token, stock market data lower than the mean would tend to expand toward the central tendency.

measuring gap. See **gap (2).**

median. See **average, statistical.**

Medical Products & Supplies. Those stocks representing companies providing instruments and equipment for medical applications.

Medical Savings Account (MSA). A trust or custodial account established to accumulate funds for the payment of qualified medical expenses, in connection with a high-deductible health insurance program. In many ways, these are similar to IRAs, but an MSA cannot be used as an IRA or combined into the same account. Two types of persons can establish such a plan: (1) an employee or spouse of a "small employer" that sponsors a "high-deductible health plan" covering that employee or spouse; and (2) a self-employed person or spouse maintaining an individual or family "high-deductible health plan," covering that person or spouse. Cash contributions begin the plan. If an employer makes contributions, an employee cannot. The tax deduction for contributions cannot exceed compensation. Distributions from an MSA can be made anytime but only those used to pay qualified medical expenses or rolled over into another MSA are not taxable, generally. Any taxable distribution from a MSA is subject to a 15% penalty, unless distribution occurs after the account holder turns 65.

MEFF Village—Financial Derivatives. See under **Global Investment Market.**

melt-down. A reference to the complete financial deterioration of a company, economy, or economic sector because of internal problems. There is a swift and total loss of investor confidence in the situation, usually leading to a massive selloff in related securities.

member bank. A commercial bank belonging to the **Federal Reserve System** subject to the System's reserve requirements, capital requirements, and so on.

member borrowings. That money, usually in the form of call loans, borrowed by the New York Stock Exchange members from commercial banks, mostly to finance customers' margin accounts and their own purchases.

member firm. An investment house that belongs to a registered exchange, subject to the exchange's capital requirements, ethics, and so on.

member short position. Those short sales by members of an exchange that offer an insight into what these professionals think about the direction of the market. If their short sales are heavy, they probably expect a drop in prices, but a rush to cover their short sales could support the market. *Barron's* publishes the New York Stock Exchange figures in their "Market Laboratory" section.

member trading. Those securities transactions by members of an exchange.

Mercasur. A trading block that is the most influential in South America. It includes Argentina, Brazil, Bolivia, Chile, Paraguay, and Uruguay. The trading bloc, ranked as the world's fourth largest, includes 227 million South Americans. Altogether, the trading partners export $13 billion to one another and $56 billion to the rest of the world.

Merchandise Trade Balance. A report issued mid-month by the Census Bureau of the Department of Commerce that includes data on total exports and imports. The list of exported and imported products is very comprehensive, but the most highly-valued components from an investment perspective are oil, agriculture, industrial supplies and materials, capital goods, automobiles, and consumer items. The report also provides bilateral trade flows between the United States and some other countries—Japan, Germany, Great Britain, and Canada are included. The largest trading partners with the United States are Canada (18%), Japan (16%), Mexico (7%), Germany (6%), UK (5%), and OPEC (5%). Actually there are four separate reports released by the Census Bureau. They are the Merchandise Trade Deficit issued monthly and limited to markets for merchandise; the Merchandise Trade Deficit issued quarterly based on balance of payments; Net Exports issued quarterly in nominal and real dollars; Current Account issued quarterly and includes financial flows in nominal dollars. When both exports and imports increase, fixed income securities tend to decrease in value, while common stocks and dollar exchange rates are not affected. When they decrease, fixed income securities rise, while common stocks and dollar exchange rates tend to remain the same. In the case of trade balances, when they grow larger, there is little effect on fixed income securities, while common stocks and dollar exchange rates tend to increase. When trade balances decline, fixed income securities tend to stay the same, while common stocks and dollar exchange rates decrease.

merger. The absorption of the assets of one or more companies, called the target(s), into a bigger one. The surviving company may buy the stock for cash or give its own shares in exchange, buy the assets of the lesser company for cash, or assume the debts of the target company. Usually over one-half, and sometimes two-thirds, of a corporation's shareholders must approve a merger or consolidation. Generally, a merger may be described as either a market-extension or a product-extension. In the case of the market-extension type, the surviving corporation increases its trade area for a similar product or service through use of the image or product created by the merged corporation. In the case of the product-extension type, the surviving corporation expands its line of products or services.

Technically, a merger involves the combining of two managements and stockholder groups, accomplished by using the surviving corporations stock in the exchange. This amalgamation usually implies that a merger involves two major corporations of similar size, whereas an **acquisition** involves the absorption of a smaller corporation into a larger one. The size differential generally exists in cases of **conglomerate** acquisitions. However, the terms *merger* and *acquisitions* are often used interchangeably in the current lexicon of finance. *See* also **consolidation mergers, pioneering mergers, talent-scout mergers, revenue-hunter mergers,** and **reverse merger.**

Merval Index. A stock index of companies in Argentina.

Metals. Those stocks representing companies engaged in the processing and manufacture of nonferrous metals such as copper, aluminum, and so on. *See* **industry stock group.**

"metrics." In securities analysis, a reference to measuring a company's data that reflects volumetric changes or magnitudes of business activities, in appraising a stock, rather than traditional valuation methods such as the Price/Earnings Multiple. For example, there is a tendency to appraise New Economy stocks, such as dot-com companies, on the basis of hits on its Web page or its subscriber growth, since in the early stages of a company's evolution, there are rarely positive earnings. Basically, the process substitutes some measure of volumetric performance for financial performance. A corollary with an Old Economy stock would be to judge a steel company by tons of steel rolled in a year versus five years prior, and making that the basis for an evaluation of the stock. Often, the analysis assumes the potential earnings from the volumetric measure, such as earnings from hits on a Web page.

Mexican Stock Exchange / Spanish. See under Global Investment Market.

mezzanine financing. In investment banking parlance, the short-term capital advanced to get a project started in the initial stages, such as beginning plant construction, until longer-term financing is arranged. Usually a commercial bank provides mezzanine financing for periods up to one year.

MFN. Abbreviation for **Most Favored Nation.**

Michigan Department of Commerce. Regulator of securities in the state of Michigan. Address: Corporation & Securities Bureau, 6546 Mercantile Way, Lansing, MI 48909. Phone: (517) 334-6200.

microcaps. Stocks of very small companies in terms of total stock market valuation, with stock market capitalizations of less than $250 million (share price × shares outstanding). They are often quoted on the over-the-counter bulletin board, operated by the National Association of Securities Dealers, or the "pink sheets," published by the National Quotation Bureau. It is important to note that the capitalization size categories are relative to the level of stock prices generally. Stock cap groups might be smaller or larger in different market environments. Institutional and mutual fund investors have popularized the size-hierarchy technique, to enable them to coordinate their research and trading expertise with the magnitude of investment funds under management, for maximum efficiencies. *See* **bulletin board, large-caps, mid-caps,** and **small-caps.**

Microsoft Decision. The first landmark legal decision of the new millennium, involving the U.S. anti-trust laws. In April 2000, a United States District Court found Microsoft guilty of violating the Sherman Anti-trust Act by maintaining a monopoly in operating systems for personal computers by carrying on practices in restraint of trade, monopolizing the Internet browser market, and requiring its Internet browser to be sold with its operating system (Windows). The case was brought by the U.S. Justice Department and 19 State Attorneys General. The trial stage required nearly two years, ending with an order by the district court to break up the company into two separate operating entities. The company has appealed the decision to the U.S. Court of Appeals in Washington, D.C. Although that court has rendered no decision, during the oral arguments it expressed dissatisfaction with the basis for the verdict. The circuit court could reverse the decision, remand the case with instructions, or uphold the trial court's decision. It is not clear whether the new U.S. Attorney General will continue to prosecute the case, but 18 of the State Attorneys General intend to do so. Another possibility is that the case will be settled through negotiation between the parties.

MidAmerica Commodity Exchange (MIDAM). Address: 141 West Jackson Blvd., Chicago, IL 60604. Phone: (312) 341-3000. *See* under **Global Investment Market.**

mid-caps. Stocks of middle-size companies, in terms of total stock market valuation, with stock market capitalizations of $2 billion up to $5 billion (share price × shares outstanding). It is important to note that the capitalization size categories are relative to the level of stock prices generally. Stock cap groups might be smaller or larger in different market environments. Institutional and mutual fund investors have popularized the size-hierarchy technique, to enable them to coordinate their research and trading expertise with the magnitude of investment funds under management, for maximum efficiencies. *See* **microcaps, large-caps,** and **small-caps.**

MIF—Interest Rate Derivatives. See under **Global Investment Market.**

minimum fluctuation or **tick.** The least variation in the prices of a security allowed by exchanges and over-the-counter dealers. Before 2000, most stock prices traded in whole numbers and fractions or 25¾ for 25.75. However, beginning in the late 1990s, under SEC prodding, exchanges have spearheaded a move to decimal pricing, meaning the minimum tick is a penny, or .01 decimalized. By the end of 2001, most stocks should be trading in this manner. But bonds will continue trading the traditional way. *See* **quote.**

mini-tender offer. An offer to stockholders of one corporation by another corporation or party to buy up to 5% of the shares of the former, within a specified time period. Unlike the case of a **tender offer,** full disclosure of the value of the offer does not have to accompany it but does have to be available on request.

Minneapolis Grain Exchange. See under **Global Investment Market.**

Minnesota Department of Commerce. Regulator of securities laws in the state of Minnesota. Address: 133 East Seventh Street, St. Paul, MN 55101. Phone (information): (612) 296-2283. Phone (complaints): (612) 296-2488.

minor. A person under 21 for whom investment transactions are not binding.

minor trend. A market move lasting a week or less. *See* **intermediate movement.**

minority interest. An ownership of less than 50% of a corporation's outstanding stock, but ownership of enough to exert influence in election of directors and corporate policy.

minus yield to maturity. A phrase describing a convertible debenture that is purchased at such a high premium above par that when it is held to maturity or redeemed early by the issuer it produces a negative average annual yield. This happens because the loss at redemption amortized over the remaining life of the debenture more than offsets the interest payments received. Investors are especially likely to get into such a predicament when the market value of the common stock into which a debenture is convertible is rising fast and causing the debenture to rise also, because of the stock profit prospects upon conversion. The danger lies in a precipitous decline in the common stock value carrying over to the debenture's value, with the result that the debenture is at a much lower price than was paid.

For example, suppose in 1995 a 5% convertible debenture maturing in a month in 1999 is convertible into common stock at $25 per share; the current value of the common stock is $20. Upon salutary near-term news, the stock's price moves toward $25, and since there is a conversion profit after the stock reaches $25, the debenture's price rises to $1,060, arbitrarily and exuberantly. At this point an investor buys debentures. Afterwards, investors become pessimistic about the common stock's prospects, and the prices of both the stock and the debentures recede. Not wishing to convert at a price higher than the stock's market value and wishing to retain the $50 annual interest per debenture, the investor holds the securities until they are redeemed at $1,000 in 1999, at a loss of $60 each. Calculating the net loss per bond, the investor would determine: ($50 – $60) ÷ $1,060 (original investment); which results in –$10 ÷ $1,060 or (–.0093) or a minus yield to maturity of .93 of 1%.

Unfortunately, there is no protection against this expensive circumstance except for the investor to become extremely cautious about paying a premium for convertible debentures when the call or maturity date is near; he should only do so if the value of the common stock seems established at a price near the conversion price beyond the date of the redemption. This stability at a price near, or preferably higher, than the conversion rate makes probable a stock market profit when the debentures are redeemed.

misappropriation rule. A rule in securities law, affirmed by the U.S. Supreme Court, pertaining to insider trading illegality. It holds that improper uses of material information by "outsiders" or those persons having no special relationship to a corporation—for example, bankers, lawyers, arbitragers, financial printers, and reporters—come under the fraud provisions of Section 10(b) of the Securities Exchange Act of 1934.

Mississippi Office of the Secretary of State. Regulator of securities laws in the state of Mississippi. Address: Securities Division, Post Office Box 136, Jackson, MS 39205. Phone: (601) 359-6364. Phone (toll free): (800) 804-6364.

Missouri Office of the Secretary of State. Regulator of securities laws in the state of Missouri. Address: Securities Division, 600 West Main Street, Jefferson City, MO 65101. Phone: (314) 751-4136. Phone (toll free): (800) 721-7996.

MITTS (Market Index Target Term Securities). Investment units issued by Merrill Lynch & Co. representing participation in an investment portfolio comprised of stocks included in the Dow Jones Industrial Average, with a maturity date and a return to investors at maturity.

mixed market. Those securities trading in which there is no general trend of price movement; some stocks higher, some lower.

MLP. Abbreviation for **master limited partnership.**

MNZ. See **money supply.**

mode. See **average, statistical.**

model. The explanation of a material event or set of events, or the anticipation of them, in a mathematical framework. A model can be used by a portfolio manager to evaluate prices of the stock market or individual securities; or it can be used by a securities analyst to forecast corporate operating results, in order to develop an earnings estimate. In a sense, a company's financial statements are models depicting various aspects of corporate progress. And a budget forecast is certainly a model. As an investor, it is important to understand the assumptions the model builder is making. It is the validity of the assumption that makes a model relevant or illogical. Probably the most important bromide about a model is that it should effectively explain the real world. *See* **forecasting or valuation model, stock market,** and **forecasting, stock price.**

moderate trading. A medium volume of share transactions, which would be 500–750 million shares per day on the New York Stock Exchange.

modularity. A reference to product design in which components are assembled as separate units and plugged or joined together into the final product. This concept allows a manufacturer to contract with others for making the sub-assemblies, saving inventory costs, or using employees on site. Besides providing a manufacturer flexibility and ease in making design changes, the technology allows for custom manufacturing to a customer's specifications. The computer industry utilizes this technique. An underlying requirement is the adoption of industry standards pertaining to connections and product performance. *See* **supply chain management.**

mom and pop shops. A reference to small, marginal business entities, in an industry that otherwise is dominated by large, well-capitalized companies. Nearly every mature industry has passed through a "mom and pop" stage. These small competitors sell their goods and services on the basis of personal attention and niche marketing. The latest such industry to produce these is the Internet Service Provider (ISP) industry. Mom and pops typically provide Internet access to 500 to 1,500 subscribers, compared with America Online, the biggest ISP, with over 17 million subscribers. There are over 5,000 mom and pop Internet Service Providers. As the technology and marketing become more standardized, mom and pops usually are squeezed out, unable to keep up with the huge demands for capital, innovation, and universal presence. Being especially vulnerable to dependence on one supplier, one contractor, or one customer, sometimes the mistakes or failure of such a key entity causes their demise. They are often bought out by bigger companies looking for special niches, or the principals tire of struggling and sell out or close down.

momentum oscillators. A reference to measurements of the tendencies of stocks to fluctuate in price and volume between overbought and oversold conditions, in reference to an equilibrium level or historical level. Oscillators are used in technical analysis, and are wave-like if charted. Overbought conditions might represent a selling signal for technical traders, while oversold conditions might signal a buying opportunity. When momentum indicators are charted, on the "Y" axis the product of daily, weekly, or monthly volume in shares is multiplied by the average price for each time period. The result is a measure of the velocity of stock momentum and, like most technical stock analysis, the measure has many variations.

momentum stocks. In stock market trading, either light or busy, those stocks that are in style with investors and generally firm to strong in price, with little regard to industry, size, region, quality, or sector. Momentum is generally measured in terms of significant share price gains on higher volume. By multiplying share volume times price in a trading session, a momentum indicator can be recorded on successive trading sessions or intervals, and compared for buy-sell timing purposes. Often in periods of market unrest, when no business bellwether stocks are stabilizing pricing and acting as stock market leaders, because of their historical and inherent financial qualities, momentum stocks take over the leadership role. Investors flock to these stocks because they are working, in terms of market appreciation. Adherence to them is sort of a "shoot first and ask questions later" philosophy, often with the same unexpected results.

The basis for the momentum in certain stocks or groups of stocks can be diverse. At times consecutive quarters of earnings draws investor attention, sometimes it is stocks that seem on the cusp of mergers or acquisitions, other times it might be stocks that represent socially conscious managements. This market form of jumping on the bandwagon can be successful, especially if some form of discipline is exercised. Professional investors usually utilize a moving average format to alert themselves to liquidation time in momentum stocks.

For example, in a ludicrously short-term situation, Charge, Inc. common stock has risen on 10 successive trading days. The time to sell the stock, using the moving average technique is when the current price falls beneath the 5-day moving average, in this case on the 11th session when the price per share is now lower than the per share moving average. It is a good idea to stipulate that the current price should remain beneath the moving average longer than one trading session. This precaution could prevent an investor jumping out of a stock on a price dip that is a temporary aberration. The reason this is a valid technique in measuring the longevity of momentum stock is that the current price is one-fifth of the moving average, in the case of the five-day interval. When it drops below the average for several sessions, the moving average will obviously follow, which illustrates the logic for using the method. This action, by definition, indicates the momentum trend is over, in the short term. *See* **momentum oscillators.**

MONEP—Equity & Financial Derivatives. See under **Global Investment Market.**

monetarist. See **monetary aggregates.**

monetary aggregates. Those categories of financial resources in a country that are analyzed in initializing, maintaining, and measuring actions in implementing an effective monetary policy. In the United States, they are, in a broad sense: currency in circulation; near-currency items such as travelers checks, savings and time deposits, and U.S. Savings Bonds; and short-term treasury debt. Specifically, they are called M1, M2, M3, L, and MZM, respectively, and are calculated and reported by the Federal Reserve System. Proponents of relying heavily on **monetary policy** in setting and attaining economic goals in a country are called monetarists, and they favor using the aggregates and their components in governmental decisions and actions as well as measuring results; while their counterparts who advocate governmental fiscal policy—taxes and manipulative spending—as the guiding light in monetary policy are called Keynesians, after the renowned British economist, John Maynard Keynes. The modern day proponent of monetarism is Milton Friedman and his disciples at the University of Chicago. *See* **money supply** and **Keynesian Economics.**

monetary base. The reserves of member banks of the Federal Reserve System plus currency in circulation, which forms the base for the money supply of the banking system.

monetary policy. A prevailing program followed by a government or central bank, but usually a central bank, in establishing actions designed to either stimulate or slow down the economy, emphasizing changes in the availability of liquid assets to banks and consumers. In essence, monetary policy involves the degree of control, or lack of it, of the money supply for use by a country's economic administrators, who are usually officials of the central bank. Either a government can do this as the supervisor of a central bank or an independent central bank can accomplish the results, as is the situation in the United States and most other industrialized nations. In the United States the Federal Reserve system is in charge of monetary policy, independent of the federal government, but it is often exhorted by members of the federal government, both the executive and legislative branches, to take action for the political ends of the politicians or for the better results the recommended action may accomplish. Those proponents of using monetary policy aggressively are called "monetarists." *See* **Federal Reserve Act, money supply,** and **fiscal policy.**

monetize, to. 1) In the financial management of a company or organization, to convert a resource into money by issuing equity or debt, and use the resources as backing for the resulting securities. Nearly always the strategy involves debt. When this action occurs, the resource in question is said to be "monetized." 2) In fiscal management by a government, to print money, represented by certain reserves, and distribute it into the banking system. Generally speaking, the term is appropriate whenever an asset or resource is converted to money.

money flows. A tool for measuring how much money is flowing into or out of the stock market or one or more particular stocks. It is calculated by comparing the number of trades occurring at an **uptick,** or price higher than the previous one, with the number occurring at a down-tick, or price lower than the previous one. As a technical indicator it is a refinement of the advance-decline ratio, in that it measures the number of times a stock or stocks gained in price versus how many times a stock or stocks declined in price.

money fund expense game or **money fund expense waiver.** The practice by some money market fund managements of waiving certain administrative fees, such as management fees and operating fees, in order to boost the yields over competitive funds for a brief period, often for one year. Usually, the fund advertises this, attracting new investors. Then the subsidizing of fees is ended, thereby reducing yields. Sometimes the strategy actually causes a fund to operate at a loss during the waiver period. Management hopes that many of the new investors will remain with the fund after subsidization ends. This practice has been questioned when the reduction in yields that are inevitable are not mentioned in the offering prospectus in clear language by money market funds that follow this practice.

money funds table. A tabulation, usually found in newspapers, of short-term money investment funds, emphasizing the size of asset base and yields.

MONEY FUNDS TABLE				
(1)	(2)	(3)	(4)	(5)
Fund	Assets	Avg Mat	7-Day Avg	7-Day Cmp
Bunker Hill	($Mil)	69	Yld (%)	Yld (%)
MMF	191.9		5.4	5.5

Explanations:

(1) name of fund/Bunker Hill Money Market Fund

(2) value of assets in fund is $191,900,000

(3) average security matures in 69 days

(4) average yields of assets past seven days was 5.4%

(5) effective compounding rate of that was 5.5%

money market. The prevailing rate of return that investors demand as reflected by yields on short-term securities, usually considered those coming due in 15 to 190 days. An exception is the federal funds rate, which is technically an overnight rate. Definitively, the money market is considered transactions in short-term securities—Treasury bills and notes maturing in less than a year, commercial paper, banker's acceptances, certificates of deposit, broker call loans, for example—while the capital market is considered transactions in long-term securities—bonds, debentures, preferred stock, common stock, mortgages, for example. The defining principle is that short-term securities are issued to raise money to operate day-to-day, while long-term securities are issued to raise money to build permanent resources, although there are many overlapping functions by each one. Psychology, money supply, habit, and competition for funds are significant factors as money shifts from one type of investment to another and, in doing so, establishes interest rates for each term or maturity.

The premiums and discounts on securities reflect how a set interest or coupon rate on its face can be adjusted to current investor demands by decreasing or increasing the actual yield. The interest rate on the issue date of a security is a fixed interest amount or cost only to the issuer as the security matures, and the yield is fixed only to the investor who holds the security until maturity. To all other investors, the interest rate varies from day to day as the price of the security changes. *See* **capital market.**

money market fund. A pool of assets invested in high-quality, short-term income securities, such as U.S. Treasury bills, commercial paper, and banker's acceptances, owned by many investors in proportion to the amounts invested. The SEC requires the funds to invest in securities having maturities of 13 months or less, with the average maturity of the portfolio not to exceed 90 days. These funds are similar to mutual funds with some important differences. Unlike mutual fund shares, money market shares maintain a constant net asset value of $1 each. Shares are priced by yields on the annualized returns of the dividend payouts of the underlying securities for the previous seven days. These funds also report "effective seven-day yields," which represents the return if dividends were reinvested. Money market funds can represent taxable or tax-free income. These funds are popular with investors who want to avoid the risk and volatility of mutual fund shares, either temporarily or permanently, while earning an investment yield. Basically, there are four types of money market funds, each offering investors different risk and yield characteristics: (1) 100% U.S. Treasury funds; (2) Government funds; (3) General Purpose funds, and (4) Tax-free funds.

MONEY MODE. See under **Web Sites for Investing Women.**

Money Purchase Retirement Plan. This plan is similar to a profit sharing plan, since an employer contributes to the fund for all participants or eligible employees. But there is a big exception. In this plan the employer is permitted to make contributions up to 25% of a participant's salary or wages, but there is no flexibility in that percentage annually. At least, it cannot be easily changed. It is funded only by the employer. Money purchase plans are favored by employers who want predictable cash flow with the maximum allowable contributions. Also, these plans can be coordinated with social security benefits by allowing a greater percentage of the contribution to accumulate to the employees in the higher income brackets. Participants vest in the contributions on a graduated basis, up to seven years. This type program fits the following situations:
- Company is for profit or nonprofit.
- Profits are dependable so that commitment to annual contribution is no problem.
- Options as to vesting schedule is important.
- Privilege of loans against employee's fund are desired.
- Part time employees can be excluded.

money-rate issues. Those stocks and bonds that very likely will maintain their dividends or interest regardless of how bad general business conditions become. If other investment yields diminish, these issues become more valuable, and in a generally faltering market they are called "defensive issues." They are called money-rate issues because they tend to move the same way short-term money-market debt securities do in response to changes in interest rates. When interest rates decrease, these securities tend to rise, thus allowing for a smaller yield, and when rates in general rise, they decline in price, thus allowing for a bigger yield. *See* **defensive stock.**

money-rate stock. A stock so likely to pay a regular dividend that it trades on a yield basis in relation to securities with similar risk characteristics. The yield demanded by investors mostly determines at what price it sells, because the constant dividend infers a quality situation. Utility stocks are the principal examples.

money supply. A nation's collective level of money and near-money assets, which is considered a controlling factor in economic growth. Under the monetary concept of economic theory, the stock of liquid assets in the form of money—readily spendable or readily convertible into spendable form—that is available to spenders in an economic region determines the growth and well-being in that region. Economists use the magnitudes of the supply in gauging future economic activity. There are six basis categories of money supply reported on by the Federal Reserve System:

1. M1, which includes currency in circulation, travelers checks, checking demand deposits, and other demand deposits;
2. M2, which includes M1, money market funds held by retail investors, savings deposits including money market deposit accounts, and certain time deposits;
3. M3, which includes M2, large time deposits, repurchase agreements, Eurodollars, and money market funds held by institutions;
4. L, which includes M3 plus U.S. Savings Bonds, short-term Treasury securities, commercial paper, bankers acceptances held by households and by firms other than depository institutions, and money market mutual funds;
5. MZM, which includes M2 minus small denomination time deposits, plus institutional money market funds.
6. There is another category, which measures total liquidity in the system. This bracket includes savings bonds, short-term treasury securities, bankers acceptances, and commercial paper. *See* **monetary aggregates.**

Money Supply, M2. See **Economic Indicators.**

monopoly. An economic situation in which there is control of the supply of or demand for a product by one or several (monopolistic competition) buyers or sellers.

Montana Office of the State Auditor. Regulator of securities laws in the state of Montana. Address: Securities Department, P.O. Box 4009, Helena, MT 59604. Phone: (406) 444-2040. Phone (toll free): (800) 332-6148.

month orders. Those stock exchange limit orders that are cancelled if they are not executed within the month.

Monthly Investment Plan (MIP). A method by which an investor may purchase shares and fractions of securities listed on the New York Stock Exchange at a minimum rate of $40 per quarter.

Montreal Stock Exchange. See under **Global Investment Market.**

Moody's Investors Service. A leading provider of independent credit ratings, research, and financial information to the capital markets. Address: 99 Church Street, New York, NY 10007. Web site: *www.moodys.com.* They also compile a stock survey index of 125 industrial stocks. *See* **stock averages** and **index numbers.**

Moore, Geoffrey H. An American economist who was a major contributor to the analysis of business cycles and economic statistics. He is considered the principle proponent of the well-known leading economic indicators, calculations considered pivotal in predicting upturns and downturns in general economic activity. These indicators have been adopted by the U.S. Department of Commerce, for use in warning of turning points in the economy. He also pioneered the use of statistical diffusion indexes, which enable the focus on each component of the leading indicators. For 30 years, he was associated with the National Bureau of Economic Research in Cambridge, Mass., a private group that designates the beginnings and ends of recessions in a quasi-official way. Dr. Moore died in 2000.

"moose on the table." A reference in business management to a sensitive topic that is openly discussed in a meeting, in spite of reluctance by the participants. Even though the subject has been unmentionable hitherto, one or more executives believe it would be beneficial for the company's success to frankly discuss the topic.

moral hazard. A relatively new concept in financial circles, it describes a situation in which investors put money in a risky entity or situation because they believe that a third party, the central government, for example, will bail them out if the investment goes broke or is unsuccessful. When the investors' benefactor fails to bail them out, perhaps because it is politically or economically unfeasible, that hazard has become a reality. An example occurred in the late 1990s, when certain Russian and Asian enterprises were not propped up by central governments, as they had been historically, when recessions struck those regions. The result was that investments by foreigners lost a great deal of their values or became worthless. Thus, the moral obligations historically assumed by the governments to keep the entities afloat financially were abandoned in favor of a market-oriented competitive standard, and the investments were abortive because of that hazard or risk.

moral suasion. The psychological pressure the Federal Reserve Board puts on member banks to raise or lower interest rates to customers. *See* **Federal Open Market Committee.**

moratorium. A legal postponement of debt payment during an emergency period.

Morgan Stanley Capital International (MSCI) indexes. Several stock and fixed-income indexes, managed by a subsidiary of Morgan Stanley investment bankers, representing market price changes in 51 countries for stock indexes and 32 countries for fixed-income indexes, and indexes for several regions, including emerging regions. An index criterion is that areas must be investable. Global investors use these indexes to monitor their asset allocations in foreign sites. Web site: *www.msci.com.*

Morgan Stanley EAFE Index. See **EAFE Index.**

Morgan Stanley Emerging Markets Index. A stock index that measures the price movement of stocks located and doing business in developing nations of the world, maintained by Morgan Stanley Investment Bankers. Companies represented tend to operate in Southeast Asia and Latin America. Because they are untested, these stocks are more volatile than their mature and more stable counterparts in developed nations.

morning loan. See **day loan.**

Morningstar ratings. A rating system for mutual funds based on one to five stars and developed by Morningstar Inc. Address: 225 West Wacker Dr., Chicago, IL 60606. Phone: (312) 696-6000. Fax: (312) 696-6001. Web site: *www.morningstar.com.*

Morris Trust transaction. A tax-free transaction (some would yell "corporate welfare") in which a corporation may split off and sell part of its business, followed by arranging a merger between either the parent or split-off entity with the purchasing company. The latter would pay stock for the merged entity. Current law allows tax-free exchanges of a subsidiary or parent corporation in exchange for an acquiring company's stock.

mortgage. A written document in evidence that title to property has been conveyed from a borrower of money to a lender until a loan is repaid satisfactorily.

mortgage banker. An individual or firm that loans money, or arranges for outside funds, to finance building loans.

mortgage bond. A bond pledging real property in the event of default.

mortgage costs. Those outlays of money required by a lender who has an interest in real estate used as security for his loaned money; for example, payment of interest and principal on the loan, maintenance of the property, property taxes, insurance, and so on.

mortgagee. A creditor to whom a mortgage is pledged.

mortgage insurance. A type of insurance that will pay off the balance due on a mortgage in the event of the death of the mortgagor or his inability to continue payments on the debt. In the first case, the heirs of the deceased then take title to the property. In the second instance, the insurer pays the lender or mortgage holder, and then takes title.

mortgage loan. A loan from a financial institution pledging real property as collateral, evidenced by a note.

mortgage trust. A type of real estate mutual fund that invests in mortgage contracts rather than real properties as Real Estate Investment Trusts (REITs) do. Like other real estate trusts, these funds must pay out 95% of their earnings in dividends.

mortgagor. A person pledging property as collateral.

most active stocks or **"stocks in the spotlight."** Those 10 or 15 stocks most traded during a session, listed with volume, close and net change. Market analysts pay particular attention to whether a majority of these closed up or down in analyzing the strength of the market.

Most Favored Nation (MFN) status. In a nation's conduct of its foreign trade, the promise to extend to one or more signatories to a treaty any favorable trading terms offered in agreements with third parties. The concept suggests that trade restrictions imposed by a **GATT** (General Agreements on Tariffs and Trade) member must be applied equally to all GATT members. The procedure, as well as the GATT concept, is being supplanted by the Permanent Normal Trade Relations status, within the framework of the World Trade Organization.

MOT. Abbreviation for **Management of Technology.**

MOTIF. Abbreviation for Management of Technology and Innovation in Financial Services. *See* **Management of Technology (MOT).**

Motley Fool, The. A Web site for investors that provides stock research, anecdotes, and useful tips on investing. *See* **Web Sites for the Inquiring Investor.**

motors. See autos.

moving average. An average calculated from a series of stock price index numbers, dropping the first of the series and adding a current index number before each calculation. Analysts often relate a 200-day moving average to a current stock index: they feel that when the current index is rising proportionately faster than the moving average, the stock market is a safe place for investment money. On the other hand, they feel that when the current index drops below the moving average for several sessions consecutively, the current market is in danger of slipping. If the trend continues, or accelerates, they begin liquidating stocks selectively, provided that other signs confirm the moving-average sell signal.

The logic for using the moving-average in this manner is as follows. Mathematically, the moving average will eventually follow the current or short-term index when it declines for several days or more. When the average begins to drop, it indicates the price trend is in that direction; the alert analyst likes to recognize this trend as soon as it manifests itself, which could be at the point where the current index falls beneath the average, or crosses over, for the first time. A graph of a 200-day moving-average of the Dow Jones industrial stocks would show the current index crossing beneath the average in April, 1953 at 280, staying until November. Then it would cross back at 275 and stay on top until late 1956 at 495 when it would pass underneath until early 1957 at 478, falling precipitously underneath again in late 1957 at 490. Therefore, observation of this moving-average would have forewarned of the declines in the economy and stock market of 1953, 1956, and 1957.

moving average crossover. On a chart using a short-term moving average and a long-term moving average to signal a change in trend or direction for a stock market or economic time series, that point on the chart at which the short-term curve moves above or below the long-term curve. At this point the observer is alerted that a change in the trend is forming. In response, an investor might sell or buy stocks in anticipation. The rational is that the long-term movement is a series of short-term movements.

moving-average method. See **"variable ratio formula"** under **formula investing.**

MROE. Abbreviation for **Marginal Return on Equity.**

MSCI indexes. See **Morgan Stanley Capital International (MSCI) indexes.**

M-squared. A reference to the measure of the investment return of a portfolio of stocks when the risk incurred is considered. The essence of the technique is to theoretically adjust a portfolio of stocks until the risk is the same as that of an index, in terms of volatility, against which its managers compare its performance. The return of the risk-adjusted portfolio is then the M-squared return. The measure is named after Leah Modigliani and her grandfather and Nobel laureate, Franco Modigliani.

 Are you ready? Let's say the Color Me Green Mutual Fund, a high-tech fund, advertises a return one year of 50%, versus a return of the S&P 500 Index of 23.5%. To find the M-squared return, the procedure would be to theoretically add ultrastable U.S. T-bills to the Color Me Green portfolio until its weighted average performance drops to the same volatility as the S&P 500. Of course, the procedure pulls down the return also. A new measure is taken of the risk-adjusted portfolio's return. After the risk adjustment, it might be under the S&P 500 return. Apples to apples, instead of apples to kumquats.

multi-jurisdictional disclosure system. An arrangement between two or more countries in which a securities registration with the proper authorities in one country is tantamount to an official registration in the other country(ies), leading to the distribution of new securities from the foreign country at a fraction of the time and costs associated with a complete initial registration in the home country. The only such arrangement in the United States is with Canada, although it was envisioned that it would include Mexico also, under the North American Free Trade Agreement (NAFTA). Recently, the SEC has expressed dissatisfaction with the Canadian agreement, on the grounds that other major trading partners—Mexico, Japan, and members of the European Union (EU)—ought also to be included. The arrangement covers the registration of share offerings, takeover offers or continuous disclosure filings as long as the information required by the SEC is included in the Canadian registration. The primary advantage of such an arrangement is in the time saved. The dual registrant can reduce the waiting time before commencing activity from approximately 60 days to five, in many cases. This is very important in volatile securities markets. During the past nine years, Canadian securities issuers have raised over $153 billion in U.S. markets, with minimal screening by the SEC, since documents required by the latter had already been filed with provincial regulators in Canada.

multilateral alliance. See **airline alliances.**

multilevel marketing. Selling products or services through more than one tier of distributors, usually in an arrangement that separates in a business organizational way the originator of the products or services from the distributors.

municipal bond debt ratio. In the credit analysis of municipal bonds, the guideline that the funded debt of a municipality should not exceed 10% of the assessed valuation of the property used as a taxing basis.

municipals, munis, or **municipal bonds.** Those bonds issued by states, towns, counties, water or school districts, or other subdivisions of a state and secured by the good faith and taxing power of the municipality, as determined by state law. The basis for taxation is a property tax, on both real and personal property, frequently supplemented by other taxes and fees. Consequently, the economic vitality of the municipality, in terms of population trends, growth in business entities, and enlightened tax policies, is essential to back a quality bond issue. However, income from specific purposes may be pledged to meet the interest payments on bonds also. Generally, the interest income is exempt from federal income taxes, which means buyers do not demand as high an interest rate from them as they do from corporate bonds. In June 1999, the $1.5 trillion in municipal bond debt represented 11% of the total bond debt in the United States. *See* **bond tables, municipal bond debt ratio,** and **tax-exempts.**

munis. Abbreviation for **municipal bonds.**

mutual company. See **stock company.**

mutual fund. A popular term for an open-end investment company. There are approximately 12,000 funds in the United States, basically investing in 14 types of mutual fund categories, depending on the characteristics of the securities invested in. One of the most attractive features of mutual funds is that interest, dividends, and capital gains are tax-deferred if a fund retains 90% of these annually for reinvestment. More detailed information can be found under some individual listings below. The SEC requires that managers of mutual funds disclose portfolio contents to shareholders at least twice a year. There are 88 million Americans invested in mutual funds, representing $6.8 trillion in 2000, versus $1 trillion in 1990. *See* **closed-end investment company, open-end investment company** and **investment trust.** The fund types are:

1. *Asset-allocation fund*—A fund in which management changes the mix of assets between stocks, bonds, and cash in an effort to focus on the most attractive segment to achieve maximum investment performance.

2. *Balanced fund*—Resources are invested in a predetermined ratio between stocks and bonds, usually 60%–40%, with stock money concentrated in quality equities and the bond portion invested in long-term taxable issues.

3. *Bear-market fund*—Commitments are timed so that investments are made in selling short individual securities on the market when their prices are considered high and vulnerable to a fall.

4. *Convertible-bond fund*—Money is invested in convertible debentures, giving this type of fund both equity and debt characteristics; such a fund has a certain amount of growth and defensive qualities, since the interest income will slow a market downturn, while the stock convertibility feature adds growth.

5. *Foreign-bond fund*—Assets are comprised entirely of bonds issued by foreign entities, subjecting the fund to both financial and political risks as well as foreign exchange risks.

6. *Foreign or international-stock fund*—Management invests exclusively in stocks domiciled in foreign countries, giving such a fund an independence from the U.S. economy.

7. *Global fund*—Investments are combined between foreign and U.S. securities, meaning that foreign results can be counteracted by U.S. events.

8. *Growth fund*—Money goes into stocks with prospects for long-term earnings growth greater than typical in the overall economy, resulting in a heavier weighting in technology stocks which are putting most of their cash flows into product research and development, and reporting little or no earnings.

9. *Hedge fund*—Assets are concentrated in securities and derivatives expected to benefit from a change in the relationships between foreign exchange rates, underlying stock, stock markets, commodities or interest rates, making these funds the most aggressive and usually limited to partners.

10. *High-expense fund*—A stock fund that charges investors over 1% of asset value in management fees, a bond fund that charges over 0.8%, or a money-market fund that charges over 0.6%.

11. *Load fund*—A fund which deducts a sales commission for a broker—usually about 5.5%—from an amount invested, before giving the investor credit in an account.

12. *Money-market fund*—Resources are channeled into short-term securities, usually quality corporate debt and Treasuries, sacrificing return for safety, and making this type of fund the most conservative.

13. *Sector fund*—Money is concentrated in the securities of certain economic sectors such as energy, financial services, health care or technology, in a sense defeating the objective of diversification.

14. *Small-cap stock fund*—Holdings are directed into stocks that have smaller stock market capitalizations than those in more established industries, usually indicating growth objectives.

mutual fund salesperson. A salesperson who handles nothing but mutual fund shares, selling the investment judgment of the fund's professional investors or money managers.

mutual fund table. The method of reporting daily mutual fund share price movements as illustrated by the following diagram, which is typical of those used in the business sections of newspapers, although tables do vary somewhat. For the meaning of complete terms and abbreviations in a stock table, refer to the glossary that accompanies it in the newspaper. *See* **mutual fund.**

MUTUAL FUND TABLE					
(1) Fund	(2) Load	(3) NAV	(4) Chg	(5) 4-Wk % Ret	(6) YTD % Ret
Am Ex	5.75	9.23	0.06		
Blue ch				−0.9	−2.1

Explanations:

(1) Name of fund: American Express Blue Chip

(2) sales load of 5.75%

(3) net asset value per share is $9

(4) change in NAV was $0.06 per share

(5) percentage return latest four weeks was −0.9%

(6) percentage return for year to date is −2.1%

mutual savings bank. See **Federal Savings and Loan Association** or **state savings and loan association.**

MVA. Abbreviation for **market value added.**

Nn

Nagoya Stock Exchange. See under **Global Investment Market.**

NAIC. Abbreviation for the **National Association of Investment Clubs.**

NAICS. Abbreviation for **North American Industry Classification System.**

Nairobi Stock Exchange. See under **Global Investment Market.**

NAIRU. Acronym for "non-accelerating inflation rate of unemployment," which is an economists' theoretical description of the level of unemployment which must exist to relieve inflationary pressures in an economy. In effect, the theory suggests that when there is an unusually low unemployment rate, inflation will accompany or follow. The NAIRU rate is the unemployment level and above that generates no inflation, according to the theory. Although the theory seemed to be valid in the 1950s and 1960s, in the 1990s it was not. The relatively low unemployment rates of around 4% in the 1990s triggered no significant inflation. Reasons cited are: rising productivity, inexpensive imports, lower-paid immigrants, less effective unions, job insecurity, and corporate mobility. *See* **Phillips Curve.**

naked option or **uncovered option.** An option contract in which the party who must deliver the underlying stock if the option holder exercises his right does not own the stock at the time of the contract. He intends to buy in the stock if and when the option is exercised.

naked shorting. A reference to selling short shares that one does not own and for which sale no arrangements have been made to borrow. This is against SEC rules, in order to prevent the sale of many more shares of a stock than are available for trading.

However, it occurs occasionally in the more unregulated online trading. *See* **Rules, SEC.**

NAM. Abbreviation for the **National Association of Manufacturers.**

Namibian Stock Exchange. See under **Global Investment Market.**

"nanocorp." A nickname for a small, entrepreneurial business using the Internet to operate and develop prospects. *See* **"e-lance economy"** and **"e-lance firm."**

nanotechnology. A reference to the emerging technology of designing systems and devices of microscopic size, with future applications in the fields of science and engineering. As the 21st century commences, this technology is in an embryonic stage, with government and university research providing most of the research and development. At this stage, the technology is considered to be a long-term, high-risk, big-payoff investment. It has not generated many commercial products yet. However, the following possibilities exist, from its "bottoms up" manipulation of atoms and molecules: materials 10 times harder than steel; new computer chips millions of times faster than today's models; solar cells twice as efficient; gene and drug delivery for detecting cancer cells; agents to detect and remove the tiniest contaminants from water.

narrow prices. Those securities with trading price fluctuations within a small range, not changing more than a fraction of a point.

narrower trading. A market session in which stocks traded at lesser fractions or with less variance than in the previous session.

NASAA. See **North American Securities Administrators Association.**

NASD. Abbreviation for the **National Association of Security Dealers.**

NASDAQ Central. A Web site featuring NASDAQ-listed stocks, including information on companies, stock screening, IPOs, portfolio tacking, and news. *See* **Web Sites for the Inquiring Investor.**

NASDAQ Composite Index. An index of average stock price changes, including in the calculations all the domestic and foreign stocks listed on the NASDAQ Stock Market. It is reported by the National Association of Securities Dealers, using approximately 5,600 large and small companies in the results. The base (100) is February 5, 1971 for the index. Current numbers should be read as a percentage of average stock prices on the base date. This index is market-weighted, a technique assuring that each issue affects the index level commensurate with its market capitalization.

NASDAQ-Japan. A joint venture between the NASD in the United States and Softbank, a Japanese venture capital firm, that provides an electronic trading system for Japanese and U.S. stocks. It commenced operations in the final quarter of 2000, with 100 U.S. stocks and several Japanese stocks trading. It is unclear how or if this system will relate to JASDAQ, where small-cap Japanese stocks are traded presently. An interesting feature of NASDAQ-Japan is that because of the time differentials between the two countries, trading could be lengthened to 21 hours, just using normal trading hours in each country. *See* **virtual global stock market.**

NASDAQ 100 Index. An index of average stock prices, representing the 100 largest and most active nonfinancial growth stocks in the NASDAQ trading system, based on stock market capitalizations. Originally launched in January 1985, the index was rebalanced on December 21, 1988 to a modified market capitalization weighted index. It reflects the largest companies across major industry groups, including computer hardware and software, telecommunications, retail/wholesale trade, and biotechnology. It is maintained by the National Association of Securities Dealers, and monitored for changes every quarter.

NASDAQ 100 Unit Trust. A depository receipt providing an investor with a proportionate interest in the holdings of a trust fund constructed to emulate the return of the NASDAQ 100

Index. This derivative security was introduced by the American Stock Exchange in 1988. Stock symbol: QQQ.

NASDAQ Stock Market (U.S.). Created in 1971, this is the largest screen-based stock market in the world, and second only to the **NYSE** in the value of transactions. Annual volume is close to 175 billion shares. Daily capacity is 6 billion shares. It is operated and regulated by the National Association of Securities Dealers. There are more than 5,500 securities firms trading 6,208 issues of 5,487 listed companies. There are two sets of listing requirements for the NASDAQ National Market, summarized below. To remain listed, a company must comply with one set, although there are also other considerations. If a company cannot maintain a listing on the NASDAQ National Market System, it may qualify for listing among NASDAQ's Small Cap Market of second-tier stocks or the OTC Bulleting Board or "pink sheets." Phone: (202) 728-8840. Recently, this exchange merged with the American Stock Exchange and the Philadelphia Stock Exchange. *See* under **Global Investment Market.**

Most Stringent Listing Requirements for NASDAQ Stock Market:
- Corporation's share price stays over $5.00.
- Corporation's total stock market value of $50 million or more.
- Corporate revenues of $50 million or more.
- Corporate assets of $50 million or more.

Less Stringent Listing Requirements for NASDAQ Stock Market:
- Corporation's share price stays over $1.00.
- Corporation owns $4 million or more in tangible assets (assets excluding Goodwill less liabilities.)
- Corporation's float or publicly traded 750,000 shares cannot include shares owned by corporate insiders or any investor owning 10% or more of stock outstanding.
- Corporation's total stock market value of $5 million or more.
- Corporation shareholders of 400 or more and two brokerage market makers in corporation's stock.

National Association of Independent Finance Advisors (NAIPFA). A professional organization of firms that specialize in providing financial advice on bond sales and financial planning on public projects of public agencies. E-mail: *email@ fiscaladvisors.com.* Web site: *www.naipfa.com/index.html.*

National Association of Investors Corporation (NAIC). A nonprofit organization composed of investment clubs and individual investors founded in 1951. It was started to increase the number of individual investors in common stocks and to provide a program of education and information for investors. Through membership, it offers several services, among them aid to the formation and sustenance of investment clubs. In 1997 there were 670,000 individual members and 33,549 investment clubs represented. Address: 711 W. 13 Mile Road, Madison Heights, MI 48071. Phone: (248) 583-6242. Fax: (248) 583-4880. Web site: *www.better-investing.org/index/html. See* **investment club** and **World Federation of Investors Corporation**.

National Association of Manufacturers (NAM). An association of manufacturers and certain nonmanufacturers formed in 1895, with the mission of enhancing the competitiveness of manufacturers and improving the living standards for working Americans by shaping a legislative and regulatory environment conducive to U.S. economic growth. Address: 1331 Pennsylvania Avenue, NW, Washington, DC 20004-1790. Phone: (800) 248-6NAM. Fax: (202) 637-3182. E-mail: *manufacturing@nam.org.* Web site: *www.nam.org.*

National Association of Personal Financial Advisors (NAPFA). The largest professional association of comprehensive, fee-only financial planners in the United States. It has 625 members with affiliates in 45 states. Address: 355 West Dundee Road, Suite 200, Buffalo Grove, IL 60089. Phone: 888-FEE-ONLY. E-mail: *info@napfa.org.* Web site: *www.napfa.org.*

National Association of Purchasing Management (NAPM). Founded in 1915, NAPM is a non-profit organization of 47,000 professional purchasing and supply managers. Its mission is to provide national and international leadership in purchasing and materials management, particularly in education, research and standards of excellence. Address: P.O. Box 22160, Tempe, AZ 85285-2160. Phone: (800) 888-6276. Fax: (480) 752-7890. Web site: *www.napm.org. See* **Purchasing Managers' Index.**

National Association of Security Dealers (NASD). An association of 5,500 securities brokers and dealers, founded in 1939, who enforce ethical standards among the members, located at 1735 K Street, NW, Washington, DC 20006. Phone: (202) 728-8840. Fax: (202) 496-2699.

national bank. A commercial bank that is supervised by the Federal Reserve System and the Comptroller of the Currency and regulated by the National Banking Act of 1863 as amended. Only such a bank may use national in its title.

"national best bid or offer" (NBBO). In the context of modern securities markets, including trading through traditional brokerages combined with trading through online brokerages and electronic networks, a trading price that represents as nearly as possible the most advantageous one to the investor. This objective is the attainment of a true national market in securities, especially stocks. It is a goal of the Securities and Exchange Commission, one that presents a definite challenge in view of the fragmentation of markets in the post-Internet period.

National Federation of Municipal Analysts (NFMA). An organization of approximately 1,000 members, formed in 1983, that provides a forum for issues of interest to municipal finance professionals, with a secondary purpose of voicing opinions on matters of concern to municipal financial analysts. Web site: *www.nfma.org.*

National Fraud Information Center (NFIC). An arm of the National Consumers League, established in 1992 to combat telemarketing fraud by improving prevention and enforcement of antifraud laws in the United States. The NFIC is the only national toll-free hotline for consumers to get advice about telephone solicitations and report possible telemarketing and Internet fraud to law enforcement agencies. Telephone: (800) 876-7600. Web site: *www.fraud.org.*

National Income and Product Accounts. (NIPA). The system that values U.S. output and shows its composition, generated by the **BEA.** The accounts also show the distribution of incomes in the United States, stemming from this production. Accounts include **Gross Domestic Product (GDP)**—the total market value of goods and services in the United States in current and real terms—National Income, Personal Income, and Corporate Profits. For the investor, this is one of the most important macroeconomic series, for it values the fountainhead from which corporations draw revenues that produce income and dividends. Fluctuations in these accounts eventually affect every corporation in the United States, and thus the stock market.

National Industrial Conference Board (NICB). An association of business organizations, trade associations, government bureaus, colleges and universities, libraries, and individuals, founded in 1916, conducting research in economics, business management, and human relations.

nationalization. The complete acquisition of foreign-owned assets by a government, usually with compensation to the owners.

National Quotation Bureau. A service that publishes daily wholesale bid-and-offer prices of 8,000 unlisted bonds and stocks in table form, both printed and electronic, with the names of the dealers making a market in those securities. The quote sheets are published on a regional basis with the color of paper indicating the region. Pink paper contains stocks traded in the Eastern sector of the country; green, the west; and white, the Pacific Coast. Yellow paper is used for bond quotations. Address: 11 Penn Plaza, 15th Floor, New York, NY 10001. Phone: (212) 868-7100. Web site: *www.nqb.com.*

national securities exchanges. 1) The eight U.S. securities exchanges registered and regulated by the Securities and Exchange Commission. *See* **American Stock Exchange, Boston Stock Exchange, Chicago Board of Trade, Chicago Board Options Exchange, Cincinnati Stock Exchange, New York Stock Exchange, Pacific Stock Exchange** and **Philadelphia Board of Trade.** 2) The securities exchanges whose members are distributed throughout the country. Geographically speaking, only the New York Stock Exchange and the American Stock Exchange are truly national in scope.

National Securities Markets Act of 1996. This act made sweeping changes in doing business for investment advisors, brokers/dealers, issuers of securities, and mutual funds. A few of the act's main provisions are:

1. Securities listed on the **NYSE,** the **ASE,** the **NASDAQ** market, mutual funds, and certain exempt securities are exempt from state registration requirements.
2. SEC is to make rules that may increase access to foreign press releases and press conferences of registered companies to U.S. investors.
3. SEC is to conduct studies of the uniformity of state regulatory requirements, the impact of technological advances, and other issues, such as developing a set of international accounting standards.
4. SEC considers whether any future regulations or rules will promote efficiency, competition, and capital formation.

National Security Traders Association. An organization whose members buy and sell securities. New York Office: One World Trade Center, Suite 4511, New York, NY 10048. Phone: (212) 524-0484. E-mail: traders@securitytraders.org. Web site: *www.securitytraders.org.*

Natural Interest Rate. See **Marginal Efficiency of Capital, company.**

NAV. Abbreviation for **net asset value.**

NBBO. Abbreviation for **"national best bid or offer."**

near money. Those assets that can quickly be converted into cash, for example, high-grade securities and certain types of inventory.

near-term investing. The investing of money in securities that are expected to appreciate within six months. Market appreciation, rather than the yield, is the investor's objective.

near-terms or **near-term bonds.** Those bonds maturing in five years or less.

Nebraska Department of Banking and Finance. Regulator of securities laws in the state of Nebraska. Address: Bureau of Securities, P.O. Box 95006, Lincoln, NE 68509. Phone: (402) 471-3445.

negative operating cycle. In a retailing business, receiving payment from a customer for merchandise sold before paying the vendor for the merchandise. This favorable situation usually is made possible because the retailer's customer charges the purchase to a credit card, which pays the retailer immediately. But the retailer waits before paying the vendor, meaning it has gotten the use of the customer's payment free for the time, until the vendor is paid, which could be 30 to 60 days. Going hand-in-hand with this billing advantage is the fact that the retailer maintains none or very low inventory levels, so that shipment to the customer is made from the distributor's or manufacturer's warehouse.

negative trade balance. See **balance of trade.**

negative yield curve. See **yield curve.**

negotiable instrument. A written document of indebtedness that may be transferred to another party by endorsement or delivery.

negotiated market. The trading of securities off an exchange so that personal negotiations determine the price rather than public auction.

negotiated offerings. Those corporate underwriting agreements (offerings) consummated privately.

Nelson Information. Foremost provider of investment research from both independent and brokerage sources. Formats include directories, catalogs, and Internet. Address: P.O. Box 591, Port Chester, NY 10573. Phone: (800) 333-6357. Fax: (914) 937-8590. E-mail: *info@netnet.com.* Web site: *www.nelsons.com.*

net assets. 1) The excess of total asset values of a company, after deducting depreciation, depletion, and amortization charges. 2) The excess of total assets over total liabilities on a balance sheet.

net asset value (NAV). 1) In reference to a share of common stock, the amount of value remaining per share after deducting from total assets the face amount of liabilities, unearned income, monetary claims, and uncollectible items in addition to liquidating values or preference rights of senior equities and then dividing by shares outstanding. This exercise is usually based on book values but can be based on market values, where such are known. 2) In reference to an asset, the amount of value remaining, after deducting accumulated depreciation, depletion, and amortization reserves applicable to that asset. 3) In pricing mutual fund shares, the market value of underlying securities less liabilities divided by the number of shares outstanding.

net change. The change in a security's closing price from one session to the next in which there has been a transaction in that security. Ex-dividend dates are considered so that if a stock closes at $145 one day and $144⁴/₈ ($144.50) ex-dividend of $.50 the next day, there is no change because new stock buyers are paying $.50 less only since they will not receive the dividend. Likewise, if a stock closed at $50 the day before a 2-for-1 split, and for $25 the next day, there would be no change since the stock price is reflecting that there are twice as many shares outstanding. Otherwise, net change is the last item in newspaper stock lists; e.g., $2²/₈ means a stock closed $2.25 higher per share than at the close of its last trading session.

net earnings. See **earnings.**

net income to net worth or **return-on-equity.** The ratio of net income divided by the total book value of preferred stock, common stock, and surplus, expressed as a percentage. It indicates how much a company is earning on the stockholders' investment. In the United States in the 1990s, the average for manufacturing corporations was 14.9%; for mining corporations, 5.9%; for retail trade corporations, 10.8%, and for wholesale trade corporations, 7.5%.

Net National Product (NNP). See **Capital Consumption Allowance** and **Gross National Product.**

net operating income or **net operating loss.** The total revenues from a firm's regular business operations minus money spent in carrying out operations; such as selling expenses, fuel and utilities costs, advertising expenses, wages and salaries, interest, depreciation and depletion, and so on.

net operating loss (NOL) carry. In filing U.S. income taxes, a net operating loss from running a business, whether a sole proprietorship, partnership, or corporation, that cannot be used to reduce taxable income in the current tax year but can be applied to prior years and then to future years, until it is used up or the time allowed to carry expires. The amount that is applied to each year can lower the taxes for that year. When the loss is applied to prior periods, it is called a carryback. When applied to future periods, it is called a carryforward. *See* **Taxpayers Relief Act of 1997.**

net present value (NPV). In cash flow investment analysis, a calculation found by adding the initial investment, represented as a negative cash flow since it is an outlay of money, to the present value of the anticipated future cash flows. If the NPV is positive, the investment is financially attractive; if the NPV is zero, the investment is neutral; if the NPV is negative, the investment is financially unattractive. The critical element in such an analysis is what interest rate or discount rate is assumed in the calculation. If the discount rate is one that makes the future positive cash flows equal to the initial cash flow or investment, an enlightened investor would not become enticed by the investment. On the other hand, if the rate makes the NPV of the future cash flows more than the initial outlay contemplated or requested, the investor becomes interested. *See* **internal rate of return.**

net profit. See **earnings.**

net property. The value of an asset such as land or buildings less amounts that have been charged off to depreciation as the property has lessened in commercial value.

net sales. The total money value of goods sold (gross sales) less purchases returned by buyers and allowances and discounts to buyers.

net to customer. A phrase used in an over-the-counter transaction meaning the amount quoted a customer is free of any deductions or additions such as commissions. The salesperson has already included both his or her own and the firm's profit in the quote.

net working capital per share. A corporation's liquid assets—those convertible into cash within one year—minus liabilities and long-term debts divided by the total common shares outstanding. This figure represents the money backing of each share of common stock for a corporate financial emergency, and tends to understate the real value backing of each share since the fixed and other assets are excluded. But it is an excellent measure of an intrinsic value of each share, since it shows the quick wealth per share.

net worth. The excess of assets over liabilities representing the net equity of the owners.

net yield. The yield from an investment after the appropriate income tax has been deducted.

Netstock Direct. A Web site offering investors an automatic investment program, with no minimum purchase required, and including investment information and news. The charge is $2 per purchase for adults and $1 per purchase for children under 18 years of age. It is comparable to the Dividend Reinvestment Plans that many corporations offer investors. *See* **Dividend Reinvestment Plan** and **Web Sites for the Inquiring Investor.**

Neuer Market. A trading segment of the Frankfurt Stock Exchange, begun March 10, 1997. Companies usually listed in this specialized marketplace are based on industries with strong prospects, which also show attractive corporate prospects. Examples of such industries are: Telecom, Biotechnology, Multimedia, and Environmental Technology. However, corporations from traditional sectors can apply for listing and quoting, if they offer new products or services or adopt an innovative approach to business. A key feature of the market is the transparency of corporate information extended to investors. The marketplace was formed in order to provide equity capital to enterprising new businesses, usually precluded from raising funds from debt markets or traditional equity markets.

neural net. In computer modeling applied to stock prices, networks that identify patterns in apparently random prices and make predictions on future prices. These models are products of chaos theory, which holds that even random events display patterns. *See* **quant.**

"neurobics." A reference to using brain teasers, puzzles, and cognitive exercises to enhance management's decision making and that of other employees. Although this technique is controversial among scientists, it still gains in popularity.

Nevada Office of the Secretary of State. Regulator of securities laws in the state of Nevada. Address: Securities Division, 555 E. Washington Avenue, 5th Fl., Las Vegas, NV 89101. Phone: (702) 486-2440. Phone (toll free): (800) 758-6440.

New Age corporation. A business that operates on fees from intangible resources—patents, services, copyrights, and services—without tying capital up in inventories or hard assets such as manufacturing plants, stores, hotels, restaurants, or other real properties, and without the encumbrances hard assets incur.

new capital. Those funds channeled into a business enterprise from a source other than the original investors.

New Economy. A reference to the economic infrastructure of an industrialized nation, after the advent of the Electronic Revolution which began in the late 20th century. In such an economy, the dominant industries are service- and high-tech–driven, rather than product-driven, as measured by their contribution to **GDP.** One of the salient characteristics of a New Economy is that production increases per worker tend to be open-ended—at least in the initial stages—such as activity now taking place as we begin the 21st century. This is because the capital is represented by advanced technology, in particular cyberspace communications. This technology, because of its communicative speed and spreading outreach to markets, seems to promote productivity growth in a geometric fashion. *See* **New Economy stocks** and **Old Economy.**

New Economy stocks. Those stocks representing corporations providing goods and services serving markets driven by technology that developed as a result of the electronic revolution, or since the late 20th century. These industries are triggering accelerated worldwide growth in developed or industrialized countries. Specifically the term refers to new industries such as computer software and peripheral hardware, digital photography, computer networking, telephony, fiber optics, dot-com technologies, e-tailing, genetics, bio-medicine, electronic encryption, digital imaging, space commerce, environmental sciences, and so on. These stocks are newer, less mature, usually pay no dividends since management advocates plow earnings into resources aimed at future growth, and tend to be more volatile in price. The additional volatility is a consequence of the lack of proven financial performance and a preponderance of short-term investment interest in such stocks. However, because the technology and markets are immature, they also tend to be more able to grow earnings than the Old Economy variety. One of the broader aspects of such stocks is that the industries represented are increasing worker productivity, as a result of capital investments in these industries. The NASDAQ Index includes many New Economy stocks, whereas the Dow Industrial Index, Dow Utilities Index, and Dow Transportation Index include mainly Old Economy stocks. *See* **Old Economy stocks.**

"new growth theory." A new economic theory, developed by economist Paul M. Romer of the Stanford Business School, ascribing high economic growth in a society related to rapid innovation in the products and methodologies used in industrial activity.

New Hampshire Bureau of Securities Regulation. Regulator of securities laws in the state of New Hampshire. Address: State

House, Room 204, Concord, NH 03301. Phone: (603) 271-1463. Phone (toll free): (800) 994-4200.

New French Exchange. See under **Global Investment Market.**

new high. 1) The sale of a security at the highest price in its trading history, taking into account altered price levels due to stock splits. For example, if a stock selling for $50 is split 2-for-l, its new market price will be $25. If $50 was its previous high, then any price above $25 on the new level will be considered a new high. 2) The highest price for a security during the current year.

new-highs-to-lows ratio. A ratio measuring daily investor confidence of those shares that traded at an all-time high price to those that traded at an all-time low on an **exchange.** If the highs exceed the lows, investor confidence is considered good.

new issue. A reference to a class of securities never before available to investors.

New Issue Index. Those stocks representing companies that have recently become public companies.

New Jersey Department of Law and Public Safety. Regulator of securities laws in the state of New Jersey. Address: Bureau of Securities, P.O. Box 47029, Newark, NJ 07101. Phone: (201) 504-3600.

new low. 1) The sale of a security at the lowest price in its trading history, taking into account altered price levels due to stock splits. For example, if a stock selling for $50 is split 2-for-l, its new market price will be $25. If $50 was its previous low, then any price below $25 on the new level will be considered a new low. 2) The lowest price for the current year.

New Mexico Regulation and Licensing Department. Regulator of securities laws in the state of New Mexico. Address: Securities Division, 725 St. Michaels Drive, Santa Fe, NM 87501. Phone: (505) 827-7140. Phone (toll free): (800) 704-5533.

new money. That capital raised through a primary offering of securities. *See* **primary offering.**

New York Board of Trade. See under **Global Investment Market.**

New York Department of Law. Regulator of securities laws in the state of New York. Address: Bureau of Investor Protection and Securities, 120 Broadway, 23rd Floor, New York, NY 10271. Phone: (212) 416-8200. Requests for information must be in writing.

New York Institute of Finance. An educational institute sponsored by a New York investment and banking group with personal or correspondence courses. Completion of their course will satisfy New York Stock Exchange registered representative requirements. Address: 37 Wall Street, New York, NY 10005.

New York Mercantile Exchange. A U.S. national securities exchange, specializing in energy, precious metals, and commodities. There are 51 clearing members. Address: 4 Trade Center, New York, NY 10048. Phone: (212) 938-2222. *See* under **Global Investment Market.**

New York Stock Exchange (NYSE). A U.S. national securities exchange, founded in 1792, with 1,427 members. There are 3,656 issues of 3,047 foreign and domestic corporations listed. Trading occurs in 85% of those stocks. Volume was 133.3 billion shares in 1997. It is the largest stock exchange in the world in terms of market valuations. Address: 11 Wall Street, New York, NY 10005. Phone: (212) 656-3000. *See* under **Global Investment Market.**

Listing Requirements of the New York Stock Exchange for U. S. Corporations: Trading
- Round-lot shareholders of 2,000 or more or total shareholders of 2,200 or more.
- Average monthly trading volume of 100,000 shares for past six months.
- Shares outstanding in public hands of 1.1 million or more.
- Stock market value of shares publicly traded, for public companies $100 million or more.

- Stock market value of shares publicly traded, for IPOs, Spin-offs, and Carve-outs $60 million or more.

Listing Requirements of the New York Stock Exchange for U.S. Corporations: Financial

- Aggregate pre-tax earnings over last three years of $6.5 million, from most recent year of $2.5 million or each of two preceding years of $2 million; or over most recent year of $4.5 million, with all three years profitable; or
- Revenues for companies with not less than $1 billion in global market capitalization, $250 million in revenues for the last fiscal year.
- For REITs with fewer than three years operating history, stockholders' equity of $60 million or more.
- For funds with fewer than three years operating history, net assets of $60 million or more.

New York Stock Exchange Composite Index. A composite stock price index of all stocks listed on the NYSE.

New York Times **bond averages.** The daily price averages of 20 rail bonds, 10 industrials, 10 utilities, and a composite average of all 140 compiled by the *New York Times*, Times Building, 229 West 43rd Street, New York, NY 10036. *See* **stock averages.**

New York Times Online. See under **Web Sites for the Inquiring Investor.**

New Zealand Stock Exchange. See under **Global Investment Market.**

next day contracts. Those stock exchange transactions calling for delivery of securities and payment the next day, instead of the regular waiting period.

NFMA. Abbreviation for **National Federation of Municipal Analysts**.

NGO. Abbreviation for **Non-Governmental Organization.**

Nicaraguan Stock Exchange. See under **Global Investment Market.**

NICB. Abbreviation for **National Industrial Conference Board.**

Nightly Business Report Online. See under **Web Sites for the Inquiring Investor.**

Nikkei Index. Japanese stock index published in Tokyo.

Nikkei 225 Index. An unweighted price index of 225 quality stocks listed on the Tokyo Stock Exchange.

NIPA. Abbreviation for **National Income and Product Accounts.**

NNM. Abbreviation for **NASDAQ** National Market.

NNP. Abbreviation for **Net National Product.**

NOL. Abbreviation for **net operating loss** as related to U.S. Tax Code.

no-load mutual fund. A mutual fund that sells its shares with no sales charge, but which usually has a redemption charge when shares are liquidated. *See* **redemption charge and quote (5).**

no-load stocks. See **direct stock plans.**

nominal dollars. See **current dollars.**

nominal interest or **stated interest.** A charge for the use of borrowed money, stated as a percentage of the borrowed principal for a year but prorated for periods less than a year. The nominal interest rate is the **real interest rate** only if the borrower has full use of the principal on which interest is charged during the loan period. If a loan is being repaid in installments, often the nominal interest rate is not the same as the real interest rate, although the dollar interest cost is the same.

nominal quotes. 1) Those over-the-counter quotes that are a representative bid and offer, but that are not firm or necessarily recent, usually listed in a newspaper. 2) Those securities prices established by trading authorities rather than actual transactions.

nominal yield. The annual income from a security, stated as a percentage of the face amount, for example, 5% of $1,000 or $50. Use of the nominal yield is realistic in indicating an investment's yield only if the investor buys a security for the face amount. *See* **current yield.**

nonassessable stock. See **fully paid and nonassessable.**

nonadmitted assets. See **admitted assets.**

noncallable bonds. Bonds that cannot be redeemed for payment of the principal or at a premium until the maturity date. *See* **callable bonds.**

noncumulative preferred stock. A preferred stock, holders of which lose rights to a dividend if the directors do not declare a dividend payment for a period.

noncumulative voting rights. Those common stock voting rights that must be distributed among each candidate for director, which prevents a corporate minority from electing a director.

Nondeductible IRA. See **Individual Retirement Accounts.**

nondetachable warrants. See **warrants.**

nondurable goods. A reference to industrial products that are used up in a relatively short time, usually under six months; for example, food, beverages, and so on. Also, goods that are bought for further processing are often called nondurable. *See* **durable goods.**

Non-Governmental Organization (NGO). A private group, usually international in scope, that contracts with one or more governments for the collection and distribution of monetary and material aid to needy people. As the NGOs have grown in size and powerful connections, there is a growing concern that they are working for governments in many cases, even though privatized, and therefore should not be considered unbiased. *See* **BINGO.**

non-qualified stock option plan. A program adopted by a company's management under which a company's stock is made available to employees at special prices and within specific periods as well as other conditions. Unlike qualified plans, these programs sometimes do not require cash up front, but can be exercised and the underlying stock sold simultaneously. Also, they can be taxed either at the date of grant or exercise, depending on when a value of the underlying stock can be determined. Usually these options are granted to select employees. *See* **qualified stock option plan.**

non-recurring items. Those expenses and revenues of a company that are not the result of normal operations and should not be included in long-term investment analysis, except as footnotes or noted adjustments, even though they might be perfectly legal and acceptable accounting practices. They should be identified in financial statements to prevent a distorted picture of a corporation's financial posture. Examples of such transactions are income from the sale of real estate or securities, changes in depreciation schedules, or increase in the value of pension fund assets. Because most stock valuation models are based on predictable results, these items should be excluded from expectations. They usually do not affect results as substantially as extraordinary items do, although there are similarities. *See* **extraordinary items** and **recurring income.**

nonrefundable. A reference to a bond issue that cannot be redeemed for payment of the principal, or more, before maturity with funds raised by issuing new bonds. This feature protects an investor who buys bonds to hold until their maturity from losing the interest income he planned on, because the issuer cannot sell new bonds at lower interest rates and redeem the older ones or exchange the new bonds for the older ones. *See* **refunding.**

nonstrategic assets. Those assets that management considers nonessential in accomplishing corporate business objectives, or those not essential to running the company's core business(es). For example, a small refinery not close to an oil and gas company's major producing properties might be sold as a nonstrategic business to raise capital for drilling more wells. *See* **downsize.**

nontaxable dividend. See **return of capital.**

no-par stock. The capital stock of a corporation, shares of which bear no official stated value. The actual value is found by dividing the total shares outstanding into net assets minus the par value of preferred stock. Some corporations issue no-par stock because some states tax the par value of issued stock.

Normal Trade Relations (NTR) status. In a nation's conduct of its foreign trade, a reference to the condition of treating commerce with any single trading partner the same way it treats commerce with all other trading partners. Specifically, the parity treatment means tariffs, imports quotas, and so on will be the applied by a nation equally to all nations enjoying this status. When the status represents a long period, it is referred to as Permanent Normal Trade Relations (PNTR). This status, under the World Trade Organization, is replacing the concept of **Most Favored Nation status.**

North American Industry Classification System (NAICS). A system developed jointly by the United States, Canada, and Mexico to provide new comparability in statistics about business activity across North America. Introduced in 1998, when assimilated it will replace the SIC code in the United States.

North American Securities Administrators Association (NASAA). The oldest international organization devoted to investor protection, having been organized in 1919. Membership consists of 65 state, provincial, and territorial securities administrators in the 50 states, the District of Columbia, Puerto Rico, Canada, and Mexico. In the United States the organization is the voice of the 50 state securities regulators supervising grassroots capital formation and investor protection. When talking to a broker, the administrators advise investors to take notes. Among other pieces of information, it says the notes should include: The broker's CRD number and report, which is a record by NASAA on a broker's and firm's registration, and disciplinary actions taken; nature of any stock recommendation (buy or sell); name of security; reason for recommendation; compatibility with investment objectives; risks in investment; and the investor's instructions to the broker. Web site: *www.nasaa.org.*

North Carolina Office of the Secretary of State. Regulator of securities in the state of North Carolina. Address: Securities Division, 300 N. Salisbury Street, #301, Raleigh, NC 27603. Phone: (919) 733-3924. Phone: (toll free for complaints): (800) 688-4507.

North Dakota Office of the Securities Commissioner. Regulator of securities laws in the state of North Dakota. Address: State Capitol, 5th Floor, 600 East Boulevard, Bismarck, ND 58505. Phone: (701) 328-2910. Phone (toll free): (800) 297-5124.

note. A written promise to pay a specific amount of money by a certain date. Legally, a note can run the gamut from a personal IOU for a few dollars to a complex commercial transaction involving millions. From an investment standpoint, however, a note is a written obligation to pay a calculated amount within a time period—usually five years or less—which is negotiable. This means it can be transferred to new holders or payees, when done in a prescribed manner. Usually, notes trade among banks, in cases of their prime customers, or among securities dealers, in cases of government or corporate obligations.

Notes in Financial Statements. See **Financial Statements and Data in Annual Report.**

notional value. The unrealized paper value of derivatives, based on the underlying securities value. This is the value shown in balance sheets, when an accounting of derivatives held by companies is required.

NPV. Abbreviation for **net present value.**

NSC. Abbreviation for **NASDAQ** Small Cap Market.

NTR. Abbreviation for **Normal Trade Relations** status.

NYSE. Abbreviation for the **New York Stock Exchange.**

Oo

obsolescence. The outmoding by new technological developments of machinery and/or equipment.

OCC. Abbreviation for Office of the **Comptroller of the
Currency**.

OCIE. Abbreviation for the **Office of Compliance Investigations
and Examinations SEC.**

odd lot. Generally speaking, a stock transaction for less than 100
shares. Actually, it is a trade for less shares than the normal unit
of trading for that stock established by an exchange. Sales of
odd lots are not printed on tapes except upon approval of a floor
official.

odd lot brokers. Those exchange floor brokers who handle all
odd lot transactions and base their prices to the public on the
stock's next round lot sale, called the effective price.

odd lot differential. The fee per share that an odd lot broker
charges a firm's customer, which is usually ⅛ of a point or 12
cents. The price differential is subtracted from the sale price or
added to the purchase price of the next round lot price of the
same stock to give an odd lot customer his actual price.
However, the Merrill Lynch investment brokerage maintains its
own market for odd lot trading, without charging a differential
as does the New York Stock Exchange.

odd lot interest. The number of shares traded during a period in
odd lot amounts. It is generally accepted in stock market inner
circles that odd lot investors are neophytes, far removed from
incisive financial information and that, consequently, they enter
the market at the end of an upward trend and sell their shares at
the bottom of a decline. For this reason many experts watch the
volume of odd lot transactions. When the volume is high these
experts rationalize that a general rise is nearly over or a downturn is nearly finished. Undoubtedly, the rationale for this derisive attitude toward odd-lotter acumen is that so many of these

small investors get interested in a stock market investment after publicity has aroused them, only to find after they buy stock that the reasons for the publicized price advance have dissipated. When the decline starts, they stoically hold their stock, hoping for a reversal. Finally, the price often gets so low, they sell impatiently.

OECD. Abbreviation for **Organization for Economic Cooperation and Development.**

OECD Online. See under **Web Sites for the Inquiring Investor.**

off or **down.** A reference to a stock average or security price that is lower than it was at the previous trade or session's close.

offered or **asked price.** The amount for which somebody will sell a security or the amount at which he offers it for sale.

"offered at." A phrase indicating at what price a class of securities is being sold to the public, expressed in dollars or as a **bond basis** price.

offering. An attempt to sell securities, either a new issue or a secondary one, by underwriters, dealers, exchange brokers, or nonfinancial corporations selling their own stock. *See* **new issue, secondary distribution, special offering,** and **underwrite.**

offering circular. 1) Technically a final **prospectus**, this document is a written presentation for prospective investors of an offer to sell certain securities for a specific price. It usually is prepared by a smaller, nonpublic or slightly public company, such as an "S" Corporation or limited partnership, that is trying to implement a growth phase through equity or debt financing. The contents include information about the company, its industry, the officers, financial statements both actual and pro forma, and legal contingencies. 2) A document accompanying an offer to sell government bonds, containing information such as the price and repayment schedule, which sets the yield; the issuing entity's credit base; the risks; legal opinions as to their taxable status, when appropriate; and refunding or retirement privileges.

Office Equipment & Supplies. Stocks representing those companies furnishing products used in the workplace generally. *See* **industry stock group.**

Office of Compliance Investigations and Examinations, SEC (OCIE). That division of the Securities and Exchange Commission responsible for enforcing laws pertaining to violations of the U.S. securities laws.

Office of Management and Budget (OMB). In the executive branch of the U.S. government, the division that prepares the president's annual budget and presents it to Congress, coordinates with the Treasury Department and the Council of Economic Advisers in shaping the federal government's fiscal program, analyzes the performance of federal agencies in relation to the administration's policies, and serves as an adviser to the president on legislation.

Office of the Comptroller of the Currency, U.S. or **OCC.** See **Comptroller of the Currency, U.S.**

Office of Thrift Supervision (OTS). The primary regulator of all federal and many state-chartered thrift institutions, with five regional offices located in Atlanta, Chicago, Dallas, Jersey City, and San Francisco. The agency, established in 1989, is a bureau of the U.S. Treasury Department. Under the Financial Institutions Reform, Recovery and Enforcement Act of 1989, the agency replaced the **Federal Home Loan Banks'** Board as supervisor of the nation's savings and loans. The OTS can issue new regulations and charter new federal savings institutions. In addition, it can supervise savings institutions insured under the Savings Association Insurance Fund. Address: 1700 G. Street, NW, Washington, DC 20552. Web site: *www.ots.treas.gov/default.htm.*

officers of a corporation. Those persons who are elected by stockholders or appointed by directors, responsible for carrying out the bylaws, objectives, and other customary duties of a corporation. *See* **management, top.**

"offshore." A description of a hedge fund, mutual fund, or other financial services business that is located in a foreign country to serve as a **tax haven** for that particular type of business operation. Besides advantages in taxation matters, the business also enjoys certain freedoms from regulation in the United States.

offshore tax haven. See **tax haven.**

Ohio Division of Securities. Regulator of securities laws in the state of Ohio. Address: 77 South High Street, 22nd Floor, Columbus, OH 43215. Phone: (614) 644-7381.

oil and gas industries. See **sector.**

Oils—Composite. Stocks representing those companies engaged in various phases of oil and natural gas exploration through marketing. *See* **industry stock group.**

Oils—Domestic Integrated. Stocks representing those oil and natural gas companies engaged in fully integrated operations in the United States. *See* **industry stock group.**

Oils—Exploration and Production. Stocks representing those oil and natural gas stocks engaged in locating and producing oil and natural gas reserves on a nonintegrated basis. *See* **industry stock group.**

Oils—International Integrated. Stocks representing those oil and natural gas companies engaged in fully integrated operations worldwide. *See* **industry stock group.**

Oklahoma Department of Securities. Regulator of securities in the state of Oklahoma. Address: Suite 860, First National Center, 120 N. Robinson, Oklahoma City, OK 73102. Phone: (405) 280-7700. Fax: (405) 280-7742.

Old Economy. A reference to the economic infrastructure of an industrialized nation, before the advent of the Electronic Revolution which began in the late 20th century. In such an economy, the dominant industries are product driven, rather than service driven, as measured by their contribution to **GDP.** One of the salient characteristics of an Old Economy is that production increases per worker is a rather predictable and a constant function of capital increases, producing an arithmetic growth rate. *See* **Old Economy stocks** and **New Economy.**

Old Economy stocks. Those stocks representing corporations providing goods and services serving markets driven by technology that was developed before the electronic revolution, or before the late 20th century. These industries triggered worldwide growth from WW II until the last decade of the 20th century, with some exceptions in electronics and biotech companies, which are generally considered New Economy stocks. Specifically the term refers to established industries such as automobiles, chemicals, utilities, oil and natural gas, retailing, insurance, air transport, railroads, food processors, beverages, and so on. These stocks are older, more mature, often pay dividends, and tend to be less volatile in price. However, because the technology and markets are mature, they also tend to be less able to grow earnings than the New Economy variety. The Dow Industrial Index, Dow Utilities Index, and Dow Transportation Index include mainly such stocks, whereas the NASDAQ Index includes many New Economy stocks. See **New Economy stocks.**

oligopoly. An economic situation in which several companies dominate the market of a product. Quality competition is more intense than price competition.

OMB. Abbreviation for **Office of Management and Budget.**

Omega Portfolio. A reference to the asset allocation in a securities portfolio that is keyed to an investor's retirement. Basically, the securities are selected to provide safety against the investor having to sell stocks after a steep downturn in prices in order to meet living expenses. The rationale for constructing such a portfolio is to estimate living expenses, reduce this by pension, social security, or other fixed retirement benefits, and invest a portion of resources available in securities with predictable income payments, such as dividends and interest payments. By selecting payment schedules that are staggered by months or quarters over a multi-year period, the retiree can supplement fixed retirement benefits with the income from the securities selected. For example, selection of high-grade preferred stocks or bonds might result in the distribution of income in each calendar month, when carefully selected. Consequently, the retiree avoids selling common stocks on an emergency basis, when prices might be depressed.

ON24 Network. A Web site for investors featuring company and industry news, technical analysis, and round tables. *See* **Web Sites for the Inquiring Investor.**

on average. A reference to rising or falling stock prices when the measurement is based on an overall average, rather than isolated stocks.

on balance. The measurement at the end of an accounting period of related business categories to determine which is greater; i.e., on balance, exports should exceed imports in a country's international trade.

on basis orders. See **Basis Price.**

on bid order. An odd lot order to sell an inactive stock at the quoted bid price, less the appropriate odd lot differential. This enables a customer to sell an odd lot in an inactive stock without waiting for a round lot sale to take place.

online broker. A stock brokerage firm that executes trades through an Internet connection, generally charging lower commissions than full-service brokers. There are over 100 such brokerages. In the fastest growing investment market today, the top five brokers in terms of daily trading volume are tabulated below. According to NASDAQ, in 2000, there were over 7 million online accounts, constituting approximately 4 percent of the retail trades processed there. The number of online brokers grew from 27 million in 1997 to 150 million in 2000. In 2000, the average daily trading volume online was 315 million shares.

online investor or **"click" investor.** An investor who uses a personal computer, the Internet, and Web sites in buying and selling investments, usually through an online brokerage firm.

Buy and sell orders are transmitted using e-mail. The true online investor carries on company and industry research independently or purchases it from a full-service online broker, taps into chat rooms and bulletin boards to gather background information, and negotiates trades electronically, although such a person is not necessarily a **day trader.** Rather, this investor might operate on a very deliberate, disciplined schedule, but believes that he or she is capable of performing the basic prerequisites to successful investing, saving money in the bargain. because the savings are due to commissions on trades being much lower online, both through using discount brokers and the online arm of traditional, full-service brokers. The time required to get executions is usually less. It is more private, although security breeches have occurred.

The two biggest criticisms of online investing are: (1) sometimes in fast-moving markets, trades are executed late, at expense to the investor; and (2) it is difficult to buy IPOs, often the most attractive securities in a healthy stock market, except in the aftermarket. Although online trading is dominated by equity issues at present, bond trading is fast catching up. In online bond trading, market participants tend to deal with one another through private electronic networks more than is the case with stock investments, although stock investors also use electronic communications networks.

Online investing is not for everybody, but for some it is a boon and a welcome benefit of digital technology. Some of the advantages of online investing are as follows:

- It allows investors to utilize personal analytical skills and judgmental values, free of conflicts with the professional research analysts employed by investment firms.
- Online commission costs are much cheaper.
- Investors can avoid the pitfalls of mob psychology, especially when rumors are swirling, into which brokers and customers sometimes lead one another.
- It encourages the making of decisions at a more convenient and sober pace, rather than while responding quickly to phone calls from brokers or salesmen during busy business days.

- It promotes a climate free of often distracting brokerage personalities and historical research biases about business entities.

On the other hand, there are disadvantages to investors relying on online investing, such as:

- It requires them to make transaction decisions alone, without the inputs of brokers who follow the markets for hours each day, sometimes a costly isolation in fast changing markets.
- It deprives them of the detailed records of traditional investment accounts regularly, useful for personal knowledge, tracing financial affairs, and income tax purposes.
- Investors may be unable to participate in new offerings, both primary and secondary issues, because they usually go to the customers on whom investment banking firms make the most money.
- The personal relationships often enjoyed in traditional investment environments are unavailable.
- Unless credible and well-known investment firms are exclusively used, it opens up the possibility of investing in untested propositions and untrustworthy relationships.

If an investor is a curious, disciplined, and independent thinker, she or he will probably take to online investing. But if one tends to follow trends and the crowd without asking "why," and is not terribly curious about how business works, conventional investing seems more in order. In a study concluded in late 1999 at the University of California at Davis, covering the period 1991 through 1996, and using the investment experience of 78,000 households, online investors were found to turn over their portfolios at six to seven times the rate of the average investor. In addition, their investment returns generally lagged behind that of the market. Those trading the most posted annual returns of 11.4%, compared with 18.5% for those trading infrequently. The annual return for the market during the period was 17.9%.

online trader. See **day trader.**

on offer order. An odd lot order to buy an inactive stock at the quoted offer price, plus the appropriate odd lot differential. This enables a customer to buy an odd lot in an inactive stock without waiting for a round lot sale to take place.

on the close. A reference to an odd lot order entered before the market closes to buy or sell at $0.12 or $0.06 away from the closing bid or offer.

on the day. A phrase used when a comparison has been made concerning the current market session so far; for example, a broker might inform his customer that at 11:00 A.M. "Prices were higher on the day."

opened. Indicates an opening trade that occurred in sequence but is reported to the tape at a later time.

open-end investment company or **open-end investment trust** or **mutual fund.** Operating under the Investment Company Act of 1940, a company organized to invest in securities that issues new shares in the investment fund as it receives new capital, so that there is never any limit to shares outstanding. The funds are invested in securities that correspond to the fund's financial objectives as described in its charter. The shares are priced by their Net Asset Values, or the value of the underlying securities less liabilities. There is nearly always a sales charge or redemption charge based on a percentage of the investment, usually 3%–5%, and an annual management fee, which is usually a fraction of 1%–2% of the fund's asset value. Mutual fund shares are not listed on exchanges, but are sold by brokers or mutual fund salespersons

Under SEC guidelines, if the mutual fund name includes a specific security type—stock or bond, for instance—then the fund must be 80% invested in that type of security. There are approximately 63 million Americans who have invested in the more than 6,270 available mutual funds. The SEC maintains a Web site that enables investors to calculate the fees and expenses charged to the shareholders through the use and reduction of a fund's assets. It can be accessed through the SEC's site at *www.sec.gov* or directly to: *www.sec.gov/mfcc/mfcc-int.htm.* For quoting information, see **quote (5)** and **Net Asset Value.**

opening. The beginning of trading in general in a securities market.

opening price. The price of the first sale of a specific stock on a given day that is **regular way** or marked "Opened Last."

operating budget. A formal company plan specifying foreSeeable revenues and expenses and cash flow from a target level of operations for the next fiscal period, usually one year. Items included are anticipated revenues, labor and wages, utilities, general and administrative expenses, amortization of capital assets, and others. In short, all costs that are used up during the budget period. *See* **capital budget.**

operating company. A company engaged in one or more manufacturing, production, or distributive processes. Its organization and style is in direct contrast to a holding company in that it turns out a product or service with all the attendant manufacturing, administrative, and marketing facilities and personnel required, whereas a holding company owns other companies, often of the operating variety, and furnishes only financing and administrative counsel.

operating costs. See **expenses** as incurred in a business.

operating income or **profit.** Total revenues of a business enterprise during a fiscal period, after deducting expenses of operating functions—wages, salaries, rent, advertising, supplies, goods or materials employed, depreciation, and so on—but before indirect expenses, such as interest and taxes. It excludes other income or deductions.

Operating Leverage. The tendency for changes in net income or profit to vary disproportionately with revenue changes when the level of fixed operating costs is changed. Operating leverage rises as the proportion of fixed costs to total costs increases, because then changes in revenues produce disproportionately greater changes in net income. The example below represents one method of calculating operating leverage.

Suppose Big Bucks Rodeo Enterprises has high fixed costs in the form of stables, grazing land, practice arena, transport trucks and so forth. Watch what happens when the company works twice as many rodeos during a year. Sales volume goes from $3 million to $6 million, while fixed costs of $2 million stay constant. In the prior year, $3 million in sales volume minus $2 million in fixed costs left $1 million in operating profit. But in the current year, sales volume of $6 million was $3 million or 100% greater. Subtracting fixed costs of $2 million leaves $4 million or an increase of 400% in operating profit. This is divided by the increase in sales volume of 100%. The operating leverage is 4 × (400 ÷ 100). *See* **Financial Leverage.**

operating parent. See **parent company.**

operating profits. Those profits made strictly from the regular operations of a business, before interest and taxes.

operating ratio. The ratio of total direct selling or manufacturing expenses to total selling or manufacturing revenues, expressed as a percentage. It does not include capital and tax expenses or any items not directly related to selling or manufacturing. This ratio is used as a measure of business efficiency in the day-to-day operations of a business, since it measures the portion of revenues eliminated by the selling or operating costs.

operating revenues. The total money receipts resulting from the sales of the regular operations of a business.

opinion. 1) An e-mailed, wired, printed or downloaded analysis of a company with a viewpoint as to the value of its stock, from a broker's research service. An opinion is more detailed than a recommendation. 2) An expression of the overall investment picture, from a research source.

opportunity costs. The costs to an investor, in terms of missing alternative opportunities, of not moving his money to a more attractive security. For example, if Durwood Drowsy is earning 5% annually in a money market fund, ignoring a stock market rising at 10% annually, on average, and it appears that the stock market's momentum will continue, his opportunity costs are 5% annually, the difference in the yield on his money market account and the possible stock market alternative. As is the case with a great many opportunity cost exercises, hindsight is better than foresight, but the investor should be ever vigilant for opportunities.

option, bond call. A bond issuer's right to call certain bonds at a specific price, after a specified date. *See* **call of bonds.**

option, market stock. The purchased privilege to buy or sell 100 shares of a stock at a specific price for a specific time. *See* **options strategy** and **options table.**

option account. An account with a brokerage firm that enables an investor to buy and sell stock options, or puts and calls, including securities derivatives such as stock indexes. Option trading involves more capital leverage than other types of securities transactions and, consequently, more risks of loss of capital. Therefore, brokers require options traders to sign a statement vouchsafing that they understand the inherent risks and are financially able to undertake them. An options account may be either a cash account or margin account. Broadly speaking, an option account includes the ability to trade commodities options also, but usually securities options and commodities options are available on different exchanges. *See* **cash account** and **margin account.**

option grant. A right to purchase specific amounts of stock in a corporation at specific prices per share within a time frame or after certain dates, granted to an employee by the company's shareholders or board of directors. The purpose of option grants is to reward employees, usually key employees, by allowing them to participate in the appreciation in stock value caused by their stewardship. Usually, management asks for shareholder approval before granting options, especially to key employees.

The NYSE and SEC have adopted rules that boards may issue "broad-based" option grants, if two key tests are met: (1) the plan must make at least 20% of employees eligible for options, and (2) at least half of them must be beneath the position of corporate officer. Among large companies, approximately 30% have broad-based option plans in effect, while approximately 11% have granted such options to certain employees. Often, executives receive more from stock appreciation than they do from salaries. According to a Federal Reserve study, 32.8% of employees at the top end of a corporation's labor force are granted options, compared to 6.7% at the lower end.

The topic of option grants and how to use and account for them equitably is one of the hottest issues in business today. Arguments turn on two points: (1) whether option grants should be expressed as expenses in the year they are exercised or accounted for in some other manner, and (2) whether it is fair to other investors for executives to receive so much equity in the corporation at advantageous prices. In respect to the first point, the FASB has decreed option grants must be delineated in the footnotes of the annual report, rather than the income statement. But this issue will not go away! In respect to the second point, a significant amount of stock dilution can be inflicted on investors in general by a munificent executive option policy.

option vesting. A reference to a company increasing a key employee's equity in a company through the use of option grants. This practice is prevalent in startup companies, because they can keep salary expenses low by compensating key employees with options or calls on future earnings. Eventually the growing number of shares can dilute future earnings and stockholder equity as earnings that must be allocated to greater numbers of shares proliferate. *See* **compensation package.**

optional dividend. A dividend payable in cash or stock at the stockholder's option. These dividends are taxable under federal income tax regulation if the stockholder may receive rights, cash, or property.

Options Clearing Corporation (OCC). Founded in 1973, the world's largest clearing organization for financial derivatives contracts. It issues and is the registered clearing facility for all exchange-listed securities options in the United States, including put and call options involving common stocks and other equities, stock indexes, foreign currencies, and interest-rate composites. There are over 135 clearing members, consisting of U.S. broker dealers and non-U.S. securities firms. OCC is dedicated to promoting stability and financial integrity in the options markets by focusing on effective risk management. It operates under the supervision of the SEC. Address: 440 S. LaSalle St., Suite 2400, Chicago, IL 60605. Web site: *www.optionsclearing.com/home.htm.*

options strategy. The use of the trading facilities of the Chicago Board Options Exchange, American Stock Exchange, Philadelphia Board of Trade, and the over-the-counter market in the United States for the buying and selling of stock options. By buying or selling an option contract, the investor can benefit from the fluctuations in the underlying stock the option represents without risking as much money as in outright stock ownership.

Options are like many other securities traded over-the-counter or on national exchanges, and the contracts are usually initiated by owners of the common stock involved, through brokers. They are similar to warrants. A call option gives the holder the right to buy 100 shares of a certain stock; a put option the right to sell. Orders to buy and sell them are handled by brokers. As in the case of stocks, listed options are traded on the floor of national regulated exchanges, where trading is conducted in a competitive, open auction market. An important difference between the market in options and common stocks is that an option is simply a contract between a buyer and a seller.

Unlike shares of common stock, there is no fixed number of options since the number depends only on the number that buyers wish to buy and sellers wish to write or sell at any time. Just as options are created by the actions of buyers and sellers, in the same manner they can be terminated. If a buyers sells an option he has previously purchased, and a seller buys back an option he has previously sold, one less option results. In practice, most options are offset in this manner so that a closing purchase or sale occurs before the expiration date. The following examples illustrate benefits of option contracts although there are many more combinations of strategies:

1. Call option: On February 1 the common stock of Beep Electronics is selling at $50 a share, or $5,000 for 100 shares, and a July 30 call option to buy 100 shares can be bought at a premium of $5 a share (premiums are limited to $5–$20 fluctuations). That would be $500 for a 100-share option. By April 1 the price of the common has risen to $56, or $5,600. The option to buy the stock at $50 becomes more attractive and the premium might be bid to $8 a share. Had an investor bought a 100-share option at $500, he would be able to sell it for $800, realizing a $300 or 60% profit, less commissions—quite a bit more leverage than buying the underlying stock for $5,000 and selling for $5,600, 60% versus 12%. Also, the buyer has limited risk. No matter how much the stock price drops, he can lose no more than the $500 premium.

2. Put option: On February 1 the common stock of HappyDaze Malt Liquor is selling for $25 a share and a July 30 put option at that price can be bought for $3 a share, $300 for a 100-share option. By April 1 the price has fallen to $20 a share. The put to sell at $25 has become more valuable and sells for $6 a share. Had an investor bought a 100-share option at $300, he would be able to sell it for $600, a $300 or 100% profit, less commissions. Leverage is again present as well as limited risk. *See* **options table** and **puts** and **calls.**

options table. A tabulation, usually appearing in newspapers, summarizing the relevant market information about issues of stock options, including information on the underlying securities. The focus of the data is to apprise investors of the attractiveness, in terms of time and money, of the options. Included in a typical stock options table are: (1) symbol of underlying stock, (2) expiration date of option, (3) option price to buy stock, (4) type of option—"p" for put, "c" for call, (5) exchange traded—"C" for Chicago Board of Trade, (6) volume of contracts last session, (7) option price, (8) change in price, (9) percentage of change, (10) stock price, (11) stock price change.

(1)	(2)	(3)	(4)	(5)	(6)	(7)	(8)	(9)	(10)	(11)
Co	Date	Strike	Type	Exch	Vol	Pr	Chg	% Chg	Pr	Chg
MCI	Fe 98	42.50	c	C	10,125	11.31	−0.25	−11.4	43.06	−0.75

STOCK OPTIONS TABLE

"Oracle of Omaha." A reference to Warren E. Buffett, the chairman and majority stockholder in Berkshire Hathaway holding company, based in Omaha, Nebraska. Many persons consider him the most influential investor in the United States. Since 1964, Berkshire Hathaway stock has recorded a 24.1% annually compounded gain. Buffet's specialty is spotting undervalued, growth-oriented businesses, using independent research and analyses.

oral stop. An unwritten stop-loss order without the broker assuming legal responsibility for its execution and not recognized as a legitimate order.

order. A directive from a customer to a broker, either in a brokerage office or on an exchange floor, or to a dealer to buy or sell a certain amount of securities.

orderly market. Those transactions on an exchange that can be carried out without enormous buy or sell pressures, causing runaway prices in one security or the market in general.

order out. To transfer stock that has been in safekeeping to a customer or his agent by an investment firm.

ordinary share. The basic unit of corporate ownership in Australia, Canada, the United Kingdom, and certain other European countries. It is very similar to a **common share** in a U.S. corporation, in terms of dividend rights, liquidation rights, new-issue rights, and voting rights.

ORDS. Abbreviation for **All Ordinary Shares Index.**

Oregon Department of Consumer and Business Services. Regulator of securities laws in the state of Oregon. Address: Division of Finance and Corporate Securities, Labor and Industries Building, Salem, OR 97310. Phone: (503) 378-4387.

organizational expense. The costs of setting up an organization that are usually subtracted from surplus during the first years of a corporation's existence and sometimes carried under "assets" on a balance sheet, for example, legal fees, printing, promotional stock, stamp taxes, and underwriting costs. *See* **promotional costs.**

Organization for Economic Cooperation and Development (OECD). An intergovernmental organization based in Paris, France whose purpose is to provide its 29 member countries with a forum to compare their experiences, discuss shared problems, and seek solutions that can then be applied within their own national contexts. There are two common denominators among member countries: commitment to the principles of the market economy and pluralistic democracy. The organization publishes social and economic data on its members. Member countries include: Austria, Australia, Belgium, Canada, Czech Republic, Denmark, Finland, France, Germany, Greece, Hungary, Iceland, Ireland, Italy, Japan, Korea, Luxembourg, Mexico, New Zealand, The Netherlands, Norway, Poland, Portugal, Spain, Sweden, Switzerland, Turkey, United Kingdom, and United States.

Original Issue Discount (ORD). A description of the method of pricing a debt security when it is sold at a discount from its par or maturity value, at the time it is originally issued. By pricing it at a discount at the time of issue, say at 70 for a $1,000 bond at maturity (when quoting a bond, the last digit is eliminated), some or all of the interest income from the security will be represented by its appreciation in value as it nears the maturity date. The most obvious example of such a security is a zero-coupon bond, or a "zero," when it is issued. Since the price of a bond is the present value of the stream of future interest payments to the investor, adjusted for any discount or premium required to convert the yield when it matures to the demands of the current capital market, the discount principle is ideally suited to bond financing. Although the rules used by the IRS in taxing this accumulation of interest income as a discounted bond matures is complicated, the underlying premise is that the accruing of interest income through the gain in the bond as maturity draws nearer is taxable as **imputed interest.** Of course this means that the accretion of the interest is taxed as ordinary income, rather than the lower capital gain rate.

originator. Generally speaking, the party who lays the groundwork and puts together the details of a financial arrangement, such as a corporate loan. In securities financing, it is a reference to the investment banker who cultivates the client, advises the client on raising money in the financial markets, engineers the type of financing appropriate to the client's situation and condition of financial markets, and, in the final stage, implements actions for going forward. The final stage might involve getting a group or syndicate together to actually raise the money in the financial markets.

orphan. A reference to a common stock that has no patronage from the research staff at investment firms in terms of oral and written presentations. Among publicly traded securities, there are opinion makers. These are generally research analysts and high-profile stock brokers who recommend buying and selling stocks on a regular basis. Stocks that are overlooked or avoided by them have little chance of sustained popularity in the marketplace. But when such a stock is embraced by an opinion maker, it can signal that the stock will become popular and enjoy market gains. However, this is not likely to happen unless the stock represents a bargain, in terms of intrinsic value or growth potential. Sometimes new management or a reorganization can instigate a change of heart among opinion makers. Astute investors should be on the lookout for these stocks. *See* **wallflower.**

Oslo Stock Exchange. See under **Global Investment Market.**

OTC. Abbreviation for **over-the-counter securities.**

OTC-BB. See **Bulletin Board.**

OTS. Abbreviation for **Office of Thrift Supervision.**

out-of-favor stocks. A reference to those stocks that Wall Street firms and investors are ignoring at present. The reasons can be mixed and they can pertain to investment characteristics, like a current stock market emphasis on yields making stocks that pay no dividends unpopular, or to business fundamentals, like an oversupply of products in a cyclical industry making that group unpopular. The topic brings up the sometimes overlooked aspect of marketing stocks to investors: There are modes, styles, and fashions in the pristine world of finance, just as there are in most other commercial endeavors. Once buying momentum begins for certain stocks, investors are in a go-go frame of mind toward such securities. This receptiveness encourages investment firms to ferret out new investment ideas that are similar. On the other hand, once disappointing results or performance has soured the market on certain stocks, investment firms tend to avoid recommending such stocks, at least until conditions improve.

For example, there are times when gold stocks are out of favor. The reasons can vary, but generally it occurs when there is too much processed gold in the world, because of overproduction or because central banks are selling some of their gold reserves. Sometimes the industrial demand for gold slackens, although this sort of things happens more to silver and some other precious metals. In the case of gold, these slack demand periods seem to occur when there is universal confidence in global trading and global currency integrity. Until there is a reversal of the situation, it is unlikely investment firms will recommend gold stocks or that investors will be receptive to owning them. Another illustration: In the late 1990s, Internet stocks went to astronomical heights in terms of conventional evaluation techniques. Stocks of some categories in this group crashed in price and have subsequently become out of favor, although this mood is one that changes fast. See **in-favor stocks.**

outside financing. The raising of funds by a company through borrowing or the sale of stock, rather than from their earnings or surplus. *See* **equity financing** and **debt financing.**

outside quote. The bid and asked price, including dealer profits, of an unlisted stock given to a regular customer. If a transaction is made on an outside quote, it is net to the customer. *See* **spread.**

outsider. See **amateur.**

outsourcing. As a manufacturer or supplier of goods and services, going outside the company, and often outside the region or country, for vital resources used in manufacturing or delivery of the final product. This practice takes advantage of lower production costs elsewhere, and eliminates having to tie up capital in easily obtainable products. For the management of the prime manufacturer, dependability of supply is a paramount consideration in making the decision to outsource.

outstanding stock. The number of shares of a corporation's authorized stock that have been actually sold or otherwise distributed to investors.

overallotment. A reference to a situation in which the underwriters of a new securities offering have the option to buy a specific number of the shares or units offered for a specified time, usually one month, in order to satisfy oversold orders. This agreement is spelled out in the underwriting agreement.

overbought. A market opinion referring to securities too high in relation to their earnings because of excessive buying.

overdiscounting by the market. In the securities or commodity markets, a situation that exists when news about the future causes traders to react so strongly that prices ultimately move in an opposite direction more than they are expected. For example, if a mutual fund buys 50,000 shares of an auto stock, so that a short market supply is expected, traders would begin buying the stock actively, hoping to sell later at huge profits. Eventually they might overbuy, causing prices to decline as sellers rushed the auto stock to the market to meet the buying demand. Thus, the market overdiscounted the scarcity expected by the mutual funds purchase, and prices were lower eventually—the opposite of what was expected.

overhang, market. A reference to a large block of stock or commodity that could be placed on the market at any time, because its holder(s) believes the price is going lower, needs to raise money or is facing a deadline on liquidating the block. The effect of this is to create a tentative market for those issues, with buyers fearing that the overhang could suddenly become sell orders, forcing down the price of their recently acquired issues, and sellers fearing that their sales might cause just enough price weakness to cause the owners of the overhang to rush the issues to market before the price declines further. This counter balance creates a nervous market for the issue, one that has no direction but tends toward price softness, especially if negative fundamental news emerges about the company. An overhang can take many forms. It can be the registration of a secondary stock distribution, a dealer's inventory that has gotten too big, company executives who are contemplating exercising their options and immediately selling the stock, a liquidation of a big commodities position, a large stock position by a disgruntled institutional investor, or an estate liquidation, to name some. *See* **overhang, options.**

overhang, options. A reference to the percentage of a company's total equity, as represented by the capital accounts, that the total number of options issued would represent, if exercised. Until the 1990s, most corporate boards were loathe to issue options in excess of 1% of the equity capital accounts in any year, which meant that the cumulative ratio seldom got above 10%. But with the advent of the new technology companies in the 1990s, that rule was blown away. In 1999, the 200 largest corporations in the United States issued options representing 2.1% of their shares outstanding. That level compares with 1.2% in 1994. In 1999 the average options overhang was 13.7%, considerably above the conventional idea of a maximum 10% cumulative overhang. Accounting guidelines require that a company indicate the options overhang in the footnotes of its annual report, both in terms of the fair value of options and the effect on earnings per share, when the options are in the money or exercisable at a price beneath the current stock price. This relatively obscure treatment has been criticized as not adequately apprising investors of the diluting effects of an overly-generous options policy. *See* **compensation package.**

override. A charge by an investment firm for a stock transaction on an exchange of which it is not a member. The firm gets a member of that exchange to negotiate the actual trade and the customer pays both the exchange member's commission and the override.

Overseas Private Investment Corporation (OPIC). A U.S. federal agency that provides investment insurance and loan guarantees against political risks to domestic companies that invest in projects or businesses in developing nations. The agency services an $18 billion portfolio and generates premium revenues and fees of over $140 million. In recent years, the insurer has focused on smaller businesses, by lowering the minimum loan size from $2 million to $250,000. The default rate on loans is less than 1%, while 95% of claims paid out are reimbursed by governments of the companies involved.

oversold. A market opinion referring to securities cheap in relation to their earnings, because of excessive selling.

oversubscribed. A reference to a new or secondary underwriting of securities that has been completely reserved by customers of the syndicate members, with demand still strong. *See* **overallotment.**

over-the-counter securities. 1) Those securities that are not traded on any exchange but that are bought and sold over the telephone or the wires by dealers for their own accounts or by brokers, **acting as principals**, for accounts. Although there are many excellent stocks of the estimated 50,000 issues traded in the over-the-counter market, and many reputable dealers of the 4,500 who trade them, it is in this loose web of the securities business that most unethical practices occur. Unlike exchanges and strict dealer associations, many salespeople operate with no supervision in a world of exaggeration. The reputation of any investment firm, exchange, or dealer should always be checked, but it is particularly important in the over-the-counter market. *See* **unlisted (1).** 2) Securities that are listed on an exchange but also actively traded over-the-counter. For quoting information, see **quote (4).**

owners' capital or **equity capital.** The dollar amount represented by a corporation's stock issues and its surplus accounts.

Pp

Pacific Stock Exchange (PSE). A U.S. national securities exchange, the third most active, specializing in trading options on small stocks. Average daily volume is 420,000 option contracts. More than 800 companies are listed for trading. Address: 301 Pine Street, San Francisco, CA 94101. Phone: (415) 393-4000. Fax: (415) 393-4018. *See* under **Global Investment Market.**

package deal. See **unit.**

pac-man defense. Named after the video game of the 1980s, a corporate strategy implemented by a company that is a takeover target. The target company turns the tables by buying shares of the acquiring company, and either directly or by inference says it will take over the latter. In the video game, any player that did not consume opponents was gobbled up. The reference is to the new corporate culture that emerged in the 1980s, in which corporate management became more aggressive and more responsive to making money for shareholders. In a way, it is the embodiment of the controversial "Greed is Good" philosophy.

"painting the tape." A reference to a group of traders, sometimes on an exchange, trading securities or derivatives among themselves to inflate the trading volume. Such a situation might occur if two or more exchanges were vying for listings.

paired shares or **Siamese shares** or **stapled stock.** A stock certificate representing ownership in the common shares of two companies that operate under the same management.

panic. A sudden, impulsive and widespread fear for the stability of the economic system, accompanied by active securities selling, bank withdrawals, and liquidation of other assets.

paper. See **commercial paper.**

Paper & Forest Products. Those stocks representing companies engaged in providing products made from wood pulp. *See* **industry stock group.**

paper clip REIT or **stapled REIT.** A tax-sheltered entity comprised of two companies—one a REIT and one an operating company—that have the same top management but different shareholders and different common stock issues. The operating company pays low taxes because it pays most of its income in rents to the REIT. And the latter pays low taxes as long as it distributes most of its income to stockholders. The objective is to maximize the income tax advantages peculiar to a real estate trust, while permitting the company to operate a business that REITs cannot normally enter.

paper profit. An unrealized gain from market appreciation of securities not yet sold. Paper profits can often beguile investors into discontinuing a critical observance of stocks that are above their costs. In reality, paper profits can disappear after the next market session, and even slip into losses. For this reason, stocks that are priced above their costs without noticeable support (active volume, high earnings) should probably be sold, or carefully watched for a sale on a downturn.

paper values. See **market valuations.**

parallel imports. Manufactured goods sold at a deep discount in foreign markets, and later imported and resold in the manufacturer's country in an unchanged condition, at a profit.

parent company. A corporation that owns the controlling interest in one or more subsidiaries. It may be an **operating company** or strictly a **holding company.**

Paris Stock Exchange. See under **Global Investment Market.**

participating preferred stock. That preferred stock that has the right to share in dividends of the common stock after it has collected its fixed dividend.

participation. The extent to which an investment banker underwrites a new issue measured by the shares or bonds he buys for resale.

partnership, general. A business arrangement whereby two or more persons combine their skill and/or capital and/or time to accomplish a business objective, with or without a written agreement. Usually, the business acts of a partner bind all partners jointly. It may be dissolved by death, mutual agreement, or transfer of assets. This form of business organization is the most intimate and, as such, it can obligate parties financially and legally beyond their original intentions. *See* **limited liability company** and **limited liability partnership.**

par value of bonds or **face value.** The principal amount that will be owed at a bond's maturity.

par value of stock. 1) The value in a corporation's charter assigned and printed on a share of stock. If stock is issued below par value, the buyer can be liable to the corporation's creditors for the amount of the discount. 2) The equity value of preferred stock in case of liquidation. Par value is more important to preferred stockholders, since they have a legal priority to the corporation assets over common stockholders, proportionate to the par value of their stock times the number of shares they own, in case of cessation of business activity. Common stock par value is meaningless as an indicator of actual value, since these stockholders divide up what is left after debts and preferred par has been paid proportionate to the number of shares owned.

passed dividend. The omission of a dividend payment that has heretofore been paid regularly. This action often results from a dire financial condition, although not necessarily a terminal one, and should be viewed as a danger signal by an investor.

passive interest. Participation in a business enterprise, such as a limited partnership, in which an investor assumes no role in working for, managing, or operating the entity and has a limited liability in the financial risks associated with it. The enterprise can be either an operating company, such as a manufacturing business, or an investment portfolio, from which come interest, dividends, or capital gains. Whatever the definition of the products or services of the enterprise, the investor participates in a strictly limited way. Under provisions of the Tax Reform Act of 1986 and the Revenue Reconciliation Act of 1993, losses and credits from passive activities are deductible only from income or gains from passive activities as long as the latter exist. *See* **working interest.**

pass-through security. A type of security in which a voluminous batch of individual debt obligations from various lending institutions has been consolidated as to principal and interest by a governmental entity into shares of a master debt security, and sold to new third-party investors. The combined debt service payments are paid to the owners of the new shares in proportion to the shares owned. Usually, the principal and income is guaranteed by the government entity that originated packaging of the original obligations. In fact, often those entities have been created for that purpose. This action can serve as a facet of a country's fiscal policy, done to promote additional financing for the purchase of important economic goods and services. It accomplishes this purpose because additional funds then become available for the institutions to make new loans. For examples, see **Collateralized Mortgage Obligations** and **Certificates of Automobile Receivables.**

payable date. A reference to the date on which a corporation's fiscal agent will mail dividend checks to stockholders of record.

payable on new shares. A reference to the payment of a dividend, with the amount based on the number of outstanding shares after a forthcoming stock split.

payable on present shares. A reference to the payment of a dividend with the amount based on the present number of outstanding shares, even though a stock split is forthcoming.

"Payday loan." A loan made to a borrower who pledges repayment by writing a check to the lender for the amount borrowed, less the interest rate charged, dating the check on a future payday. Usually the payday is the next one. When the borrower receives a paycheck, s/he takes it to the lender who cashes it or extends the loan for another pay period, possibly at a higher interest rate. Interest rates on average payday loans average 500%, on an annualized basis. These loans are made to borrowers who tend to remain perpetually in debt. Such loans are criticized by consumer-protection organizations as keeping borrowers in a constant state of debt.

paying agent. A bank or trust company designated as a bond issuer's agent for paying interest and principal on bonds.

payment for order flow. The practice by a brokerage firm of paying one or more other brokerage firms for passing along for execution a portion or all of their orders to buy or sell stocks or derivatives, such as stock options. By reviewing the order flow as it comes in, the brokerage firm paying for the order flow has the opportunity to fill the orders internally. Although this is a legal practice, regulators are beginning to wonder whether it is compatible with the trend toward transparent markets that electronic trading has created. Since the order flow is only seen by the executing broker, the trades are not shared with the broad stock market.

payoff. See **kickback.**

pay-to-play. A reference to the situation when public officials select an investment firm on the basis of political contributions benefiting those officials. The SEC proposes new rules limiting this activity.

PBGC. Abbreviation for **Pension Benefit Guarantee Corporation.**

PC. Abbreviation for **professional corporation.**

P/E. Abbreviation for **price/earnings.**

peak and trough. The high level and low level respectively in a business cycle. The complete cycle occurs when the level of business activity rises from the trough to the peak, in approximate terms, and returns to the trough again.

peer group. Several stocks issued by companies that are engaged in the same or similar business operations. In evaluating a company's stock, analysts usually compare it to others in the group, in order to recommend the best ones, eliminate the worst ones, or find the ones that best meet specific investor needs, such as dividend income. It is very useful to develop a composite of the peer group, so that any company's performance in critical standards, such as return on equity and capital, growth, and revenue stability, can be measured against the industry averages.

PEG. Abbreviation for **Price/Earnings Growth Multiple.**

pegged to the market. A phrase indicating the price of a new stock offering or secondary offering will be based on the prevailing market price of the old shares in the same corporation, although usually slightly beneath the price of the old shares as an incentive to buyers.

PEGY. Abbreviation for **Price-Earnings-Growth-Yield Ratio.**

penalty bid. A bid to buy stock by an underwriting syndicate at which price the salesperson is penalized by losing his or her profit in a recent sale of new stock. This is done by a syndicate in a weak underwriting to prevent a salesperson from selling the shares to customers who will sell it back immediately, causing additional weakness in the underwriting.

Pending Litigation or Contingencies Item of the Annual Report. See **Commitments and Contingencies Section of the Annual Report.**

Pennsylvania Securities Commission. Regulator of securities laws in the state of Pennsylvania. Address: Eastgate Office Building, 1010 N. 7th Street, 2nd floor, Harrisburg, PA 17102. Phone: (717) 787-8061. Phone (toll free): (800) 600-0007.

penny stock. A highly speculative stock selling under five dollars per share, which is the price definition used by the Securities and Exchange Commission for regulatory purposes. In a popular and historical sense, these are stocks priced under one dollar per share, but the real defining characteristic is that the company represented is usually a startup, a pioneer in a new industry or market, or one that is not growing financially but seems on the brink of breaking out of the doldrums. Many of them are listed on an exchange, such as the NYSE, ASE, or NASDAQ, while some trade on the OTC Bulletin Board. Information and transactions in others are not posted anywhere, but represent stocks that are bought and sold through stockbrokers known to trade them. It is the latter stocks that pose special pitfalls for investors, for they have no professional investment sponsorship that promotes liquidity of principal and investment ethics. On the other hand, many of today's most prestigious companies began life as penny stocks. Some that have recorded huge gains for investors started as penny stocks. The important investment principle to follow is that such stocks should have a story that makes sense, if economic events work out to their benefit. They should represent management with sound business plans, even if the product or service is innovative, in terms of realistic expectations for revenues and earnings. And most importantly, the investors and brokers comprising the market for a stock should be serious about making money on the company's future operating prospects, and should have good business reputations. Otherwise, it's a craps shoot, a rank speculation!

Pension Benefit Guarantee Corporation (PBGC) or **Pen Ben.** The administrator of employer programs providing employee retirement benefits, in general, established by the **Employee Retirement Income Security Act of 1974 (ERISA).** Its purpose is to encourage the growth of defined benefit pension plans, provide timely and uninterrupted payment of pension benefits, and maintain pension insurance premiums at the lowest level necessary to fulfill the corporation's obligations. The Corporation is financed through premiums collected from companies that sponsor insured pension plans, investment returns on its assets and recoveries from employers responsible for underfunded, terminated plans. Within its purview are 42 million American workers covered by 45,000 defined benefit pension plans, plans that provide specified monthly benefits at retirement, often based on a combination of salary and wages and years of service. PBGC pays monthly retirement benefits to about 206,000 retirees in 2,510 terminated plans, with another 260,000 persons awaiting payment when they reach retirement age. Address: 1200 K Street NW, Washington, DC. Web site: *www.pbgc.gov.*

pension plan or **retirement plan.** Any plan, fund, or program that provides retirement income to employees or results in a deferral of income by employees until the termination of employment or beyond. There are basically two types of pension plans, traditional defined benefit and cash benefit. Over a long employment period, say 30 years, and when employees begin working at an early age, say 25, there is not a great deal of difference in the long-term benefits of the two plans. But as workers begin a plan at older ages, receiving higher compensation and working for shorter periods, the traditional plan tends to be much more rewarding.

1) *Traditional defined benefit plam.* In this plan, the employer contributes an amount that rewards seniority. The contributions increase in percentage for each year of employment. Such plans are based on formulas, for example, taking the average of the highest five years of annual compensation multiplied by 1.5% multiplied by the number of years worked, to get the annual pension benefit. Therefore, if Charlie Hustle's average income for his top five years is $50,000, over his 25-year employment period his annual pension would be $18,750 ($50,000 × 0.015 × 25 = $18, 750).

2) *Cash balance plan.* In this plan, the employer contributes a fixed amount each year, usually 3% to 10% of the employee's annual compensation. The percentage of annual contribution is usually based on the employee's age and length of service. But regardless of a worker's length of service, it compounds at a certain interest rate. That return is often linked to a U.S. Treasury Bond yield. To illustrate, if Charlene Bustle's company contributes 4.5% of her annual salary, which averages $25,000 over 25 years, to her pension plan each year, and compounds the principal at 5.0%, the pension fund would accumulate to approximately $28,125 plus a compounded growth of 5.0% each year. That could be estimated at 5.0% of the average account balance of $14,062.50, or $703.13 per year, or $17,578.13 over 25 years. The total pension fund would be $45,703.13, distributable as an annuity over Charlene's life or payable as a present value immediately.

Sponsoring companies may show gains from pension funds in their financial reports, such as lower administrative costs or capital appreciation of securities therein, but they cannot spend the money for anything but pension benefits. Usually, information on the inclusion appears in footnotes to the financial statements. *See* **Employee Retirement Income Security Act, 401(k) Retirement Plan, 403 (b)(7) Retirement Plan, Money Purchase Retirement Plan, Retirement Planning, Profit-sharing Retirement Plan, Simplified Employee Pension IRA or SEP-IRA Plan** and **SIMPLE IRA Plan.**

percent (%). A portion of any amount measured in 100ths of that amount. To calculate a percentage of one number to another, express them as a fraction, with the numerator the number you want to represent as the percentage of the denominator. Then divide the numerator by the denominator to arrive at the percentage. To express it as a whole number, multiply by 100. For example, to calculate the percentage of business miles flown of 35 million to total miles of 100 million, an airline would divide 35,000,000 by 100,000,000 for .35 × 100, or 35%.

performance, investment. In terms of monetary gain or loss, the results of an investment experience. Basically, it is a measure of the rate of return each investment decision provides. This topic is one of the most controversial for today's investor, simply because there are many ways to look at the subject and many ways to calculate investment results. Should the procedure measure performance in an absolute sense or relative to an index? Should it be time weighted? Should the measure incorporate risk? It is impossible to treat the subject exhaustively, in the limited space available here.

The Association for Investment Management and Research has developed the most comprehensive quantitative measures, ones that are becoming the standards for the professional investment community. Research providers such as Value Line, Morningstar, and Standard & Poor's also report on performances, often with different and more qualitative wrinkles.

For purposes of this discussion, the basic AIMR formula for measuring total return is used, although it is not time weighted as suggested for AIMR members. Keep in mind, there are many variations in measuring performance, but the formula below will keep you humble:

$$TIR = (MVE - MVB) \div MVB \times 100$$

where:
TIR = total investment return;
MVE = market value at end of period, including dividends received;
MVB = market value at beginning of period;
100 = factor for converting to percentage expression.

performance portability, investment. The degree to which a portfolio manager takes along past investment performance in a new professional association, in respect to the latter's advertising and descriptive materials. The Association for Investment Management and Research (AIMR) has established that performance is the record of the firm, not the individual, and that performance results of a prior firm may not be used to represent the historical record of a new affiliation or a newly formed entity. However, using the performance data from a prior firm or affiliation as supplemental information is permitted.

"permatemp." An employee who is hired as a temporary or contract worker but who actually remains an employee on a long-term or permanent basis. As a temporary, the employee works without the benefits of regular workers, such as paid vacations, insurance, paid sick leave, stock options, and pension fund interests. The period after which the status changes from "temporary" to "permanent" is not fixed but is regarded by many managers to be six months, since that is usually the term after which permanent employees become eligible for benefits. The practice of hiring temporaries became popular among managers with the corporate downsizing of the 1980s and 1990s, in order to reduce expenses such as those associated with the benefits listed above. The practice has carried over into the millennium. Although it remains popular as a strategy, a U.S. Circuit Court decision in 1997 found for temporaries in a class action suit against Microsoft, in which temporary employees who worked alongside full-time employees were granted rights to buy company stock at a discounted price, retrospectively. The settlement, reached in 2000, cost Microsoft $97 million. The decision by the Ninth Circuit in San Francisco was considered to be a signal that other cases might be forthcoming. Some employers are putting clauses in employment contracts that would indemnify them against losses from a similar law suit.

perpetual bond. A bond issued with no definite maturity date but, instead, with an option date after which the bond issuer (borrower) can call in the bond for payment, often at a premium. Generally, such bonds bear high interest to compensate investors for the indefinite liquidity date.

personal disposable income. The money people have left to support themselves after paying living expenses and federal income taxes.

personal holding company. A holding company declared by the IRS to have been formed by an individual or group to hold securities and receive income from them, for the express purpose of reducing the income tax liabilities per individual. For such a company, the tax liability on income received is 85% on the first $2,000 and 75% beyond that, with regular personal taxes assessed when the remainder is distributed to the owners. Once the IRS classifies a company as a holding company, the tax advantage is lost. Dividend distributions received by an operating company (what investors wanted to be) receive an 85% tax credit, but a personal holding company does not.

personal income. A phrase used by government statisticians to describe the total sum of wages, salaries, rental income, interest, dividends, and other payments received by individuals and unincorporated business proprietors. *See* **Personal Income and Consumption Expenditures Report.**

Personal Income and Consumption Expenditures Report. A report issued in the last part of the month by the Bureau of Economic Analysis of the Department of Commerce. Personal consumption data is the most important part of the report, and is modified to show real and inflation-adjusted figures of the market values of all goods and services purchased by individuals. Since the compensation portion represents data from wages, salaries, proprietor income, rental income, dividend, and income and transfer payments—social security, veteran, welfare, unemployment benefits—it is extremely useful in projecting future spending and personal savings. The prime importance of compensation to economists and industry analysts is that it represents over half of GNP. Because the series is only moderately volatile, it is fairly easy to predict. When personal income rises, fixed securities tend to retreat, while common stocks and dollar exchange rates improve in price.

Personal Income Less Transfer Payments. See **Economic Indicators.**

personal property. Personal belongings of value, excluding real estate.

personalization technology. Information systems that divide and distribute data tailored to the special needs of users. In some cases, the systems are consumer-based, providing information to Web sites for customers or subscribers. Others may deliver data internally to customers over an intranet or to important customers over an extranet.

phantom bid or **"spoof bid."** Among veteran stock traders, a reference to the practice by some traders of putting in orders to buy certain stocks on electronic trading systems and then withdrawing or canceling those orders. The purpose of such maneuvers is to draw other investors into bidding up those stocks through actual purchases, thinking that investor interest is spreading. When the price of the shares rises, the phantom bidders begin selling any shares they own. Usually, this forces the prices of the stocks in question down. In New York, the term used is "phantom bid," while in London "spoof bid" is the term applied.

phantom loss. A loss resulting from a transaction without any economic purpose except to avoid taxes. Generally, the Federal Tax Court has found these are not legitimate losses for corporate income tax purposes.

phantom stock. Provision for issuing corporate stock to key individuals if certain performance or profit measures are accomplished, usually by a private corporation.

Pharmacogenomics. A new applied science of customizing drugs for patients based on their genetic codes.

Philadelphia Board of Trade. Address: 1900 Market Street, Philadelphia, PA 19103. Phone: (215) 496-5555. Fax: (215) 496-5653.

Philadelphia Enquirer Online. See under **Web Sites for the Inquiring Investor.**

Philadelphia Stock Exchange (PHLX). A U.S. national securities exchange, founded in 1790 as the first organized stock exchange in the nation. Over 2,800 companies are listed. It has discussed plans to become a companion exchange with NASDAQ. Address: 1900 Market Street, Philadelphia, PA 19103. Phone: (215) 496-5102. Fax: (215) 496-5653. *See* under **Global Investment Market.**

Phillips curve. A plotted chart curve, depicting in graphic form the theory that there is a direct correlation between employment and inflation. Specifically, as the unemployment rate in a country declines through a level known as the natural rate of unemployment, the rate of inflation begins to rise. The theory was developed by the British economist A.W. Phillips in the late 1950s, and was contributed to by economists Milton Friedman and Edward Phelps in the late 1960s. In the 1990s, the theory came under disrepute, because unemployment dropped below the assumed natural rate of approximately 4%, but inflation did not occur. This prompted many economists to offer subtheories such as: the natural rate of unemployment had decreased as a result of greater worker mobility and job accessibility; greater worker productivity restrained inflation;

or better matching of workers and jobs through technological advances had kept unemployment low.

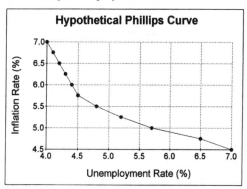

PinkBull. See under **Web Sites for Investing Women.**

pink sheets. A quoting service for over-the-counter stocks with small capitalizations, published by the **National Quotation Bureau.**

pioneering merger. A style of corporate merger in which two companies combine to enter a market neither was prepared to enter alone.

pivotal stock. A listed stock that influences by its movements the price direction of the market. Examples include steel, autos, rails, and such.

"Plain English" initiative. A reference to the rule adopted by the SEC in 1998 to get the contents of prospectuses written in a clear, understandable fashion. The SEC suggests the following writing tenets should be followed:
- Use active not passive voice
- Use short sentences
- Use concrete, everyday words
- Whenever possible, use "bullets" for explaining complex material
- Avoid legal jargon or highly technical business terminology
- Avoid multiple negatives

"plain vanilla" derivative. See **derivative.**

plan sponsor, retirement. The business enterprise, nonprofit organization, or government entity that implements an employee's retirement program by registering it with the IRS, selecting the type of plan available for a tax-sheltered status and making required reports annually to the IRS and the participants, once the program is in operation. In addition, a sponsor arranges for deductions from salaries or wages of participants in the plan, sometimes on a tax-deferred basis. Often, the sponsor will also make contributions to the retirement fund.

"plastic bonds." A reference to bonds of the pass-through variety, which are collateralized by packaged credit card installment debt, with interest and principal paid from the consolidated installment payments. *See* **asset-backed securities** and **Collateralized Mortgage Obligations.**

plateau. A period in which business activity is relatively unchanged.

player. A reference to an investor, trader, or speculator who is vying for a controlling block of stock in a corporation, with the goal of taking over the management through controlling the election of the board of directors of the company or selling the block at a profit to another interested party.

playing the stock market. A phrase meaning to invest in common stocks expecting high profits or heavy losses, with no thought of a conservative middle ground.

PLC. Abbreviation for **private liability company.**

plowing back profits. An expression describing the use of earnings for business expansion rather than for dividends.

plurality of issues traded. A phrase followed by "gained," "lost," or "remained unchanged" indicating the measure of daily investor confidence in stable or rising stock prices. If the plurality, or greatest number of stocks that traded, gained in price, confidence is good; if they lost, confidence is waning; or if they remained unchanged, indifferent. Pluralities are figured from the stocks that traded on an exchange during a session.

plus accrued interest or **and accrued interest.** A phrase indicating a bond seller will receive whatever interest has accrued since the last interest payment besides the bond's purchase price from the buyer. The buyer will then receive a full interest payment from the issuer's paying agent on the next interest date. *See* **quote (2).**

point. 1) In stock and corporate bond trading, a point is $1. 2) In government bonds, it is 1% of $1,000, or $10. 3) In the stock and bond averages, it is an arithmetical point.

point-and-figure chart. A system of plotting a stock's daily closing prices on graph paper by using Xs and Os. Usually a minimum recording fluctuation is established, selected for convenience in view of the stock's price level and price volatility, so that a mark is not made until the difference in a close is of a certain magnitude above or below the last recorded close. In choosing minimum fluctuations, higher priced stocks are assigned larger ones. When the price changes by at least the minimum amount, as measured on the graph's vertical axis, an X or O is entered at the closing price.

Successive closes in the same direction are recorded in the column. When a reversal occurs—the price changes direction by the minimum amount or more—it is represented by an X or O at the closing price, in the next column on the graph. As long as the reversal continues, new Xs or Os are recorded. If another reversal occurs, a new column is begun. Usually, Xs are used in upward columns and Os for downward, but charting is a many-splendored thing, and every style is unique. Chartists are like doodle aficionados; they have a compulsive need to invent and scribble.

In the event there is no price change during a session or the change is a fraction of the minimum, no entry is made. The passage of time is indicated on the graph by months in the following manner. On the first day of the month, the numeral corresponding to the month's chronological position in the year is used in lieu of a figure; i.e., on January 1 a 1 is entered, on February 1, a 2, and so on. Some chartists use an H for heavy volume, M for moderate, L for low, or an S for a stock split, in place of the X, or they use any other notation that reflects an event likely to affect future price movements of the stock.

```
                Point and Figure Chart on Doodles Inc.
                              X     X
 $60                      X O X O
                      H O X       L O
                      X O             O
                      X O             O
                                      O
 $50              X O        M X O        X O X
                  X              O X O X O X O X O
                  X              O X O X O X O X O
              X O X                   O X O X O
              X O M                   O X O X O
 $40  X L X                           A X O X O
      X O X                               X H
      X                                     O
      X                                     O
      X                                     B
 $30  H
      X
      X
      1

 $20
                              2001
```

As the price movements form patterns on a point-and-figure chart, the chartist prognosticates future movements based on what he reads on the chart about buying and selling pressures at various prices. This is another way of saying the chartist delves into the supply and demand for a certain stock, and attempts to make money on the conclusions. Intrinsic stock values are generally ignored, which is the main criticism leveled at stock charting. *See* **price patterns.**

poison pill. See **antitakeover strategy.**

Ponzi or **pyramid scheme.** A type of money-raising plan, illegal in the United States, whereby money contributed by investors is used to pay artificially high distributions to earlier investors. As long as new money flows in, everybody is happy. But as word gets out that the money is being used to develop a beefstake mine that only W. C. Fields could visualize, new money dries up and the scheme collapses like a house of cards. Usually, the promoters abscond with a great deal of the money. These schemes cause both federal and state securities regulators constant headaches. *See* **sucker.** (Only kidding!)

"poof" roll-up. See **roll-up.**

pooled shares. Those shares of stock belonging to owners who have formed an agreement whereby their shares will be manipulated in a market or voted together to their particular benefit. This is illegal in theory in the United States, but prevalent in Canada.

pooled trust fund. See **common trust fund.**

pooling of interests. An accounting technique often used in consolidating corporate acquisitions and mergers. Using its capital stock as payment, an acquiring corporation "purchases" the assets of another corporation and consolidates them at the book value carried by the acquired corporation, adjusted for accommodation to the acquirer's accounting methods. This results in assets and liabilities being transferred at book values, along with retained earnings. The capital stock accounts of the acquired corporation are eliminated.

When the price paid is above book value, as represented by the total market value of the acquiring corporation's stock, the technique avoids establishing a **Goodwill** account on the survivor's balance sheet, which normally would be written off through charges to annual income flow. In order to accomplish a pooling of interests, the stockholders of the acquired corporation must maintain an equivalent amount of control, proportionate to the size of their company in the combination, after the consolidation. This is accomplished by issuing to them stock in the surviving corporation.

The technique is in contrast to a cash "purchase," leading to a merger in which the capital accounts of the acquired corporation are eliminated. The net assets are transferred at current market values and, in the event more is paid for them in the form of cash, stock, or debt securities, a Goodwill account is established on the survivor's balance sheet. Subsequently, when this intangible asset is written down through charges to operating income, earnings available to stockholders are penalized. This is the primary reason managements prefer the pooling treatment when acquiring another company.

Under accounting rules, after a company merges using pooling of interest, it may not buy back its own shares for a period of six months nor may it sell the acquired company for two years. The FASB has voted to discontinue allowing companies to account for mergers as pooling, after July 1, 2001. But as a palliative to those opposing having to write off Goodwill as the purchase method dictates, and thus reducing earnings over the amortization period, FASB is considering a compromise that would require the elimination of the pooling method while allowing Goodwill or the premium paid over book value to remain on the balance sheet (unless assets representing the premium in the acquired corporation become impaired or worth less, in terms of economic value). For the accounting purists, the problem here is that "impairment" can be subjective, and under the control of a management not wishing to amortize Goodwill.

popular market indicators. Those **stock averages** or indexes that the investing public looks to in order to consolidate broad market price movements into simplified indications. Also, indicators such as short interest, margin buying, odd lot buying volume, and so on, which indicate when compared with past activity in the same category whether professionals are dominating the market and, if so, what position they are taking.

portfolio. A listing of securities held by an investor, including the number of units of each security held, dates purchased, costs, and present market values of the securities. *See* **business portfolio.**

portfolio turnover. A measure of securities trading activity in a mutual fund, calculated by dividing the lesser of the dollar amount of securities purchased or securities sold by the average monthly value of securities owned during the year. This calculation does not include securities with maturity dates at acquisition of one year or less. When a 100% turnover ratio occurs, a fund's trading during a fiscal year is equal to its assets. Although a relatively low turnover ratio reflects the payment of lower trading costs, it should not be attained at the risk of holding unattractive securities.

position. 1) The clarification of a trader's situation in a certain transaction. If he owns the securities he sold, his position is long; if he does not own the securities he sold, his position is short. 2) An investor's holdings, especially in connection with market timing. For example, a position of speculative stocks in a bear market is risky. Also see **position, securities claims.**

position, securities claims. A reference to the relative seniority each category of securities legally possesses in a corporation's capital structure in the event of a liquidation, reorganization, or some other impairment of a company's operating viability. Basically, securities give holders claims on two resources: the revenue stream and assets. These claims are determined by formal agreements, in the case of debt instruments, and state laws and common law, in the case of equity shares. In some cases, however, state laws, federal laws, and agreements apply. Securities law is a broad practice. Usually, claims are backed up by the collateralization of a specific property, such as a building, or by the general credit of the issuer and where the claimant is placed legally in the tiers of general credit claimants. At the top are the contractual or indentured claimants, represented by senior bonds, and at the bottom are the residual securities, represented by equity interests. As an investor, it is important to know where securities reside in the claims hierarchy. By understanding this internal risk, as opposed to the external risk the securities markets represent, an investor can better gauge the suitability of a security and a reasonable return to expect.

positive trade balance. See **balance of trade.**

positive yield curve. See **yield curve.**

postponed offering. A primary or secondary underwriting that is held from a public distribution, often until market conditions improve.

post. A booth on an exchange floor where a certain stock is traded.

power of attorney. An authorization, notarized and in proper written form, for another party (agent) to act in a customer's (principal's) behalf in securities transactions or the management of other assets. In the event the principal is declared incompetent, the agent's power to act is terminated under a regular power of attorney. A power can either be full (general) or special (specific), the latter type pertaining to making decision for the principal concerning certain matters. Usually, powers of attorney that are granted to investment advisers and brokers are regular powers of limited scope. *See* **agency** and **power of attorney, durable.**

power of attorney, durable. A power of attorney arrangement, but one that remains in effect if the principal is declared incompetent or becomes disabled. *See* **power of attorney.**

PRARS. Abbreviation for **Public Register's Annual Report Service.**

predation. See **predatory pricing.**

predatory pricing or **predation.** In the legal context of maintaining free competition, the sacrificing of profits by a company or companies for as long as it takes to eliminate competition, and then raising prices sufficiently to recover the losses suffered, without attracting more competition.

preemptive right. A stockholder's right to purchase a corporation's new stock before others, usually at a favorable price.

preference share. In the corporate structures of Australia, Canada, the United Kingdom, and certain European countries, a stock share taking precedence over the ordinary shares of the same company, in regard to dividends from profits and liquidation distributions. It is similar to **preferred stock** in the United States.

preferred creditor. A lender who is entitled, under law in bankruptcy or estate settlement situations, to have his claims settled first.

preferred stock. That stock taking precedence over other stock of the same corporation in regard to dividend liquidation distributions and usually carrying no voting rights, except in cases where the preferred stock category has been created to attract new capital to a floundering corporation. In regard to dividends, the annual rate of payment is usually a percentage of the stock's par value. When there is more than one class of preferred stock, it is generally called "first preferred," "second preferred," and so on, according to the claim on asset and earnings priority of each issue. *See* **convertible preferred stock** and **stock table.**

preferred stock ratio. The ratio of the par value of the outstanding preferred stock to the total capitalization, expressed as a percentage. Using new securities issues as a gauge, from 1990 to 1996 nearly 15.5% of total new stocks were preferred, while new preferred equities were slightly more than 2% of all corporate stocks and bonds issues in that period. Utilities usually have the highest preferred stock ratios, because their stable dividend coverage makes the preferred stock attractive to income-minded investors. In addition, the regularity of utility revenues makes the cash flow for the dividends reliable.

preholiday liquidation. The increased selling of stocks on a market day prior to a holiday because of the apprehension market traders have about adverse news events developing while the markets are closed. Such events could affect stock prices drastically on the next opening, before traders can act. This selling is extremely heavy if unfavorable news seems likely.

pre-IPO stock. A reference to stock granted or sold to investors immediately before other shares of the stock are registered for a sale to the public for the first time. In stock markets where there is a big demand for the type of stock represented, such as dotcom company shares in the late 1990s and early 2000s, this stock is particularly attractive because shortly after the initial distribution the stock often is worth a great deal more.

preliminary prospectus. See "**red herring.**"

premium, bond. The amount over the face value for which a bond or preferred stock is selling. *See* **money market.**

premium, conversion. The amount over its conversion value for which a convertible bond or convertible preferred stock is selling. To determine whether a convertible bond or stock is selling for a **discount** or premium, calculate the value of an underlying share in the current market. From that value, subtract the cost of a share through buying the convertible security and exercising the conversion feature. A plus amount represents a discount, a minus amount represents a premium. Illustrating, a convertible debenture of Whee! Corp., convertible into 20 shares of common stock, is selling for $1,500 per debenture, or $75 per common share equivalent ($1,500 ÷ 20). The common stock is currently quoted at $70 per share, meaning the premium stock is $5 per share ($75 – $70). In other words, it would cost $5 more per share, or a 7.1% premium, to own the shares through purchasing the convertible debenture and converting it. However, it is important to factor in the interest yield from the debenture, which might compensate an investor for some or possibly all of that premium, if the debenture is held long enough.

premium, option. The amount for which an option contract is selling over the underlying value. For example, the premium on a July call option selling for $1 on 100 HOWL at 25 would be $100 (100 units times $1).

premium stock. Stock that a borrower (short seller) must pay interest on because of its scarcity.

prenuptial agreement, corporate. An agreement between two merging corporations that outlines certain events and preconditions necessary for the business union to occur, usually adopting a longer schedule for completion than other mergers. The objective is a more complete blending of the two companies, including working out specific problems foreseen by the managements in developing a smooth-operating merged entity.

prenuptial agreement, personal. A legal contract that defines how the partners to a marriage want their assets and liabilities divided, in the event of a divorce or death. Although this is a legal contract, some parts can be declared illegal later, such as in a probate settlement. Experts say that the following conditions are a valid basis for a prenuptial agreement before marriage: there are children from a previous marriage; business ownership is involved; one party is a partner in a business; there are significant assets; one party is putting the other through college; and one party is in a potentially lucrative career.

present value. See **discounted value.**

"present value of one formula." See **annuity.**

preservation of capital. In investment analysis, a reference to the reasonable assurance that invested funds will retain their original or greater value when converted back to cash at a later date.

pressure. A downward force on securities prices. *See* **under pressure.**

pretax income or **earnings.** The amount of money on which corporate income taxes are paid. It is calculated on the tax rate of net revenues after deducting operating expenses, interest, and other taxes and including other income and deductions but before income tax credits and net operating losses from prior periods are considered.

pretax profit margin. The gross profit margin with income taxes added back. This indicates how effective management is in minimizing income tax expenses through the use of tax credits and tax deductions. A ratio under the current corporate income tax rate is considered effective. *See* **under ratio.**

price. See **quote.**

price competition. A market condition in which vendors strive to increase their market shares through offering consumers lower prices than rival establishments. Usually, this happens when products are similar in quality—but not always, since service competition and quality competition can play a role in where customers purchase goods also. Refined petroleum products are an example, among others, of price competition. *See* **quality competition** and **service competition.**

Price/Earnings Growth Multiple or **PEG.** The current price of a stock divided by its expected growth rate for the next fiscal year. To illustrate, analysts estimate earnings on a share of Finnegan's Irish Stew, Inc. will increase by 25% next year, because of management's bold plan to dye the ingredients green. Currently priced at $30 per share, the price/earnings growth multiple is 1.2 ×, or ($30 ÷ 25%). By using this valuation technique, the investor places the emphasis on expected growth rate rather than earnings per share. The procedure tends to make high-growth stocks with exorbitant P/E multiples more reasonable, since the gain in earning power is emphasized. *See* **Cash-Adjusted Price/Earnings Multiple** and **Price/Earnings Multiple.**

Price-Earnings-Growth-Yield Multiple or **PEGY.** The current price/earnings multiple of a stock divided by the sum of its expected earning growth rates over five years, plus its dividend yield.

> The formula is below:
> PEGY = P/E + ((SumI$_{1-5}$) + Y)
>
> Where:
> P/E = Price/Earnings Multiple;
> I = Earnings growth rates for five years, expressed as whole numbers;
> Y = Dividend Yield, expressed as a whole number.

Proponents of this method of stock evaluation believe that a ratio under 1.0 represents a stock bargain. For example, the price of Sing Sing Cell Phones, Inc. stock is $40 per share. Expected earnings for the current year are $5.00 per share, making the P/E multiple 8×. The growth rate over the next five years is expected to be: 7%, 10%, 12%, 15%, and 20%. The current dividend of $2.00 yields 5%. The PEGY is: (8 ÷ 69 = .12), indicating it is reasonably priced since it is below 1.0. Remember not to decimalize the percentage.

Price/Earnings (P/E) Ratio or Multiple. The market price of a stock divided by its annual earnings per share, based on the trailing four quarters, the latest fiscal year, or an estimated future year for earnings. The quotient is called the price/earnings ratio or multiple, and is used as a gauge in describing the relative value of a stock, in terms of its earnings per share for a particular period. Although between 12× and 15× is a preferred multiple for trailing four quarters, there is no standard since projected earnings and dividends can bid the multiple higher. For example, Patience! Inc., an Internet service provider's stock, is selling for $50, is expected to earn $2, and has a P/E Multiple of 25× or ($50 ÷ $2). That seems high historically for most stocks. But a sound investment approach would be to find the average price/earnings multiple over the prior 5–7 years, to determine if the current one is too high or low. By doing this, you are probing into how investors tend to value the shares under different circumstances. Possibly 25× is typical, possibly it is way out of line, unless really new factors have appeared. ("There is nothing new, under the sun"—*Ecclesiastes.*) *See* **Cash-Adjusted Price/Earnings Multiple, Price/Earnings Growth Multiple,** and **Forward Price/Earnings Multiple.**

price/earnings reciprocal. See **earnings yield.**

Price/Fantasy Multiple. A somewhat facetious reference to rationalizing a high stock price for a company by using an extremely optimistic number in the denominator of the ratio. For example, the stock of InternetsUnlimited.com, a gateway to information on tennis tournaments throughout the world, is priced at $100 per share, while losing $5 per share in the current year. Investors begin feeling the stock is too high. But an enterprising broker forecasts that in three years the earnings will be $5 per share, assuming tennis becomes the number one spectator sport in the world by then. The Price/Fantasy Multiple could be considered to be $100 ÷ 5 = 20×. Not bad for a high growth stock.

price level accounting. An accounting concept that gained favor in the inflationary periods of 1946–48, 1950–51, 1956–55, and from 1965 to the early 1990s. The idea was developed to prevent the overstatement of earnings or profits during and following a period of rising prices, an overstatement that occurs because of the accounting convention of charging only the historical cost of the consumption of physical assets (for example, fixed assets and inventory). When inflation is eroding the purchasing power of the dollar, the charging off during operating periods of historical costs, representing earlier, lower prices, and establishing like reserves, is inadequate for the replacement of those assets being consumed.

Advocates claim that proper accounting requires a restatement of costs in current dollars because only when costs and revenues are measured in equivalent dollars (current dollars) can the difference in those costs and profits be fairly determined. In making such an adjustment, an index of general price increases such as the Consumer Price Index or Gross Domestic Product Deflator may be used, or a more specific price-level index where greater differentiation is desired.

price patterns or **price formations.** The various formations
made by recorded stock prices on a **chart.** Although chartists of
both the bar and point-and-figure breed develop personal techniques in chart making and chart interpretations, most of them
agree that whenever a stock's price range breaks out of one of
the basic price formations accompanied by significant trading
volume, the move indicates a buy or sell sign. If the price breakthrough is above the formation, a buy sign is indicated; if
below, a sell sign is present. The rationale of this method is that
during the interval of the price formation, buyers and sellers are
confining their transactions to predictable price limits, holding
the fluctuations down because of a lack of conviction about
financial progress or slipping of the corporation represented by
the stock. Then, when financial news becomes known by active
investors, resultant substantial buying or selling causes the price
to break out of the formation, a confirmation that a new investor
attitude is forming toward the stock.

Many chartists claim that the extent of the price move will
be similar to the previous move in the opposite direction on the
chart, although others follow the gap theories explained under
gap. The important point about price formations is that trading
activity of a stock is graphically exhibited, indicating when
investor outlook is indecisive, as in a rectangular formation;
changing in an orderly way, as in a rounded pattern; drawing to
a climax in a downward or upward trend, as represented by the
restrained price fluctuations in a triangular or wedge formation;
or limited by past trading trends, indicating impassable levels,
as in a double and triple top or bottom formation. The head and
shoulders pattern is a special case in which the extent of the
breakout is supposed to match the previous move in the opposite direction or the move in the middle portion. The crucial
point is when the price pierces the formation limits of a previous low or high price, for then a new pattern is in the making.
The chartist hopes to spot the breakthrough immediately and
buy on the upside or sell on the downside, always ready to take
the opposite position when the new movement slows down and
a price reversal on substantial volume seems imminent.

Obviously, the chartist is a trader expecting to make money by buying and selling at exactly the right time without studying intrinsic stock values or becoming sensitive to rumors and stock market patter. The most studied price patterns are: **ascending triangle, ascending wedge, descending triangle, descending wedge, double top, double bottom, head-and-shoulders, rectangle, rounded top, rounded bottom, symmetrical triangle, triple top,** and **triple bottom.**

primary earnings per share. Net income divided by shares outstanding, without regard to residual securities—warrants, options, convertibles and so forth—which might reduce earnings per share were they exchanged for common stock. *See* **fully diluted earnings per share.**

primary market. The distribution to the public of a new issue of securities.

primary offering. The solicitation by underwriters, dealers, or salespeople of orders to buy at a fixed price an issue of securities never before offered to the public.

prime manufacturer. A maker of goods that are bought by other businesses for marketing under their brand names.

prime rate. The interest rate commercial banks charge their surest and most continuous borrowers, usually from $1/2$% to 2% lower than general rates.

Primex Trading. An electronic trading network formed by the four largest U.S. securities firms—Solomon Smith Barney, Morgan Stanley Dean Witter, Goldman Sachs, and Merrill Lynch—that offers auction trading for a broad listing of securities as well as interactive negotiations for them to all brokers and dealers. It commenced operations in the summer of 2000.

principal. 1) The stated amount of a debt on which the interest is calculated. 2) *See* **"acting as principal."**

principal denominated in principal bonds or **PRINs.** When a debtor is experiencing severe financial problems, the repayment of a portion or all of debt when due with bonds or notes.

principal paying agent. A bank or trust company named by a bond issuer to pay interest and principal to bondholders from funds deposited for such purposes.

principal underwriter. The investment banker in a syndicate that has furnished the largest share of money, usually the syndicate manager.

PRINs. See **principal denominated in principal bonds.**

private, going. As a public corporation with stock outstanding in the public's hands, the act by the board and others included of recapitalizing whereby the company buys back its public stock and issues new stock to the principals who put up the money, thus putting the company in private hands. Usually, other company accounts, such as debt outstanding, remain intact. The purpose of going private is to escape the public spotlight or to eliminate the financial and clerical requirements of public registration, both with the SEC and an exchange, such as filing lengthy documents. There is also an escape from the hazard of liability from share-holder suits. Officers of private corporations also have such a vulnerability, but one that is not as great or varied. In going private, a corporation can even be taken down to a partnership, but hardly ever does one devolve into a sole proprietorship.

Another condition that can lead to going private is investment strategy. Often when a company is in a weakened financial position, it is vulnerable to absorption by another company at an unrealistically low price because its public shareholders want to dump their shares and move on. Financiers organize a leveraged buyout and take the company public—out of harm's way—until its operations and financial positions improve materially. The cash flow and other money usually has paid off the debt incurred to go private. Then they do a reverse buyout, and take the company public again, frequently making huge profits on the higher stock price. *See* **leveraged buyout** and **reverse leveraged buyout.**

private bank. An investment or commercial bank that furnishes all financing and/or other banking services to a business in return for exclusive patronage or other concessions.

private brand. An item manufactured especially for a store to sell under its own name.

private enterprise. The financing of a project with personal funds rather than governmental funds.

Private Export Funding Corporation. See **agency securities.**

private limited company (PLC). A British company chartered by the government to carry on certain business pursuits, and authorized to sell shares to the public. Investors have limited liabilities, in regard to company affairs. The abbreviation PLC must appear in the company title, in order to assure limitations on liability for investors. Basically, this organizational designation informs the public that shareholders and officers are limited to their direct investment in the entity. This form of business structure is much like the American corporation.

private placement or **direct placement.** A direct sale of securities between an issuer (corporation) and investor, usually a financial institution, without using regular channels of the public market or having to register as completely with the SEC. However, an investment firm active in the public markets usually organizes and negotiates the financing for a fee of 3%–10% of the value, through its special corporate financing staff. The securities involved might be common stock, partnership units, preferred stock, debentures, bonds, or notes or some hybrid of these. Also, they might include equity kickers or be convertible into other securities. This latter feature makes them attractive to financial institutions, since they can take a role in customizing speculative investments in which they are interested. Typically, large financial commitments—$500,000 to $1 million and up—are required.

Private Securities Litigation Reform Act of 1995. A landmark Congressional act intended to curb questionable lawsuits for fraud involving securities. The law requires investors to prove much more when they make accusations of fraud against corporate managements. Also, the law includes a "safe harbor" provision that protects managements when they make predictions about future results.

private stock offering. A reference to the sale of corporate shares to individual investors without the lengthy registration process required for public offerings. The issuer of the stock is usually a start-up or near start-up company, seeking $3 million to $25 million in financing. This is often the second stage or mezzanine financing stage in the evolution into a public company. Under SEC rules, investors must have a $1 million net worth because of the high risk associated with these deals.

privatize. As a government, to distribute assets in a state-owned enterprise to private investors in exchange for payment and sometimes operating concessions. Usually, privatization occurs when a country reorganizes under new economic philosophies, either voluntarily under an election mandate or involuntarily under creditor demands.

privileged issue. Those securities carrying the right to buy additional securities of the same corporation at lower than the market price for a limited period.

pro. A floor broker, odd lot broker, specialist, or stock exchange member who trades for his personal account. Thus, in a strict sense, a pro is close to market transactions, trading often and for quick results.

pro forma. 1) A financial report or projection adjusted for a contemplated change in the corporate structure. By way of illustration, if a stock report on Going Out of Business Stores, Inc. showed earnings of 50 cents per share on present stock outstanding, to reflect a forthcoming 2-for-1 split, it would adjust the earnings to 25 cents per share on a pro forma basis. This adjustment would indicate how much earnings would be after twice as much stock was outstanding. 2) A management concept of adjusting financial results in the best light possible by restating items such as earnings as though some event did or did not take place, usually the former. Some consider the restated accounts "hypothetical." The practice leads to ignoring damaging occurrences like natural disasters or legal judgments on the grounds they are nonrecurring and should not influence investors unduly. The result is that the item makes the total picture more palatable. Although there are no hard rules governing the use of this charitable practice, the SEC has asked for opinions from financial executives. (The SEC does not accept pro forma statements in filing with it.) Generally, executives feel the pro forma results should be accompanied by the actual results and should be within the guidelines of Generally Accepted Accounting Practices. For example, suppose the cookie monster gobbled up the entire inventory of Not-So-Famous Otis Oatmeal Cookies, causing a write-off of $1.0 million or $0.50 per share for the year. This brings down EPS to $0.25. Management decides that's a lot of dough. They might rationalize the nonrecurring write-off by releasing a pro forma adjustment not including the affair that showed EPS of $0.75, restoring the amount of the write-off. As long as both versions are displayed, it would be ethical under present practice.

Producer Price Index (PPI). A monthly index, including subindexes, of producer or wholesale prices, published mid-month by the Bureau of Labor Statistics of the Department of Labor. It is important to economists and analysts, partly because it represents the first monthly indication of inflation. Besides its sequential difference—it measures producer or upstream prices—the PPI differs from the CPI in that it excludes services, focusing only on commodities. Another important difference is the PPI measures changes in the prices of capital equipment besides prices of wholesale consumer goods, while the CPI measures only consumer goods and services. Also, the PPI measures only domestic goods, while the CPI includes imports. Although there is a relatively high correlation between the PPI and CPI over time, in short-term periods they can act differently. The composition of the PPI is as follows: Finished Consumer Goods (40%), Food (26%), Capital Equipment (25%), and Energy (9%). Usually, in the context of inflation, the PPI of finished goods is the reference. The methodologies in calculating PPI are similar to that used in the Consumer Price Index. When data in the Producer Price Index rises, fixed income securities tend to fall, as do common stock prices, while dollar exchange rates are unpredictable. When the index drops, fixed income securities tend to escalate as do common stocks, while dollar exchange rates are unpredictable. *See* **chain-weighted price index** and **Consumer Price Index.**

production. A reference to physical industrial output, expressed in specific units.

production costs. Those expenses incurred during a manufacturing process. *See* **expenses.**

product mix. The integration of diverse products under one management, with the resultant balance achieved in planning, scheduling, production, and marketing.

professional corporation (PC). A special status corporation organized by individuals practicing a public service requiring licensing or other legal authorization, such as accounting, law, medicine, dentistry, or architecture. The main advantage to such a form lies in taxability similar to that of a partnership, without some of the fiduciary risks. However, personal professional responsibility or privilege is not changed, nor is malpractice liability through incorporation.

professional investor. A person who invests for a living or who manages investments as a career for institutions, mutual funds, private accounts, and so on.

profit. See **earnings.**

profit and loss account. In accounting practice, a ledger account into which balances from revenue, income, profit, expenses, and losses are entered at regular intervals. Its balance is then transferred to retained earnings or another proprietary account for reporting purposes. Over time the phrase has come to mean any item of gain or loss charged to a particular accounting period.

profit margin or **margin of profit.** 1) Profit margin, gross. The ratio of operating profits (total operating revenues less total operating expenses, including depletion, depreciation, and amortization but not income taxes or interest paid) to net sales, expressed as a percentage; the profit portion of total sales or revenues from just running the business. This ratio establishes the operating efficiency since it means that for every dollar of sales, the corporation has a fraction (cents) left after paying both direct and indirect costs of operating. From this sum, after adding other income, must be paid bond interest, taxes, and preferred and common stock dividends, in certain cases. This ratio is the converse of the operating ratio. In the United States over the past 15 years, the average gross profit margin for corporations has been 11.2%. Generally speaking, when the margin is low, a large sales volume is required for reasonable net profits or income. 2) Profit margin, net. The sum of the gross profit margin and interest and income taxes. This is the bottom line figure that Wall Street focuses on, or perhaps lives and dies on, in the equity markets. In the United States over the past 15 years, the average net profit margin for business has been 2.3%.

Profit Sharing Retirement Plan. A type of retirement plan popular because it is easy for all parties to understand. An employer can make discretionary contributions from profits of up to 15% of salary or wages for all eligible employees. In addition, the employer may change the level from one year to the next, making this type of plan one of the most flexible. Employers are allowed to base the percentage contribution on the profitability of the business enterprise. This type of plan is funded only by employers. It may be started prior to fiscal year end. Participants vest on a graduated schedule, in up to seven years. Because the plan may be coordinated with an employee's social security benefits, it allows for a greater portion of contributions to go to the higher paid employees. This type of plan is ideally suited to the following business situations:

- Company operates either for profit or is nonprofit.
- Maximum flexibility of contributions annually is an objective.
- No future size limitations for the company.
- Options on vesting schedule desirable by employer.
- Loan and hardship withdrawal privileges are wanted.
- Exclusion of part-time employees is important.

profit squeeze. A smaller percentage of net profits than in a corresponding past period, caused by higher operating costs or lower selling prices.

profit taking. A phrase describing active selling of a security that has risen in price as sellers realize their profits, depressing the price in the process, since more shares become available.

program trading. Generally speaking, any securities trading program that is computer assisted. These programs can range from predetermined portfolio structures, in which selling or buying occurs when a market index reaches a certain level, to options trading, in which buying or selling occurs when a derivative contract and the underlying stock or commodity get out of line. In all cases, computers enable lightning reactions to imbalances in securities trading and initiate activity in a manner that will benefit or protect the users of the program. On the NYSE, where there is no options trading, program trading involves a broad range of portfolio strategies in which there is a purchase or sale of at least 15 stocks from the S&P 500 Index or a basket of stocks worth $1 million or more. In December 1997, program trading accounted for 16.9% of NYSE volume.

progressive convertible preferred stock. A type of preferred stock that can be converted into common shares on a progressively higher basis of exchange. Usually, such a stock also entitles holders to the same cash dividend received by common share holders and to stock dividends above the rate that matches the accelerating conversion schedule. For example, a hypothetical conversion schedule might be as follows:

NUMBER OF COMMON SHARES FOR EACH SHARE OF PROGRESSIVE CONVERTIBLE	
Year	Preferred (3% Acceleration)
1977	1.0
1978	1.3
1979	1.7
1980	2.1

Since the exchange basis is compounding at 3%, the holders would be entitled to any stock dividend on the common shares above 3% that would protect them against dilution of equity pursuant to the conversion. Without obligating themselves to pay fixed cash dividends, a corporation issues this form of pre-ferred stock to attract investors looking for a form of fixed return; however, whether income-minded investors generally will accept a capital growth increase of common shares as a fixed return in view of fluctuating stock values is uncertain, since this form of financing is a new concept.

progressive tax system or **graduated tax system.** An income tax plan that imposes higher taxes as income rises, by increasing tax rates. In the United States, federal income taxes are based on this concept. However, in recent years there has been an effort to move to a **flat tax system** by eliminating many of the tax rate brackets. The system might now be called a modified progressive tax system. This system is criticized by many economists on the grounds that its rising taxes for higher incomes discourages the wealthy from investing in new plant and equipment. At present, there are six tax brackets and a tax surcharge. The brackets are: 10%, 15%, 25%, 28%, 33%, and 35%.

projection. An estimate of the magnitude of future business or economic events—developed by securities analysts, economists, credit analysts, and corporate planners—such as an earnings projection, sales projection, GDP projection, and so on. Technically, a projection is an extension of a statistical model, a quantitative estimate rather than a subjective forecast. In other words, a projection is a disciplined estimate based on empirical evidence, whereas a forecast is a combination of empirical evidence and intuitive expectations, based on personal knowledge or past experience. For example, in a model that estimates that a stock will increase earnings by 15% annually over the next three years, a projection would simply add 15% to the prior year's earnings, to estimate or project earnings during that period. On the other hand, a forecast would inject a subjective notion into the 15% increment, fine tuning the estimate for events like accounting charges or potential legal liability. In the economist's vernacular, a forecast allows for the "fudge factor" or guesswork.

promissory note. A written promise to pay a sum of money on a specific date.

promoters. Those organizers and salespeople who create a legal corporation and then sell the capital stock to the public. *See* **promotion costs.**

promotion costs. Those charges by corporation organizers and its stock salespeople who are distributing a new issue. Usually they receive a cash portion of the sale of each share, options to buy stock at a low price, and sometimes free stock. All of these dilute the public shareholders' equity. *See* **dilution of equity.**

property taxes. Annual assessments on real estate and/or personal property by a city or county.

proportional voting power or **proportional representation.** In corporate governance, a method of voting for the board of directors in which stockholders have a right to elect a ratio of directors in proportion to the number of shares owned. For example, when cumulative voting is practiced, a form of proportional representation, the shareholders with 10% of the common stock outstanding could elect 10% of the board by concentrating their votes on one person. If 10 vacancies existed on the board they could elect one director, whereas under statutory voting rights they could not. In the latter case, they would have to cast their votes for each vacancy, allowing the majority shareholders to choose the board. Another example is when preferred stockholders have the right to elect a certain proportion of the board if the corporation allows certain events to occur, such as failing to pay preferred dividends. *See* **cumulative voting right** and **statutory voting right.**

Proprietary Drug Industry. The makers of drugs and medicines that can be bought without a physician's prescription.

prospectus. The official literature that must accompany an offering of securities. Under Securities and Exchange Commission regulations, it must contain a full disclosure of the company's financial status and prospects as well as the nature of the securities being offered. It also should contain information about corporate officers and legal matters of significance, the nature of the industry, and markets served by the issuer. For security offerings not interstate in nature or offerings related to corporations capitalized at under $300,000, prospectus contents are regulated by state agencies, but the completeness required varies. Under rules adopted by the SEC in 1998, mutual fund prospectuses and offering documents of other companies should emphasize **"Plain English"** in descriptions of securities in the cover page, summary, and risk factor sections of stock and bond offering documents. It is important to note that the SEC and state agencies do not warrant the merits of securities offered by a prospectus, but only the completeness of the information. In the case of new offerings, there are usually two prospectuses—the preliminary prospectus, or **"red herring,"** and the final prospectus, or statutory prospectus or **offering circular.**

protected from dilution. A reference to the automatic feature of a convertible security to increase the units into which it can be converted, proportionate to any increase in stock outstanding.

proxy statement. An authorization giving to a corporation's directors, or to a group opposing them, the right to vote the shares held by an absent stockholder. The authority covers corporate matters such as the election of directors and approval of mergers and acquisitions, when required by the charter.

proxy valuation. In evaluating a share of common stock, the use of some measuring stick(s) other than the conventional ones or commonly accepted ones in securities analysis in establishing some value for a share. Generally, this technique is employed when examining a new or fledgling industry. Such stocks often have not had an opportunity to prove themselves in terms of traditional methods of valuation, such as P/E Multiple, Dividend Yield, Profit Margin, and so on. An example would be a new sales company that is chalking up fast-growing revenues but not showing earnings, since the revenue receipts are less than needed for expenses. In such a case, a promoter for the stock might publicize the Price/Revenues ratio per share, making the stock look reasonable using an unorthodox technique. The problem is that management might not have the foggiest notion of how to manage earnings out of the impressive sales revenues at any stage of the company's development.

Another example of the use of proxy valuation is in the appraisals of Internet stocks or dot-com stocks. In the late 1990s, when these stocks were not yet reporting earnings but were very popular, investors began to look for gauges like "page hits per quarter," "eyeballs per quarter," "questions per quarter," or "unique visitors per quarter." These are all expressions denoting visits to the Web site of the company and are, generally, a rationale for buying a stock that is very speculative in that the chances of making money are no better than 50-50. One purpose the exercise does serve, however, is to ferret out the most popular or well-known of the group, which is a reasonable argument for buying shares in an unproven group in which an investor is determined to invest.

"prudent man rule." An investment principle developing from the policy of recognizing that growth common stocks should be included in a trust portfolio. It was adopted by New York in 1950 and is now recognized by several states. Generally, the rule allows a 35% investment in common stocks, preferred stocks, and bonds not on a **legal list,** providing a "reasonable man" would select them. This is considered a stricter fiduciary requirement than the facetious "brokers' prudent man rule," which is, "I would not even invest your money in those securities."

PSE. Abbreviation for the **Pacific Exchange.**

public, going. As a partnership or corporation with a limited number of owners, to make the legal and financial arrangements to recapitalize and distribute new stock to the public. This action usually involves retaining an investment banker(s) who puts together a group that will sell the stock to the public through their brokers. However, in a limited number of cases, corporate officers have managed the distribution of the new stock themselves, using direct selling of the shares to brokers and wealthy investors. Usually the value of the new corporation exceeds the original value because of the public spotlight, so the original owners receive shares worth a great deal more than their original stakes. The additional shares are sold to the public, although the original owners can arrange to sell all or a portion of their shares at the same time. When the shares are sold to the public for the first time it is called an **initial public offering.** There are three reasons that persuade private owners to go public, although there are undoubtedly others, such as income tax angles: (1) The owners are at retirement age and want to leave the management of company affairs. (2) The owners wish to diversify their estates in order to pass on to their heirs long-term assets in the form of shares in the new publicly traded corporation. (3) The original owners have built a valuable entity and want to take profits for other ventures or pursuits. *See* also **private, going**.

public corporation. 1) A reference to a corporation's stock that is available to the public at large. 2) A corporation created by Congress or a state legislature—although not necessarily owned by the government—to achieve something on the public's behalf. An example is the Federal Deposit Insurance Corporation.

public investors. 1) Those individuals or associations who invest private funds that have been deposited with them or paid to them in exchange for such instruments as annuities. Insurance companies are examples. These institutions are sometimes called fiduciaries and intermediaries. 2) Those investors, excluding the Federal Reserve Banks, who buy U.S. Treasury securities.

Public Register's Annual Report Service (PRARS). See under **Web Sites for the Inquiring Investor.**

Public Utility Holding Company Act of 1935. A Congressional act placing the supervision of certain gas and electric holding companies that own or control operating subsidiaries engaged in interstate generation and distribution of power under the Securities and Exchange Commission in matters related to securities and financing. The statute's main thrust is to simplify the corporate structure of public utilities and applies to both electric and gas power companies. Normally, public utility operating companies are regulated by state commissions and, to a lesser extent, the localities they serve. The purpose of the statute was to protect investors, consumers, and the general public from the deleterious effects of complex holding companies. Some of the abuses of this economic concentration were watered stock, financial irregularities, manipulations of the stock and bond markets, misleading advertising about securities issued, and irresponsible management. So powerful were the holding companies that at one point 10 of them controlled most of the delivered power in the United States.

Important features of the act are the following:

1. Holding companies operating between states must register with the SEC, as must persons controlling such companies, and furnish information on their business organizations, financial matters, and the types of control exercised.

2. The SEC supervises the financial and operating processes of registered companies and must approve all securities offerings.

3. The act requires the establishment of uniform accounting standards approved by the SEC and requires the filing of regular management and financial reports as well as reports delineating ownership by officers and directors, while prohibiting interlocking directorates with commercial or investment banks.

4. It allows only one intermediate company or layer between a holding company and its operating subsidiaries. *See* **securities laws.**

Publishing. Those stocks representing companies publishing books and periodicals other than newspapers. Often, they also operate other media businesses. *See* **industry stock group.**

Publishing—Newspaper. Those stocks representing companies publishing newspapers, although they often are multimedia companies. *See* **industry stock group.**

Pujo Committee. A committee of the House of Representatives established in 1912 to study financial practices, especially banking control, and whose recommendations contributed to the Clayton Act and Federal Reserve System.

pump-and-dump. In a plan to defraud investors, the stages that follow establishing the **rig.** The rig is the scheme by which the con artists intend to bilk investors out of money through selling them shares in the rig corporation. The group hires persons such as questionable public relations consultants and "analysts" to pump up the price of the stock through releases and statements to the media or the Internet. However, no filings of company progress are made to regulatory agencies. Often, the promoters will enlist the aid of a broker-dealer to sponsor the shares, and thus gain a listing on the Over-the-Counter Bulletin Board. These persons usually are working for a piece of the action, or shares in the sales receipts. Sometimes newsletters are used. Whatever the means employed, the message is exaggerated claims of future profits or capital gains.

As this happens, aggressive salespeople, posing as legitimate brokers, pitch the stock to unwary investors over telephones or the Internet for huge commissions, in proportion to the cost of the shares. The shares are nearly always **penny stocks** selling for one dollar or less. This activity is aimed at driving up the price of the stock in a fictional market. This stage of the fraud continues until the promoters are able to sell, or dump, their shares at big profits or the scam is discovered and closed down by law enforcement officials. The more audacious ones actually try to sell the shares short, if the truth comes out and the share price collapses. *See* **grease** and **rig.**

purchase accounting (in accounting for a merger or acquisition). See **pooling of interests.**

purchase agreement. See **underwriting agreement.**

Purchasing Managers' Index. An index reflecting a survey managed and published by the National Association of Purchasing Management, released on the first working day of each month under *Report on Business.* It is the first comprehensive look at the manufacturing sector and, therefore, very important for analysts and economists. It is basically a diffusion index, so that marks above 50 represent expanding manufacturing activity, while those below 50 reflect declining activity. In compiling the survey, NAPM polls 250 industrial executives in 21 industries in 50 states. Those participating answer a questionnaire revealing changes in production, orders, commodity prices, inventories, vendor performance, and employment. In calculating the composite diffusion index from the sub-indexes, various weights are applied. When the index rises, fixed income securities tend to go down, while common stocks and dollar exchange rates go up. *See* **National Association of Purchasing Management.**

purchasing power of the dollar. The amount of goods and services a dollar will buy compared with a base period, expressed as a percentage or index number. In determining the dollar's purchasing power, the reciprocal (index divided into 1) of the

Consumers' Price Index of the Labor Department is used. If the index is 1.25, prices are 25% higher, or 125% of themselves, in the selected base period, and the current purchasing power of the dollar is 80% or .80—the reciprocal of 1.25—in relation to the base period. To equate a fund such as life insurance benefits into current purchasing power, divide the principal by the index; viz., $125,000 of insurance is worth $100,000 (125,000 ÷ 1.25) in the purchasing power of the year used as a base period.

"push the envelope, to." In a business or financial transaction, a reference to testing a situation to the extreme limit or beyond the limit expected when it was first conceived. For example, when an investment banker brings a new initial public offering to market during a highly-speculative period, the firm might price the IPO at a valuation based on the average for the year or "push the envelope" to a new level. If the average IPO had come to market at 25 times cash flow, and the banker priced the latest one at 50 times, it would represent pushing the envelope. The risk of such an action is that the market could soften suddenly, leaving many units unsold or requiring the banker to withdraw the IPO until market conditions improved, whereas if the valuation had been within the annual range, it probably would have been sold out. The term comes from aeronautical engineering parlance and in that context means to exceed the design specifications of an aircraft.

put. A written contract to sell a certain security (100 shares) at a specific price by a stated date, often in 30, 60, or 90 days, or 6 months. The buyer of a put anticipates the decline of that security's price, so he buys cheaply at the market then executes his put, or sell, option for a profit after the cost of the put is deducted. The commission on the transaction is not paid until the option to sell is exercised. Put options, sold over-the-counter historically, were introduced on the Chicago Board Option Exchange and American Stock Exchange in 1976.

put bonds or **bullet bonds.** Corporate bonds that give the holder the right to sell the bond back to the issuer if interest rates rise within a certain time period. The issuer bets that the company can save enough in interest expense in the initial stage to lower the overall interest expense, even if the bonds are put back. This type of bond comprises only approximately 10% of the corporate bond market, so it's not for every CFO. *See* **synthetic put bonds.**

put-call notes. See **synthetic put bonds.**

put in play. As an investor, trader, or speculator who holds the controlling interest in a corporation, to communicate to the financial community that the company is for sale to the highest bidder.

"putting together." The phrase used when brokers are looking for investors to buy or sell shares in order to make up a large block transaction, such as buyers for a secondary offering, in which case brokers are putting together the secondary.

put warrant. A warrant sold by a corporation to outside investors giving them the right, for a limited time, to sell shares back to the company at a specific price—called the "strike price"—beneath the market price at the time the warrants are bought. The advantage for the issuing company is that it can sell the puts and thereby receive cash flow not subject to income tax, since a company's dealings in its own stock are tax-free. The advantage for investors is that they can sell the stock to the company for more than the current market price, after a decline in the stock's market value. Often a company can improve its operating results by selling put warrants at the expense of future dilution in the stockholders' equity. A company's reliance on selling puts is sometimes hard to spot because the revenues from such a sale are not broken out in the income statement. However, they do appear in the Cash Flow statement. Some companies report the outstanding warrants as liabilities on the Balance Sheet, since the agreement to buy shares back is a potential liability if the market price of the company's shares falls below the strike price. *Caveat emptor!*

pyramid. See **Financial Pyramid.**

pyramiding. 1) The practice of purchasing a security at intervals, if the price is rising, to prevent commitment of total funds into a questionable security. 2) The gaining of leverage by pyramiding in a margin account; that is, the additional buying power from rises in stock bought on margin is used to buy additional stock.

pyramid scheme. See **Ponzi.**

Qq

QFR. Abbreviation for **quarterly mutual fund review.**

Q Ratio, The Tobin. A concept to describe whether the stock market is priced too high or too low developed by Professor James Tobin, economics professor emeritus at Yale University and Nobel Laureate. Briefly, the theory suggests that when prices of stocks are generally above their replacement values in terms of net assets represented, the market is overpriced and due for a drop or a period of stagnation. On the other hand, when prices are below replacement values, stock buying will be set off by bargain hunters and mergers and acquisitions strategists. This will raise prices. When stock prices are at parity with replacement values, or 1-to-1, the Q Ratio is one. When above, say 25%, the Q Ratio is 1.25. When below, say by 75%, the Q Ratio is .75.

In calculating the replacement values, only tangible resources are considered. And this is the rub! Critics of the theory say by ignoring intangibles such as brainpower, high-tech stock growth generated by research and development activities is completely eliminated from investment commitments. Big mistake!

quadratic mean. See **average, statistical.**

qualified endorsement or **restricted endorsement.** An endorsement on a check or other commercial instrument limiting the liability of the endorser or requiring a certain course of action be taken in processing the instrument. Examples are "For Deposit Only," protecting the endorser if the instrument is misappropriated and "Without Recourse," limiting the endorser's liability if the obligation of the maker is not fulfilled. *See* **endorsement.**

qualified opinion. In a company's financial statements, such as those in the annual stockholders' report, a statement by the independent auditor that certain portions of the statements do not completely reflect the financial or operating situation or that the statement is limited in scope. This opinion is not as critical as an adverse opinion, because the former indicates some possibility of a damaging event, such as losing a law suit, whereas the latter indicates the event has already occurred but is not reflected in the statements. *See* **adverse opinion.**

qualified retirement or **pension plan.** An arrangement between an employer, also called a sponsor, and employees, at least those who are eligible to participate in the plan, under which participants may choose to defer part of their salary or wages through contributions to a fund that is invested and accrued to their benefit upon retirement or severance from the employer. In order to receive certain tax benefits and be considered a "qualified" plan, it must be registered and approved by the IRS. The employees' contribution is a pretax reduction in the compensation shown on their W-2 forms. That amount is paid into the plan's fund by the company. The prededuction, or gross salary or wages, can still be considered an employee's compensation for other elements in an employer's fringe benefits package, such as vacation, life insurance, medical benefits and other pension programs.

The employee's contribution is tax-sheltered until the assets in the retirement fund are withdrawn upon retirement or when leaving the employer's service. This is advantageous in the case of retirement because that portion of career earnings is transferred to a time of life when tax rates are generally lower. An employer can also contribute to the employee's retirement fund, either matching the employee's contribution, adding a set amount or basing the contribution on a fixed percentage. As an incentive, employers receive income tax benefits for contributing. Assets in the retirement fund are placed under the management of one or more fiduciary institutions—investment firm, bank, mutual fund, insurance company—under a trust arrangement, usually.

There are three fundamental responsibilities that plan sponsors must assume: they must offer employees adequate choices of investments in their retirement funds, reflecting at least three core investment structures or programs; they must empower participants by giving them control of the assets in their accounts; and they must provide participants with the information to make informed investment decisions concerning securities included in their accounts.

qualified stock option plan. A program adopted by a company's management under which a company's stock is made available to employees at special prices and within specific periods as well as other conditions. There are two categories of qualified stock option plans: incentive stock option plans (ISOs) and employee stock purchase plans (ESPPs). Qualified plans require the receiver to pay cash up front in the transaction. Generally, but not always, they are not taxed when granted or when exercised. *See* **nonqualified stock option plan.**

quality competition. A market condition in which vendors strive to increase their market shares through offering consumers better products or services than rival establishments. Usually, this happens when products are higher priced—but not always, since price competition can still play a role in where customers purchase goods. There is a great deal of quality competition in the applied technology industries (such as audio equipment), among others. *See* **price competition** and **service competition.**

quality issue. See **investment quality stock.**

quant. A money manager, trader, or consultant who employs mathematical and statistical methods in making investment decisions. These methods usually lead to a macromanagement style, with ideas passing from the top down for individual stock and portfolio actions. The alternative is the traditional money manager who employs fundamental research methods in organizing portfolios. The latter results in a micromanagement style, with ideas passing from the bottom upward for portfolio actions. The quant looks to models for guidance, while the traditionalist looks to brokers and their company reports or in-house research and sometimes Divine Guidance. The quant is inclined to be introspective, independent, and a loner. The traditionalist is inclined to be extroverted, convivial, and a mixer. As the number and volume of securities trades proliferates, the quant is becoming more effective. This is because statistical and mathematical methods lend themselves better to large universes.

quant shop. A trading or money management firm that uses statistically and mathematically trained persons to direct the commitment of funds into stocks, bonds, options, currencies, or commodities, based on computer models. *See* **quant, inefficiencies, statistical arbitrage, neural net,** and **random walk.**

quarter (q). A period of three months into which most corporations divide their fiscal year for financial reporting.

quarterly fund review or **QFR.** A quarterly review or audit of a mutual fund's performance, in terms of its results relative to benchmark stock indexes and fund competitors, usually conducted by the Chief Executive Officer of a management company with fund managers.

quarterly report or **interim report.** A report issued by the management of a company after the close of each fiscal quarter, except the fourth quarter, which is often encapsulated in the annual report. The quarterly report includes a summary of important financial and operating information and relevant events that transpired during the period. Summary financial statements are included. However, as a document it is not as comprehensive as the annual report, tending to treat interim matters only, rather than the overview of industry conditions that the annual report usually encompasses. *See* **Form 10-Q filing.**

quasi-corporation. The legal term for a public or private enterprise having some of the characteristics of a corporation. For example, a **limited partnership** is not taxed as a corporation but assures **limited liability** to the general partners. Under certain state laws and a provision of federal tax law, a business enterprise may operate as a corporation but elect to be taxed as a partnership, thus preventing the taxing of business profits twice. *See* **"S" Corporation.**

quasi-reorganization. A business recapitalization, the focus of which is the elimination of a deficit without creating a new corporate entity. An operating deficit or a capital deficit is absorbed, and a new earned income or earned surplus account is set up. There is no court action involved. *See* **reorganization.**

"questions per day." See **dot-com stock.**

quick assets. That cash or property easily convertible into cash. Usually, this consists of current assets less inventory, plus cash and marketable securities.

Quicken online. Web site for investors providing information and news on investing, mortgages, insurance, taxes, banking, and retirement. *See* **Web Sites for the Inquiring Investor.**

quick ratio. The ratio found by dividing the **current assets** on a balance sheet by the current liabilities. This measure, when the quotient is one or greater, establishes that the company is solvent on a short-term basis. That is, the liquid assets on hand will cover the current or near-term liabilities.

"quiet period." Under federal securities law, an interval covering the period of a company's registration of its stock for an initial public offering and the actual distribution of the stock. During that period, company management and the underwriters and distributors of the stock must remain silent about the company or the stock's prospects, although there is an indication that the principals can clarify some details about the offering itself. The idea of the law is to prevent promotion of the stock by interested parties, thus allowing a new issue to settle at a consensus market price. The SEC has never issued a specific rule about how long the period should last, instead leaving the decision to attorneys for the investment bankers. But it is generally understood that the period covers an interval between the date on which the issuing company employs an underwriting investment banker until 25 days after the distribution of the **initial public offering.** Like a great deal of federal securities law, the SEC has the power to enforce the spirit of the securities laws in the United States as they pertain to not manipulating or promoting an initial public offering. Consequently, that agency has left itself room to take action on violations, regardless of the specific time covered. *See* **effective date.**

quietperiod.com. An Internet site providing hard-to-find information on companies in the so-called **"quiet period."** *See* **Web Sites for the Inquiring Investor.**

QUIPS. See **Cumulative Quarterly Income Convertible Preferred Securities.**

quote or **quotation** or **price.** The current or latest transaction price, or the current bid and asked price, of a security. 1) For listed stocks and listed closed-end investment companies, shares are now quoted in whole numbers and decimals—10.35 for $10.35—after trading in whole numbers and fractions—$10^{3}/_{8}$ for $10.37—for many years. The conversion to this decimal system is expected to be completed by the year 2002. *See* **stock table.** 2) For corporate bonds, quotes represent a percentage, usually $^{1}/_{10}$ of the value, and after converting the fraction portion to decimals should be multiplied by 10 for the entire dollar value. Thus, if a corporate bond is quoted at $90^{1}/_{4}$, and the fraction is converted to the decimal .25 and then the entire number is multiplied by 10, the quote becomes 902.50 or $902.50 (90.25 × 10). To this amount accrued interest is added, unless the bonds are trading flat. A baby bond ($100 face or par value) is quoted the same as stocks. *See* **bond table.** For U.S. Treasury bonds, prices are quoted as $^{1}/_{10}$ of the price, but the fractions are expressed as thirty-seconds of one hundred. Thus, a quote of 98.24, when the $^{24}/_{32}$ is converted to .75, represents a price of 98.75 × 10, or 987.50 or $987.50 per bond. 4) Municipal and agency bonds are quoted the same way corporate bonds are. 5) For over-the-counter securities and unlisted closed-end investment company shares, a quote includes both the bid and asked price. *See* **inside quote** and **outside quote.** 6) When mutual fund shares are quoted, the bid price represents the asset value per share and the asked price represents the asset value plus the sales load. If there is a redemption charge, rather than a sales load, the bid price represents the asset value less the redemption charge and the asked price represents the asset value. Also see **mutual fund table** and **options table.**

Rr

Raging Bull Investor Revolution Page. See under **Web Sites for the Inquiring Investor.**

raider. See **corporate raider.**

Railroad Retirement Act. A federal act of 1935 that created a social security program for railroad workers in the United States. Benefits are provided for: (1) workers who retire because of age or disability, (2) eligible spouses and divorced spouses of retired employees, (3) surviving widows, widowers, divorced spouses, children, and dependent parents of deceased employees, (4) unemployed workers, and (5) workers who are sick or injured. Among other requirements, the eligible employee must have 10 or more years of railroad service and have earned at least $2,125 in railroad wages in calendar year 1995, $2,163 in calendar year 1996, and $2,226 in calendar year 1997. A worker who does not qualify might qualify for Social Security benefits.

Railroads or **Rails.** Those stocks representing companies operating railroad transportation services to the public. *See* **industry stock group.**

rally. A rapid rise in stock market prices after a sharp decline, usually accompanied by a stirring cavalrylike bugle charge in most brokerage offices and shrieks of delight in the club room of the Beardstown Ladies. *See* **seasonal rally.**

R & D. Abbreviation for **Research and Development.**

Random Walk Theory of stock market prices. A reference to the hypothesis developed by researchers at the Graduate School of Business of the University of Chicago that stock markets efficiently value prices and that the history of a stock's price changes cannot be used in a meaningful way to predict the stock's future prices; the future direction of the price level of a stock is no more predictable than the pattern of a series of cumulative numbers. This theory, substantiated with voluminous mathematical and statistical evidence showing an independence of stock prices in relation to past price patterns and, to a lesser degree, in relation to the intrinsic value assigned a stock, has caused a controversy over the value of making investment decisions based on stock charts or intrinsic value analysis. *See* **quant.**

range, statistics. In statistics or in measuring the volatility of stock prices, the calculation of the maximum and minimum values in the dispersion, or scatter, around an average value, or central tendency of price changes, for one or more stocks. It is used in measuring the risk of selected stocks, as measured by their volatility. For the preferred measure of risk, see **standard deviation.** *See* also **average deviation, range, variance,** and **volatility.**

range, stock price. A stock's opening, high, low, and closing prices for a period. Daily ranges are often used by investors who want to enter limit orders. The historical range helps them decide at which price they can reasonably expect an advantageous limit order to be executed, because it shows the extent of the fluctuations and the market action when they occurred previously. The range is also an indicator of the volatility of stock prices. *See* **standard deviation.**

Rare Metals. Those stocks representing companies that extract, process, and develop ore that becomes a metal of enormous economic value, usually because of lightness, strength, or resistance to heat; for example, beryllium is being developed for spaceship nose cones because of its heat-resistant properties.

RASDAQ Stock Market (Romania). An electronic system for trading stocks, dealer-operated, in Romania. It is organized and operated much like the NASDAQ system in the United States. *See* under **Global Investment Market.**

rate of return. The method an investor selects to measure the cash flow or monetary gain from an investment. The Association of Research & Management (AIMR) recognizes 11 different methodologies, depending on the circumstances. For individual investments, that association recommends the internal rate of return. *See* **internal rate of return.**

rated. A word followed by letters and/or numerals indicating certain securities, usually bonds, have been appraised for investment merit by an investment service. This rating is based on a scale designating the quality of the securities. In the case of bonds, ratings are based on the ability of the issuer to pay interest when due and set aside amounts periodically, in cases of sinking fund bonds, that will protect the principal and enable the issuer to retire the bonds on time.

Ratings on preferred stocks are similar to bonds, substituting preferred dividend for interest payments. Common stock ratings emphasize growth and stability of earnings and dividends. The basic difference between bond ratings and common stock ratings is that a bond rating keys on credit worthiness, while a common stock rating emphasizes earnings growth and stability. An aphorism of investment management is that one should look for reasons *against* buying a bond but look for reasons *for* buying a common stock. These ratings are especially useful to institutional investors who must be certain of the quality of securities they buy or on which they lend money. Moody's Investors Service, Dun & Bradstreet, Fitch Publishing Co., Duff & Phelps, and Standard & Poor's Corporation plus others rate securities. Below is the Standard & Poor's rating scale for common stocks and corporate bonds.

STANDARD & POOR'S COMMON STOCK RATINGS	
Rating	**Characteristics**
A+	Highest
A	High
A–	Above Average
B+	Average
B	Below Average
B–	Lower
C	Lowest
D	In Reorganization
r	Derivative or hybrid/ highly volatile

S & P Corporate Bond Ratings

Rating	Characteristics
AAA	highest grade/safety of principal and interest/interest rate sensitive
AA	high grade/safety of principal and interest/interest rate sensitive
A	upper medium grade/considerable safety but vulnerable to economic and trade conditions/prices sensitive to interest rates and economic conditions
BBB	borderline between sound and speculative/adequate asset coverage and earning power/susceptible to changing conditions/more sensitive to business conditions than interest rates
BB	lower medium grade/interest narrowly earned in business downturns/deficits possible
B	speculative/interest cannot be assured under difficult economic conditions
CCC	speculative/interest payments questionable
CC	highly vulnerable to non-payment
C	income bonds on which no interest is being paid
D	default bonds

Note: Plus (+) or minus (–) may modify ratings AA through CCC to show relative standings within major category.

Under commercial bank regulations, bonds rated in the top four categories are generally regarded eligible for bank investment. Most services rate bonds under a plan that assigns the first four letters of the alphabet and numbers, in various combinations. Ratings have become very important in the age of electronic information, because there is less time for investors to closely examine each bond decision.

ratio. The relationship of two meaningful business figures, expressed as one to the other or as a fraction, quotient, or percentage, and used to measure a company's current and past business achievements. There are three basic types of ratios: (1) profitability ratios, or those measuring how efficiently and profitably a business is operated; (2) liquidity ratios, or those measuring how well the business can meet its financial obligations; and (3) leverage ratios, or those measuring how much risk is present in the business or capital structure. For example, if current assets are $15,000,000 and current liabilities $10,000,000, the current ratio is 3-to-2, 3/2, 1.5 or 150% ($15,000,000/$10,000,000). Broadly speaking, this indicates that for every $1 of short-term liabilities, there is $1.50 of short-term assets to keep the business solvent. As you might have guessed, this is a liquidity ratio. If a year ago the ratio was 1-to-1, then this aspect of business solvency has improved.

Ratios are also useful in analyzing various companies in the same industry by comparing ratios representing their respective operating efficiencies, capitalizations, asset strengths, and so on. Usually, the figures needed in constructing significant ratios appear on company balance sheets, cash flow statements, equity statements, or income statements.

Another use for ratios is found in estimating future performance for companies. By calculating averages of current and past measures, some idea can be gleaned of future performances, given some assumptions about revenues or capital infusions. For example, Hungry Bull, Inc. arranges to issue one million shares of common stock at $10 per share to the public, or $9.50 per share to the company after underwriting and offering expenses are deducted. That is an equity capital infusion of $9.5 million. Over the past 10 years, the company has reported a 15% average return on equity, with no sharp deviations from that average. It would be reasonable to assume, therefore, that the return starting the year after the infusion would produce income of $1.4 million before taxes (15% of $9.5 million). Of course, when carrying the incremental earnings produced by the capital infusion to the per-share level, the million additional shares outstanding would need to be factored in, in order to detect any possible dilution of earnings resulting from the new financing. *See* **Marginal Return on Equity.**

For information on other key financial and operating ratios, *See* **acid test, accounts receivable turnover, book value per share—common, cash flow ratio, combined or overall coverage, common stock ratio, current ratio or working capital ratio, dividend coverage, dividend pay-out, dividend return or dividend yield, dividends per share—common, earnings per share—common, earnings per share—preferred, equity**

ratio, fixed charge coverage, interest coverage, inventory
turnover, liquidity ratio, long-term debt ratio, net income to
net worth, net working capital per share, operating ratio,
preferred stock ratio, pretax profit margin, Price/Earnings
Ratio (P/E), profit margin—gross, profit margin—net, quick
ratio, return on invested capital, sales to fixed assets, sales to
inventories, and working capital turnover.

reacquired stock. See **company stock purchases.**

reaction. A sudden downturn of a stock's price after demand has
bid the price up sharply, usually caused by profit taking; or vice
versa, in which case it is a sudden upturn after oversupply has
depressed the price to a point where bargain hunters start buying.

real dollars or **inflation-adjusted dollars.** In reporting an economic or business time series, such as the Gross Domestic
Product (GDP) or Corporate Earnings over a span of months,
quarters, or years, the adjustment of the actual values for those
periods to reflect the effects of inflation or deflation (rarely
occurs) on the actual values or on the comparative buying power
of the original values, compared to some base period in the past.
Usually, the adjustment is accomplished by dividing the actual
values by an index of price change since the base period. For
example, if prices double over a 10-year period, what are $50
billion in corporate profits worth in capital expenditures or rein-
vesting? Prices are 200% of their level 10 years ago, or the index
is 2.00. Dividing $50 billion by 2.0 gives a quotient of $25 billion—the current value of corporate profits, expressed in the
buying power 10 years ago. Another use in adjusting a series to
real dollars is that it creates the ability to estimate the change in
physical output, since the difference due to price change has
been removed. When a series is not adjusted for the effects of
price changes, it is stated in current dollars or nominal dollars.

real estate or **real property.** A reference to land, including
improvements such as buildings on it.

real estate investment trust (REIT). A company organized to
pool investors' funds and buy, develop, and sell real estate, operating under a revision in the federal income tax laws of 1960,

which allows tax exemption on 95% of investment income if it is distributed to the owners. There must be 100 or more owners. There are approximately 300 publicly traded REITs in the United States, which generally specialize in hotels, malls, nursing homes, offices, or apartments. These trusts are restricted to income from sources such as mortgage lending and leasing their properties. Also, they can operate passive real estate ventures, such as office buildings and apartments, but not more active ventures, such as casinos, hotels or race tracks. Although a REIT can own such properties, it must lease them to a non-REIT entity to manage.

real estate mortgages. Those mortgages secured by liens or titles to land or buildings.

real income. The actual goods and services that can be bought with income received during a period, usually expressed as a percentage of buying power during a base period.

realizing a profit. 1) The actual receipt of money from the sale of personal or real property that is in excess of that property's cost. 2) Taking in revenues by providing a product or service in excess of the costs of operations during a fiscal period.

reallowance. The amount of money per share that is deducted from the profit established for a member of an underwriting or selling group if that member sells shares in a current under-writing to a dealer, rather than the public.

real property. See **real estate.**

real wealth. An economic term meaning the ability to produce a flow of goods or services, without using up something else of value. This can be accomplished by increases in labor or capital productivity. It is not the result of switching money from spending to investment but rather the consequence of getting more out of the same capital resources in generating the same level of market wealth or the exchange value of a certain output.

recapitalization. An agreement by stockholders, bondholders, and creditors of a corporation to surrender their claims. A new corporation is created, usually under bankruptcy laws, to settle the general debts and carry on business.

recapture. In the U.S. Tax Code, the restoration to the IRS of taxes that were previously avoided through amortization charges against an asset that is later resold at a gain. This situation most often arises when a taxpayer takes amortization charges such as accelerated depreciation against a resource over one or more tax periods, fully depreciating or depleting the asset. In the event that the taxpayer then sells the asset for an amount greater than the assumed residual value or scrap value, the IRS would want to recapture or reclaim the depreciation charge and tax it as ordinary income, since it was really not an expense at all. The amount realized in excess of the recaptured charge would be taxed at capital gain rates. Another situation where this deferred tax collection is likely to occur is in the case of a tax credit taken on a gain that exceeded the credit taken.

receiver. An independent person appointed by a court to take charge of a business, receive funds, pay expenses, and so on, usually in cases of bankruptcy.

receiver's certificates. Certificates of indebtedness with first lien on the earnings of an enterprise, issued to raise money for the operation of an insolvent enterprise by a court-appointed receiver.

recession. A gradual decline in business activity—shorter and less severe than a depression. Technically, a recession is defined as a decrease in Gross National Product for two consecutive quarters or more. It is referred to as a contraction in the business cycle, versus expansion, and represents declining general business activity. The National Bureau of Economic Research delineates business cycle periods. Historically, in the United States contractions have lasted 11 months, expansions 50 months.

reclamation. The repossession from an investment house of securities delivered in error for delivery on a sale.

reclassification of stock. An adjustment in the number of issued stock shares to reflect changes in par value, authorized shares, or other corporate changes, usually involving an exchange of stock by shareholders.

recommended list. Those securities recommended for purchase by an investment firm, usually published with current P/E multiples, expectations for earnings growth, dividends, and future prices as well as other information about securities included. *See* **"buy," "hold,"** and **"sell."**

record date or **Date of Record.** The date on which an investor must legally own units of a security issue in order to be entitled to items such as a declared dividend, stock split, or special distribution. It is the date on which a stockholder or bondholder must be listed in the corporate register to receive forthcoming distributions or privileges. On the trading tape, the Latin word *cum* followed by the action indicates when transactions are made that include the item.

recourse paper. Those promissory notes that the present holder may collect on from the original creditor in the event of default by the debtor, even though the present holder bought the notes.

recovery. A market or single stock's return to a prior price level after a decline.

rectangle. A price pattern made by recorded high-low-close bars on a stock bar chart or Xs and Os on a point-and-figure chart. Chartists maintain that the long period of restricted price fluctuations indicates that important news about the stock or the market in general must precede a breakout. In other words, it's stuck and needs something to happen to motivate investors one way or the other.

recurring income. In financial reporting by a company, income that occurs from its normal operations and is likely to be repeated in future fiscal periods. It excludes one-time transactions, such as securities gains, increment in pension assets, or reduced depreciation charges, even though the latter may be perfectly legal and fall within acceptable accounting standards. However, such nonrecurring items can enhance the company's net worth or stockholders' equity. Investors should be careful to include only recurring or repetitive earnings as part of the company's long-term growth trend, since they are predictable and, therefore, most suitable for stock valuation models. *See* **extraordinary items** and **non-recurring items.**

red chip. 1) A speculative stock in a company that has recently moved to a strong financial position with possibilities of achieving a dominant position in its industry. This is the second step in becoming a blue chip stock. For the first step, see white chip. 2) A stock of a company in mainland China that is often partly government-owned, trading on the Hong Kong Stock Exchange.

redemption. 1) The buying back of an obligation by a debtor by paying its value or a prearranged amount to the creditor. 2) The liquidation of mutual fund shares. Sometimes a fee is deducted from a shareholder's cash value when he liquidates his shares. Generally, mutual funds with redemption charges have no sales load.

"Red hell." An expression referring to the chaotic financial situation in the late 1990s in Russia, in which there occurred run-away-inflation, huge deficits, and the constant threat of currency devaluation (ruble). This was accompanied by government instability. The reference derived from the feeling experienced by investors holding Russian securities, not knowing whether or how much they would be repaid. The meltdown occurred simultaneously with the **"Asian flu,"** although from different causes. However, ultimately the economic problems in any region will affect those close by, and many far away.

"red herring" or **preliminary prospectus.** A prospectus issued while a security issue is in the process of Securities and Exchange Commission registration, subject to change and not containing the offering price of the security, underwriter fees, concessions, and so on. It is not legally an offer to sell but can be used to appraise investor interest. *See* **prospectus** and **underwriting agreement.**

rediscount. To make a discount loan using a note that has already been discounted once as collateral. *See* **discount (5).**

refinancing. See **refunding.**

reflation. A condition in a country or region whereby, after a sharp contraction of economic activity, accompanied by falling commodity prices and industrial output, there is a coordinated effort to halt falling prices through investment and expanded output, in order to resume growth. Usually, government's monetary powers are used to increase the supply of money in the initial stages. So that no harm is done by the inflationary effort, wages and prices are increased in tandem.

refundable. A reference to an agreement enabling a debtor to refund bonds. *See* **refunding.**

refunding or **refinancing.** 1) The prolonging of a debt, such as bonds represent, by exchange. One way to accomplish this would be by substituting new bonds for older ones before or at the maturity of the older ones. 2) The paying off of holders of old bonds before or at their maturity with funds received from the sale of new bonds. The debtor's purpose before maturity is usually to sell the new bonds at a lower interest rate than the old ones bear, thus reducing borrowing expenses.

regional exchange. A securities exchange whose members are mostly in a locale rather than distributed over the country. Geographically speaking, all stock exchanges but the New York Stock Exchange and the American Stock Exchange are regional, even though several are called "national" because of registration with the Securities and Exchange Commission and national and international trading arrangements. *See* **national securities exchanges (1).**

"registered as to principal only." A phrase meaning that any holder of certain bonds may collect interest by presenting the attached coupons, but only the registered owner can collect the principal.

registered bonds. Those bonds whose owners are registered in the issuer's books and on the bond. Registration is a safeguard against loss but it also slows down liquidity. The interest and principal when due are paid to the registered owner, to whom interest is sent. These bonds must be endorsed when transferred.

registered exchange. A securities exchange doing interstate business whose members and securities traded are registered with the Securities and Exchange Commission. There are presently 12 registered exchanges in the United States.

registered representative. 1) An associate of an investment firm who is authorized by an exchange to transact business in its listed securities. 2) An associate of an investment firm who is registered with the National Association of Security Dealers.

registered secondary. A secondary offering of a stock required to be registered with the Securities and Exchange Commission before it is sold to the public. If the total value of the stock offered for sale is $100,000 or more, registration with the Securities and Exchange Commission is required. *See* **registration.**

registered securities. 1) Securities that are registered with the Securities and Exchange Commission, disclosing financial structure and capital strength of the issuing companies. All corporations whose stocks are listed on national exchanges are required to register with the Securities and Exchange Commission, as are companies whose stocks represent capitalization of $2,000,000 or more and are traded in the over-the-counter market. 2) *See* **listed stocks.**

registered trader. A member of a national stock exchange registered with the Securities and Exchange Commission who buys and sells stock for his personal account. A registered trader is required to aid in the stabilization of market prices.

registrar. An officer or agent of a corporation named to keep a record of its securities and to certify that each certificate holder is bona fide. The registrar acts as an auditor of the transfer agent.

registration. The furnishing of financial information to the Securities and Exchange Commission before a new stock issue, in order that the regulatory body can ascertain that all pertinent information is available in the prospectus to a prospective investor. The information is made available by the issuing corporation and is usually prepared and submitted by an investment underwriter. Registration is required of new stock issues in companies capitalized at $300,000 or over, with fewer than 500 stockholders or less than 1 million in gross assets and which will be sold through the mails or interstate commerce. However, exemption to registration is granted public offerings by persons other than issuers, underwriters, or dealers. But an issuer includes a person in control of the corporation when an underwriter aids in a distribution. Also, private offerings are exempt from registration. In determining whether an offering is public or private, the following tests apply: (1) number of offerees and their relationships to each other and to the issuer, (2) number of units offered, (3) size of the offering, and (4) manner of the offering. *See* **multi-jurisdictional disclosure system.**

regression analysis. A statistical method of testing for a mathematical relationship between two or more variables with the objective of explaining the value of one, the dependent variable, in terms of one or more of the others, the independent variable or variables. Basically, the regression equation establishes whether or not the changes in the dependent variable can be explained by the changes in one or more independent variables. If affirmative, the equation can be used to predict changes in the dependent variable, predicated on changes in the independent ones. The testing is performed by analyzing changes over a meaningful period in the past, or "regressing" the variables. Then assumptions are made about what to expect in the future. As an application to investment or securities analysis, its main use is in forecasting some business activity or financial performance.

For example, an investor might wish to use a good regression to predict the value of an oil company's revenues from expected changes in automobiles registered, in the case of a simple regression calculation, or from expected changes in auto registrations, airline passenger miles, and transport truck traffic, in the case of a multiple regression. When the relationship between the dependent and independent variables is based on arithmetic changes over time it is called a linear regression; if it is based on geometric or power changes over time, so that changes between the variables are disproportionate but still related, it is called a curvilinear or nonlinear regression. A regression test based on more than one independent variable is called a multiple regression. *See* **forecasting.**

regressive tax. 1) A tax program that is based on reducing the percentage of tax as the tax base or property value increases. For example, if the county tax assessor levies a tax of 5% on property valued at $10,000 to $15,999, 3.5% on property valued at $16,000 to $25,000, and 3% above $25,000, it would be called regressive. 2) A tax program that falls heaviest on lower income taxpayers by taxing items for which they spend proportionately more of their income at the same rate as higher income earners pay. A flat tax, including the income tax and property tax varieties, is regressive in this context. This characteristic of the flat income tax is the most effective argument used against adopting it in the United States.

regular way transaction. A reference to the settlement of a securities trade in the normal time interval, four business days after the transaction on the New York Stock Exchange, which usually applies to over-the-counter trades also.

regulated investment company. An investment company that is supervised by state and federal agencies, and has elected to distribute at least 90% of dividend income each year to avoid its own tax liability.

Regulation A, Fed. The policy adopted by the Federal Reserve System outlining the procedures by which it will make loans to member banks and others, in the practice called using the discount window. *See* **discount rate, Fed,** and **discount window.**

Regulation A, SEC. The SEC procedures for registering securities issued by small corporations—recently set at $1.5 million in assets—for public distribution. Generally, it is much simpler to register these securities than ones representing larger issuers. Securities issued under these guidelines are allowed to distribute a shorter prospectus. In addition, officers and directors are less vulnerable for misleading and defrauding investors.

Regulation D, Fed. The basis for the Federal Reserve Bank's control of the ratio of reserves to deposits that member banks must maintain. The Fed is a fractional reserve system, so that the ratio is one of the tools that can be used to control money in circulation, or the money supply, through influencing the level of lending funds in the system, in effect. The ratio usually centers around 15%.

Regulation D, SEC. The SEC procedures dealing with privately placed securities, and how they can be traded in public markets. Also, this regulation takes up some concepts of who can participate in private placements.

Regulation S, SEC. A rule that exempts a company that sells securities in foreign countries from the requirement to register them with the SEC as long as the buyers agree not to sell them in an American market for a period of 40 days. This period could be extended to one year, under a recent proposal.

Regulation S-P, SEC. A rule, required by the Gramm-Leach-Bliley Act of 2000, that governs the use and protection of non-public confidential, personal information by brokers, dealers, and investment companies, as well as investment advisors registered with the SEC. It restricts the dissemination of such information to third parties. In general, such a financial firm must provide notice of its privacy policies and practices in a "clear and conspicuous manner." The notice must be provided to: (1) consumers, before a firm discloses any non-public personal information to a non-affiliated third party; and (2) customers at the time that relationship is established. The distinction between consumers and customers under the act is that a consumer obtains a financial product or service that is to be used primarily for personal, family, or household purposes, while a customer intends a continuing relationship with a firm for providing financial products or services. Although the SEC is only concerned with the act in connection with investment firms, the law also applies to banks disseminating non-public personal information.

Regulation T, Fed. A portion of the Federal Reserve Board's securities credit document that controls investment firm credit to customers for securities purchases. *See* **margin.**

Regulation U, Fed. A portion of the Federal Reserve Board's Securities credit document limiting commercial bank loans for purchases of securities. The regulation prohibits a bank from allowing a customer to borrow money secured by stocks and using a portion of that money that exceeds the legal credit allowable on listed stock purchases in buying additional listed stocks. For example, let's say a bank's customer borrows $800 on stocks valued at $1,000, and the legal credit limit established by the Federal Reserve Board in buying listed securities is 30% of market value; the customer can be required to sign a statement saying he or she will not use more than $300 (30%) to buy listed stock.

Regulation Z, Fed. A reference to the applications of the Credit Consumer Protection Act of 1968 that the FED participates in.

rehypothecation. See **margin agreement.**

reinvest funds. Those securities proceeds available for the purchase of other securities, for example, money received from a maturing bond used to buy another bond.

REIT. See **real estate investment trust.**

rejected bid. A refusal by a perspective bond issuer to accept an offer on his bonds made by one or more underwriters. See **bid (2).**

relative market action. A measure of a change in a stock's price or a stock group's price in relation to a broad price index, in order to compare the isolated price action to that of the general market. Here's an illustration. Flour Power Tortillas Corp. climbed from $10 per share in 1990 to $89 in 1998, a compounded annual growth rate of 27.5%. During the same period, a popular stock index rose from 500 to 1,480, a compounded annual growth rate of 12.8%. The differential of 14.7% (27.5 − 12.8) reflects the appreciation potential of a dynamic stock, compared to stocks on average. For a more vivid comparison, many analysts show the differentials on a graph.

relative value. In securities analysis, the concentration on how a stock compares to others in categories such as price/earnings multiples, dividend yield, return on equity, return on capital, growth rate, and other performance measures, in selecting the most attractive stocks to buy or sell. In other words, if RamJet, Inc. earnings are compounding at 25% per year and the stock is selling for 10 times earnings, while It's Superman! Inc. earnings are compounding at 20% annually but the stock is selling for 25 times earnings, RamJet would be selected as the better buy, based on relative P/E multiples. The caveat in relying on this investment method is that some stock is always a good buy, even though all stocks might be overvalued and due for a correction. *See* **intrinsic value.**

released. See **released from registration.**

released from registration or **released.** The authorization by the SEC for a registered security issue to be sold to the public. This is not an endorsement of the securities but only an expression that complete financial information is available to the investor in the prospectus.

remanufacturing. Designing and making the components of a product so that they can be reused by the original manufacturer in turning out a new like product. This process differs from recycling in that in the latter the used product is destroyed or sent to a land fill after reusable parts are removed and sold at discounts, often by independent manufacturers, whereas in remanufacturing the components are refurbished and reinstalled in the products for resale at regular prices. The technique is gaining popularity among original equipment manufacturers, because it is more cost effective and reduces environmental damage. For the latter reason, the Environmental Protection Agency supports the trend.

renting-a-fund-manager. See **subadvising.**

"reoffered at." See **"offered at."**

reoffering. The reselling of securities to the public by an underwriter after buying them from a corporation, municipality, or a group of stockholders. Stocks are reoffered at dollar amounts, whereas bonds are reoffered at basis prices, which can be converted to dollars with a bond basis book. *See* **offering, underwrite,** and **bond basis.**

reorganization. A retirement of outstanding securities in a corporation and their replacement by new ones, resulting in a significant change in the rights and interests of securities holders. Often, this is accompanied by a change in management and/or a change in business policies or objectives. It can occur in a merger, recapitalization, or consolidation. *See* **quasi-reorganization.**

reorganization and divestment. See **divisive reorganization.**

replacement cost or **replacement value.** The amount of money required to replace a company asset with one of equal or like performance capability at current prices. This concept is used when the historical cost—the traditional accounting valuation technique—is considered insufficient to estimate the replacement value. Differentials between historical cost and replacement cost can arise because of an asset's technological obsolescence or a rise in its price.

replacement cost accounting. The practice of estimating and accounting for the outlay required to replace an asset with another of equal or like performance at current price levels and technological advances. It is accomplished by charging supplementary depreciation or depletion expenses against revenues, thus building up the accounting reserve to replace the asset.

replacement cost insurance. A casualty or property insurance policy that replaces damaged or destroyed property with no deductions for depreciation, so that the insured is usually assured of new total or partial resources that can perform similarly to those damaged or lost, within the monetary limits set by the declarations of the contract. The alternative is to set out specific reimbursement values for the resources.

replacement of capital. The allowing for depreciation and/or depletion of a company's assets by withholding from earnings enough to replace the assets at regular intervals.

report. A reply to a broker from an exchange upon an order's execution, giving the exact selling or buying price.

report form of balance sheet. See **balance sheet.**

Report Gallery—Online Library of Financial Reports. See **Web Sites for the Inquiring Investor.**

repricing, stock options. As a corporate board of directors, to lower the exercise price at which executives can buy stock in the corporation that employs them, usually because shares have dropped in price and the options are not currently as valuable. Another way to adjust the value of the options is to extend the period at the exercise price. Either way, other stockholders are likely to get riled by this generosity, especially when sub-par management performance of those same executives has caused the stock's unpopularity and price atrophy. In order to enforce openness in financial reporting, the FASB is considering the requirement that when a company reprices options, it treats as an operating expense the difference between the new lower price and a subsequent rise in the share price. *See* **"under water."**

Research and Development (R & D). That portion of corporate disbursements used for improving and discovering marketable products. Companies that stress growth need to maintain these expenditures under the assumption new products and services will create new markets and allow for greater penetration of older markets. However, payoffs from the expenditures must be high to amortize the high costs of products generated, sometimes requiring a period of several years. Usually, R&D expenditures are not expensed on the income statement. Instead, they are accumulated in capital accounts until they begin producing revenues, at which time amortization charges begin, thus lowering income.

Sometimes the R&D expenditures are reported in the annual reports, in special sections or in the notes. This concentration of charges is the main reason that the payoff from R&D must be high. The stock market takes a neutral stance on the value of these outlays. In a study at the University of Illinois at Urbana-Champaign, for each year from 1975 to 1995, the authors divided stocks into those that reported R&D outlays and those that did not. Then they checked each stock's performance for the ensuing three years. The return on the companies reporting R&D was 19.7%, while for those that did not, it was 19.5%. In industries where there is significant R&D spending—say software for computers, it can amount to 15% to 20% of a company's total sales.

Research in Process. In a transaction in which a company pays more than book value for an acquisition, that portion of the excess that is attributed to research and development efforts on products not yet marketable. *See* **Goodwill.**

reserve requirements. The fraction of a commercial bank's deposits that it must withhold from loans or investments to maintain a protective reserve. This is determined by federal agencies or state laws.

reserves. The systematic setting aside of funds in advance to meet property value decreases, expected losses, and other liabilities. Money is transferred from surplus or undistributed profits to various reserve accounts such as contingency reserve, debt reduction reserve, depletion reserve, depreciation reserve, valuation reserve, and so on. When the actual decrease is recorded, it only affects the reserve account rather than the income stream.

reset, to. In the terms of a convertible bond issue, the inclusion of a provision that promises to investors that the conversion price will be renegotiated within a certain period, usually one to two years after the issuing date of the bonds, in the event the market price of the issuing company's stock drops from its price on the issuing date of the bonds. This is an unusual provision, generally included when the issuing company's credit rating is in the speculative category—"C" ratings, by the rating agencies—and/or the stock is considered fully valued or overpriced. It is an inducement to investors who otherwise might shun straight debt or equity or even a regular convertible bond issue. For example, NOZAMA.com Internet Books, Inc. stock is priced at $100 per share. The company has never reported earnings, although revenues are rapidly expanding. The company wants to raise $500 million in new capital, but does not want to create an oversupply of its stock, which might push share values down. In consultation with its investment banker, management elects to issue 500,000 convertible debentures, each convertible into common stock at $100 per share or 10 shares per debenture, beginning in three years. In the event the price drops to $75 per share from one to two years after issuance, the reset provision will trigger a renegotiation between NOZAMA.com and investors, presumably leading to the conversion price decreasing to $75 per share or 13.3 shares per debenture. In this manner, the investor receives interest income, providing the company covers the debt service requirements, and a protected equity participation in future growth. *See* **convertible debenture.**

residual security. A security that entitles the holder to ownership of common stock through exercise of some privilege. Convertible debentures, convertible preferred stocks, warrants, and debentures with warrants attached are examples.

resistance area. A level that stock averages or an individual security price has moved to, but not through, in the past. When that level is above the current averages or price, it is known as a ceiling or supply area, because the large quantities of stock offered for sale will form a barrier to higher prices. Two failures to penetrate the area constitute a double top, and three, a triple top.

The chief reason this price level is an obstacle to rising prices is that sometime in the past investors bought heavily at this point, anticipating a further rise. Instead, buying and prices tapered off, and those disillusioned investors are waiting for prices to return to that level so they can sell, recouping their money. Below current prices, a support area is often formed because investors feel prices will not decline through that point, either for reasons based on past market performance or because at that point the yield and/or earnings are so attractive a wave of buying will halt the downturn.

Broadly speaking, a resistance area is any price level that will most likely halt a market direction, temporarily. When a price breaks through a resistance area, it is often a record high or low. Chartists pay particular attention to these areas, for if they see volume increasing each time prices approach the level, a breakthrough is indicated. When the level is below it is called a support, demand, or buy area because the large numbers of buyers will halt the downturn. Two failures to penetrate the area constitute a double bottom and three, a triple bottom. *See* **price patterns.**

resolution. The passage of a piece of business or policy by a corporation's directors and/or stockholders under its charter and bylaws.

restatement of results. Reporting of previously reported financial results adjusted for changes that more accurately explain corporate operations. Usually a restatement goes back five years in order to present a long-term perspective to the changes.

Restaurants. Those stocks representing companies operating public eateries. *See* **industry stock group.**

restricted account. See under **margined account.**

restricted endorsement. See **qualified endorsement.**

restricted list. A list of securities and dealers guilty of questionable or unethical business practices, according to the Securities and Exchange Commission.

restricted shares or **restricted stock.** That corporate stock with limitations either as to its issuance or use after issuance To the regret of many employees, certain stock issued under employee option plans is restricted as to when it can be sold or how it can be used after issue, or in some other way.

retail industries. See **sector.**

Retail Sales Report. A report issued mid-month by the Bureau of the Census of the Department of Commerce, considered important by economists and analysts because in a modified form, excluding services and automobiles, it represents approximately 40% of GNP. However, there are drawbacks such as services are omitted, prices are real rather than adjusted for inflation, and the series is very volatile. Approximately 65% of retail sales are non-durable goods, while 35% are durable in the data collected from a random sampling of retail establishments, including automotive. When the report signals an upturn, fixed income securities tend to decrease in value, common stock prices rise and dollar exchange rates are little affected. When the report is lower, fixed income securities tend to appreciate, common stocks decline and the effect on dollar exchange rates is minimal.

Retail Stores—Composite. Those stocks representing companies engaged in general retailing operations. *See* **industry stock group.**

Retail Stores—Department. Those stocks representing companies engaged in department store operations. *See* **industry stock group.**

Retail Stores—Drugs. Those stocks representing companies engaged in drug store operations. *See* **industry stock group.**

Retail Stores—Food. Those stocks representing companies engaged in grocery store operations. *See* **industry stock group.**

Retail Stores—General merchandise. Those stocks representing companies engaged in broad and discounted merchandise operations. *See* **industry stock group.**

Retail Stores—Specialty Apparel. Those stocks representing companies engaged in merchandising specialty clothes. *See* **industry stock group.**

Retail Stores—Specialty. Those stocks representing companies merchandising special categories of products. *See* **industry stock group.**

retained earnings. That portion of earnings cumulatively retained after the board of directors declares dividends or elects not to declare them, usually accumulated by a company for reinvestment purposes and reported in the financial statements.

retirement, asset. The removal of a fixed asset from service by a company, either because it has completed its useful life or it is has been sold. Adjustments are required to the asset and the depreciation reserve accounts.

retirement, debt. Paying off the principal of a bond or shorter term debt to the holder, or legal owner in the case of registered bonds, at maturity or regularly through installment payments to a retirement fund called a sinking fund.

retirement, stock. The cancellation of shares reacquired by a corporation. They are not reissuable.

retirement account. A program of regular money contributions by a worker, employer, or self-employed person, usually administered by a financial or investment institution, designed to provide funds for living expenses and savings after the worker retires. *See* **individual retirement account** and **401(k) plan.**

retirement planning or **estate planning.** Although there are differences, the distinctions between retirement and estate planning are dimming with the increased applications of professional skills such as law, taxation, financial analysis, accounting, and financial management to effect successful financial planning for greater numbers of people. This is the result of a public awareness in the United States of the impending inadequacies of the Social Security System, in view of the extraordinarily large age group called Baby Boomers who will begin retiring in the early part of the 21st century. Tax breaks by the federal government and employee perks by employers have accentuated the emphasis among workers on adequate financial resources for the future.

Technically, retirement planning is a process designed to systematically save, insure, and invest during one's productive years, in order to live comfortably after retirement. Estate planning is the preservation of the economic resources at one's disposal and distribution of them in a predetermined way during a lifetime or upon death. As similar professional skills and services come to bear on each function, the end result is the joining of the strategies engendered by the accumulation and management of economic resources during retirement planning and the preservation and enhancement of them during estate planning. In either case, the underlying thesis is to maximize, through the use of law, taxation, and financial management, the resources on which one will retire and pass on resources to heirs.

The sections below provide frameworks for developing a basic planning tool for retirement planning and estate planning. During the processes, insurance serves as an umbrella of protection for income producers or assets. It is important to plan systematically, otherwise the result could be an abortive effort at either retirement planning or estate planning. *See* **Pension Plan.**

I. *Net Worth.* The important point in calculating your net worth or estate is that the assets and liabilities should be appraised and listed at their current market values, or discounted present values in the case of assets not yet matured, rather than their original costs. The formula for estimating net worth is: Assets minus Liabilities equals Net Worth. List your assets, then subtract liabilities to get net worth. Hopefully, assets are greater than liabilities and increasing that excess, providing a growing, positive net worth. At the very least, your plan should be moving in a positive direction. By updating the analysis regularly, say at the end of each year, a planner becomes aware early on of imbalances or deficiencies and can adopt the financial strategies necessary to adjust in the accumulation of retirement resources. In the interim, insurance should be used to protect the income producer and the resources in the ongoing process.

II. *Retirement Planning.* This tool is basically an analysis of your cash flow needs or desires during working years and leading into retirement years, and the adequacy of your expanding retirement resources or estate to provide them. Like the net worth analysis, this tool should be used regularly during working or accumulation years and continued during retirement years. In establishing this procedure, you can anticipate cash needs during retirement years early and implement the financial changes required to accomplish those goals. It is important that you are moving in the direction of living within your means as you fashion ideas about how you want to live and where you want to live during retirement. Ideally, a retiree should strive for a positive cash flow from working and/or investment income before retirement and investment and pension income afterwards. Remember, planning is a large part of accomplishing any financial result. In estimating expenses and cash flow items, it is better to forecast on the conservative side. That is, lower cash sources and raise cash outflows slightly when estimating, especially when in doubt about the future.

retirement or **estate planning Web sites.** The table below gives several Web sites that assist in retirement planning.

RETIREMENT PLANNING HELP ON THE INTERNET

Web Site	Web Host	Contents
www.aarp.org/programs/retire	American Association of Retired Persons (AARP)	General retirement planning help.
www.asec.org/bpk-comp.htm	American Savings Education Council	Simple, fast ballpark worksheet estimates of savings needs.
www.CFP-Board.org	Certified Financial Planner Board of Standards	General advice, brochures and name of CFP in your area.
www.dtonline.com	Deloitte & Touche Accounting	Internal search engine finds articles and other information.
www.metlife.com	Met Life & Snoopy	Retirement planning primer.
www.nasd.com/it5c.html	National Association of Securities Dealers (NASD)	Worksheet for estimating savings needs to fill gap in pension savings.
www.pueblo.gsa.gov	Consumer Information Center of U.S. General Services Administration	See "Money" section for help with retirement planning.
www.asec.org	American Savings Education Council and securities dealers	Help with ballpark estimates on cash you will need each year in retirement.
www.ssa.gov	Social Security Administration	Guideline for Social Security and earnings and benefits estimates statements.

retrospective yield. The average annual yield of a stock, considering the dividends or income and the market appreciation from the time of purchase to sale. This measure of yield can only be calculated after the stock is sold.

By way of example, suppose a share of preferred stock cost $100, its annual dividend is $5 and the annual appreciation of the stock is $2 over five years. Substituting in the formula develops a retrospective yield of 4.8%: (($5 ÷ $100) + ($5 ÷ $108)) ÷ 2. The calculation actually measures the mean of the yield from the dividend based on the original cost of the stock and the lesser yield from the same dividend based on more money invested.

return. 1) Technically, the annual income from an investment. *See* **yield.** 2) In popular usage, the amount of money an investor receives from an asset over its investment cost. For example, "The real estate returned $5,000 in rent and resale over what it cost." 3) In corporate jargon, the profits from sales or revenues. *See* **expected return.**

return of capital or **nontaxable dividend** or **liquidating dividend.** A dividend, or portion of one, which under IRS interpretation is not subject to a federal income tax because: (1) it represents earnings accumulated before March 1, 1913, (2) it represents a payback of savings or deposits, (3) it represents a sale of corporate assets that has diluted the stockholder's equity and is a return of part of the money they invested. If a profit was made on the sale, generally it is taxable, but each case can vary and a corporation usually labels such a dividend nontaxable.

return-on-equity. *See* **net income to net worth.**

return on invested capital. The net income plus fixed charges (interest, rentals, and so on) divided by par value of bonds and preferred stock, common stock stated values, and surplus or retained earnings accounts. This percentage reflects operating and capitalization efficiency, or how well management has done with the capital invested. For all industries in the United States, the median return on capital was 11.4% over a recent five-year period, with the range 4.6% for the metal industry and 17.3% for the health industry

revenue bonds. Those bonds sold by a municipality or government agency to raise money for building a project that will apparently earn enough money to pay the bond interest and principal when due, for example, a toll bridge. Note: The bondholders do not always have the right to look to general taxation funds of the issuer for payment, which would vitally effect the safety of such a bond. *See* **industrial revenue bonds.**

revenue-hunter merger. A type of corporate merger in which the acquiring company simply wants to grow bigger through adding the revenues of the other with a minimum of forethought involved.

reversal. A sudden change in prices to an opposite direction by a stock, stock group, or the market in general.

reverse auction. As a buyer of materials and parts used in manufacturing a product(s), to make bids for those inputs through the Internet using special software designed by business-to-business companies.

reverse leveraged buyout. A reference to an action by financiers who have taken a corporation private through a leveraged buyout that involves taking the company public again. The financiers are optimistic that the new shares will be better received by the market, because the company has repaid or paid down its debt and is presumably in a better financial position, with better prospects. They are paid with the proceeds of the public offering, after appropriate underwriting fees, and stand to make huge profits because their stakes have increased in value in the investment public's eyes. *See* **leveraged buyout; private, going;** and **public, going.**

reverse merger. A reference to a complex and unusual financial arrangement whereby a company absorbs one or more other companies, in order to use the status of one of the latter one(s) as a publicly-held company to initiate, expand, or operate its own business as the surviving corporation, without going through a registration and public offering procedure under the scrutiny of the Securities and Exchange Commission. After the merger, the assets of the merged company(s) are spun off to stockholders, the surviving company, or sold for cash or equivalent. The survivor corporation can then issue and sell additional shares, without filing for an initial public offering. Often it sells them as a private placement initially. An example of such a merger was the creation of a public company by Muriel Siebert's Brokerage by acquiring a furniture company and selling its assets. *See* **merger.**

reverse mortgage. A type of mortgage loan in which a homeowner receives payments and accumulates a loan balance as the payments continue, with the home collateralizing the nonrecourse loan. The loan is repaid when the house is sold. During the schedule, the homeowners' loan liability rises, while the equity in the home declines.

reverse split or **split-down.** A stock split whereby the number of authorized shares is reduced, usually 1 share for 2 shares.

reversionary trust. A special trust whereby there is a transfer of property to a beneficiary with the stipulation that the property rights revert back to the donor upon the death of the beneficiary or after a fixed period of time. This is useful in conveying income properties to beneficiaries in low tax brackets while retaining a vested interest. An attorney should be consulted for complete information.

"Revlon rule." In reference to the landmark opinion of corporate law as it applies to corporate takeovers, the ruling by a Delaware chancery court that the so-called established corporate culture of a company—management, organization, policies, and so on—cannot be the overriding consideration by its management in deciding whether to accept an acquisition offer. Rather, the court found in Revlon, Inc v. MacAndrews & Forbes Holdings, Inc. that the management representing the object of the takeover must place the interests of its shareholders first, especially when the monetary offer itself is superior to others. It requires directors to obtain the highest price for the benefit of stockholders. In making this decision, the court apparently took the position that the phrase "corporate culture" was not relevant in following proper corporate governance, although the court has confused the question somewhat with an apparently conflicting opinion.

revocable or **living trust.** A document designed to allow the maker to own some or all his or her property while alive and make provisions for its disposal after death, while avoiding the probate process but not escaping estate taxes. *See* **irrevocable trust.**

revolving door. A reference to the tendency for high government officials to join private companies as executives after serving on a federal regulatory body or in a high government post in Washington, D.C. Thus, government service often serves as a revolving door to a lucrative position in the private sector.

Companies that are federally regulated or do business using federal procedures like to recruit executives from government posts and regulatory bodies because these persons are familiar with traversing the sometimes circuitous paths to approvals and backing from leaders in Washington, D.C. Examples are officials leaving the Food and Drug Administration (FDA) to join pharmaceutical companies or commissioners leaving the Federal Communications Commission (FCC) or the Securities and Exchange Commission (SEC) to join media companies or law firms, respectively.

Rhode Island Department of Business Regulation. Regulator of securities laws in the state of Rhode Island. Address: Securities Division, 233 Richmond Street, #232, Providence, RI 02903. Phone: (401) 277-3048.

riding it out. A term describing an investor who decides not to sell a stock when it goes down, because of a conviction that its price will rise again.

rig. In a fraudulent strategy by which a group of stock promoters intends to defraud investors, the rig is the scheme or plan by which they intend to accomplish the fraud. There are basically three ways to create the rig. They are: (1) to gain control of a struggling or marginal business that is already a corporation, sometimes through strong arm tactics; (2) to gain control of an inactive corporation; or, (3) to create a new corporation through selling the stock directly to prospective investors, usually from phone banks or on the Internet, using exaggerated financial claims. The stock involved is nearly always a **"penny stock,"** selling for one dollar or less a share. Whichever method to create the plot is employed, after getting control of a corporation is accomplished, the group engages fellow conspirators—such as questionable public relations firms and "analysts"—to create an image of the stock as one with an extraordinary product, value, process, or resource that will be a goldmine for the ground floor investors once the word gets out and excited buyers drive the price up. Often, the promoters will enlist the aid of a broker-dealer to sponsor the shares, and thus gain a listing on the Over-the-Counter Bulletin Board. Usually, those putting out stock recommendations or false press releases are sharing in the receipts from the aggressive sales of the stock to the public. The final stages are the **"pump and dump."** *See* also **grease.**

rights or **subscription rights.** See **rights offering.**

"rights off." See **rights offering.**

rights offering. An offering by a corporation to current stock-holders of the opportunity to buy additional shares for a definite price, usually under the current market price, within a relatively short time limit (usually within 30 to 60 days). Rights may be sold but as a practical matter would only be desired by stockholders of the corporation or prospective stockholders, since the rights can only be expressed in proportion to the shares already owned.

Before the rights are issued, their value is determined by finding the difference between the stock's market price, including the rights, or "rights on," and its price to a rights recipient. This difference is divided by the number of old shares it is necessary to own to get a new share plus one. The quotient is the value of one right.

For example, if rights enable the owner to buy one share of new common stock for every nine shares of old stock he owns at $25 per share, and the price of current shares is $30, the value of each right is calculated as follows: Value of a right = ($30 – $25) ÷ (9 + 1) = ($5 ÷ 10) = $.50. When the rights have been issued and distributed, the old shares begin trading without the rights, or "ex rights," or "rights off." Often a market continues to exist for the rights separately. In this case, to find the value of a right do not add one to the ratio of rights required for a share. Value of a right = ($30 – $25) ÷ 9 = $.56

Rio de Janeiro Stock Market/Portuguese. See under **Global Investment Market.**

risk. In broad financial terms, risk is the cost of being wrong about the outcome of an investment. In evaluating an invest-ment decision, both the probability of the outcome and the con-sequences of being wrong should be evaluated.

There is a difference between risk and uncertainty, although the differences in the two are often clouded by investors. Risk is the expected outcome of an event or events that would diminish the value of an investment, as defined by a probability distribution of its occurrence. On the other hand, uncertainty is having no basis for assumptions about the outcome of an investment.

Experts say three factors need to be considered by an investor: (1) total assets to be placed at risk, (2) the particular needs of the investor, and (3) the length of time before some or all of the assets will be needed. Simply stated, if the investor will likely need the invested resources in the near future, this factor is more important than how much more could be gained by staying in the stock market. If wrong, the consequences could be disastrous for the investor, while the benefits of being right would be marginally beneficial at best.

Quantitatively, absolute risk is the measure of dispersion around a mean or average performance, as in a standard deviation; relative risk is the measure of difference with an index or other benchmark measure, as in Beta Values. It should be noted that investment risk is measured ex post, which means that you are anticipating events in the future (an ex ante mind set), using data from the past (an ex post mind set). This is an interesting paradox. *See* **Alpha Value, Beta Value, M-squared, standard deviation, variance,** and **volatility.**

risk capital. Those funds invested in an enterprise in which there is a great chance of loss and a small chance of enormous gains. *See* **venture capital.**

risk/reward expected outcome. In making a decision about whether to buy a particular stock, a way to calculate the expected gain or loss using a simplistic probability analysis. For example, the stock of Sour Grapes Vineyards, Inc. is $35 per share, representing a P/E multiple of 35× its $1.00 earnings per share. The stock pays no dividend and is at an all-time high. It has moved from $10 to its present price in three successive years of gains. Of all the wineries, this is the highest priced, in terms of the P/E. Furthermore, there has just been released a medical report that indicates sulfites—preservatives used in wines—could be detrimental to health. The manager of Good Times Mutual Fund, a fund specializing in entertainment stocks, believes the party is over for Sour Grapes.

The money manager asks the research analyst covering distilled spirits to come up with a risk/reward expected outcome for the next six months. Jack Daniels, the analyst, goes to work. He rationalizes that the winery is the best managed in the industry, tops in measures such as profit margin, return-on-equity, and customer loyalty. Consequently, he believes the stock will always command a premium P/E multiple over the industry average of 20×. On the other hand, the sulfite report has lowered his spirits. He decides the stock will tumble to at least an industry P/E of 20×, or $20 per share. He assigns a 90% probability to this happening. But wait! From a corner of his mind comes the memory that medical reports come and go. This one might be a false alarm. The stock might remain a winner, due largely to expected earnings next year of $1.25. Capitalized at its premium of 35×, it would sell for $43.75 for a gain of $8.75 per share. He assigns a 10% probability to this occurring. Notice the chance of the stock price staying the same is ignored, because that would represent null consequences. The objective is to calculate an expected value of holding the stock, which is really a weighted average of the investment outcomes using probabilities as the weights. Below is the shorthand memo from Jack Daniels:

Upside Potential = 10% × $43.75 = + $4.38
Downside Risk = 90% × $25 = − $22.50
Expected Gain/Loss = − $18.12 (Downside Risk–Upside Potential)

The loss predicted seems overwhelming, in this circumstance. The money manger sells. Risk/reward probability analysis is tricky business, because there are usually subjective evaluations of complex situations. For example, how reliable are the probabilities assigned? How reliable is the earnings assumption? How influential is the sulfite report? But working in an objective way is more likely to get successful investment results than operating by the seat of the pants.

risk/reward ratio. In making a decision about whether to buy a particular stock, a calculation of the gain if the stock price goes up versus the loss if it goes down. For example, assume the stock of Peaks and Valleys Steel Corp. is priced at $25, or 5× its $5.00

earnings per share for the trailing four quarters, and pays a $1.25 dividend, which yields 5.0%. In the past, during business cycle expansions the stock has climbed to a P/E of 7.5×. The estimated earnings for the next fiscal year are $6.00 per share, which could be capitalized at $45 per share. On the other hand, because of the well-covered dividend it is felt the price would not drop below $20, where the yield would be an attractive 6.3%, and historically high. The risk is considered to be $5; the reward, $20—for a risk/reward ratio of .25 (5 ÷ 20), meaning the potential risk is only 25% as great as the potential reward. Some investors put the reward potential in the numerator instead. Doing so in the present example, the ratio would be 20:5, or four; the reward expectation is four times the risk. In this method of risk/reward analysis, probabilities of outcomes are inferred but not actually quantified. Even so, the same proscriptions regarding assumptions apply in this method as in risk/reward probability analysis. *See* **risk/reward expected outcome.**

"road show." See **"dog and pony show."**

"rock." In a business manufacturing operation, a problem that is not apparent until demand for a company's products rises to a level which strains efficiency, and cannot be sustained profitably unless the process is modified. The name derives from an ocean tide going out, representing unused capacity, and thereby exposing rocks that must be removed in order to use the dry beach, representing no unused capacity.

"rocket scientists." A nickname given to the young investment strategists, educated in financial mathematics, who guided Wall Street firms and their customers into the use of computers for building decision models to manage derivative securities in the 1980s. These strategists are concentrated in hedge fund management, and have been criticized for their unfailing confidence in the predictive ability of their models.

roll out, to. As a business manager, to expand a business from one to multiple locations.

rollover. A collective term applied to the principle of units of debt that are extended beyond their original maturity dates. The rollover in January is often large because so many bonds mature in that month. *See* **refunding**.

roll-up. A business enterprise that has been formed by the combination of a group of businesses from the same industry under the direction of a venture capitalist or investment banker. When one company is the acquirer of the others, it is called a consolidator. The owners of the acquired companies receive shares or some other units of ownership in the surviving enterprise. A rolled-up company continues to grow in this manner. When the surviving company is a brand new enterprise, it is called a "poof" roll-up, so named because it is created seemingly out of a magician's hat. In this case, the new shares are issued to the combined company's owners as payment. But cash might also be used. One advantage of this type of company creation is that proven management is often available in one or more of the combined entities. Usually the combined companies are small and unknown. The ultimate purpose for the venture capitalist is to take them public at great profit.

"rose glasses." A reference to the viewpoint of an investor reading financial information, usually about shares of stock in a favorite company, with an overly-positive bias. This can lead to unwarranted optimistic assumptions about future prospects, followed by a loss of money in purchasing an over-priced stock. *See* **"black glasses."**

rotation. As an investor, especially an institutional investor, to buy and sell stocks so that industry sectors that are currently experiencing profitable operating results, or are expected to experience them, are emphasized in commitments. For example, as a business cycle peaks, the Look Sharp Fund might start selling cyclical stocks, such as metals, construction materials, machinery makers, and so on, and begin buying stocks in the Food & Beverage sector, because when economic tempos slow down, such consumer stocks are usually relatively stronger. This is because people must eat, while they can postpone durable purchases such as automobiles or appliances.

Roth IRA. See **Individual Retirement Accounts.**

Roth IRA Web Site. A Web site for investors offering information and news in using a Roth IRA in retirement planning. *See* **Web Sites for the Inquiring Investor.**

rounded bottom. A price pattern made by recorded high-low-close bars on a stock bar chart or Xs and Os on a point-and-figure chart. Chartists warn that volume should increase as the price rises for an orderly pattern to exist on the recovery. Otherwise, the price rally might fizzle out.

rounded top. A price pattern made by recorded high-low-close bars on a stock bar chart or Xs and Os on a point-and-figure chart. Chartists believe that volume should increase as price declines for an orderly pattern to exist as the price falls. Otherwise, a panic-type price collapse could ensue.

round lot. The normal unit of trading in a security, usually 100 shares, on which quotes are based. Round lots can be less than 100 shares if an exchange so decides. The number of shares constituting a round lot is based on its popularity and price. All over-the-counter quotes are technically for 100 shares unless specified otherwise, although odd lot trades can generally be made at the same price.

round trip cost or **in-and-out cost.** The total commission cost, taxes, and fees of buying and later selling a security on an exchange.

royalty. The payment of a user for rights to exploit mineral lands, patents, manuscripts, music renderings, and so on.

Rubbers. Those stocks representing corporations making finished rubber or rubberized synthetic products. *See* **industry stock group.**

Rules, SEC. The following rules promulgated by the Securities and Exchange Commission in their regulation of U.S. securities markets are important ones, frequently encountered, but are only summarized here, and descriptions are only meant to impart their general meaning. *See* **Regulation A, SEC; Regulation D, SEC;** and **Regulation S, SEC.**

Description	Rule Number	Summary
Short selling defined	Rule 3B-3	A short sale is defined as one in which the seller does not own the security sold or it is borrowed to make delivery. In addition, the meaning of ownership is defined from the standpoint of conventional securities, convertibles, stock options, and stock warrants.
Short sale restrictions	Rule 10a-1	Prohibits a short sale for less than the previous regular transaction, and at that price only if it was above the previous different price. After a security goes "ex" for any type of distribution, short sales price restrictions may be lowered by the value of the distribution.
Solicitation of orders on primary or secondary distribution	Rule 10b-2	Parties who are working in a primary or secondary distribution of a security cannot solicit orders except through presenting the offering circular or final prospectus.
Tender short sales banned	Rule 10b-4	Short sales cannot be used in response to a tender offer.
Trading during a securities distribution	Rule 10b-6	Issuers, underwriters, brokers-dealers, or others working in a securities distribution cannot purchase same or rights to it or convertible into it during the distribution period unless the transactions are to implement the distribution process.
Stabilizing the market	Rule 10b-7	Explains what issuers and underwriters of securities may do toward stabilizing the market during offerings.
Right offerings manipulation	Rule 10b-8	Prohibits manipulation of market prices in rights offerings.
Information on trade confirmation	Rule 10b-10	Outlines minimum information that must appear on a trade confirmation to a customer, which includes disclosure of whether a broker-dealer acted as a principal (independent dealer) or agent (broker) in the trade.
Purchasing security during tender offer	Rule 10b-13	Disallows a person making a cash or equity-exchange tender offer from taking a position in the tendered security, or one convertible into it, until expiration of the tender offer.
Margin transactions	Rule 10b-16	Covers general terms related to interest charges on margin accounts and disclosure required by brokers about credit terms and conditions.

Description	Rule Number	Summary
Protection from market manipulation action	Rule 10b-18	Protects companies from legal action for market manipulation when they repurchase shares of their own stock immediately after a market-wide suspension of trading.
Floor trading procedures	Rule 11A	Includes rules related to floor trading procedures in regard to precedence and priority of trades.
Mutual fund fees	Rule 12b-1	Treats miscellaneous fees assessed by mutual funds.
Acquiring big positions	Rule 13d	Requires disclosures for a person who acquires beneficial interest of 5% or more of outstanding units of any class of a registered security. Generally, these regulations were adopted from the Williams Act of 1968, which enacted the requirement that corporate takeover objectives be identified.
Going private	13e	Establishes regulations for issuers of securities or their affiliates on "going private," and prohibits them from buying their shares during a tender offer.
Proxy solicitations	Rule 14a	Explains information to include with proxy requests sent to shareholders of a public corporation.
Tender offers	Rule 14d	Procedures required in public tender offers, such as disclosures of information. Generally, these regulations were adopted from the Williams Act of 1968, which enacted the requirement that corporate takeover objectives be identified.
Safekeeping of hypothecated securities.	Rule 15c2-1	Sets the rules for the safekeeping of customers' securities in margin accounts by prohibiting commingling of accounts without permission and commingling with noncustomer securities. It also restricts broker borrowing, using customers' collateralized securities, to the amount of total customer borrowing.
Capital requirements of brokers and dealers	Rule 15c3-1	Establishes the mandatory net capital amounts required for brokers and dealers in various categories.

Description	Rule Number	Summary
Free credit balances	Rule 15c3-2	Requires notification of customers with free credit amounts in their accounts that those balances may be withdrawn on demand.
Excess customer securities	Rule 15c3-3	Deals with management by broker-dealers of fully paid securities and excess margin securities (which are securities valued in excess of margin requirements) belonging to customers. The broker-dealer must segregate fully paid securities, and make weekly deposits to a special bank account for the interest of those customers.
Laundering money	Rule 17a-8	Makes unlawful the use of broker-dealers to launder money obtained from illegal activities.
Missing or stolen securities	Rule 17f-1	Directs commercial banks, transfer agents, exchanges, clearing firms, and others responsible for safeguarding public security certificates to inform the SEC and appropriate legal agencies when they become aware securities are missing, lost, counterfeit, or stolen. Also, they are instructed to check out new securities received with the SEC in order to ascertain whether such a problem exists.
Mutual fund trading ethics	Rule 17j-1	Gives directors more responsibility in overseeing personal trading by investment managers and other insiders at mutual funds. Also requires pre-clearance of purchases of securities sold in initial public offerings and private placement transactions by mutual fund employees as well as disclosure of ethical codes by mutual funds.
No fixed commissions	Rule 19b-3	Incorporates Securities Act Amendments of 1975 into prohibition of exchanges establishing fixed commission rates for members.
Trading listed securities off exchanges	Rule 19c-3	In conformance with the Securities Act Amendments of 1975 requiring experimentation with a national securities market, allows trading in securities listed on exchanges off the exchange by member firms.
One-share-one-vote	Rule 19c-4	Restrains the NASD or any exchange from listing or quoting prices on a stock issue with more voting clout than other common shares of the same corporation.

Description	Rule Number	Summary
Selling private placement securities	Rule 144	Delineates the conditions under which securities obtained through a private placement, or letter securities, may be sold publicly without registering. There is a two-year wait for securities received through a private placement. After that, during any three-month interval, if listed securities, the greater of 1% of outstanding units or average trading volume during four previous weeks; if unlisted securities, 1% of outstanding units. All sales must involve brokers.
New securities sale without registration	Rule 144-A	Eliminates the need for approval of new high yield-debt issues that are bought by qualified institutional investors—such as mutual funds and insurance companies—which eliminates delays that can take up to 30 days on broader placements.
Selling securities obtained through corporate change	Rule 145	Enables investors selling securities obtained through transfers of corporate resources, mergers and acquisitions, consolidations, or reclassifications to dispose of them without registration, under specific guidelines.
Mutual fund sales literature	Rule 156	Guards against investment companies or mutual funds from distributing misleading or exaggerated sales literature.
Simplified registration for small issues	Rule 254	Simplifies registration for small security issues of $1.5 million and less, by providing for a shorter registration procedure and prospectus.
Registering now for future issues	415	Allows public corporations to file registration information currently for future securities issues. This enables companies to wait for more favorable market conditions and to be ready to go to market when they occur.
Penny stock investor protection	419	Requires investor funds to go into escrow, for the interest of the investors, when used to buy new issues of penny stocks involving companies that have not yet commenced operations or purchased or combined with unspecified businesses.

Rule of 70 or 72. The quick method of finding how fast money will double while compounding at an annual rate. Divide the compounding rate into either 70 or 72 to determine the number of years until the principal will double. For example, if there is $1,000 in a savings account drawing 5% interest annually compounded, it will double to $2,000 in 14 years (70 ÷ 5). If an investor's $5,000 account will compound at 6%, the money will double to $10,000 in 12 years (72 ÷ 6). Note this short cut does not encompass a program in which there are additions to the compounding deposit throughout the period. For a formula and more details, *See* **compound interest.**

Rule 127. On the NYSE, a procedure allowing a trade executed outside the present quote under the following conditions: (1) it represents 10,000 shares or more, and (2) it represents a value of $200,000 or more.

Rule 155. On the AMEX, a procedure allowing a trade of a block of stock, executed outside the current market at a single "clean-up" price.

runaway gap. See **gap (2).**

run-up. A security's rapid appreciation in market value.

Rural Electrification Administration (REA). See **agency securities.**

Rural Telephone Bank. See **agency securities.**

Russell 2000 Index. A popular stock price index that includes the smallest 2,000 companies in the U.S. stock market in terms of market capitalizations, representing many industries. These stocks tend to be more volatile than larger ones. It represents 11% of the total market capitalization, with a range of $288 million to $746 million.

Russian Stock Exchange. See under **Global Investment Market.**

Russian Trading System. See under **Global Investment Market.**

Ss

SA. Abbreviation for **société anonyme**, the equivalent of the U.S. corporation.

"safeguard clause." See **"dumping."**

"safe harbor." Provisions in an act that exempt certain activities from liability, when conditions are met.

Safe Harbor for Forward-looking Statements. See **Forward Looking Statements in Annual Report.**

safekeeping of securities or **customer safekeeping.** A service performed by investment firms and commercial banks whereby securities can be left in their custody. When a brokerage firm performs this service the securities are registered in the firm's name. Therefore, all dividends, subscription rights, financial reports, proxy statements, and so on are sent to the brokerage firm, who should then notify the customer and follows his or her instructions as to further disposition, often crediting dividends to the customer's account automatically.

safety net. The system put in place by a securities exchange to prevent calamitous stock market collapses. Among other items, the system usually includes temporary trading halts, cessation of program trading, efforts to match sell orders with buy orders, and other efforts to mollify the panic. See **collar (2).**

salary deferral savings plan. A 401(k) plan in which an employee is given the option of deferring a portion or a specific amount of pay in favor of contributions to a retirement fund. Contributions are made directly by the employer, based on the employee's choice.

sale and leaseback. A financial arrangement whereby an operating company sells an expensive resource to another party, usually a financial company, with the agreement to lease the resource back at a specific price for a specific time period, usually a long-term one such as 20 years. This is a popular strategy for companies that have limited cash reserves and are housed in or using valuable capital facilities. Usually, the selling company has a need for the cash that is tied up in the resource, such as an airplane, ship, or building, and the buying company has ample cash reserves but not much need for expensive operating facilities. The seller gets operating cash and the continued use of the needed facility, while the buyer is assured a steady cash flow and perhaps a residual value for the resource after the lease has expired. *See* **buy-sell-leaseback.**

sales finance company. A business that buys the accounts receivables of retail merchandisers for a discount, which provides working capital to the retailer.

sales load. In the purchase of mutual fund shares, the percentage of the investment deducted to compensate sales personnel. This amount varies, but it is generally from 5% to 8%. *See* **front-end sales load.**

sales to fixed assets. The ratio of annual sales to the sum of the book values of plant, equipment, and land, before depreciation. It indicates whether funds used to expand output facilities have increased sales to the point expected. Over a recent 15-year period in the United States, the average sales to fixed assets was .99 or almost 1 to 1.

sales to inventories. The ratio of annual sales divided by year-end inventories. This is also called inventory turnover and indicates whether inventory investment is too high. Over a recent 15-year period in the United States, the average inventory turnover rate was 12.4.

Sallie Mae. Abbreviation for **Student Loan Marketing Association.**

SAM. Abbreviation for **shared appreciation mortgage.**

same. See **unchanged.**

same store sales. A reference to evaluating the sales revenues for a fiscal period of a merchandising business, usually retail in nature, by comparing those revenues with the revenues of an identical number of the company's outlets or units in the prior year or quarter. When outlets have been updated or remodeled during a period, they are considered part of the same number count. Retail managers and securities analysts use this comparison in appraising the change in sales due strictly to achieving greater output with the same asset base. It disallows the false impression of a company's revenue change from internal operations when more outlets in one of the periods is used. The comparison is used for all manner of retail operations, including department stores, specialty stores, grocery stores, restaurants, discount stores, and so on.

For example, in comparing two retailing companies, Hi Ya'll Grits to Go, Inc. reports fourth quarter revenues of $10 million, versus $9 million for the same period one year earlier. On the other hand, Kansas City Steak Outs, Inc. reports fourth quarter revenues of $15 million, compared with $10 million one year earlier. Hi Ya'll Grits increased sales 11.1%. But Steak Outs grew revenues 50%! On closer examination, however, the inquiring investor discovers that Steak Outs increased franchised outlets from 15 to 30, while Hi Ya'll Grits added no new stores. So from the same number of units, Steak Outs had no gain in revenues. Hi Ya'll Grits did a better merchandising job, with the same number of stores. That's what I like about the south.

SARs. Abbreviation for **stock appreciation rights.**

SaveWealth.com. A Web site for investors providing advice, information, and news on estate planning, retirement planning, reducing taxes, and workshops, including related links. *See* **Web Sites for the Inquiring Investor.**

Savings and Loans. Those stocks representing companies accepting deposits for the purpose of investing in mortgage properties or other related investments. *See* **industry stock group.**

savings bonds, U.S. See **Series E Savings Bonds.**

SBA. See **Small Business Administration.**

SBIC. See **Small Business Investment Company.**

scalability. In the business world, a reference to the ability of a system or process to adjust to changing customer demand or supply or materials without suffering financial penalties.

scale down buying or **scale down support.** A pattern of market activity whereby buying increases as prices get lower.

scalp. In online trading, to buy and sell securities rapidly for small gains, frequently holding a position for under a day.

scalp, to. As a person recommending the purchase of certain stock shares, to sell shares in the same issue while others are buying as the stock's price rises, without disclosing the action. This can be fraudulent under U.S. securities laws.

"scared money." In online trading, a reference to the frantic buying and selling at the end of a session in an effort to recoup losses.

scatter diagram, regression. A plotting of dots on graph paper or on a computer printout that shows the degree of relationship between changes in the values of two variables—one independent of the other for its changes and the other dependent on the former for its changes—at the same intervals over a period of time. It is a graphic representation of a statistical relationship or a lack of relationship. When the value of each variable is plotted, setting the observations for the independent variable along the X axis and those for the dependent variable along the Y axis, a line or curve is drawn amidst the dots so that it come as close to each dot as possible. When the dots are close to the line, it is a sign of a close relationship and the basis for a formal regression analysis. When the dots are scattered in a random manner about the line, it indicates no statistical relationship exists. A diagram is a tool for ascertaining the likelihood that deeper analysis would provide an important, predictive relationship. In securities or stock market analysis, the technique is used in predicting dependent variables, such as earnings, shipments, and expenses from independent series such as demographics, Gross Domestic Product, and interest rates. *See* **forecasting.**

scenario. In making an investment decision or recommendation, the broad set of assumptions about economic, political, and financial conditions that have led to that conclusion.

Schedule K-1. The notification form used by a limited partnership to advise an investor of the portion of the partnership's income, loss, deduction, and tax credits that can be used on the investor's personal income tax filing.

"S" corporations. In the context of small business organizational strategies, a special corporation in the U.S. Tax Code called a Subchapter "S" corporation, or "S" corporation, which does not pay income taxes itself on most types of income; instead, all income, credits, and deductions are flowed through to the personal filings of the shareholders and are taxed accordingly. Under certain circumstances, it may own subsidiaries. It may only issue one class of stock and the maximum number of shareholders is 75, all of whom must be U.S. citizens or U.S. residents.

scrip. Those certificates issued by a company as in a stock dividend instead of fractional shares of stock. The certificates can usually be sold to the issuer or held until a full share can be issued.

"scrub" the books, to. As the management of a company, to review the accounting entries for a fiscal period, in order to eliminate or adjust those items that are questionable, either from the standpoint of acceptable accounting practices or accurate reporting.

SDRs. Abbreviation for **special drawing rights.**

seasonal fluctuations. The regular variations in business activity in certain industries caused by a changing seasonal demand for their products.

seasonal rally. A reference to the erroneous belief that there are seasonal upturns or patterns in general stock market prices. Actually, stock prices, as represented by the S&P 500 Stock Index, are not seasonal statistically and, therefore, not seasonally adjusted by the Bureau of Economic Research in preparing economic indicators. *See* **rally.**

seat. The trading membership on a securities exchange that often is bought and sold, providing membership requirements are met. A seat is worth whatever a prospective member of an exchange will pay, which depends on the desirability for a securities businessman to transact on an exchange. New York Stock Exchange seats have sold for $17,000 in 1942, $625,000 1929, to over $1 million in the 1990s. *See* **member firm.**

SEC. Abbreviation for the **Securities and Exchange Commission.**

SEC fee. A fee levied on the seller of securities on any registered exchange or on over-the-counter trades of listed issues by the SEC. It is $0.01 for each $300 or fraction thereof of the principal amount of money involved in sales.

SEC filings. See **Form-3, Form-4, Form-5, Form 8-K, Form 10-K, Form 10-KSB, Form 10-Q, Form-12B-25, Form S1, Form S-4,** and **Form 5500.**

secondary distribution or **secondary offering.** The sale of a large block of listed stock off an exchange by underwriters through their salespeople. Its price is usually pegged close to market price and offers a generous concession to stock salespeople. However, frequently the price is below the market price, so a buyer can save on the actual purchase plus not pay the regular exchange commission. *See* **registered secondary.**

secondary market. The market that exists for a security after shares from its initial underwriting are in public hands.

secondary offering. See **secondary distribution.**

"Section 1031 exchange." See **Starker exchange.**

sector. A group of industries that are engaged in different phases of preparing products or services for the same primary market or markets. Often they perform vertically related activities, such as different elements of the oil and gas sector do. In that industry, activities from the top down are: exploring and developing oil and gas production, transporting and storing the crude oil or raw materials, refining or processing the materials, and transporting the refined products to distributors and marketers that distribute the products to the final users.

Sectors can also be organized horizontally, such as financial services sometimes are. Banking companies might interact with both insurance brokers and stockbrokers to increase service to their customers, for example. Usually, but not always, industries in a sector are affected in the same way by changes in general economic conditions. In macroeconomics sectors are even broader, composed of industries that focus on broad sections of the overall economy—consumer durables, consumer nondurables, capital goods, consumer services, and transportation, for example. In investment research, sometimes the lines get blurred. S&P in-depth research sectors include: Basic Materials, Capital Goods, Communication Services, Consumer Cyclicals, Consumer Staples, Energy, Health Care, Technology, Transportation, Utilities, and Financial. Note the absence of New Economy sectors, due to their immaturity.

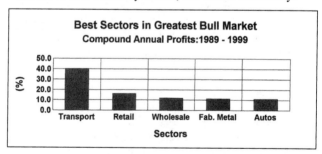

sector fund. A mutual fund that specializes in certain industry sectors. *See* **sector.**

sector rotation. See **rotation.**

Securities Act of 1933. A federal act requiring disclosure of significant information about securities offered to the public through the mails or sold in interstate commerce to allow investors to make informed decisions. It came almost literally in the wake of the Crash of 1929 and the onset of the Great Depression in the United States, when Americans became disillusioned about capitalism. A wobbly government was desperate to restore confidence in the way America invested. This law and others that followed represented a new look at the importance of the protection of investors from unscrupulous practices if free enterprise was to work.

Classes of securities exempted from provisions of the act, except the antifraud provisions, which apply to any sale of securities, are:

1. securities issued or guaranteed by the United States, any state or territory thereof, or any political subdivision or any public instrumentality of one or more states or territories or any national or state bank
2. commercial paper arising from current transactions, having a maturity at the time of issuance of not more than nine months
3. securities issued by certain nonprofit organizations
4. securities issued by building and loan associations and similar institutions, provided that the issuer does not take more than 3% of the face value of the security as a withdrawal fee
5. securities issued by common carriers subject to the Interstate Commerce Act
6. certificates issued legally by a receiver or by a trustee in bankruptcy
7. insurance policies
8. securities issued in reorganizations approved legally
9. securities exchanged by the issuer with its existing security holders exclusively, where no commission or other remuneration is paid or given for soliciting the exchange
10. securities that are part of an issue sold only to residents of the state in which the issuer is incorporated and doing business

State regulatory securities laws, or "Blue Sky Laws," were not abrogated by this act. *See* **Securities Acts Amendments of 1975**; **Securities Exchange Act of 1934; Securities and Exchange Commission; Form** definitions; **Regulation, SEC** definitions; and **Rules, SEC.**

Securities Acts Amendments of 1975. This is considered by many to be the most important securities legislation since the **Securities**

Act of 1934. It was a blockbuster for the securities industry because it ended fixed commissions among exchange members. It also began action toward the establishment of a national market system and gave to the SEC the ultimate approbation before the adoption of rules by any self-regulatory organizations.

Securities and Exchange Commission (SEC). A federal commission created by the Securities Exchange Act of 1934 to regulate registered national exchanges, the activities of brokers and dealers in national over-the-counter markets, the issuance of new stock and to protect the public from unethical acts in securities markets. Five members, appointed by the president and confirmed by the Senate, comprise its body. The SEC considers its most important mandate to be the ensuring of a full disclosure of the activities surrounding the issuance and trading of public securities. Federal laws administered by the Commission are the **Securities Act of 1933,** the **Securities Exchange act of 1934,** the **Trust Indenture Act of 1939,** the **Public Utility Holding Company Act of 1935,** the **Investment Advisers Act of 1940,** and the **Investment Company Act of 1940.** Address: Judiciary Plaza, 450 5th Street, NW, Washington, DC 20549. Phone: (800) SEC-0330. For important corporate filings required and securities markets rules, see under **Form** definitions, **SEC,** and **Rules, SEC.**

The Securities and Exchange Commission's Regional Offices:

Northeast Regional Office
Securities and Exchange Commission
7 World Trade Center, Suite 1300
New York, NY 10048
Phone: (212) 748-8000
E-mail: newyork@sec.gov

Central Regional Office
Securities and Exchange Commission
1801 California Street, Suite 4800
Denver, CO 80202-2648
Phone: (303) 844-1000
E-mail: denver@sec.gov

Boston District Office
Securities and Exchange Commission
73 Tremont Street, Suite 600
Boston, MA 02108-3912
Phone: (617) 424-5900
E-mail: boston@sec.gov

Fort Worth District Office
Securities and Exchange Commission
801 Cherry Street, Suite 1900
Fort Worth, TX 76102
Phone: (817) 978-3821
E-mail: dfw@sec.gov

Philadelphia District Office
Securities and Exchange Commission
The Curtis Center, Suite 1005
E. 601 Walnut Street
Philadelphia, PA 19106-3322
Phone: (215) 597-3100
E-mail: philadelphia@sec.gov

Salt Lake District Office
Securities and Exchange Commission
500 Key Bank Tower
50 South Main Street,
Suite 500 Box 79
Salt Lake City, UT 84144-0402
Phone: (801) 524-5796
E-mail: saltlake@sec.gov

Southeast Regional Office
Securities and Exchange Commission
1401 Brickell Avenue, Suite 200
Miami, FL 33131
Phone (305) 536-4700
E-mail: miami@sec.gov

Pacific Regional Office
Securities and Exchange Commission
5670 Wilshire Boulevard, 11th Floor
Los Angeles, CA 90036-3648
Phone: (213) 965-3998
E-mail: losangeles@sec.gov

Atlanta District Office
Securities and Exchange Commission
3475 Lenox Road NE, Suite 1000
Atlanta, GA 30326-1232
Phone: (404) 842-7600
E-mail: atlanta@sec.gov

San Francisco District Office
Securities and Exchange Commission
44 Montgomery Street, Suite 1100
San Francisco, CA 94104
Phone: (415) 705-2500
E-mail: sanfrancisco@sec.gov

Midwest Regional Office
Securities and Exchange Commission
Citicorp Center
500 W. Madison Street, Suite 1400
Chicago, IL 60661-2511
Phone: (312) 353-7390
E-mail: chicago@sec.gov

securities analysis. The art and craft of determining the investment status, in terms of being favorable or unfavorable for investors, of one or more securities. This is accomplished by analyzing important financial and operating measures present that are pertinent to the category of securities being analyzed—common stocks, preferred stocks, bonds, debentures, warrants, and so on—and measures pertinent to the issuers of the securities under scrutiny. In other words, there is a difference in focus depending on the class of securities. Securities analysis includes judging financial performance based on factors such as operating ratios and balance sheet ratios, to name just two, and reviewing the progress in them from year to year. It also includes judging management's success in its record of operating measures, such as labor productivity and utilization of plant capacity. Finally, these financial and operating appraisals are compared with others in the industry in order to select the most likely issuers to achieve the investment potentials of that class of securities. Also analyzed in conjunction with a company appraisal are the general economic conditions and industry prospects during the contemplated holding period of the security. No stock is an island.

In analyzing fixed-income securities, such as bonds and preferred stocks, the emphasis should be on the adequacy of the issuer's cash flow in covering interest and sinking fund payments or dividend distributions, among many other considerations. In analyzing equities, the emphasis should be on growth of earnings and shareholders' equity to provide the possibility of future dividends or capital appreciation of the shares, as well as other elements. In simplified terms, it is said that an analyst should find reasons to buy a stock, and reasons not to buy a bond. As a general rule, the emphasis in securities analysis should be on determining the probability of the issuer accomplishing specific investment expectations—interest payments, dividend payments, or earnings growth, for example—over the projected holding period.

Last but certainly not least, securities analysis involves recognizing how the securities marketplace is evaluating financial and operating performances. Are there expectations for high yield, low yield, high growth, stable growth, and so on? This propensity is essential if investment assumptions are to be realistic, for it determines the basis on which market players are evaluating corporate business results. Are P/E Multiples high or low? Are book values important? The caveat applies more to the short term than the long term, because historical norms resume to investment decision making sooner or later.

There are times when either pessimism or exuberance rules, making strict adherence to historical norms in securities analysis out of fashion. It is during such times that discipline must be used, for times will change. In either environment, an analyst must continue to search out the best values among issuers in the securities category under examination. The idea can be summed up by saying securities analysis is in context with the current market conditions, with the proviso that it should always stress cognizance to changes in these conditions. An investor should decide when to sell upon buying a security, if possible. Finally, as John Maynard Keynes said, "There is nothing so tragic as a rational man in an irrational market." *See* **ratio.**

securities analyst. A professional practicing securities analysis, often after having passed a series of exams demonstrating his or her competence. *See* **chartered financial analyst.**

Securities Exchange Act of 1934. A federal law that established the Securities and Exchange Commission to oversee the trading of securities in the United States along the following guidelines:
1. It makes manipulation and other abusive acts in issuing securities illegal.
2. It requires registration of stock exchanges, brokers and dealers, and the securities listed on exchanges.
3. It requires disclosure of financial information about securities and insider activity, officers and directors of a corporation, and those owning 10% or more of outstanding stock.
4. It establishes supervision of trading practices on stock exchanges and over-the-counter markets.
5. It establishes SEC subpoena authority in investigations and in enforcement.
6. It requires solicitation of shareholder votes by proxies on corporate matters.

   Under this law, the SEC was given the authority to monitor exchanges and brokers. It also charged the SEC with enforcing the Securities Act of 1933. An amendment in 1938 included over-the-counter markets to be regulated by the SEC, working with self-regulated organizations. *See* **Securities Acts Amendments of 1975; Securities Act of 1933; Securities and Exchange Commission; Form** definitions; **Regulations, SEC** definitions; and **Rules, SEC.**

securities factor. A financial firm or individual who loans money to speculators in order for them to buy stock. Often, they loan as much as 60% to 70% of the cost of the speculative stock, at exorbitant interest rates. They are not regulated by the Securities and Exchange Commission or the Federal Reserve Board. *See* **clearance transaction.**

Securities Industry Association (SIA). An organization of about 800 securities firms throughout North America that share a common interest in the continued growth and development of capital markets in a professional and ethical manner. It includes investment bankers, broker-dealers, specialists, and mutual fund companies who are active in all phases of corporate and public finance, and account for approximately 90% of securities firms' revenues of $100 billion. Members manage the accounts of more than 50 million investors directly and millions more indirectly through corporate, thrift, and pension plans. The group was formed in 1972 through the merger of the Association of Stock Exchange Firms and the Investment Banker's Association. Address: 120 Broadway, 35th Floor, New York, New York 10271-0080. Phone: (212) 608-1500. Fax: (212) 608-1604. E-mail: *info@sia.com.* Web site: *www.sia.com.*

Securities Investor Protection Corporation (SIPC). A federally chartered corporation, created in 1970, composed of all firms registered under the Securities Exchange Act and all entities that are members of a national securities exchange. Its purpose is to afford certain protection against financial loss to customers of broker-dealers that fail. The limits of protection are $500,000 per account, except that claims for cash are limited to $100,000 per account. Money required to protect customers beyond what is available from the property of the failed broker-dealer is advanced by SIPC from a fund built up primarily from assessments on the securities business of members. Additionally, the SEC has authority to lend SIPC up to $1 billion, which it would borrow from the United States Treasury.

Since its founding, the SIPC has returned $3.4 billion in cash and securities to customers of 282 liquidated brokerage firms. Of those distributions, $233 million has been cash. Even though the corporation was created by Congress to protect investors against fraudulent losses, there is ample evidence to suggest the SIPC tries numerous legal tactics to restrain payments to customers, through using the many exceptions established under the law and raised by its interpretations.

Address: 805 Fifteenth Street, NW, Suite 800, Washington, DC 20005-2207. Phone: (202) 371-8300.

securities laws. The laws that regulate the issuance and trading of public securities in the United States. Basically they include six statutes enacted and amended by Congress as well as state laws, sometimes called Blue Sky Laws. This term is now somewhat outmoded with the passage of Uniform Securities Laws in most states. All federal securities laws are administered by the Securities Exchange Commission, which was created by the Securities Exchange Act of 1934. Most states have adopted the Uniform Securities Act, under which they regulate intrastate securities matters. In every state there is an administrator of securities laws in that jurisdiction. *See* **under each state for information on the securities regulator there.** For the six Congressional acts regulating interstate securities affairs, see **Securities Act of 1933, Securities Exchange Act of 1934, Public Utility Holding Company Act of 1935, Trust Indenture Act of 1939, Investment Company Act of 1940,** and **Investment Advisers Act of 1940**. Also see **Uniform Securities Law.**

securities market. See **market.**

securities salesperson. Although the factors distinguishing securities salespeople, dealers, and brokers are often vague, generally speaking, salespeople never buy stocks or bonds to maintain their own business inventory for resale as do dealers, nor do they always negotiate for customers on a commission basis as do strict brokers, but they would sell shares in a new stock issue for a portion of each share price. In short, and strictly speaking, security salespeople take no financial risks in their selling. Sometimes they act as principal for their employer, sometimes as brokers, but their primary function is to sell to the public shares of stock or bonds, often on a new underwriting for a specified portion of the underwriting profit. *See* **mutual fund salesperson.**

securitization. A reference to the packaging of individual loans into units that are used as the financial backing of bonds sold to investors. The interest and repayments on the loans are used collectively to pay the debt service on the bonds. Since the loans must be the source for payments on the securitization bonds, only loans suitable for that purpose are packaged. Often this procedure is used in raising money in order to rescue banks from nonperforming loans, for example, certain real estate loans made in Japan during boom times there and held by Japanese banks in the late 1990s. In 1999 the bad debt held by Japanese banks was estimated to be between $766 billion and $957 billion.

security. A certificate showing debt or financial ownership that can be transferred when properly endorsed from one owner to another, for example, bonds, debentures, stocks, promissory notes, and so on.

seed capital. See **venture capital.**

segregated account. A cash balance or securities in the possession of an investment firm, but owned by a customer. The firm cannot use these assets for its own investment purposes, even though they appear on the firm's balance sheet.

seigniorage. As a central bank or government holding reserves in a foreign currency, to receive interest payments on that portion of those reserves held in the form of bonds issued by that foreign country. See **seigniorage profits.**

seigniorage profits. Profits made by a central bank or government from printing its currency for use by another nation or government. These can be from the difference in the cost of bullion brought to be minted plus minting expenses and its value as money, comprising a source of revenues for the minting government, or from interest payments or capital appreciation on the foreign country's bonds held as reserves. See **seigniorage.**

Selected Financial Data Section in Annual Report. The section of the annual reports, usually one or two pages, that enables an investor to compare historical results. Generally, five years is covered, sometimes 10 years. Operating data is often also

included. The data chosen is in a summary format and is meant
to provide a scan of the progress, or lack of it, made by the
company over the years. There is a wise saying in statistics—
"The best estimate of the future is the past"—and this section
implements that insight. For unless extraordinary events are present or impending, results for the next fiscal period will
resemble the last one. Of course, the inquiring investor should
always look for potential change in appraising securities, but the
selected data in this section can form the basis for an educated
guess about the presence of a financial trend. *See* **Annual
Report to the Stockholders.**

selective disclosure. A reference to one or more corporate officials communicating significant information about the financial
or operating affairs of a company to a selected group of
investors, rather than disclosing the information over public
channels. This is accomplished through conference calls,
closed-door meetings, or personal conversations. The complaint
about this procedure is that those privy to the key information
often take actions that affect the price of the company's stock,
thus leaving uninformed investors in the dark or apprised too
late to protect their positions. Although the SEC has condemned
the practice, that agency did little to discourage its occurrence
until late in the year 2000. *See* **full disclosure.**

Self-Directed Investment Retirement Account (SDIRA). An
Investment Retirement Account that provides the investor max-
imum flexibility with a full menu of investment choices. *See*
Investment Retirement Account.

"sell." A stock recommended for immediate sale by an investment
firm, together with its removal from the firm's recommended
list. This is never a popular commentary on a stock, because it
alienates the firm and the company's management. That can
mean the loss of corporate business in the future. Also, the sell
advice might imply the analyst was wrong in recommending the
stock in the first place. Generally, if the stock is removed from
the recommended list because it has appreciated in price, it will
be reclassified a "hold." This keeps everybody happy.

sell order. See **order.**

seller's option, futures contracts. In any month, the first day on which a delivery fulfilling a futures contract is to be made. Deliveries under these contracts are at the seller's option, so it can be any day as long as complete notice is given.

seller's option, securities. The sale of securities in which the **delivery date** is optional with the seller, within a three- to 60-day range.

selling concession. The amount of profit from an underwriting that goes to the underwriting group and the selling group. It is always stated as so much per share. For example, stock brought out at $20 might have a profit of 75 cents to the firm in the underwriting group, 50 cents to the selling group, and 25 cents reallowance. The salesperson receives a fraction of the concessions, usually from one-third to one-half.

selling group or **syndicate.** The security dealers that are organized by an underwriting or syndicate manager to sell a new issue without any underwriting on their part at less profit to them than the underwriting group receives. *See* **underwriting agreement.**

selling group concessions. See **dealer concessions.**

selling short. As an investor, to sell stock that he or she does not own presently, but is borrowed indefinitely by a broker to make delivery on the sale. In the transaction, the seller must put up a margin of equity and the sale can only be executed at a price higher than the last different sale price or as high as the last bid, depending on the rules of the market where the transaction occurs. Certain securities, usually those of high investment quality, are exempted from rules but not margin requirements.

selling pressure. See **under pressure.**

selloff. A heavy selling volume triggering low prices.

senior equity. Stock that sometimes takes precedence over other shares in corporate matters such as voting, dividends, or liquidation, for example. Preferred stock, preference stock, and certain classes of common stock are illustrations.

senior issue. A class of stock or bonds that enjoys priority to another of a corporation's securities in the matter of income, interest or dividend payments, or in a liquidation distribution of assets. In a corporation's hierarchy of multiple securities, there is always one most senior and another most junior, but in evaluating the position of each, it is usually in relation to all those more senior and all those most junior. In other words, the important point is how much of cash flow and asset values will be available to the category in question. *See* **junior issue** and **position, securities claims.**

senior mortgage. In mortgage financing, a debt secured by a mortgage on real property that is higher in rank than one or more other mortgages in terms of priority in settling the lender's claim in the event of a default by the borrower. Sometimes there is a second and third mortgage on the same property, leading to senior and junior mortgages. Mortgages are satisfied in the order of their seniority in the event of nonperformance by the borrower. *See* **junior mortgage.**

senior subordinated issue. In a multiple corporate debt structure, a debt issue that enjoys a priority to most securities but is junior to at least one other. *See* **junior issue** and **senior issue.**

SEP—IRA. Abbreviation for **Simplified Employee Pension—Investment Retirement Account.**

serial acquirer. A company buying up other companies at a rapid rate, usually competitors or operators in the same industry, using its common stock as payments. The opportunity to become a serial acquirer most often occurs in a bull market, leading to a rise in the acquirer's stock price as each buyout expands earnings and their capitalized value, and thus a more valuable security with which to make the next acquisition. It is a cycle that can end with acquisitions not performing as well as expected and that, when coupled with a downturn in the stock market, can lead to considerable losses for the serial acquirer's stock. Frequently, the terms and accounting gets very complex in these deals, and their rapidity can obfuscate whether the strategy is beneficial for stockholders. For example, Waste Management bought as many as 100 companies each year during its high-growth period. First Union Corporation has made more than 70 acquisitions since 1985.

serial bonds. A group of bonds issued simultaneously and scheduled to mature at regular intervals over a period of several years. This feature meets a borrower's need for capital that can be repaid at a convenient rate.

series bonds. Those bonds that are issued in a group, usually with the same maturity date and interest rates, and identifiable by a letter, for example, Series A bonds. This identification aids investors when there is more than one bond issue by a corporation.

Series E Savings Bonds. Savings bonds issued by the U.S. Treasury Department in denominations of $50 to $10,000. They were issued from 1941 to 1979. These savings bonds have paid interest continuously for 30 to 40 years from their issue date. Specifically, those bonds issued from 1941 to November 1965 have a life of 40 years, while those issued afterwards through 1979 mature in 30 years. In 1980, Series EE Savings Bonds, ranging in denominations from $50 to $10,000, and Series HH Savings Bonds, ranging from $500 to $10,000, were substituted for them. Series E and EE bonds in denominations of $500 or greater that are outstanding may be exchanged for Series HH bonds, which is the only method of obtaining the latter series. Once savings bonds have matured, interest is not paid on them, so they become a barren investment, except for the past interest earned; but holders are not notified of this by the U.S. Treasury, so it is important for investors to keep track of these bonds. Those bonds issued on May 1, 1997 or later, held less than five years, are penalized three months of interest. Currently savings bonds pay interest ranging from 4% to 6%. The highest yield paid was 7.5%. The yields on savings bonds are set twice a year, on May 1 and November 1.

State and local taxes are not applied to savings bonds, and federal income taxes on Series EE bonds are not due until bonds are redeemed. To accomplish this, maturing Series EE bonds must be exchanged for Series HH bonds. Individuals with modified Adjusted Gross Income between $50,850 and $65,850 and married couples filing jointly with income between $76,250 and $106,250 can save for higher educational outlays with complete or limited income-tax exemption by purchasing Series EE bonds. For information on interest, maturities, and other topics contact the Savings Bond Wizard Web site, developed by the Treasury Department, and download the free program. Web site: *www.savingsbonds.gov.* Also, contact the U.S. Government Printing Office, phone (800) 927-1901 for a windows program that sells for $20, or write to Bureau of the Public Debt, P.O. Box 1328, Parkersburg, WV 26106-1328. *See* **I-bonds.**

Series EE Savings Bond. See **Series E Savings Bond.**

Series HH Savings Bond. See **Series E Savings Bond.**

Series 7 registration. The process of passing an exam and background check by the national Association of Securities Dealers, preparatory to becoming a licensed stockbroker.

service competition. A market condition in which vendors strive to increase their market shares through offering consumers more support in association with purchases of goods or services than rival establishments. Usually, this happens when products are similar in price or quality—but not always, since quality competition and price competition can also play a role in where customers purchase goods or services. Insurance providers are examples, among others, of service competition. *See* **price competition.**

settlement date. 1) The date on which a seller must deliver securities and a buyer must pay for them, usually four business days after a transaction, unless otherwise specified. *See* **cash contracts, next day contracts** and **seller's option, futures contracts.** 2) On "when-issued" contracts, the date set by an exchange on which the actual certificates that the when-issued trade represents must be delivered to the rightful owner.

sexenio. A reference to the economic crisis in Mexico that has followed its election of a president every six years for the past 25 years. The crisis is apparently precipitated by a lack of confidence in the new government by foreign investors, which causes currency devaluations and business recessions. It has become more pronounced as other parties have challenged the dominant Institutional Revolution Party (PRI) in recent years, because of possible radical reforms such opposition could trigger. Since 1976, there have been four devaluations of the peso, all in election years. Also destabilizing, and adding to the prophecy, was the nationalization of the banks in 1982, an election year.

SFAS. Abbreviation for **Statement of Financial Accounting Standards.**

shake-out. A reference to a period of market adjustment when stocks that are overpriced, based on their earning prospects, are sold off to lower levels and remain there until earnings improve.

Shanghai Securities Exchange. A stock exchange in Shanghai, China. Address: 5 Huang Pu Road, Shanghai 200080.

share (of stock). A certificate of proportionate ownership in the earnings and assets of a corporation. Each shareholder of a certain class of stock enjoys privileges and rights proportionate to the number of shares of that stock he owns.

shared appreciation mortgage (SAM). A type of real estate mortgage in which the borrower receives a lower rate of interest and sometimes makes a lower equity payment than on a conventional or adjustable rate mortgage, in exchange for sharing any appreciation when the house is sold with the lender. Typically, the lender gets an interest of 30 to 60% in the appreciation for funds at half or more the conventional rate.

Shared Foreign Sales Corporation. The creation of a corporation of 25 or less exporters which combine to reduce costs and get the tax advantages of a Shared Foreign Sales Corporation. *See* **Foreign Sales Corporation (FSC).**

shareholder. See **stockholder.**

shareholder advocacy. The exercise of influence and pressure by stock owners, usually in unison, to persuade the management of a corporation representing stock they own to adopt policies that enhance the value of the stock. This might take the form of selling off questionable assets, moving in a new business direction, or spinning off shares. It is a strategy once employed mostly by big investors—such as government pension funds—but is growing popular with money managers and analysts who feel the need to take more seriously their voting on proxies.

shareholders' equity. The value of the stockholders' ownership in a corporation, found by subtracting the liabilities plus the liquidating rights of any senior stocks to the ones being analyzed from the net value of the assets. Divide by the number of remaining shares outstanding to get the equity represented by each share. If assets are $1,000,000, liabilities are $500,000, total liquidating or stated preferred stock par value is $20,000, and there are 100,000 shares of common stock outstanding, then common shareholders' equity is ($1,000,000 − $500,000 = $500,000) − $20,000 = $480,000 ÷ 100,000 = $4.80. Bingo!

Shareholders' Equity, Statement of. A detailed accounting of the capital contributions to a corporation's treasury in terms of par values for each category of capital stock, capital raised in excess of par values, earnings retained historically, and deficits and other adjustments affecting shareholder capital positions. *See* **Balance Sheet, Cash Flow Statement,** and **Income Statement.**

Sharpe Ratio or **Sharpe Index.** A mathematical measure that relates the return on an investment, such as a common stock, to an investor's risk exposure incurred in holding that investment, originated by Professor William R. Sharpe of Stanford University. It is a relatively simple method of adjusting return for risk incurred. Three elements are used in calculating the ratio: (1) the average return of an investment over a given period; (2) the rate of riskless return the investor could have gotten over the period as, for example, by holding U.S. Treasury bills, and (3) the standard deviation of the investment's return or its volatility. The result must be compared with results of other investment strategies in order to be useful. In doing so, the higher the ratio, the higher the risk-adjusted return. Using the average of the annual returns obtained from the stock investment below of 10.53% for FlibberJibbit, Inc. and calculating the average return on Treasury bills was 5.65%, the investor's net return was 4.88%. (10.53% – 5.65%.) Assuming the standard deviation, or dispersion around the number, on the stock's average return was 6.25%, the Sharpe Ratio or risk-adjusted return was .78 (4.88% ÷ 6.25%). In order for the results to be meaningful, it must be compared with alternative investments. The ones with higher ratios are more efficient, in terms of combining investment return and safety. *See* **Standard Deviation.**

ANNUAL RETURN OF FLIBBER JIBBIT, INC.						
Year	**2000**	**2001**	**2002**	**2003**	**2004**	**2005**
Annual Return (%)	15.50	12.25	10.50	6.35	5.90	12.70
Average Annual Return = 10.53%						

shelf registration. A registration procedure with the SEC whereby the registrant may issue any of several categories of securities up to a designated valuation. A more detailed supplement to the prospectus would be filed with each issue.

shell corporation. A solvent corporation with assets and liabilities and financial presence but no current operations. Often, such an entity can be drained of its assets and operating capabilities through a planned liquidation calling for an acquiring corporation to issue stock for the stock of that shell. Usually, the purpose of such a strategy by the acquiring corporation is to increase the number of its stockholders for exchange listing privileges and/or to utilize some tax breaks available, while not paying more than the liquidating value of the prospective acquisition, or paying only a nominal amount if the liquidation is complete.

    Obviously, the corporation acquired would be unattractive as a continuing enterprise to the exchanging stockholders. Otherwise, they would demand more for their equity in the defunct enterprise than the other would be willing to pay, since they would place a value on future earning power. On the other hand, the acquiring management would not intend to operate the enterprise and would place no value on earning power. It is not unusual for the name of the surviving corporation to be the corporation acquired so that its corporate identity can be retained, a protection of the listing privilege. Later the corporate name and charter would be amended and the new name (original name of acquiring corporation) changed on the exchange list. Thus, the merging corporation has become listed without a new stock issue or the expense and time that often are attendant upon a listing. Although, most plans follow this framework, there are many variations. A hypothetical example follows.

The acquiring company, Sly Corp., wants an exchange listing for an upcoming stock issue. The board votes to acquire Hazben Corp, the nonoperating shell and a NYSE listed stock. Sly issues 1,000,000 shares to pay the 10,000 Hazben stockholders in exchange for their 10,000,000 Hazben shares. The Hazben shares are valued at $5,000,000 by Sly, since they represent the net assets' worth of $5,000,000. Sly receives $5,000,000 in cash from the sale of these assets, meaning it paid virtually nothing for Hazben, except for future share dilution. The company then merges into Hazben, and gets a listing on the NYSE. Hazben shareholders get $5,000,000 and ownership in a successful operating company, now possessing the prestige of a NYSE listing. Later, the stockholders rename the entity Sly Corp., and approve a budget calling for development of the first intergalactic Web browser; the rest is history, as they say.

Sherman Act. See **antitrust laws.**

She's Got It Together. See under **Web Sites for Investing Women.**

shop. A brokerage office.

shopping. As an over-the-counter investor, getting quotes on a stock from various dealers, and then trading on the best terms possible.

short bonds. In trading bonds, a reference to those securities maturing in 15 years or less.

short interest. The number of accumulated shares that have been sold short and are still on a borrowed status published monthly by the New York Stock Exchange. Market analysts study this figure because sooner or later the stock must be bought to pay back that borrowed, and this buying pressure could halt a downward trend.

short-interest ratio. Among technical analysts, a measure of the near-term price cushion afforded the general stock market by the number of shares that must be bought to cover delivery on NYSE prior short sales. The ratio is derived by dividing the total short interest or uncovered short sales by the average daily trading volume for the preceding month.

For example, a short interest of 9,000,000 shares and average daily trading volume of 6,000,000 shares of Jazzed-Up Juices, Inc. would produce a short interest ratio of 1.50 (9,000,000 ÷ 6,000,000), or one-and-a-half days of average trading volume. Market analysts consider a ratio of 1.25 or greater a sign of technical market strength, less than 1.25 a signal of weakness. The rationale employed is that sizeable buying to cover short positions on inactive days can buoy prices up dramatically while the same buying activity on high-volume trading sessions would be absorbed without affecting prices noticeably.

short-sale account or **Type 5 account.** A brokerage account operated by a customer for the express purpose of selling shares not owned, but borrowed through the brokerage firm, in order to profit from those shares falling in price. Those shares thereby become available to the short seller at favorable prices to pay back the shares and cover the earlier short sale. This activity is regulated by the Federal Reserve regulations and requires a margin by the customer.

short sales or **shorts.** See **selling short.**

short seller. An investor who sells stock short as an investment strategy, either occasionally or frequently—depending on the tolerance for high anxiety—anticipating a fall in the market price of stocks selected. At the time of the short sale, he or she borrows the stock from a broker. The seller repays the stock when he or she buys an equivalent amount of stock in the market later, hopefully at a lower price than the earlier short sale. The seller will thereby produce a capital gain from the two transactions, after commissions, taxes, and fees are considered. The short seller is not really a backward person, but the strategy may seem backwards. In order to accomplish the traditional investment objective of buying low and selling high, most investors buy first. However, the short seller sells first. In either case, the objective is to buy low and sell high. See **sell short, to.**

short-term capital gain or loss. See **capital gain.**

Siamese shares. See **paired shares.**

SIC. Abbreviation for **Standard Industrial Classification code.**

"sidecars," program trading. A NYSE curb which delays trading for five minutes when the S&P 500 Futures Contract, traded on the Chicago Mercantile Exchange, rises or falls at least 12 points over or under its current opening price for the day. After five minutes, program trading can be executed only when it does not cause the market to go up or down. A 12-point move in the S&P 500 Futures Index is equivalent to approximately 95 points in the DJIA.

"sidelines." A position of having no money invested in fluctuating stocks because of uncertainty toward their market performance.

side of the market. A phrase indicating either the number of shares buyers want and their bids and/or the number of shares sellers want and their offers. The bid side of a popular stock is usually larger than the offer side.

sideways movement. A price movement on a horizontal plane, if charted, either because of no fluctuations or steep movements up and down that average out to little change over a period of time.

signature guarantee. A verification of a financial institution on the back of a security certificate, which assures that the certificate is endorsed by the actual owner.

SiliconInvestor. A Web site offering an investment message board, research, news, and securities markets information. *See* **Web Sites for the Inquiring Investor.**

SIMPLE IRA Plan (Savings Incentive Match Plan for Employees). This tax-favored retirement plan is feasible for small businesses with less than 100 employees and the self-employed. Workers who are eligible to participate may choose to defer part of their salary or wages to the retirement fund, and the employer must contribute matching amounts or nonelective amounts. The employer may contribute 100% of employee's compensation up to $6,000. Both employee and employer contributions are tax-deductible. Earnings in accounts grow on tax-deferred basis or until they are withdrawn or liquidated. Employee vests in both employer and employee contributions immediately. These plans are not burdened by complicated testing that other retirement plans, such as 401(k)s, require. They can be established anytime. This type of plan is recommended for the following employer situations:
- A low cost retirement plan needed.
- No other plans are offered.
- There are no more than 100 employees who earned $5,000 or more during the preceding calendar year.

simple interest. That interest figured as a percentage of the original principal only. In other words, interest is not calculated on interest in a payment schedule. *See* **compound interest** and **interest.**

Simplified Employee Pension—Investment Retirement Account (SEP—IRA). A tax-deferred retirement plan sponsored by sole proprietors and/or small businesses. Usually, the pensioners have no other retirement plan. They must be at least 21 years old. An employer can contribute up to 15% of each employee's total compensation, limited to a $24,000 ceiling, and the participant vests 100% in the employer's contributions immediately. Note that only employers can make contributions, but pensioners can also open regular IRAs. For the employer, it is the simplest plan to administer, which makes it appropriate for small businesses. The plan can be started anytime prior to filing taxes, including extensions. An employer cannot deny participation to part-time employees or exclude those who have worked for the company in three of the past five years. Experts consider the plan suitable for employers under the following circumstances:

- Business is for profit or nonprofit.
- Maximum flexibility in contribution level is important.
- Business has fewer than 25 employees.
- Lower cost option than profit sharing or money purchase plan is preferable.
- No problem with employees investing 100% immediately.
- No problem that employees have access to their retirement funds once contribution is made.
- Avoidance of annual IRS filings on plans is important.

Singapore International Monetary Exchange (SIMEX). Address: 1 Raffles Place, OUB Centre 07-00, Singapore 0104, 65-535-7282. *See* under **Global Investment Market.**

Singapore, Stock Exchange of. 1 Raffles Place, OUB Centre 07-00, Singapore 0104. Phone: 65-535-7282. *See* under **Global Investment Market.**

sinking fund. Those monies systematically allocated out of earnings for a specific objective, usually the retirement of a bond debt. In the case of bond debt, the issuer makes payments to a trustee or purchases an equivalent amount of the bonds in question for deposit to the trustee. This process provides additional assurance to bondholders that all bonds will be redeemed by their maturity, since operation of the sinking fund beings that process early.

"sin tax." A tax levied on items or practices that many consumers enjoy and buy but which have negative public connotations, usually because they are harmful to one's health or society's welfare. Because the enjoyment of such items is habitual, and in some cases addictive, taxing authorities are vigilant for opportunities to levy revenue-raising taxes on them when they become unpopular enough. The items or activities can be expensive, so tax proceeds can be huge. Soon the taxing authority becomes addicted! There is an irony in most of these situations. It is that the taxing authorities need the revenues the taxes generate, while often having to condemn the items or practices as immoral to rouse public support for the punitive taxes. Examples are taxes on liquor and cigarettes. Politics make strange bedfellows.

SIPC. Abbreviation for the **Securities Investor Protection Corporation.**

six sigma (∞). In corporate operations, a reference to the goal of attaining near perfection in performance—from product development to manufacturing to billing. The procedure derives its name from combining the effort to reach a higher goal of useable results, or a higher yield, with the statistical symbol for a standard deviation—sigma—in the analysis of a bell curve. One sigma represents a range within which 66.7% of all observations fall, two sigmas 95%, and three sigmas 99%. Six sigmas would indicate a 99.96%, or near-perfect, ratio. The object of the six-sigma model is to reach higher in achieving results, since conventional wisdom considers three sigmas acceptable in quality control.

size of market. The number of shares wanted at the bid price and the number available at the offering price at the current market price in a specialist's books.

skinny, Wall Street. A reliable viewpoint in the investment community, but not yet generally known, regarding an upcoming merger, acquisition, lawsuit, financial report, or other information of great importance to the performance of one or more stocks.

"skunk camp." A reference to a conference or seminar organized and conducted to teach aspiring corporate innovators to establish a special group or team to develop products and services through innovation, called a "skunkworks." *See* **"skunkworks."**

"skunkworks." A reference to the internal program or plan selected by a major corporation intended to make itself more innovative immediately, when that program involves creating a special team of visionaries who are allowed to work at developing innovative products and services without the daily pressures and constraints of the company's mainstream business(s). Such teams are staffed to possess attitudes of meanness, leanness, and flexibility as well as expertise. They are usually given stock options or some other form of equity stake in the results of their work or in the corporation. For this reason, they are selected on the basis of an intrapreneurial spirit. In a sense, these enclaves become small mobile companies within the big company. Many believe they present the best hope for the corporate behemoth struggling with the costs of coordinating internal activities to compete effectively against the swift entrepreneurial innovators of today. Both IBM and Apple Computer used skunkworks to develop the first PC and the Macintosh computer, respectively. Modern managers say that the number one problem with creating these teams is that other employees often resent exclusion. One remedy is to establish advisory panels that include non-team members, to implement progress made in the team throughout the company. Critics of the skunkworks approach say that the formation of such a group is an admission that the main company has failed at innovation. *See* **"skunk camp."**

sleeper. A slang term for an ignored stock with excellent earnings and/or growth potential, making it vulnerable to sudden market action when it draws attention.

slush fund. A sum of money available for investing without delay.

SLS. Abbreviation for the Salt Lake Stock Exchange.

Small Business Administration (SBA). An independent agency of the U.S. government, created by Congress in 1953, for the purpose of aiding small business development in the United States. There are many programs to foster this broad objective, the most important of which are: (1) to lend money to small business entities unable to arrange financing through regular commercial channels at reasonable costs; (2) to help small businesses sell their products and services to the federal government; (3) to lend money to small business firms impaired by natural disasters; (4)

to license and regulate private investment companies **(SBICs)** that lend money to small businesses; (5) to improve the managerial skills of prospective and active small business operators; and (6) to furnish aid and support to women and minority groups and encourage their participation in owning small businesses. The director of the SBA is appointed by the President, with the advice and consent of the Senate. *See* **agency securities.**

Small Business Investment Company (SBIC). An investment company operating under the Small Business Investment Act of 1958 as amended June, 1960, chartered and regulated by the **Small Business Administration (SBA).** The act provides that private investors can organize an investment company by furnishing $150,000 with the balance borrowed from the Small Business Administration to establish the $300,000 minimum capitalization of such a company. The company can then buy convertible debentures or make loans to small business concerns. There are certain tax benefits and exemptions from Securities and Exchange Commission regulations to those owning or selling Small Business Investment Company stock. The purpose of the act is to provide long-term financing to small businesses. *See* **loss on small business stock** and **venture capital.**

small business stock. See **loss on small business stock.**

Small Cap Analyst, The. See **Web Sites for the Inquiring Investor.**

Smallcapcenter.com See **Web Sites for the Inquiring Investor.**

Small Order Execution System (SOES). An over-the-counter trading network developed by NASDAQ for the use of individual investors.

smart money. A broad slang term for investors and speculators with a keen knowledge of events that could affect future market trends.

Social Security. A federal retirement, health, and disability insurance program for working Americans or their survivors, created by the Social Security Act of 1935, as amended and administered by the Social Security Administration. Each year

44.2 million persons receive benefits totaling $383 billion. Reserves to fund the program are collected by payroll taxes— Federal Insurance Contribution Act (FICA) taxes.

Under an expanded concept, these taxes fund the federal government's old-age, survivors, and disability benefits program (OASDI), and its health insurance program Medicare (HI). Employees and employers each pay half these taxes, which amount to 12.4% on annual incomes up to $72,600 for social security benefits and 1.45% on annual incomes up to $130,200 for Medicare benefits—a combined FICA payroll tax of 13.85% on wages. The self-employed also pay the taxes but at higher percentages—15.3% of self-employed income as a sole proprietor with no employees, and 7.65% per employee.

The original Social Security plan, a key part of President Franklin Roosevelt's "New Deal," was never intended to finance retirement completely, but to act as a supplement to savings, family support, private pension funds, or direct investments. As it was in the beginning for philosophical reasons, it remains controversial today for other reasons. They pertain more to the likelihood that the fund will be financially inadequate in the first half of the 21st century, when the Baby Boomers retire en masse. This is because it is not actuarially funded, meaning there is no correlation between contributions made per capita and funds needed to meet that person's retirement. Contributions are invested entirely in fixed-income U.S. government bonds. Many experts believe some of the contributions should be allocated to common stocks and other growth securities, to enable the reserves to grow faster. For some reason, this viewpoint is highly popular on Wall Street. Historically, the average return on stock investments in the United States has been about 7% above the inflation rate, versus 3% above it for bonds.

As amended in April of 2000, the Act now allows individuals who work past the "normal retirement" age of 65 to do so without reducing their Social Security benefits. However, the retirement age begins to rise gradually for those born in 1938 and after, and will reach 67 for those born in 1960 and after. Those who retire early, at ages 62 through 64, are eligible for retirement benefits, but will have the benefits reduced by one dollar for every two dollars they earn elsewhere in excess of $10,080 in the year 2000 and thereafter, until they reach the retirement age.

société anonyme (SA). An international company chartered by a government to carry on certain business pursuits and authorized to sell shares to the public. Investors have limited liabilities in regard to company affairs. The abbreviation "SA" must appear in the company title. This form of business structure is much like the American corporation.

Société de la Bourse de Luxembourg. A stock exchange in Luxembourg. Address: 11 Avenue de la Porte-Nueve, BP 165 L-2011 Luxembourg, 352-477-3961. *See* under **Global Investment Market.**

SOES. Abbreviation for **Small Order Execution system.**

soft asset. In a company's portfolio of resources, an asset that does not have a physical or mechanical function. Examples are: copyrights, patents, mineral rights, royalties, software programs, and Goodwill. From an investment viewpoint, the value management places on these in a balance sheet is usually dependent on an outside party who is exploiting the resource the asset represents, and paying the owner from the proceeds. Consequently, it is important for the inquiring investor to check out the likelihood of success by the user of the assets if that party is different than the asset owner. There is no reason that such assets are less valuable than other assets but, because they often represent new technologies or intellectual properties, they might not have proven values to another business in case the owner has to raise capital suddenly. There is also the danger of claims on the rights to the assets by others. *See* **hard asset.**

soft currency. That money not freely convertible into foreign exchange.

soft dollars. Monies paid by investment managers for research materials that are based on securities trading commissions. For example, an independent research firm, Fearless Eagle, arranges to sell a report to the Asian Tigers Forever Mutual Fund recommending an investment in a new theme park—Forbidden City. In exchange for the research, Asian Tigers Forever agrees to generate big bucks in commissions with Wealth Brokers. Wealth Brokers in turn pays Fearless Eagle a predetermined amount for producing the research. Under current securities regulations, such research must benefit the investors who ultimately pay for it, in this case, the mutual fund shareholders. However, there are many abuses, arising because some investment managers and brokers use the payments for their personal advantages. Continuing to spotlight poor old Asian Tigers and Wealth Brokers, the former might pay the latter a lot more in commissions than the research producer receives in exchange for a rebate of some kind or in exchange for paying another bill. The SEC has brought civil fraud charges in certain cases of the abuse of soft dollar commissions.

In a comprehensive report on the subject in 1998, the SEC did the following:

- Restated the legal principles and requirements governing soft dollar arrangements
- Alleged that many brokers and advisors engaged in soft dollar practices were not within the "safe harbor" provided by Section 28(e) under the Securities Exchange Act of 1934
- Recommended that the SEC adopt enhanced record-keeping rules for brokers and advisors relating to soft dollar arrangements
- Urged the SEC to amend Form ADV, the investment advisor registration statement, to require expanded disclosure of soft dollar practices
- Encouraged brokers, advisors, and investment companies to enhance their compliance procedures relating to soft dollars

softness in the market. A lessening of demand for a type of security in relation to its supply, generally accompanied by a price decline.

"soft patent." An exclusive right to the use of an idea or process that is not based on a physical invention, as granted by the U.S. Patent and Trademark Office. Software used by computers can be included in this category, as can methods of accomplishing some useful task, such as training workers. Until recently, the Patent office did not grant such rights, but recent court decisions have required them to do so. From the investor's point of view, the stated values of assets represented by these are questionable, since they are in a gray area legally. *See* **soft asset.**

sokaiya. The word in Japan for a high-profile corporate extortionist.

sold last. A transaction that occurs in sequence but is reported to the tape at a later time. There are no intervening trades between the time the transaction occurs and when it is reported.

sold sale. A transaction that is reported to the tape at a later time than it occurred, with other trades taking place between the time of the transaction and its report time.

sole proprietorship. The ownership of a company's assets by one person.

solicitation fee. A charge to a corporation by a stock exchange for requesting stock tenders through its members. *See* **tender.**

Soros Fund Management. See **power of attorney** and **Tiger Management Investment Company.**

Sources and Applications of Funds Statement. See **Cash Flow Statement.**

South Carolina Securities Division. Regulator of securities laws in the state of South Carolina. Address: Post Office Box 11350, Columbus, SC 29211. Phone: (803) 734-1087.

South Dakota Division of Securities. Regulator of securities laws in the state of South Dakota. Address: 118 West Capitol Avenue, Pierre, SD 57501. Phone: (605) 773-4823.

spam. A broad reference to unsolicited e-mail sent over the Internet, which can include recommendations to buy certain stocks. These messages sometimes mention unfounded events or opportunities for the subject companies in glowing terms and can be misleading to investors. Many investors are bilked or conned into phony investment schemes through following such advice. Often the messages include the qualifications that they are prepared from independent analyses, when in fact the messengers are being compensated by the companies in some fashion. Such misrepresentations are infractions of SEC rules.

special bid. A procedure for filling an order on the floor of an exchange to buy a large block of stock at a fixed price. The buyer pays a special commission to the broker who represents him, but the seller pays no commission. The bid may not be below the past regular sale price of the security or the current bid, whichever is higher. Member firms may sell their customers' block of stock directly to the buyer's broker during trading hours.

special drawing rights (SDRs). The unit of account for the IMF, created in 1969 and used in its transactions and operations. The units are created by the IMF for a period of five years, when it determines there is a global need to supplement existing reserve assets or those of a member. The value of an SDR is determined by the inclusion in it of currencies of the five leading exporters in the world for the five previous years, currently the United States, Germany, Japan, France, and the United Kingdom. The interest rates to borrowers are based on the rates in those same countries.

special power of attorney. See **power of attorney.**

specialist. An exchange member, stationed at a booth, who handles limit orders in certain assigned stocks and maintains an orderly market by buying and selling those stocks, when necessary, for a personal account.

specialist's block purchase. The buying by a specialist for his own account of a large block of stock outside the regular exchange market, if the purchase could not be made in the regular market within a reasonable time at reasonable prices, and when it will help him keep a fair and orderly market.

specialist's block sale. The opposite of specialist block purchase.

specialist's book. The record in which a specialist keeps track of limit orders given to him to execute.

special miscellaneous account (SMA). A special bookkeeping account set up by brokerage houses to reflect the amount of additional buying power accruing to stocks bought on a margin, because of a rise in their market value and dividends, interest, and so on credited to those stocks. The buying power is found by dividing the current margin figure established by the Federal Reserve as the credit limit into the market gain of the stock plus dividends, interest, etc. For example, if the current margin requirement is 70% and certain stocks costing $1,000 have risen in value to $2,000, .70 divided into 1,000 (1,000 ÷ 70), or about $1,428, indicates the amount available to buy additional stocks without more money being required.

special offering. The sale of a large block of stock on an exchange floor during trading hours by special announcement. Only the seller pays a commission and the price is pegged to the last regular trade in that security. The counterpart of a special bid.

special situation. A security that is acting independently, price-wise, of the general market.

special subscription account. A margin account whereby a stockholder can buy additional shares with his subscription rights, partly on credit of about 25%.

specific pool. A securities offering by a limited partnership in which management has disclosed the exact properties to be purchased. In evaluating such an arrangement, investors can estimate return on investment and other factors beforehand. Most often, this situation accompanies real estate financing. On the other hand, in a **blind pool** assets have not yet been purchased.

speculation. The commitment of capital with its appreciation rather than its preservation and income as the primary objective. Generally, an **investment** in which the probability of gain is 50% or less is considered a speculation.

speculation fever. An attitude predominant among investors that causes them to flout income investments in favor of highly speculative ones. High income tax schedules with more advantageous capital gains treatment have contributed to this mood.

spendthrift trust. A trust placing a dollar limit on the income from a trust the beneficiary may spend. An attorney should be consulted for complete information.

"spiders (SPDRs)." A nickname for Standard & Poor's 500 Depository Receipt. This is an investment product consisting of a unit representing a proportionate ownership of the stocks in the Standard & Poor's 500 Stock Index. Their form is a depository receipt issued by the SPDR Trust, a long-term investment trust arrangement that trades like a stock. Spiders can be purchased for 10% of their market values, which make them a popular and inexpensive way to buy and sell the "stock market." They are traded on the American Stock Exchange.

spin-off. The distribution of stock and transfer of assets of a subsidiary corporation to shareholders of the parent corporation. Under the U.S. Tax Code, the distribution can be tax-free only if the parent and the spin-off do not have business dealings after the distribution. *See* **divisive reorganization.**

split-coupon bonds. See **zero-coupon convertible bonds.**

split down. See **stock split.**

split-off. A parent corporation's distribution to its stockholders of stock of a subsidiary corporation for total or partial surrender of the parent company's stock. *See* **divisive reorganization.**

split-up (of a corporation). An exchange of all of the stock in an old corporation for stock in two or more newly created corporations accompanied by a transfer of assets to the new corporations. The old corporation ceases to exist. *See* **divisive reorganization.**

split-up (of stock). See **stock split.**

sponsor. An investment firm that recommends a security or underwrites an issue. *See* **touting a stock.**

sponsor, plan. See **plan sponsor, retirement.**

"spoof bid." See **phantom bid.**

"spot." In the pricing of stocks in decimals, a reference to the jargon used in quoting that part of the price represented by decimals. For example, 35-spot-10 means $35.10.

spot secondary offering. A block trade initiated by a company selling its own stock through an underwriter, generally after a shelf registration with the SEC. The underwriter buys the shares at a discount, although sometimes it must pay a premium, and resells them immediately. These block offerings are riskier because the underwriter takes the entire block for resale. There is no syndicate. For the stock issuer, the advantage is an immediate infusion of cash and avoidance of the arduous **"dog and pony show."**

Spousal IRA. See **Individual Retirement Accounts.**

spread. The amount of money between the bid price and the asked price of an over-the-counter stock. There are two different quotes for each bid and asked price, unless a salesperson is charging a commission. The first quote is given by a dealer who actively buys and sells the stock. The second occurs when the salesperson reduces the bid side of the dealer's quote or increases the asked side to the public, in order to make a margin of profit.. The salesperson will not give a quote on the stock without knowing that there is a dealer who will buy it from or sell it to him or her at a better price than the one quoted to the public.

Here's how it works. Let's say a salesman has a customer interested in Zapper Zippers Corp. stock. He knows a dealer's quote is $15 bid and $16 asked. He also knows the customer wants to sell Zapper. Therefore, he bids the customer $14.50, intending to resell the stock to the dealer for $15, making 50 cents per share for himself. On the other hand, if the customer wanted to buy Zapper stock, the salesman would offer it at $16.50, knowing he could buy it from the dealer for $16 and resell it for $16.50. Thus, the salesman would profit 50 cents either way. The quote from the dealer to the salesman of $15 to $16 is an inside quote. The quote from the salesman to the customer of $14.50 to $16.50 is the outside quote. See **wide spread.**

"spread products." Corporate and mortgage-backed bonds that provide higher yields for investors than U.S. Treasury bonds. The yield differential is the spread, described in basis points or in hundredths of one interest point. In many cases, these debt securities offer higher returns, without a great deal more risk than U.S. Treasuries.

squeeze. 1) A demand for repayment of stock that a short seller has borrowed, forcing him to cover his sale regardless of the current market price. 2) See **profit squeeze.**

stabilizing the market. See **syndicate bid.**

stag. A short-term investor, who buys and sells quickly for a fast profit.

stagflation. In a nation's economy, a combination of high inflation, high unemployment, and relatively slow economic growth. Often, this condition is due to low or no gains in worker productivity. This was a condition of the U.S. economy in the 1970s. The opposite was true in the U.S. during the 1990s, when high-tech electronic advances prompted increased worker productivity. *See* **inflation.**

stair-step promoting. A stock promotion practice of offering new stock to the public in a series of separate blocks or classes, each priced slightly above the other to give the impression of a rising demand and values. *See* **promoters.**

"stalking horse." In a situation where several buyers exist for a target corporation, a potential buyer that has agreed to make a tender offer in order to elicit offers from the other interested parties.

stamped shares. Those shares of stock or depository receipts that have been stamped to indicate some condition under which they were issued. Beware of this sort of condition. For example: "These shares will not participate in any dividends prior to October 1, 2005."

stamps. The federal and state stamps affixed to stock certificates signifying payment of transfer taxes by the seller.

Standard & Poor's (S & P). The leading publisher and provider of investment and credit information in the world for institutions and individuals. S&P is a subsidiary of McGraw Hill Company, Inc. Address: 55 Water St., New York, NY 10041-0003. Telephone: (212) 438-3516. E-mail: *sp_global@standardandpoors.com.* Web site: *www.standardandpoors.com.*

Standard & Poor's Blue List. A listing of more than 8,000 municipal and corporate bond offerings, updated daily by 750 bond dealers. Web site: *www.bluelist.com.*

Standard & Poor's Equity Investor Services. An investor source for financial news, S&P indexes performance statistics, a listing of the S&P 500, and links to other S&P investor services. Web site: *http.stockinfo.standardpoor.com/index.html.*

Standard & Poor's 500 Depository Receipts (SPDRs). See **"spiders."**

Standard & Poor's 100 Stock Index or **S&P 100**. The daily price index of a composite of 100 stocks, compiled by Standard & Poor's Corporation.

Standard & Poor's 500 Stock Index or **S&P 500.** The daily price index of a composite of 425 industrial stocks, 25 railroad stocks, and 50 utility stocks compiled by Standard & Poor's Corporation. In compiling the index, the price of each stock used is multiplied by the number of shares outstanding, thus weighting the average to represent more accurately price changes in terms of share volume rather than company volume. Such a statistical procedure makes large companies more dominant than small ones in categorizing market fluctuations. This index is the most popular in measuring overall stock price changes, and is the one most often used by professional money managers in evaluating the performance of their portfolios. *See* **index numbers.**

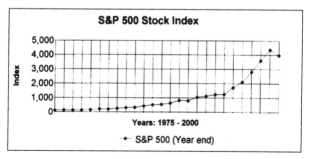

Standard Deduction. In filing personal income taxes, the use of an average in reducing Gross Income by certain household living expenses, such as medical and dental costs, sales and excise taxes, charitable giving, mortgage interest, and miscellaneous expenses such as unreimbursed employee expenses, tax preparation fees, certain legal and accounting fees, IRA custodial fees, investment expenses, and losses from casualty or theft of income-producing property. The standard deduction is indexed to adjust covered expenses for inflation. The alternative to using the standard deduction is to itemize the included types of expenses and using the greater of that total or the standard deduction. When a taxpayer has experienced an extremely high level in an allowable expense, such as expensive medical costs, it is worth considering the itemized version. *See* **Gross Income** and **Adjusted Gross Income.**

standard deviation (SD). A statistical measure of the dispersion of a set of observations or events about their arithmetic mean or central tendency. It reflects to what extent an arithmetic mean or other measure of central tendency represents a group of numbers or values. While there are other measures for expressing central tendency, such as calculating a range or average deviation or variance, in securities investing the standard deviation has become the standard for measuring the risk or price volatility of a group of common stocks that comprise a portfolio, or of the broader market, in the case of a stock index. The important point is that investment performance is more commendable when returns are accomplished with the least volatility possible. From the standpoint of investment risk, it is much better that an investor hold 10 stocks that gain 15%, on average, with an average price change of twice that, than hold 10 stocks that gain 15%, on average, with an average price change five times that. The first investor is less exposed to forced losses from having to sell at inopportune times than the second one is. That critical differential is the sort of stuff a standard deviation measures. The formula for calculating it is below. *See* **volatility.** Also, see **average deviation, beta value, range,** and **variance.**

As you are probably aware, there are zillions of software applications that will compute a standard deviation. But in case you are a zealot or still using a slide rule or abacus, here is an example. Assume that a group of 10 stocks have moved up or down over the past 10 days. (Remember, standard deviations have no signs.) The arithmetic mean of the 10 price changes for the 10-day period was 9.7%. And from the calculations in a standard deviation formula, the price dispersion or volatility for the 10 stocks in the portfolio was 15.2%. That was the basic risk for that 10-day period. If another investor's portfolio had gained 9.7% in the same period, but experienced a volatility or standard deviation of only 12.5%, the risk would have been less and the accomplishment greater, since if a forced sale had been required, the likelihood is the loss would have been less in the second portfolio.

Standard Industrial Classification System (SIC). A code, comprised of a series of up to four digits, used to classify industries. The code is employed by the federal government to measure economic progress in the United States, and is under the direction of the Office of Management and Budget.

standby underwriting. An agreement by investment bankers to purchase new corporate issues for resale if current stockholders do not buy them through the issue of rights.

stapled stock. See **paired stock.**

Starker exchange or **"Section 1031 exchange."** A reference to a real estate transaction completed under the guidelines of the section of the IRS code that allows a tax deferral on the sale of rental real estate property by rolling the proceeds over into another rental property.

Stat-USA Internet. See under **Web Sites for the Inquiring Investor.**

state banks. Those banks chartered only by the state in which they operate and examined by state auditors. However, state banks may apply for membership in the Federal Reserve System.

state bonds. Those bonds issued by states for road construction, bridge construction, or other such state improvements, usually pledged by the state's general taxing power and, therefore, considered sound.

stated value. A value assigned to stock shares for incorporation purposes and having no relation to actual value.

statement of account or **statement, investors.** A regular or special notification from an investment firm to a customer showing his financial activity, including such items as securities in safekeeping, interest owed for margin loans, recent purchases and sales, rights available, and dividends created to his customer safekeeping account.

statement of additional information. A document of information mutual funds are required to provide only to investors who request it.

Statement of Financial Accounting Standards (SFAS). When followed by a number, the official communiqué from the Financial Accounting Standards Board that outlines the methodology recommended to accountants and auditors for reporting certain transactions in company financial reports.

state of the art. A reference to a company's manufacturing, processing, or product technology that is the very latest. As such, the company would be expected to have a competitive advantage over those not so well situated in terms of lower costs or higher quality control in manufacturing or processing or the ability to realize better pricing or product acceptance in marketing.

state savings and loan association (S&L). A mutual savings bank created under state charter to make loans to its members as well as general mortgage loans, distributing profits to depositors as dividends.

static industry. A field of business in which projected earnings and dividends of companies included are not upward, generally because product demand is not increasing.

statistical analysis. In reference to the practice of securities analysis, the collecting, organizing, and interpreting of numeric data on a company, industry, or economy. The object is to identify whether trends, cycles, or randomness dominates an investment situation. The situation can reflect markets, operating costs, raw materials, and so on. Once the nature of the data is determined, the degree of predictability can guide a securities analyst in forming judgments about the outlook for a security and its place in the investment spectrum.

statistical arbitrage. Discovering and buying or selling for profits those securities that exhibit disparities in the prices computer models predict for them. The arbitrageur looks to make money when the market corrects the disparities. *See* **quant.**

statutory prospectus or **final prospectus.** See **prospectus** and **underwriting agreement.**

statutory voting right. The most popular form of electing a corporate board of directors, in which each share of stock entitles a shareholder to one vote per vacancy on the board. In this procedure, holders of a majority of the stock outstanding can elect all the directors. And, of course, a majority stockholder can elect all the directors as well. In an effort to allow minority stockholders to elect at least one director, some corporations have adopted the **cumulative voting right.**

steels. The stocks representing companies that process and sell ferrous metal products.

"sterilized" currency interventions. Actions taken by a nation's central bank aimed at enhancing the value of the country's currency in international exchange markets along with offsetting actions to effect a neutral result. For example, if a central bank buys securities denominated in its currency, thus supporting the currency in international markets, but then lowers interest rates, thus making it less attractive to buy securities denominated in its currency, the results will tend to "sterilize" its interventions.

sticks. A slang expression meaning the financial areas away from New York City, where investors must depend on widely distributed research reports rather than direct corporation or analyst contact for investment intelligence. However, with the advent of electronic information and trading, the lines between Wall Street and the rest of the planet are becoming obscured.

stock. A certificate representing ownership in a corporation that is usually sold to raise money to begin or expand a business. Stockholders have a claim on corporate earnings and assets after equity holders and debt holders senior to them have their claims satisfied. They also have a right to examine the corporation's books and records, at a convenient time and manner, but not excessively or in a frivolous way. *See* **common stock** and **preferred stock.**

stock ahead. The report to a customer on a limit order when his price is one at which there are prior bids or offers to his order.

stock appreciation rights (SARs). Rights to purchase shares of stock in a corporation at a price related to the appreciation in the value of the stock, usually granted to key employees as incentives to exert their efforts to enhance share values.

stock-based compensation. A company plan that makes payment of its common stock to employees under specific terms. FASB encourages companies to adopt a fair value-based method of accounting for such plans, such as the "intrinsic value" method. Under this method, a company records no compensation expense for stock options granted, when the exercise price is equal to the fair market price of the common stock on the day of the grant. When the exercise price is lower, an expense of the difference is recorded. The rationale is that the company could have sold the stock in the market for more, so the difference is a compensation expense, in effect.

stock buyback. See **buyback, stock.**

Stock Clearing Corporation. A securities clearing house operated by the New York Stock Exchange to keep members' trading balances recorded systematically.

"stock coming to me." A dealer's message meaning he is getting ready to lower his bid on a certain stock because supply outweighs demand.

stock company. A form of business organization whereby shares in a firm are sold to investors and owners who exclusively share in the profits from operations such as is done in corporations or limited partnerships. This is in contrast to cooperatives or mutually owned insurance companies in which the members share in profits and actually own the assets of the firm. The liability of investors in a stock company is usually limited to the paid-in cost of the stock purchases.

stock distribution. The issuing to stockholders of additional stock as a result of a stock split, stock dividend, etc.

stock dividend. The payment to stockholders of additional shares of stock, which requires a cash transfer from earnings or surplus to the capital account. Stockholders own the same proportion of the same assets, but the strategy is useful for corporations that desire to buy productive assets with money otherwise available for cash dividends and at the same time reward stockholders with tangible evidence of earnings or surplus. A stock dividend requires no change in par value of stock and so usually can be declared by a board of directors. Under New York Stock Exchange policy, any stock dividend requiring an issue of 25% or more stock is a stock split. Generally, stock dividends are not taxable when received (unless in lieu of cash or property, or in the case of preferred stock), so, they are popular with stockholders, who hold them hoping to get a capital gain tax advantage.

stock exchange. See **exchange.**

stock index futures. Derivative securities that represent contracts to buy or sell a microcosm of a popular stock index such as the Dow Jones Industrial Average or the S&P 500 Stock Index, on a specified date for a specified price. These securities combine elements of stocks and commodities and are traded on either stock or commodity exchanges, including NASDAQ, and can be traded before the settlement dates. Just as investing in a certain stock index represents a proportionate investment in that index, committing funds into stock index futures enables one to speculate on the direction of that general index, at a low initial cost or with a great deal of leverage. Trades are settled in cash, since delivery of a minute fraction of an index would be impossible. Under the law that established regulations for stock index futures in 1982, trading futures contracts on individual stocks is not permitted. However, that restriction could be changed in the near future. The most popular stock futures contract is the S&P 500 Stock Index or the S&P Composite. It trades in four quarterly cycles, with settlement based on the closing price on the last trading day of March, June, September, and December. There are many variations to accommodate different contracts and trading sites, but a contract for 100 shares usually costs a price of $50 to $250 times the stock index level at the time of purchase. For example, if the S&P Composite were 1,500, the price of a futures contract could be $75,000 (1,500 × $50). It is important to keep in mind the difference between a futures contract and an option contract, which is that the former represents an obligation to buy or sell the underlying entity, while the latter represents the privilege of buying or selling the underlying entity. *See* **futures** or **forward contracts** and various **options** topics.

stockholder or **shareholder.** The owner of one or several certificates of ownership in a corporation.

Stockholder Information in Annual Report. The section of a company's annual report that includes relevant information on the administrative matters relating to stock ownership in the company. Such matters as the time and place of the annual meeting, the company's registrar and transfer agent—usually a bank that processes stock clerical matters—information on how to obtain an annual report or 10-K report, and the person to contact at the company regarding stockholder inquiries. This section is the place to look when Uncle Ned left you 100 shares of the company and you want to find out what to do next. *See* **Annual Report to the Stockholders.**

"stockholder of record." An abbreviation for "stockholder as of the record date." A stockholder whose name appears on a corporation's records on the record date and is therefore entitled to dividend payments, stock splits, subscription rights, and so on through that date.

stockholders' equity. See **shareholders' equity.**

Stockholm Options Market (SOM). Address: Box 16305, S-103 26, Stockholm. Phone: (46) 8-700-0600.

Stockholm Stock Exchange–Stockholms Fondbors. Address: Box 1256, Kallargrand 2, S-111 82, Stockholm. Phone: (46) 8-613-8800.

stock index or "average." A measure of the representative changes in daily, weekly, or monthly stock prices of one or more selected companies in investable business fields, such as industrials, railroads, or utilities; geographic locations—countries or regions; economic sectors—natural resources or telecommunications; or securities markets—the New York Stock Exchange, NASDAQ, or others.

Really, an index can be constructed to represent about any economic series that investors can use in gaining insights as to investment timing and their own investment performances. In the latter case, the index becomes a benchmark against which investors would measure their average results. However, an index can be used to measure more than comparative capital changes. It can also measure and compare investment indicators such as dividend yields, returns on equity, debt leverage, and so forth. Here, it is important to compare apples and apples, so that an investor's portfolio rich in small-cap stocks is compared to an index of small-cap stocks.

Price changes in the various groups are expressed as a single average or index, and usually allow for value changes caused by dividends, stock splits, and so on, as well as trading volume in stocks used, in the case of weighted indexes. They are compiled by various organizations and attempt to register relative changes in the market value of securities in general by showing average price changes of a few stocks that are considered representative by investors. Technically, only an index measures the price change as a percentage of a base price level, although any arithmetical representation of price change is referred to as an index or average in popular usage.

A simplified example of a stock index is as follows: At the market close on Monday, the total of the closing prices per share of 100 preselected industrial stocks is $3,000, making for an average price of $30 per share. A value of 100 is assigned the $30 level or the base level. On Tuesday, the same stocks close at an average price of $31, and dividing $31 by $30 (1.033), an index of 103 is calculated (1.033 × 100), which is an average price rise of approximately 3% from the base level on Monday, excluding adjustment for stock splits, dividends, or trading volume. *See* various **Dow Jones Averages,** various **S&P Indexes, Russell 2000 Index, Wilshire 5000 Stock Index, EAFE Index, stock market indexes,** and **index numbers.**

stock market. See **market.**

stock market indexes. A reference to various statistical methods for measuring changes in the prices of a universe of stocks generally, such as the NYSE broad market, or a universe of stocks in particular, such as industry, geographic, or sector stock groups. Although stock market index data fluctuate widely, such data exhibit definite and measurable general price tendencies when incorporated into indexes. This characteristic is their contribution to the investment process. *See* **stock indexes** or **"average."**

MAJOR STOCK MARKET INDEXES IN U.S.

Stock Market Index	Symbol
10 Year T-Note Interest Rate (× .10)	$TNX
30 Year T-Bond Interest Rate (× .10)	$TYX
AMEX Composite Index	$XAX
AMEX Major Market Index	$XMI
AMEX Oil & Gas	$XOI
Dow Jones Utilities Average	$UTIL
Dow Jones Industrial Average	$INDU
Dow Jones Transportation Average	$TRAN
Mexico Index	$MEX
Morgan Stanley High Tech Index	$MSH
NASDAQ High Technology Index	$IXCO
NASDAQ 100 Index	$NDX
NASDAQ Composite Index	$COMPQ
NYSE Composite Index	$NYA
PHLX Gold & Silver Index	$XAU
PSE High Technology Index	$PSE

Russell 2000	$RUT
Russell 3000	$RUA
Russell 1000	$RUI
S&P 100 Stock Index	$OEX
S&P 400 MidCap Stock Index	$MID
S&P 500 Stock Index	$SPX
Semiconductor Index	$SOX
Toronto 35 Index	$TSE-TC
TSE 300 Composite Index	$TT-TC
TSE 100 Index	$TOP-TC
Value Line Index (Geometric)	$XVG
Value Line Index (Arithmetic)	$XVL
Wilshire Small Cap Index	$WSX

stock message board. An Internet site where subscribers may post news, comments, opinions, and questions about stocks. In the rapidly expanding Internet stock market, these chatter sites are creating some problems, due to efforts at stock manipulation through postings for personal gain. This practice is unlawful but difficult to enforce, because real identities are often not used.

stock options. See **option grant.**

stock pools. See **pooled shares.**

Stock Prices, 500 Common Stocks. See **Economic Indicators.**

stock price index. See **stock averages.**

stock quote. See **quote.**

stock report. A formal document recommending some action on a stock investment, usually distributed by a brokerage firm for the use of its customers and others in the investment community. It is a professional evaluation of a company's past and future profit-making ability, net asset value, and other business factors, in relation to competitors in the same industry and operating under similar economic conditions, leading to an opinion about the worth to investors of stock representing the company. It can also be useful in appraising other securities issued by the company. In many cases, the analysis sections contain adjustments to the reported financial statements that accentuate a company's investment values and progress. The report is generally produced attractively, in colors, and is definitely a sales piece advising some investment action. It is a fuller-blown version of a **stock analysis**. Before a stock report is issued to the public by a brokerage firm, the investment ideas and concepts included are usually reviewed by an investment committee or similar group in established and traditional investment firms.

stock right value. See **rights offering.**

stock salesperson. A security salesperson who just sells shares of stock, usually new issues. *See* **securities salesperson.**

stock split or **split-up and split-down.** A legal change in the charter of a corporation that allows for a reduction or increase in authorized stock. An example of a split down would be an exchange of one share for each two shares outstanding. An increase in authorized stock (split-up) would be, for example, an exchange of two shares for each one share outstanding. There is a proportionate change in par value. The significance to investors of a split-up is that frequently it causes a stock to move into popular buying range, since the stock market price is reduced proportionate to the split. Technically, stockholders approve true stock splits (where the par value is changed), but recently, stock dividends are being declared solely by directors, which accomplishes practically the same results, without shareholder approval. *See* **stock dividend.**

"stock stopped at." The report on a market order indicating the order can be executed at the stopped price, but the floor broker is trying for a better price. To illustrate, "stock stopped at 40" on a sell order means there is a bid of 40 on the specialist's books, but the floor broker might feel he can get an oral bid on the floor of 40.25 if he waits awhile. The specialist has agreed to reserve the sale of a specific number of shares for the floor broker at 40. However, he will not wait too long, because the specialist must take off the stop if another broker will sell at 40 and the reserved buy order is next on the books. *See* **stopping stock.**

stocks in the spotlight. See **most active stocks.**

stock table. A tabulation of investment and trading information for common and preferred stocks, most often appearing in newspapers, and usually reflecting activity on a specific exchange or market. Basic information is similar but some media publish more comprehensive data than others. For the meaning of terms and symbols in tables, refer to the glossaries, which are usually found at the end of the tables.

NEWSPAPER STOCK TABLE					
(1)	(2)	(3)	(4)	(5)	(6)
Stock	Div	P/E	Vol	Close	Chg
Disney	0.21	63.0	59,333	27.09	(0.93)

Explanations:

(1) name of company

(2) annual dividend

(3) Price/Earnings multiple

(4) daily volume in 100s

(5) closing price

(6) change during last trading session in dollars and cents

stokvel. The term describing a black investment club in South Africa.

stop-loss order. See **stop order.**

stopped stock. See **stopping stock** and **"stock stopped at."**

stopping stock. The courtesy by a specialist to a floor broker of agreeing to buy or sell his customer's stock at either the bid or offered limit price on his books if the floor broker cannot do better as other brokers come up with orders. *See* **"stock stopped at."**

stop order or **stop-loss order.** A limit order to buy or sell a quantity of stock that becomes a market order as soon as the stock rises or declines through the limit specified by the customer.

stop order, Securities and Exchange Commission. An order by the Securities and Exchange Commission suspending the registration of a security issue because of false, misleading, or incomplete information. The effect of such an order is to prohibit the sales of a certain security.

storefront. A reference to the Web site of a business entity, where transactions occur between that entity and new or established customers.

Stores. The stocks representing corporations engaged in retail selling. *See* **industry stock group.**

story. A plausible but probabilistic investment thesis or scenario advanced by a securities analyst or salesman. It is a slightly facetious expression, since "story" implies some fiction could be present, which is not altogether inaccurate, because such an investment forecast includes subjective attitudes and statements that depend on personal insights. These insights usually vary with the professional competency of the storyteller. The reference is generally used when an analyst anticipates that a certain company(s) or industry is on the verge of recovering from business doldrums, and that related securities could score big capital gains in the process. But the story could also pertain to a new company. Always on the prowl for new ideas, the analyst's employer—usually a brokerage firm —dispatches the analyst to spread the good news throughout the land, trying to convince investors to take their positions early.

"storytelling." A new planning tool used by company management to look ahead at the possible effects on business and culture its major corporate goals will produce in the distant future—25 to 50 years. Sometimes a group of companies will participate. Usually, a symposium is held at which outside experts and observers present various scenarios expected from the company's present actions. The purpose is to re-think present policies or missions in terms of profitability and social responsibility. The procedure differs from a forecast in that it is subjective and imaginative, whereas a forecast is usually objective and quantitative.

straddle option. A purchased option to buy or sell 100 shares of a specific stock at a certain price for a specified time. It is a combination put and call. If the stock can be bought at the market and sold for a profit at the option price, or bought at the option price and sold at the market for a profit, after figuring the amount paid for the option, it is generally exercised. If not, when the time limit lapses, it expires and the holder loses what he paid for the option. For instance, an investor buys a straddle option to buy or sell 100 shares of Two Worlds, Inc. stock at $50 per share. Option costs are $2 per share. The market price rises to $55 per share, so he buys 100 shares on the option at $50, resells for $55, and makes a $3 profit per share after deducting the option costs but excluding commission costs.

straight-line depreciation. A depreciation method of reducing an asset's value by identical amounts each year. *See* **depreciation allowance** and **sum of digits depreciation.**

stranded costs. In the regulation and deregulation of electric power companies, those costs representing past expenditures for generating plants that are no longer economic to operate and, therefore, subject to a request by management to a regulatory authority that it be allowed to recover the costs by amortizing or charging them off gradually. This is usually accomplished by including the costs in the power company's rate base, for billing purposes. Such costs arise because of shifts in market or technological conditions. The question usually arises: Should management have foreseen the shifts?

strangle option. A reference to buying or selling a put and a call option on the identical underlying security or commodity, expiring at the same time and with strike prices out of the money by the same amounts. Because both derivatives are out of the money, strangles tend to sell for lower prices than straddles do. In order to make money, the underlying security's price must change markedly. The investor must make money on the price moving enough in one direction to more than offset the loss on the companion option. *See* **straddle option.**

strategic assets. Those corporate assets considered essential by management to accomplishing corporate business objectives.

strategic alliance. See **airline alliance.**

Street, the. A reference to a semiofficial consensus among professional investors about the condition of the stock market and related financial topics. That consensus is disseminated by an electronic network emanating from the southern tip of Manhattan Island in New York City, where the financial capital known as Wall Street actually is, out to branch brokerages and media. Sometimes the appellation has an awesome connotation, conjuring up the vast billions of money traded daily and the wisdom that represents its central purpose and direction. Other times, there is an irreverent tone to the nickname, reflecting the rumor mill that spawns hundreds of financial misadventures monthly. The Street is many things to many people, but it is where the investment action is in the United States.

StreetFusion. A Web site for investors featuring access to corporate conference presentations, Webcasts, and other special events. *See* **Web Sites for the Inquiring Investor.**

street loan. A call loan in the vicinity of New York City's financial district. *See* **brokers' loan** and **call loan.**

street name. A reference to the registration of securities that are owned by a customer in an investment house.

"street teams." See **guerilla marketing.**

stress testing. When using computer-derived models for managing investment decisions, incorporating in the variables during model-building the likely effects of extraordinary financial events on the predicted outcomes. The term usually applies to risk management models in buying and selling derivative contracts. For example, if Risky Is Frisky Decision Management, Inc. develops a model that predicts what happens to the price of tapioca under 100 possible variables, but overlooks financial chaos in the pudding market as one of them, the model has not been stress tested.

"stretch-out IRA." The use of a bona fide Investment Retirement Account (IRA) as an estate-planning strategy by naming one or more beneficiaries of the account's resources, so that when its creator dies the tax-deferred distributions generated by the account will pass to them. This can be accomplished whether or not the creator dies before the mandatory date for the beginning of distribution (generally, April 1 of the year following the year in which the creator reaches age $70\frac{1}{2}$). But there are different rules pertaining to the number of years of deferment allowed when that death occurs before the mandatory distribution date and afterwards. For details, consult a tax professional. *See* **estate planning.**

stricken from the list. A phrase indicating a stock is no longer trading on an exchange, usually because certain exchange trading requirements—number of shareholders, geographic distribution of shareholders, adequate financial reporting, and so on—are not present.

strike price. The amount of money that the holder of a buy option contract must pay to buy shares of the underlying stock or that a sell option holder would receive in selling shares of the underlying stock.

strip. As a securities issuer or sponsor, to separate a security into two entities. One security represents its principal or par portion—in the case of bonds—its preferred stocks, or its stated value or equity value portion in the case of common stocks. The other security represents its interest or dividend payments for purposes of selling each portion separately to investors. This procedure allows investors to choose between the capital gain potential of the par, or equity portion, and the income or yield portion, and gives the investment firm two products instead of one to sell.

STRIPS, Treasury or **Treasury Investors Growth Receipts.** A reference to U.S. Treasury bonds or notes on which the semiannual interest income and principal repayment at maturity have been separated and sold to investors as separate securities. Technically, each claim on an interest payment is an individual security as are the claims on the maturity payment. The Treasury does not issue stripped securities, but allows brokers and dealers to issue them on certain Treasury notes and bonds they hold. Usually, underlying Treasury issues are for 10 years or longer. This is so because a longer maturing period attracts investors, since those investing in the income pieces can count on it longer, and those buying the maturity pieces have greater chances to get capital appreciation when the strips mature or when the investor sells them. Investors who need steady cash flow buy the interest strips, while investors who need a certain amount at a future date buy the maturity strips. For example, a retiree might roll over funds in an IRA account into an interest strip for living expenses. On the other hand, parents planning to send a child to college in 15 years might buy a bond strip that matured in 15 years into an amount they judge they will need in the first college year. Both pieces of a strip are guaranteed by the U.S. government.

"structural remedy." A legal solution to anti-competitive behavior, involving breaking up the guilty company, such as requiring divisions to separate completely. *See* **"conduct remedy."**

structured note. See **derivative security.**

stub. A stamped stock certificate indicating that the corporation it represents is being liquidated and an initial liquidation distribution of money has been made to stockholders. The holder of the stub is entitled to remaining distributions.

Student Loan Marketing Association. (SLMA). See **agency securities.**

style, investment. The rationale or concept for investing in a current stock market by aggressive investors looking for short-term results, more interested in riding the current vogue in piggyback stock buying, rather than using fundamental analysis on untried situations. The basic stock styles are: (1) buying momentum stocks or stocks in vogue, (2) buying long-time value stocks, (3) buying favorite growth stocks, (4) buying micro-cap stocks, (5) sticking with blue chippers, and (6) timing purchases of cyclical stocks.

sub-advising or **renting-a-fund-manager.** As an institutional investment advisor, with in-house trading and research capabilities, providing management services to a mutual fund manager on a fee basis. This practice enables the mutual fund manager to begin a new fund with a track record related to the sub-advisor, rather than having the expense of having to wait for one to be established with its own personnel and facilities. Also, the practice can yield better investment performance than in-house management. The administration of the fund and relations with the shareholders is retained by the mutual fund company.

sub-prime loan. A loan, usually collateralized by a real estate mortgage, made to a borrower with insufficient income or an adequate credit history to qualify for a conventional loan. In recent years, predatory lending practices have led to regulatory examinations of the sub-prime lending industry, representing loans of $280 billion. Such practices include deception about fees and cost by loan officers; excessive loan charges, whether or not the borrower's credit history is questionable, and other misrepresentations, especially in relation to adjustable-rate loans.

subscription rights. See **rights.**

subsidiary. A company owned and managed completely or partially by another company, through control or ownership of a majority of all of its outstanding voting stock.

subsidy. A program of governmental aid to domestic businesses because they cannot profit against world competition or because their products are of a public necessity. In recent years the bulk of these programs have been carried on by the federal government purchasing products at an artificial high price and reselling them in world markets at a loss. The practice is more often used in foreign countries than in the United States.

substitution bias. See **fixed-weighted index.**

"sucking-in." An investment slang phrase referring to amateurs who begin buying stock after a rumor has caused it to rise sharply and lose money when it falls back because professionals, who bought it cheap, sold their stock on the rise and want no more, thus eliminating the big demand.

suitability rule. An SEC requirement of investment advisers, in general, and a New York Stock Exchange requirement of member brokers that selection by them of securities for investors be compatible with investors' circumstances and means. This applies even when the customer has the investment idea, rather than the broker in the case of the NYSE firm. On the other hand, the National Association of Securities Dealers does not require a suitability test for the customers of its members. A customer has no legal recourse for an inappropriate investment recommendation, unless the NASD broker makes the recommendation on his or her own. According to the NASD, suitability questions are at the core of 29% of their arbitration cases. Suitability is one of the strongest efforts of the SEC, in protecting investors.

sum of digits. A depreciation method whereby an asset is reduced in value by computing its useful life in years and assigning each year a digit, using the inverse order of the life. The depreciation each year is that year's digit divided by the sum of all the digits. It depreciates larger amounts in earlier years. Here's an example. A truck valued at $15,000 is estimated to have a life of five years. Each year is given a value—the first year "5," second year "4," and so on. Their sum would be 15. And so, after the first year, depreciation is $5/15$ or $5,000, after the second year, $4/15$ or $4,000, and so on until the truck is fully depreciated.

Super Bowl Indicator. A somewhat whimsical belief that if a football team from the old National Football League wins the Super Bowl, stocks will rise during that year, while if a team from the old American Football League wins, stocks will decline. This indicator has proven accurate 87% of the time.

"Super-montage." A reference to the electronic display planned by the NASDAQ stock market, in response to the SEC requirement that all quotations be posted for stocks listed, including limit orders. This would include bids and offers on stocks listed on NASDAQ as well as those quotations from Electronic Trading Networks (ECNs).

supply area. See **resistance area.**

supply chain management. A reference to a manufacturing process in which the manufacturer maintains a completely neutral and flexible attitude about whether functions of production are performed by its employees or outsiders, whichever makes economic sense. It is a form of outsourcing, introduced by Dell Computer in the 1980s. The premise is in direct antithesis to the vertical integration methodology exemplified by Ford Motor Company in the 1950s. The advantages are flexibility in design— usually the components of the finished product are modular, and can be changed easily—and the cost advantages of maintaining minimum investment in materials inventory. See **integrated company (2), modularity,** and **outsourcing.**

support area. See **resistance area.**

"surgical solution." A reference to an anti-trust legal action that demands the divestiture of certain divisions of the offending company or a breakup of the offending company into smaller companies, in order to restore competition to markets. From the Justice Department's point of view, this is a desirable solution when the requirement to monitor a lesser solution would be onerous, if not impossible. Only twice in its 110-year history has the federal government successfully cause the breakup of a major corporation—Standard Oil of New Jersey in 1911 and AT&T in 1984. The Justice Department requested a district court to break up Microsoft in 2000, in a case that will probably be appealed, if not settled.

surplus. 1) Generally, a reference to a portion of earnings, past and/or present, allocated to a "surplus account" of a balance sheet. 2) Capital surplus or paid-in surplus. The surplus to a corporation from a sale of its stock or gifts of its stock received by a corporation.

surplus, appraisal. The surplus from revaluation of corporate property.

surviving company. The company whose name emerges as the name of a new company after a merger. Usually, administrative control of the merged assets also passes to the surviving company.

suspended from trading. A phrase indicating a security is no longer to be traded on an exchange for any of the following reasons. 1) The issuing corporation has substituted another security because the suspended one has expired. 2) A corporation has changed its name or place of incorporation. 3) Irregularities have developed concerning the security or its market.

suspension. 1) The revoking of a member's trading privileges temporarily by an exchange. 2) The removal of a security from trading by an exchange or other market. When a security is suspended, all orders in the hands of odd lot dealers and specialists expire at the close the day before the suspension is effective.

swap. A derivative contract in which two parties agree to make payments to one another on specified dates, based on formulas that determine the amounts of the two payments. These contracts are used by corporations and institutions, but not individual investors. There is a drawback to them, since they are not guaranteed by a clearing house and can be defaulted. As protection, some parties require collateral or a mark to the market periodically. The most common one is an interest rate swap, in which one party promises to pay an amount based on a fixed interest rate, in return for receiving an amount based on a floating rate from the other party. It is a hedge against a change in interest rates, in this case, and is an offspring of strategies using forwards.

swap fund. See **Centennial-Type mutual fund.**

swapping checks. See **exchanging orders.**

swaptions. The option but not the commitment to negotiate a swap on specific terms by a certain date.

sweetener. See **kicker.**

swings. A reference to continuous short-term general stock price movements, up and down alternatively.

Swiss Options and Financial Futures Exchange (SOFFEX). Address: Neu Mattstrasse, CH-8953 Dietikon. Phone: (41) 1-740-30-20. *See* under **Global Investment Market.**

switching. 1) The liquidation of one security to buy another. 2) The practice of selling a security at a loss for tax purposes, and using the proceeds to buy stock of a company that is merging with the one whose securities were sold. Thus, the switcher can generally sell his original stock for about what their exchange into the new stock will be worth under the merger agreement, buy stock in the surviving company, and still have a tax loss. He ends up with shares (less commissions) in the surviving company proportionate in value to those that he would have had if he held the old shares, but by selling first he also established a loss.

Sydney Futures Exchange. Address: 20 Bond Street, Sydney, NSW 2000. Phone: 61-2-2570000. *See* under **Global Investment Market.**

Sydney Stock Exchange. Address: 20 Bond Street, Sydney, NSW 2000. Phone: 61-2-2570000. *See* under **Global Investment Market.**

symbol. A price pattern. *See* **symmetrical triangle** and **ticker symbol**.

symmetrical triangle. A price pattern made by recorded high-low-close bars on a stock bar chart or Xs and Os on a point-and-figure chart. Chartists believe that the price move after the breakout will be similar to the distance of the back of the triangle. If the backside rise is a $12 distance, the price will climb $12, after the breakout.

sympathetic buying. The purchase of stock because good news has developed about another corporation in the same or a related industry.

syndicate. 1) A temporary partnership of investment bankers who have agreed to buy securities from certain stockholders, a municipality, a state, a corporation, an authority, etcetera for a certain price and to resell them at a profit to the public, in compliance with state and federal security laws. 2) A group of investors merging their funds to buy securities that they intend to hold to centralize voting power to accomplish an objective.

syndicate bid. A syndicate manager's bid to buy stock being sold to the public to keep the price up, called stabilizing the market. The practice can last until all the stock is sold. *See* **in syndicate.**

syndicate lending. In cases of exceptionally big loans or high-risk loans, the formation of a large group of banks to share in providing the funds in order to relieve the burden on only one or a few banks. Usually, the lead bank or biggest lender forms the syndicate.

syndicate manager. The investment banker or firm who organizes a syndicate, arranges for underwriting terms with the stock issuer, allocates underwriting participation to members, manages promotion expenses and keeps track of a new issue's distribution until the books are closed. *See* **principal underwriter.**

syndicate real estate investing. The commitment of funds into a company that buys, rents, and/or sells real estate. The investment is generally represented by collateral trust notes issued by the company. The formation of a syndicate allows small investors to put their money to work in large tracts of real estate. *See* **real estate investment trust.**

synergies. A reference to the economic gains that result from a merger or acquisition. For example, when two companies merge, the consequence might be more cash flow through savings in operating costs such as wages and salaries. Generally, incremental cash flow is considered the most important synergy in a merger or consolidation.

synthetic put bonds or **"put-call notes."** Corporate put bonds or corporate put notes with two elements: 1) a short to medium-term instrument that gives the holder the right to sell the bonds or notes back to the issuer, if interest rates rise within a certain time period; and 2) separate put options on the principal amount. The notes are sold to traditional fixed-income investors, while the options are sold into the derivatives market. The issuer bets that the company can save even more in interest expense than through issuing straight put bonds. *See* **put bonds.**

synthetic short stock. See **synthetic stock.**

synthetic stock. A block of stock that can be developed for trading, even though it is not owned outright but can be materialized through the use of options. A long call option and a short put option is a synthetic long stock, while a long put option and a short call option is a synthetic short stock.

systemic risk. A reference by financial experts to the tendency of financial or securities market failures in one country to react chain-like through the world economy, creating problems in other countries. *See* **Asian flu** and **"Red hell."**

Tt

T+1. A reference to the number of days after a securities trade until settlement, referring to when delivery of securities sold or payment for securities purchased is due. Historically, the number of days until settlement was five business days. However, with the advent of electronic trading and the acceleration in trading steps that has introduced, an acceleration in the settlement date worldwide is occurring. In the United States it has been T+4 until recently, and is now T+3. Although T+2 and T+1 will encounter many barriers worldwide, T+1 is the goal of a great many exchanges.

T+2. See **T+1.**

T+3. See **T+1.**

T+4. See **T+1.**

T+5. See **T+1.**

tactical alliance. See **airline alliances.**

take out or **take out price.** In a proposal by one company to acquire the stock of another, the price to be paid.

takeover. The acquisition by one company or party of the control of another company, through (1) a formal merger or acquisition, (2) a proxy battle, in which one faction tries to influence voting for a corporation's board of directors, possibly gaining control, and (3) insiders taking the company private.

"take time." A phrase used by a broker in wiring an order to buy or sell a large number of shares. It indicates to the floor broker the customer wishes to move slowly so that the stock's price will not be greatly affected by the order.

talent-scout merger. A type of corporate merger in which one of the companies purchases the other to gain access to the latter's resources, such as patents, copyrights, processes or personnel.

tangible asset value per share. The value of a corporation's total assets less intangible assets (such as Goodwill and patents) less liabilities and par value of preferred stock divided by common stock outstanding. Theoretically, it represents the realistic value per share in case of the liquidation of the corporation.

tape. The paper ribbon in a ticker tape machine, used by an exchange to transmit printed data on trades, quotations, and other market information to members. This form of communication became archaic with the advent of electronic tickers.

tape trading. The practice of buying and selling securities solely by an interpretation of trades on the ticker or tape. To use an example, suppose a trader is watching the market action of JET stock. At 10 o'clock, she sees a trade of 100 shares at 25; at 10:15 she notices a 200-share trade at 25.25; at 10:30, a 10,000 block trades at 26. Her reasoning might be that rumor about the accelerated future earnings of the corporation is prodding anxious buying, since the price is higher on higher volume. Furthermore, she concludes the 10,000-share block was a purchase by an institutional investor, probably a mutual fund, which substantiates the feeling that optimistic news is soon to be revealed. Consequently, the trader buys 1000 shares of JET, knowing very little about the intrinsic value of the stock, but convinced by her interpretation of the tape that the stock is going to rise.

target corporation. In a merger or acquisition action, that company which is being acquired.

target stock. See **tracking stock.**

tax abatement. The temporary waiver of all or a portion of a company's property taxes for a specific period by a municipality, in exchange for the additional jobs and economic activity the company will create in the area.

tax anticipation bill or **tax certificate.** A short-term, interest-bearing obligation issued by federal, state, or local government to be purchased by businesses with money accumulated as tax reserves. Businesses present the notes as tax payments when taxes are due and can draw interest on otherwise idle funds, while governments can accomplish a more steady inflow of tax revenues. *See* **reserves** and **income tax.**

tax brackets or **marginal tax brackets.** A reference to the levels of federal income tax liability for each tax period into which taxpayers fall in a progressive tax system, expressed as percentages of taxable income. Each base amount of taxable income places the taxpayer in a specific bracket. Any amount of taxable income over the base amount is taxed at the rate apropos to the bracket. Under the IRS code for the year 2001, there are six new brackets for individuals: 10%, 15%, 25%, 28%, 33%, and 35%. For corporations there are four basic brackets: 15%, 25%, 38%, and 39%. *See* **Economic Growth and Tax Relief Reconciliation Act of 2001, income tax,** and **corporate income tax** for base amounts.

tax capitalization. In referring to the valuation of a security, a calculating technique that takes into account the after-tax proceeds from buying and selling the security.

tax certificate. See **tax anticipation note.**

tax-cost basis. The cost assigned to an item by a tax payer in reporting a capital gain or loss from its sale for income tax purposes. The purchase price of securities entered on an income tax form when figuring capital gains.

Tax Court, U.S. Part of the Federal Judiciary System, the Tax Court decides controversies between taxpayers and the Internal Revenue Service involving the alleged underpayment of federal income, gift, and estate taxes. Its decision may be appealed to the federal courts of appeal and the United States Supreme court. There are 19 tax court judges, appointed by the President for a term of 15 years, as well as special judges. The judges elect one of their group to serve as chief judge for two years, including administrative responsibilities and a case load. The Tax Court hears cases in approximately 80 cities. Its headquarters are in Washington, D.C. Web site: *www.uscourts.gov/about.html.*

tax-deferred investment. A special investment security or account in which the accumulating income, in the form of interest, dividends, or capital gains, is not taxable under the U.S.

Tax Code until the investor actually realizes it in the form of payments or distributions. *See* **Individual Retirement Account** and **mutual fund.**

tax efficiency, mutual fund. Management of a mutual fund's transactions to maximize its ability to reduce taxes for its investors, both income taxes from dividends and capital gain taxes from selling stocks at gains. In the latter case, efficient management would optimize offsetting tax gains with losses. This leaves more money for investment and deferred taxation when investors cash out their shares. A mutual fund's portfolio turnover is considered a rough indicator of the ability of a fund's tax efficiency; low turnover of stocks keeps capital gain taxes to a minimum.

tax-equivalent yield. In reference to comparing the yields from bonds subject to federal income taxes to municipal bonds exempt from federal income taxes, the pretax annual rate of return required on a bond subject to taxes to produce the equivalent rate on a tax-exempt one. The pretax yields are made equal for comparative purposes. This procedure enables an investor to compare the yields on tax-exempt bonds with taxed ones with similar financial characteristics and to compare the after-tax compensation received for capital risks in the two categories. By indicating how much a taxable bond must yield pretax before being considered competitive with a tax-exempt, the calculation provides a hurdle rate for taxable yields before they become attractive to an investor. It also tells the investor whether he or she is paying too much for the tax-exempt bond—in cases where the taxable equivalent yield is higher—or is getting a bargain— in cases where the taxable equivalent yield is lower. As tax rates become higher in the tax code, the comparison is more important, because more taxes can be saved on the tax-exempt variety as they do. At present, there are six basic, marginal tax brackets: 10%, 15%, 25%, 28%, 33%, and 35%.

Let's work one out. Manana, the newest sexy singer, is in a high and rising tax bracket, currently 33%. Her manager, Constance Worry, wants to put a chunk of Manana's savings into bonds for long-term retirement purposes. (It's not like Manana is retiring tomorrow!) Connie can get plenty of tax-exempts yielding 3.5% and lots of corporate taxables at 7%, of roughly similar quality and maturity, although comparisons on this score can be tricky. Which is the better deal for her client?

> Equivalent taxable yield = (tax-exempt yield) ÷ (1.00 − .33)
> Equivalent taxable yield = 3.5 ÷ (1.00 − .33)
> Equivalent taxable yield = (3.5 ÷ .67)
> Equivalent taxable yield = 5.2%

Or the taxable bonds must yield 5.2% or better pretax to be the equivalent of the 3.5% tax-exempts. Their yields at 7% are 1.8% higher, so Connie plans to buy the taxable bonds. Manana plans another tour to Spain. For changes in the year 2001, see **Economic Growth and Tax Relief Reconciliation Act of 2001.** Also see **tax-exempts.**

tax-exempts. Those municipal and state bonds paying interest that is exempt from federal income tax, as determined by the Internal Revenue Service. Technically, under the U.S. Constitution, the federal government cannot tax state and municipal governments, hence the exemption. However, the proliferation of bond-issuing authorities created by state legislatures to finance some exotic and extra-governmental projects in recent years has caused the IRS to place some restrictions on the exemption. Also, certain bonds issued by federal agencies are exempt. Federal Land Bank bonds are an example. This exemption from federal income taxes becomes more important the higher an individual's tax bracket becomes. *See* **tax-equivalent yield.**

tax-free exchange, IRS Code Section 368(a)(1)(B). Under the U.S. Internal Revenue Code, the section that allows investors to exchange their stock in a corporation being acquired, or the target, to the acquiring corporation tax free in exchange for the acquirer's voting common stock. After the exchange, the acquiring corporation must control the acquired corporation, but the control does not have to occur on the exchange. Under this exchange, there must be a "continuity of interest" among all parties. Before shareholders agree to such an exchange, it is important that they are apprised of an opinion by the IRS that the exchange has been designated "tax free." Otherwise, they could owe a capital gains tax on the transfer.

tax-free exchange, IRS Section 1031. Under the U.S. Internal Revenue Code, the section that allows investors to exchange real property for a "like kind" piece of property without reporting a gain or loss on the exchange. "Like kind" property must be similar in nature but not necessarily of the same grade or quality. In order to qualify, the property exchanged must be in the United States and must be held for productive business or trade purposes or for investment. The following property does not meet the requirements of this section: (1) primary residence; (2) partnership interests; (3) foreign property, money, securities, and inventory held for resale.

Tax Guide for Investors. A Web site for investors providing information and news on retirement tax planning. *See* **Web Sites for the Inquiring Investor.**

tax haven. A reference to a country in which laws, regulations, traditions, or treaties make it possible for companies or individuals to reduce their overall tax burdens. When located on a remote island(s), they are referred to as offshore tax havens. Contrary to popular belief, these do not exist to launder "dirty money" or for merely "banking" money after it is earned, but, rather, to provide a place where nearly any international business can benefit legitimately. However, this is not so because there are loopholes around international fiscal procedures. According to one estimate, wealthy individuals keep over $6 trillion in offshore havens. It is also important to consider the type of asset or transaction one is trying to shelter from taxes in choosing a tax haven site. There are basically four types:

1. Complete tax haven—countries with no income, capital gains, or capital (accumulated wealth) taxes, and that allow the formation and incorporation of trusts. There are charges for documentation and other nonoperating fees. Examples are Bermuda, the Bahamas, and the Cayman Islands.
2. Foreign income tax haven—countries that only tax income earned locally by individuals and corporations. Examples

are Panama, Liberia, Jersey, Guernsey, the Isle of Man, and Gibraltar.

3. Reduced-tax haven—countries that tax corporate income but that favor treaties with high-tax countries, eliminating double taxation. Examples are the British Virgin Islands and Cyprus.

4. Special tax haven—countries with most taxes in effect, but ones that allow tax concessions to certain types of businesses (shipping or movie production, for example) or special categories of corporate organization for tax purposes. Examples are Liechtenstein, the Netherlands, and Austria.

tax loss. A loss on the sale of a security to offset a capital gain or reduce taxable income.

tax losses carried forward. The current business losses from operations or property sales deducted from future taxable earnings, under Internal Revenue regulations. In the search for corporate expansions, a company with a tax-loss carried forward is often an attractive acquisition, since the acquiring company can use the tax loss to offset its own high revenues or capital gains, thereby increasing net income after taxes. Of course, whether or not the tax-loss company will be profitable in its own right is also important. Under current regulations, a company first must apply the losses to the previous three tax years, thus establishing tax credits. If the losses are not used up, they may then be used to offset profits in the succeeding five years. *See* **capital loss.**

tax-managed fund. A type of mutual fund that attempts to maximize after-tax gains rather than gross returns on investment.

tax selling. A wave of security sell orders triggered by income tax considerations at year end, usually for the purpose of limiting profits or establishing losses to offset gains.

tax shelter, investment. An investment vehicle or security which provides advantages under U.S. tax laws. For example, an investment in a foreign mutual fund which can reinvest all its income, without paying a tax, could incur only capital gains taxes to an American holder, when he or she liquidated the fund shares. Also, investors in domestic mutual funds can avoid tax liability on dividend income received by the fund, if 90% of it is reinvested by the fund management, resulting in investors paying only capital gains taxes. Units of beneficial interests in limited partnerships and shares in "S" Corporations are considered tax-sheltered investments, because losses from the operating business can be flowed through to the investor's tax filing and deducted from that taxable income, under certain conditions. Therefore, it becomes a tax shelter to the investor's other income. For other investment tax shelters, see **income reserved trust, uniform gifts to minors acts,** and **reversionary trust**.

tax shelter, operating. Any provision under the U.S. tax laws that allows for a reduction in taxable income, either for corporations or individuals, as a result of certain costs in normal operations. For example, both depreciation and depletion expenses can be used as tax shelters. Depreciation represents the wearing out of an asset, such as buildings or machinery, while depletion represents the using up of a resource, such as mineral deposits or oil and gas deposits. Taxable income may be reduced by the amounts of each expense annually. The process is called a "shelter," because when the book cost of the asset or resource is fully depreciated or depleted tax-wise, any income produced by the asset is fully-taxed. In reality, most businesses establish reserves to replace wasting assets. In this way, new capital improvements begin new depreciation and/or depreciation schedules, meaning that there are always tax shelters in operation. The government can affect the amount of capital expenditures in a year as well as the level of business income taxes, by changing the allowable methods of calculating depreciation and depletion. In addition, certain industries can be given a stimulus through preferential depreciation and depreciation strategies. To illustrate, for years the oil and gas industry was allowed to deduct 27.5% of wellhead revenues as the annual depletion allowance, regardless of how many barrels or cubic feet were actually produced or depleted in a given year. The code has since been changed, eliminating that preferential treatment. *See* **Accelerated Depreciation** or **Accelerated Cost Recovery System (ACRS).**

tax switch. The practice of selling securities that have declined in market value, in order to establish a tax loss for the year, and using the proceeds to buy another depressed security. Thus, taxes are lessened by the loss, and the switcher owns other securities with equivalent market appreciation potential. Commissions and the investor's tax bracket must be considered, however.

Taxpayer Relief Act of 1997. Before 2001, this statute was the latest significant tax law enacted by the U.S. Congress, representing the biggest tax cut since 1981, and establishing the most significant decreases in tax rates on capital gains and ordinary income since 1986. It was included in a bill to balance the federal budget. Some of its provisions were modified by bills in 1998. Provisions of the tax act affect taxes on capital gains, home sales, medical insurance, education expenses, student loans, and retirement funding. However, the statute added complexity to a tax code that many were trying to simplify as evidenced by the tax simplification reforms of 1986. Small businesses and the self-employed benefitted from the act, including an alternative minimum tax (AMT) exemption, for which they lobbied vigorously and a phase-in of a 100% deduction for health insurance premiums for the self-employed. The reduction in capital gain tax rates is expected to stimulate profit taking among securities investors. The act included increases in airline, cigarette, and FUTA (Federal Unemployment Taxes) taxes. The following were highlights of the Act:

1. *Reduction in Capital Gains Taxes.* The maximum tax rate dropped from 28 to 20% on gains realized after July 28, 1997, on property held more than 18 months, and on gains between May 7, 1997 and July 28, 1997, on property held longer than one year.

2. *Exclusion of Gain on Personal Residence.* On a gain realized from the sale of a principal residence, individuals may exclude up to $250,000 and married couples up to $500,000. During two years of the five years preceding the sale, a taxpayer must have owned and used the property as a principal residence. In the case of taxpayers who cannot meet these qualifications, due to employment changes,

health problems, or other unexpected circumstances, they may be eligible for scaled down exemptions, keyed to the actual length of time they did live in the residence when compared to the two-year requirement.

3. *Tax Credit for families with Children.* Beginning in tax years after 1997, taxpayers are entitled to a tax credit of $500 for every qualifying dependent under the age of 17 years.

4. *Hope and Lifetime Learning Credits.* For general education expenses incurred starting in 1998, a Hope income tax credit is available for qualified tuition and related costs for the first two years of post-secondary education for a taxpayer, taxpayer's spouse, or dependent. This includes tuition and fees but not room and board or books. The credit is provided on up to 100% of the first $1,000 and 50% of the next $1,000 of eligible expenses.

5. *Deduction for Student Loan Interest.* On qualified education loans made after 1997, a phased-in deduction on amounts up to $2,500 is available for interest paid that is due.

6. *Taking Money from IRAs for Education.* Beginning after 1997, taxpayers may take out amounts from IRAs and apply them to education expenses of a spouse, child, or grandchild, without penalty.

7. *Contributing to Education IRAs.* Beginning in 1998, contributions to an IRA of up to $500 annually for children under 18 are allowed. While these contributions are not deductible, withdrawals from them used to pay qualified education costs, including room and board, generally are tax-free. Earnings not used for a qualified educational purpose are generally taxable, including a 10% penalty.

8. *Traditional IRAs.* For the tax years starting in 1998, income limitations on deductible contributions to traditional Individual Retirement Accounts are graduated upward from $50,000 to $60,000, for single taxpayers; and $80,000 to $100,000, for couples filing jointly. Individuals may withdraw up to $10,000 from any **IRA**, in order to use the withdrawal in purchasing a first home, and any withdrawal amount in paying for qualified higher education expenses.

For the spouses of taxpayers who are participating in an employer-sponsored retirement program, deductions may be taken for contributions to traditional IRAs. For taxpayers with **AGIs** between $150,000 and $160,000, deductions are phased out. Gold coins and bullion may be used as IRA resources.

9. *Creation of Roth IRA.* Starting with the 1998 tax year, taxpayers may make non-deductible contributions up to $2,000 each year to a Roth IRA, but no more than $2,000 per year may be contributed to all the IRAs maintained by that taxpayer. Distributions later on are tax-free, if they occur after the taxpayer reaches age $59\frac{1}{2}$ and five years have elapsed since the first contribution was made. Other IRAs may be switched to Roth types before 1999, by taxpayers with AGIs less than $100,000, with amounts converted treated as taxable income over four years, on a pro rated basis. For joint filers with AGIs between $150,000 and $160,000 and single filers with AGIs between $95,000 and $110,000, the $2,000 maximum contribution is phased out.

10. *Unified Gift and Estate Tax Unified Credit Increased.* Starting with the 1998 tax year, there is an increase in the unified tax credit applying to estate and gifts from $600,000 to $1 million dollars. In addition, the $10,000 annual exclusion for gifts and various other gift and estate tax provisions are indexed for inflation.

11. *Family-owned Businesses Get Special Estate Tax Treatment.* For deaths occurring after 1997, another estate tax exclusion is available for an estate deriving from a qualified family-owned business interest; when combined with the unified credit the exclusions may not exceed $1.3 million.

12. *Increased IRS Acceptance of Home Office Expenses.* Starting in 1999, home offices can qualify as the principal business place, when used exclusively and regularly by a taxpayer to carry on management or administrative functions of a business or trade. However, there can be no other fixed location where the claimant conducts such activities.

13. *Reinstatement of Provision Allowing Contributions of Stock.* Retroactively to June 1, 1997, contributions of "qualified appreciated stock," generally considered to be publicly-traded corporate stock, to private foundations is deductible at its fair market value.

14. *Raising of Estimated Individual Tax.* Beginning in 1998, individual estimated tax minimum raised from $500 to $1,000.

15. *Increase in Health Insurance Deductibles for Self-employed.* Starting with 1997, the portion of health insurance premiums for the self-employed is raised.

16. *Repeal of AMT for Small Businesses.* Starting in 1998, the corporate alternative minimum tax (AMT) for small business is ended. A small business is defined as one with average gross receipts for the three years following 1994 of $5 million. Corporations meeting this test will continue exempt from the AMT as long as gross receipts do not exceed $7.5 million.

17. *Changes in Business Credit Carryovers.* For general business credits, the carryback period is shortened from three years to one year and the carryforward period is lengthened from 15 to 20 years. This change began in 1997.

18. *Changes in NOLs.* Beginning in 1998, the carryback period for net operating losses (NOLs) was reduced from three to two years, while the carryforward period was increased from 15 to 20 years.

19. *Restriction of Tax-free Spinoffs.* Beginning April 17, 1997, it is more difficult for corporations to get tax-free status for certain spinoffs. When a spinoff is part of a plan or series of related transactions where 50% or more of the vote or value of stock of either the distributing corporation or the controlled corporation is spunoff, corporate level gain is recognized for tax purposes.

20. *Extension of FUTA.* The temporary surtax on businesses for income for the unemployed that was scheduled to expire in 1998 was extended through the year 2000.

21. *No Penalties for Failure to File Taxes Electronically.* Those companies supposed to file income taxes electronically

because their federal tax deposits in 1995 exceeded $50,000 are excused from penalties for not doing so between July 1, 1997 through June 30, 1998.

22. *Deductibility of Business Meals for Certain Parties.* When away from home, certain airline employees, truckers, railroad employees, and sailors, while performing duty that is subject to limits by the U.S. Department of Transportation, may increase tax deductions for the cost of food and drink graduated upward from 50 to 80%, starting in 1998.

23. *Introducing Constructive Gains on Short Sales.* Gains but not losses are recognized on short sales or an offsetting notional principal contract transaction, of any appreciated position in a stock, partnership interest or certain debt instruments, effective on June 9, 1997.

24. *Extension and Increase of Aviation Taxes.* Excises taxes levied under the Airport and Airway Trust fund are extended through September 30, 2007. Furthermore, the 10% tax rate for commercial airline passengers is replaced with an ad valorem and flight segment tax that gradually phases to a 7.5% rate plus a segment tax of $3 per flier. And the $6 per passenger international departure tax was jacked up to $12 and extended to arrivals from out of the country. Generally, these provisions went into effect on October 1, 1997.

25. *Increase in Tobacco Taxes.* The excise tax on cigarettes was raised by 10 cents per pack on January 1, 2000, and will increase an additional 5 cents per pack on January 1, 2002. There are increases in other tobacco products as well. In the event of future federal legislation implementing the proposed tobacco industry settlement, amounts equal to these tax hikes will be credited against payments required.

technical indicators. Those statistics that measure significant changes in various categories of stock market activity. This data is used by analysts in evaluating basic price trends or market moods; however, the indicators are not usually effective in predicting exact price changes. Generally, the data measures stock prices, trading quantities, or meaningful ratios; their changing relationships to each other are what make them analytically useful. Analysts select only those indicators to study that in the past have shown a relevance to market price direction. This relevance makes observers reasonably confident that when several measurements are similar to their levels of previous periods, the basic psychology of investors en masse is the same, a similitude that generally shows whether a "sell" or "buy" mood prevails, and furthermore, just how intense this mood is.

Normally, investment professionals create a practical application of technical indicators by expressing two of them as a ratio and plotting the ratio on a graph with other key ratios or with a price index, but they can use individual stock statistics too. When they observe that one or more indicators are moving in a pattern like ones that preceded a price reversal in the past, they become acutely anticipatory of a current change in the price level, ready to buy or sell as similar price behavior develops. Of course, technical indicators do not move in great repetitious cycles advertising symmetrical price directions but, when discriminately chosen and interpreted, they are extremely effective in measuring the degree and quality of current investor activity, measurements that often signify how long a current price trend or market condition will continue.

Although technical indicators can be used by the skillful to measure the condition of the market for individual stocks, the application of these statistics is usually restricted to broader price movements. Undoubtedly, the reason for the universal application is that statistics on individual stocks are not as accessible as they are on comprehensive groups, such as the New York Stock Exchange Index of its listed stocks.

The following examples present popular statistics used in stock market analyses. There are other statistics in use, but the ones tabulated show quite well the sort of relationships that exist as a result of trading activity and, consequently, those that technicians use. There are other technical indicators included in this dictionary under separate headings, where the names are proprietary. Most of the indicators appearing are published in some form in hard copy and on line. *Barron's Financial Weekly* and *Barron's*

Online, Equity Analytics, Ltd. Online, and Telescan Online are excellent sources, as are the financial pages of some search engines and Web browsers. The information presented can be from any sizable database, the NYSE list, the AMEX list, the NASDAQ list, or other sources. Also, technical indicators are usually measurements of activities during one trading session, but sometimes a week or month is covered. The measurement horizon can be longer when historical implications or cumulative data, such as short sales, are desired. Also see **odd-lot interest.**

1. *The Dow Jones Industrial Average (DJIA).* This figure is covered thoroughly under a separate listing. When considered with the technical indicators, it is usually compared with one to analyze how the latter is changing in relation to the price level. More often, a ratio of the DJIA to the **Standard & Poor's 500 Stock Index** is used as an indicator. When the quotient decreases, or high-grade stocks as reflected in the DJIA are rising slower than the broader market as reflected by the S&P 500, the market is said to be a speculative one, subject to a sharp selloff.

2. *Volume of 20 Most Active Stocks.* The ratio of the share volume of the 20 stocks most actively traded to the total volume is important as an indicator of the concentration of stock trading. If the percentage of share volume of this group is high, the analyst can assume that trading is focused on selected stocks. This concentration can mean that wide spread confidence in the market is lacking.

3. *20 Low-Priced Stocks Volume.* When the volume of 20 lower-priced stocks is high, there is a widespread interest in the market, especially in speculative issues. If prices are advancing while the volume of the lower priced stocks is increasing, investors are most likely enthusiastic about a continuation of the trend. On the other hand, when prices are falling, active volume in this group indicates a general abandonment of the market by speculative investors.

4. *20 Low-Priced Stocks Volume as Percentage Volume to Dow Jones Industrial Volume.* This percentage involves the total volume of stocks used to compile the Dow Jones Industrial Average and is complementary to the share-volume figure

explained above. When the percentage is high in relation to the Dow Jones industrial stocks, speculative shares are being traded more rapidly than the more conservative Dow Jones stocks.

5. *Short Sales, Number of Shares.* From this indicator the technical analyst learns how strong the feeling is that prices are destined to decline in the near future, because traders who sell short intend to buy stock for delivery later at a lower price. Therefore, when short sales are increasing, traders believe prices will decline. It should be noted, however, that when the total short interest on the New York Stock Exchange reaches a prodigious quantity, the analyst regards such a magnitude as a cushion against further declines. The reason is that many shares have to be bought eventually, in order to cover the short sales. Recent short-sellers, who sold at near current prices, are more likely to underpin prices, since they cannot hazard a purchasing delay if the market turns upward even slightly. Consequently, a high short interest can convert into dynamic buying power, whenever a price descent seems likely to reverse.

6. *Member Trading As Percentage of Total Trading.* The percentage of member trading reflects how active professional investors are. It is what the smart money is doing. To the analyst, the percentage reveals whether rational investors are stabilizing trading activity or whether amateur investors are changing prices inordinately, leaving the market vulnerable to sudden opposite movements. Historically, member trading has comprised a shade over 20% consistently, indicating this level is normal.

7. *Member Purchases.* This statistic indicates the outlook on the market price level by professionals. When they are buying more, their outlook is optimistic.

8. *Member Sales.* This statistic indicates the outlook on the market price level by professionals. When they are selling more, their outlook is pessimistic.

9. *Member Short Sales.* This measure is a qualitative approach to the interpretation of short sale data. All that was said in the former explanation of short sales applies here, reinforced

by the fact that knowledgeable professionals are responsible for changes in this indicator.

10. *Confidence Index.* Of all the indicators, a Confidence Index is probably the one that is considered most anticipatory of price direction. It is a ratio of high-grade bond yields to average bond yields. Adherents of this ratio indicator claim that its trend precedes the actual "average" price level of stocks by 60 to 90 days. (Since the index is predicated on the belief that bond investors are more aware of capital markets than stock investors often are about almost everything, activities in that market are presumed to precede actions in the stock market.) As the quotient of the Confidence Index gets larger, the analyst realizes that more professional money is being used to buy high-grade bonds, forcing down their yields. This flux often has downward repercussions on riskier stock values, leading to lower prices.

11. *Yields on Dow Jones Averages.* (Yields indicate better than any other measure when prices are relatively high or low, for they tell analysts what stock buyers are getting as an actual return—a cash payment that is the very essence of investing.) Unfortunately, yields by themselves do not reveal a great deal of what investors think about the price level. (The same criticism can be leveled at the price/earnings ratio.) Consequently, yield figures are usually expressed as a ratio with another yield figure. For example, the ratio of the average yield of speculative stocks to high-grade stocks. When the quotient gets smaller, speculative interest is thought to be dominating the market, a condition that often leads to price downturns.

12. *Price/Earnings Multiple.* Simply stated, the price/earnings multiple is the number of times the earnings per share of a stock have been increased or capitalized in the stock trading process to form the current market price. The higher this multiple becomes, the more speculative in nature investors are considered to be, since grossly inflated multiples in general are contingent upon a rate of economic growth unlikely in a reasonable time interval. Like the yield figure, the price/earnings multiple reflects dependably when prices are

relatively high or low; the multiple does not indicate how investors intend to react to current prices. Most analysts assume a range of yield and price/earnings multiples that investors are anchored to historically, and this belief in the innate traditionalism of most investors causes analysts to isolate levels of these two indicators, which in the past have harbingered a return of stock prices to more typical levels. So, when the levels reappear the market is headed for a reversal, according to these analysts.

13. *Issues Traded.* The popular name for this category is "Breadth of the Market" indicators. As the name implies, these indicators measure the extensiveness of market activity. The more general a price advance or decline is, the more convinced a technician becomes that the direction is not of a temporary nature. When total issues traded is at a high level there is an indication that the market is dynamic, attractive to shareholders of all types. When issues that have advanced in price outnumber those that have declined, or when stocks that have sold at new high prices outnumber those that have sold at new low prices, the market is thought to be primed for further price rises. Naturally, a reverse situation would indicate a faltering market. When the issues that have remained unchanged in price are abnormally high, the market is considered stagnant, indecisive about financial prospects of listed corporations.

14. *Advance-Decline Ratio.* In measuring the strength or weakness in a stock market, the calculation of the number of listed stock issues trading that are higher in price at the close of a trading session divided by the number of issues lower in price. For example, if on a given day 3,500 issues on the Roller Coaster Stock Exchange were higher and 3,000 were lower, the Advance-Decline Ratio would be 1.17 or 117% $(3,500 \div 3,000 \times 100)$. When the ratio is greater than one, the market is considered healthy, since that indicates a majority of individual issues trading advanced in price.

Several points should be remembered in analyzing technical indicators. First, they are only relevant when considered over a period of time. A spasmodic reference to them is apt to lead to misinterpretations. They do not enlighten the analyst instantly, but do show him significant trends over a period of time. Second, indicators are effective only when several are used together. By using just one or two, there is a probability that market analysis will be distorted. In the same vein, indicators should be used to substantiate each other. When a majority of them do not indicate the same market condition, they are likely invalid indicators, or they should be studied further in anticipation of changes.

Finally, there are times when certain indicators seem to refute logical stock market analysis, deviating inexplicably from a pattern. The experienced analyst does not become dismayed at such an aberration, for he knows that market analysis is a behavioral semi-science, at best—unlike the natural laws of the orderly Universe. The lax laws of the stock market are subject to human impulsiveness, which can make the most probing analysis appear fatuous. But in the gigantic trading process, the analyst can observe relationships that reflect investor attitudes, and as long as he stays alert for outside events that can suddenly nullify a trend, he can do a creditable job of anticipating price movements.

technical movement. A price change caused by internal market pressures such as a rush to cover short orders, rather than a change in prevailing investor psychology.

technical reversal. A reference to an inevitable change in the price direction of a stock or the general market, purely due to momentary trading moves in the opposite direction by investors who want to realize profits or investors who want to buy favorite stocks at bargain levels. When this happens, there is no change in basic investor psychology, even though there is a short price reaction. For example, if a stock reaches new highs on growing volume on 10 consecutive days, and declines in price the 11th day in the absence of derogatory news, a technical reversal would be presumed, especially if the reversal occurred on diminished volume.

technological breakthrough. The development of a major scientific discovery that opens the door to heretofore impossible products.

Technology. Those stocks representing companies engaged in the research, development, and marketing of products in biotechnology, telecommunications, Internet infrastructure, Internet software, hand-held digital communications, and medical equipment among others. *See* **sector.**

TED Spread. An acronym for Treasuries over Eurodollars, it represents the spread, or difference, between futures interest rates of U.S. Treasury bills and Eurodollars. The widening and narrowing of the spread reflects confidence in the U.S. economy as well as global economic conditions. Among interest-rate traders, a narrow spread suggests high confidence in the U.S. economy and financial markets in general, while a wide spread suggests the opposite. The rationale for this inference is that similar rates between different key currencies indicates stability, since no one or more currencies is out of line with potentially serious problems with the government represented. Traders buy and sell currencies and interest rate futures, based on the spread.

"teenie." A reference to the stock trading jargon for $\frac{1}{16}$ of a dollar on the New York Stock Exchange, used before decimal quotes became standard.

Telecommunications—Long Distance. Those stocks representing companies providing long distance voice, data, and picture telephony services. *See* **industry stock group.**

telephone (T). The nickname for American Telephone and Telegraph Company, world's largest utility company.

Telephone—Local. Those stocks representing companies providing local access voice, data, and picture telephony services. *See* **industry stock group.**

teletype. A machine connected to a "wire" circuit that prints financial news throughout a market day.

10-K Wizard. Web site highlighting keywords in researching company SEC filings. *See* **Web Sites for the Inquiring Investor.**

10-share units. See **round lot.**

tenancy in common (TIC). In securities or other personal property ownership, a tenancy of two or several persons in which the property(s) belonging to each co-owner(s) in the tenancy becomes part of that person's estate for probate upon death. It does not pass to the survivor's in the tenancy as is the case with a joint tenancy with rights of survivorship. *See* **joint account, joint tenants** and **joint tenancy with rights of survivorship.**

tender offer. A public offer to buy stock of a corporation from its stockholders, made by another corporation or buyer at a certain price, generally provided that a minimum number of shares are presented for sale within a specified period. Usually, tender offers must be inclusive of all shareholders and must be accompanied by information or full disclosure regarding the value of an offer. *See* **escrow agent** and **minitender offer.**

Tennessee Department of Commerce and Insurance. Regulator of securities laws in the state of Tennessee. Address: Securities Division, Volunteer Plaza, #680, 500 James Robertson Parkway, Nashville, TN 37243. Phone (information): (615) 741-3187. Phone (complaints): (615) 741-5900.

Tennessee Valley Authority (TVA). See **agency securities.**

term bonds. Bonds issued simultaneously and that mature at the same time.

term certain annuity. An annuity contract guaranteeing income to the annuitant or an estate for a specified period of time, in exchange for a single or multiple payment in advance.

term trust. An investment unit with terms stated in advance, providing an investor a portion of regular dividends and the return of principal at a future time, in theory. The fund can be invested in taxable or nontaxable securities, from adjustable-rate mortgages to zero-coupon bonds. In practice, these trusts have been unpredictable as to the amounts of dividends and principal, mainly because of interest rate fluctuations.

test a low or high. In reference to a stock average or an individual security price, to move to a previous low or high price level. In the case of a low, if the price or average does not go beneath the level, investor confidence usually returns, stimulating buying. In the case of a high, if the price or average does not penetrate the level, investor confidence wanes.

testamentary trust. A trust arrangement created by a will and taking effect upon the death of the maker of the will.

tested high. A level above the current one that a stock average or an individual security price has gone to, stopped at, and turned downward often enough for it to be considered an impenetrable high point for the period or until some news impacts the stock's performance image.

tested low. A level below the current one which a stock average or an individual security price has gone to, stopped at, and turned upward often enough for it to be considered a support point for the period or until some news impacts the stock's performance image.

Texas State Securities Board. Regulator of securities laws in the state of Texas. Address: P.O. Box 13167, Austin, TX 78711. Phone: (512) 305-8332.

Textile Apparel Manufacturers. Those stocks representing companies making clothing items. *See* **industry stock group.**

The Street. A term for the Wall Street area of New York City, denoting the securities and financial area of that city. *See* **Street, the.**

theta. The measure of how much an option's value decreases each day as it nears its expiration date.

thin market. A market in which few shares (under 25,000 in some listed stocks but this figure must be based on historical evidence) are being traded daily in a security with wide fluctuations in price. This is an explosive situation because when demand increases sharply it is not satisfied by a proportionate increase in stock available, and the price can jump. When demand wanes, buyers are scarce and prices might fall. The situation amounts to a few people trading with each other, eliminating the gradual price changes of a broad market.

Three "C"s, banking. A reference to the three main tenets used in evaluating a loan to a bank customer: Credit, Capital, and Character. When a loan officer takes a loan application to the loan committee for approval, s/he emphasizes these characteristics, garnered from information on the loan application as well as data on the customer from the bank's data base. "Credit" represents the information related to the customer's record in borrowing and repaying money. Preferably, there is some record and, if so, bank officers favor applicants who have paid off past obligations regularly and in a timely manner. "Capital" represents the financial resources owned or accessible to the applicant. These can be stocks, bonds, real estate, savings, and so on. Although the assets might not be used as collateral or security for the loan, banks like to see financial resources at the disposal of the customer, in case they are needed to get the applicant over a difficult financial period without jeopardizing a loan from the bank. "Character" represents that intangible trait of honesty and dedication to objectives, such as paying off a loan. It is the reputation of the applicant in the community, pertaining to business and financial matters. Personal and business references usually are included in the application or might be contacted by an officer. Sometimes the applicant is so well known, that is unnecessary. Obviously these Three "C"s rely more on quantitative than qualitative analyses.

Three "C"s, Internet companies. A reference to the three ingredients that investment analysts like to see present in an Internet provider. They are: Commerce, Content, and Community. Because there is a very short financial and operating history for most Internet providers, these Three "C"s are more qualitative than quantitative, compared to the three "C"s of banking. "Commerce" represents a company's ability to generate traffic to its Web site. This involves attractive design and effective promotions to entice visitors, including persuasiveness in converting shoppers to buyers. "Content" represents the nature of products or services offered to the visitor, in terms of desirability, in order to make the shopper a buyer. "Community" represents the size and degree of interest in the body of prospects that visit the site. The larger and more intense, the better. Some measure of this is from the frequency of visits by prospects and the extent of their repetitious buying . Also, factors like active community chat groups sponsored by the company are indicative of "Community."

"throwing good money after bad." A reference to trying to bail out a bad investment by putting more money into it, in the form of capital equipment, salaries, and such, on a crash basis. It is generally conceded such action is not a remedy unless a complete reorganization, recapitalization, and redirection occurs.

tick. A slang expression meaning a **minimum fluctuation** of price allowed in a stock market. The name derived from the "tick-tick" noises the old ticker tape machines made as they rattled out quotes and the news.

ticker. The electronic panel on which a record of securities trades, quotations, and other information related to securities trading on an exchange is transmitted to member firms.

ticker symbol. A combination of capital letters, sometimes with additional lowercase prefixes and suffixes, that identify the issuer of a specific security. These are imaged on moving tapes for the purpose of reporting trades in those securities during trading sessions and quotes after trading closures. Most symbols are in three or four letters, not including prefixes and suffixes, and unless otherwise noted, most trades represent 100 shares for stocks. Some examples are: "BEAM" stands for Summit Technology (lasers), "BUD" stands for Anheuser-Busch Companies, and "CAKE" for the Cheesecake Factory. *See* **ticker trading symbol suffixes.**

ticker tape. See **tape.**

ticker trading symbol suffixes. Symbols attached to stock trading reports and other phrases on the ticker tape indicating special trading information.

TICKER TRADING SUFFIX SYMBOLS

Description	Suffix Symbol
Class A	A
Class A Called	ACL
Class A Convertible	ACV
Class A When Issued	AWl
Class B	B
Class B Called	BCL
Class B Convertible	BCV
Class B When Issued	BWI
Called	CL
Certificate	CT
Convertible	cv
Convertible Called	CVCL
Ex-Dividend	xl)
Ex-Rights	XRT
Without Warrants	xW
Part Called	PTCL
Preferred	PR
Preferred A through Preferred Z	PRA through PRZ
Preferred Called	PRCL
Preferred When Issued	PRWI
Rock Island Certificate UP	CTUP
Rights	RT
Rights When Issued	PRWI
Special	sP
Stamped	SD
Warrants	WS
Warrants Class A	WSA
Warrants Class B	WSB
Warrants When Issued	WSWI
With Warrants	WW
When Distributed	WD
When Issued	WI

Tiger Cub. The nickname for any one fo the 13 hedge funds in the U.S. managed by alumni of Tiger Management Investment Company. *See* **Tiger Management Investment Company.**

Tiger Management Investment Company. The name of one of the two best known and biggest hedge fund management companies in the United States, the other being Soros Fund Management. In the late 1990s, at their peaks, each one had under management approximately $23 billion. *See* **hedge fund** and **Tiger Cub.**

TIGERS. Abbreviation for **Treasury Investors Growth Receipts.** *See* **STRIPS, Treasury.**

tightening bias. In reference to the quarterly meetings of the Open Market Committee of the Federal Reserve system, a prevailing attitude toward restricting credit and money creation. This is accomplished through the sale of securities into the system's commercial bank system. The process reduces bank reserves, which are the basis for credit creation in the form of loans to bank customers.

tightly held. See **closely held.**

tight money. Lendable funds that have a high interest rate because of heavy demand in relation to the supply.

TIM. Abbreviation for Telecommunications and Information Management. *See* **Management of Technology (MOT).**

time contract or **acceptance.** The purchase of a piece of merchandise on credit, payable in installments, with the total payout amounting to the retail price plus finance charges. Usury laws are not applicable to the amounts charged for credit. These contracts are often bought at discounts, in which case they are acceptances.

time diversification. See **diversification (3).**

time value of money. In investment theory, a phrase indicating that there is a direct relationship between the use of money as an investment and (1) the length of time it is used, and (2) the rate of return expected. Basically, the concept is used to establish a value of money at various points in time during an investment program or process, providing a structure to the investment operation, although its dependability varies with the nature and duration of the investment vehicle. In essence, the concept establishes that a present amount is worth a greater amount in the future, after it has compounded at a certain interest rate for a specific period; a future amount is worth a lesser amount in the present, before it has had time to compound. An amount in hand today is worth more than a greater amount tomorrow, because it is available for use immediately.

The time value of money is the basis for all contractual investing such as bonds or annuities. It is also used in evaluating the present values of future streams of cash flows or earnings, including the case of common stocks. In this context, $1.00 of earnings five years from now is worth $0.62 today, assuming the interest rate is 10% annually. Therefore, earnings that grow to $5.00 per share in five years are said to be worth five times the present value of $0.62 or $3.10 per share today. If the current stock market is appraising earnings of similar stocks at 20 times earnings, the valuation of the stock would be $62 per share. *See* **Capital Asset Pricing Model.**

TIME VALUE OF $1.00 OVER FIVE YEARS						
Present Value Today	Assumed Interest Rate	Year 1	Year 2	Year 3	Year 4	Year 5
$0.62	10%	$0.68	$0.75	$0.83	$0.91	$1.00

time-weighted value of money. The value of a sum of money, taking into account the rate of return it will earn and the length of time for which it will be used.

times fixed charges earned. See **fixed charge coverage.**

timing. A reference to the important question of when to buy and sell securities. Generally speaking, the best time to invest in common stocks is at the outset of a long period of business and economic advance. On the other hand, the best time to invest in selected securities is just before an unusually good report is revealed by a company, such as high earnings, a major product development announcement, a beneficial merger, a lucrative contract announcement, and so on. When unfavorable news about the company, its industry, or the economy is impending, sales should be contemplated. Since the emergence of institutions as trading giants, many investors take their cues from them. Bonds and preferred stocks are good buys, usually when their yields are more attractive then other securities, but they often fall in price if common stock yields become much better and constant. A long-term investor should not be as concerned with timing as with permanent quality of her securities, in terms of her investment needs.

tip. A slang expression for a little known rumor about a certain company that allegedly will drastically affect its market price.

TIPS. See **Treasury Inflation-Protected Security.**

TIPS Fund. A mutual fund principally invested in TIPS. *See* **Treasury Inflation-Protected Security.**

"Titanic stock." In an otherwise sea of clear sailing for the stock market, a stock that is doomed to crash for obscure reasons. The opposite of a "Good-Ship-Lollipop stock."

TMT. An acronymn for Technology, Media, and Telecommunications Stocks. These are the equities in the forefront of the advent of the New Economy, with its emphasis on the benefits of applied science products and processes, multimedia publishing products and services, and broad electronic and digital communications services and products, emphasizing wireless telephony.

"to the market." See **margin to the market.**

Tobaccos. The stocks representing corporations engaged in processing tobacco for consumer smoking products. *See* **industry stock group.**

tombstone advertisement. A newspaper or magazine advertisement that is published when a company goes public or otherwise issues new securities to the public, enumerating summarily basic information such as the type of securities in the offering—common stock or corporate notes, for example—the nominal interest rate for debt securities or preferred stock, the price of the securities on the date of issue, the name of the issuer, the size of the securities offering in terms of money value, and the names of the principal underwriters of the deal. It also includes the firms that are members of the selling syndicate supporting the underwriters, arranged in brackets denoting the size of their participation. The tombstone is not an offer to buy or sell the subject security, as the prospectus or offering circular is distributed for that purpose, but rather a record that the distribution has taken place, usually several days before the tombstone appears. Underwriters are nervous about the offering price being mentioned, for it could be above the security's current market price, and nobody on Wall Street likes a riot during business hours. In addition, investment bankers sometimes run tombstones reflecting private financing arrangements or acquisitions and mergers they have managed. And other types of business corporations often do the same, reflecting acquisitions or mergers they have negotiated.

tontine. A financial plan, such as an insurance policy or annuity, in which investors own shares and rights in a common fund. Upon the demise or default of any participant, his rights are distributed among the others until only one remains. At that time, the balance of the fund goes to that person. An alternative to such an action would be an agreement that the remainder be distributed to survivors, after a certain period of time had elapsed. A "tontine" insurance plan accumulates no earnings or surplus to a policy, unless it stays in force for a definite period of years. Only those who remain active in the plan or their beneficiaries reap the benefits. This concept is more prevalent under French financial practices.

toony. Nickname for Canadian two-dollar coin.

top-down decision strategy. In making decisions about the most attractive securities to buy or sell, the use of broad macroeconomic, sector, and industry data and trends in making selections of specific securities. This technique is based on the assumption that the big picture is the place to start in forecasting investment dynamics, rather than many company snapshots. *See* **bottoms-up decision strategy.**

"Top hat" pension plan. A reference to an agreement with a top executive of an organization promising to provide a special pension to that person, in addition to a regular pension that person is owed by the plan sponsor. *See* **"bad boy" clause.**

top out, to. As a security currently enjoying rising prices, to meet resistance and decline or move sideways at a particular market price. Teki Technician might say: "High Risers has topped-out four times at 50."

total enterprise value. The calculation of the value of a corporate entity, found by multiplying the earnings before interest, federal income taxes, depreciation, depletion, and amortization by a multiple representative of the industry.

total market fund. A mutual fund that is designed to track the broad stock market or the broad spectrum of securities in a country. In the United States, such a fund mirrors the **Wilshire 5000 Index.** Unlike the S&P 500 Index, which includes 500 of the biggest American companies, the Wilshire 5000 Index includes both large- and small-cap companies. Thus stability and growth are combined. Actually, it now includes 7,200 U.S. stocks. Like the S&P 500, the Wilshire 5000 is weighted by the market capitalizations of the stocks included. Therefore, funds replicating the Wilshire 5000 are similar to those replicating the S&P 500. In fact, in mid-1999, S&P stocks comprised 80% of the value of the Wilshire 5000. Total market funds are noted for maintaining low expense ratios.

total-return swap. A short-term arrangement whereby an investor or speculator pays a brokerage a set interest rate for a block of stock that the brokerage controls, based on the price if it were purchased outright. In return, the brokerage agrees to pay the stock borrower the value of any dividends paid and any capital gain. However, if the stock decreases in value, the investor or speculator agrees to pay the brokerage the amount of the capital loss. This tricky maneuver is sometimes called an exotic swap. It might be used by a speculator who wants control of a block of stock.

touting a stock. A slang expression for the promotion of a stock by a salesperson, dealer, or broker, based on its speculative profit potential. It is often a reference to a securities salesperson recommending a stock in which he or she has a financial interest, such as shares or options, or one representing a company that has paid a fee for promoting the stock. The views on the stock's prospects are often exaggerated. It is not unlawful to promote a stock in which one has a financial interest, but it is unlawful not to disclose that fact.

tracking stock or **target stock** or **lettered stock.** A relatively new form of security, usually issued by a conglomerate or large holding company to its stockholders, which is designed to give holders of the tracking shares an interest in a specific economic segment of the diversified issuer. Although the holders of the true or original stock of the issuer are the owners of the assets represented by the tracking shares, benefits like earnings and the sale of assets can accrue to the tracking stock owners. Only 15 companies in the United States have issued tracking shares. The first company to do so was General Motors in 1984. Each one is different in benefits to shareholders, making it risky to generalize about them. A prospective buyer of such shares should investigate the terms of the issue. Tracking stock must be registered with the SEC, and it can be used to make acquisitions. Issuing this type of stock is something just short of spinning off a division or subsidiary to shareholders. A corporation must wait several years after issuing tracking stock before the same entity can be spun off.

From the standpoint of the management of the issuing corporation, tracking shares present these advantages: (1) A spin-off of a business segment that will do business with the parent can be accomplished without incurring tax liabilities for the recipients of the shares, as would be the case in a true spin-off of a segment that would do business with the parent; (2) Additional capital can be raised with the new class of stock to operate the business or make acquisitions, often at a better rate than the oversized parent can manage. From the standpoint of shareholders, they gain the economic advantages of participation in a specific segment of the parent company.

trade. A securities transaction. One specific order, an agreement between a seller and a buyer, or their agents, to exchange specific securities at a mutually agreeable price.

trader. 1) An investor who buys and sells continuously during a market session, usually for many quick profits. 2) A securities dealer working for an investment firm and splitting trading profits with it. *See* **dealer.**

trading. Buying or selling securities.

trading at par. A reference to a bond or debenture selling at its face value or convertible value.

trading bloc. See **common market.**

trading collar. See **collars (3).**

trading exchange. A reference to a high-tech business exchange, or B2B electronic marketplace, in which multiple buyers and sellers with common industrial interests conduct purchasing and selling activities with each other, through the use of shared industry-wide computer systems, or networks, accessed over the Internet. The initial focus of such an exchange is to lower transaction costs between the participants, such as computer manufacturers, but ultimately to support collaboration in product development and act as a coordinator of the supply chain that links members of the exchange. In 2000, Hewlett-Packard Co., Compaq Computer Corp., Gateway Inc., and nine other original equipment manufacturers, suppliers, and distributors began such an exchange.

"trading on the equity." See **Financial Leverage.**

trading privileges. The authorization to transact orders on an exchange.

trading restrictions removed. See **free market.**

trading stock. A popular stock that fluctuates continually in price because of an uncertain financial future for the corporation it represents.

trading stopped. The halting of trading by exchange authorities in one or more securities or in all those listed for many reasons, but usually because the market is not orderly and an accumulation of buy or sell orders has made prices vulnerable to steep rises or drops. *See* **short circuits.**

traditional pension fund. See **pension fund.**

tranche. 1) In reference to a financial structure, a segment or level of the entire amount. Usually, each segment or tranche of the structure is represented by a different investment security and time period, but the ultimate objective of the plan is to accomplish some financing project from the initial short-term money to the final long-term capital and equity. In this context, the placement of all the tranches in a financing must be accomplished in order for the project to be finished. The financing of each tranche is dependent on the others. 2) In Europe, especially the UK, successive issues or distributions of the same or similar securities, representing fixed rates of interest and terms, to investors. Also, the word can mean parcels of a big deposit, with similar financial terms, that are sold to many investors.

transactions. See **trade (2).**

transfer agent. A bank or trust company that transfers stock from one owner to another as an agent for a corporation.

transfer tax. A federal or state tax imposed on the transfer or sale of securities borne by the seller or transferor. New York and Florida have transfer taxes.

translux. A small portable screen device that magnifies a ticker tape, manufactured by the Translux Corporation.

transparency. In securities markets, a reference to the extent to which important information and prices are visible to all participants—individual investors and institutional professionals. This represents an important principle used by the SEC in its market surveillance, the purpose of which is to guard against fraud and stock price manipulation.

Transportation. Those stocks representing companies providing rail, truck and road transportation services. *See* **industry stock group.**

transportation industries. See **sector.**

Treasuries. A reference to those debt securities issued by the U.S. Treasury sold to finance the primary operations of the federal government. They are direct obligations of the U.S. Treasury, as opposed to the debt of U.S. agencies that includes other remedies in the event of default. Treasuries are negotiable instruments. These securities come in three basic maturities classes: (1) bills or short-term obligations, (2) notes or intermediate-term obligations, and (3) bonds or long-term obligations. All Treasuries are secured by the full faith and credit of the federal government. As such they are considered the safest investments in the world, and the interest rate paid on these securities is considered the "pure" interest rate, for all securities with similar maturities. In investment theory, the true interest rate or cost of money is the rate on any other security less the rate of Treasuries for that class. In other words, if the Treasuries rate is 5% and a corporation's rate is 8.5%, the corporation's true cost or premium is 3.5% (8.50 – 5.00). The corporation has to pay 3.5% more than the basic cost of money. Although interest income on Treasuries is federally taxable, it is exempt from state and local income taxes. *See* **Treasury bill, U.S., Treasury bond, U.S., Treasury Direct,** and **Treasury note, U.S.**

Treasury bill, U.S. or **T-bill.** A short-term federal obligation of the U.S. Treasury in bearer form sold at a discount when issued, usually for a term of 91 days, but recently for 13 and 26 weeks. *See* **Treasuries.**

Treasury bond, U.S. A federal long-term debt obligation of the U.S. Treasury, issued in registered or bearer form in denominations of $1,000 up to $500 million, in maturities of 10 to 30 years. These bonds are callable within five years of maturity. Interest is payable semiannually. In mid-1999, this market amounted to $3.2 trillion, 23.7% of the total bond debt in United States. *See* **bond tables** and **Treasuries.**

Treasury Direct. The name of the program sponsored by the U.S. Treasury whereby small investors can buy its bills, bonds, and notes by simply debiting a bank account, and sell them without going through a bank or broker—commission free. These securities can now be purchased in denominations as low as $1,000, an amount comparable to the entry level of many mutual funds. There are 825,000 investors who hold accounts in the system, valued at $83 billion. Of those, 85% are over 55 years old. Investors in the program may reinvest maturing securities or make purchases by dialing (800) 943-6864 or over the Internet. For purchasing and more information visit their Web site: *www.publicdebt.treas.gov.*

Treasury Inflation-Protected Securities (TIPS) or **indexed securities.** A reference to U.S. Treasury bonds and notes, introduced in 1997, that are indexed to the inflation rate in the United States, as measured by the Consumer Price Index (CPI). As such, the nominal interest rate on these securities is adjusted every six months for the inflation that has occurred during that period by accreting it to the principal at maturity. For example, if an investor held five-year, inflation-protected notes that yielded 3.91% in January and the CPI inflation rate for 1998 was 1.6%, the Treasury would adjust the yield to 5.6% currently by adding the inflation rate to the nominal rate through an increase in the principal at maturity.

These types of securities are more popular during periods of moderate to high inflation, although they do get out of sync in terms of yield differentials in the market from time to time and can represent selling or buying opportunities then. They are compared to Treasury 10-year conventional notes when measuring yield differentials. For example, when conventional notes are priced to yield 6.15%, the inflation rate is running at 1.00% annually, and the indexed notes are priced to yield 5.15%, the markets are in equilibrium as far as yields are concerned. This is the case because the indexed notes will soon be yielding 6.15% also, after the upcoming inflation adjustment. Another way to look at the yield differential is the "breakeven inflation rate." To get this rate, the investor subtracts the indexed yield rate from the conventional rate. The difference is what the actual inflation rate would have to be for the investor to break even on either security in terms of yield. In the case above, subtracting the 5.15% indexed rate from the 6.15% conventional rate produces a 1.00% breakeven inflation rate. If the annual inflation rate is 1.00%, the securities are identical in terms of only the yields. If inflation turns out to be greater than 1.00%, the index bonds will yield more because of the adjustment greater than 1.00%. If inflation is less than 1.00%, the indexed securities will yield less for the opposite reason.

When the securities were introduced, investor demand was slack, because inflation was invisible. But since then the market for these issues has expanded to $70 billion. These securities can be purchased directly from the U.S. Treasury through a Federal Reserve Bank in $1,000 increments. For income tax purposes, indexed securities are taxed under the IRS Original Issue Discount system. Under this treatment, taxpayers must pay income taxes on the semiannual interest payments as well as accretions to the principal at maturity, reflecting the inflation adjustments, each year. *See* **Original Issue Discount.**

Treasury Investors Growth Receipts or TIGERS or STRIPS. A type of zero-coupon bond issued by the U.S. Treasury. The original bonds are stripped of their coupons and sold separately at a deep discount. The same is done with the coupons. Under IRS regulations, even though bondholders receive no interest until the accumulation of interest at maturity, they are subject to filing "imputed interest" each year on the accumulated amounts, as though they were conventional bonds. The same procedure is used with the separated coupons. Because the interest liability is imputed on this type of bond, they are recommended for tax-sheltered programs, such as retirement plans. This is because in such programs there is no tax liability, imputed or otherwise. *See* **imputed interest** and **zero-coupon bonds.**

Treasury note, U.S. A federal debt obligation of the U.S. Treasury issued in registered or bearer form in denominations of $1,000 up to $500 million, in maturities of more than one year up to seven years in duration. *See* **Treasuries.**

treasury stock. That stock that has been issued by a corporation but subsequently reacquired by that corporation. It is not unissued stock and can subsequently be distributed. When kept active, the cost of the stock is subtracted from the capital accounts on the balance sheet.

trend. A well-defined movement of stock prices, either up or down. This concept has undergone a change in the popular lexicon in recent years. Statistically and historically, the expression has denoted a period of 10 years or more, during which time a normal passage of events would occur that would enable an observer to draw inferences about patterns of change, such as growth or decline in some economic or business series—stock prices, for example. With the advent of the electronic revolution, however, the meaning has come to mean short-term directions or movement, events statisticians refer to as seasonality, cyclicality, or irregularity. *See* **intermediate movement, major swing,** and **minor swing.**

trend-line method. See **variable-ratio formula** under **formula investing.**

triple bottom. 1) A price pattern made by recorded high-low-close bars on a stock bar chart or Xs and Os on a point-and-figure chart. Chartists believe the level at which the bottoms occur is even more supported by buyers than double bottom levels. Investors indicate the stock's "junk" value is at that level, and some event might increase prospects for the company and the stock's price. 2) See **resistance area.**

triple top. A price pattern made by recorded high-low-close bars on a bar chart or Xs and Os on a point-and-figure chart. Chartists say the level at which the tops occur is even more vulnerable to selling pressure than a double-top level. Investors indicate the stock is overpriced above that level.

triple witching hour. The last hour of stock market trading on the third Friday of March, June, September, and December. During that time, stock-index options, options on individual stocks, and stock-index futures contracts expire on market indexes used by program traders to hedge their position in stocks. The simultaneous contract expirations frequently trigger heavy buying and selling of options, futures, and the underlying stocks, creating a Damien-like unleashing of unnatural forces on the trading floor—the witching hour!

Truckers. Those stocks representing companies providing over-the-road transportation. *See* **industry stock group.**

trust. The conveyance of property or funds to a supervisor (trustee) by a donor (trustor) for the use of a third party (beneficiary) under certain conditions and time limits. *See* **testamentary trust.**

Trust Indenture Act of 1939, the. One of the six federal acts that regulate securities affairs in the United States. The statute was enacted to protect investors purchasing certain kinds of bonds, usually corporate bonds, by requiring that the trust indenture or contract be approved by the SEC. Furthermore, the act specifies an indenture contain protective clauses and exclude exculpatory clauses (clauses that would excuse a bond issuer from requirements under the statute). It also calls for the appointment of a financially responsible corporate trustee who will look after the interests of bondholders. This person must have no conflicting interests with the security holders and be independent of the issuer of the bonds. In a typical indenture, the following provisions are present: (1) names of the parties; (2) consideration and grant or assignment in trust; (3) conditions applicable to the issuance of bonds—amount and limitations, conditions, certification and registration; (4) definitions of terms used; (5) particular covenants of the indenture; (6) provisions in the case of pledged securities; (7) information related to redemption of bonds; (8) remedies of trustee and bondholders; (9) provisions pertaining to releases of corporate property from the indenture; (10) matters such as consolidations, mergers, and purchases affecting the borrower; (11) agreement related to the trustee;

and (12) execution, acknowledgment, recording, and affidavits of good faith. *See* **securities laws.**

trust—originated preferred security. A security that has characteristics of both debt and equity in that interest payments are tax deductible although they may be deferred. The security does not have to appear as debt on the balance sheet, instead appearing in a position between debt and stockholders' equity in the position of "minority interest."

trustee. A person or firm legally made responsible for the management of funds or property allocated to a particular use by those owning such funds or property.

turnover, market. 1) The total number of shares issued by companies listed on an exchange divided into the shares traded during a day or any other period to give the percentage of total shares listed that traded. 2) The number of shares traded in a session. 3) For **inventory turnover,** see **sales to inventory.** 4) See **capital turnover.**

turnover rate. A ratio calculated from the number of shares traded in a year or shorter period divided by: 1) the total shares listed on an exchange, or 2) the total shares outstanding of a corporation, or 3) the total shares held in an institutional portfolio, expressed as a percentage. The idea is to determine how important the shares turned over are in relation to the overall stock activity on the exchange, corporation, or portfolio. For example, on the NYSE the January 1999 monthly turnover ratio was 89% versus 68% in June. Therefore, January was much busier than June, in terms of share volume. Looking at another illustration, if only 10% of a company's outstanding shares trade in a year, it is very inactive, a tendency that might be troublesome for corporate management when it comes time to raise new equity capital.

12-b-1 fee. A fee assessed shareholders by some mutual fund managements to reimburse the fund for promotion, distributions, marketing expenses, and in some cases broker commissions. This fee should be disclosed in the prospectus and should be included in the fund's stated expenses ratio. It is usually less than 1% of the fund's assets under management. Although a bona fide "no-load" fund does not charge this fee, some calling themselves "no-load" do.

two-dollar broker. A broker on an exchange floor who executes orders in the name of commission-house broker for a fee.

"type I account." See **cash account.**

Uu

UGMA. Abbreviation for **Uniform Gifts to Minors Acts.**

ultra vires acts. Those business acts engaged in by corporate officials or employees that exceed their legal authority or that violate a corporation's charter or bylaws. Generally, the culpable individuals are personally responsible for damages to others caused by such acts.

UIT. See **unit investment trust.**

unacceptable accounts. The people for whom stock exchange firms cannot transact orders, for example, minors or incompetents.

unchanged or **same.** A reference to a stock average or security price that closed at the same figure as it did at the close of the previous session.

uncovered option. See **naked option.**

uncovered short sales. The number of shares borrowed and sold but not yet purchased by the seller.

underlying. In options trading, the security or commodity one has the right to buy or sell under the option contract.

underlying bonds. Those bonds which take priority over others in satisfying the claims of creditors.

under-margined account. A margin account in which the market value of the securities has decreased to a point where the customer's equity (percentage of ownership) is less than when he purchased them. This puts certain restrictions on withdrawing proceeds from sales or securities out of the account.

under pressure. A reference used when heavy offerings of a security or securities cause depressed prices in that security.

under the rule. A phrase used when the officers of a stock exchange purchase or sell securities to complete a transaction begun by a tardy member. The member who has failed to deliver or accept securities is charged with any difference in price. Also, sales or purchases under the rule may be made by the exchange officers to settle disputes, or complete other unsettled matters.

"under water." A reference to stock options whose exercise price is above the current market price of the stock which they can be used to purchase. For example, options with an exercise price of $15 per share are under water when the stock obtainable is priced at $10 per share. This situation is particularly acute for executives with option grants in their compensation packages, since they probably accepted less salary in lieu of the options. *See* **compensation package, option grant, repricing,** and **stock options.**

underwrite. To agree to purchase and resell new securities or an old block, although an underwriter takes title only to those shares he cannot resell.

underwriter. An investment banker who buys part or all of a securities issue for resale to the public at a profit. By working through an underwriter, a corporation or stockholder group can raise capital immediately or in the near future in exchange for accepting less than the public will pay for their securities. Thus, underwriters perform the vital function of financing big blocks of public securities.

underwriting agreement or **purchase agreement.** The basic document of understanding between a managing underwriter and a company issuing new securities to the public, covering such items as the commitment of the underwriting group to purchase the securities from the issuing company and resell them to the public; the offering price of the securities to the public; the underwriting spread, or amount between the offering price and the proceeds to the issuing company; all discounts and commissions; the net proceeds for the benefit of the issuer; and the settlement date of the deal. The managing underwriter acts as agent for the underwriting group—the other investment bankers putting up money for the purchase of the securities from the issuing company—in the transaction. In the event greater distribution of the securities is an objective or if increased demand for the securities is needed, the underwriter group can put together a selling group or syndicate, which participates at a lower margin. The manager(s) also establishes the period during which insiders cannot sell their stock, usually 180 days, in order to avoid a disruption to an orderly distribution.

In the agreement, the issuer agrees: (1) to make all SEC filings in a timely manner; (2) to observe all provisions of the Securities Act of 1933; (3) to take responsibility for full and legal disclosures of all information in the registration statement and prospectus; (4) to comply with state securities laws, where applicable; (5) to insure the underwriters against liabilities arising out of omissions or failure to carry out responsibilities; (6) to spend the proceeds in the manner stated; and (7) to make every effort to register the securities on the exchange agreed upon. The underwriting group commences with the distribution as soon as the SEC accepts the filing, or at some date agreed to.

The issuing company pays for registration with the SEC, including legal fees; the preliminary prospectus, or **"red herring"**; the final prospectus, or statutory prospectus, including required copies for the sales forces of the underwriters and selling syndicate, if applicable; and the public financial presentation, or **dog-and-pony show,** when appropriate.

underwriting discounts and commissions. The total costs to a corporation and/or selling stockholders by underwriters in selling securities to the public. Actually, it is the difference in what the underwriters agree to buy the securities for from the issuer and the price the public pays to compensate the underwriters for expenses and risks in financing an issue. *See* **underwriting agreement.**

underwriting group. See **underwriting agreement.**

underwriting spread. See **underwriting agreement.**

unearned dividend. A declared dividend that impairs the capital of a corporation. However, if earnings are in near-money form, money may be borrowed for a dividend. Otherwise, an unearned dividend is illegal in most states.

unfavorable trade balance. In international trading, a country's excess in the value of its imports of goods and services in relation to the value of its exports of goods and services. *See* **balance of trade.**

Uniform Gifts to Minors Acts (UGMAs). The state laws enabling the transfer of stocks, bonds, or other securities to a minor by registering the securities in the name of a parent, guardian, grandparent, brother, sister, uncle, or aunt, acting as custodian until the minor reaches seniority, either 18 or 21 in every state. However, in New York, where the legal age is 18, a donor may specify a transfer of this gift at age 21. The custodian is appointed by the donor, who may name himself or herself to this role. If the donor dies before the property is transferred to the minor, the value of the property is included in the donor's taxable estate, even though the property belongs to the minor as soon as the gift is made. No formal trust instrument is required nor are the restrictions that are applicable to assuming a formal guardianship for a minor's property, and income from the gift is taxable to the child, usually at a lower tax rate, providing it is not used to support him. Under present laws, if income from this arrangement is under $600, there is no income tax liability arising from the gift, and the custodian may manage the income to enlarge the minor's gift. In most states, gifts under this act can be lifetime gifts or by a benefactor's will. Lifetime gifts of this nature qualify for the $10,000 gift tax exclusion annually. Furthermore, under the Taxpayers Relief Act of 1997, tax-free gifts will be adjusted for inflation in increments of $1,000. An attorney should be consulted for complete information. All states have adopted a UGMA. *See* **Taxpayers Relief Act of 1997** and **Uniform Transfers to Minors Act (UTMA).**

Uniform Practice Code. A set of operational rules and procedures adopted by the National Association of Securities Dealers (NASD) pertaining to consistent methods in handling over-the-counter securities transactions—delivery of securities, settlement dates for trades, dates when securities go ex-dividend, ex-rights and ex-warrants, as well as other "ex" dates. The code also stipulates procedures in the matter of using arbitration in securities disputes, under the direction of Uniform Practice committees.

Uniform Securities Act. Developed under the aegis of the Uniform Commercial Code adopted in the United States for state governments, the Uniform Securities Act is a model securities law first adopted by commissioners in 1956 and amended in 1988. Basically, it recommends a blueprint for each state to adopt and use in regulating securities matters within its borders. Of course, most states modified their versions somewhat, but the laws in each state are comparable today. Basically the model has 13 sections, dealing with the following topics: definitions, exempt securities and transactions, stock broker licensing, investment advisers and firms, securities registration, notice filings of federally covered securities, securities fraud and other prohibited practices, judicial review, enforcement, remedies, liabilities, and penalties. *See* **securities laws.**

Uniform Transfers to Minors Acts (UTMA). Those laws adopted by every state in the United States that accomplish what the Uniform Gifts to Minors Acts do, except they apply to gifts besides cash and securities. Also included are real property, patents, royalties, and works of art. Another difference is that these acts prohibit a minor from assuming control until age 21, with the exception that in California the age is 25. *See* **Uniform Gifts to Minors Acts.**

"unique visitors per quarter." See **dot-com stock.**

unissued stock. The stock authorized for issue under a corporate charter but not distributed. It is not included in the capital stock outstanding of a corporation and receives no dividends. Often such stock is held in reserve for mergers and acquisitions or stock bonus programs.

unit. An investment sales package usually consisting of two securities, such as a debenture and one share of common stock or a share of detachable stock that can be sold separately after a certain period.

unit investment trust (UIT) or **"unitrust."** A security that is sold to investors, usually in $1,000 denominations, which is registered with the Securities and Exchange Commission under the Investment Company Act of 1940. A manager and trustee are named—the manager responsible for the securities included in the portfolio, and the trustee responsible for vouchsafing that the terms of the trust are followed. The arrangement concludes when the trust expires, either because bonds mature, as in the case of a municipal bond investment trust, or on a certain date. Investors are entitled to an undivided interest in the income and principal accruing to the trust. Until the late 1900s, these trusts usually held municipal bonds but shifted to equities afterwards. Realistically, the trusts can invest in corporate, municipal, or government bonds; mortgage-backed securities; or common and preferred stocks, but investors must be apprised of the intentions. In the case of common stock unit trusts, stocks representing stock indexes like the Dow Jones Industrials or the S&P 500 have been popular. Brokerage commissions range from approximately 1–2% on equity trusts and 4% for municipal bond units.

unit of trading. The number of shares of a stock that constitute a regular transaction, under the rules of a stock exchange.

"unitrusts." A marketing reference to units of investment trusts.

units of participation. See **commingled investment account.**

universal bank. An institution that offers services and products in all three of the major financial categories: banking, insurance, and investing, under one roof or management structure. In Europe and certain other regions, this has been the prevalent financial institution for a long time. However, in the United States, beginning with the Glass-Steagall Act or the Banking Act of 1933 and the Banking Act of 1956, these three types of institutions have been separated in an effort to prevent a repetition of the debilitating effects of the stock market crash of 1929. At that time there were interrelationships between these products and services, within the same institution in many cases. The Glass-Steagall Act restricted income originating from the securities business to 10% or less for a bank, a restriction that made the securities business uneconomic for banks. Even so, there has been a functional melding of sorts taking place in modern times in certain instances of mergers between major companies, under a holding company concept in which operating partitions between the three functions were erected. This was the concept of the "Chinese Wall," applied to quasi-universal banking institutions.

With the repeal of the Glass-Steagall Act and amendments to the Bank Holding Company Act of 1956 enacted in 1999, universal banking is once more legal in the United States. It will take a while for the implications of this historic change to become obvious, but one change is clear. There will be companies that offer banking, insurance, and investing products and services, with certain restrictions on consumer privacy. The regulation will remain under the U.S. Comptroller for federally chartered banks, the Federal Reserve Bank for bank holding companies and state banks that have joined the Federal Reserve System, and the Securities and Exchange Commission for public securities issued by these entities. *See* **Bank Holding Company Act of 1956, "Chinese Wall," and Glass-Steagall Act.**

universal life insurance. A life insurance policy with both an investment element and a death benefit, on which the policyholders has the right to increase or decrease the investment element.

unl. Abbreviation for **unlisted** securities.

unlisted. 1) Securities—those securities not traded on an exchange, but in the over-the-counter market. 2) Investment firms—those dealers that hold no exchange membership and who deal exclusively in over-the-counter issues.

unlisted trading privileges (u). The status of a company when its stock is admitted for trading on an exchange without the company being required to publish regular financial reports. The New York Stock Exchange grants no unlisted trading privileges.

unremitted income. The earnings from a company's foreign subsidiaries or divisions that are known but not yet transferred to United States banking accounts.

unrestricted account. A margin account in which the market value of the securities has remained the same or increased so that the customer's equity (percentage of ownership) is the same or more than when he purchased them, which means he can immediately withdraw proceeds from sales in an amount equal at least to the percentage of his equity. *See* **under-margined account.**

up. A reference to a stock average or security price that is higher than it was at the previous session's close.

upgrade, to. As an investment firm, to raise the investment expectations and attractiveness of a stock issue on its recommended list. As a practical matter, a firm's analysts would rather upgrade a stock than downgrade one, for companies receiving favorable comments and opinions are apt to be rewarded with corporate finance business.

upside. A reference to a general rise in security market prices during a session. For example, "Stocks closed on the upside."

upside potential. A reference to the possibility of a security rising sharply in market price. Usually it is accompanied by an estimate of the potential higher price, based on some quantitative measure like a P/E multiple or Asset Value. For example, suppose that over a period of five years Wobble Construction, Inc. has frequently sold at 15 times its annual earnings. Currently priced at $25, its EPS estimate for the current year is $3.00. The upside potential could be said to be $45 or $15 higher per share. *See* **downside risk.**

uptick or **plus-tick.** A rise in the trading price of a stock, versus the previous transaction in that stock.

U.S. Treasury bonds. See **Treasury bond, U.S.**

USA Today: **Money Online.** See under **Web Sites for the Inquiring Investor.**

"use-it-or-lose-it." A rule, usually in relation to taxing policy by a government, whereby the beneficiary of a tax break, such as a credit, must use it or forfeit the opportunity.

usury. An illegal rate of interest on loaned money under state laws.

Utah Department of Commerce. Regulator of securities laws in the state of Utah. Address: Securities Division, P.O. Box 45808, Salt Lake City, UT 84145. Phone: (801) 530-6600. Phone (toll free): (800) 721-3233.

utilities. Those stocks representing companies engaged in furnishing the public electric power, natural gas, and water. These companies are regulated by the states and municipalities in which they operate and the federal government, when interstate sales are involved. These stocks are usually "money rate" stocks, trading largely on how their yields compare with securities with similar risk characteristics. *See* **industry stock group.**

utility industries. See **sector.**

UTMA. Abbreviation for **Uniform Transfer to Minors Acts.**

Vv

validation board. A committee, usually international in membership, which determines the present value of old, apparently defaulted bonds. These have become valuable because someone has accepted responsibility for the debts. The board supervises registration of those claiming to have these bonds, and determines bona fide owners.

valuation. The process in which some worth is assigned to a company's resource or a share of its common stock.

valuation model. See **forecasting.**

valuation reserve. In managing a going-concern business, the establishment of a reserve account for all items that wear out, are used up, or are overvalued on the books, in order to reduce their values over time by reducing earnings and the item's stated value systematically. In the process, the same amounts are added to the reserves until the value of the item eliminated has been replaced by the reserve. In this way, assets can be replaced, bad debts removed, and Goodwill eliminated from the balance sheet in a predictable way.

value added. In processing or manufacturing, the process of taking in raw materials or worked on materials, adding to their completion, and passing them along to another entity for further enhancement or for final distribution.

value added tax (VAT). A tax that is assessed at each stage of production or processing, based on the amount of value added or marginal value at that stage, and on the consumer at the time of final purchase. However, it does not levy as much on the consumer as, say, the flat sales tax, because the prior costs of materials and supplies is removed before the tax is assessed in the VAT. This tax revenue plan is popular in Europe, especially with the newly formed European Union. In the United States it is controversial. Proponents claim it would raise significant revenues in an efficient way and would allow the government to reduce income taxes. Opponents say the tax amounts to a national sales tax and is regressive in that it falls heaviest on lower income consumers who can afford it least.

Value at Risk (VAR). A single, summary statistical measure of potential financial losses in a foreign exchange or derivatives portfolio. It is a measure of expected losses emanating from normal market activity. Losses exceeding the VAR expectations are stated at specific levels of probability. There are three mathematical methods of calculating a VAR: historical simulation, delta-normal approach, and Monte Carlo simulation. The requirement by the SEC that U.S. companies quantitatively disclose their market risks can be satisfied by a VAR as one of three options.

value chain management. A relatively new concept of manufacturing management, stimulated by the Internet and Intranet applications of computers in business planning and operations. The essence of this technique is to create consumer value in a globally competitive economy. At the core is the integration of marketing guidance systems with the process of new product and service development, materials transformation, assortment, and geographical dispersion. Also included is an awareness of environmental impact, so that an earth-to-earth supply chain is the focus. Many different business entities might share in the planning and execution. Underlying the thinking is that breakthroughs in business productivity and quality must be process-based, leading to cross-organizational relationships replacing traditional business methodology, such as a manufacturing operation vertically integrated in a single company. This interdependence means information sharing between partners participating in the research, development, manufacturing, marketing, and evaluation of a product or service. That trusting relationship seems to be the present objection to the management style. While a small number of companies participate fully in value chains at present, many participate on a limited basis and report good results in effects on profits. Through sharing data with informal partners along the supply-and-demand chain, many manufacturers report increased sales, faster cash-to-cash cycles, and order to shipment lead times in purchasing materials. Industries successfully engaged in chain value management are: Aerospace, Automotive, Chemicals,

Consumer Durables, Consumer Packaged Goods, Industrial Machinery and Equipment, High Tech, Pharmaceuticals, and Printing and Publishing.

value investing. A style of investing in which fundamental worth—yield, book value, low debt, and other vanishing species—are stressed in portfolio selections.

Value Line. An independent evaluator of stocks and mutual funds, founded in 1931 and employing 100 investment professionals. Its best-known resource is the *Value Line Investment Survey,* the most widely read investment information service worldwide. Other publications include: *Options and Convertibles Surveys, OTC Special Situations Service, The Value Line Mutual Fund Survey, The Value Line No-Load Fund Advisor,* and the *Value Line Investment Survey Expanded (Small-caps).* Also, the advisor provides electronic data services to investors. Address: Value Line, 220 East 42nd Street, New York, NY 10017. Phone (toll free): (800) 634-3583. Web site: *www.valueline.com/profile.html.*

Value Line Composite Index. An unweighted price index of 1,700 stocks, maintained by the Value Line Publishing company.

VAR. Abbreviation for **Value at Risk.**

variable annuity. A life insurance annuity contract with premiums mostly converted into units of growth stocks to provide appreciation potential for the annuitant or a surviving beneficiary, rather than only a fixed income. It was the realization that fixed-income annuities were losing purchasing power in the rise of cost-of-living since World War II that prompted most insurance companies to issue variable annuity contracts.

Variable Costs. Those costs that fluctuate with the volume of production or because of management decisions. Examples are labor, raw materials, and advertising. They are sometimes called direct costs. *See* **Fixed Costs.**

variable income investment. The employment of funds in securities or an enterprise in which the return, whether dividends, interest, or capital gains, increases proportionately to high profits from business and economic growth. Examples are common stock, mutual funds, and variable insurance annuities.

variable life insurance. A life insurance policy for which the performance of the underlying reserves, selected by the policy holder, determines the premium payments.

Variable Rate Mortgage (VRM). See **Adjustable Rate Mortgage.**

variable rate preferred stock. See **adjustable rate preferred stock.**

variable ratio formula. See **formula investing.**

variable ratio write. A reference to an options strategy in which a trader writes multiple contracts with different strike prices.

variance. In statistical analysis and expressing the volatility of stock prices, the measure of the average distance between each observation value and the mean in a data point set, equal to the sum of the squares of the deviations from the mean. It is also the square of the standard deviation of the values in the observations. *See* **average deviation, range, standard deviation,** and **volatility.**

VAT. Abbreviation for **value added tax.**

vega. The measure of change in the price of an option contract resulting from a change of 1% in its volatility.

velocity of money. In macroeconomic theory, the number of transactions experienced by each unit of money in a fiscal period. It is a measure of how fast people are spending money, which can affect the size of a Gross Domestic Product (GDP). In the case of the National Income and Product Accounts in the United States, it is the ratio of the total money supply, defined as bank deposits and cash in circulation, divided into GDP.

For example, the money supply of $1,076.0 billion and GDP of $8,110.9 billion in 1997 in the United States represents a ratio or velocity of 7.5 × ($8,110.9 ÷ $1,076.0). By contrast, in 1990 the money supply of $825.8 billion and GDP of $5,743.8 billion represents a velocity of 6.9 × ($5,743.8 ÷ $825.8). Professor Irving Fisher of the University of Chicago originated this concept in the 1920s. The Federal Reserve Bank uses the theory, to a degree, in determining when to change money supply in the banking system. Since a change in velocity tends to produce similar results to a change in money supply, it is useful for the board to take velocity into account before acting. In recent years, the concept has become clouded by the introduction of so many consumer credit facilities, or "plastic," which has produced several "money supplies." *See* **money supply.**

vendor hub. A reference to an Internet group that offers goods or services to many vendors that are transacting with only one or a few buyers through a product or service procurement business. *See* **customer hub.**

Vendor Performance, Slower Deliveries Diffusion Index. See **Economic Indicators.**

venture capital or **risk capital** or **seed capital.** Funds allocated for startup enterprises or those in the early stages of development or in turnaround situations, with high risks and rewards potential.

venture capital firm. An investment firm or investment banker that specializes in raising seed or initial capital for prospects they cull out of many screened each year. Typically such an investment firm is a partnership or limited partnership backed by several wealthy investors or institutions. When they find a worthy candidate to market as a venture capital entity, they structure the deal into a corporation or special corporation or perhaps a limited partnership. In many cases the fledgling enterprise is already structured, so the venture capital firm builds on that. When the means of distributing investment units in the new enterprise is ready, the venture capitalists market the idea to investors who are receptive to participating in venture capital securities—pension funds, miscellaneous investment partnerships, and corporations such as Small Business Investment Companies, wealthy individuals and family trusts, endowments and foundations, and insurance companies and banks. However, many venture capitalists ferret out their own seed capital candidates without the help of investment firms. But as an investor, it is reassuring to know there is an established and reputable firm bringing others into the arrangement.

Venture capitalists fill the critical gap between the original capital supplied by the founding entrepreneurs and the middle and eventual bigger capital injections, usually comprising equity and then debt, since commercial banks shun risk capital commitments except through special subsidiaries or affiliates. Ultimately, the goal is to take the new company public in order to raise permanent capital comprised of equity and debt. In order to do that, the enterprise must be further along the road to success. Usually, this means it must display a revenue stream that is growing, positive cash flow, and embryonic earnings. When the entity does go public, or reaches a higher stage in the capital formation ladder, the original investors are assured of an advantageous position. In 1997, nearly $9.7 billion was raised for venture capital limited partnerships. *See* **angel fund, Small Business Administration (SBA),** and **Small Business Investment Company (SBIC).**

Vermont Department of Banking, Insurance and Securities. Regulator of securities laws in the state of Vermont. Address: Securities Division, 89 Main Street, Drawer 20, Montpelier, VT 05620. Phone: (802) 828-3420.

vertical integration. See **integrated company (2).**

vest, to. As an employee and potential beneficiary of a profit-sharing plan or stock option plan, to reach a point in service that invests all or a portion of the ownership rights and privileges of the plan.

vested, fully. As an employee and potential beneficiary of a profit-sharing plan or stock option plan, to be at a point in service that invests all, or 100%, of the ownership rights and privileges of the plan. Even so, the benefits might not take place until a future date.

veto stock. A class of stock that entitles the holder to cast a vote on certain corporate business but not on electing the board of directors.

viatical settlement. See **death future.**

Virginia State Corporation Commission. Regulator of securities laws in the state of Virginia. Address: Division of Securities and Retail Franchising, P.O. Box 1197, Richmond, VA 23209. Phone: (804) 371-9051.

virtual global stock market. A reference to the instant accessibility by an investor to the most important securities exchanges and electronic trading systems in the world through the use of a personal computer and the Internet—the World Wide Web or other online networks. On the Web pages of the exchanges and trading systems, an investor can find important information on brokerages that are members, information on securities listed, trading information, stock indexes and charts, and business news of the particular country or region represented. Often it is possible to find the conversion rates of major currencies of the world. The latter data are extremely important, since they affect capital when it is transferred out of or back to the United States. *See* **Global Investment Market.**

volatile stocks. Those stocks that rise and fall sharply in price because of an inactive market or sudden speculative buyer and seller interest.

volatility. In risk management, which investment management ultimately becomes, the measure of the price changes in securities owned or followed, usually within a certain period of time. There are two principal measures of volatility in use today: (1) percentage of trading days in a year when daily prices changed more than 1% from the preceding day, and (2) a high standard deviation of daily price changes, compared to a historical average. However, volatility can also be measured over other time frames. It is important to note that volatility refers to both ups and downs in prices; one is as indicative of risk as the other when changes are rapid and sizeable.

    The point in measuring the degree of risk is to ascertain whether one is being adequately rewarded, in terms of investment return, for the chance that securities will have to be sold at a time when prices have dropped sharply. To amplify on the two measures of volatility cited above, the Dow Jones Industrial Average has moved 1% or more daily 17.2% of the time since

1940. In the case of standard deviations, the median level for daily changes in the S&P 500 since 1940 is 0.72%. Another look at volatility—in 1999 the annual volatility of the S&P 500 was about 15%. Summarily, when volatility climbs above those benchmarks, the market has become riskier; when below, the market is safer, in a statistical sense. (This distinction is made because traffic collisions around a broker's office might have trebled, making visits riskier!)

The **standard deviation (SD)** measures dispersion of data about the arithmetic mean. Signs are ignored in these calculations. Good news—most calculators and database software programs calculate these descriptive statistics readily. Say, for instance, during 10 trading days, the average change in a stock's price is 1.9% and the standard deviation or dispersion about the 1.9% is .71%. Another way of looking at such a result is that prices changed within a range of 1.9%, plus or minus 1 SD or plus or minus .71%, or prices changed + 2.61% to – 2.61% most of the time, defined statistically as 65% of the time. (± 1.9% ± .71%). By using two SDs, the investor can increase the probability of the dispersion to 95% of the time and, by using three SDs, to nearly 98%. *See* **average deviation, range,** and **variance.**

CALCULATING VOLATILITY	
Trading Session	**Price Change (%)**
Day 1	– 2.40
Day 2	– 1.70
Day 3	1.00
Day 4	1.50
Day 5	– 2.30
Day 6	3.00
Day 7	– 2.80
Day 8	2.20
Day 9	1.40
Day 10	– 1.00
Mean	1.90
Standard Deviation	0.71

volume. 1) The total of shares traded on an exchange, usually during a trading session. The rapidity of trading since 1980 has been explosive. In that year, the average volume was 45 million shares per day. Now that figure is probably in excess of 500 million shares per day. Furthermore, the NYSE is making plans for 6 billion-share days in the new century. 2) The total shares traded in an individual security, usually during a trading session.

voting right. A right of a stockholder to vote, by proxy or in person, at a called meeting, on corporate matters presented by management and on members of the board of directors. In a corporate charter and by laws, matters needing only the board's approval and those needing stockholders' approval are spelled out.

voting by proxy. See **proxy statements.**

voting stock. That common stock entitling the owner to vote in corporate business.

voting trust. An arrangement whereby all or a substantial portion of a corporation's voting shares are transferred to trustees for a specific purpose and time.

vulnerable market. See **vulnerable prices.**

vulnerable prices or **vulnerable market.** A description of security prices that have been forced up by erratic, low-volume buying in spite of unfavorable economic news and that could fall suddenly if widespread selling commenced.

vulture investor. An investors who focuses on situations in which there are financial problems, such as nonperforming bank loans, bankruptcy proceedings, or debentures and bonds in default, in an effort to acquire equity interests and controls. This is done in a manner that satisfies the contending parties and assures profits.

Ww

waiting period. The time required before corporate directors, officers, or other insiders must wait before selling their shares received in a public offering by corporation. The waiting periods are established by both the SEC and some underwriting agreements. *See* **insider** and **underwriting agreement.**

wallflower. Like an **orphan,** this is a reference to a common stock that has no patronage from the research staff at investment firms in terms of oral and written presentations. Opinion makers, generally research analysts and high-profile stock brokers, recommend buying and selling stocks on a regular basis. Stocks that are avoided by them have little chance of sustained popularity in the marketplace. But when such a stock is embraced by an opinion maker, it can signal that the stock will become popular and enjoy attractive market gains. Nevertheless, this is not likely to happen unless the stock represents a bargain in terms of intrinsic value or growth potential. Sometimes new management, reallocation of assets, or a corporate reorganization can instigate a change of heart among opinion makers about a stock that has been shunned. Positive promotion will likely begin. Astute investors should be on the lookout for these stocks. The difference between a wallflower and an orphan is that a wallflower is shunned for investment reasons, while an orphan either is simply overlooked or shunned for investment reasons.

Wall Street. Nickname for the financial district on lower Manhattan Island, New York City, where the New York Stock Exchange, American Stock Exchange, and New York Mercantile Exchange are located as well as the headquarters for major national brokerages and investment bankers. It is one of the most influential financial districts in the world, if not the most influential. *See* **Street, the.**

Wall Street Journal Interactive Online. See under **Web Sites for the Inquiring Investor.**

war chest. A stash of cash reserved by a corporation for a capital intensive event, such as the acquisition of a competitor.

warehouse receipt. A document representing the existence and availability of a specific quantity and quality of a commodity in storage for security. These are frequently used in settling cash and futures transactions, instead of the delivery of the actual commodities.

warehouse securities. Securities which have been accumulated or will be accumulated by a fund or trust in order for an administrator to issue depository receipts representing them to investors for investment purposes. Examples of such securities are mortgages or stocks backing an index fund.

warrants. Those certificates authorizing to the holder the privilege of buying additional capital stock at a specified price within a time limit, which is generally longer, often by several years, than the time limit specified in a "right" option. Warrants are also issued with bonds or preferred stocks, and, if they can be sold separately after a specified time period, are called detachable; if not, they are nondetachable.

wash. Any trading situation in which one action cancels the effect of another one.

wash sale. 1) Or **matched order,** when a fictitious sale of stock between two parties without a change in beneficial ownership is used to establish a tax loss or to create an impression of market activity in that stock. This practice is prohibited by securities laws and exchange rules. 2) The sale of securities to establish a tax loss, followed by a repurchase of the same securities. Tax regulations prohibit a purchase of identical securities within 30 days of a tax-loss sale.

Washington Department of Financial Institutions. Regulator of securities laws in the state of Washington. Address: Securities Division, P.O. Box 9033, Olympia, WA 98507. Phone: (360) 902-8760.

Washington Metropolitan Transit Authority. See **agency securities.**

***Washington Post* Online.** See under **Web Sites for the Inquiring Investor.**

wasting asset. 1) In a business enterprise, an asset with a limited life, such as a copyright or patent, that is not being developed and marketed. 2) In investing, a security with a limited life, such as an options contract that is out of the money.

watch list. A group of securities under scrutiny by a brokerage, exchange, or research service for possible irregularities, violations, or credit change.

watered stock. 1) The stock issued as fully paid par value stock with the par value greater than the amount paid to the corporation for the stock, which causes each share to have an exaggerated value. 2) The stock representing assets that have been greatly exaggerated in value in corporate financial statements.

"wealth effect." In the principles of economics, the tendency for rising stock prices to persuade consumers to increase amounts for the purchase of durable and nondurable items. This propensity is caused by greater cash availability from stock market profits and more borrowing, often using the rising stock prices as collateral. The effect can be positive when stock prices are rising, and negative when they are falling.

Web, the. See **Internet.**

Web Sites for the Inquiring Investor Financial Markets and Investment Ideas, Data, and News

---

WEB SITES FOR THE INQUIRING INVESTOR
(FINANCIAL MARKETS AND INVESTMENT IDEAS, DATA, AND NEWS)

Name of Site	Web Address
10-K Wizard	*www.10kwizard.com*
AboutYourBroker	*www.nasdr.com/2000.htm*
ACCESS Online Magazine	*www.accessmediakit.com*
Allexperts.com	*www.Allexperts.com*
Alternative Investment Market (AIM)	*www.londonstockex.co.uk*
Associated Press "Wire" Online	*http://wire.ap.org*
bankrate.com	*www.bankrate.com*

Barron's Online	*www.barrons.com*
BestCalls.com	*www.bestcalls.com*
bigdough	*www.bigdough.com/free*
Bloomberg Online	*www.bloomberg.com*
Bond Market Association	*www.bondmarkets.com*
Bureau of Economic Analysis (BEA)	*www.bea.doc.gov*
BusinessWeek Online	*www.businessweek.com*
BuyandHold.com	*www.buyandhold.com*
CBS MarketWatch	*www.CBS.marketwatch.com*
CNNfn: Financial News	*www.cnnfn.com*
CNBC Business News	*www.cnbc.com*
Chicago Tribune	*www.chicagotribune.com*
CiberCentro for Latinos	*www.bancointernet.com*
CNET Investor: Coalition of Black Investors	*www.cobinvest.com*
CNET Investor News	*http://investor.cnet.com*
Department of Commerce, U.S.	*www.doc.gov*
Douglas Gerlach's Invest-O-Rama	*www.investorama.com*
Dow Jones Business Directory	*http://businessdirectory.dowjones.com*
EarningsWhispers.com	*www.earningswhisper.com*
Economic Calendar: The Dismal Scientist	*www.dismal.com*
Economist, The	*www.economist.com*
EDGAR Online	*www.edgar-online.com*
E-Line Financials	*www.financials.com*
Federal Reserve Board (Beige Book)	*www.federalreserve.com/fomc/ BeigeBook2001.com*
Financial Engines Investment Advisor	*www.financialengines.com/ advisor*
Financial Web: Research and Financial Topics	*www.financialweb.com*
Forbes Magazine	*www.forbes.com/magazines*
Fortune	*www.fortune.com*
FreeEdgar	*www.freeedgar.com*
Holt Stock Report	*http://holtreport.com*
GE Center for Financial Learning	*www.financiallearning.com*
Individual Investor Online	*www.iionline.com*
InfoSeek: Personal Finance	*www.infoseek.com/Stock_exchanges*
Investor Home	*www.investorhome.com*
Investor Relations Information Network	*www.irin.com*
Investorguide.com	*www.investorguide.com*
Investor's Business Daily	*www.investors.com/web_edition/today*
Investorville	*www.investorville.com*
IPO.COM	*www.ipo.com*

IPO Maven	*www.ipomaven.com*
IRS Digital Daily, The	*www.irs.gov*
kidstock	*www.kidstock.com*
Kiplinger Online	*www.kiplinger.com*
Los Angeles Times	*www.latimes.com*
Mercury Center	*www.sjmercury.com*
(The San Jose Mercury News)	
Money.Com	*www.money.com*
Motley Fool, The	*www.Fool.com*
MSN MoneyCentral	*http://moneycentral.msn.com*
MULTEX Investory Network	*http://hoovers.multexinvestor.com/home*
Netstock Direct	*www3.netstockdirect.com/index*
New York Times, The	*www.nytimes.com*
Nightly Business Report	*www.nightlybusiness.org*
OECD Statistics	*www.oecd.org/statistics*
ON24 Network	*www.on24.com*
Philadelphia Inquirer Online, The	*www.phillynews.com*
Public Register's Annual Report Service	*www.annualreportservice.com*
Quicken	*www.quicken.com*
Quietperiod.com	*www.quietperiod.com*
Raging Bull Investor Revolution Page	*www.ragingbull.com*
Report Gallery Online	*www.reportgallery.com*
Library of Financial Reports	
Reuters Limited	*www.reuters.com*
Roth IRA Web Site	*www.rothira.com*
SaveWealth.com	*www.savewealth.com*
SiliconInvestor	*www.siliconinvestor.com*
Small Cap Analyst, The	*www.small-capanalyst.com*
smallcapcenter.com	*www.smallcapcenter.com*
Smart Money	*www.dowjones.com/smart*
Stat-USA Internet	*www.stat-usa.com*
Street.com, The	*www.thestreet.com*
StreetFusion	*www.StreetFusion.com*
Tax Guide for Investors	*www.fairmark.com*
University of Iowa College of Law	*http://uiowa.edu/ifdebook*
(Int. Finance Info)	
USA Today: Money	*www.usatoday.com/money/mfront.htm*
Wall Street Journal Interactive, The	*www.wjs.com*
Washington Post, The	*www.washingtonpost.com*
westergaard broadcasting network.com	*www.wbn.com*
Yahoo! Finance	*http://finance.yahoo.com*
Zacks Investment Research	*ww.ultra.zacks.com*

Web Sites for Investing Women. These sites offer information from beginning to research and management.

WEB SITES FOR INVESTING WOMEN	
Name of Site	**Web Address**
Cassandra's Revenge	*www.cassandrasrevenge.com*
iVillage Moneylife	*http://ivillagemoneylife.com*
Ka–Ching	*www.ka-ching.com*
Money Mode	*www.womenswire.com/money*
PinkBull	*www.pinkbull.com*
She's Got It Together	*www.shesgotittogether.com*
Wife.Org	*www.wife.org*
womenCONNECT.com	*http://WomenConnect.com*

webcast, investment. A regular presentation over the Internet, using what is called streaming video technology, by a financial services firm that features securities analysts discussing industry trends and attractive stocks or other products and services offered by the financial services firm. The presentation emanates from a Web site of the financial services firm. Access to the site is often open to the general Internet, while more detailed discussions are restricted to linked sites for a firm's customers or through a trial subscription. However, procedures and regulations are evolving daily in the burgeoning e-commerce markets. Topics often can be downloaded by viewers. For the investor, this practice has blurred the lines with news broadcasting over radio and television, historically the source of such information. Consequently, the investor should be on guard to distinguish webcast information as emanating from parties with an interest in the use of the information. Under SEC regulations, the recommendation of specific stocks cannot be done over the broad Internet, but must be accomplished through links or an intranet operated by the financial services firm for a select audience such as institutional investors.

WEBS. Abbreviation for World Equity Benchmark Shares, an investment product in the form of a unit representing a package of shares in foreign companies. It is based on the

Morgan Stanley Capital International (MSCI) Indexes and
trades on the ASE.

week order. A limit order in effect during the week it is entered. If
it is not executed by the week's end, it is cancelled.

weight, to. To calculate a mean or central tendency of a data set in
order to allow mathematically a certain characteristic to influence
the results in proportion to its significance in each item of the
data set. The result is a weighted average, which incorporates the
significance of that characteristic among the group into the
average. For example, suppose you want to calculate the average
performance of five stock portfolios, but there is a great deal of
difference in their sizes financially, a fact that persuades you to
use a weighted average in order to inject greater importance to
the performance of the larger portfolios. That procedure more
accurately reflects the return of money invested, generally, in
those five portfolios.

A weighted mean can best be described by the formula:

Weighted Average = (Sum of Weights × Numbers Weighted) ÷ Sum of Weights

DIFFERENCE IN WEIGHTED AVERAGE AND ARITHMETIC MEAN IN ANNUAL RETURN			
(1) Portfolio Style	(2) Financial Assets or Weights ($Millions)	(3) Annual Return (%)	(4) Col. 2 × Col. 3
High Growth	5.1	37.5	191.3
Income	22.5	15.8	355.5
Growth & Income	35.7	15.5	553.4
Derivatives	3.5	10.3	36.1
Bonds	20.8	8.5	176.8
Totals	87.6	87.6	1,313.0
Weighted Average (Col. 4 total ÷ Col. 2 total)		15.0	
Arithmetic Mean (Col. 3 total ÷ Col. 5)		17.5	

weighted mean. See **weight.**

weighted shares outstanding. See **average number of shares outstanding.**

westergaard broadcasting network.com. See **Web Sites for the Inquiring Investor.**

West Virginia State Auditor's Office. Regulator of securities laws in the state of West Virginia. Address: Securities Division, State Capitol Building, 1900 Kanawha Boulevard East, #W-118, Charleston, WV 25305. Phone: (304) 558-2257.

WFIC. Abbreviation for **World Federation of Investors Corporation.**

"What did the market do?" A request for a summary of stock market activity in a concluded session.

"What's the market doing?" A request for a market summary during trading hours. See **market summary.**

"what traffic will bear." As a company pricing its services and products for distribution, to sell them for whatever buyers will pay, usually through an informal market testing process, as opposed to setting prices based on the costs of providing them. Often, companies practicing predatory pricing base their pricing on this technique; companies barely surviving use this approach until they can recover. See **predatory pricing.**

"when distributed (WD)." A short form of **"when, as, and if distributed."** A reference to the indicator (WD) in reporting securities transactions on tape or in the media to securities that are not yet distributed, although they have been issued and are outstanding (held by investors). They represent a secondary distribution of closely-held securities or scattered securities that dealers are consolidating for resale, in a secondary distribution.

"when issued (WI)" or **"when, as, and if issued."** A reference to the indicator (WI) in reporting securities transactions on tape or in the media to securities that are not yet issued, although they have been authorized. This is done to accommodate investors who want to begin trading in the forthcoming issue. If the securities are canceled, an investor loses the commissions paid to buy the anticipated securities.

when-issued contracts. A general reference to the category of transactions involving the buying and selling of securities and commodities contracts, such as futures contracts, that are not yet issued, and will not be considered complete until such securities or contracts are delivered to their rightful owners.

"whisper number." The amount analysts believe a "hot stock" company can earn per share in a fiscal period in a best-case scenario. In an effort to show public restraint, the amount is circulated to clients vocally, but not published.

whistle blower. An employee who publicly reports unethical or illegal activities, usually in relation to government purchasing contracts or subsidies involving the employer.

white chip. A stock representing a valid speculation in a company, usually developing new products through heavy borrowing with a better-than-average chance of success. This is the first step in becoming a blue chip stock. For the second step, see **red chip.**

whole life insurance. A type of insurance that provides death benefits during an individual's entire life, rather than a specific period. There is also a savings component, called cash value, that increases over time.

Wholesale Financial Entity or **woofie.** A commercial bank that does not engage in retail banking activities, such as making car loans, and one that only accepts large deposits—over $100,000. Although deposits are not insured, the banks are members of and regulated by the Federal Reserve System as well as the Comptroller of the Currency and state regulatory agencies. Technically, these megabanks are commercial banks for big depositors and corporations that have been proposed at various times when the Congress has been debating the reform of the laws governing financial institutions.

wide spread. A difference that is considered large between the bid and asked prices of a stock. Such a spread is risky, because if an investor buys at the asked price and wants to sell immediately afterwards, he loses too much by selling at the bid price. A wide spread is generally the result of a dealer getting too much of a stock about which he is uncertain, so to discourage sellers he lowers the bid. In other words, he likes what he has (if he does not lower the asked price), but he is not eager to buy more. Also, a wide spread can indicate future market weakness for a stock if the dealer is aware of impending bad financial news about a stock that the public has not heard and has reduced his bid but maintained the asked price to give the appearance of strong demand for a stock.

widow-and-orphan-stock. A nickname for an extremely stable stock, usually paying dividends, in an industry that represents a long-term, if unspectacular, growth trend.

Wife.org. See under **Web Sites for Investing Women.**

wildcat strike. A work stoppage while a union contract is in effect.

will. A legal document, usually typed, witnessed, and notarized, by which a person passes on his or her property at death to others. A handwritten will is called a "holographic will." It is also legal to create an oral will, but there can be severe restrictions.

Williams Act. A federal law enacted in 1968 requiring that all shareholders receive the same price in a public tender offer. The law also addressed corporate takeovers, and was later incorporated into SEC rules. *See* **Rules, SEC #13d.**

Wilshire 5000 stock index. A stock price index that is the most comprehensive of all U.S. indexes, encompassing small-cap, mid-cap, and large-cap stocks. Actually, this index is comprised of approximately 7,200 stocks. It is considered a better representation of total market performance than the S&P 500.

windfall. An unexpected profit resulting from unforeseen circumstances.

window. In implementing corporate strategies, a reference to the opportunity to take advantage of a temporary situation. It could be such things as low interest rates in relation to a bond issue, purchase of capital equipment before a tax credit expires, or purchase of a futures contract before the price reflects the effects of a weather catastrophe on the supply of the commodity represented.

window dressing. Among financial institutions sensitive to public approbation, the effect created by shedding underperforming stocks and acquiring top-performing, popular stocks at the close of a reporting period in order to create the impression that stock selections have been outstanding during the entire period. The effect on the portfolio is minuscule, since they have been owned such a short time, but often the public is impressed because the high performances of the stocks are well known. The association makes the institution look good.

wire house. A brokerage firm that is a member of one or more national exchanges and has branches connected by a wire communications system.

Wisconsin Office of the Commissioner of Securities. Regulator of securities laws in the state of Wisconsin. Address: P.O. Box 1768, Madison, WI 53702. Phone: (608) 266-3431. Phone (toll free): (800) 472-4325.

witching hour. See **double witching hour** and **triple witching hour.**

withdrawal from margin account. See **undermargined account.**

with interest or **cum interest.** A reference to the requirement that a bond buyer must pay the seller accrued interest from the prior interest payment date up to, but not including, the settlement date.

"without recourse." See **qualified endorsement.**

without warrants or **sans warrants.** In reference to a securities transaction, not including warrants.

with warrants or **cum warrants.** In reference to a securities transaction, including the attached warrants.

womenCONNECT.com. See **Web Sites for Investing Women.**

woofie. Nickname for a **Wholesale Financial Entity.**

working capital. That money used to meet current business expenses; for accounting purposes, it is the total current assets minus the total current liabilities.

working capital loan. A short-term loan meant to finance corporate activities until amounts due are collected, billings are out for shipments, or long-term financing is in place.

working capital ratio. See **current ratio.**

working capital turnover. The net sales divided by working capital at year-end. This ratio indicates how much sales the highly liquid assets generated. In a recent 15-year period for the United States, the working capital turnover on average was 2.1.

working control. A reference to the situation when one or more shareholders, though owning less than half of a corporation's voting stock, have control in voting due to decentralized ownership of outstanding shares.

working interest. A direct participation in the financial affairs of a business enterprise in which an investor assumes a role in working for, managing, or operating the entity, with unlimited financial liability and risk in the outcome of the business enterprise or the financial risks associated with it. Under provisions of the Tax Reform Act of 1986, investors with working interests in drilling partnerships, such as General Partners have, may use losses from the working interest to offset other income of all types. The opposite of a **passive interest.**

workout. A reference to an unresolved corporate issue, such as the terms of corporate bonds during a bankruptcy of the issuer.

work-out quote. An over-the-counter quote for which the price is not firm and the quoter will have to negotiate to find buyers or sellers.

World Bank. Supported by member countries, the World Bank is actually a group of financial organizations comprised of the International Bank for Reconstruction & Development (IBRD), the International Development Association (IDA), the International Finance Corporation (IFC), the Multilateral Investment Guarantee Agency (MIGA), and the International Center for Settlement of Investor Disputes (ICSID). It was conceived in 1944 at Bretton Woods, New Hampshire, by the Allies to help the war-ravaged economies of Western Europe and Japan rebuild. Loans are made to governments of developing countries to finance investments and promote economic growth through (1) infrastructure projects, (2) economic reform packages, and (3) technical assistance. Today loans have been expanded to Africa, Central Europe, Latin America, the Middle East, and the former Soviet Union. The largest single loan provider in the group is the International Bank for Reconstruction & Development. In fiscal 1997, it approved loans totaling $14.7 billion for 141 projects. Its bond rating is AAA and the bank is consistently profitable. Web site: *www.worldbank.org.*

World Bank Bonds. Those bonds issued by the International Bank for Reconstruction and Development to raise money to loan its members. The AAA bonds are sold in the capital markets of the world and are payable in a variety of currencies. Many are traded on the New York Stock Exchange. *See* **World Bank.**

World Economic Forum. An annual conference held in Davos, Switzerland, attended by currently active, highly placed government officials, influential journalists and academics, and powerful corporate executives who can contribute to the global free market exchange that prevails there.

World Federation of Investors Corporation (WFIC). Originally called the World Federation of Investment Clubs, this association was organized in 1960 to assist investment club associations around the world and to encourage wider ownership of investment shares. Its goals also are to advance investment education on a worldwide scale for the benefit of individuals, families, and nations. This is implemented through a mutual exchange of investment and economic knowledge, and the mutual exchange of information and assistance between the member countries and between individuals and groups in each of the countries. There are 16 nations represented, with 200 to 300 attendees at annual congresses. Web site: *www.wfic.org.* *See* **investment club** and **National Association of Investors Corporation.**

world market. The competition with foreign businesses in the manufacturing, producing, and selling of goods to worldwide buyers.

World Trade Organization (WTO). The only international body dealing with the rules of trading between nations. The essence of the organization is defined in two agreements, negotiated and executed by most of the trading countries in the world. These documents are essentially contracts binding governments to abide by agreements. Although governments spearheaded the formation of the overlying agreements, two important objectives are to aid producers of goods and services negotiate agreements through forums and to help exporters and importers conduct their business in a free-flowing trade atmosphere. As a related function, the World Trade Organization settles disputes between trading nations. There are other goals coincident with promoting world trade. The WTO was established January 1, 1995 in Geneva, Switzerland and has 132 member countries, an operating budget of $93 million and a staff of 500. It superceded the **General Agreement on Tariffs and Trade (GATT).**

World Wide Web. See **Internet.**

Worth Online. See under **Web Sites for the Inquiring Investor.**

wrap. A company's annual report that is a copy of the SEC 10-K filing enclosed in a commercial cover, usually including a few pages of management's spin on corporate progress and expectations.

wrap fee. A brokerage charge for an investment program that bundles together a suite of products and services, part of which is trading commissions.

Wright Investors' Service. An investment management and research service, in business over 35 years. Address: 1000 Lafayette Boulevard, Bridgeport, CT 06604. Phone: (203) 330-5000. Fax: (203) 330-5001. Web site: *www.wisi.com.*

write down. To transfer a portion of an asset's value to an expense account or to the profit and loss account and a reserve account simultaneously in order to show a reduced value of the asset in the balance sheet. It is usually done to reduce the value of inventory in periods of rapid price fluctuations, while keeping money through the reserve account in the treasury to maintain net worth. However, the process can be applied to any overvalued asset.

write-off, restructuring. In corporate accounting, a reduction or charge to current earnings representing the monetary values involved in the elimination of certain assets that are deemed no longer valuable to the company. The process is used to build a reserve, against which the charge is ultimately made. According to current accounting rules, a company must specifically identify and disclose the costs involved in a restructuring write-off and amplify on its anticipated effects on future profits. Restructuring information, such as which facilities will close down, including locations, and which departments will dismiss personnel, would have an effect on future profits. Generally, the management of the company taking the write-off must be certain the action will take place. This specificity is required in order to guard against the manipulation of earnings through the use of restructuring write-offs that set up reserves that are used to conceal other expenses that are not necessarily complimentary to management.

write off. To deduct fixed amounts from an asset's value to show its diminished value on a balance sheet and to show these amounts as expenses so that money is set aside out of current earnings for the assets replacement or elimination without lowering net worth. The write-off might take place over several years, as opposed to a write-down, which is usually a one-time, nonrecurring event.

writer. An investor who contracts to sell, in the case of a call option, or buy, in the case of a put option, the underlying security at the exercise price.

WTO. See **World Trade Organization.**

Wyoming Secretary of State. Regulator of securities laws in the state of Wyoming. Address: Securities Division, State Capitol Building, Cheyenne, WY 82002. Phone: (307) 777-7370.

Xx

X or **XD.** Symbols used in ticker tapes, newspapers and magazine stock tables, indicating that a stock is selling without the latest dividend or a bond without the latest interest payment or a mutual fund without a recent capital gain or dividend distribution.

XR. A symbol used in newspaper and magazine stock tables, indicating a stock is trading without certain rights attached.

XW. A symbol used in newspaper and magazine stock tables, indicating that a stock is trading without certain warrants attached.

Yy

Yahoo! Finance. A Web site offering investment and financial information on international securities markets, including message boards. *See* **Web Sites for the Inquiring Investor.**

yankee bonds. Bonds denominated in U.S. dollars, in which the interest and principal are paid when due.

Y-bond. See **Z-bond.**

year-end dividend. A dividend declared by the Board of Directors at the close of the fiscal year, usually based on unusual earnings or an extraordinary gain through a sale of corporate assets. It is not a regular dividend and is non-recurring.

year-end rally. An alleged rise in security prices the last few days of the year after factors such as tax selling have forced many issues downward to attractive prices. This event is highly conjectural, since studies show that stock prices lack seasonality.

year-to-date (YTD). A reference to the period from the beginning of a corporation's fiscal year through the latest quarter or year. It is used when reporting and comparing a company's financial or operating results.

"Yellow fever." See **Asian flu.**

yellow sheets. See **National Quotation Bureau.**

yen bond. A reference to a bond denominated in Japanese currency. In banking usage, it refers to a Japanese bond held outside Japan.

"yen-carry trade." Among international investors and traders, the strategy of borrowing undervalued yen, in terms of the dollar, at very low interest rates in Japan, converting the yen to overvalued dollars, in order to buy bonds in the United States. When the trade is attractive, the bonds pay much higher interest rates than the yen loan costs, so the trade is a free-carry as far as interest rates are concerned, and possibly more. However, in the event the yen spikes upward in value, in terms of the dollar, the ploy might not work, because when the bonds are sold and the dollars are converted back to yen, it is for fewer yen, and more have to be furnished to repay the loan. This discrepancy might eliminate the yield advantage. In addition, a change in price of the securities purchased can affect the profitability of the trade. When their price falls, less currency is available on conversion back to repay the loan. But when their price rises, the reverse is true. *See* **carry trade** and **"gold-carry trade."**

yield. The annual income in dividends, rent, or interest that an investment returns, expressed as a percentage of the purchase price or face value and found by dividing the annual dividends, rent, or interest by the purchase price, although this method is only applicable to stocks, strictly speaking. For example, a stock bought for $40 per share, paying an annual dividend of $2, yields .05 or 5% (($2.00 ÷ $40) × 100), expressed as a percentage. Market appreciation of property is not considered yield. Since yields fluctuate because of the changing supply of investment money and changed investor attitudes, no set yield prevails, but investments associated with identical risks of loss tend to bear similar yields. Securities should be earning a yield comparable to current yields on investments of similar quality. If they are not, indications are that the dividends have not kept pace with market price. Often, such securities should be sold to buy ones with better current yields and similar risks.

By way of illustration, if an investor paid $50 per share for a stock with a $2 dividend, his yield would be 4% as long as the dividend remained $2. But, suppose the price rises to $75, still on the basis of a $2 dividend. At this point, the current yield on the stock is 2.65%. If the original buyer sells his stock at a $25-per-share capital gain and buys one of similar risk currently yielding 4%, he is probably not only selling an overpriced stock but earning more with his dollars simultaneously. On the other hand, if the original stock increased its dividend to $3 during the price rise, the yield of 6%, based on the original investment price, is probably commensurate with similar stocks. The stock seems reasonably priced and probably worth retaining. *See* **current yield, nominal yield,** and **retrospective yield.**

yield burning. As a securities dealer, to arrange a sale of income securities, such as U.S. Treasury bonds, to a client at inflated prices in order to lower the yield to the client. This practice is usually used when a client's yield must be lowered for legal reasons, such as retaining tax-exempt status for bonds issued by states and municipalities. In the process, the dealer makes money on the U.S. Treasury bond mark up.

yield curve. A graph depicting the term structure of interest rates on which the average yields of bonds of like quality, with maturities ranging from near-term to long-term, are plotted. The curve indicates whether short-term rates are higher or lower than long-term rates, and whether there are imbalances in the supply and demand for money and capital over the time horizon plotted. When short-term rates are lower, the yield curve is called positive. When short-term rates are higher, it is called a negative curve. When the curve is straight, the yield curve is called flat. The reason that the curve is called negative when near-term rates are higher is that investors usually expect higher rates when the investment period is longer to compensate them for the greater time risks. When the rates are higher short term, a reversal in investment logic is indicated, caused by an imbalance in the supply and demand for investment funds. *See* **inverted yield curve.**

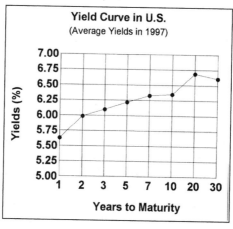

yield equivalence. See **tax-exempts.**

yield spread. The fluctuations between the yields on high-grade U.S. Treasury bonds and high-risk junk bonds with the same maturity dates. In speculative periods, this spread tends to narrow as investors bid up junk bond prices in trying to lock in their higher yields, bringing down the yields and, in doing so, pull money out of higher grade bonds, thus lowering their prices and raising the yields. In the process, the two yields move closer together but never equate because the risk differential is always present. Many stock market observers use the yield spread to ascertain whether the stock market is risky. They rationalize that when the spread is wide, investors generally are very cognizant of risks, and this caution has lowered the stock market to realistic levels. On the other hand, when the yield spread is narrow, they are apt to find the market vulnerable to a correction as investors restore historical balances. Broadly speaking, a yield spread can apply to the differences in yield between any two or more types of securities, such as common stocks and bonds, with the purpose of identifying one or more that is out of line. Such an anomaly might indicate that one type is overpriced or underpriced. A **yield curve** is the yield on various maturities of the same or an equivalent bond, while a yield spread is the average yield of different issues of securities at one point in time over a time frame.

Yield to Average Life. In the case of bonds that are required to be redeemed by a sinking fund at regular intervals, under the terms of the indenture—the contract between the issuer of bonds and the investors, administered by a trustee, usually a bank—the practice in the market of trading them on an average life basis. This is an alternative to using Yield to Maturity and Yield to Call. Traders believe the sinking-fund purchases give the bonds additional price support, since bonds selling below par will be snapped up by the sinking-fund trustees. The yield on these bonds is calculated as the yield to maturity is, except that the average life is substituted for the maturity date. For a bond maturing in 20 years, with its indenture requiring one-tenth of the issue to be redeemed by the sinking-fund trustees each year beginning after the 10th year, the average life is 15 years. Five years before sinking fund plus midpoint of sinking fund, or five years, equals 10 years. *See* **Yield to Call** and **Yield to Maturity.**

Yield to Call. The rate of annual interest that will be earned when a bond is held to its first call date. Technically, it is the interest rate that will make the present value of the cash flows from interest payments equal to the price paid for a bond if it is held to the first call date. This calculation is the same as yield to maturity, except that the maturity date is replaced by the first call date and that the redemption value at maturity is replaced by the first call price. *See* **Yield to Average Life** and **Yield to Maturity.**

U.S. TREASURY BOND YIELDS (30-YEAR MATURITIES)			
Year	**Yields**	**Year**	**Yields**
1980	9.81	1991	8.47
1981	12.96	1992	7.84
1982	13.92	1993	6.81
1983	10.93	1994	7.40
1984	13.44	1995	6.57
1985	10.45	1996	7.06
1986	7.57	1997	6.77
1987	8.57	1998	5.70
1988	9.00	1999	6.04
1989	8.27	2000	5.93
1990	8.46	2001*	5.65

Source: Federal Reserve Board of Governors.
*Note: June of each year, except April in 2001.

Yield to Maturity (YTM). The rate of annual return that will be earned when a bond is held to maturity or the **internal rate of return** on a bond. In calculating this yield, interest income, redemption value, interest earned on interest, as well as the cash flow timing are considered for the period from purchase to maturity. It is assumed that interest payments are reinvested in the calculated yield to maturity, so that the YTM is only realized when a bond is held to maturity and all interest from it invested at exactly the YTM rate. An approximation formula follows. (Remember that percentage amounts are stated as hundredths that are decimalized.)

$$YTM = [(100 - P) T] + (I + P)$$

where:

P = Price paid, expressed as a quote, or $\frac{1}{10}$ the real price;

T = Years to maturity;

I = Rate of interest, expressed in tenths.

Let's say that KCS Energy 8⅞s of 2008 were purchased on January 1, 1998 for 97⅝ or 97.60 decimalized on the NYSE. Translation: The KCS Energy bonds paying interest of $88.40 annually and maturing at the close of 2008 were bought for $976.00 (97.60 × 10), a $24.00 discount under the redemption value of $1,000. What is the yield to maturity? The newspaper table said the yield was 9.1%, but that did not incorporate the discount as the YTM formula will do; therefore, the newspaper quote should be called the **current yield.**

$$\begin{aligned} YTM &= [((100 - 97.60) \div 10) \div 100] + (8.84 \div 97.60); \\ &= [(2.40 \div 10) \div 100] + .0906; \\ &= (.24 \div 100) + .0906 \\ &= .0024 + .0906 \\ &= .0930 \text{ or } 9.3\% \end{aligned}$$

See **Yield to Average Life** and **Yield to Call.**

yo-yo. A stock whose price moves up and down continuously. This usually means there is no bona fide investment support for the issue, and that its price is in the hands of speculators and traders who are using it to make fast bucks.

YTD. See **year-to-date.**

Zz

Zagreb Stock Exchange. See under **Global Investment Market.**

zaitech. 1) In a narrow sense, a reference to a company or individual who violates securities anti-fraud laws, often, but not always, by using the Internet to offer fraudulent securities. The name comes from litigation in 1996 between the SEC and Zaitech Holdings, Inc., in which the latter was restrained from continuing its fraudulent operations in a civil action. The defendant offered promissory notes to investors claiming falsely they were secured by U.S. government securities and that the annual returns would range from 12–22%. The offering was made available through news group bulletin board postings and through advertisements on the Web. The SEC asserted the Internet provides promoters with access to millions of prospective investors worldwide, with great speed and ease, minimal expense, and virtual anonymity. 2) In a broad sense, a reference to Japanese corporations that were highly profitable in the late 1980s, coinciding with reduced capital spending requirements or opportunities. Consequently, they became increasingly proficient at sophisticated corporate finance strategies or playing financial games internationally. The root of the word is "zai," the Japanese word for finance. One of the ploys was to use burgeoning stock prices in Japan to issue convertible bonds, which were exchanged for shares rising in price, and made for very cheap financing. Ultimately the borrowed funds were invested in international projects. The practice led to borrowing money excessively, although at a diminishing rate from banks, in order to invest in hot spots globally, with the result that debt cascaded into many layers. When one layer experienced financial problems, such as currency devaluation, it could set off a chain reaction. In the late 1990s in Asian economies, and in the early 1990s in Japan, this type of money management caused financial panics and huge losses.

Z-bond. A reference to the bottom tier, or bottom tranche, or bonds in a Collateralized Mortgage Obligation (CMO) bond structure. The position of a tranche in the bond structure usually determines when bondholders will be repaid. The "Z" bondholders are the very last to receive consolidated payments from the huge universe of mortgagers that lead to a payoff of their bonds, in a typical CMO structure of "A" (earliest paid), "B" (next paid), "C" (last paid, except for tiers below), and sometimes "Y" (last paid, except for "Z"). Because the "Z" bonds participate in the distribution of the cash flow, and are discounted to set the market price like the others, they are a combination of income (from regular interest form mortgage payments) and zero-coupon bonds (because part of the yield is deferred until the bonds mature), in terms of return. In the case of Z-bonds, they are entitled to the cash flow after the higher tiers are paid off, including interest on principal. However, sometimes there is a sinking fund for "Z" and "Y" tranches. In packaging thousands of mortgage contracts, as is done in a CMO with diverse mortgage payment schedules and maturities, it is necessary to assign the cash flow to the various tranches for administrative purposes. The tranche is not a mortgage bond quality designation. *See* **Collateralized Mortgage Obligation (CMO)** and **pass-through security.**

Zeitgeist industry. A reference to the industry emerging in the Internet age in which marketing of products and services, as well as profits, are keyed to consumer reactions to a particular personality or name. As the economy enters the new millennium, this phenomenon is used more and more to explain valuations on common stocks that are not based on traditional values of securities analysis, but on valuations that, in many cases, are ethereal and extremely high, relatively. It is possible that this industry or phenomenon will become more integral to economic growth than conventional ones such as autos, airlines, drugs, and even those in businesses employing high technology. Curiously, such an industry might not even show up in GDP. The expression is borrowed—zeitgeist industry derives from the same German word, meaning the spirit of the times or the cultural preferences of a generation. Examples of Zeitgeist stocks are Martha Stewart, World Wrestling Federation or WWF, and Koop.com.

zero-base budgeting. A system of financial management in which every budget outlay must be rationalized in the new budget period, including those already approved in prior periods. In this way, all budgetary items begin each fiscal period on an equal footing and must justify their use of monies in the coming budget period. There are no sacred cows.

zero-beta portfolio. A reference to a securities portfolio that includes only risk-free securities, in terms of the general stock market and is totally divorced from stock market performance. While this characteristic is beneficial when markets are weak or in disarray, it can eliminate the opportunities during strong stock markets. Usually stocks in this category are too new to display a trading history or represent products and services completely independent of the general economy and business conditions.

zero-coupon bonds. Bonds bearing investors no regular cash interest payments. Instead, investors must wait until maturity, when they are paid what represents the accumulated interest from the gradual appreciation of the bond through interest accumulation to its face value at maturity. In essence, the investor pays the present value of the face value of the bond at maturity, discounted by a rate of interest that will grow that present value to the face value over its term. They are sold to investors at a large discount under the face value, so that the cash return is delayed. However, under tax laws in the United States the **imputed interest** accruing as the bond matures is taxable each year. This taxing procedure follows the **Original Issue Discount** rule of the IRS on taxing imputed interest income. For that reason, they are best used in tax-sheltered retirement programs, such as IRA accounts.

Because the entire yield is accumulated and paid at maturity, interest rate changes affect these bonds more dramatically than regular interest-bearing bonds. This is because the entire yield must be accounted for in the difference between the discounted price and the matured face value. On the other hand, a conventional bond receives contributions from both regular interest payments and changes from the level of the current price to its face value in adjusting its yields to a competitive rate. It has a limited exposure to interest rate changes. Frequently, the U.S. Treasury issues this type of bond, called Certificates of Accrual on Treasury Securities (CATS) and Treasury Investors Growth Receipts (TIGERS) or STRIPS. *See* also **bond table.**

zero-coupon convertibles, corporate. Zero-coupon debentures issued by corporations. They are convertible into common stock of the issuing corporation at specified prices and within specified time periods. These securities were originally issued and called Liquid Yield Option Notes or LYONs. There is an option to put the bonds back to the issuer, usually within three years from the date of the original offering, which is why they are also called notes. Because they include an equity participation, they tend to yield less than a straight convertible of similar quality would.

zero-coupon convertibles, municipal. A municipal bond that has a zero coupon but is convertible into an interest-bearing bond at a future date before its maturity. An example could be a 12-year zero-coupon municipal bond, sold at a deep discount because all the interest income compounds and accrues at maturity, that is, convertible into an interest-bearing bond at maturity. It is useful to investors who want to assure themselves an interest rate at a low cost, since the bonds are selling at deep discounts, compared to conventional bonds with similar financial characteristics. Various investment firms market these types of securities. One popular variety is called Growth and Income Securities or GAINS, while another is sold as Future Income and Growth Securities or FIGS.

zero-coupon security. Any security that is purchased at a price that includes and accumulates the total investment return or yield to a future date when the face value is paid at maturity. There are no semiannual interest payments, as there are in most corporate bonds. Under current tax laws in the United States, the imputed interest accruing as the bond matures is taxable each year. For that reason, they are best used in tax-sheltered retirement programs, such as IRA accounts. *See* **zero-coupon bonds.**

zero-coupon split bonds. Zero-coupon bonds issued by a municipality that are convertible into interest-bearing bonds under
certain circumstances.

zero downtick. See **zero-minus tick.**

zero-minus tick or **zero downtick.** A transaction representing no
change in the price of a stock versus the previous trade in that stock,
but lower than the preceding different price trade in that stock.

zero-plus tick or **zero uptic.** A transaction representing no change
in the price of a stock versus the previous trade in that stock, but
higher than the preceding different price trade in that stock.

zero-sum game. 1) In a business context, a condition in which one
company's market or financial gains are the consequence of a
competitor's proportional losses. For example, in a two-company
market, the demand for diapers is limited to the number of babies
born each year. If the High Fashion Diaper Corp. expects to
increase sales next year, the company must capture sales from
Goo Goo Diapers Unlimited. 2) In a commodities or derivatives
market sense, a situation in which the winners' gains are matched
by the losers' losses. This is because for every buyer contract,
there is a seller contract; and some will make money and some
will lose money. For example, if Nervous Purvis exercises his
call to buy 100 shares of Gorilla Tearooms, Inc. at $25 per share
when the current market is $50 per share, he has made $25 per
share or $2,500. On the other hand, Fearless Freddie, who wrote
the call, loses $25 per share or $2,500 on the transaction. The
result is a washout or zero sum.

zero uptic. See **zero-plus tick.**

Zimbabwe Stock Exchange, The. Address: 2nd Floor, 65
Samora Machel Avenue, Harare, Zimbabwe. Web site:
www.zse.co.zw.

zombies. A reference to companies that are managing to stay in
business even though they are experiencing severe financial and
operating problems. Often they are actually operating under a
court's protection, such as under a bankruptcy order. Stocks of
these companies frequently are worthless. However, some

investors shop for bonds of such companies, which are usually trading at steep discounts due to the problems. They are betting that subsequent reorganization can lead to the elimination of the original equity interests and the issue of new equity shares to the bondholders in exchange for the bonds at very favorable average costs per share because of the discounted bond purchase price.

zoning ordinance. A municipal law that creates a board or panel that is responsible for establishing and maintaining a code or set of standards that designates the uses to which real property and buildings can be put within the municipality. Examples of zones are industrial, light industrial, residential, and commercial. Once these are established, future property uses must be in accordance with the code, unless exceptions are granted. However, usually grandfather exemptions are created by city councils, under which those uses in effect before the ordinance are allowed to continue for as long as the user is present there.

For real estate investors, keeping up with zoning changes in a municipality is a paramount activity, for changes might alter the value of a parcel of real estate. Even exemptions to the laws might alter the value of real estate. For securities investors, zoning insights are less critical, but do have a role to play. Where a company owns real estate as its core business, as a Real Estate Investment Trust does, zoning laws can affect the rental values and resale values of its properties. Obviously, zoning trends are a prime consideration. For companies that own real estate as an adjunct to doing business, as a hotel company might unless it leases its properties, zoning changes can impact market values on the balance sheet. Although such assets are generally carried on the books at the book value or historical cost, a nonreflected value change as a result of zoning changes would be an investment consideration for an analyst who was digging deep into asset values. This rationale could go into his or her appraisal of the stock. And it is important for investors to learn how opinion makers in the stock market think, especially when contemplating a commitment of funds into a stock group.

Zurich Stock Exchange. See **Swiss Exchange** under **Global Investment Market.**